THE HISTORICAL AND INSTITUTIONAL CONTEXT OF ROMAN LAW

The Historical and Institutional Context of Roman Law

GEORGE MOUSOURAKIS
The University of Auckland

Routledge
Taylor & Francis Group
LONDON AND NEW YORK

First published 2003 by Ashgate Publishing

Published 2016 by Routledge
2 Park Square, Milton Park, Abingdon, Oxon OX14 4RN
711 Third Avenue, New York, NY 10017, USA

Routledge is an imprint of the Taylor & Francis Group, an informa business

British Library Cataloguing in Publication Data
Mousourakis, George
The historical and institutional context of Roman law. –
(Laws of the nations series)
1.Roman law 2.Roman law – History
I.Title
340.5'4

Library of Congress Cataloging-in-Publication Data
Mousourakis, George.
The historical and institutional context of Roman law / George Mousourakis.
p.cm. – (Laws of the nations series)
Includes bibliographical references and index.
ISBN 0-7546-2108-1 (alk. paper) – ISBN 0-7546-2114-6 (pbk. : alk. paper)
1. Roman law. 2. Civil law–History. I. Title. II. Series.

KJA147 .M68 2002
340.5'4–dc21

2002026137

ISBN 13: 978-0-7546-2108-9 (hbk)
ISBN 13: 978-0-754-62114-0 (pbk)

Contents

Preface

The law of ancient Rome, as transmitted through the sixth century codification of Emperor Justinian, has been one of the strongest formative forces in the development of what we now think of as the Western legal tradition. It furnished the basis of the Civil law family of legal systems – one of the major groups of legal systems in the world today – and supplied an almost inexhaustible reservoir of legal concepts, doctrines and principles the influence of which can be traced in any body of law, both national and international, and in any system of courts and procedures. The history of ancient Roman law spans a period of more than twelve centuries. Initially the law of a small rural community, then that of a powerful city-state, Roman law became in the course of time the law of a supranational empire which embraced a large part of the civilised world of its time. During its long history Roman law went through a remarkable process of evolution. It passed through different stages of development and underwent important transformations, both in substance and in scope, keeping up with changes in society, especially with those changes brought about by Rome's expansion in the ancient world. During this long process the interaction between custom, enacted law and case law led to the formation of a highly sophisticated system, gradually built up from layers of different elements. But the great bulk of Roman law, especially Roman private law, was not a result of legislation but of jurisprudence. This unenacted law was not a confused mass of shifting customs, but a steady tradition developed and handed down by specialists, at first members of the Roman priestly class and later by the jurists. In the closing stages of this process, as law-making became more and more centralised, this law, together with statutory law, was compiled and then 'codified'. The codification of the law both completed the development of Roman law and became the means by which Roman law was subsequently transmitted to the modern world.

The aim of this book is to show how Roman law emerged, how it became a universal system and how it was transmitted to the modern world. The book traces the evolution of Roman law from the primitive law of a small rustic community in Italy into a highly refined system continuously adapting itself to the needs of a commercial society extending over a vast empire and embracing many different races. It examines the development of the various sources of Roman law in their social and political setting and attempts to explain how in practice a source was made effective. And since so much of Roman law hinged upon forms of legal process, the book also discusses the evolution of Roman legal procedure and outlines the mechanisms by which legal judgements were put into effect. Although the growth of Roman criminal law is also considered, the emphasis is upon the development of Roman private law. This is largely because private law was the chief interest of the most creative makers of law, the Roman jurists, but partly too because the later influence of Roman law has been predominantly in this field. In this survey I have tried to encompass the history of Roman law as a whole and to convey it in such a way as to avoid the fragmentation which has become usual in the subject. While principally concerned with the historical development of Roman law, I have made a sincere effort to combine the perspectives of social, political and economic history with those of legal history. In the foreground are those historical events which had the strongest impact on Roman law. Special emphasis is placed on the development of the Roman political institutions and the historical evolution of the Roman state. In the final chapter of the book attention is paid to the factors which, in later times, warranted the preservation and continuing influence of the Roman legal inheritance in continental Europe.

This introductory book on the history of Roman law has been written primarily for law students whose course of studies includes Roman law, legal history and comparative law. It is also designed to meet the needs of the general reader of history who would like to know about the main features of Roman law and the social, political and cultural processes that contributed to its development. However, the details of the development of particular legal doctrines or branches of law are not within the scope of this book. There is abundant material available in English and other languages to enable the student to examine selected topics in depth. But any detailed study in Roman law should be carried out only when some understanding of the system as a whole has been attained. It is hoped that this book will provide an accessible historical introduction to the development of Roman law and will encourage students of all kinds to carry out further work in this area of study.

I am grateful to a number of people who have helped me in the preparation of this book. First I should like to thank my colleagues and students at the University of Auckland for their encouragement and constructive criticism. I also wish to thank Professor Alberto Burdese of the University of Padova, Professor Pietro Costa of the University of Florence, Professor Vito Mangini of the University of Bologna, Professor Alfons Bürge of the University of Munich and Professor Nikolaus Benke of the University of Vienna, who enabled me to spend several months in Italy, Germany and Austria as a Research Scholar and to make use of the libraries and facilities of their Institutions. Mr Ian McIntosh, with his eye for detail and acute insight, has been a superb editor and has made a number of helpful suggestions for improvement. Finally, I wish to thank Chapman Tripp law partnership for one year's financial grant towards the research for this book and my publishers for their courteous assistance.

Abbreviations

Bas	*Basilica*
Bruns, *Fontes*	*Fontes iuris romani antiqui*, ed. C. G. Bruns, Tubingen 1909, repr. Aalen1969
C	*Codex* of Justinian
C Th	*Codex Theodosianus*
D	*Digest* of Justinian
FIRA	*Fontes Iuris Romani Anteiustiniani*, I-III, ed. S. Riccobono, J. Baviera and V. Arangio-Ruiz, Florence 1940-1943, 2nd edn, 1968
G	*Institutes* of Gaius
Girard, *Textes*	*Textes de droit romain*, ed. P. F. Girard and F. Senn, 7th edn, Paris 1967
Inst	*Institutes* of Justinian
MGH	*Monumenta Germaniae Historica*
Nov	*Novels* of Justinian
SZ	*Zeitschrift der Savigny Stiftung für Rechtsgeschichte*
P.Oxy.	*The Oxyrhynchus Papyri*, ed. B. P. Grenflell, A. S. Hunt, et al., London 1898
PS	*Pauli Sententiae*
UE	*Tituli ex corpore Ulpiani* in FIRA II, 261-301
XII T	*Twelve Tables*

1 Introduction

Divisions of Roman Legal and Constitutional History

The history of Roman law may be divided into periods in different ways, depending on the nature of the developments taken to provide the requisite historical landmarks. Although these divisions have facilitated the study of Roman law, one must bear in mind that Roman law evolved gradually and therefore no clear-cut lines separate the different stages of its development. The sources of Roman law were, in varying degrees of strength from period to period, all present and in force at one and the same time, and in various ways qualified the influence of each other.

In general, Roman history falls into three major periods that correspond to Rome's three successive systems of political organisation:

(i) The Monarchy – from the founding of Rome in the eighth century BC to the end of the sixth century BC.
(ii) The Republic – from the end of the sixth century BC to the battle of Actium in 31 BC, or the transformation of the Roman constitution under Augustus in 27 BC. The republican era is subdivided into two phases: the early Republic (509 BC to 367 BC), and the later Republic (from 367 BC to 31 or 27 BC).
(iii) The Empire – this period begins in 31 or 27 BC and ends, for the western Roman empire in 476 AD with the overthrow of the last emperor of the West, and for the eastern Roman empire in 565 AD with the death of Emperor Justinian. The imperial era is subdivided into two parts: the Principate (from 31 or 27 BC to 284 AD), and the Dominate (from 284 AD to 476 AD for the western empire and to 565 AD for the eastern empire).

According to one approach, Roman legal history follows these divisions as the various legal institutions adapted themselves to the type of government in power.

Roman legal history may also be divided into periods by reference to the modes of law-making and the character of the legal institutions that came to prevail in different epochs. In this respect, the history of Roman law may be divided, roughly, into four phases:

(i) The archaic period – from the eighth century BC to the third century BC. This period includes the Monarchy and the earlier part of the Republic.
(ii) The pre-classical period – from the third century BC to the beginning of the Principate in the first century AD. This phase covers the later Republic and the early years of the Principate.
(iii) The classical period – from the first century AD to the middle of the third century AD.
(iv) The post-classical period – from the middle of the third century AD to the middle of the sixth century AD. This period covers the later part of the Principate and the Dominate.

The above divisions will provide a suitable framework for the discussion of Roman legal history as presented in this book. Before we proceed to examine the development of Roman society and its law in some detail, an outline of the general features of each historical period will be offered in the following paragraphs.

The archaic period

The earliest Rome was an agricultural community which differed little in its social and political organisation from its neighbours in central Italy. The mass of the population was composed of small freeholders and economic life was based largely on cattle-raising and the cultivation of the land. Political power was in the hands of a landowning aristocracy, the patricians, which dominated the most important political body, the senate, out of which the highest magistrates of the state were chosen. Social life revolved around the family (*familia*), the basic social unit, whose head (*pater familias*) had absolute authority over all persons and all property in his family group. A turning-point in the history of this period was the overthrow of the Monarchy, Rome's earliest system of government, at the close of the sixth century BC and the establishment of an aristocratic Republic. During the period from the sixth to the mid-third centuries BC Rome's social and political organisation underwent a series of important changes – a process marked by the 'struggle of the orders', the internal political strife between the old aristocracy, the patricians, and the lower classes, the plebeians. By the middle of the third century BC a precarious equilibrium between the classes had been established and the Roman state came to be dominated by a new nobility composed of both patrician and wealthy plebeian families.

During the earlier phase of the archaic period Roman society was governed by a body of customary norms of a largely religious nature. There appear to have been no written laws, although the jurist Pomponius, who lived in the second century AD, does allude to certain *leges regiae* (laws of the kings) in his description of the state of the law during this period. In the archaic era the formulation and articulation of the law was in the hands of the priestly class, the *pontifices*. In their capacity as custodians of religious law (*ius divinum*) the pontiffs were concerned with, among other things, the punishment of violations of religious norms and the regulation of the calendar; at the same time they supervised the application of private law (*ius civile*). They alone were acquainted with the technical forms employed in the making of the typical transactions of private law, and they alone were entitled to give official advice and authoritative opinions on questions of law. Like the law of other primitive societies, the Roman law of the archaic period was characterised by its extremely formalistic nature. A legal transaction or procedure could not produce the desired results unless it was performed in accordance with strictly prescribed rituals. And once the prescribed ritual had been observed, the transaction was regarded as binding irrespective of the parties' real intentions. A momentous event that marks the development of Roman law during this period was the codification of the customary norms that governed the life of the Roman citizens by the Law of the Twelve Tables, enacted around 450 BC. With the introduction of this law, the first binding written record of the rules and procedures by which justice might be done, a new source of law came into existence, in addition to the unwritten customary law. In the years that followed the promulgation of the Law of the Twelve Tables legal development was based largely on the interpretation of its text, a task carried out by the pontiffs and, in later ages, by the jurisconsults. Moreover, in this period the office of praetor was introduced (367 BC), a new magistracy entrusted with the administration of the private law. In the course of time the praetor's edict became one of the strongest formative forces in the development of Roman civil law and provided the basis for a distinct source of law known as *ius praetorium* or *ius honorarium*.

The pre-classical period

This period witnessed Rome's ascendancy as the dominant power in the ancient world. By the middle of the third century BC Rome had conquered most of the Italian peninsula and, by the end of the first century BC, she held sway over the entire Mediterranean basin. It was during this period that the Romans came into direct contact with the Greek world and were fully exposed to the influence of the Greek and Hellenistic culture. But Rome's rapid growth in territory, wealth and political influence had far-reaching consequences for the social and economic life of the later

Republic. The new conditions brought about by Rome's expansion generated a social and political crisis which was accompanied by an increasingly violent internal strife, both between rival factions and individuals within the ruling classes and between the aristocracy and various disadvantaged groups. This state of affairs degenerated into an almost permanent state of civil war which led to the erosion and final collapse of the republican system of government.

The legal history of this period is marked by the emergence of the first jurisconsults (*iurisconsulti* or *iurisprudentes*), a group of jurists who, without being members of the pontifical college, acted as interpreters of the law. Like the pontiffs, these secular jurists were members of the Roman aristocracy. They were men actively engaged in public life and many of them were elected to the highest offices of the state. The main focus of their activities was the giving of legal advice on difficult points of law to judicial magistrates, judges and parties at law. They were also engaged in drafting legal documents, such as contracts and wills, and in advising state organs on legal matters. At the closing stages of this period there appeared the first systematic treatises on civil law – a development associated with the influence of Greek philosophy and rhetoric or Roman legal thought. The legal history of the pre-classical period is marked also by the development of the *ius honorarium* or magisterial law as a distinct source of law. As was mentioned before, early Roman law was rigid, narrow in scope and resistant to change. As a result of the changes brought about by Rome's expansion, the Romans were faced with the problem of how to adjust their law so that it might meet the challenges imposed upon it by new social and economic conditions. In response to this problem the law-dispensing magistrates, and particularly the praetors, were given the power to mould the law in its application. A new flexible system of legal procedure was developed, known as the *per formulam* procedure, under which the magistrates were given much more discretion in deciding whether to grant or to refuse a legal action. Although the magistrates had no legislative authority, by making an extensive use of their right to regulate legal process they did in fact create a new body of law which was progressive and free and subject to continual change and development.

The classical period

The classical period of Roman law largely coincides with the first part of the imperial era, referred to as the Principate. With the establishment of a new form of government under Augustus in the late first century BC the political and social upheaval that marked the closing years of the Republic came to an end. During the first two centuries of the Empire Rome consolidated its position as the dominant power in the Mediterranean world and, under the conditions of peace and security that prevailed within the boundaries of the empire, trade and industry flourished and Roman culture reached its highest level of achievement. However, the first symptoms of a new crisis began to appear in the second century AD and became more apparent in the closing years of that century: a weakening of Rome's political system and the rise of the army as the decisive power factor, lack of economic equilibrium and economic stagnation, social unrest, and the emergence of new enemies on the empire's frontiers. All these and other factors interacted to intensify and spread the crisis during the third century. In the closing years of that century, under a line of strong emperors, the crisis was finally checked and a temporary revival materialised, but only at the cost of establishing a despotic government and a rigidly regulated society.

Roman law reached its full maturity in the classical period and this was largely due to the creative work of the jurists and their influence on the formulation and application of the law. From the early years of the Principate it became customary for the emperors to grant to the most influential jurists the right to give opinions on questions of law (*ius respondendi*) and to deliver them by the emperor's authority. In the later half of the second century the opinions of the jurists who had been granted this right, when in agreement with each other, came to be regarded as authoritative sources of law and as legally binding. Besides dealing with questions pertaining to the practical application of the law, the jurists were also engaged in the teaching of law and the writing of legal treatises. Most of the fabric of Roman law, as it is known to us today, was built upon the writings of the leading jurists of this period. During the same period the resolutions of the senate and the decrees of the emperors came to be regarded as authoritative sources of law. On the other hand, the influence of the magisterial law (*ius honorarium*) on the development of Roman law gradually weakened as praetorian initiatives became increasingly rare. The final codification of the praetorian edict in 130 AD put an end to the *ius honorarium* as a distinct source of law.

The post-classical period

The unity of the Roman state, badly shaken by the crisis of the third century, was gradually restored in the later half of that century by a line of capable emperors elevated to the throne through the support of the army. The work of these emperors was completed by Diocletian (284-305 AD), whose rise to power is traditionally taken to mark the beginning of a new phase in Roman history known as the Dominate. Under Diocletian and his successors the imperial government was transformed into an absolute monarchy of an Oriental-Hellenistic type. The administration was reorganised and measures were introduced aimed at the stabilisation of the economy and the strengthening of the empire's defences. But most of these measures proved short-lived and, as the empire's problems escalated, the forces of dissolution gathered momentum. In the later part of this period civil wars, invasions and economic decay plagued the empire, which was finally divided into an eastern and a western part in 395 AD. Within less than a century the western Roman empire finally succumbed to the invading Germanic tribes (476 AD). The eastern empire was transformed into the medieval Byzantine empire and, with Constantinople as its capital, survived for another 1100 years as an essentially Greek state.

The legal history of this period is marked by the general decline of jurisprudence. The interpretations of the jurists ceased to be a living source of law and earlier juristic works came to be regarded as a body of finally settled doctrine. The only effective source of law was imperial legislation, largely concerned with matters of public law and economic policy. At the same time custom began again to play a part as a secondary source of law – a development which, in the western provinces in particular, led to what is referred to as the 'vulgarisation' of Roman law. As the body of imperial legislation continued to grow, there emerged the need for the codification of the law. In addition to that, direction needed to be given concerning the use of the classical literature – a vast body of legal materials stretching back over hundreds of years of legal development. The process of codification began with the publication of two private collections of imperial law which appeared at the end of the third century AD: the *Codex Gregorianus* (291 AD) and the *Codex Hermogenianus* (295 AD). These were followed by the *Codex Theodosianus*, an official codification of imperial statutes published in 438 AD. The process of codification came to an end in the middle of the sixth century AD with the great codification of the Roman law – both of juristic law and imperial enactments – under Emperor Justinian.

Sources of Roman Legal History

Our knowledge of the history of Roman law is derived from a number of different sources. Depending upon the nature of the relevant historical material a distinction is drawn between literary sources, epigraphic evidence and the unwritten archaeological record. Of particular importance for our reconstruction of Roman legal history are documents of a specifically legal nature, such as various legislative texts, the surviving body of juristic literature, records of legal transactions and statutes inscribed on tablets of bronze, stone or copper.

Juridical literature

Of the literary sources of particular importance are the surviving works of the Roman jurists of the pre-classical and classical periods. Most of these works have come down to us in a fragmentary form and only indirectly through the codification of Justinian and other post-classical compilations of law. But questions arise as to whether many of the surviving fragments accurately reflect the original sources from which they were derived, as they may have been simplified and in various ways adapted to the needs and purposes of the post-classical compilers. The only juristic work from the classical period that has survived in its entirety is the Institutes of Gaius, a textbook dating from the middle of the second century AD. Although the manuscript containing this work dates from the fifth or early sixth century AD – more than three centuries after Gaius's time – it is believed that it is a faithful reproduction of the original text. This was confirmed after the discovery in 1933 in Egypt of fragments of another manuscript of Gaius's Institutes, probably of the late fourth century, matching the text of the first manuscript. About a tenth of the manuscript's content is lost or totally illegible, but some of the missing parts have been reconstructed from extracts included in later compilations.

Another important source of juristic literature is the so-called Vatican Fragments (*Fragmenta Vaticana*), a general collection of juristic opinions and imperial legislation discovered in the Vatican library in 1821.[1] A further collection, known as the *Collatio legum Mosaicarum et Romanarum* (A Comparison of Mosaic and Roman Law), dates from the late fourth or early fifth century AD and was first published in Paris in 1573.[2] This collection has been particularly helpful in reconstructing the *Pauli Sententiae*, an important work based on the writings of the classical jurist Paul. Extracts from the latter work, which was produced by an unknown author in about 300 AD, have been included in a number of post-classical compilations besides the *Collatio*, as well as in the Digest of Justinian. In this connection the *Ulpiani Epitome* may be mentioned as well. This was probably an abridgment of the *liber singularis regularum*, a

---

1 This collection was published in Rome in 1823. See chapter 10 below.

2 The original title of this manuscript is *Lex dei quam praecipit dominus ad Moysen* (The divine law which the Lord gave to Moses). It appears that in this work the author wanted to demonstrate that Roman law agreed with or possibly even was based on Mosaic law. See chapter 10 below.

work of the jurist Ulpian, produced by an unknown author at the beginning of the fourth century AD. A manuscript of Ulpian's *Epitome* dating from the tenth century and first published in 1549 is now kept in the Vatican library. An additional source of juristic literature is the *Consultatio* (*consultatio veteris cuiusdam iurisconsulti* or 'a Consultation with an Ancient Jurisconsult'), first published by Cujas in 1577.[3] In this work a number of legal questions are defined and then answered on the basis of statements drawn from classical and post-classical authorities. These include various passages from Paul's *Sententiae* and extracts from collections of imperial legislation (the Gregorian, Hermogenian and Theodosian Codes). Among the main surviving sources from the eastern part of the Roman empire are the *Scholia Sinaitica* [4] and the Syrio-Roman Book of Law. The former consists of extracts from a commentary in Greek on Ulpian's *libri ad Sabinum*, probably of the late fifth century. The Syrio-Roman Book of Law consists of imperial constitutions and juristic writings and appears to have been used at the law schools of the East as a textbook for students.[5]

Important sources of information on the development of Roman law are also the legal codes of the post-classical period. Among the earliest of these codes were two private collections of imperial laws, the *Codex Gregorianus* and the *Codex Hermogenianus*, compiled at the end of the third century AD. Although neither has survived, parts of these codes have come down to us through other post-classical compilations.[6] The first official codification of imperial legislation was the Theodosian Code (*Codex Theodosianus*), published in 438 AD. Fragments of this code have been included in later collections, such as the Code of Justinian and the *Lex*

---

3 Cujas, who taught at the University of Bourges, was one of the leading representatives of the Humanist School of the sixteenth and seventeenth centuries. See chapter 11 below.

4 So called because the relevant manuscript was found, in 1880, at the monastery of St Catherine of Sinai, in Egypt.

5 Most of the surviving legal literature of the pre-Justinianic period can be found in a number of easy-to-use collections produced by modern scholars. See e.g., T. Baviera & J. Furlani, *Fontes Iuris Romani Anteiustiniani* (FIRA) II, *Auctores*, Florence 1940, repr. 1968; P. Girard & F. Senn, *Textes de droit Romain* I, 6th edn, Paris 1937, repr. 1967; O. Lenel, *Palingenesia Iuris Civilis* I-II, Leipzig 1889, repr. Graz 1960 – a reconstruction of the texts of the classical Roman jurists; Lenel also produced a reconstruction of the praetorian Edict entitled *Das Edictum Perpetuum*, 1927, repr. 1966 and 1985. For more on modern sources see chapters 8 and 10 below.

6 Extracts can be found in the Code of Justinian, the Vatican Fragments, the *Collatio*, the *Consultatio*, and in Germanic codes of Roman law, such as the *Lex Romana Visigothorum* and the *Lex Romana Burgundionum*.

Romana Visigothorum. Moreover two manuscripts, one dating from the fifth and the other from the sixth century, have been found containing parts of the code's original text. Several important reconstructions of the Theodosian Code have been published since the sixteenth century.[7] Another collection of imperial laws is the so-called Sirmondian Constitutions (*constitutiones Sirmondi*).[8] This contains a number of imperial constitutions dating from the first half of the fifth century AD. Besides the above compilations of Roman origin, important sources are also the Germanic codes of Roman law (*leges Romanae Barbarorum*) issued by Germanic kings after the fall of the Roman empire of the West for use by their Roman subjects. These compilations include the *lex Romana Visigothorum*, also known as the Breviary of Alaric (*Breviarium Alarici*), the *lex Romana Burgundionum*, and the *Edictum Theodorici*. Although the Roman law contained in these compilations is but a crude and diluted version of the law of the classical period, their importance for the study of Roman law today is great. Besides offering a vivid account of the stage of the law and society at the beginning of the early Middle Ages, these codes have preserved valuable legal records from earlier times which cannot be found in any other sources.[9]

But the most important source of our knowledge about the historical development of Roman law, especially during the late classical and post-classical periods, is the great codification of the law which was carried out in the middle of the sixth century on the orders of Emperor Justinian. It was Justinian who finally succeeded, at a moment when the ancient world was dissolving, in putting together, in a form which could survive, the vast literature of Roman law stretching back over hundreds of years of legal development. The Justinianic codification is made up of four parts: a) the Digest (*Digesta*), containing a large number of excerpts from the works of the classical jurists;[10] b) the Code (*Codex*), a collection of imperial constitutions from the time of Emperor Hadrian (middle of the second century AD); c) the Institutes (*Institutiones*), an introductory textbook on law based on the Institutes of Gaius and d) the Novels (*Novellae leges*),

---

7 One of the earliest editions of the Theodosian Code is that of Gothofredus, published in Lyons in 1665.

8 So called from the fact that it was first published by Sirmond (J. Sirmondus) in 1631.

9 For more on the character of these works and for information about modern reconstructions see chapter 10 below.

10 The earliest surviving copy of the Digest dates from the middle of the sixth century AD. This manuscript, which provided the basis for the modern editions of the Digest, is kept in Florence (it was moved there from Pisa at the beginning of the fifteenth century), and is known as '*Codex Florentinus*'.

containing enactments of Justinian subsequent to the publication of the Code. The term *Corpus Iuris Civilis*, by which the Justinianic codification is known, was first introduced by Dionysius Gothofredus, who edited the work in 1583.[11]

Other literary sources

Much of what we know about the history of Roman law is derived from the surviving works of Roman and Greek historians, geographers, grammarians and lexicographers, orators, poets and philosophers. These sources provide valuable information about the socio-economic, political and cultural context within which the Roman legal institutions developed. The beginning of Roman historical writing coincides with the emergence of Latin literature at the end of the third century BC.[12] The earliest Roman historians, referred to as 'annalists', are believed to have had access to Rome's official records (*annales maximi* or *tabulae pontificum*) which, from an early age, were under the supervision of the *pontifex maximus*, head of the most powerful of Rome's priestly colleges. These records chronicled important events, such as eclipses and other natural phenomena of a religious significance, wars and the names of the elected magistrates, on a year-by-year basis. But almost all documentary evidence for the period preceding the fourth century perished – according to some annalists this occurred during the sack of Rome by the invading Gauls in c. 390 BC. As a result, the annalists tended to describe Rome's remote past by filling in the scanty documentary evidence at their disposal with materials derived largely from the oral tradition, which consisted chiefly of folk-tales and the traditions of the Roman nobility. Although these stories tell us much about the cultural framework of the early Roman society, their value as sources of historical information is regarded as highly questionable. And since later Roman historians relied on the annalistic inheritance for their own reconstructions of Rome's early history, their accounts are not taken at face value but are viewed in the light of the findings of modern scientific archaeology, linguistics and comparative philology. Moreover, one has to keep in mind that, as most of the leading historians were members of the Roman upper classes, the world-picture they convey is often affected by their ideological and family bias and their political affiliations. Of

---

11 For a closer look at Justinian's codification and information on modern editions see chapter 10 below.

12 Among the earliest writers of Roman history were Fabius Pictor and Cincius. On the origins of Roman historical writing see M. L. W. Laistner, *The Greater Roman Historians*, London 1947, repr. 1977, ch. 1.

particular importance are the works of Greek historians who, insofar as they can be seen as outside observers, probably offer a more disinterested description of events than Roman writers.

Of the Greek and Roman historians of the late Republic and early Empire, the following are among the most important: Polybius of Megalopolis (c. 208-118 BC), whose Universal History offers a vivid account of Rome's wars of expansion from 220 to 145 BC;[13] Diodorus Siculus (c. 80-20 BC), who composed a general history of the world from the earliest times down to the first century BC;[14] Dionysius of Halicarnassus (first century BC), author of the Roman Antiquities, a comprehensive narration of Roman history down to the middle of the third century BC;[15] Posidonius of Apamea (first century BC), also a celebrated scientist, geographer and philosopher, who wrote a history of Rome from 145 BC down to his own times;[16] Plutarch (c. 46-120 AD), author of the Parallel Lives, a work that compares the lives of famous figures of Greek and Roman history; Sallust (c. 87-35 BC), whose subsequent reputation as one of the foremost historians of his time rested mainly upon his Histories, an exhaustive account of the period 78-67 BC, and to a lesser extent on his monographs on the Catilinarian conspiracy (*Bellum Catilinae*) and the Jugurthine War (*Bellum Iugurthinum*);[17] Livy of Padua (Titus Livius, 59 BC-17 AD), whose monumental history of Rome (*Ab urbe condita*), covering the whole span of Roman history from the foundation of Rome down to the early years of the first century AD, was well-known all over the Roman world;[18] Tacitus (Publius Cornelius Tacitus, c. 55-123 AD), author of a series of famous works providing valuable information about

---

[13] But only the first five books of Polybius's work, covering a period down to 216 BC, have come down to us complete. Of the rest only fragments have been preserved through later historical works.

[14] Of the 40 books of Diodorus's World History only books 1-8 and 11-20 are fully preserved; of the rest we have only fragments.

[15] Of the 20 books of the Roman Antiquities only the first 10 survive complete.

[16] Only fragments of Posidonius's works have survived.

[17] Of Sallust's Histories very little has come down to us, but both his shorterworks have survived.

[18] Of the 142 books of Livy's history only books 1-10 (covering the period 753-243 BC) and 21-45 (covering the period 218-167 BC) have survived complete; from the lost books we have fragments as well as two sets of abridgments. Livy viewed historical writing as a literary category based upon the narration of dramatic events. He was interested not so much in historical research as in digesting materials taken from earlier sources and then preserving them in his own unique literary style.

the history of the early imperial era;[19] Dio Cassius Cocceianus (c. 155-235 AD), who composed a general history of Rome from the beginning of the archaic era down to 229 AD;[20] Pliny the Younger (Gaius Plinius Caecilius Secundus, c. 61-114 AD), whose Letters include an account of speeches he made as an advocate in extortion trials before the senate; Suetonius (Gaius Suetonius Tranquillus, c. 70-150 AD), whose writings include the Biographies and the Lives of the Caesars (*De Vita Caesarum*).[21] Another source of information is the *Historia Augusta* (probably the work of six authors), a collection of biographies of Roman Emperors, Caesars and usurpers from 117 to 284 AD.

Among the best known historians of the later imperial period are: Ammianus Marcellinus (c. 330-395 AD), whose History (*XXXI Libri Rerum Gestarum*) covers the period 96-378 AD;[22] Flavius Josephus (c. 38-95 AD), who in his work the Jewish Antiquities, a history of the Jews from the Creation to 66 AD, has preserved many Roman edicts and rescripts as well as information about several Roman emperors taken from authoritative Roman sources; Lactantius (c. 240-320 AD), author of a work describing the trials of the Christians under Emperors Diocletian and Galerius;[23] Eusebius, Bishop of Caesarea (c. 260-340 AD), who composed a Church History covering the period down to 324 AD, as well as

---

19 The earliest of Tacitus's five works, entitled *Agricola* and *Germania*, were written in 98 AD. The first is a short biography of Agricola, his father-in-law, who played an important part in the Roman conquest of Britain. In this work Tacitus gives us a clear picture of the moral beliefs and political ideas prevailing among the members of the newly formed imperial aristocracy. The second work is a description of the geographical, social and cultural characteristics of Germany. Between the years 104-109 AD Tacitus wrote his Histories, an account of the period 69-96 AD in five books. About 107 AD he wrote his Dialogue on Orators (*Dialogus de Oratoribus*), a treatise of literary criticism discussing the decline of forensic eloquence in his times. His famous Annals, probably written between 115-117 AD, cover the history of the period 14-68 AD.

20 But many parts of Dio's work are lost. Of the 80 books of his Roman History we have only books 36-60 complete; the others are known through the summaries of the Byzantine historians Zonaras (twelfth century), who prepared an epitome of books 1-21, and Xiphilinos (eleventh century), who wrote an epitome of books 36-80.

21 Suetonius's Lives of the Caesars contains the biographies of Rome's rulers from Julius Caesar (first century BC) up to Domitian (late first century AD).

22 Of this work only books 14-31 (dealing with the period 353-378 AD) survive.

23 Lactantius's work is entitled On the Deaths of the Persecutors.

comprehensive chronological tables of the Greek and Roman history;[24] Cassiodorus (c. 490-538 AD), writer of numerous works, including the *Chronica*, a summary of the Roman history down to 519 AD; and Procopius (sixth century AD), thanks to whom we have a vivid account of the age of Justinian.[25]

Besides the historical works, important sources of Roman legal history are the writings of political and forensic orators, such as Cato the Elder (Marcus Porcius Cato, 234-149 BC), Cicero (M. Tullius Cicero, 106-43 BC), known also for his writings on philosophy and political theory,[26] the philosopher Seneca (Lucius Annaeus Seneca, 4 BC-65 AD) and Pliny the Younger, mentioned before.[27] Our sources include also the works of Greek and Roman geographers, such as Strabo of Amasia (64 BC-21 AD), whose *Geographica* survived almost intact;[28] biographers, such as Cornelius Nepos (first century BC), and Plutarch and Suetonius, mentioned before; antiquarians and philologists, such as Varro (Marcus Terentius Varro, 116-27 BC),[29] Aulus Gellius (second century AD),[30] and Valerius

---

24 Eusebius' chronological tables, which have survived both in Latin and in an Armenian translation, provide us with valuable information about ancient chronology.

25 Procopius wrote the History of the Wars of Justinian in 8 books. As he was among the officials who accompanied Justinian's generals in their campaigns, he gives us a first-hand account of events. Besides his historical writings, Procopius produced a number of other works, including a book called the *Anekdota* or Secret History in which he criticises the private lives of Justinian and his wife Theodora.

26 Cicero expressed his views on ethics, politics and law in a series of celebrated treatises. In his *De re publica* (On the State), a work inspired by Plato's Republic, Cicero delineates the actual constitution of the ideal state. His famous works *De legibus* (On the Laws), *De officiis* (On Duties) and *De senectute* (On Old Age) reflect Cicero's political, ethical and philosophical thinking. Besides his oratorical and philosophical works, Cicero left an extensive collection of letters which contain valuable information about Roman society and politics during the last century of the Republican era.

27 Orations, one of the chief weapons employed in political contest, were addressed to political bodies, such as the senate or the assemblies of the Roman people. Among the greatest orators of the republican period were the Gracchi brothers, Lucius Licinius Crassus and Quintus Hortensius Hortalus.

28 In this Strabo describes the countries of the Roman world, their geographical characteristics, their peoples and their histories. Besides his Geography, Strabo also composed an extensive historical work from which only some fragments survive.

29 Varro's main work, Antiquities, did not survive, however. Only parts of his treatises On the Latin Language and On Rural Conditions have come down to us.

Maximus (first century AD). Of some importance for the study of Roman legal life during the pre-classical period are the comedies of Plautus (c. 254-184 BC) and Terentius (c. 190-159 BC), although it is difficult to say whether their works give an accurate picture of life in Rome or they reflect the Greek models upon which they are based. Finally, information relevant to the history of Roman law is derived from the works on agriculture of Cato (Marcus Porcius Cato, second century BC) and other writers.[31]

Epigraphic sources

Besides the various literary sources, valuable information about the development of Roman law is derived from a variety of authentic records of Roman date. These include inscriptions on tablets of stone or metal, inscriptions on the walls of arches, temples and other buildings, writings on leaves of papyrus or parchment and other documents. A large number of epigraphic texts reproduce statutes, decisions of the senate, imperial decrees, municipal charters, calendars and official records, speeches of the emperors, judicial decisions, military discharge certificates and agreements concerning private transactions. To this category of sources belongs, for example, the *Res Gestae Divi Augusti*, a text recording the most important events of the reign of Augustus. This is also known as *Monumentum Ancyranum*, because a copy of it was found inscribed on the wall of a temple in Ankara, Turkey.[32] Other examples of documents of this kind include: an inscription from Cyrene containing four edicts of Augustus and a senatorial decree concerning matters of procedure in extortion cases;[33] a bronze plaque found in Lyons with the text of a speech delivered by Emperor Claudius;[34] and an inscription reproducing the text of a law conferring on Emperor Vespasian the same legal powers as his predecessors (the famous *lex de imperio Vespasiani*).[35] An important

---

30 Author of a book on literary criticism entitled Attic Nights (*Noctes Atticae*).

31 A collection of extracts from the various literary sources concerning Roman law can be found in C. G. Bruns, O. Gradenwitz, *Fontes iuris romani antiqui*, Tubingen 1909, repr. Aalen 1969; see also P. F. Girard & F. Senn, *Textes de droit romain*, 6th edn, Paris 1937, repr. 1967.

32 For the text see P. A. Brunt & J. M. Moore, *Res Gestae Divi Augusti: The Achievements of the Divine Augustus*, Oxford 1967; J. Gagé, *Res gestae divi Augusti*, Paris 1950; H. Volkmann, *Res gestae divi Augusti* , Berlin 1969.

33 These can be found in F. De Visscher, *Les édits d'Auguste découverts `a Cyrène*, Louvain and Paris 1940.

34 See H. Dessau, *Inscriptiones Latinae Selectae*, Berlin 1892-1916, 212.

35 See P. A. Brunt, 'Lex de imperio Vespasiani', *Journal of Roman Studies* lxvii 1977, 95-116.

document dating from the early fifth century AD is the *Notitia Dignitatum*, an official list of all administrative and military posts in the empire from provincial governors upwards. This document provides important information about the organisation of the imperial administration during the late imperial epoch.[36] Another inscriptional text from the same period offering us a picture of the social and economic conditions of the times is the famous Edict of Prices (*Edictum de pretiis*, 304 AD) of Emperor Diocletian who, in an effort to stabilise the currency, stipulated maximum prices and wages over a detailed range of goods and services.[37] Information on the social and economic conditions that prevailed at different stages of Roman history is derived also from inscriptions on tomb-stones and mausoleums of various ages.[38] A rich source of information about every aspect of Roman life are, moreover, the numerous letters and other documents which have been preserved on leaves of papyrus, parchment and on clay and wooden tablets. Recorded on leaves of papyrus are, for example, records of legal proceedings, legal decisions, tax records, official memoranda, leases, sales, petitions to the imperial government, contracts and wills, private accounts and letters. This category includes also ostraca, bits of broken pot on which are recorded, for instance, tax receipts and receipts for military rations.[39]

---

36 For the text see O. Seeck (ed.), *Notitia Dignitatum, Accedunt notitia urbis Constantinopolitanae et latercula provinciarum*, Berlin 1876, repr. 1962.

37 The text of this law can be found in M. Giacchero (ed.) *Edictum Diocletiani et Collegarum de pretiis rerum venalium*, Genoa 1974; see also S. Lauffer, *Diokletians Preisedikt*, Berlin 1971.

38 Modern collections of inscriptional texts include: *Corpus Inscriptionum Latinarum*, Berlin: Deutsche Akademik der Wissenschaften 1863; H. Dessau, *Inscriptiones Latinae selectae*, Berlin 1892-1916; A. Degrassi, *Inscriptiones Latinae liberae rei publicae*, vls 1-2, Florence 1957-1963; A. E. Gordon & S. Joyce, *Album of Dated Latin Inscriptions*, Berkeley 1958; E. H. Warmington, *Remains of Old Latin*, London 1940; R. Cagnat, J. Toutain, P. Jouguet, G. Lafaye, *Inscriptiones Graecae ad res Romanas pertinentes*, 1,3,4, Paris 1906-1927, repr. Rome 1964. And see L. Keppie, *Understanding Roman Inscriptions*, London 1991; J. E. Sandys, *Latin Epigraphy: An Introduction to the Study of Latin Inscriptions*, Cambridge 1926, repr. Chicago 1974; B. W. Jones & R. D. Milns, *The Use of Documentary Evidence in Roman Imperial History*, Sydney 1984.

39 Modern collections of this type of material include: L. Mitteis & U. Wilcken, *Grundzüge und Chrestomathie der Papyruskunde*, Leipzig 1912, rep. Hildesheim 1963; P. M. Meyer, *Juristiche Papyri*, Berlin 1920, repr. Chicago 1976; A. S. Hunt & C. C. Edgar, *Select Papyri* (text and English translation), London 1932, 1959, 1963; W. L. Westerman & A. A. Schiller, *Apokrimata – Decisions of Septemius Severus on Legal Matters*, New York 1954. And see V.

The unwritten archaeological record

Finally, an important source of information about the historical framework of Roman law is archaeological evidence – the evidence of buildings and structures surviving above ground or brought to light by archaeological excavations, together with the artifacts and other finds connected with them. By comparing remains from different sites and from different periods of the same site archaeologists can reconstruct, by reference also to other sources of historical information, the social and cultural history of a region. Of special interest for the legal historian are coins, commemorative medallions and seals, illustrations and sculptures. Coins, in particular, often used for propaganda purposes in both the Republican and imperial epochs, can supply valuable information about the political and economic conditions that prevailed at the period of their issue.[40]

Fundamental Concepts and Distinctions

Fas and *ius*

During the earliest phase of Roman history[41] social life was governed by a body of customary norms, the *mores maiorum* or 'the ways of our forefathers', which the Romans had inherited from their ancestors. Some of these norms were regarded as being of human creation, whilst others derived their binding force from their supposed divine origin. The divine

---

Arangio-Ruiz, *Studi Epigrafici e Papirologici*, Naples 1974; R. Taubenschlag, *The Law of Greco-Roman Egypt in the light of the Papyri*, Warsaw 1955. See also R. Cavenaile, *Corpus Papyrorum Latinarum*, Wiesbaden 1958; E. G. Turner, *Greek Papyri: an Introduction*, Oxford 1968. Collections of legislative acts and private transactions taken from various literary and epigraphic sources can be found in the *Fontes iuris romani anteiustiniani* (FIRA) I, *Leges*, by S. Riccobono (ed.), Florence 1941, repr. 1968, and III, *Negotia*, by V. Arangio-Ruiz (ed.), Florence 1943, repr. 1969. See also C. G. Bruns (ed.), *Fontes iuris romani antiqui* I, *Leges et negotia*, Tubingen 1909, repr. Aalen 1969. Many of the legislative enactments contained in these collections have been translated into English by A. C. Johnston, P. R. Coleman-Norton & F. C. Bourne in *Ancient Roman Statutes*, Austin 1961.

40 See M.H. Crawford, *Roman Republican Coinage*, Cambridge 1974; H. Mattingly, *Roman Coins from the Earliest Times to the Fall of the Western Empire*, 2nd edn, London 1960, repr. 1967; M. Grant, *Roman History from Coins*, 2nd edn, Cambridge 1968.

41 The Monarchy and early Republic.

element in this system was signified by the word *fas*.[42] The norms associated with *fas* occupied a higher plane and had a fuller scope and wider range than man-made rules. These norms demanded, for example, that no military operation or other public undertaking should be embarked upon without the sanction of the divine will (as revealed through the prescribed religious rituals). They enjoined hospitality to foreigners because strangers were regarded as being under the protection of the gods. They punished murder as an offence against the gods. They forbade the displacement of boundary stones, for boundary stones were regarded as being under the protection of the gods. Conduct that violated the divine law was referred to as *nefas*, and was regarded as disrupting the harmonious relationship between the community and its gods (the Romans believed that such conduct could arouse the wrath of the gods and that the whole community could be struck by misfortune as a result). The enforcement of the norms of *fas* was entrusted to the priests who discharged their task in their own way by means devised and administered by them. The breach of a rule associated with *fas* rendered the offender impious and the punishment inflicted upon him was expiatory in character. Its purpose was to heal the condition of collective impurity and thus to restore the state of harmony (*amicitia*) between the community and the gods.

Behaviour that caused no harm to others was regarded as conforming with *ius*, the man-made norms of social conduct governing human relations. The term *iniuria* was used to denote any violation of the *ius*. The word *ius* originally signified that which is due in human relations, the power of a human being to act with reference to other human beings. In historical Latin the word *ius* was taken to mean 'right' or 'power'.[43] With the gradual differentiation of human and divine law and the development of Roman legal thinking the term *ius* came also to denote what we mean by the word 'law' in a broad sense: the entire system of norms, whether written or unwritten, by which the rights and concomitant powers of the members of a community are defined, protected and enforced. In this respect *ius*, or law in a broad sense, was distinguished from morals (*mos*, *mores*). The latter referred to the rules of conduct which are addressed to the conscience of a person and which are not formally enforceable.

But in the archaic period the two spheres of *ius* and *fas* largely overlapped. The link between the two concepts is evident from the fact that for a very long period the interpretation and application of the norms of *ius*

---

42 The word *fatum* denoted that which has been decreed by the gods and which, for that reason, must inevitably occur.

43 Such as a person's right to seize by force a thing justly claimed or a person liable to retributive punishment.

was in the hands of the priesthood. Their connection is manifested also by the fact that, during the regal era, the king performed functions pertaining to both human and divine law. Every important act of a Roman citizen, whether of a public or a private nature, assumed a religious character and its validity was made to depend upon the determination of the divine will. Even after the Romans began to distinguish between divine and human law, in the later archaic period, the connection between *ius* and *fas* continued to exercise an influence on Roman legal thinking and practice. Thus, both legislative acts and private agreements usually began with some reference to the gods and ritual continued to play an important part in legal transactions.

Moreover, the term *ius*, besides its purely descriptive function, was always perceived as embodying a strong normative element reflecting the relationship between law and justice (*iustitia*). Thus, *ius* has been defined by classical jurists as 'the art of good and equitable',[44] and as that which is always 'just and fair'.[45] The same relationship is also reflected in Ulpian's definition of jurisprudence as 'the knowledge of things divine and human, and of what is just and unjust'.[46] From this viewpoint, Ulpian says that *ius* requires living honestly, harming no-one and giving each one his due'.[47] *Ius*, in this broad normative sense, is not the same as morality nor, of course, the same as posited law; rather, it is right law, or posited law as it ought to be in the light of what morality and justice ordain.[48] The impact of morality on law is evidenced by the fact that, in the administration of justice, reference was often made to general moral standards, as in cases where legal transactions were declared null as being contrary to generally accepted moral norms (*contra bonos mores*).

But the Romans interpreted the term *ius* in more than one way, depending upon the context in which the term was used or the legal relationship it referred to. Sometimes it was used to denote a specific public or private right or power granted to an individual by law for the pursuance of a legally recognised interest.[49] *Ius* also indicated the personal

---

44 '*Ius est ars boni et aequi.*' See D. 1. 1. 1. (Celsus).

45 D. 1. 1. 11. (Paulus).

46 '*Iurisprudentia est divinarum atque humanarum rerum notitia, iusti atque iniusti scientia*'. See D. 1. 1. 10. 2; *Inst.* 1. 1. 1. Ulpian defines justice as the constant and perpetual will to give each one his due ('*iustitia est constans et perpetua voluntas ius suum cuique tribuere*'). See D. 1. 1. 10; *Inst.* 1. 1.

47 '*Iuris praecepta sunt haec: honeste vivere , alterum non laedere, suum cuique tribuere*'. D. 1. 1. 10. 1; *Inst.* 1. 1. 3.

48 This meaning of *ius* is better conveyed in English by the word 'right' as a noun.

49 For example, the phrase *ius in re aliena* denoted a right in another person's property, such as a servitude or a pledge. The term *ius honorum* signified the

legal status of a person, as in the phrases *persona sui iuris* (a person in charge of his own affairs), and *persona alieni iuris* (a person under the power of another). Moreover, in procedural language the term *ius* denoted the place where a Roman magistrate performed his judicial functions.[50] In a similar way, the word *iniuria* was capable of several interpretations, depending upon the nature of the violation of *ius* it was used to describe. In general, any act that was done contrary to *ius* (*contra ius*) was called *iniuria*. The same term was used to signify a specific offence against one's person or reputation.[51]

Ius and *lex*

Ius, as defined above, was distinguished from *lex* (plural *leges*). The latter term refers to a law enacted by a competent legislative organ in accordance with a prescribed procedure. In the archaic and pre-classical periods the term *leges* was used to denote statutes enacted by the Roman popular assemblies.[52] In the classical and post-classical periods the term *leges* referred to laws originating from a number of sources, such as decrees of the senate and imperial constitutions. Sometimes the term *leges* was used to signify the entire body of posited law, irrespective of its sources.

A *lex*, which by definition pertained to a specific type of legal relationship, drew upon *ius* but was not identified with it. The normative principles of *ius*, under which the question of lawfulness or unlawfulness was decided, were not reducible to the body of formally enacted laws. These principles were perceived of as pre-existing and transcending the enacted law, which merely prescribed how *ius* was to be implemented under certain circumstances. Unlawfulness was defined primarily in relation to *ius*, for an unlawful act was taken to encroach upon the principles of *ius* which informed the particular legislative enactment under which the act was subsumed. From this viewpoint, the word *iniuria* signified any infringement of the law as an act done '*contra ius*'. Furthermore, the application of a *lex* was typically strict ('*dura lex sed lex*'), for an act or dispute was dealt with according to the letter of the law, without reference to the circumstances of the individual case. Thus, under the system of *legis actiones* (actions based on the law) of early law, a person suing another had to make his claim strictly according to the

---

right of a Roman citizen to stand for public office. The term *ius intercessionis* referred to the power of a higher magistrate or a tribune to block by veto official acts of other magistrates.

50 D. 1. 1. 11. (Paulus).

51 *Inst*. 4. 4. pr.

52 G. 1. 3.

formula prescribed by the statute he was relying upon. If the wrong formula was used the action was rejected.[53] On the other hand, the application of *ius* was seen as flexible and thus adaptable to the circumstances of each particular case. Whereas the implementation of a *lex* was based on purely formal criteria, the implementation of *ius* was based on its intrinsic rightness. As we will explain later, it is the modification and refinement of enacted law, through the application of equitable principles – principles pertaining to *ius* – that characterises the praetors' and, in later years, the jurists' contribution to the development of Roman law.[54]

In the post-classical era the term *ius* came to denote the entire body of law based on the works of the leading jurists of the classical period. *Lex*, on the other hand, signified the law contained in the enactments of the emperors, the principal source of law of this period.

Ius non scriptum, ius scriptum

The Romans distinguished between two general categories of *ius*, or law in a broad sense, unwritten law (*ius non scriptum*) and written law (*ius scriptum*). In the category of unwritten law belonged the customary law of the archaic period. Custom (*consuetudo*) was a source of norms which derived their binding force from the tacit consent of the people and their long-standing practice within the community.[55] As was noted earlier, during the Monarchy and the early years of the Republic there appears to have been no written law in Rome. Knowledge of law was handed down as a tradition (*mos maiorum*) in the patrician families. But as legal relations grew more complicated and the population increased in size, the role of

---

53 See chapter 4 below.

54 The distinction between and interrelationship of posited law and right (as a noun) is a characteristic feature of Continental European legal systems based on the Roman legal inheritance. The Germans distinguish between *Gesetz* and *Recht*, the French between *loi* and *droit*, the Italians between *legge* and *diritto*, the Greeks between *nomos* (Nomos) and *dikaeon* (Dikaion). *Ius* in the sense of right (like the words *Recht*, *droit*, *diritto*, *dikaeon*) is a normative concept emphasising the relationship between justice and sound (posited) law. On the concept of *ius* see A. A. Schiller, *Roman Law: Mechanisms of Development*, New York 1978, 224 ff; M. Kaser, *Römische Rechtsgeschichte*, Göttingen 1976, 59 ff; F. Wieacker, *Römische Rechtsgeschichte*, Munich 1988, 267 ff; A. Guarino, *Storia del diritto romano*, Naples 1996, 124 ff, 420 ff.

55 See D. 1. 3. 32. (Julianus); *Inst.* 1. 2. 9. Consider also Cicero, *de invent.* 2. 22. 67. Besides *consuetudo* , custom was also referred to as *usus* or *mos*. None of these terms had a fixed or specific meaning however. The term *mos regionis* was used in later years to signify local custom, although no clear distinction between this and general custom seems to have been recognised.

custom as the main source of social regulation began to diminish. The existing customary norms, often uncertain and difficult to prove, could no longer provide the certainty and security which a complex system of social and economic relations required. Thus, the need arose for the development of legislation, i.e. the organisation of law by public authority. The decline of custom and the emergence of legislation was accompanied by the strengthening of the role of the state and the improvement of the position of the lower classes. But the introduction of written law did not eliminate the role of custom as a source of social regulation. Customary norms continued to govern aspects of social life left outside the state's sphere of control. In addition to that, custom played an important part in the interpretation of the law[56] and many of the laws which the state, through its organs, formally enacted were based on existing customary norms. Many of Rome's social, political and legal institutions were derived from custom, such as the family and clan structures, the institution of patronage and clientship, the earliest forms of property ownership and property transference and a great deal of the formalities associated with legal procedure. Some of these institutions have had their origin in customs whose roots lay in the most remote past of Roman history while others in customs that emerged later, during the formative years of the Roman state. Many of these later customs reflected the strong Etruscan and Greek influence on aspects of Roman social and cultural life. Although custom has always had an indirect influence on law, for a very long time, especially during the classical period, it was not included among the sources of law, having been entirely superseded by legislation. Custom began again to be regarded as a source of law during the post-classical period.[57]

In the category of written law (*ius scriptum*) fell the statutes (*leges*), the resolutions of the plebeian assembly (*plebiscita*), the decrees of the senate (*senatus consulta*) and the edicts of those magistrates who possessed the *ius edicendi* (the right of issuing binding ordinances). To these were in later times added the imperial constitutions (*constitutiones principum*) and the written answers of those jurists whose opinions on questions of law had been recognised as authoritative (*responsa prudentium*).[58] The publication of the laws of the Twelve Tables, in the middle of the fifth century BC, marks the starting-point in the development of written law.[59]

---

56 The jurist Paul referred to custom as 'the best interpreter of laws'. See D. 1. 3. 37.

57 See *Inst.* 1. 2. 9-10.

58 G. 1. 2; *Inst.* 1. 2. 3.

59 On the distinction between *ius non scriptum* and *ius scriptum* see A. A. Schiller, *Roman Law: Mechanisms of Development*, New York 1978, 254 ff; R. Monier,

Ius civile, ius gentium

The term *ius civile* denoted, in a broad sense, the law which governed a political community and prescribed the rights and obligations of its members.[60] Thus, with respect to the Roman state, *ius civile* signified the entire body of Roman law, irrespective of its sources. This understanding of the term was associated with the principle of the 'personality of the laws' – a principle widely recognised in antiquity. According to this principle, it was nationality rather than place of residence that determined a person's legal status. A person lived under the law of the state or political community to which he belonged. In this respect, the Roman *ius civile* (also known as *ius Quiritium*)[61] was the law that applied only to Roman citizens (*cives Romani*), and the term *ius civitatis* was used to denote the legal rights to which only Roman citizens were entitled.[62] The Romans drew a distinction between two categories of such rights: public rights (*publica iura*) and private rights (*privata iura*). The former category included, for example, the right of voting in a popular assembly (*ius suffragii*), the right of standing for public office (*ius honorum*) and the right of appealing from a magistrate to the people's assembly against sentences involving death or the loss of personal freedom or citizenship (*ius provocationis*). In the category of private rights fell the right of contracting a regular Roman marriage (*ius connubii*), the right of acquiring, owning and transferring property according to law (*ius commercii*) and the right of making or inheriting under a Roman will (*ius testamenti factio*). A person entitled to all the rights of the citizenship was referred to as *civis optimo iure*. But not all Roman citizens were *cives optimo iure* (for example, Roman women did not enjoy the *ius suffragii* and the *ius honorum*). The primary rights of the citizens entailed a number of derivative rights or privileges. For example the *ius itineris*, i.e. the right of a person to go through another person's property, was a secondary right with respect to *ius commercii*. The *ius intercessionis*, i.e. the right of the

---

Manuel élémentaire de droit romain, Aalen 1977, 7; A. Guarino, *Diritto privato romano*, Naples 2001, 136 ff.

60 According to Gaius 'the rules enacted by a given state for its own members are peculiar to itself and are called civil law' (G. 1. 1.).

61 *Quirites* was the name by which the early Romans called themselves in early times (*populus Romanus Quirite* or *populus Romanus Quiritium*).

62 Hence the description of the Roman *ius civile* as '*ius proprium Romanorum*'. On the notion of *ius civile* see A. A. Schiller, *Roman Law: Mechanisms of Development*, New York 1978, 366 ff, 525 ff; M. Kaser, *Römische Rechtsgeschichte*, Göttingen 1976, 130 ff; A. Guarino, *Diritto privato romano*, Naples 2001, 128 ff.

higher magistrates to veto official acts of other magistrates, was a secondary or derivative right with respect to the *ius honorum*.[63]

From an early period, communities affiliated with Rome were granted limited rights under the Roman *ius civile*. The members of these communities occupied an intermediate position between Roman citizens and foreigners. Thus, what was referred to as Latin law (*ius Latinum* or *ius Latii*) applied to certain groups who enjoyed some of the rights of Roman citizenship. These groups included the inhabitants of communities in Latium, colonies founded by Romans and members of other Latin states (*coloniae Latinae*), as well as certain categories of freedmen. The term *peregrinus*, on the other hand, was used to denote any free person who was not a citizen of Rome.[64] Initially foreigners (*peregrini*) living in Rome had no rights under Roman law.

From an early period the Romans came to realise that certain institutions of their own *ius civile* could also be found in the legal systems of other nations. As contracts of sale, service and loan, for example, were recognised by many systems, it was assumed that the principles governing these were everywhere in force in the same way. These institutions which Roman law had in common with other legal systems were thought of by the Romans as belonging to the law of nations (*ius gentium*) in a broad sense. But this understanding of the *ius gentium* was of little practical value for the Roman lawyer, for the specific rules relating to the operation of such generally recognised institutions differed considerably from one legal system to another. Related with the above understanding of *ius gentium*, as the legal principles observed by all nations, was the development of a body of law which was of particular importance to the Roman lawyer. As the number of foreigners living in Rome continued to increase, especially after the third century BC, the need arose for formulating rules to regulate legal transactions involving foreigners living in Roman territory. What emerged as a response to this need was a distinct body of law which, although thoroughly Roman in origin and content, lacked the rigidity and complexity of the Roman *ius civile*. Thus, by contrast with *ius civile* as the law that applied exclusively to Roman citizens, the term *ius gentium*, in a narrow, practical sense, came to signify that part of Roman law governing relations between citizens and foreigners and between foreigners belonging to different states. This body of law was built upon the edicts of the *praetor*

---

63 The words *facultas* and *potestas* were also used to denote a specific right or power based upon a primary right.

64 But the term *peregrini* did not apply to all foreigners indiscriminately, but only to those who had some sort of relationship with Rome (for example, citizens of states in alliance with Rome). Those who had no connection with Rome were usually referred to as *barbari* (or *hostes*, if they were at war with Rome).

peregrinus, the special magistrate appointed to deal with legal disputes involving foreigners and, to a lesser degree, upon the edicts of provincial governors.[65] Dealing with disputes involving people of diverse nationalities and customs would have been difficult without appealing to generally recognised and understood principles. Thus, what characterised *ius gentium* was its simplicity and adaptability and its emphasis upon general principle rather than form. For that reason not only foreigners but also Roman citizens often relied on it as a means of resolving legal disputes. Moreover, elements of the *ius gentium* entered the edict of the *praetor urbanus* (the magistrate in charge of the administration of the *ius civile*) and, through it, the domain of *ius proprium Romanorum* (i.e. the domestic Roman law). But not all legal institutions associated with the Roman *ius gentium* belonged to the 'law of nations' in a broad sense, for certain institutions open to both citizens and foreigners alike had no place in any other system except the Roman. For example, the form of verbal contract known as *stipulatio*, although not found outside Roman law, was available to both citizens and foreigners alike.[66]

Ius naturale

The second century AD jurist Gaius defines *ius gentium* as 'the rules prescribed by natural reason for all which are observed by all nations alike'.[67] And in the Institutes of Justinian is stated that 'the laws of nature, which all nations observe alike, being established by divine providence, remain ever fixed and immutable'.[68] These statements may be taken to suggest that, in the eyes of Roman jurists, *ius gentium* was associated with the philosophical ideal of natural law (*ius naturale*, *ius naturae*), understood as a set of precepts valid everywhere in the world. But this

---

65 Disputes involving Roman citizens only fell within the jurisdiction of the *praetor urbanus*, the magistrate entrusted with the administration of the Roman domestic law (*ius civile*).

66 On the concept of *ius gentium* see W. Kunkel, *An Introduction to Roman Legal and Constitutional History*, 2nd edn, Oxford 1973, 77; H. F. Jolowicz and B. Nicholas, *Historical Introduction to the Study of Roman Law*, 3rd edn, Camridge 1972, 102 ff; B. Nicholas, *An Introduction to Roman Law*, Oxford 1962, repr. 1991, 54 ff; H. J. Wolff, *Roman Law, An Historical Introduction*, Oklahoma 1951, 82-84; M. Kaser, *Römische Rechtsgeschichte*, Göttingen 1976, 134 ff; *Ius gentium*, Cologne, Weimar and Vienna 1993; R. Monier, *Manuel élémentaire de droit romain*, Aalen 1977, 5-6; A. Guarino, *Diritto privato romano*, Naples 2001, 128 ff.

67 G. 1. 1.

68 *Inst.* 1. 2. 11.

connection has been far from clear, as no generally accepted definition of *ius naturale* can be found in the sources, and the meaning of the term appears to vary depending upon the point of view from which it is contemplated.

Cicero and other Roman thinkers embraced the idea of the Stoic philosophy that the world is permeated and governed by a universal soul, a divine reason, whose dictates constitute an 'eternal law' (*lex aeterna*). This eternal law is reflected in the law of nature (*ius naturale*). The law of nature, as the embodiment of divine reason, is everlasting, immutable and universal, knowing no limitations by people, place or time, and transcending the laws of any particular state or political community.[69] It is engrafted in the souls of all human beings, directing them by a kind of innate apprehension, since they all participate in the universal rationality.[70]

---

69 This understanding of natural law had its origin in the thought of Zeno and other Greek and Roman philosophers who belonged to the Stoic school of philosophy. It was also influenced by the Platonic and Aristotelian philosophies, although it differs from them in some important respects. For a closer look at the origins and claims of Stoicism see E. V. Arnold, *Roman Stoicism*, London 1958; F. H. Sandbach, *The Stoics*, London 1989; C. J. Friedrich, The *Philosophy of Law in Historical Perspective*, 2nd edn, Chicago 1963, 27 ff; A. Erskine, *The Hellenistic Stoa: Political Thought and Action*, London 1990; R. M. Wenley, *Stoicism and its Influence*, New York 1963; W. Ebenstain, *Great Political Thinkers: Plato to the Present*, 4th edn, New York 1969, 139-48.

70 Cicero, writing in the first century BC, expounded the philosophers' conception of natural law as follows: 'True law is right reason in agreement with nature, diffused among all men; constant and unchanging, it should call men to their duties by its precepts, and deter them from wrongdoing by its prohibitions; and it never commands or forbids virtuous men in vain, while its rules and restraints are lost upon the wicked. To restrict this law is unholy, to change it illicit, to repeal it impossible; nor can we be exempt from it by the order either of senate or of popular assembly; nor need we look for anyone to clarify or interpret it; nor will it be one law at Rome and a different one at Athens, nor otherwise tomorrow than it is today; but one and the same law, eternal and unchangeable, will bind all peoples and all ages; and God, its designer, expounder and enactor, will be as it were the sole and universal ruler and governor of all things; and whoever disobeys it, because by this act he will have turned his back on himself and on man's very nature, will pay the heaviest penalty, even if he avoids the other punishments which are considered appropriate for his conduct'. (*de re publica* 3. 22. 33.) A different definition of *ius naturale*, attributed to the third century jurist Ulpian, is found in Justinian's Digest (D. 1. 1. 1. 3.) and Institutes (1. 2.). According to this 'the law of nature is that law which nature teaches to all animals. For this law does not belong exclusively to the human race, but belongs to all animals, whether of the air, the earth, or the sea. From this law

This universal ability to reason and the fact that the law of nature is applicable everywhere resulted in the Stoic emphasis on equality and the unity of humanity, and the ideal of a world state governed by one system of law based on reason. The Stoics viewed natural law as the source of fundamental ethical principles governing human conduct and human relations and as furnishing the standards to which the institutions of positive law should conform. But *ius gentium* and *ius naturale*, in the sense the philosophers understood it, did not necessarily concur. For example, whereas under natural law all people were born free, slavery was widely recognised in antiquity as an institution of the law of nations.[71] The obvious problem here is that *ius naturale* alludes to law which ought to be observed, whereas *ius gentium* refers to law that was actually in force among nations. Considering this, the most one can say is that, from a philosopher's point of view, the universal recognition of a legal institution or principle as part of the law of nations might be taken to imply that such an institution or principle has its origin in natural reason.[72]

Now, the philosophers' conception of *ius naturale* had no direct effect on Roman law, for the Roman lawyers were practical and down-to-earth in their attitude, preferring to deal with legal problems on a case by case basis instead of attempting to construct general philosophical theories of law.[73]

---

comes the union of male and female, which we call marriage, and the begetting and education of children. For we see that all other animals are likewise governed by a knowledge of this law'. This definition, which probably derives from the Pythagorean philosophers, appears to confuse between animal instincts and the demands of reason and law on human conduct. See B. Nicholas, *An Introduction to Roman Law* , Oxford 1962, repr. 1991, 54 ff.

71 As stated in Justinian's Institutes, 'The law of nations is common to all mankind, for nations have established certain laws, as occasion and the necessities of human life required. Wars arose, and in their train followed captivity and then slavery, which is contrary to the law of nature; for by that law all men are originally born free'. (*Inst*. 1. 2. 2.)

72 In the words of C. J. Friedrich, 'the most that can be admitted is that there is a presumption in favor of the contention that a legal institution found in diverse *civitates* is part of the law of nature'. *The Philosophy of Law in Historical Perspective*, Chicago 1963, 32.

73 As H. J. Wolff points out, 'the Roman jurists. for all their philosophical and rhetorical education, never showed more than a superficial interest in purely philosophical problems. The originality of their approach lay in their interest in, and intimate connection with, the practical application of Roman law as it was. Their efforts were directed not at building a purely theoretical jurisprudence, but at demonstrating from every possible angle the practical use to which the institutions of their law could be put'. *The Western Idea of Law*, S. C. Smith and D. Weisstub (eds), London 1983, 322.

Although they were aware of the distinction between positive law and law as it ought to be, they took little interest in linking philosophical speculation with everyday disputes and mundane practices, or in questioning the validity of positive law on the grounds that it conflicted with a higher law. This does not mean, however, that the concept of *natura* was of no significance to them. But for the Roman lawyers its content was defined not so much by reference to divine reason, or God's plan for the universe, but by reference to the qualities of things worldly, to states of affairs and modes of thought and action that were commonly accepted as reflecting the realities of everyday life.[74] From their viewpoint, working out the appropriate course of action, or arriving at an acceptable legal solution, presupposed reasonable familiarity with the nature of things on the ground (*natura rerum*), including human nature (*natura hominum*), and with the ordinary expectations that social and legal relations entailed. Hence the Roman lawyers spoke of the nature of an obligation (*natura obligationis*), the nature of a contract (*natura contractus*), etc. The term *natura hominum* or *natura humana*, in particular, referred to the physical and mental qualities and the psychological characteristics and attitudes common to all human beings. In this respect, the postulates of nature emanated not from metaphysical speculation, but from the findings of common sense and the need for order in human relations.[75] This understanding of *natura* was of great importance to the Roman lawyers, for legal rules were constructed, interpreted and applied by reference to the nature of the things or legal relationships with which the rules were concerned. Thus, in the eyes of the Roman lawyers, it was 'natural' that certain things found in the open should belong to the person who found them;[76] or that a structure built on a person's land with materials belonging to another should belong to the owner of the land.[77] It was the nature of certain things, such as the open sea or the air, that precluded their being subject to private ownership;[78] and one

---

[74] As Ernst Levy explains, 'nature is here the order inherent in the conditions of life as the Romans saw it'. *Studia et Documenta Historiae et Iuris*, 15 (1949), 9.

[75] In Levy's words, "natural' was to them not only what followed from physical qualities of men or things, but also what, within the framework of that system, seemed to square with the normal or reasonable order of human interests and, for that reason, not in need for further evidence'. Ibid at p. 7.

[76] *Inst.* 2. 1. 18: 'Precious stones, gems, and other things, found upon the sea-shore, become immediately by natural law the property of the finder'.

[77] *Inst.* 2. 1. 29: 'If a man builds upon his own ground with materials of another, he is considered the proprietor of the building, because everything built on the soil accedes to it'.

[78] *Inst.* 2. 1. 1: 'By the law of nature these things are common to mankind – the air, running water, the sea and consequently the shores of the sea'.

could not legally own animals that are wild by nature unless he was able to exercise physical control over them.[79]

Did the philosophers' conception of *ius naturale* have any influence on Roman legal thought? Our evidence suggests that the Roman jurists, as members of the educated higher classes of society, were familiar with Greek philosophy and the ideas of natural law and natural justice. And although they did not view *ius naturale* as a juristic category, nor did they regard it as capable of invalidating positive law, by recognising it as a source of universally applicable principles they were doing something more than simply conveying their philosophical views: they were calling attention to the important relationship between legal rules and ethical principles – between positive law and justice as it relates to *ius* in a broad normative sense.[80] The impact of *ius naturale*, as a philosophical idea, can be traced not so much in specific legal doctrine or in the technical aspects of the law but, rather, in the general spirit and method of Roman jurisprudence, as reflected in the legal literature of the classical period. The philosophers' conception of *ius naturale*, despite its lack of a precise definition, came to play a part in the working out by the classical jurists of the principles of justice in the light of which the rules of positive law should be interpreted and applied. The jurists sought to express these principles in the form of general maxims capable of guiding the application of law in different situations. Principles such as equity (often referred to in the texts as *naturalis aequitas*), good faith (*bona fides*), humanity (*humanitas*) and others were now perceived as stemming from an all-embracing ethical and logical scheme.[81] These principles, which in earlier times were attributed only an instrumental value, came to be regarded as universal principles transcending and qualifying the norms of positive law. Furthermore, the Stoic notion of the unity of humanity under natural law, as an element of the ideological foundation upon which the political theory of the empire was built, played a part in the process towards the universalisation of Roman law. Notwithstanding the fact that the *Pax Romana* was established by conquest and the use of violent means

---

79 *Inst*. 2. 1. 14: 'Bees also are wild by nature. Therefore, bees that swarm upon your tree, until you have hived them, are no more considered to be your property than the birds which build their nests on your tree'.

80 Hence Paul's definition of natural law as 'that which is always just and right' (*quod semper est bonum et aequum*). See D. 1. 1. 11. pr.

81 According to Wolff, 'for the first time, the Roman lawyers were really able to see their system as a whole. Familiarity with Greek logic and ethics made them more fully aware of the sociological function of legal institutions and, consequently enabled them to look behind and overcome the rigid formalism of the old *ius civile*'. Supra note 73, 324.

(contrary to Stoic principles), Rome as a world empire governed by one system of law moved Stoic universalism from the plane of philosophical speculation to that of political reality.[82]

Ius civile, ius honorarium

By reference to the sources of law, the term *ius civile* was used to denote that part of Roman law which was derived from statutory enactments (*leges* and *plebiscita*), the resolutions of the senate (*senatus consulta*), the interpretations of the jurists (*responsa prudentium, interpretatio prudentium*) and imperial enactments (*constitutiones principis*). *Ius civile*, in this sense, was distinguished from the *ius honorarium*, i.e. the law derived from the edicts of the magistrates, especially the praetors (*ius praetorium*). According to Roman jurists, the role of the *ius honorarium* was to assist, correct and supplement the *ius civile*.[83]

Ius publicum, ius privatum

With respect to the scope and range of the law, Roman lawyers drew a distinction between public law (*ius publicum*) and private law (*ius privatum*).[84] Public law was concerned with the administration of the affairs of the state and the interests of the Roman people as a whole.[85] Roman jurists associated public law with what is now known as *ius cogens*, i.e. law that cannot be changed by agreement between private individuals.[86] To the category of *ius publicum* belonged, for example, the law governing the functions of magistrates and other state organs. Sometimes the law regulating relations between private citizens was associated with *ius*

---

82 On the idea of *ius naturale* see A. A. Schiller, *Roman Law: Mechanisms of Development*, New York 1978, 556 ff; M. Kaser, *Römische Rechtsgeschichte*, Göttingen 1976, 137-38; A. Guarino, *Diritto privato romano*, Naples 2001, 128 ff.

83 D. 1. 1. 7. 1. (Papinianus). On the category of *ius honorarium* see in general A. A. Schiller, *Roman Law: Mechanisms of Development*, New York 1978, 422 ff; M. Kaser, *Römische Rechtsgeschichte*, Göttingen 1976, 138 ff; W. Kunkel/M. Schermaier, *Römische Rechtsgeschichte*, Cologne 2001, 102 ff; A. Guarino, *Diritto privato romano*, Naples 2001, 93 ff; M. Talamanca (ed.), *Lineamenti di storia del diritto romano*, Milan 1989, 153 ff.

84 The technical distinction between private and public law was for the first time elaborated by the jurists of the imperial period.

85 *Inst.* 1. 1. 4; D. 1. 1. 1. 2. (Ulpianus).

86 D. 2. 14. 38. (Papinianus). The term *ius cogens* does not belong to the Roman legal terminology.

publicum, when a general public interest concurred with a private one. Private law, on the other hand, was concerned with the interests of private citizens (their legal status, property, transactions between them etc.).[87] Roman jurists adopted a division of private law into three parts: the law of persons, the law of property and the law of actions.[88] It was private law that Roman jurists were primarily interested in, and it was in the sphere of private law that their contribution to the development of Roman law for the most part lay.[89]

In connection with the distinction between public and private law judicial proceedings were divided into *iudicia publica* and *iudicia privata.* The former were concerned, in particular, with wrongful acts affecting the interests of the community as a whole (*crimina publica*), such as treason, murder, embezzlement of public funds and abuse of power by state officials. But Roman criminal law was narrower in scope than modern-day criminal law, for many wrongdoings which are today treated as criminal offences, such as theft and damage to property, were regarded, under Roman law, as affecting the interests of the individual alone. These wrongdoings were referred to as *delicta privata* and fell in the sphere of private law. In contrast with the *iudicia publica*, the object of the *iudicia privata* was the resolution of private disputes between individuals, such as disputes relating to property rights, the fulfilment of contractual obligations or the question of compensation for personal harm. While the state had no direct interest in the outcome of these disputes, it guaranteed the stability of social and commercial life by supplying the organs and procedures required for their resolution.[90]

Ius commune, ius singulare

Roman law recognised a distinction between *ius commune*, i.e. the law that applied to all Roman citizens indiscriminately, and *ius singulare*, i.e. the law applying to a specific category of persons, things or transactions. The term *privilegium* was used to denote a legal enactment concerning a specific person or case and creating an exception from a generally

---

87 D. 1. 1. 1. 2. (Ulpianus); *Inst.* 1. 1. 4.

88 According to Gaius, 'The whole of the law by which we are governed relates either to persons, or to things, or to procedure'. (G. 1. 8.)

89 The term *ius civile*, which originally denoted domestic Roman law in general, came to be used as synonymous with private law.

90 On the distinction between *ius publicum ius privatum* see M. Kaser, *Römische Rechtsgeschichte*, Göttingen 1976, 128-29; A. Guarino, *Diritto privato romano*, Naples 2001, 123 ff; R. Monier, *Manuel élémentaire de droit romain*, Aalen 1977, 6-7.

applicable rule. The Law of the Twelve Tables included a provision which prohibited the introduction of special rules for the purpose of granting privileges or imposing restrictions to particular persons.[91]

Interpretatio

The word *interpretatio* signified the intellectual process through which the true meaning of a legal rule, term or institution was brought to light. As has been noted, the first interpreters of the law were the pontiffs. In the second century BC the first secular jurists (*iurisprudentes* or *iurisconsulti*) appeared on the scene. The activities of these jurists consisted in giving advice or opinions on questions of law to magistrates, judges and litigating parties, drafting legal documents and assisting litigants on points of procedure. The earlier jurists occupied themselves with practical questions of law arising from given situations and did not attempt to develop a systematic approach to law or a theoretical analysis of its concepts. Their chief concern was with the letter of the law and its technical application in individual cases. But in the later pre-classical period, under the influence of Greek rhetoric and philosophical logic, the jurists began to apply in the interpretation of the law the dialectical method for purposes of definition and classification. This was a form of logical analysis that both distinguished between the various concepts and, at the same time, subsumed concepts sharing the same essential characteristics under common heads. By applying the dialectical method the jurists were able to systematise legal knowledge and to explain the nature of the various legal institutions through general organising concepts.[92] The later jurists did not confine themselves, like their predecessors, to the discussion of isolated cases, but sought to bring to light the logical connections between their institutions as parts of an all-embracing logical system. They arrived at the contents of the law by means of deduction from extant sources, but also by intuitive insight into the nature of legal problems, although that insight was prepared by a close study of legal decisions and juristic responses of the past. From this knowledge they drew general principles and then applied them to the case at hand. In interpreting legal rules the jurists sometimes

---

91 XII T. 9. 1. See Bruns, *Fontes* I, p. 34; and see Cicero, *de leg*. 3. 4. 11. and 3.19. 44. On the notions of *ius commune* and *ius singulare* see A. Guarino, *Diritto privato romano*, Naples 2001, 138 ff.

92 For instance, the jurist Scaevola, in his comprehensive treatise on the *ius civile*, written about 100 BC, first defined the general nature of institutions such as possession, guardianship, partnership, sale etc., and then described the various categories (*genera*) of these recognised by the law. Consider G. 1. 188. And see B. W. Frier, *The Rise of the Roman Jurists*, Princeton 1985, 95 ff.

gave a rule a broader meaning and sometimes a narrower one depending upon the nature and function of the relevant rule and the legislator's intention. They also utilised, although to a limited degree, the method of interpretation by analogy. This allowed them to apply a legal rule to cases that fell outside the scope of the rule, provided that these cases were in some important respects similar to that which the rule was intended to cover. Moreover, in the work of interpretation the jurists relied upon general ethical principles, such as equity (*aequitas*), good faith (*bona fides*), legitimate interest (*utilitas*) and, in later ages, humanity (*humanitas*), to ensure that the law was interpreted and applied in a way that accorded with common values and expectations.[93] Although the Roman jurists did not develop a comprehensive theory of interpretation, some principles of juristic interpretation can be found in various parts of Justinian's Digest. Many of these principles emphasise the importance of the purpose and spirit of the statute.[94] Principles of interpretation relating to legal acts (both unilateral and bilateral) proceed from the assumption that priority should be given to the parties' real intentions (*voluntas*) over the words or form in which a legal act had been expressed (*verba*).[95]

Aequitas

In juristic literature the notion of *aequitas* is associated with justice or fairness, as the substance of *ius*, or law in a broad normative sense.[96] It is

---

93 In the words of J. Declareuil, the *interpretatio* of the jurists 'organised and classified the means by which every legal problem could be brought to a solution which should at the same time satisfy the mind and the sense of equity'. *Rome, the Law-Giver*, London 1927, repr. 1996, 26.

94 See, e.g., D. 1. 3.13. (Ulpianus): 'Whenever a law provides something, there is a good opportunity to add further rules which aim at the same benefit through interpretation or jurisdiction' ; D. 1. 3. 17. (Celsus): 'To know the laws means to adhere not to their words but to their force and sense'; D. 50. 16. 6. 1. (Ulpianus): 'The term 'according to law' (*ex legibus*) should be understood as meaning 'according to both the sense and to the words [of the laws]'.

95 See, e.g., D. 50. 17. 96. (Marcianus): 'If ambiguous utterances occur, the intention of the person who used them should be taken into consideration'; see also D. 34. 5. 21. (Paulus); D. 32. 25. 1. (Paulus). On the nature of juristic interpretation see also chapters 4, 6 and 8 below.

96 The concept of *aequitas* had its origin in Greek philosophical thought. Aristotle defined equity (*epieikeia*) as a principle of justice aimed at the correction of the positive law where the latter is defective owing to its universality. (*Nic. Ethics* 5. 14.) According to Cicero, 'the law is the established *aequitas*'. (*Top.* 9.) And the jurist Celsus speaks of the law as 'the art of finding the good and the just' ('*ius est ars boni et aequi*'). (D. 1. 1. 1. pr.)

also linked with the notion of *lex naturae*, the command of an inner voice through which speaks the *ratio* of the *natura rerum* immanent in things (hence it is often referred to as *aequitas naturalis* and as being connected with *naturalis ratio*). Recourse to *aequitas* permitted the infusion of moral values into the law and, as such, it constituted an effort to go beyond the formal sources of law and to reach for a higher, enduring, normative plane. When the existing norms of positive law became inadequate to meet the social and economic needs of the times the notion of *aequitas* was relied upon to make the necessary corrections. In this respect, *aequitas* is compared and contrasted with the law in force (*leges* or *ius* in a descriptive sense).[97] In the eyes of the Roman jurists *aequitas* coexisted with positive law, amending, and supplementing it, but was not viewed as an independent source of law.[98] It postulated the interpretation of the law in terms of its purpose, the interpretation of a legal act by reference to the real intention of the parties or, more generally, an interpretation that would produce a fair result.[99] The incorporation of principles of equity into the law through the praetorian edict and the interpretations of the jurists enabled the Romans to break free from the rigid formalism of the old *ius civile* and to develop a system of law that could meet the needs of a constantly changing society. After the Christianisation of the empire in the fourth century AD the notion of *aequitas* was considered in the light of Christian ethical principles. This new approach to the meaning of *aequitas* is reflected in the Justinianic codification, where *aequitas* is linked with notions such as piety (*pietas*), affection (*caritas*), humanity (*humanitas*), kindness (*benignitas*) and clemency (*clementia*).

---

97 Law which accords with the principles of *aequitas* is called *ius aequum*; its opposite is *ius iniquum*.

98 As J. A. Crook explains, equity 'was not so much a source of law as a principle by which cases could be judged and the law be interpreted and developed'. *Law and Life of Rome*, London 1967, 27.

99 But no single straightforward definition of *aequitas* can be found in juristic texts. See W. W. Buckland (revised by P. Stein), *A Text-Book of Roman Law from Augustus to Justinian*, Cambridge 1963, 55; see also J. M. Kelly, *A Short History of Western Legal Theory*, Oxford 1992, 52. On the concept of *aequitas* see in general A. A. Schiller, *Roman Law: Mechanisms of Development*, New York 1978, 551 ff; A. Guarino, *Diritto privato romano*, Naples 2001, 135-36; F. Wieacker, *Römische Rechtsgeschichte*, Munich 1988, 506 ff.

Bona fides

The concept of good faith (*bona fides*) was of Roman origin and, initially, it appears to have been linked with the notion of *fas*, or divine law. In the sphere of private law *bona fides* was understood in two ways:

(i) From an objective point of view, *bona fides* was associated with the general expectation that persons should behave honestly and fairly in legal transactions.[100] Acting dishonestly was considered to be *contra bonam fidem*.

(ii) From a subjective point of view, *bona fides* pertained to a person's belief that what he was doing was just and lawful and did not violate another person's legitimate interest.[101]

A number of general rules based upon the concept of *bona fides* are included in the sources (e.g. '*bona fides* requires that what has been agreed upon must be done',[102] '*bona fides* demands equity in contracts').[103] The concept of *bona fides* was particularly important in the field of the law of contracts, because for certain types of contract to be valid the requirement of *bona fides* had to be met at both the conclusion and the execution of the contractual obligation.

Utilitas

The term *utilitas* was used to denote the idea of a social or common interest (*utilitas publica* or *communis*). A number of legal rules were regarded as having been established *utilitas causa*, i.e. either for the good of the community as a whole, or for the good of certain groups or categories of persons (e.g. minors, lunatics, absent persons). The term *utilitas privatorum* was used to signify the personal interests of private individuals.

Humanitas

Humanitas, as an ethical principle based on the idea of benevolence towards others, played a part in the development of Roman law during the later classical and post-classical periods. The principle of *humanitas*, which had its origin in Greek philosophical ethics, postulated that human beings

---

[100] See, e.g., D. 18. 1. 68. pr. (Proculus).
[101] See D. 18. 1. 27. (Paulus).
[102] D. 19. 2. 21. (Iavolenus).
[103] D. 16. 3. 31. pr. (Tryphoninus).

should be valued and respected as such, irrespective of their social or economic status. Like *aequitas*, *humanitas* was a general guiding principle pertaining to both the interpretation of the law and judicial decision-making. After the Christianisation of the empire in the fourth century AD, the idea of *humanitas* was regarded as particularly important in the fields of criminal law, family law and the law of succession. In the post-classical period imperial constitutions often included references to the notion of *humanitas*.

2 Monarchy and Early Republic

Introduction

Among our chief sources of information on the earliest period of Rome's history are the works of Greek and Roman historians, such as Livy of Padua, Plutarch and Dionysius of Halicarnassus. These writers drew their information from earlier sources – the records of the annalists of the third and second centuries BC. But, as has been noted earlier, due to the lack of documentary evidence from the period preceding the fourth century BC, the annalists could only record what was preserved in an oral tradition much coloured by myths and legends. Moreover, the later historians tended to construe events that occurred in the remote past in the light of the social conditions and beliefs of their own age. For that reason their accounts of Rome's early history are usually assessed by modern scholars in the light of information supplied by other disciplines, such as scientific archaeology, comparative philology and linguistics.

The *Latins*

Archaeological evidence suggests that the territory of Rome was not permanently inhabited until about 1000 BC. The first people who settled around the Tiber valley and in the area that was later to become Rome were the Latins and the Sabines, two of the Indo-European peoples referred to collectively as Italians, who drifted down from the North across the Alps into the Italian peninsula at the close of the second millennium BC.[1] The people of Latium, as this area became known, lived in small fortified villages and were engaged mainly in pasturage and the cultivation of the land. Although they were divided into several independent groups of people (*populi*) forming separate communities, the Latins saw themselves as members of the same broader family, sharing the same cultural and

---

1 It is believed that the Latins arrived first, at the close of the Bronze Age (i.e. before 1000 BC); the Sabines moved into Latium in the early Iron Age (after 1000 BC) and gradually amalgamated with the Latins. For a closer look see M. Cary & H. H. Scullard, *A History of Rome*, 3rd edn, London 1975, 31-94; E. Gjerstadt, *Early Rome. The Written Sources*, 3rd edn, Lund 1973, 35-36. See also M. Pallottino, *A History of Earliest Italy*, London 1991; R. R. Holloway, *The Archaeology of Early Rome and Latium*, London and New York 1994; R. Palmer, *The Archaic Community of the Romans*, Cambridge 1970.

religious inheritance and having largely common interests. This is manifested by the formation of religious associations, or leagues, between the various Latin communities, which provided the framework for their later political unification. The Latins' culture and conditions of life underwent very little change until the end of the seventh century BC when they came into contact first with the Etruscans, who occupied the neighbouring territory of Tuscany, and later with the Greeks and the Carthaginians. But it was mainly to the Etruscan influence that the people of Latium owed much of their political and cultural development.

The *Etruscans*

Although historians, both ancient and modern, agree on the uniqueness of the Etruscan civilisation, the origins of the Etruscan people has been a matter of a long-standing controversy. According to the Greek historian Herodotus (fifth century BC), the Etruscans immigrated to Italy from Lydia in Asia Minor by sea in the early Iron Age (tenth or ninth century BC). Herodotus's account was accepted by most Roman writers, as well as by the Etruscans themselves, and provided the basis for the so called 'Asianic theory'. But Dionysius of Halicarnassus, writing in the first century BC, drew attention to the important differences between the Etruscan and Lydian languages and institutions of his day and concluded that the Etruscans must have been of Italian origin. A theory which has gained ground in recent years claims that the Etruscans were either immigrants from the Danube basin, or a fusion of continental, eastern and indigenous races.[2] Archaeological evidence suggests that the Etruscan civilisation grew out of the earlier Villanovan culture of central Italy. This early Iron Age culture took its name from the village of Villanova, in the district of Bologna, where its remains were first discovered.[3]

The Etruscans, unlike the Latins and the Sabines, were a city-dwelling people. Their fortified cities, which were situated on hilltops and other easy to defend positions, formed strong political and commercial centres. Each city was politically independent and, until the sixth or early fifth century BC, was governed by a king who was chosen from among a small number of noble families. Although the kings were in later years replaced by annually elected magistrates, the Etruscans' social and political

2 For more on the origins of the Etruscan people see H. M. Last, *Cambridge Ancient History*, vol. 7, Cambridge 1928-39, ch. 12; M. Pallotino, *The Etruscans*, London 1975; E. Macnamara, *The Etruscans*, London 1990. See also G. & L. Bonfante, *The Etruscan Language*, Manchester 1983; T. J. Cornell, *The Beginnings of Rome*, London 1995, 45 ff.

3 Important Etruscan cities, such as Veii, Cerveteri, Tarquinia and others seem to have evolved from earlier Villanovan settlements.

organisation remained predominantly aristocratic in character. Economic life was based on agriculture and cattle-rearing, as well as on industry and commerce.[4] The Etruscans were also a powerful maritime people and their involvement in sea-trade brought them into contact with other Mediterranean peoples, such as the Greeks and the Phoenicians. The Greek influence on their culture is reflected in their art and architecture and is evidenced by the thousands of tomb-inscriptions which they left behind. These inscriptions indicate that the Etruscans had adopted a Greek alphabet (probably from the Greek city of Cumae in Campania) before the end of the seventh century BC.

In the closing years of the seventh century BC the Etruscans began their territorial expansion in Italy by conquering neighbouring Latium. With the occupation of Latium began the move towards the urbanisation of the rural communities in the area around the river Tiber that was later to become the city of Rome. By the middle of the sixth century BC, the Etruscans had gained control over a large territory extending from the Adriatic coast in the east to the Alps in the north, and from the Arno river to the bay of Naples on Italy's western coast. But the Estruscans' domination over Italy was short-lived, largely due to the rigidity of their aristocratic system of government, which did not permit the peaceful assimilation of subject populations, and the lack of an effective political alliance between the Etruscan city-states that could secure their territorial gains.[5] In the late sixth century BC the Etruscan power declined rapidly following a series of military setbacks and armed uprisings of subject populations. But, despite the decline of Etruscan power, the Etruscan culture continued to progress and remained productive and influential for several centuries.

The *Greeks*

From as early as the eighth century BC Greek colonies began to be established in the shores of southern Italy and Sicily. The colonists brought with them the contemporary Greek culture and systems of government, but each colony was an independent city-state owing no political allegiance to its mother city in mainland Greece. The presence of the Greek element in Italy stimulated the cultural and political development of other Italian communities and it was largely through the Greek cities that the Etruscans and, later, the Romans came into contact with the more advanced civilisations of the eastern Mediterranean.

---

4 The Etruscans were skilful artisans and their excellent black pottery, bronzes, jewellery and other products were famous all over the Mediterranean world.

5 Although a loose confederacy of Etruscan cities had been formed, mainly for religious purposes.

The beginnings of Rome

Roman tradition, combining earlier Latin and Greek folk-tales and myths, ascribed the actual founding of Rome to a group of Latins from the nearby settlement of Alba Longa, headed by Romulus, a descendant of the Homeric hero Aeneas. According to writers of the Augustan era, such as Varro, Livy and Virgil, Rome was founded in the year 753 BC. Although the story of Rome's founding, as related by these authors, lacks a concrete historical basis, the date 753 BC is important for the study of Roman history as the Romans used to reckon time from that date. Moreover, archaeological evidence has confirmed the presence of a number of settlements from the ninth to the seventh century BC in the area where Rome was later on established. These settlements were transformed into a city under Etruscan influence in the seventh century BC. It was the Etruscans who, recognising the strategic importance of the site, drained the marshy land between the hills, built temples and reservoirs and erected a city-wall. Under an Etruscan ruling elite, the various groups that had settled in the area were unified into a single community and were organised according to the Etruscan system of political and military organisation. Notwithstanding the Etruscans' role in the formation of the city of Rome, the influence of the Etruscan civilisation on early Roman culture, and the fact that Rome's population was the result of a fusion of different elements (Latins, Sabines, Etruscans and probably even some indigenous elements), the Romans and their social institutions remained predominantly Latin in character.[6]

Early Roman Society

The Roman family

The cornerstone of Roman society was the household (*familia*), a closely knit unit characterised by its social and economic cohesion. The Roman family was organised on a strictly patriarchal basis – something common to all peoples of Indo-European descent. The head of the family (*pater familias*) had absolute control over all persons and all property within his household. Under his control (*patria potestas*) came his lawful wife (*cum manu*),[7] all his legitimate male children, married or unmarried (*filii*

---

6 For a closer look see: R. M. Ogilvie, *Early Rome and the Etruscans*, London 1976; A. Alföldy, *Early Rome and the Latins*, Ann Arbor 1963; T. J. Cornell, *The Beginnings of Rome*, London 1995, 48 ff; J. Poucet, *Les origines de Rome. Tradition et histoire*, Brussels 1985.

7 The word *manus* denoted the power of a husband over his wife.

familias), his daughters-in-law and their children (*nepotes*), his unmarried daughters (*filiae familias*) and any adopted children he may have had.[8] The authority of the *pater familias* extended to all his descendants, however remote, such as his grandchildren and great-grandchildren. Moreover, the *pater familias* was the only person within the family capable of holding rights under private law. A person under paternal control (*in potestate patris*) could not, for example, acquire or convey property or incur debts without his father's consent.

The head of the family was also in charge of the religious observances within his household and, as a judge, he inflicted punishments for breaches of family discipline. Although his *partia potestas* gave him the power of life and death (*ius vitae et necis*) over his wife, children and slaves (he could, without breaching any law, imprison a child, sell him as a slave or even put him to death), in practice this power was limited by custom, religion and public opinion. Thus, in cases involving serious violations of customary norms the *pater familias* was required by custom to put the matter before a domestic court (*consilium familiae*) which was composed of the nearest relatives of the family. Since Roman respect for public opinion was always great, it is probably unlikely that a *pater familias* would have often disregarded the judgement of a family council, although he was not strictly bound by it. In later years the *pater familias*' power of life and death over his family members gradually fell into abeyance and during the republican period the arbitrary killing of a child by his father, although not strictly forbidden by law, came to be regarded as an 'abhorrent' act.[9]

No matter how old a person was, he remained under the control of his *pater familias* until the latter died or his *patria potestas* was extinguished in one of the legally prescribed ways. Release from the *patria potestas* was usually effected through the formal method of *emancipatio*: a son was freed from paternal control and became master of his own affairs (*sui iuris*) following his fictitious sale by the *pater familias*. The *patria potestas* could also be terminated in a number of other ways such as, for example, when the *pater familias* was deprived of the Roman citizenship (*capitis deminutio*), when a daughter passed into the control of her husband following a formal marriage and when a son or daughter assumed certain religious positions.

---

8 See A. Watson, *Rome of the XII Tables*, Princeton 1975, 47-51. R. Paribeni, *La famiglia romana*, Rome 1948; J. A. Crook, *Law and Life of Rome*, London 1967, 107 ff; D. Johnston, *Roman Law in Context*, Cambridge 1999, 30; M. Kaser, *Römische Rechtsgeschichte*, Göttingen 1976, 26-27.

9 See, e.g., Seneca, *de clem.* 1. 14. 15.

The *gentes*

Families claiming descent from a common ancestor formed a broader social group, the clan or *gens*. Each *gens* was distinguished by its own name (*nomen gentilicium*), which was borne by all its members (*gentiles*),[10] and each celebrated its own religious rites (*sacra gentilicia*). The members of a *gens* held meetings in which various matters of private or public nature were discussed and passed resolutions that were binding within their *gens*. The Law of the XII Tables (c. 450 BC) provided that when a person died intestate, his inheritance had to go to the members of the *gens* to which he belonged. The same law provided, further, that a person's guardians or tutors had to be appointed from among the members of that person's family or *gens*. But during the early Empire the so called *ius gentilicium* – the law concerning the members of a *gens* – fell into desuetude and the *gentes*, although they continued to exist, ceased to have any legal significance. This was the result of the gradual weakening, largely due to the social conditions of the times, of the sense of unity that once prevailed among the clan members.[11] Although the *gentes* never played a direct part in Roman politics, gentile solidarity was one of the key elements upon which the

---

10 The Romans, especially those belonging to the upper classes, bore three names: a) the *praenomen*, or first name, by which an individual member of a family was distinguished, b) the *nomen gentilicium*, indicating the *gens* to which an individual belonged and, c) the *cognomen*, or family name. For example, in the name *Gaius Julius Caesar*, *Gaius* is the *praenomen*, *Julius* is the *nomen gentilicium*, and *Caesar* is the *cognomen*. In later years the expansion of a family could result in its subdivision into a number of separate branches or sub-families, each being distinguished by its own name. A member of such a sub-family bore two *cognomina* or family names, the name of the original family and that of the family branch to which the individual belonged. The *cognomen* should be distinguished from the *agnomen*, a largely complimentary title added to a person's ordinary name. The *agnomen* was used to commemorate some noble task accomplished by the person to whom it was applied, and was confined strictly to its bearer. When a person passed from one *gens* to another by adoption he assumed the names of his adoptive father with the addition of an epithet indicating his former *gens*. The women of a family had no *praenomen* or *cognomen*, bearing only the name of the *gens* to which they belonged (e.g., *Julia* was the name of *Gaius Julius Caesar*'s daughter). Slaves were called by a first name only.

11 According to R. Sohm, 'When the consciousness of the mutual connection between the *gentiles* was lost, the word dwindled into a mere designation for a group of persons with a common name, without possessing any legal importance'. *The Institutes of Roman Law*, Oxford 1892, 359.

ruling families of Rome relied when seeking to further their social and political influence.[12]

Patricians and plebeians

Early Roman society was marked by the division of the population into two distinct classes: the patrician nobility and the rest of the citizenry referred to as plebeians or *plebs*. Several theories have been put forward attempting to explain the origins of this division, but very little can be said with certainty. A theory accepted by many modern scholars claims that the patricians were the descendants of the early clan patriarchs (*patres*) who formed the senate (*senatus*), the powerful council of elders which nominated and gave advice to the kings. The families which provided the early *patres* assumed a noble status as a class distinct from the rest of the population. This view seems to draw support from the fact that the term '*patres*', which was originally confined only to senators, came in later years to be used as synonymous with the term '*patricii* ' (members of the patrician class). But the distinction between patricians and plebeians may also be explained as having an economic basis. With the progressive differentiation of wealth, which began well before the city of Rome was founded, those few families which came to control large tracts of land assumed a predominant position in society and formed the inner circle of Roman nobility from which the 'fathers of the state' were chosen. Of course this does not preclude the possibility of ethnic differences being one of the reasons behind the accumulation of land in the hands of a few families.[13]

The early patrician aristocracy formed a closed order in society with clearly defined privileges based upon birth and the ownership of landed property. The members of this class enjoyed all the rights of the Roman citizenship (only they were Roman citizens in a full sense, or *cives optimo*

---

12 For more on the Roman *gentes* see *Cambridge Ancient History*, 2nd edn, vol. 7, Cambridge 1989. Consider also M. Kaser, *Römische Rechtsgeschichte*, Göttingen 1976, 32-33; F. Wieacker, *Römische Rechtsgeschichte*, Munich 1988, 196 ff; W. Kunkel/M. Schermaier, *Römische Rechtsgeschichte*, Cologne 2001, 6.

13 For an overview of the various theories that have been proposed on the origins of the Roman social classes see F. Ferenczy, *From the Patrician State to the Patricio-Plebeian State*, Amsterdam 1976, 15-16. See also J. C. Richard, *Les origines de la plèbe romaine. Essai sur la formation du dualisme patricio-plébéien*, Rome 1978; T. J. Cornell, *The Beginnings of Rome*, London 1995, 242 ff; R. E. Mitchell, *Patricians and Plebeians: the Origins of the Roman State*, Ithaca and London 1990. And see M. Kaser, *Römische Rechtsgeschichte*, Göttingen 1976, 29 ff; W. Kunkel/M. Schermaier, *Römische Rechtsgeschichte*, Cologne 2001, 5 ff; M. Talamanca (ed.), *Lineamenti di storia del diritto romano*, Milan 1989, 51 ff.

iuris), and monopolised all political power through their control of the senate, the popular assembly and the various state and religious offices. Although the patrician nobility was initially a closed order, new families began to be admitted into it from the late sixth century BC. The opening up of Rome's privileged class continued throughout the early Republic, as manifested by the distinction between older or major patrician houses (*patres maiorum gentium*) and new or minor ones (*patres minorum gentium*).

The plebeian class, which constituted the great majority of Rome's population, was made up largely of small farmers, labourers, artisans and tradesmen. Although its members were regarded as free Roman citizens, initially they did not enjoy any of the public rights (*iura publica*) which the Roman citizenship entailed, such as the right to hold public office (*ius honorum*), whether political, military or religious. It is believed that they first acquired the right to vote in the assembly (*ius suffragii*) in the later years of the regal era (late sixth century BC), when they were included in the Roman *classes* as a result of the constitutional reforms attributed to king Servius Tullius. The important right of appealing from the magistrates to the assembly against certain severe forms of punishment (*ius provocationis*) was probably first given to them shortly after the establishment of the Republic, in the late sixth century BC. Of the private rights (*iura privata*), the plebeians enjoyed the right of acquiring, holding and transferring property (*ius commercii*). But it appears that they did not have the right of contracting a regular Roman marriage (*ius conubii*) and, as a result, intermarriages between plebeians and patricians were forbidden.[14]

During the early part of the republican period the plebeian class continued to grow, whilst the old patrician aristocracy rapidly declined in numbers. And although, in general, the gap between the rich and the poor grew bigger, a number of plebeian families acquired considerable wealth and, from a position of strength, began to challenge the patricians' monopoly of political power. For nearly two centuries after the establishment of the Republic Rome's internal history is marked by the

---

14 As was stated in the Law of the XII Tables (c. 450 BC). It has been argued, however, that the rule forbidding intermarriages between patricians and plebeians was for the first time introduced by the Law of the XII Tables by the patricians in order to preclude wealthy plebeians from entering the senate. See A. Watson, *Rome of the XII Tables*, Princeton 1975, 20 ff. This prohibition was finally removed by the *lex Canuleia* in 445 BC. The right of contracting a regular Roman marriage was subsequently extended, first to the Latins, then to the Italians (by the *lex Iulia* of 90 BC and the *lex Plautia Papiria* of 89 BC), and finally to all the free inhabitants of the Empire in the early third century AD (under the *constitutio Antoniniana* of Emperor Caracalla).

struggle between the two classes. In the course of this contest (referred to as 'the struggle of the orders') the plebeians gradually removed all obstacles that stood in the way of their political emancipation and, with regard to civil rights, placed themselves on an equal footing with the patricians. But, as we will see later, it was only a political division of a particular kind that was removed, whilst the more fundamental division between the rich and the poor remained on the whole unaffected by the plebeians' success. In the years that followed the conclusion of the struggle of the orders the meaning of the term *plebs* gradually changed. During the last century of the republican era this term came to denote not a politically distinct social group but simply the whole mass of lowly and poverty-stricken citizens, in contradistinction with Rome's new nobility of wealth and office.[15] However, the old distinction between patrician and plebeian clans retained some importance. Although the highest offices of the state were now open to both patricians and plebeians alike, there were certain magistracies, such as that of the tribune of the plebeians (*tribunus plebis*), which remained, as a matter of constitutional principle, closed to men of patrician descent. At the same time, certain offices of a religious character[16] could only be held by members of traditional patrician clans.

Patronage and clientship

Another social institution whose origins, like those of the division between patricians and plebeians, remain obscure was that of patronage and clientship (*patronatus* and *clientela*). The term clients (*clientes*) referred to a body of people who were in a position of complete personal dependence upon the patrician clans (*gentes*) to which they had attached themselves. The individual or family members under whose protection these people had placed themselves were termed, in relation to their clients, *patronus* or *patroni* respectively. The clients may originally have been foreigners who, after their tribes were subjugated by the Romans, settled in the area of Rome. As they did not enjoy any of the rights of the Roman citizenship, they placed themselves under the patronage of powerful patricians, offering them their services and receiving protection from them in return.[17]

---

15 During the late Republic and early Empire the word *plebs* was often used contemptuously by members of the nobility as synonymous to mob or rabble.

16 Such as that of the *rex sacrorum*.

17 But the clientship was not an original Roman institution, as it seems to have been widespread throughout the Greek world and existed also among the Sabines, the Etruscans and other Italian peoples. However, its role in Rome's social and political development was much more decisive than anywhere else in antiquity.

Notwithstanding their inferior status, the clients were in the eyes of the law free persons. The relationship between them and their patrons, which was hereditary on both sides, was based on a reciprocity of certain socially defined duties and obligations. A patron was expected to protect his client's life and bodily and moral integrity, to watch over his financial interests, to advise him on legal matters and to represent him in the courts of law (in which a client could not appear alone). In return, a client was expected to stand by his patron on all occasions and to further his interests by every means, whether material or moral, in his power. More specifically, a client had to assist his patron in his political endeavours,[18] to raise money for his patron's ransom if the latter was taken prisoner, to contribute to any legal costs, such as fines and damages, which his patron may have incurred, to contribute to any expenses involved in the holding of any public office by his patron, and even to provide a dowry for his patron's daughter, if his patron was unable to do so.[19] Although the obligations which the patron-client relationship entailed were not enforceable by law, both parties were under a strong moral duty not to violate the quasi-religious principles upon which their relationship was founded. Since the interests of patron and client were presumed to be identical, there could be no legal dispute between the two, nor could either of them testify against the other in a court of law. A patron's misbehaviour towards his client or the breach of trust that the client-patron relationship entailed was strongly condemned by custom and public opinion as being contrary to established social and religious norms.[20]

During the later republican period large numbers of poor and underprivileged citizens, largely members of the plebeian class, and even entire communities, sought to place themselves as clients under the protection of powerful Roman families or individuals in high office. In this form clientship had a profound effect on Rome's social and political life especially during the closing years of the Republic.[21] Although during the

---

18 This entailed, among other things, that clients were expected to be of the same mind with their patrons when it came to voting in a political assembly.

19 The various benefits which the clients received from their patrons were termed *beneficia*. The various services which clients rendered their patrons were called *officia*.

20 On the client-patron relationship see Dionysius 2. 10. And see A. Watson, *Rome of the XII Tables*, Princeton 1975, 98 ff; A. Wallace-Hadrill (ed.), *Patronage in Ancient Society*, London and New York 1989; M. Kaser, *Römische Rechtsgeschichte*, Göttingen 1976, 28-29.

21 According to writers of the Augustan era (first century BC - first century AD) there was no real distinction between plebeians and clients during this period; the term *plebs* simply denoted Rome's subordinate class in general, whilst the term *clientes* referred to members of the same class in relation to the various

Empire the *clientela* phenomenon lost much of its earlier force, the client-patron relationship may be regarded as one of the most distinctive and enduring features of the Roman society.

Roman religion and the role of the priesthood

The religion of the early Romans, characteristic of a primitive society, was based on a combination of animism – the belief that the phenomena of the natural world were inhabited and governed by spiritual beings, whose powers the Romans called *numina* – and a practical materialistic attitude overlaid with a simple and rather stern morality. In the sixth century BC, under the influence of the Etruscan culture, the *numina* began to be associated with deities with distinct characteristics and powers,[22] and the first temples were erected on Etruscan models. But there was very little room for religion to be viewed as a private matter in a society in which the group, in the form of the family, the clan and, later on, the state, predominated over the individual. Moreover, neither emotion nor morality in an abstract sense played a significant part in this religion. It was material goods, such as rich crops, bodily vigour and victory in war, rather than spiritual blessings, that the Romans asked their gods for. The emphasis in early Roman religion was on individual deities and their distinctive powers and ways of interfering in human affairs. It was not until the Romans came into contact with the more advanced religious systems and philosophies of the East that they began to embrace a more universal perception of the divine forces and their relation to man.[23]

One of the defining characteristics of early Roman religion was ceremonial formalism and the quasi-contractual nature of the relationship

---

noble houses under whose protection they had placed themselves. This description may be accurate in view of the social conditions of the later Republic, when a great portion of the client population had been incorporated into the *plebs*, but circumstances were different in earlier ages. The nature of the patron-client relationship, as traditionally understood, would never have permitted the clients to rise, either collectively on individually, against their patrons in the way the plebeians did; nor would it be possible for a patrician to treat another patrician's client as ruthlessly and tyrannically as the plebeians were so often treated during the archaic era for, as has been noted, a client enjoyed the protection of the *gens* to which his patron belonged.

22 The association of these forces with specific deities (gods or *dei*) represents a more advanced phase in religious evolution, referred to as 'deism'. Among the earliest personified deities were Jupiter, Janus, Vesta and Mars.

23 For more on the development of Roman religion see G. Dumezil, *Archaic Roman Religion*, 2 vols, Chicago 1970; R. M. Ogilvie, *The Romans and their Gods*, London 1969; M. Beard, J. North, S. Price, *Religions of Rome*, Cambridge 2000.

between man and the gods. The Romans believed that if the prayers and other forms of worship were carried out according to the proper ritual, the gods were bound to treat them favourably. And one was no longer obliged to continue his worship if the gods paid no attention to his prayers, although this was often attributed to some mistake or omission in the performance of the relevant ritual. Religious ritual usually involved the performance of certain acts, such as the covering of one's head with a garment, the raising of the right hand to the lips or the turning of one's body in a certain direction. Of vital importance for the success of the prayer was the use of the appropriate phraseology, for the Romans believed that words possessed a power quite distinct from the attitude or feelings of the person who uttered them.[24] It was only through correct ritual that 'divine peace' (*pax deorum*), that is balance in nature and harmony between gods and men, could be warranted. As Roman society progressed, the idea of balance in nature began to take a distinctively moral flavour and the norms and forms of conduct which aimed at securing harmony between men and gods were gradually extended to relations between men.[25] It was beliefs and practices of a religious origin and nature that furnished a great deal of the raw materials from which early Roman law was formed.

During the early archaic age religious worship revolved around domestic life and the farm, and was carried out under the supervision of the *pater familias*, who acted as the family priest. But as the early settlements moved closer to becoming a city, religious ritual began to broaden and new ceremonies were introduced through which citizens evoked the support and protection of the gods in their collective undertakings.[26] Just as the well-being of individuals and families depended on their gaining the gods' favour by discharging their religious duties with care, so the welfare of the community as a whole depended on the state's fulfilling its obligations towards its divine patrons. Finding out which these

---

24 As we will see later, a similar attitude is reflected in the formalism that characterised archaic Roman law.

25 It is worth noting here the special place which certain moral qualities, such as *fides* (trust), *honos* (honour), *pudor* (decency), *concordia* (harmony) etc., occupied in Roman religion.

26 Under Etruscan influence new rites were introduced through which priests aimed at discovering the will of the gods by observing and interpreting natural phenomena. The Romans, like most ancient peoples, did not embark on any undertaking, whether of a private or public nature, without first seeking to determine the gods' attitude towards their plans. The discipline by which the will of the gods was believed to become known was called *divinatio*, and the various signs by which it was manifested were referred to as *omina*. With regard to public affairs, the process of *divinatio* was carried out by a special college of priests, the *augures*. Most of the rules governing this process had been borrowed from the Etruscans.

obligations were and how they were to be carried out was the concern of the divine or sacred law (*ius divinum*, *ius sacrum*), a special branch of Roman public law. During the Monarchy the king (*rex*), as the head of the Roman state, occupied a position analogous to that which the *pater familias* occupied in relation to the religious affairs of the family, although most of the relevant duties and powers were delegated to special colleges of priests whose members were chosen exclusively from the patrician class.

The Roman priests were, in effect, state officials who, often in addition to their duties as senators or magistrates, were responsible for the religious branch of public administration.[27] Of the various religious bodies the most influential was the college of the *pontifices*. According to Roman tradition, the institution of the *pontifices* was first introduced by Romulus's successor, the priest-king Numa Pompilius (late eighth century BC).[28] Originally, this religious body was made up of five members drawn exclusively from the patrician class (four ordinary *pontifices* headed by a *pontifex maximus*).[29] As guardians and interpreters of the divine law (*ius divinum*), the *pontifices* exercised general supervision over a wide range of matters associated with public religion and set the rules governing the conduct of religious ceremonies and rituals (*ius sacrum*).[30] They gave instructions to state officials on the performance of public acts of a religious nature and punished wrongdoings regarded as disrupting the *pax deorum* – the harmony between the community and its gods. The duties of the *pontifex maximus* included the publishing of the decisions and opinions of the college (referred to as *decreta* and *responsa*) on any matter, whether

---

27 There were two general classes of priests in Rome: those who exercised general supervision over all religious matters, without being attached to one particular god, and those who were associated with the worshiping of particular gods. Of the former the most important were the *pontifices*, the *augures*, the *quindecemviri sacrorum* and the *epulones*; the latter included the *flamines*, the *salii* and the *vestales*.

28 See Livy 1. 20; Dionysius 2. 73.

29 Under the *lex Ogulnia* of 300 BC their number was increased to nine, with the our additional *pontifices* being drawn from the plebeian class, and subsequently to fifteen. The term *cooptatio* referred to the way in which the members of the pontifical college were chosen in early times. In short, new members were selected by the existing *pontifices* and were formally admitted (*inauguratio*) after the interpretation of the auspices had indicated the approval of the gods. But in the later republican period the position became elective (under the *lex Domitia* of 103 BC), and the pontiffs were elected by the tribal assembly (*comitia tributa*). During the Empire the selection of the *pontifices* was in the hands of the emperor who headed the college as *pontifex maximus*.

30 The law governing the activities of the pontiffs was termed *ius pontificium*, and was created and regulated by the pontiffs themselves.

secular or religious, that was put before them, and the recording of the most important events of the year in the *annales maximi*. The latter should be distinguished from the *libri pontificum*, the archives of the pontifical college, accessible only to its members, containing norms and decisions relating to matters of both religious and secular law. Moreover, the *pontifex maximus* was entrusted with the regulation of the calendar, the fixing of the dates of public ceremonies and festivals (*dies festi*), and the setting of the days of each month on which alone legal transactions, trials and other business could take place (*dies fasti*).[31]

The interconnection of religion and law in the archaic period accounts for the important role of the *pontifices* in the formulation, interpretation and application of the law. During this period all legal knowledge was confined to their college and was handed down to new members by tradition and instruction. In their capacity as custodians and interpreters of the customary law, they gave opinions on questions of law put before them by state bodies, magistrates and private citizens. Their opinions were based on precedents of which they alone had knowledge. To these precedents, based on ancestral custom, the pontiffs added interpretations and developed formulae or instructions for the performance of legal acts. After the publication of the Law of the XII Tables in the middle of the fifth century BC an important part of the pontiffs' work was to explain and give shape to its provisions and at times, under the cover of interpretation, they extended the law to cover new situations. Thus a body of jurisprudence was gradually built which furnished the basis for the subsequent development of Roman legal science. With the gradual separation of law and religion the priesthood began to lose its monopoly on matters of law and in time was almost entirely superseded by the civil magistracy.[32]

Economic Conditions

In the early years of the archaic period the city of Rome occupied an area that did not exceed the sixty square miles. But by the close of the sixth century BC the Roman territory had increased to about four hundred square miles. Economic life during this period was based on cattle-rearing and agriculture. Indeed, for many centuries the cultivation of the land was regarded as one of the most important activities for a free-born Roman citizen. It seems more likely that, initially, the pasture-land remained largely undivided, while the arable land gradually became open to private

---

[31] A distinction was drawn between the *dies fasti*, the days on which the courts of justice were open and legal transactions could be carried out, and the *dies nefasti*, the days on which the courts were closed.

[32] See chapters 4 and 6 below.

ownership. But there is little agreement among historians as to the scope of the institution of private property, or the process by which it was established in early Roman society. According to one theory, initially only moveables, such as domestic animals, farm implements etc., could be privately owned, whereas immovables were subject to collective ownership by the members of the Roman *gentes*.[33] Considering the etymology of certain terms of the Roman law of property may be of some assistance here. For example, the derivation of the term *mancipatio*[34] from the phrase *manu capere*, which meant holding or seizing by hand, might be taken to suggest that, initially, only objects which could be delivered by hand, i.e. moveables, could be privately transferred.

Under the influence of the Etruscans the Romans began to take an interest in commerce and industry, a development precipitated by the transformation of their settlements into a city-state. Archaeological evidence from the seventh and sixth centuries BC has confirmed the presence of a ceramic industry as well as the working of bronze, copper and other materials in the area of Rome. Moreover, the growth of trade in the sixth century BC is evidenced by the fragments of Greek pottery and other artefacts found on the site of the city. It is believed that payment for the various imports was made in kind (probably in timber, salt, cattle etc.), as coinage was not introduced in Rome until the later part of the fourth century BC. Instead of coins the early Romans used in their transactions pieces or ingots of bronze (*aes*), whose value was determined according to their weight.[35] After the introduction of a written alphabet at the end of the sixth century BC the Romans began to record their customary rules relating to property and to draft legal documents for certain economic transactions, such as contracts and wills.

---

33 See G. Diòsdi, *Ownership in Ancient and Preclassical law*, Budapest1970, 19 ff.

34 A formal method of transferring property on certain things (*res mancipi*) based on an imaginary sale and delivery. In the category of *res mancipi* were included lands and houses (*praedia*), slaves and domestic animals.

35 An ingot of bronze was called *stipes* or *stips* (hence the word *stipendium*: pay); the term *libripens* was used to describe the person who weighed the bronze on a pair of scales (*libra*). This ancient practice provided the form in which certain legal transactions of Roman law were dressed (e.g. the transference of certain kinds of property by *mancipatio*).

Political Organisation of the Regal Period

The *populus Romanus*

As was noted before, the population of early Rome was made up, for the most part, of three elements, the Latins, the Sabines and the Etruscans, with the Latin element being the predominant one. For military and political purposes the entire citizen body, referred to as *populus Romanus Quirites* (or *populus Romanus Quiritium*),[36] was divided into three tribes (*tribus*), the *Ramnes*, the *Tities* and the *Luceres*. Each tribe was headed by a tribal commander (*tribunus*). The tribes were subdivided further into smaller groups known as *curiae* (wards or brotherhoods of men), each consisting of a number of clans or groups of families (*gentes*). There were thirty *curiae* in all, ten in each tribe.[37] Membership in these groups was probably hereditary. Each *curia* was distinguished by a different name and had its own place of assembly (also called *curia*) where its members held their religious ceremonies (*sacra*), settled disputes over the legitimacy of a person's membership in their group[38] and witnessed the formalities relating to adoptions and testaments. These meetings were presided over by the head of the *curia* (called *curio*). The meetings of all thirty *curiae* were headed by the *curio maximus*, chosen out of the heads of the thirty *curiae*, while a *flamen curialis* supervised the common worship of the members of the *curiae*. The *curiae* originated from the prehistoric organisation of the Italian tribes into groups of clans, probably bound together by blood-ties and united for common defence. Besides kinship, territorial proximity between different clans must also have played a part in the formation of these groups. The division of the Roman people into *curiae* furnished the basis for Rome's earliest popular assembly, the *comitia curiata*.[39]

---

36 The early Romans called themselves *Quirites*. Although this term was in later ages superseded by the term *Romani*, it continued to be used in the official phraseology to signify those who enjoyed full Roman citizenship. As to the origin of the name *Quirites* very little can be said with certainty. According to an explanation found in the Institutes of Justinian, the name comes from *Quirinus*, a name by which Romulus, the legendary founder of Rome, was known (*Inst.* 1. 2. 2.). The same name might also be linked with the goddess Juno, often referred to as *Quiritis*, or the god Ianus, who was also called *Quirinus*. Other possible associations include the verb *quiritare*, by which a citizen appealed to another for assistance in battle.

37 According to Dionysius, each *curia* was subdivided into ten *decuriae*, or groups of ten, each group being headed by a minor officer termed *decurio*. See Dionysius 2. 7.

38 And hence indirectly determined whether that person was a Roman citizen.

39 Consider on this T. J. Cornell, *The Beginnings of Rome*, London 1995, 114 ff; W. Kunkel, *An Introduction to Roman Legal and Constitutional History*, 2nd

The king

According to Roman historical tradition, during the first two and a half centuries after the founding of the city Rome had been governed by a succession of seven kings.[40] Of these the first four (Romulus, Numa Pompilius, Tullius Hostilius and Ancus Marcius) are believed to have been of Latin or Sabine origin, whilst the last three (Tarquinius Priscus, Servius Tullius and Tarquinius Superbus) were Etruscans.[41] Roman kingship, especially during the earlier phase of the regal era, was closely associated with religion. As the chief priest of the state, the king (*rex*) acted as an intermediary between the community and its gods and exercised general supervision over all matters relating to public worship. But the Roman kings, although they were often attributed magic powers, did not profess to be of divine descent, nor did they claim any special connection with the gods other than through the taking of the auspices. Moreover, many religious ceremonies and rituals were conducted not by the king himself but by special officiators and priests acting under the king's authority.[42] Besides his purely religious duties, the king was responsible for the maintenance of public peace and had the power to issue decrees and inflict punishment for offences against the gods or the state. He was also in charge of the state's foreign affairs and could declare war on or conclude treaties with other states in the name of the community. In times of war, as commander-in-chief of the army, he called the people to arms and led them in the battlefield. Moreover, only he had the right to convene and address the assembly of the people and the senate and to put proposals before them. Thus, although in principle legislative power rested with the Roman

---

edn, Oxford 1973, 9-10; J. M. Rainer, *Einführung in das römische Staatsrecht*, Darmstadt 1997, 22 ff; F. Wieacker, *Römische Rechtsgeschichte*, Munich 1988, 200 ff; M. Kaser, *Römische Rechtsgeschichte*, Göttingen 1976, 33-34.

40 See, e.g., Tacitus, *Ann.* 1. 1.

41 According to Livy, the kingship played a vital role in the consolidation of the early Roman state, for it provided the necessary cohesive element at a time when the people of Latium were in the process of establishing their political identity (Livy 2. 1.). And see D. 1. 2. 2. 1. (Pomponius).

42 After the fall of the Monarchy, at the close of the sixth century BC, the religious functions of the king were assigned to a special priest, referred to as *rex sacrorum* or *rex sacrificus*. The creation of this office appears to have been based on the belief that certain religious duties which once were performed by the king could only be discharged by a person who, in religious matters at least, had the authority of the king. According to W. Kunkel, the *rex sacrorum* 'was not a new office, different from the kingship, but was the old kingship itself; for as long as a Roman state cult remained it continued to exist in its sacral function because only a king possessed the necessary magic power'. *An Introduction to Roman Legal and Constitutional History*, 2nd edn, Oxford 1973, 13-14.

people, the king exercised a strong influence on legislation by virtue of his exclusive right to propose laws.[43] The royal power seems to have increased considerably under Etruscan influence with the introduction of the principle of *imperium*, or supreme command.[44] But the king's power was not absolute, for its exercise was tempered by custom and public opinion (expressed through the assembly of the people and the senate).

With respect to the administration of justice, the king had jurisdiction over matters of both public and private law. With regard to the latter, however, his authority was limited by established customary norms and the coexisting jurisdiction of the *pater familias* over the affairs of his household. In general, it seems that the king rarely interfered in private disputes and, when his intervention was deemed necessary, he confined himself to pronouncing the general norm pertinent to the matter at stake, leaving the case to be determined by regular judges or specially appointed arbiters (*arbitri*).[45] But in relation to the administration of public law he had much wider jurisdiction. As protector of the community's interests, he acted as supreme judge in criminal trials concerned with various offences against the state and its gods, such as treason, sacrilege and unjustifiable homicide.[46] But when an important case was brought before him for trial it was customary for him to seek the advice of the senate (*regium consilium*).[47] Moreover, the king did not always try capital or other important cases in person; he could, if he so wished, delegate a case to specially appointed officials. These were termed *quaestores parricidii*, when dealing with charges of murder (*parricidium*), and *duoviri perduellionis*, when dealing with charges of treason (*perduellio*).[48]

---

43 However, the kings' contribution to the development of private law was minimal as in early Rome the principal source of private law was not legislation but custom.

44 Among the various external symbols of the king's *imperium* were the lictors (*lictores*), twelve attendants each bearing a bundle of rods with an axe in the middle (*fasces*), symbolising the king's power to punish, the *sella curulis*, an ivory chair fitted on a chariot, and a special cloak (*toga*). All these insignia were probably of Etruscan origin.

45 See, e.g., Cicero, *de re publica* 5. 2. 3.

46 Those found guilty of such crimes were punished by death (inflicted by hanging, beheading or the hurling of the offender from the Tarpeian rock), exile or the offender's being declared an outlaw (*sacratio capitis*). The *sacratio* entailed that the wrongdoer was no longer under the protection of the laws and could be killed by anyone with impunity. And see chapter 4 below.

47 Although it is not clear what powers the *regium consilium* had, it seems unlikely that the king was bound by its opinions. According to Livy, the unpopularity of Rome's later kings was partly due to the fact that they no longer sought the advice of the senate in criminal matters (Livy 1. 49.).

48 See, e.g., Livy 1. 26.

According to Cicero, a citizen sentenced to death or some other form of capital punishment (*poena capitalis*), such as loss of liberty or citizenship, could appeal against the sentence to the assembly of the people (*provocatio ad populum*).[49] The latter could suspend the sentence, but could not re-try the case. In the course of time, the right of appealing to the people against decisions of magistrates involving capital punishment came to be regarded as one of the most important rights associated with Roman citizenship (*ius provocationis*).

The Roman kings were not hereditary but elective and, although they held office for life, they could not nominate their successors. The person who was to serve as king was chosen from among the heads of Rome's noble families through a process in which both the senate and the assembly of the people played a part. Upon the death of a king supreme power (*summa potestas*, *imperium*) passed to the senate, which appointed one of its members as a temporary king, or *interrex*. The *interrex* was entrusted with the duties of the regal office. He also nominated the new king (usually with the senate's consent) and supervised the procedure leading to his confirmation. Depending on the time required for deliberation, up to ten *interreges* might be appointed in succession, each *interrex* remaining in office for up to five days. The person nominated as a king by the *interrex* was presented to the curiate assembly for confirmation and, if he was approved by the people, was elected king.[50] But the election of a king was not complete before the end of the religious rituals through which the gods' approval of the new king was ascertained (*inauguratio*).[51] Shortly after his election the king re-convened the assembly and proposed a special law, known as *lex curiata de imperio*,[52] by which the people conferred upon him supreme authority (*regium imperium*, *regia potestas*) and the right of taking the auspices (*auspicia*) – a right associated with the king's role as the community's chief priest. With the passing of this law and the ratification of the people's decision by the senate (*patrum auctoritas*) the whole process came to an end.[53]

---

49 Cicero tells us that the archives of the pontiffs contained evidence suggesting that the right of appeal had been recognised before the fall of the Monarchy (*de re publica* 2. 31.) If this information is correct, the right of appeal must have belonged exclusively to members of the patrician class. This right was first granted to the plebeians at the close of the regal period by the *lex Valeria* of 509 BC.

50 The period between the death of a king and the appointment of his successor was termed *interregnum*.

51 See Livy 1. 18. 6 ff; Plutarch, *Num*. 7.

52 See Cicero, *de re publica* 2. 13. 17. 18. 21.

53 On the powers and duties of the Roman kings see in general T. J. Cornell, *The Beginnings of Rome*, London 1995, 119 ff; J. M. Rainer, *Einführung in das*

The senate

The Roman senate (*senatus*) had its origins in the gatherings of the heads of the Latin clans (*gentes*), the groups of families around which primitive society was organised prior to the formation of the state.[54] During the regal era the members of the senate (*patres*, *senatores*) were selected by the king himself from among the heads of the patrician houses. According to Roman tradition, Romulus, Rome's first king, set up a council of clan elders made up of one hundred members.[55] In later years the number of senators was increased to two hundred and, at the end of the Monarchy, it had reached three hundred members. Although membership was neither hereditary nor for life, a man once appointed senator usually served for as long as he lived. In the closing years of the Monarchy and during the early Republic a distinction was made between senators representing the 'greater' or long-established patrician clans (*patres maiorum gentium*) and those representing the 'lesser' or newer ones (*patres minorum gentium*). The sources speak of a decimation of the senate during the calamitous rule of Rome's last king, Tarquinius Superbus. After the fall of the Monarchy, one hundred and sixty-four new senators were added to the existing ones for the purpose of restoring the senate's size to three hundred members. These were chosen from among the most prominent families of Rome and included both patricians and plebeians alike.[56] The senators who were drawn from plebeian families were referred to as *conscripti*, whilst those of patrician descent continued to be called *patres*.[57]

Cicero tells us that the chief function of the senate during the regal era was to provide counsel to the king and assist him in the exercise of his duties (hence its designation as *regium consilium*).[58] But, as a political institution, the senate occupied a position subordinate to the king, except during the interval between the death of a king and the election of another

---

römische Staatsrecht, Darmstadt 1997, 28 ff; W. Kunkel, *An Introduction to Roman Legal and Constitutional History*, Oxford 1966, 13-14; W. Kunkel/M. Schermaier, *Römische Rechtsgeschichte*, Cologne 2001, 18-19; M. Kaser, *Römische Rechtsgeschichte*, Göttingen 1976, 34 ff; F. Wieacker, *Römische Rechtsgeschichte*, Munich 1988, 208 ff; A. Guarino, *Storia del diritto romano*, Naples 1996, 104 ff; M. Talamanca (ed.), *Lineamenti di storia del diritto romano*, Milan 1989, 19 ff.

54 Bodies similar to the Roman senate existed in most city-states in Greece, Italy and elsewhere.

55 Livy 1. 8. 7; Dionysius 2. 12. 1; Plutarch, *Rom.* 13.

56 See Livy 2. 1; Tacitus, *Annales* 11. 25.

57 Hence the later description of the senate as *patres et conscripti*. See Livy 2. 1; Dionysius 5. 13.

58 Cicero, *de re publica* 2. 9; See also Livy 1. 32; Dionysius 2. 14; Plutarch, *Rom.* 27.

(*interregnum*). Thus, it was within the king's discretion whether to summon the senate or not, and what questions to put before it for discussion. And although the king was required by custom and public opinion to seek the senate's counsel on matters of great importance for the state, he was not formally bound to do so, nor was he obliged to accept the senators' opinions or to follow their advice. The king, often for reasons of convenience, delegated to the senate the conduct of state affairs, but the senate was bound to act within the limited authority granted to it by the king. Besides its role as the king's advisory council, the senate played a part in the legislative process through the exercise of its power to ratify the measures passed by the popular assembly before they became law (*patrum auctoritas*).[59] As to the judicial functions of the senate, the sources tell us that a council of senators, or the senate as a whole, assisted and advised the king when the latter sat as a judge in important criminal cases. Of the political functions of the senate probably the most important was the running of the government of the state during the period between the death of a king and the election of another (*interregnum*) through a succession of senators acting as temporary kings (*interreges*).[60]

The assembly of the people (*comitia curiata*)

According to Roman tradition, the curiate assembly (*comitia curiata*), Rome's oldest popular assembly, was established by Romulus himself shortly after the founding of the city.[61] The assembly was made up of the thirty *curiae* or wards in which the whole citizen body (*populus Romanus*) was divided. Its functions were probably of a largely religious nature and included the inauguration of the king and the election of priests. The assembly also met to consider important matters concerning the community as a whole, such as the declaration of war or the conclusion of peace and the admission of a new *gens* into the existing ones. Although the curiate assembly, strictly speaking, did not have any legislative power, one of its most important functions was the formal sanctioning of the laws proposed

---

59 Originally legislative enactments were ratified by the senate subsequent to the people's vote but, after the passing of the *lex Publilia Philonis* in 339 BC, the senate was required to ratify proposals that were to be put to the assembly in advance. See chapter 3 below.

60 On the character and functions of the early Roman senate see M. Kaser, *Römische Rechtsgeschichte*, Göttingen 1976, 36-37; W. Kunkel/M. Schermaier, *Römische Rechtsgeschichte*, Cologne 2001, 25 ff; A. Guarino, *Storia del diritto romano*, Naples 1996, 102 ff; M. Talamanca (ed.), *Lineamenti di storia del diritto romano*, Milan 1989, 47 ff; F. M. D' Ippolito, *Aspetti di storia costituzionale romana*, Naples 2001, 17 ff.

61 Dionysius 2. 14.

by the king in exercise of his *imperium*.[62] Moreover, as was noted before, following the election of a new king it granted him his *imperium*, or supreme command, by a special law, the *lex curiata de imperio*. Although the political role of the assembly during the regal era seems to have been, in general, a passive one, the idea that political authority rested ultimately with the Roman people as a whole proved to be of great importance in the development of Roman political theory.

With respect to private law the *comitia curiata* performed two important functions: they ratified the admission of a person into an existing *gens* (*adrogatio* or *adoptio per populum*), and witnessed public testaments (*testamentum calatis comitiis*). When an individual passed by adoption from one clan to another the sanctioning of the curiate assembly (*auctoritas populi*) was deemed necessary for, once the adoption was complete, the person adopted was no longer obliged to observe the religious rituals (*gentilicia sacra*) of the clan to which he originally belonged but only those of the clan into which he was adopted. The sanctioning took the form of a legislative act and the relevant procedure was supervised by the *pontifex maximus*. Moreover, the *comitia* were often invited to witness and confirm the making of wills. A will made before the people amounted to a formal declaration of the way in which the testator wanted his property to be disposed of after his death.[63] When it was discharging this latter function the assembly was presided over by the *pontifex maximus,* and was referred to as *comitia calata*. Finally, as was mentioned before, the curiate assembly acted as a final court of appeal with respect to sentences involving death or the loss of liberty or citizenship (*provocatio ad populum*).

The curiate assembly was summoned by the king through a herald (*calator*).[64] In the later part of the regal era an official known as *lictor curiatus* gave notice of a forthcoming meeting of the assembly to the members of the *curiae* (there were thirty lictors, one for each *curia*). During the period of the *interregnum* the assembly was convened by the *interrex* with the approval of the senate. The *curio maximus* or a pontiff could also convoke the assembly for the purpose of carrying out certain religious functions. The meeting of the assembly was preceded by the taking of the auspices and no meeting could take place if the auspices were deemed unfavourable. Voting in the curiate assembly was conducted in two stages. First, voting took place within each *curia* separately – a citizen could cast his vote only within the *curia* to which he belonged. The

---

62 D. 1. 2. 2. 2. (Pomponius).

63 Such a public declaration was needed so that the contents of a person's will could easily be proved, if a dispute arose, at a time when written documents were not in use. See Aulus Gellius, *N. A.* 15. 27; G. 2. 101.

64 See *lapis niger*, FIRA I, pp. 19-20; Bruns, *Fontes* I, addit. 14.

majority of the members of a *curia* determined the vote of that *curia*. Then the votes of all the *curiae* were cast and the majority of the *curiae* determined the vote of the assembly. But no debate took place during the proceedings. The assembly's vote simply took the form of a 'yes' or 'no' and the proposal put before them could only be accepted unconditionally and without any modifications.[65]

The 'Servian reforms' and the decline of the curiate assembly

According to Roman historical tradition, the military and political organisation of the Roman citizen body underwent an important change during the reign of king Servius Tullius (c. 578-535 BC). The early Roman army consisted of the infantry (*pedites*) and the cavalry (*equites* or *celeres*), the latter being drawn from among the wealthiest citizens. Each of the three Roman tribes supplied a thousand foot-soldiers (a hundred from each *curia*) and a hundred horsemen (ten from each *curia*). In battle the Roman soldiers fought not so much as an organised body but as individuals, often entering into heroic contests with enemy soldiers. Servius enlarged the army and, drawing upon Etruscan and Greek models, introduced new battle tactics in order to improve its effectiveness. The reformed army was based on a heavily armed and well-disciplined infantry (*hoplites*), whose members fought in a regular line of battle according to the principles of the Greek *phalanx*.[66] The army was organised, further, into centuries, or groups of a hundred soldiers (there were 193 centuries in all). In order to recruit and equip these units the entire citizen body was divided into five classes on the basis of wealth, with each class supplying a set number of centuries. The first class, which was made up of the wealthiest citizens – those who could equip themselves with horses and heavy armour – provided most of

---

65 The *curia* which was called to cast its vote first was probably determined by lot. As there were thirty *curiae* in all a split vote appears to have been possible, but we have no information on how the matter was resolved in such cases. On the *comitia curiata* see T. J. Cornell, *The Beginnings of Rome*, London 1995, 114 ff; H. F. Jolowicz and B. Nicholas, *Historical Introduction to the Study of Roman Law*, 3rd edn, Cambridge 1972, 18-19; W. Kunkel, *An Introduction to Roman Legal and Constitutional History*, 2nd edn, Oxford 1973, 9-10; M. Kaser, *Römische Rechtsgeschichte*, Göttingen 1976, 37; W. Kunkel/M. Schermaier, *Römische Rechtsgeschichte*, Cologne 2001, 11; F. Wieacker, *Römische Rechtsgeschichte*, Munich 1988, 200; A. Guarino, *Storia del diritto romano*, Naples 1996, 91 ff; M. Talamanca (ed.), *Lineamenti di storia del diritto romano*, Milan 1989, 43 ff; F. M. D' Ippolito, *Aspetti di storia costituzionale romana*, Naples 2001, 22-23.

66 For a closer look at the military organisation of early Rome see L. Keppie, *The Making of the Roman Army*, London 1984.

the centuries.[67] These developments led to the gradual decline of the role of the *comitia curiata* and the formation of a new political body based upon the division of citizens into classes and centuries. This new body, known as *comitia centuriata*, became Rome's chief popular assembly during the republican period. An account of the constitution and main functions of this assembly will be offered in chapter 4 below.

Another significant change that appears to have taken place in the same period was the replacement of the three original tribes (the Tities, Ramnes and Luceres) with a number of purely territorial tribes. The city was divided into four districts, or urban tribes (*tribus urbanae*),[68] and the remainder of the Roman territory into sixteen rural tribes (*tribus rusticae*).[69] Those who owned land were enrolled in the rural tribes or districts in which their property was situated, while the landless citizens were included in the four urban tribes.[70] Both patricians and plebeians were included in these tribes. With the establishment of the new system mere domicile in a geographical tribe, not membership in a *curia*, became the basis of Roman citizenship, which was extended to many immigrants attached as clients to various patrician households.[71]

The end of the Monarchy

The Monarchy came to an end in 509 BC, with the expulsion of king Tarquinius Superbus who, as his name suggests, was of Etruscan origin.[72] The fall of the Monarchy was connected with the general breakdown of the Etruscan power in Italy and was brought about by an internal uprising against the king. The revolt appears to have been instigated by the patrician

67 Livy 1. 43; Dionysius 4. 16; 7. 59.

68 The names of these urban tribes were *Suburana*, *Palatina*, *Esquilina* and *Collina*. See Dionysius 4. 14.

69 The number of the rural tribes was gradually increased to reach a total of thirty-five tribes in the middle of the third century BC. See L. Ross Taylor, *The Voting Districts of the Roman Republic*, Rome 1960.

70 Livy 1. 43; Dionysius 4. 14. 15.

71 On the 'Servian reforms' see T. J. Cornell, *The Beginnings of Rome*, London 1995, 173 ff. Consider also M. Kaser, *Römische Rechtsgeschichte*, Göttingen 1976, 49 ff; M. Talamanca (ed.), *Lineamenti di storia del diritto romano*, Milan 1989, 63 ff; F. M. D' Ippolito, *Aspetti di storia costituzionale romana*, Naples 2001, 41 ff.

72 Shortly after the expulsion of Tarquinius Rome was taken by Porsenna, the Etruscan king of Clusium. But Porsenna was defeated by an alliance of Latin and Greek cities and was compelled to leave the city.

aristocracy whose privileged position had been threatened by the last king's disregard of established customary norms and the authority of the senate.[73]

Social Developments during the Early Republic: the Conflict of the Orders

With the ousting of the Etruscan dynasty in 509 BC begins a new period in Roman history, known as the Republic (from *res publica* or commonwealth). The first two centuries of this period witnessed the gradual transformation of Rome's social and political institutions. This transformation was brought about in part by the necessity of modifying the system of government to meet the needs of a rapidly growing community, and in part by the internal political struggle between the patrician aristocracy and the plebeian class.

As has been noted, the downfall of the Monarchy was brought about by an uprising of the patrician aristocracy against the authority of the king – an uprising probably inspired by similar movements in neighbouring cities and facilitated by the general weakening of the Etruscan power in Italy. During the early years of the Republic the political power of the patrician class appears to have increased. The plebeians, on the other hand, continued to be denied access to state offices and remained, both socially and economically, subordinate to the patricians. But the patricians' monopoly of political power was soon challenged by the plebeians who, having defined themselves as an independent social order, began to press for political equality. As the burdens which the plebeians were called on to bear became heavier (especially with respect to the defence of the state), the plebeians could no longer remain a silent majority in politics and the patricians found themselves under increasing pressure to make political concessions.[74] In the conflict between the classes, which lasted more than two centuries, the rich plebeians were looking for a share in the government, while the poor were more interested in improving living conditions and in securing protection from the arbitrary power of the

---

73 But the overthrow of the Etruscan dynasty did not mean the expulsion of all Etruscans from Rome (many of the leading Roman families were of Etruscan origin).

74 After Rome's military reorganization the state came to rely increasingly upon the plebeian class for its military strength. During the military campaigns of the early republican period, many plebeians gained a share of the *ager publicus* – the new lands acquired by Rome in the course of the wars. The number of the wealthy plebeians continued to increase with the expansion of Roman territory and this led to the strengthening of the position of the plebeian class in Roman political life.

patrician magistrates. But this conflict never resulted in an outright civil war because the patricians gradually, although not without resistance, agreed to meet the plebeian demands and, by the middle of the third century BC, all political distinctions between the two classes had disappeared. A brief description of the main events marking this process is offered in the following paragraphs.[75]

In 494 BC, according to the traditional dating, the plebeians refused to serve in the army and left the city, establishing their own settlement on a nearby hill (*Mons Sacrum*).[76] In order to avoid civil war, a compromise was reached and the plebeians were granted the right to elect officials of their own (*tribuni plebis*) to act as their spokesmen and to protect them against arbitrary acts of patrician magistrates. These officials were declared to be sacrosanct (*sacrosancti*) and inviolable.[77] Although not regarded as magistrates, the tribunes of the plebeians had the right to veto acts of magistrates threatening the interests of the plebeian class (*ius intercessionis*) and the power to protect the plebeians against abuses of patrician officials (*ius auxilii*). The tribunes were elected by the plebeians' own assembly, the *concilium plebis*. In 471 BC, under the *lex Publilia Voleronis*, the plebeian assembly was accorded legal status and was reorganised on a tribal basis. The plebeian assembly met to elect the tribunes and to vote on various measures put before it.[78] But the plebeian assembly was not regarded, in this phase, as an element of the Roman constitution, since it was not for nearly another two centuries that its resolutions came to be recognised as having the full force of laws.

In 462 BC the plebeians demanded, through their tribune Terentius Harsa, that the customary law of the land which guided magistrates and judges in their decision-making should be written down and made public. As was noted earlier, until that time the law was largely unwritten and known only to the patricians. As the plebeians did not know what their rights were, they had little chance of obtaining justice under the prevailing informal enforcement of customary laws. This demand, although at first strongly resisted by the patricians, was finally accepted and a special commission was appointed to carry out the codification of the law.[79] The

---

[75] For a more detailed account of the conflict of the orders see T. J. Cornell, *The Beginnings of Rome*, London 1995, 256-92, 327-44; G. Alföldy, *The Social History of Rome*, London 1985, 13 ff; F. R. Cowell, *The Revolutions of Ancient Rome*, London 1962, 30 ff, 38 ff, 47 ff.

[76] An event described as the 'secession of the plebeians'. See Livy 2. 32. 2. Cicero, *de re publica*, 2. 33. According to tradition, five such secessions took place in the period between 494 and 287 BC.

[77] Livy 2. 33. 3; Cicero, *de re publica* 2. 34.

[78] Livy 2. 58.

[79] Livy 3. 32. 6. 7.

code, which was probably modelled on similar codes of law enacted by Greek city-states some two centuries earlier, was finally published about 450 BC. After its enactment it was set up in public on twelve wooden tablets and for that reason it became known as the Law of the Twelve Tables (*lex duodecim tabularum*). But the Law of the Twelve Tables was neither a constitution nor a comprehensive code of laws – it was simply a compilation of basic customary civil and criminal laws and rules of procedure. Important areas of the law, such as constitutional law, were not included and remained under the exclusive control of the patricians.[80] Moreover, existing customary norms, such as the ban on the intermarriage between the patricians and plebeians and the rule pertaining to the right of creditors to imprison and sell into slavery their insolvent debtors, now received legislative recognition. Furthermore, the interpretation of the provisions of the Law of the Twelve Tables remained within the exclusive competence of the pontiffs who, as was noted earlier, were members of the patrician class. Yet the publication of the law proved advantageous to the plebeians, for the law was now accessible to all and not, as before, only to the patricians. Ordinary citizens were now able to defend themselves against exploitation by the powerful through recourse to explicit legal rules and procedures and judges were bound to give their decisions according to written laws.[81]

In 449 BC the right of Roman citizens (both patricians and plebeians alike) of appealing to the assembly of the people (*provocatio ad populum*) against sentences involving capital punishment was confirmed by the *lex Valeria Horatia*.[82] The same law also gave some legislative power to the plebeian assembly by enacting that 'what the *plebs* assembled in tribes ordered was binding on the whole people',[83] but the scope of this provision is not clear. It is more likely that this law recognised the right of the plebeian assembly to enact legislation, even though such laws did not become binding until approved by the senate and the assembly of the people (*comitia centuriata*). The same enactment confirmed the inviolability of the plebeian tribunes and their right to block by veto acts of magistrates they considered detrimental to the interests of the plebeian class (*ius intercessionis*).

The ban on the intermarriage between patricians and plebeians, which had been included in the Law of the Twelve Tables, was finally removed by the *lex Canuleia* of 445 BC. This law had far-reaching social and

---

80 See A. Watson, *The State, Law and Religion: Pagan Rome*, Georgia 1992, chs 2 and 3.

81 For more on the Law of the Twelve Tables see chapter 4 below.

82 This right was probably first recognised by a *lex Valeria* in 509 BC and was reconfirmed by another *lex Valeria* in 300 BC.

83 Livy 3. 55. 3.

political implications, as wealthy plebeian families, who were leading the fight for political equality, now began to contract alliances by marriage with patrician families with which they shared potentially common economic and political interests.

The plebeians had another success in their struggle for political equality in 367 BC with the passing of the *leges Liciniae Sextiae*, a series of laws proposed by the tribunes Lucius Sextius Lateranus and Gaius Licinius Stolo.[84] One of these laws recognised the right of the plebeians to hold the consulship, the highest office of the state, by providing that at least one of the two consuls elected each year should be chosen from the plebeian class.[85] At the same time the office of praetor was introduced, as an office open only to the patricians, to take over the judicial duties of the consuls.[86] By the close of the fourth century BC the plebeians had gained access to all the highest magistracies of the state (the dictatorship in 356 BC, the censorship in 351 BC and the praetorship in 337 BC).

Moreover the *leges Liciniae Sextiae* sought to improve the position of those without property and to address the problem of debt which gave rise to the condition of servitude to which large numbers of plebeians had been reduced. Thus it was provided that the portion of public land (*ager publicus*) that could be held by individuals could not exceed the 500 *jugera* (about 330 acres). As a result of this measure, large tracts of public land became available for distribution among the impoverished plebeian peasantry. Another provision reduced existing debts by providing that the interest paid should be deducted from the sum due and that the remainder should be paid in three annual instalments.[87] Another important enactment designed to improve the position of the poor was the *lex Poetelia Papiria de nexis* of 326 BC. This law abolished the early rule (sanctioned by the Law of the Twelve Tables) which allowed creditors to sell their insolvent debtors into slavery (*nexum se dare*).[88]

In 326 BC the plebeians were admitted to the most important priestly colleges, those of the *pontifices* and the *augures*, by the *lex Ogulnia de auguribus*. This law increased the number of the pontiffs by four and the augurs by five and provided that the new members were to be chosen from the plebeian class. Through their membership in the college of the pontiffs, the plebeians gained access to the formulae used in legal transactions and members of their class acquired the right to act as interpreters of the law.

---

84 Livy 6. 35. 3. ff.

85 But this law was resisted by the patricians and was not observed on several occasions in the years that followed. It was however re-confirmed in 342 BC and, from that time, one of the two consuls appointed each year was a plebeian.

86 Livy 6. 37-42.

87 Livy 6. 35. 4.

88 Livy 8. 28. 1. ff.

The conflict of the orders came to an end in 287 BC with the introduction of the *lex Hortensia de plebiscitis*. Under this law the enactments of the plebeian assembly (*plebiscita*) were given the full force of laws binding on all Roman citizens.[89] From that time the senate's sanction was no longer required for the resolutions of the plebeian assembly to be regarded as legally valid.

The plebeians' success in the conflict of the orders and the elimination of the political division between the two classes did not result in the eradication of social and economic inequalities. Instead, a new type of nobility (*nobilitas*) emerged in the place of the old patrician aristocracy. This new nobility was based on wealth and the participation in the government of the state through the holding of high office. The political rights which their success in the struggle of the orders guaranteed for the plebeians allowed wealthy plebeian families access to the highest offices of the state through which membership in the nobility was secured.[90] In the course of time (especially from the beginning of the third century BC) Roman government came to be monopolised by a small number of patrician and plebeian families from which almost all the high magistrates and members of the senate were drawn. Thus, the fundamentally aristocratic character of the Roman state did not change. What changed was the constitution of the aristocracy in power: the old patrician aristocracy was replaced by a new patricio-plebeian nobility based on wealth and office-holding. This new nobility soon became exclusive and its members treated with suspicion or even overt hostility members of lower classes who sought to attain high office.[91]

---

89 G. 1. 3.

90 As F. Adcock remarks, 'the social equalisation of patrician and plebeian notables was translated into a sharing of political power…A nobility, conferred on members of leading families by holding office, made aristocracy secure by broadening its basis'. *Roman Political Ideas and Practice*, U. of Michigan Press 1975, 28. And see T. J. Cornell, *The Beginnings of Rome*, London 1995, 340-344; G. G. Alföldy, *The Social History of Rome*, London 1985, 31 ff; R. Develin, 'The Integration of Plebeians into the Political Order After 366 BC', in K. A. Raaflaub (ed.) *Social Struggles in Archaic Rome*, London 1986.

91 Persons belonging to families whose members had occupied the consulship and other high magistracies were called *nobiles*. These had, by custom, the right to display in public figures (*imagines*) representing their distinguished ancestors (*ius imaginum*). The standing of a family, or clan, among the nobility depended on the number of such images they could exhibit. Those few 'outsiders' who could penetrate the barriers and reach the highest offices of the state (like Cato the Elder and, later, Marius and Cicero) were referred to as 'new men' (*novi homines*). All the others were collectively referred to as *ignobiles*.

The Roman Expansion in Italy

While the Roman state was undergoing the internal changes described above, Rome was gradually establishing herself as the dominant power in Italy. Shortly after the expulsion of the kings an alliance was formed between Rome and a league of city-states in Latium for the purpose of suppressing the threat posed by the Etruscans and the neighbouring mountain tribes of the Aequi and Volsci (493 BC). Although Rome had been recognised as the dominant city in the alliance and had the leadership in war, the Latin cities retained their independence. By the end of the fifth century BC the Aequi and Volsci had been driven back and Rome had conquered a large part of the Etruria. But about 390 BC Rome suffered a serious setback, when invading Celtic tribes from Gaul defeated the Romans and their Latin allies and captured the city. The invaders were finally bought off with gold and withdrew, but the Gallic occupation survived in the memory of the Romans as one of the most tragic events of their early history. In the years that followed Rome retained and consolidated her earlier conquests and continued her territorial expansion. In 338 BC the Romans, aided by Samnite forces, defeated the Latins, who attempted to break free from Roman domination, and dissolved their alliance. Rome's position as the dominant power in Latium was secured not only through the annexation of territory and the forging of alliances, on her own terms, with individual cities, but also through the implementation of effective new policies, such as the granting of Roman citizenship to members of Latin communities and the planting of Roman colonies among them. In 327 BC Rome embarked upon a long struggle with the powerful Samnite tribes for the control of cental Italy. The Samnites were finally subdued in 295 BC and, like the Latins and the Etruscans, were gradually incorporated in the Roman state through their admission to the Roman citizen body.

Not long after the end of the Samnite wars, Rome's rapidly growing power and influence brought her into conflict with Tarentum, the most powerful of the Greek cities of Southern Italy. In 280 BC the Tarentines and their allies, aware of Rome's military strength, summoned to their aid king Pyrrhus of Epirus, an ambitious ruler and capable general, who wished to unite the Greeks and form a Greek empire. Although Pyrrhus won several victories over the Romans, he was finally driven from Italy in 275 BC and Tarentum was forced to surrender in 272 BC. Along with the other Greek cities of Southern Italy it then became a Roman ally, agreeing to supply Rome with naval forces in return for Rome's military protection. With the submission of the Greek cities the unification of the entire Italian peninsula under Roman control was only a matter of time – it was completed a few years later, in 264 BC.[92] But the unification of Italy did not result in the formation of a single state. Rather, Italy was a conglomeration of many communities and individual city-states under Roman domination.

In the third century BC the Italian communities fell into two broad groups: those whose territories had been annexed by Rome and those which retained their independence but were bound to Rome by various kinds of treaties. Some of the conquered communities were granted full Roman citizenship (*civitas optimo iure*) while others were given partial citizenship only. The members of the latter communities had the private rights of citizenship, including the right to trade and hold property in Rome (*ius commercii*) and the right to intermarry with Romans (*ius conubii*), but not the political rights of voting (*ius suffragii*) and holding public office (*ius honorum*) in Rome. To this category belonged the inhabitants of towns in Latium, Etruria and Campania. These communities, which were called *municipia*, retained local self-government but their external relations were controlled by Rome. At the same time their members shared the obligations of Roman citizenship, paid taxes to Rome and served in the Roman armies. In general, the granting of partial citizenship was regarded as the first step towards the acquisition of full citizenship and the municipal system served as a means of incorporating foreign communities into Rome without the dissolution of their political and social institutions and customs. On the other hand, those cities in Italy which retained their independence paid no taxes to Rome but were individually bound to her by treaties of alliance under which they were obliged to provide military aid and to surrender control over their foreign affairs. Under these treaties their members enjoyed some of the private rights of Roman citizenship (without being regarded as Roman citizens) and might individually gain citizenship by becoming permanent residents of Rome.

Besides the two types of communities described above, a large number of colonies (*coloniae*) had been established throughout Italy on conquered territories by Roman citizens and members of Latin communities to whom plots of land had been allotted for cultivation. A distinction was drawn between Roman colonies (*coloniae civium Romanorum*) and Latin colonies (*coloniae Latinae*). The former were formed by Roman citizens and were linked directly to Rome, while the latter were usually made up of both Romans and Latins. The Latin colonies had their own systems of government, modelled on that of Rome, but were subject to Roman control and had to pay taxes to Rome and assist her militarily. Their members enjoyed some of the rights of the Roman

---

92 For a closer look at the earlier phase of Rome's expansion see T. J. Cornell, *The Beginnings of Rome*, London 1995, repr. 1997, chs 12 & 14; M. Cary and H. H. Scullard, *A History of Rome*, 3rd edn, London 1975, chs 8 & 10.

citizenship, such as the right to own property according to Roman law (*ius commercii*).[93] The colonies safeguarded Rome's conquests and at the same time facilitated the diffusion of the Roman culture in Italy.[94]

---

93 Before the first century BC the term *Latini* was used to describe those communities in Latium whose members enjoyed partial Roman citizenship. The term *ius Latii* denoted the legal position of the inhabitants of these communities and of the citizens of colonies founded by the Romans as Latin colonies. After the granting of the Roman citizenship to all Italians (89 BC) the same term referred to the legal status of the inhabitants of communities outside Italy who possessed some of the private rights of the Roman citizenship.

94 On the organisation of Italy during the Republic see also chapter 5 below.

3 The Constitution of the Roman Republic

Introductory

Our knowledge of the form and development of the Roman system of government during the early years of the Republic is incomplete due to the scarcity of authentic records and the gaps in the ancient historical sources. According to a widely accepted view, put forward by the German historian Theodor Mommsen, after the fall of the Monarchy the power of the king was transferred to two supreme magistrates who acted as heads of state, whilst the senate continued to function as a mainly advisory body.[1] Another theory claims that the government of the infant Republic was most likely in the hands of the senate, out of whose ranks one or more functionaries were appointed, whenever the need arose, to deal with urgent matters of the state.[2] This view draws support from the fact that, as regards the earlier phase of the Republic, the sources speak of different colleges of magistrates (*praetores*, *iudices*, *consules*, *decemviri legibus scribundis*, *tribuni militium consulari potestate*), as being entrusted with a variety of political, judicial and military tasks. During this period, the chief magistrates were referred to as *praetores*.[3] Later, probably after the introduction of the *leges Liciniae Sextiae* (367 BC), they began to be called

---

1 T. Mommsen, *Römisches Staatsrecht* I, Leipzig 1887, repr. Graz 1971. See also H. F. Jolowicz and B. Nicholas, *Historical Introduction to the Study of Roman Law*, 3rd edn, Cambridge 1972, 8.

2 W. Kunkel, *An Introduction to Roman Legal and Constitutional History*, 3rd edn, Oxford 1973, 14-15; F. Wieacker, *Römische Rechtsgeschichte*, Munich 1988, 223-224.

3 *Quod populo praeirent*: those who lead the people. The *praetores* were headed by a *praetor maximus*. See Livy 7. 3. 5. It should be noted here that in Etruscan cities, after the expulsion of the kings (*lucumones*), power was transferred to magistrates called *zilath*, a title translated in Latin as *praetor*. The head of this body of magistrates was referred to as *zilath purthna*, a title corresponding to that of the Roman *praetor maximus*.

praetores consules or, simply, *consules*.[4] Under the *leges Liciniae Sextiae* the institution of the magistracy (*magistratus*) was given a more definite form.

The republican constitution was based upon three interdependent elements: the magistrature (*magistratus*), the legislative assemblies of the Roman people (*comitia*), and the senate (*senatus*). Of these three elements the latter appears to have been the prevalent one, for the approval and support of the senate was, in practice, a necessary condition for the efficient functioning of both the magistrature and the assemblies.

The Senate

During the Republic the senate (*senatus*), the great council of the state, played a pivotal role in Roman political life. Although it had no legislative functions, operating mainly as an advisory body to the highest magistrates of the state, it was the most important stabilising factor of the republican system of government. This was largely due to its prestige and influence in society, the stability of its constitution and the experience of its members in the conduct of public affairs. Its resolutions, referred to as *senatus consulta*, although not legally binding, were usually treated with great respect and carried special weight in the eyes of the magistrates and other state organs. These resolutions were regarded as reflecting the accumulated experience and wisdom of the ruling aristocracy out of whose ranks the political, religious and military officers of the state were drawn. Moreover, since the consuls' term in office was limited to one year, the senate, as a permanent body, exercised much more influence on them than it had exercised on the kings and, despite its internal conflicts, was capable of pursuing long-term policies with continuity and consistency.

At the beginning of the republican period the senate was composed of three hundred members, chosen exclusively from the patrician class. Leading plebeians began to be admitted to the senate after the passing of the *leges Liciniae Sextiae* in 367 BC. From that time the senators were drawn from among those who had occupied the highest offices of the state.[5] Senators representing plebeian families were referred to as

---

4 *Consulere reipublicae*: those who deliberated for the well-being of the state. See G. Rotondi, *Leges publicae populi Romani*, Milan 1912, repr. Hildesheim 1966, 216 ff.

5 In 81 BC Sulla raised the number of senators to six hundred by drawing new members from among the most distinguished elements of the equestrian class. Under Caesar the number of senators was increased to nine hundred and, in the closing years of the Republic, there were as many as one thousand senators. But

conscripti (enrolled), whilst patrician senators were called *patres.*[6] The senators were selected first by the consuls and, from 443 BC, by the censors (*censores*). The latter were entrusted with the task of drawing up the senators' list (*album senatorium*), filling up vacancies caused by death or the removal from the senate of persons who, because of some misconduct, were deemed unworthy of holding the position of senator (*nota censoria)*. Initially the criteria that applied in the selection of senators were not specified by legislation but rested largely on custom. But the discretionary power of the censors in preparing the senators' list was limited after the passing of a *plebiscitum*, the *lex Ovinia de senatus lectione*, in the late fourth century BC. Under this statute, which probably simply confirmed existing practice, the censors were required to choose new senators from among the most prominent citizens.[7] This in practice meant that the senators had to be selected from among those who had occupied the highest offices of the state, such as the consulship, the praetorship and the censorship.[8] To these were added, in the later Republic, those who had held the positions of tribune, aedile and quaestor.[9] The procedure through which senators were selected was termed *lectio senatus*. The person whose name was placed at the top of the list of senators was called *princeps senatus* and, although he enjoyed no special privileges, his position carried special prestige.[10]

As was mentioned above, when revising the list of senators the censors had the right to omit the names of senators found guilty of conduct entailing personal disgrace (*infamia*) and could deny admission to candidates whom they considered unworthy of the position of senator.[11] As

---

the six-hundred member senate was restored by Augustus at the beginning of the Principate. See Dion Cass. 52. 42; 54. 13. 14; Suetonius, *Div. Aug.* 35.

6 Hence the phrase *patres et conscripti*, by which the senate was usually addressed.

7 See Festus '*praeteriti*', in Bruns, *Fontes* II, p. 26.

8 These were referred to as *magistratu curules*, as they alone were entitled to sit on a *sella curulis*, a special ivory chair used in public ceremonies as a symbol of their authority.

9 Moreover, it most likely that, during the last two centuries of the Republic, no person below a certain age could be considered for a position in the senate. The relevant age limit (*aetas senatoria*) was probably determined according to the *lex Villia Annalis* of 180 BC, by which the minimum age required for election to the higher offices of the state was fixed. Under this law the minimum age for consuls was forty-three, for praetors forty and for the aediles thirty-seven. See Cicero, *de off.* 2. 17.

10 See Livy 27. 11; 34. 44.

11 Those passed over the censors in the selection process were referred to as *praeteriti*. See, e.g., Livy 39. 42; 41. 27.

membership in the senate was regarded as a position of honour (*dignitas*), certain occupations, such as that of gladiator or actor, precluded admission to the senate. Emancipated slaves (*libertini*) and their immediate descendants were also excluded by custom. Moreover, senators were not allowed to engage in any commercial activities, other than the selling of the produce of their estates.[12] As the holding of public office was the principal condition for admission to the senate, persons who did not belong to the nobility but who, because of their exceptional ability and political influence, had been elected magistrates could be appointed senators. These 'outsiders' (*novi homines*), although not always welcome by the traditional senatorial aristocracy, were usually very wealthy and shared the same conservative attitudes with their senior colleagues in the senate. Although there is no evidence that during the Republic admission to the senate depended upon the possession of certain amount of property,[13] there is no doubt that the senatorial class (*ordo senatorius*) as a whole represented the wealthiest element of society.

Although the senate did not function as a legislative body, resolutions passed by the assemblies of the people could not acquire the full force of laws without their subsequent ratification by the senate (*patrum auctoritas*). The *lex Publilia Philonis* of 339 BC provided that the approval of the senate had to be given in advance (i.e. before a proposal was put to the vote of the people).[14] Furthermore, under the *lex Maenia* (early third century BC) candidates for the highest offices of the state had to be approved by the senate before they were formally elected by the assembly. Although, as a result of these enactments, the granting of the senate's approval came in most cases to be regarded as a mere formality, the senate continued to exercise a strong influence on legislation for neither the magistrates nor the assemblies could easily disregard its opinion when discharging their functions.

The senate had, moreover, complete control over foreign policy. It received envoys of other states, conducted negotiations with foreign powers, appointed ambassadors (*legati*) out of its own ranks, concluded treaties and alliances and intervened in disputes between cities in alliance with Rome. With the senate appears to have rested the ultimate responsibility of declaring war and concluding peace, although in principle this power belonged to the people. Proposals on such matters were

---

12 Under the *lex Claudia* of 213 BC senators were prohibited from owning vessels that could carry more than three hundred amphorae, that is, vessels that could be used for large scale trade.

13 Such a qualification was for the first time introduced in the early years of the imperial period.

14 Dionysius 7. 38; 9. 41; See also Cicero, *de re publica* 2. 32. 56.

submitted to the assembly on the senate's initiative and any attempt to by-pass the senate amounted to a violation of an important constitutional principle. In times of war, the senate supervised the conduct of military operations and ensured that the army received the necessary supplies of provisions. After a victory, it organised thanksgiving ceremonies (*supplicationes*) and triumphs (*triumphi, ovationes*) and made arrangements regarding the administration of conquered territories. During the later Republic the senate was responsible for the government of the Roman provinces overseas. It named the various Roman provinces and designated their boundaries, appointed their governors (*proconsules, propraetores*) and fixed the number of troops that were to be placed under their command. It also received delegations from the provinces and dealt with their requests and protestations.[15]

Within the senate's province fell also various duties relating to the administration of public finances, such as the fixing of the budget assigned to each magistrate, the management of public lands (*ager publicus*) and the imposition of special taxation (*tributum*) to cover the expenses of war. Moreover, with the assistance of the pontiffs and other priestly colleges, the senate exercised general supervision over the religious affairs of the state and dealt with matters relating to public morals. Thus it fell upon the senate to ensure that acts of state organs were carried out in accordance with the prescribed religious forms and to take measures against foreign cults regarded as threatening the established religious and moral order.[16] In

---

15 One of privileges which senators enjoyed was that when a senator decided to leave Italy in order to pursue his own private business he was given, by a decree of the senate, a title similar to that of an ambassador (*legatio libera*), by virtue of which he was entitled to the same privileges as those who represented the Roman state overseas. See, e.g., Cicero, *ad Att.* 2. 18; *pro Flacc.* 34; *de leg. agr.* 1. 3; 2. 17.

16 Such a measure was the famous *senatus consultum de Bacchanalibus* of 186 BC, the earliest senatorial decree that we know in its original form, under which severe penalties were provided for the followers of the eastern cult of the Bacchantes. The adherents of this cult, which was based on the worship of the wine-god Bacchus, had formed secret associations and were engaged in orgiastic religious rites. After a number of cult members had been found guilty of criminal and immoral conduct the senate declared that these associations constituted a threat to the state and ordered their dissolution. During the persecutions that followed more than four thousand people were put to death. The senate's action seems to have been motivated by genuine aversion to conduct that was taken to offend public morals and reflected a policy against religious associations operating in secret (the worshipping of Bacchus and other deities was permitted if done in the open and under official supervision). See Livy 39. 8-19; Cicero, *de legibus* 2. 37; For the text of the *senatus consultum de*

times of crisis the senate could declare a state of emergency, passing a special resolution (*senatus sonsultum ultimum*) by virtue of which the consuls were authorised to apply any extraordinary measures deemed necessary to avert the danger.[17] The principle that the salvation of the state outweighed any law justified the extension of the consuls' powers (*imperium*) and the temporary suspension of certain constitutional norms, such as that relating to the right of citizens to appeal to the assembly against capital sentences (*ius provocationis*).[18]

Only the highest magistrates of the state (*magistratus maiores, magistratus cum imperio*) had the right to convoke and preside over the senate (*ius agendi cum senatu*) and to submit proposals to it (*vocare* or *cogere senatum*). These included the consuls, the praetors, the dictator and the tribunes of the plebeians.[19] Before the commencement of the proceedings, the presiding magistrate saw that the auspices were taken and sacrifices offered, as custom required.[20] Then the magistrate proceeded to the presentation of the proposal or issue requiring discussion (*relatio*), always beginning with some reference of religious significance.[21] He then

---

Bacchanalibus see FIRA I, 30; A. C. Johnson, P. R. Coleman-Norton, F. C. Bourne (eds), *Ancient Roman Statutes*, Austin 1961, No. 28. Another example of a similar measure was the *senatus consultum de philosophis et rhetoribus* of 161 BC, under which the praetor was entrusted with the task of expelling from Rome philosophers and rhetors whose teachings were deemed morally harmful.

17 See, e.g., Livy 3. 4; 6. 19. And see B. Rödl, *Das Senatus Consultum Ultimum*, Bonn 1969.

18 On the various responsibilities of the senate see Polybius 6. 13; Livy 30. 17; 31. 11.

19 Aulus Gellius, *N. A.* 14. 7; Cicero, *de leg.* 3. 4. The senators were usually notified of a forthcoming meeting by means of a public notice (*edictum*). In circumstances of emergency, a magistrate would call an urgent meeting of the senate with the help of lower officers (*viatores*) and public criers (*praecones*). A regular meeting of the senate was termed *senatus legitimus*, while an extraordinary one *senatus indictus*. See, e.g., Livy 3. 38; 28. 9; Attendance was, in principle at least, obligatory, and those absent without an excuse could be fined, although it seems that a penalty was very rarely imposed in practice. Moreover, for the proceedings to be valid a certain number of senators had to be present. The requisite number varied at different times during the Republic and was probably connected with the nature of the issue under consideration.

20 Aulus Gellius, *N. A.* 14. 7.

21 A magistrate could summon the senate in order to put a matter to it for discussion (*rem ad senatum referre*), or only to impart some important news to the senators (*rem ad senatum deferre*). The magistrate could introduce further subjects for consideration but only after the conclusion of the debate for which the meeting of the senate had originally been called. See, e.g., Cicero, *Phil.* 7. 1; *pro leg. Man.* 19. Although individual senators were precluded from bringing

sought the opinion of the senate (*consulere senatum*), by inviting each member individually (*nominatim*) to express his views (*sententiam rogare*).[22] If the proposal consisted of more than one part the magistrate could, at the senators' request, divide it into clauses and then seek the opinion of the house on each clause separately. After all the speeches had been delivered and all views had been heard the presiding magistrate put the matter to the vote.[23] The senate's decision was expressed in the form of a resolution referred to as *senatus consultum* or *senatus decretum*.[24] The resolutions of the senate were, however, subject to tribunician veto (*intercessio*). Besides the tribunes, any magistrate equal or superior in rank to the magistrate on whose initiative a proposal had been submitted to the senate could prevent the relevant senatorial resolution from being validated (*intercessio collegae*).[25] *Senatus consulta* approved by the majority of the senators but rendered ineffective by tribunician veto had no legal force and

---

forward questions, it was not uncommon for the senate as a whole to invite the presiding magistrate to initiate discussion on any subject outside the set agenda. Consider Tacitus, *Ann.* 13. 49; Livy 30. 21; 42. 3.

22 First were called to speak those elected consuls for the following year (if the election process had been completed). (Besides the consuls-elect, no other magistrate-elect seems to have enjoyed such a privilege.) Next in the order of speakers was the *princeps senatus*, then those members who had served as consuls (*consulares*), then the former praetors (*praetorii*) and then those who had occupied lower magistracies according to their rank (*gradatim consulere*). Senators belonging to the same class usually spoke in order of seniority, although the presiding magistrate could call upon a senator to speak at any stage of the proceedings. Inviting a member to speak at the early phase of the proceedings was considered to be a great honour and a mark of respect. See, e.g., Livy 28. 45; Cicero, *Phil.* 5. 13; *ad Att.* 1. 13; 12. 21. A senator could refrain from delivering a formal speech, only expressing his assent or dissent to the proposal under consideration, or simply casting his vote without making any comment.

23 In cases of emergency, when there was no time for debate, the presiding magistrate could put the matter to the vote without obtaining the opinion of each senator separately. (Hence the distinction between *senatus consulta per relationem* and *senatus consulta per discessionem* - the second term denoted resolutions upon which the senate had voted, no matter whether its vote had been preceded by a debate or not).

24 The term *senatus consultum* was broader than the term *senatus decretum* (senatorial order), as a *senatus consultum* often included more than one *decreta*.

25 Aulus Gellius, *N. A.* 14. 7. Although individual senators lacked the power to block the passing of a resolution upon which the majority of the senate agreed, they could obstruct or delay its formal introduction by making use of the procedural rights to which they were entitled. See, e.g., Cicero, *ad Att.* 5. 4.

were regarded as mere expressions of the senate's views.[26] To a tribunician veto the senate could respond by calling upon the consuls to intervene and try to persuade the tribunes to withdraw their veto (*agere cum tribunis*). In extreme cases the consuls could seek the senate's advice on whether stronger action needed to be taken, such as putting the matter to the vote of the people, or even dealing with it themselves after having been invested with extraordinary powers.[27]

The Magistrature

Under the republican system of government executive power was divided among a number of annually elected magistrates (*annui magistratus*).[28] In the earliest period of the Republic the offices of the state were filled exclusively by members of the patrician class. But after the political barriers between the patricians and the plebeians were removed any free-born Roman citizen could, in principle at least, be a candidate for public

---

26 A non-binding resolution of the senate was referred to as *senatus auctoritas*.

27 For a closer look at the powers and functions of the senate during the Republic see F. E. Adcock, *Roman Political Ideas and Practice* , Ann Arbor 1975, ch.3; P. Willems, *le Sénat de la république Romaine* I-II, Louvain 1878-1885, repr. Aalen 1968; T. Mommsen, *Römisches Staatsrecht*, Leipzig 1887-8; H. F. Jolowicz and B. Nicholas, *Historical Introduction to the Study of Roman Law*, 3rd edn, Cambridge 1972, 30ff; M. Bonnefond-Coudry, *Le Sénat de la république romaine. de la guerre d'Hannibal à Auguste: pratiques délibératives et prise de décision*, 'Ecoles francaises d' Athènes et de Rome, vol. 273, Rome 1989; H. H. Scullard, *Roman Politics, 220-150 BC*, Oxford 1973; I. Shatzman, *Senatorial Wealth and Roman Politics*, Brussels 1975; A. Burdese, *Manuale di diritto pubblico romano*, 3rd edn, Turin 1987, repr. 1994, 74 ff; M. Kaser, *Römische Rechtsgeschichte*, Göttingen 1976, 52-55; W. Kunkel/M. Schermaier, *Römische Rechtsgeschichte*, Cologne 2001, 25-27; F. Wieacker, *Römische Rechtsgeschichte*, Munich 1988, 354 ff, 408 ff; A. Lintott, *The Constitution of the Roman Republic*, Oxford 1999, ch. 6; J. M. Rainer, *Einführung in das römische Staatsrecht*, Darmstadt 1997, 129 ff; A. Guarino, *Storia del diritto romano*, Naples 1996, 214 ff; F. M. D' Ippolito, *Aspetti di storia costituzionale romana*, Naples 2001, 67-68; G. Crifò, *Lezioni di storia del diritto romano*, 3rd edn, Bologna 2000, 89; M. Talamanca (ed.), *Lineamenti di storia del diritto romano*, Milan 1989, 187 ff.

28 The word *magistratus*, which was probably derived from the term *magister populi* (chief, leader of the people) by which the king was in earlier times described, referred to both the official and his office.

office.[29] No special knowledge or ability was formally required and, until the passing of the *lex Villia Annalis* in 180 BC, no specific law existed prescribing a minimum age for magistrates.[30] It was recognised as a general norm, however, that a person could not be appointed to the highest offices of the state without first having passed through the lower ones – a process known as *cursus honorum*.[31] But, during the early Republic at least, this norm does not appear to have received legislative recognition.[32] The *lex Villia annalis*, mentioned above, probably included provisions setting out rules concerning the regular succession of the offices (*certus ordo magistratuum*). The lowest office in the order was the quaestorship (*quaestura*); above it in the scale was the aedileship (*aedilitas*), then the praetorship (*praetura*) and then, highest of all, the consulship (*consulatus*).[33] The censorship (*censura*) and the dictatorship (*dictatura*) were not included in the *cursus honorum*. The magistrates of the Republic received no remuneration for their services. Appointment to state office reflected the people's confidence in the person elected and, as such, it was regarded as being the greatest of all honours.

As was noted before, the Roman magistrates' tenure of office was limited to one year, with the exception of the censors, who were appointed

---

29 Liberated slaves (*libertini*) and their sons were not eligible for public office. This norm, which seems to have been based on custom rather than on positive law, was not without exceptions however. See, e.g., Livy 9. 46.

30 According to Tacitus, 'in the days of our ancestors.every good and able citizen was entitled to compete for office. At the beginning there were no restrictions even of age, which prevented a man in his early youth from being elected to the consulship or even to the dictatorship'. (*Ann.* 11. 22.) See also Cicero, *Phil.* 5. 17; Livy 25. 2; 26. 18; 28. 43; Polybius 10. 4. Under the *lex Villia* the minimum age required for election to the consulship was forty-three, to the praetorship forty and to the curule aedileship thirty-seven. See on this Cicero, *de off.* 2. 17; *de leg. agr.* 2. 2; *Phil.* 5. 17. According to Polybius, the minimum age for election to the quaestorship was twenty-seven (for a person to be eligible for that office he should have completed at least ten years of military service, and most Romans entered the army at the age of seventeen). See Polybius 6. 19.

31 Livy 39. 39; 22. 26; Cicero, *de leg.* 3. 3.

32 In the sources we find a number of cases in which the rules governing the succession of the offices had not been observed.

33 The *lex Villia* was supplemented by the *lex Cornelia de magistratibus* of Sulla in 81 BC. This law provided that the office of quaestor had to be held before the praetorship, and the latter before the consulship. See Appian, *B.C.* 1. 100, 101; Cicero, *Phil.* 11. 5; *pro Planc.* 21. In the last century of the Republic it was recognised, moreover, that there had to be a lapse of two years (*biennium*) between the aedileship and the praetorship, as well as between the latter and the consulship.

for eighteen months, and the dictators, whose term in office did not exceed six months. The principle of annuality served as an important constitutional safeguard against the danger of abuse of power which a long term in office entailed. But in the early years of the Republic this principle meant little, as a person could be re-elected to the same office for several years in succession. This practice, which was often followed by the tribunes, although it had been condemned by a senatorial decree passed in the middle of the fifth century BC,[34] did not come to an end until 342 BC, when it was enacted that no one could lawfully be re-elected to the same office unless ten years had passed from the time he was first elected to office. By the same legislation it was decreed that no one could occupy two magistracies in the same year.[35] Furthermore, under a law passed probably in the first half of the second century BC, no one was allowed to hold the consulship twice.[36] Notwithstanding these restrictions, the assembly and the senate reserved the right, when circumstances so demanded, to suspend the relevant rules or to introduce exceptions to the law in favour of certain individuals.[37]

The magistrates were responsible to the Roman people and their assemblies by which they were elected (*per suffragia populi*).[38] Upon entering office, a magistrate had to swear that he would abide by the law (*iurare in leges*); when his term in office expired (*abdicare se magistratu, magistratu deponere*), he was similarly required to swear that he had not deliberately transgressed the law (*eiurare magistratum*). After leaving office, a magistrate could be held liable for any offences he committed while in office, especially for abuses of power committed against Roman citizens, members of allied communities or provincials. In other words, a

---

34 Livy 3. 21; Cicero, *de leg*. 3. 3.

35 Livy 7. 42; 10. 13; 39. 39. But one was not precluded from holding an extraordinary magistracy together with an ordinary one in the same year. See, e.g., Livy 23. 24. 30.

36 Livy, *Epit*. 56. The official lists of the magistrates show that, between 151 and 104 BC, no one held the office of consul twice, with the exception, under special circumstances, of Scipio the younger.

37 Cicero, *pro leg. Manil*. 21; *Phil*. 11. 5; Livy, *Epit*. 56. For example, during Hannibal's invasion in Italy, in the course of the second Punic war, the senate and the assembly decided to suspend all legal restrictions relating to the re-election of the consuls until the threat was removed. See Livy 27. 6.

38 See Polybius 6. 15.

magistrate's responsibility, which during his term in office was only political, became legal after his return to private life.[39]

Among the magistrates' main duties were the implementation of the decrees of the people and the senate and the administration of the laws. But from an early period it became clear that state officials could not operate efficiently unless they were given a sufficient degree of freedom in the execution of their duties. Thus it was recognised that, within the confines of their authority, the magistrates could issue edicts or ordinances (*edicta magistratuum*) for the purpose of facilitating the application of the law. Although the magistrates were in no sense regarded as law-makers, their edicts played an important part in the development of the law and, in the later Republic, came to be regarded as a distinct source of law (*ius honorarium*).

The term *potestas* was used to denote the executive power with which every Roman magistrate was invested as soon as he was elected to office. By virtue of this power a magistrate was able to carry out the various duties and responsibilities of his office. In exercise of his *potestas* he could issue executive orders (*ius edicendi*) and employ any coercive or punitive measures he considered necessary for the enforcement of his orders (*ius coercendi, coercitio minor*).[40] He could also call the citizens together in order to make announcements relating to the way he intended to discharge his duties (*ius contionem habendi*).

Besides the *potestas*, with which all state officials were invested, the highest magistracies (i.e. the consulship, the praetorship and the dictatorship) were accompanied by a special power known as *imperium*.[41] The word *imperium*, which originally signified the king's supreme military command, denoted, in a strict sense, the power of the higher magistrates to recruit and command troops, to appoint junior officers and to make arrangements for the distribution of war booty. Only magistrates with *imperium* (*magistratus cum imperio*) could assume command of an army, convene and preside over the assemblies of the people (*ius agendi cum populo*), summon and preside over the senate (*ius agendi cum senatu*) and celebrate triumphs after victory in battle (*ius triumphandi*). Moreover, only these magistrates had the full power of *iurisdictio*, that is, the power of

---

39 The legal responsibility of magistrates for abuses of power was the subject of various programmes of legal and judicial reform introduced during the later Republic.

40 Cicero, *de re publica* 2. 35; Dionysius 10. 50; Aulus Gellius, *N. A.* 11. 1.

41 The *imperium* was conferred upon a magistrate by a special law of the curiate assembly (*lex curiata de imperio*). In the last century of the Republic the granting of *imperium* by the curiate assembly had become a mere formality. See Cicero, *de leg. agr.* 2. 10-12.

setting out the legal principles upon which legal disputes were decided[42] and could impose severe penalties for violations of their orders, including capital punishments (*ius coercendi*, *coercitio maior*). As a sign of their supreme authority and their power to inflict severe punishments the magistrates with *imperium*, when appearing in public, were accompanied by officers, called lictors (*lictores*), carrying a bundle of rods (*fasces*) surrounding an axe (*securis*). Although outside the city of Rome a magistrate's *imperium* was regarded as absolute, within the city limits (*pomerium*) it was limited by the principle that supreme authority belonged to the Roman people and their legislative bodies.[43] A further restriction upon the *imperium* of the higher magistrates, also based upon the presumed supremacy of the people, was the institution of the *provocatio ad populum*, pertaining to the right of a citizen to appeal to the people's assembly against a capital sentence imposed upon him by a magistrate (*ius provocationis*).[44] But outside the city limits the magistrates' power to inflict such punishments remained absolute until the passing of the *leges Porciae* in the early second century BC. Under one of these laws the institution of *provocatio* was extended to protect citizens as well as soldiers from punishments imposed upon them by magistrates outside Rome.

As has been noted, a magistrate's term in office was limited to one year. But during the period of Rome's expansion it became evident that recalling a consul or praetor whose year in office had expired while he was still in command of an army engaged in military operations was both inconvenient and dangerous. Thus it was established that in times of war the assembly of the tribes (*comitia tributa*) could prolong the military command of a magistrate until the completion of the operation in which he was engaged. This extension of the period of *imperium* by an act of the

---

42 *Ius dicere*: the law. In the higher magistrates' jurisdiction fell the resolution of disputes between citizens (*iurisdictio inter cives*) and the confirmation of personal legal acts, such as adoptions, emancipations etc. (*iurisdictio voluntaria*). Lower magistrates, i.e. magistrates without *imperium*, (*magistratus minores*), had limited *iurisdictio*.

43 Under the *lex Valeria* of 509 BC, the lictors had to remove the axe from the *fasces* while the consuls remained in the city and, when they appeared in the assemblies, they had to lower the *fasces* as an acknowledgment of the supremacy of the Roman people. See Cicero, *de re publica* 2. 31.

44 The *provocatio ad populum* was regulated by the *lex Valeria de provocatione* of 300 BC. The sources make reference to two earlier statutes dealing with the same issue, the *lex Valeria Horatia de provocatione* of 449 BC and the *lex Valeria de provocatione* of 509 BC. See Livy 2. 8; 3. 55; Cicero, *de re publica* 2. 31. 53-54.

people was termed *prorogatio imperium.*[45] But in these cases the people reserved the right to rescind their own act (*abrogare imperium*) at any time.[46] When the *imperium* of a consul or praetor was prolonged, he continued to exercise the relevant powers, even though he no longer held office. In time the titles of proconsul and propraetor were introduced to describe those who were invested with the powers of the consul or praetor respectively. As a general rule, however, only a person who had occupied the consulship or the praetorship could be appointed as a proconsul or propraetor.[47] The *imperium* of a proconsul or propraetor differed in some important respects from that of the ordinary consuls and praetors. For instance, a proconsul could not exercise his *imperium* outside the particular district or province where he was appointed. And when a victorious proconsul or propraetor returned to Rome to celebrate a triumph, he had to remain outside the city limits until his entrance was approved by the senate and the assembly of the people and a special *plebiscitum* was passed allowing him to retain his *imperium* within the city on the day of the triumph. An ordinary consul, by contrast, could exercise his *imperium* anywhere outside the city limits. And although within Rome his *imperium* fell in abeyance, he could leave and re-enter the city as often as he needed, without having to apply each time for its renewal.

Besides annuality, another important principle governing the institution of the magistrature was that of collegiality (*collegium*). The same magistracy was held by more than one person[48] each of whom had equal *potestas* and, with respect to the higher magistrates, equal *imperium.* The division of the magistracies facilitated the carrying out of the various duties which each office entailed with greater speed and efficiency.[49] But,

---

45 The term *prorogare imperium* should be distinguished from the term *continuare consulatum*. The latter term referred to the election of the same person to the consulship for two consecutive years.

46 Like the *prorogatio imperium*, the *abrogatio imperium* required the passing of a *plebiscitum* by the assembly of the tribes.

47 This rule was not without exceptions, however. See, e.g., Livy 26. 18; Cicero, *pro leg. Man.* 21; *Phil.* 11. 8.

48 With the exception of the dictatorship and, until 242 BC (when the office of the *praetor peregrinus* was created), the praetorship.

49 With regard to the magistrates with *imperium*, the word *provincia* was used todenote the sphere of action pertinent to each magistrate. The *provinciae* of the consuls (*provinciae consulares*), that is, the various tasks assigned to the consuls, were determined by the senate (*nominare provincias*). After the tasks had been identified their allocation was usually left to the consuls concerned (*comparare inter se provincias*) or, if they could not reach an agreement, was decided by lot (*sortiri provincias*). In times of war one of the consuls assumed command of the army while the other remained in Rome to carry out the

more importantly, the principle of collegiality was intended to serve as a barrier against abuses of power by state officials, as a magistrate could not enforce a decision or order without the consent or acquiescence of his colleague. A magistrate could prevent the execution of a decision of his colleague either in advance (*prohibitio*) or after its publication (*intercessio*, *ius intercessionis*). Moreover, the *lex Villia annalis* (180 BC) provided that higher magistrates could prevent the performance of official acts of lower magistrates by *prohibitio* or *intercessio*. Of particular importance was the right of the tribunes (as was noted earlier, these were not regarded as magistrates) to veto official acts not only of other tribunes but of any magistrate.

As magistrates remained in office for a limited time only, it would have been difficult for them to carry out their duties efficiently without the help of advisers and experienced technical staff. Thus, when discharging his judicial functions, a magistrate was usually assisted by a council of experts (*consilium*). The daily routine and most of the clerical work was carried out by salaried civil servants (*apparitores*) or slaves (*servi publici*, *ministeria*). Moreover, a magistrate could perform some of his duties through delegates acting in his name, but could not appoint another person in his place.[50]

---

everyday business of the state. Under extraordinary circumstances the senate reserved the right of assigning a particular duty to one of the consuls or to both (*dare provinciam extra ordinem*). Similar procedures applied with regard to the allocation of the *provinciae* of the praetors, with the drawing of lots (*sors*) being the most common method of determining who was to serve as *praetor urbanus* and who as *praetor peregrinus* (hence the terms *sors urbana* and *sors peregrina* by which the relevant positions were described). But no matter how the various *provinciae* were distributed, their boundaries were strictly defined and it was considered a grave breach of the constitutional order if a magistrate, without formal permission, overstepped the limits of his *provincia*. During the turbulent period of the later Republic there were cases in which the assembly of the tribes (*comitia tributa*), acting under the constitutional principle that all power stemmed from the people, assigned *proviniae* to their favourite leaders without taking into account the opinion of the senate.

50 When a magistrate with the power of *iurisdictio* delegated this power to another person the Romans spoke of *iurisdictio mandata*. As stated in the Digest, 'The person who assumes *iurisdictio mandata* has no right of his own but exercises the jurisdiction of his mandator' (D. 1. 21. 1. 1.). And in D. 1. 21. 1. pr. we read: 'That which is assigned to a magistrate by statute, *senatus consultum* or imperial constitution as a special assignment cannot be transferred to another as a *iurisdictio mandata*'.

Categories of Roman magistrates

The most important offices of the state during the Republic were the consulship (*consulatus*), the praetorship (*praetura*), the censorship (*censura*), the aedileship (*aedilitas*), the quaestorhip (*quaestura*) and the dictatorship (*dictatura*). To these may be added the tribunate (*tribunatus*), although the tribunes were not formally regarded as magistrates. Depending upon their functions and powers by which they were accompanied these magistracies were classified in a number of different ways.

(i) *Magistratus cum imperio and magistratus sine imperio*

The power of *imperium* was conferred by a special enactment of the *comitia curiata* (*lex curiata de imperio*) upon the consuls, the praetors and the dictator. These officials were referred to as *magistratus cum imperio*; all the other magistrates possessed *potestas* only and were described as *magistratus sine imperio*. A consul's *imperium* was regarded as being superior (*imperium maius*) to that of a praetor, but inferior (*imperium minus*) to that of a dictator.

(ii) *Magistratus maiores and magistratus minores*

To the category of higher magistrates (*magistratus maiores*) belonged the consuls, the praetors and the censors, that is those magistrates elected by the assembly of the centuries (*comitia centuriata*). On the other hand, the aediles, the quaestors and other lower state officials, who were elected by the assembly of the tribes (*comitia tributa*), were classified as *magistratus minores*.

(iii) *Magistratus curules and magistratus non curules*

The magistrates entitled to use a *sella curulis*, a special ivory chair, as a symbol of their authority were the consuls, the praetors, the aediles, the censors and, probably, the dictator. These were referred to as *magistratus curules*, in contrast with the quaestors and other officials who were described as *magistratus non curules*. Citizens who could include among their ancestors persons who had occupied curule offices were termed *nobiles* and it is by these that the Roman aristocracy (*nobilitas*) was, for the most part, formed.

(iv) *Ordinary magistrates and extraordinary magistrates*

Of the Roman magistrates some were elected at regular intervals and for a set period of time, whereas others were appointed only under special circumstances or for specific purposes. To the category of ordinary magistrates belonged the consuls, the praetors, the censors, the curule aediles, the quaestors and the tribunes. Extraordinary magistrates were the dictator and the *interrex*.[51] To this category one might include the *decemviri legibus scribundis* and the *tribuni militares consulari potestate*, although at the time these were appointed the distinction between ordinary and extraordinary magistrates was not fully recognised.[52]

The consuls

During the Republic the highest executive office of the state was held by two annually elected officials originally called *praetores* or *iudices* and later, probably after the passing of the *leges Liciniae Sextiae* (367 BC), *praetores consules* or simply *consules*. The relevant magistracy was termed *consulatus*. The consuls were elected by the assembly of the centuries (*comitia centuriata*), which was convened for that purpose by one of the highest magistrates (consul, dictator or *interrex*). In the earliest period of the Republic the consuls were chosen exclusively from the patrician class. The plebeians gained access to the consulship in 367 BC, with the passing of the *leges Liciniae Sextiae*. This law, which provided that one of the consuls should be elected from the plebeians, was re-confirmed in 342 BC (by a *lex Genucia*) and, from that time, the rule that one of the consuls should be a plebeian was fully recognised and implemented.

The consuls had the same authority and exercised the same powers, both civil (*imperium domi*) and military (*imperium militiae*), as the kings.[53] But, as was noted before, the consuls' power was limited by two important constitutional principles, annuality and collegiality. Under the principle of annuality, a consul's term in office was limited to one year (*annuum*

---

51 During the Republic *interreges* were appointed by the senate when both consuls died or abdicated to supervise the election of new consuls.

52 The prefect of Rome (*praefectus urbi*), who seems to have been a *magistratus ordinarius* during the Monarchy, became *extraordinarius* during the early Republic (a prefect was appointed when all higher magistrates were absent). The office disappeared after the introduction of the urban praetorship in 367 BC but was re-introduced as a permanent one in the early imperial period.

53 Cicero, *de re publica*, 2. 32; *de leg*. 3. 3. The religious duties of the king were entrusted to a specially appointed priest called *rex sacrorum* or *rex sacrificus*.

imperium). After the expiry of his term a consul had to appear before the senate to assume responsibility for his official acts and, if accused of abuse of power, he could face trial before the people's assembly. Under the principle of collegiality, both consuls had full *imperium* (*imperium duplex*) and both had the power to block each other's actions, as well as those of lower magistrates, by *prohibitio* or *intercessio*.[54] Moreover, a judicial decision pronounced by one of the consuls could be appealed against before the other (*appellatio collegae*), who had the power to quash his colleague's verdict (*intercessio collegae*). However, as frequent conflicts between the consuls could be detrimental to the interests of the state, it was accepted as a common practice that each should assume in turn, usually for a period of one month at a time, the responsibilities of government.[55] And when both consuls were put in charge of an army they would divide the troops between them, each acting as commander-in-chief on alternate days, unless it had been agreed from the outset that one of them would have the overall leadership.[56] If a dispute or uncertainty arose as to how responsibilities were to be divided the matter was usually settled by lot.[57] In the event of the death or resignation of one of the consuls the other was required to summon the assembly for the election of a substitute for the remainder of the year (*subrogare* or *sufficere collegam*).[58]

Initially the powers of the consuls were very broad but in later years, especially after the passing of the *leges Liciniae Sextiae* in 367 BC and the creation of the praetorship and other offices, some of their duties were transferred to other magistrates. Despite the narrowing down of the consuls' sphere of action, however, the consulship remained the highest office of the state.[59] As bearers of *imperium domi*, the consuls were in charge of the government at home and exercised control over all other state

---

54 When the exercise of veto led to a deadlock the consuls were expected by custom to seek the advice of the senate (especially when important matters of the state were at issue).

55 Cicero, *de re publica* 2. 31; Livy 2. 1; Dionysius 5. 2; Valerius Maximus 4. 1. 1; Plutarch *Publ.* 12; Aulus Gellius, *N. A.* 2. 15.

56 See, e.g., Livy 3. 70; Polybius 3. 110; 6. 26.

57 Livy 2. 8.

58 Hence the distinction between *consul suffectus*, i.e. a consul who had beenelected to replace another who died or resigned before his year in office expired, and *consul ordinarius*, i.e. one who had been elected in the usual way. But we find cases in the sources in which the rules relating to the substitution of consuls had not been followed.

59 The importance of the consulship is manifested by, among other things, the practice of naming the year after the consuls in office – a practice which continued for centuries after the fall of the Republic.

officials, with the exception of the tribunes. They convened the senate and the assemblies, presided over them as chairmen and put forward questions for discussion to the first and legislative proposals for voting to the second.[60] Besides introducing bills, the consuls proposed to the assemblies the candidates for the highest magistracies of the state (*magistratus maiores*). In addition to ensuring that the decisions of the assemblies and the senate were properly carried out, they were responsible for the maintenance of law and order in the city and could order the expulsion from the city of foreigners whom they considered undesirable. Before the introduction of the praetorship in 367 BC, they were in charge of the administration of justice in relation to both civil and criminal matters.[61] And until 443 BC, when the office of censor was created, they were responsible for the formal enrolment and classification of the citizens. Moreover, as bearers of *imperium militiae*, the consuls acted as commanders-in-chief of the army and could inflict severe punishments (*coercitio*) to soldiers disobeying their orders. However, decisions relating to the declaration or termination of war and the conclusion of treaties could only be made by the senate and the assembly of the centuries. Furthermore, when war broke out, it lay with the senate to determine the number of soldiers needed to be recruited and to fix the cost of the operation and the amount of supplies required.

The praetors

The praetorship (*praetura*) was introduced in 367 BC as a concession to the patricians for acceding to the plebeians' demand that one of the consuls should be a plebeian. Originally one praetor was elected, exclusively from the patrician class. The plebeians gained access to the praetorship in 337 BC.[62] To the new magistracy were transferred the duties of the consuls relating to the supervision of civil litigation (*iurisdictio*) in disputes between Roman citizens (*qui inter cives ius dicit*).[63] In the third century

---

60 Laws proposed by the consuls were referred to as *leges consulares*.

61 A consul had the right to call any person to appear before him for questioning (*vocatio*) and could, if the latter refused, order his being brought forward by force (*prehensio*).

62 Livy 6. 42; 7. 1; 8. 15.

63 It has been suggested that, before the establishment of the praetorship, the task of declaring the law and supervising civil litigation fell to the pontiffs. See A. Watson, *The Law of the Ancient Romans*, Dallas 1970, 24-25. See also D. 1. 2. 2. 6. (Pomponius). The most widely accepted view, however, is that, before the office of praetor was created, this task was entrusted to the consuls. See H. F. Jolowicz and B. Nicholas, *Historical Introduction to the Study of Roman Law*,

BC, as the number of foreigners (*peregrini*) living in Rome continued to increase and transactions between them and Romans multiplied, an additional praetor was appointed (c. 242 BC) to supervise litigation in disputes between foreigners (*iurisdictio inter peregrinos*), and between foreigners and Roman citizens (*iurisdictio inter cives et peregrinos*). The new praetor (*praetor peregrinus*) was distinguished from the original one who, as having jurisdiction over disputes between Roman citizens only (*iurisdictio urbana*), was termed *praetor urbanus* or *praetor urbis*.[64] As the Roman territory continued to expand, two further praetors were added in 227 BC and two more in 197 BC. These were appointed as governors of the newly formed Roman provinces overseas (*praetores provinciales*).[65] Under Sulla (82 BC) the number of praetors in Rome was increased to eight. Of these the *praetor urbanus* and the *praetor peregrinus* continued to supervise the administration of the civil law in Rome and Italy,[66] while the remaining six served as chairmen of the newly established criminal courts (*questiones perpetuae*, *praetores quaesitores*). Eight more praetors were added by Caesar in the second half of the first century BC.[67]

Like the consuls, the praetors were elected annually by the assembly of the centuries (*comitia centuriata*) and, although they were inferior to the consuls to whom they were regarded as junior colleagues (*minores collegae consulum*), they were invested with the same power of *imperium*.[68] As bearers of *imperium*, besides being capable of assuming military command, they had the right of summoning the senate and the assembly (*comitia tributa*), and could introduce questions for discussion to the first and propose laws to the second. As has been noted, the praetors had the full power of *iurisdictio*, that is, the power to regulate legal proceedings and to declare the legal principles on the basis of which disputes were resolved. Associated with this power was their right of

---

3rd edn, Cambridge 1972, 48. And see F. Wieacker, *Römische Rechtsgeschichte*, Munich 1988, 429-34.

64 The province of the *praetor urbanus* was termed *provincia* or *sors urbana*, while that of the *praetor peregrinus* was known as *provincia* or *sors peregrina*.

65 The first two were appointed governors of the provinces of Sicily and Sardinia, while the other two of those of Hither and Farther Spain. But from 148 BC provincial governors were chosen from the ranks of ex-consuls and ex-praetors.

66 Outside the city these were represented by lower jurisdictional magistrates referred to as *praefecti iuri dicundo*.

67 Suetonius *Caes*. 41. The allocation of the various duties among the praetors was usually done by lot under the supervision of the senate.

68 Livy 7. 1; 8. 32; 10. 22; 27. 35. While a consul was usually accompanied by twelve lictors, a praetor was accompanied only by two within the city, or by six when he was overseas.

issuing binding regulations, or edicts (*ius edicendi*). The edict, which the praetor of each year issued upon taking office, specified the principles which he would observe in enforcing the law and the conditions under which he would allow prosecutions and suits. As it was intended that it should be valid throughout his year in office, it was called continuous edict (*edictum perpetuum*). If occasions arose, the praetor might issue additional edicts at any time during the year (such an edict was called *edictum repentinum*). Originally, a praetor was not legally bound to adhere to the directions set out in his edict, although he was required to do so by custom. But in the last century of the Republic a law was enacted – the *lex Cornelia de iuris dictione* of 67 BC – which forbade praetors from departing from their edict. Moreover, although each praetor's edict was valid only during his own term, it became customary for a newly elected praetor to incorporate into his own edict the bulk of his predecessor's edict, making only limited alterations.[69] In the course of time the praetorian edict became one of the most important factors in the development of Roman private law and provided the basis for a distinct source of law known as *ius praetorium* or *ius honorarium*.

The praetors appointed as provincial governors (*praetores provinciales*) exercised, by virtue of their *imperium*, broad civil and military powers. They decided on all matters relating to the internal administration of their provinces and warranted the peace and security of the various communities within their borders. They commanded the military forces, both Roman and auxiliary, stationed in their provinces and, when the need arose, could recruit fresh troops locally (*delectus provincialis*). Furthermore, provincial governors exercised general supervision over the administration of the law, both civil and criminal, within their territories. Although the majority of cases were tried before local courts, a party had the right to lodge an appeal with the governor. Moreover, the governor, assisted by a committee of advisers (*consilium*), visited the main towns of his province at least once a year to hear cases in specially set up tribunals. In criminal cases he had the power to impose punishment, including capital punishment, on both locals and Roman citizens residing in his province.[70]

As was noted before, the praetors entrusted with the administration of criminal law (*praetores quaesitores*) were introduced after the

---

[69] The part of a praetor's edict which he adopted from the edict of his predecessor in office was termed *edictum tralaticium*.

[70] Roman citizens, however, retained the right of appealing to the assembly in Rome (*provocatio ad populum*, *ius provocationis*) if found guilty of capital offences.

establishment of the permanent criminal courts (*quaestiones perpetuae*) in the later republican period. A *praetor quaestitor* conducted the preliminary investigation into a criminal charge, presided over the court trying the case and directed the relevant proceedings. Before proceedings began he had to swear that he would abide by the law by which his court was established and could be subject to punishment if found guilty of corruption or abuse of power.[71]

The censors

As a result of the reforms which Roman tradition attributes to King Servius Tullius property became the basis of Rome's military and political organisation. This necessitated the registration of the whole citizen body at regular periods so that both the age and property of the citizens would be recorded as required for the purpose of determining the amount of property tax (*tributum*) which each citizen had to pay and the class (and hence the century in the assembly of the centuries) to which he belonged. In the earliest period of the Republic the taking of the census (*censum agere*) was carried out by the consuls. But from 443 BC this task was assigned to a new magistracy, the censorship (*censura*).[72] Two censors were appointed exclusively from the patrician class until the passing of the *lex Publilia Philonis* of 339 BC which provided that at least one of the censors had to be a plebeian.[73] Although the censors belonged to the *magistratus maiores*, they did not have *imperium*, being invested with *potestas* only. Nevertheless, the censorship was regarded as one of the most important offices of the state, as manifested by the fact that only persons who had previously served as consuls (*consulares*) were normally considered eligible for this office, and its holders were treated with great respect and deference. The significance of the office lay in the fact that, by assigning the citizens to the appropriate classes, the censors determined also, in a definite way, the political and social position of each individual citizen. By the end of the fourth century BC the censors were entrusted with the additional tasks of compiling the roll of the senators (*album senatorium*) and of filling vacancies in the senate through the procedure of *lectio senatus*. In doing so they were bound by the *lex Ovinia* (318-312 BC) which ordained that only the worthiest men of every class should be

---

71 For more on the *quaestiones perpetuae* see chapter 6 below.

72 Livy 4. 8. 2; Dionysius 11. 63.

73 Livy 8. 12. 16. Two plebeian censors were elected for the first time in 131 BC. See Cicero, *de leg*. 3. 3; Livy 7. 22; 8. 12; 10. 8.

appointed as senators. The censors were also responsible for the enrolment of citizens into the local tribes (*tribus*).

Like the consuls and the praetors, the censors were elected by the assembly of the centuries (*comitia centuriata*), which was summoned for that purpose by the consuls.[74] Unlike other magistrates, whose term in office was fixed to one year, the censors were elected originally for a five-year term, as the census was traditionally taken every five years (*lustrum*). But in 434 BC the duration of the censors' term in office was limited to eighteen months by the *lex Aemilia.* The introduction of this law had probably been motivated by the fear that political freedom might be endangered if the same individual exercised the extensive powers of the censorship for a long period of time.

As has been noted, the chief duty of the censors was the registration of the Roman citizens and their property and the determination of the class and century to which each citizen belonged and the amount of tax which each citizen had to pay. The registration was preceded by a special edict of the censor by which he announced the rules governing the registration process (*lex censoria*).[75] When carrying out the census the censors relied upon declarations (*professiones censualis*) submitted under oath by the citizens who were summoned for that purpose (*censendi causa*) by tribes. A declaration included the name and age of the person concerned, his family status and the amount of property in his possession.[76] Moreover, a person had to state if he was a free-born Roman citizen (*ingenuus*) or a freedman (*libertinus*).[77] One should note here, however, that only those who were legally independent and in full control of their own affairs (*sui iuris*) were included in the censors' lists (*ius censendi*). Thus, a son under the control of his father (*in patria potestate*), or a wife under the control of her husband (*in manu mariti*) were not enrolled independently but together with the persons to whose power they were subject. Orphans (*orbi orbaequae*) and unmarried women outside their parents' control (*viduae*) were placed under guardians (*tutores*) and were enrolled together under a separate category. Evading the census was a serious offence and the

---

74 When convened to elect the censors this assembly was usually referred to as *comitia censoria* or *comitia censoribus creandis.*

75 These edicts or ordinances came to be regarded as a form of code binding upon all those entering the censor's office. The term *lex censoria* was also used to denote the special edict in which the censors prescribed the terms and conditions under which state property could be sold or leased.

76 These declarations provided the basis for the registration of citizens into publicregisters called *tabulae census* or *libri censorii.*

77 See Cicero, *pro Flacc.* 32; *in Verr.* 1. 18; Livy 39. 44. See also the *lex Iuliamunicipalis*, lines 145-148, in Bruns, *Fontes* I, no. 18.

transgressor (*incensus*) suffered confiscation of his property and could be sold as a slave by the consuls (*deminutio capitis maxima*).[78]

In the course of time the censors acquired the right to look into the public and private conduct of citizens, when carrying out the census, and to single out those whose behaviour violated generally accepted moral norms. Thus the censors came to be recognised as supervisors of public morals and upholders of the moral standards of society (*regimen morum*, *cura morum*). With respect to matters of public morality, they exercised quasi-judicial functions and could stigmatise those found guilty of morally reprehensible acts, irrespective of whether these acts amounted to legal offences or not. Conduct likely to incur the censors' disapprobation included, for example, maltreating one's family members or clients, neglecting one's religious duties, acting against good faith in private transactions or being engaged in a disreputable trade. Likewise, abuses of power by magistrates, the taking of bribes by judges or jurors and cowardice in battle were subject to censure. The censor's disapproval was expressed in the form of a note added next to the culprit's name in the register (*nota censoria*).[79] The censors were under no obligation to conduct a formal investigation before passing judgement but, if in doubt, they could give the person whose character was in question an opportunity to defend himself.[80] It was required, however, that the reason for the *nota censoria* must always be stated (*subscriptio censoria*) and that both censors must have agreed in affixing it. A person whose conduct was stigmatised by a censor (*notatus*) was branded with ignominy or infamy (*ignominia*, *infamia*) and, as a result, was deprived of certain political rights and privileges or fell from a position of honour. Thus, senators and members of the equestrian class branded with ignominy could be expelled from their respective orders. For an ordinary citizen the effect of a *nota censoria* was his removal from the tribe to which he belonged and thus the loss of his right of voting in the assembly (*ius suffragii*).[81] It was accepted, however, that censors could

---

78 The forfeiture or suspension of a citizen's social and political rights as a punishment for an offence he committed was termed *deminutio capitis*. Depending upon its seriousness the Romans distinguished between three degrees of *deminutio capitis*: *maxima*, *minor* and *minima*. See G. 1. 159-163; D. 4. 5. 11. (Paulus). On the evasion of the census as a reason for a *deminutio capitis maxima* see Cicero, *pro Caec*. 34; Livy 1. 44.

79 See, e.g., Cicero, *pro Cluent*. 46.

80 Livy 24. 18. But no appeal against the censors' decisions could be raised before the assembly or any other court.

81 Citizens deprived of the *ius suffragium* on such grounds were termed *aerarii* because, notwithstanding their inferior status, they were still required to pay taxes (*aerarium*: public treasury). Sometimes a citizen branded with *ignominia*

remove the *notae censoriae* of their predecessors and reinstate those who had been stigmatised in their former position.[82]

A further duty entrusted to the censors was the collection of the Roman public revenues (*publica*). These came mainly from taxes paid by Roman citizens and provincials and the exploitation of lands, mines and other property belonging to the state. The public revenues were not collected by the state directly, but were let or leased to contractors – tax-farmers (*publicani*) and collectors of other public revenues – who undertook, at their own risk and cost, to levy the dues and to pay a fixed sum annually into the Roman public treasury. The job of the censors was to lay down the framework of these contracts, or leases, by setting out the conditions under which these were granted, and to let them out to the highest bidder.[83] In connection with this task the censors exercised a form of *quasi* jurisdiction when disputes arose between the state and collectors of public revenues, when the demarcation lines between public and private lands were called into question, and in cases involving the unlawful occupation of public lands by private individuals. In the latter cases they could order the expulsion of persons who illegally occupied property belonging to the state.

In the last century of the Republic the office of censor was stripped of most of its powers and, during the civil wars that mark the end of this period, appears to have fallen in abeyance. Augustus' attempt to revive the censorship was met with little success and the office, in its original form, finally disappeared by the close of the first century BC. As we will see later, during the imperial era both the supervision of public morals and the selection of senators were undertaken by the emperors, while the other functions of the censors were divided among other state officials.

The aediles

The aedileship (*aedilitas*) was introduced in the middle of the fifth century BC, probably under Greek influence.[84] Its original functions were

---

was transferred from a rustic tribe into one of the four urban tribes which were regarded as less honourable partly because they contained all the liberated slaves.

82 Livy 4. 31; Cicero, *pro Cluent.* 42; Val. Max. 2. 9. 9.

83 The conditions under which these contracts were concluded – usually for a period of five years – were referred to as *leges censoriae*. It should be pointed out here that the censors' duties did not include the administration of public finances which, as was said earlier, fell in the senate's sphere of responsibilities.

84 Magistrates exercising the same functions as the Roman aediles existed in many Greek city-states.

associated with the supervision of temples and other religious sites (*aedes sacra*) and the care of records and public money.[85] At first two aediles were elected as exclusively plebeian officials (*aediles plebis*) by the assembly of the plebeians (*consilium plebis*) to serve as assistants of the tribunes.[86] Under the *leges Liciniae Sextiae* of 367 BC two additional aediles were introduced. These were referred to as *aediles curules* for, although they were included in the *magistratus minores* and, as such, they lacked *imperium* (they had *potestas* only), they were entitled to use a curule chair (*sella curulis*), which had been a prerogative of the higher magistrates. The *aediles curules* were chosen first probably by the assembly of the centuries (*comitia centuriata*) and, subsequently, by the assembly of the tribes (*comitia tributa*) from both the patrician and the plebeian orders.[87]

Although the curule aediles were deemed superior to their plebeian colleagues, they all shared similar duties. These included the supervision and maintenance of public roads and buildings, such as altars and temples (*procuratio aedium sacrarum*),[88] the keeping of public records, the supervision of the supply of corn and other essential goods to Rome (*cura annonae*) and the organisation of public games (*ludi*).[89] Moreover, as custodians of the city (*curatores urbis*), the aediles were entrusted with police duties and were responsible for the maintenance of order in the area of Rome. They had criminal jurisdiction over cases involving minor offences and could inflict punishment on those disobeying their orders (*coercitio*).[90] One of the aediles' earliest and most important functions was

---

85 D. 1. 2. 2. 21. (Pomponius).

86 Although the plebeian aediles were not regarded as magistrates, they were treated as sacrosanct and inviolable, like the tribunes under whom they served.

87 Aulus Gellius, *N. A*. 13. 15; Dionysius 9. 49; Livy 9. 46; 25. 2.

88 It also fell upon them to ensure that public baths, taverns and other public houses operated according to the required standards and that public works were carried out in accordance with the conditions stipulated by the censors in the relevant contracts.

89 Of the public games, the most important (*ludi romani*) were organised by the curule aediles, while the less important (*ludi plebei*) were organised by the plebeian aediles.

90 The sources speak of prosecutions initiated by the plebeian aediles, acting under the authority of the tribunes, against private individuals illegally occupying public lands, tenants of public pastures (*pecuarii*) whose flocks exceeded the legal limit, and money-lenders (*feneratores*) who demanded interest in excess of the legally prescribed amount. See, e.g., Livy 7. 28; 10. 13. 23. 31. 47; 30. 39; 33. 42; 34. 53; 35. 10. 41; 38. 35.

the supervision of activities in the market place.[91] In their capacity as market officials they issued edicts (*edicta*) concerning the sale of goods and ensured that the prices charged were reasonable and that the measures and weights used complied with the prescribed standards. The edicts of the aediles and the limited civil jurisdiction which these magistrates exercised in the market place played an important part in the development of the Roman law of sale.

The quaestors

The quaestorship was the first step in the regular *cursus honorum* (*primus gradus honoris*), the process through which an individual could gain access to the highest offices of the state. Like the aediles, the quaestors belonged to the *magistratus minores* and thus they were invested with *potestas* only. During their year in office they had the right to attend the meetings of the senate and ex-quaestors could be considered for permanent senatorial posts, although priority was given to those who had held higher magistracies.[92]

Officials bearing the title of quaestor (*quaestores paricidii*) first appeared in the period of the kings. The *quaestores paricidii* were extraordinary officials who were appointed to investigate cases of homicide. Similarly, in the early years of the Republic quaestors were appointed by the consuls to carry out the prosecution of criminal offences before the assembly of the centuries.[93] As an ordinary magistracy the quaestorship was established in the middle of the fifth century BC, probably in imitation of a similar office found in the Greek cities of Southern Italy and Sicily. Until 421 BC the quaestors were appointed by the consuls, exclusively from the patrician class, to assist them in matters pertaining to the administration of public finance.[94] From that time they were elected by the assembly of the tribes (*comitia tributa*) from both the patrician and the plebeian orders. The number of the quaestors was originally two, but in 421 BC it was increased to four.[95] Of these two remained in the city where they served as public treasurers (*quaestores urbani* or *aerarii*), while the other two (*quaestores militares*) accompanied the consuls in military campaigns and performed the duties of quartermasters in charge of supplies, the payment of troops and the

91 Greek historians refer to them as *agoranomoi* (those in charge of the marketplace).

92 See Livy 23. 23; Val. Max. 2. 2. 1.

93 See, e.g., Livy 2. 41; 3. 24. 25; Dionysius 8. 77; D. 1. 2. 2. 23. (Pomponius).

94 D. 1. 2. 2. 22. (Pomponius); Tacitus, *Ann.* 22; Livy 4. 4; Plutarch, *Publ.* 12.

95 Tacitus, *Ann.* 11. 22.

distribution of war booty.[96] Around the middle of the third century BC the number of quaestors was again increased to eight. In the last century of the Republic Sulla raised their number to twenty, and Julius Caesar to forty.[97] Of these the provincial quaestors (*quaestores provinciales*) served in the Roman provinces overseas, where they acted as assistants to the governors in financial and other administrative matters.[98] The allocation of the various duties among the quaestors was usually done by lot, although the senate had the right of assigning a specific duty to a particular individual.

The *quaestores urbani* were in charge of the public treasury (*aerarium*) which also served as a public records office. In this were kept the account books of the quaestors, the lists of taxpayers drawn by the censors, the contracts by which public revenues were leased, the reports of provincial magistrates as well as the military standards of the Roman army.[99] In the *aerarium* were also kept the statutes (*leges*) passed by the assemblies, the resolutions of the senate (*senatus consulta*) and the official list of those who were chosen to serve as jurors in criminal trials (*album iudicum*). Moreover, magistrates, whether civil or military, retiring from office were required to deposit in the *aerarium* all records connected with their offices.[100] Besides supervising the *aerarium*, the quaestors were entrusted with the collection of all public revenues derived from taxation and other sources and the financing of various public projects, such as public works and military operations. In discharging these duties they acted under the authority of the senate, under whose overall control the administration of public finance lay.[101] All financial transactions involving public money which took place in the provinces were carried out by the provincial quaestors who were responsible to the senate either directly or indirectly, through the *quaestores urbani*. Finally, the quaestors dealt with claims by private individuals contesting debts and other financial obligations to the state.

---

[96] Livy 4. 43; Tacitus, *Ann.* 11. 22.

[97] Tacitus, *Ann.* 11. 22; Suetonius, *Caes.* 41.

[98] Cicero, *pro Muren.* 8; *in Vatin.* 5; Tacitus, *Ann.* 4. 27.

[99] These standards were handed over by the quaestors to the general in command of an army before embarking on a military expedition. See Plutarch, *Publ.* 12; Livy 3. 69; 4. 22; 7. 23.

[100] In doing so they had to take an oath before the quaestors as to the authenticity and accuracy of the relevant documents. See Livy 29. 37; Val. Max. 2. 8; Appian, *B.C.* 1. 31.

[101] Consider, e.g., Livy 4. 15; 5. 26; 24. 18; 33. 42; 38. 60; 42. 6; 44. 16; Dionysius 5. 34; 7. 63; 8. 82; Cicero, *Phil.* 9. 7; 14. 14; Val. Max. 5. 1. 1; Polybius 6. 13.

The tribunes

As was mentioned in chapter 2, the tribunate was introduced in 494 BC as an exclusively plebeian office. At first two tribunes were appointed, but their number was subsequently increased to five and, around the middle of the fifth century BC, to ten. These officials were elected by the assembly of the plebeians (*concilum plebis*) and, in later years, by the assembly of the tribes (*comitia tributa*), under the supervision of one of the tribunes in office.[102] To be eligible for the office of tribune one had to be a free-born Roman citizen (*ingenuus*) and a member of a plebeian clan by birth or by adoption.

The tribunes were not regarded as magistrates (they acted as representatives of the plebeians only) and, unlike the regular magistrates, had neither *imperium* nor ordinary *potestas*. Yet they exercised such wide powers (*tribunicia potestas*) that their decisions had a strong impact on the affairs of the whole community. They had the right to intervene on behalf of any member of the plebeian class who sought their assistance (*auxilium*) and could invalidate acts of magistrates by simply pronouncing the word *intercedo* or *veto* (I forbid).[103] By exercising their right of veto against magistrates presiding over meetings of the senate and the assemblies they could prevent these bodies from functioning. Although they did not possess the *ius vocationis*, i.e. the right of summoning citizens to appear before them, they could order the arrest and prosecution of any person who, in their presence, encroached upon the rights of the plebeians (*ius prehensionis*).[104] Moreover, they had the right to convene and preside over the assembly of the plebeians (*concilium plebis*) and, in later years, the assembly of the tribes (*comitia tributa*), and to submit laws to them (*leges tribuniciae*). They could also call and preside over meetings of the senate (*ius agendi cum senatu*).[105] As the office and person of a tribune was

---

[102] Livy 2. 33. 44. 58; 3. 30; 4. 16; Cicero, *de re publica* 2. 34. 59; Dionysius 6.89; 9. 41. The ten tribunes formed a college or association known as *collegium tribunorum plebis*.

[103] Livy 6. 35. They could do so either in advance (*prohibitio*) or after the other magistrate's order had been issued (*intercessio*).

[104] Like the ordinary magistrates, the tribunes were usually accompanied by *viatores*, lower officials whose role was to carry out the orders of their superiors. In the sources we find cases in which tribunes ordered the arrest even of consuls and other high magistrates. See, e.g., Livy 2. 56; 4. 26; Cicero, *in Vatin.* 9; *ad Att.* 2. 1; Val. Max. 9. 5. 2.

[105] From the end of the second century BC persons who had held the office of tribune began to be admitted as members of the senate. On the relation of the

regarded as sacrosanct and inviolable (*sacrosanctus*, *sancrosancta potestas*),[106] tribunes were not subject to coercion by magistrates. Any person who impeded a tribune in the execution of his duties or assaulted his person was treated as accursed (*sacer*) and could be put to death without trial.

However, the power of the tribunes was not free from limitations. Not only did they lack *imperium*, and hence the ability to command an army, but their civil powers as well as their independence from consular control did not extend outside the city limits.[107] A further restriction on the tribunician power resulted from the right of the tribunes to block by veto each other's acts. Moreover, the granting of assistance (*auxilium*) to a citizen by a tribune was conditional upon the consent of his colleagues. This took the form of a public declaration (*decretum*) made by one of the tribunes on behalf of all (*pro collegio sententia pronuntiare*). Further restrictions on the tribunes' power were imposed in times of emergency, when the government of the state was put into the hands of a dictator, or by special legislation.

On many occasions, especially during the later Republic, the tribunes' power of veto played in the hands of members of the senatorial aristocracy who, by winning over one or more tribunes and inducing them to use their *prohibitio* or *intercessio* against the rest, frustrated legislative initiatives they regarded as detrimental to their interests.[108] In the closing years of the Republic the tribunate lost much of its earlier prestige as many of its holders became mere organs in the hands of political factions and military leaders fighting for political supremacy. After the fall of the Republic the office was used as one of the chief instruments by which Augustus and his successors sought to secure their power.

The dictator

In times of emergency, when the security of the state came under threat, the Roman constitution provided for the appointment of a special magistrate,

---

tribunes to the senate see Dionysius 10. 31; Aulus Gellius, *N. A*. 14. 8; Livy 4. 1.

106 This was confirmed by the *lex Valeria Horatia* of 449 BC. The *potestas sacrosancta* of the tribunes was often opposed to the *imperium* of the higher magistrates.

107 Dionysius 8. 87; Livy 3. 20; Cassius Dio. 51. 19. In certain exceptional cases the tribunes could be invested with extraordinary powers, extending even beyond the city limits, by a special decree of the senate. See Livy 9. 36; 29. 20.

108 During the later Republic many patricians sought to join the plebeian class (*translatio ad plebem*) so that they could be elected to the tribunate.

the dictator (or *magister populi*, as he was called in earlier times), in whose hands all state power was concentrated.[109] The defence of the state against external enemies and the quelling of internal insurrection were the main objects for which a dictator would usually be appointed.[110] In later times, however, nominating a dictator came to be regarded as a convenient way of dealing with problems of government resulting from the inability of the ordinary magistrates to perform their duties. For example, when both consuls were absent from the city, a dictator could be appointed to supervise the annual elections of magistrates by the assemblies. A dictator could also be entrusted with the tasks of organising public games and festivals, presiding over important trials, filling vacancies in the senate and disciplining magistrates who overstepped the bounds of their authority.[111]

Unlike the ordinary magistrates, the dictator was not elected by a popular assembly but was nominated, with the approval of the senate, by one of the consuls or, in exceptional circumstances, by a magistrate who had been invested with the powers of the consulship (e.g. a *tribunus militaris consulari potestate*).[112] Originally only members of the patrician class who had previously held the office of consul (*consulares*) were eligible for the position of dictator. The first plebeian dictator was appointed after the passing of the *leges Liciniae Sextiae* (367 BC), in 356 BC. Shortly after his nomination the dictator was invested with supreme power (*imperium*) by a special law of the curiate assembly (*lex curiata de imperio*). At the same time he named a deputy, called *magister equitum* (master of the horse), who carried out his orders and acted as his representative when he was absent. During a dictatorship the ordinary

---

109 The institution of the dictatorship (*dictatura*) was of Latin origin. The first dictator was probably appointed before the close of the sixth century, shortly after the fall of the Monarchy, to protect the newly established Republic against attempts at restoring the Etruscan dynasty to power. As the term *magister populi* suggests, the dictator's primary function was to act as military commander. See Livy 2. 18; 4. 56; 6. 38; Cicero, *de re publica* 1. 40; 2. 32; *de leg*. 3. 3; Dionysius 5. 70-73.

110 It appears, however, that as a matter of constitutional principle, no one was allowed to assume the extraordinary powers of the dictator outside Italy. In the course of the first Punic War there had been one exceptional case in which a dictator was put in charge of the military operations in Sicily (c. 249 BC).

111 Consider, e.g., Livy 7. 3. 28; 8. 18; 9. 26. 28; 23. 22; 27. 33; 30. 24.

112 On the procedure through which a dictator was appointed see, e.g., Livy 4. 21. 26; 7. 19. 21; 8. 12. 23; 9. 38; 23. 22; 27. 5. In one exceptional case, shortly after the destruction of the Roman army by Hannibal in the battle of the lake Trasimene (217 BC), when Rome was left without a consul, the assembly of the centuries elected Q. Fabius Maximus as *prodictator*. See Livy 22. 8.

magistrates continued to exercise their regular functions but were subject to the dictator's authority.

During his term in office the dictator had unlimited powers and his decisions were not subject to the *intercessio* of the tribunes and other magistrates.[113] He was free to introduce any measures he considered necessary without having to seek the consent of any other state organ or the approval of the senate. Moreover, his judicial decisions were not subject to appeal before the assembly (*provocatio ad populum*).[114] But the dictator's power was limited by the fact that he was expected to resign as soon as the emergency situation was over, or the task for which he had been appointed was fulfilled. In any event, a dictator could not remain in office for more than six months and this rule appears to have been followed without exceptions.[115] Moreover, if appointed for a specific purpose, a dictator could use his extensive powers in pursuance of that purpose only and might be lawfully resisted if he attempted to interfere in matters unrelated to it.[116] And if he was entrusted with the conduct of ordinary constitutional proceedings, such as the supervision of the annual elections of magistrates, he was obliged to act in accordance with the established constitutional norms.[117] Finally, it appears unlikely that the dictator was allowed to handle public finances without the consent of the senate.[118]

During the earliest period of the Republic, when the constant wars between Rome and her neighbours posed a real threat to the city, the Romans often resorted to appointing dictators as a means of dealing with emergency situations. But after the Roman conquest of Italy and the subjugation of Carthage at the end of the second Punic war (218-201 BC) the institution of the dictatorship appears to have fallen in abeyance.[119] During the later Republic, whenever a great emergency (*ultima necessitas*)

---

[113] However, some cases can be found in the sources in which the tribunes were asked to intervene against dictators whose actions went beyond the bounds of the specific task for which they had been appointed. See, e.g., Livy 7. 3. 21; 9. 26.

[114] By contrast with the ordinary magistrates, a dictator could not be impeached for his actions after his term in office expired.

[115] See on this Livy 3. 29; 9. 34; 23. 23; Cicero, *de leg*. 3. 3.

[116] Consider Livy 3. 29; 4. 46; 6. 29; 7. 3; 9. 26. 34; 23. 23.

[117] Livy 7. 21.

[118] Livy 22. 23.

[119] The decline of the dictatorship as an institution began before the second Punic war, as manifested by the fact that from the middle of the third century to 217 BC no dictator had been appointed for the prosecution of a war. Only in the course of the second Punic war, and especially during Hannibal's invasion of Italy, the office of dictator was temporarily revived.

occurred, the senate could pass a special decree (*senatus consultum ultimum*) arming the consuls with additional powers and authorising them to take any extraordinary measures required, including the temporary suspension of certain constitutional norms. The perpetual dictatorships of Sulla and Caesar, in the last century of the Republic, were established by special statutes and should be considered as departures from the traditional constitutional norms at a time when, as a result of factional strife and civil wars, the republican system of government was on the verge of collapse. At that time the dictatorship, as originally understood, no longer existed.

Other extraordinary magistrates

The decemvirs (decemviri legibus scribundis)

One of the most important events of the early republican period was the codification of the until then unwritten customary law by the Law of the Twelve Tables. The task of codification was entrusted to a board of ten magistrates, referred to as *decemviri legibus scribundis*, who were chosen exclusively from the patrician class. According to Roman tradition, two such commissions were successively appointed.[120] During the two years that took the decemvirs to complete their work (451-449 BC) the powers of all state officials were suspended and the government of the state was in the hands of the commissioners, who had been vested with consular *imperium*.[121]

The military tribunes with consular power (tribuni militum consulari potestate)

Magistrates bearing the title of military tribune with consular power were for the first time appointed in 444 BC, five years after the end of the decemvirate, in the place of the consuls. At first three consular tribunes were appointed but their number was subsequently increased to six. The introduction of these magistrates is associated with two measures proposed in 445 BC by C. Canuleius, a tribune of the plebs, one permitting intermarriage (*connubium*) between patricians and plebeians (contrary to an earlier rule included in the Law of the Twelve Tables), and the other

---

[120] The traditional account of the decemvirate, however, contains a number of anachronisms and inaccuracies and some modern historians have dismissed the second decemvirate as a fiction.

[121] Cicero, *de re publica* 2. 36. 61. For a closer look at the Law of the Twelve Tables and the role of the decemvirs see chapter 4 below.

opening up the consulship to the plebeians. Although the first of these measures was successfully carried in the same year (*lex Canuleia*), the implementation of the second was blocked by the patricians. Faced with the discontent of the plebeian population the patricians devised a compromise in terms of which the two consuls were to be replaced by three (later six) magistrates invested with consular power, chosen from both orders. But the traditional account, which derives from sources of a much later period (first century BC), contains a number of inaccuracies and contradictions and therefore is not very reliable. An alternative explanation accepted by some modern writers is that the military tribunes with consular power were introduced to provide more military commanders at a time when Rome was facing war on several fronts.

It was probably up to the senate to determine annually, by decree, whether the magistrates for the following year should be ordinary consuls or consular tribunes. The preservation of internal order and the defence of the state against external enemies must have been the main considerations upon which the senate's decision was based. The consular tribunes were elected by the assembly of the centuries (*comitia centuriata*) according to the procedure followed in the election of ordinary magistrates. Their functions and powers were not different from those of the consuls.[122] Thus one of them remained in the city to carry out the everyday business of the state (he supervised the administration of justice, summoned and presided over meetings of the senate and the assemblies, introduced laws and supervised the procedures relating to the election of magistrates etc.) while the others were entrusted with the conduct of military operations, each acting as supreme commander of the army on alternate days.[123] As the administration of justice was traditionally regarded as a patrician prerogative, the consular tribune who remained in the city was probably always a member of the patrician class.[124] The practice of electing military tribunes with consular power was abandoned in 366 BC, after the passing of the *leges Liciniae Sextiae*, and the dual consulship was restored.[125]

---

[122] Livy 4. 7.

[123] Livy 5. 13. 52; 4. 31. 36. 45. 46. 49; 6. 1. 30.

[124] Although no clear evidence of this can be found in the sources.

[125] For a closer look at the consular tribunate see T. Mommsen, *Römisches Staatsrecht*, II, Leipzig 1887, 182-193; R. E. A. Palmer, *The Archaic Community of the Romans*, Cambridge 1970, 222 ff.; J. Pinsent, *Military Tribunes and Plebeian Consuls*, Wiesbaden 1975. On the Roman magistrature in general see H. F. Jolowicz and B. Nicholas, *Historical Introduction to the Study of Roman Law*, Cambridge 1972, repr. 1978, 45 ff.; W. Kunkel, *An Introduction to Roman Legal and Constitutional History,* 2rd edn, Oxford 1973, 14-19; A. Lintott, *The Constitution of the Roman Republic*, Oxford 1999,

The Popular Assemblies

Introductory

The earliest popular assembly in Rome was the curiate assembly (*comitia curiata*), whose origin lay in the period of the kings. As we saw in chapter 2, this assembly was based on the division of the Roman people into thirty *curiae*, or brotherhoods of men, whose members were believed to be bound together by ties of blood. The curiate assembly was superseded by the new political bodies that emerged as a result of the military and political reforms of the late sixth and early fifth centuries BC. These were the assembly of the centuries (*comitia centuriata*) and the assembly of the tribes (*comitia populi tributa*), both comprising the entire citizen body. The *comitia centuriata*, Rome's main legislative assembly, consisted of the citizens organised, on a property basis, into classes and centuries (*centuriae*: groups of a hundred citizens). In the *comitia tributa* the people were divided into tribes (*tribus*) according to their place of residence. Another type of assembly was the *concilium plebis*, the assembly of the plebeians.

The Roman assemblies could not meet to discharge their functions unless formally summoned by one of the higher magistrates (the right of magistrates to call the people together was referred to as *ius agendi cum populo*). The *comitia centuriata* and the *comitia tributa* were summoned by a written proclamation (*edictum*) which was issued by the magistrate usually twenty-four days before the day on which the assembly was to meet.[126] When a magistrate submitted a proposal to an assembly he was

---

ch 7; T. R. S. Broughton, *Magistrates of the Roman Republic*, New York 1951-2; W. Kunkel/M. Schermaier, *Römische Rechtsgeschichte*, Cologne 2001, 19 ff; J. Bleicken, *Das Volkstribunat der Klassischen Republik*, Munich 1968; J. M. Rainer, *Einführung in das römische Staatsrecht*, Darmstadt 1997, 41 ff; M. Kaser, *Römische Rechtsgeschichte*, Göttingen 1976, 38 ff, 40 ff; A. Magdelain, *Recherches sur l' imperium. La loi curiate et les auspices d' investiture*, Paris 1968; A. Burdese, *Manuale di diritto pubblico romano*, 3rd edn, Turin 1987, repr. 1994, 55 ff.; F. de Martino, *Storia della costituzione romana*, 2nd edn, Naples 1972-5; F. M. D' Ippolito, *Aspetti di storia costituzionale romana*, Naples 2001, 60 ff; M. Talamanca (ed.), *Lineamenti di storia del diritto romano*, Milan 1989, 127 ff; G. Crifò, *Lezioni di storia del diritto romano*, 3rd edn, Bologna 2000, 79 ff; A. Guarino, *Storia del diritto romano*, Naples 1996, 222 ff.

[126] This period was called *trinundinum* as it covered three consecutive market days (*nundinae*: the period of time, i.e. eight days, between two consecutive markets). The relevant practice was confirmed by the *lex Caecilia Didia* of 98

said to 'consult' or 'ask' the people. Thus, the word *rogare* (to ask, to request) was often used in conjunction with the object upon which the people were invited to vote, as in the phrases *rogare (populum) legem* (to propose a law), *rogare (populum) magistratus* (to propose magistrates), *rogare (populum) consules* (to propose consuls), *irrogare (populum) poenam* (to ask the people to impose a penalty), etc. By the same token, the word *rogatio* (question) was used to denote a legislative proposal or bill submitted to an assembly. A *rogatio*, after its passing (*lata est*) in the assembly, became a law (*lex*).[127] What are today known as 'private members bills' were not permitted, as the magistrate alone could decide what motions should be put to the vote.[128] Moreover, the people could only accept or reject the proposal put before them by the magistrate, without prior debate or the possibility for amendment. Before a proposal was submitted to the people it was usually discussed in the senate, whose approval was often regarded as vital, and in informal gatherings of citizens (*contiones*).[129]

In all Roman assemblies voting was done by units or groups rather than by individuals. For example, in the assembly of the centuries (*comitia centuriata*) decisions were reached by considering the number of centuries that voted for or against a proposal, the vote of each century being determined by the majority of the individual voters it comprised. Similarly, in the *comitia curiata* and the *comitia tributa* questions were decided by the majority of the *curiae* and *tribus* respectively. During the early Republic voting was done orally. The method of voting by ballot (*per*

BC and the *lex Licinia Junia* of 62 BC. Consider Livy 3. 35; 35. 24; Aulus Gellius, *N. A.* 13. 15.

127 Sometimes the words *rogatio* and *lex* were used interchangeably, like the words bill and law are often used today. In the Roman legal vocabulary the verb *rogare* was used as a basis of many technical phrases, such as *legem abrogare* (revoking a law), *legi derogare* (revoking a law but only in part), *legem subrogare* (adding new clauses to a law) etc. The phrase *ferre legem* referred to the actions of a magistrate in proposing a law and in presiding over the proceedings through which the law was passed. The phrase *creare magistratus* described the procedure through which a state official was elected by the people, following a magistrate's proposal. See, e.g., Livy 1. 60; 2. 2; 3. 55; 25. 2.

128 See, e.g., Aulus Gellius, *N. A.* 13. 15-16; Cicero, *de leg.* 3. 4; *in Vatin.* 7; Livy 42. 34.

129 Consider Aulus Gellius, *N. A.* 13. 15; Livy 39. 15; Cicero, *pro Sest.* 50. A *contio* could be summoned by a higher magistrate (including a tribune of the plebeians) for the purpose of calling the citizens' attention to various matters of public interest. Only the presiding magistrate and those who had obtained his permission to speak could address the meeting.

tabellas) was introduced in the later Republic by a series of laws referred to as *leges tabellariae*.[130] The *lex Gabinia*, enacted in 139 BC, introduced the secret ballot in elections of magistrates. This was followed by the *lex Cassia* in 137 BC which provided that the secret ballot should be used in all cases heard before the assemblies when these acted as courts of justice (*iudicia populi*), except in those involving treason (*perduellio*). In 131 BC the *lex Papiria* introduced the use of the ballot in voting on legislative matters. Finally, the *lex Caelia* of 107 BC extended the use of the ballot to trials for treason, thus removing the exception provided for by the *lex Cassia*. The number of citizens needed to be present for holding a lawful meeting was not fixed by law. It appears, however, that if the number of the citizens in attendance was very low the presiding magistrate could postpone the meeting.

When an assembly was convoked to decide on a legislative proposal each voter-member was given two wooden tablets (*tabellae*). The tablet representing a positive vote was inscribed with the letter *V*, which stood for the phrase *uti rogas* ('as you propose', 'as you ask');[131] the other tablet bore the letter *A*, which stood for the word *antiquo* ('I maintain things as they are'), and indicated a vote against the proposed measure.[132] In judicial assemblies (*iudicia populi*) the tablet with the letter *L* (*libero*: 'I absolve') was used to indicate a vote for acquittal; the tablet with the letter *D* (*damno*: 'I condemn') expressed a vote for condemnation. It is not clear how the voting was conducted in elections of magistrates. It seems likely that each voter wrote on a blank tablet the initials of the name of his preferred candidate.[133] The votes were cast into the balloting urn (*sitella*) and were collected and counted by tellers, called *rogatores* or *diribitores*.[134] After the vote of each unit (*centuria*, *tribus*) became known it was reported to the presiding magistrate who made a formal announcement. When the votes of all the *centuries* or *tribus* had thus been

---

130 Livy 10. 13. 22; 29. 22; Cicero, *de leg*. 3. 15-16.

131 Cicero, *ad Att*. 1. 14; *de leg*. 3. 17.

132 Hence the expression *antiquare legem* (to reject a law).

133 But outvoting one's opponents did not by itself warrant one's election to office. To get elected a candidate had to win the votes of a certain number of *centuriae* or *tribus*. In consular elections, if a candidate obtained the requisite number of votes, and thus was elected to office, he was given the right to name his colleague without further meetings of the assembly being necessary. A similar practice was probably followed in the election of tribunes.

134 *Diribitio*: the sorting of votes. Very little is known about the procedure that was followed when voting was done orally. It seems probable that each individual voter notified his vote to the teller (*rogator*, *diribitor*) who then put it down, in the form of a mark, on a wooden tablet.

reported and counted the magistrate notified the final result to the assembly. In the case of an inconclusive vote, or if the election procedure was interrupted for some reason, the assembly was convened again and again until a decision was finally reached.[135] After the conclusion of the proceedings and the announcement of the final result the presiding magistrate declared the meeting closed and asked the citizens to disperse.

The *comitia curiata*

The *comitia curiata* continued to operate during the republican period, although its significance as a constitutional organ was greatly diminished. The main function of this assembly during the Republic was the granting of *imperium* – and the associated right of taking the auspices (*auspicia*) – to the higher magistrates of the state (*magistratus cum imperium*), i.e. the consuls and the praetors, following their election by the assembly of the centuries. Moreover, the curiate assembly bestowed *imperium* on the dictator after his nomination by the consuls. The conferment of *imperium* to these magistrates was done by a special law, the *lex curiata de imperio*, which was proposed to the curiate assembly by the magistrate upon whom the power of *imperium* was to be bestowed.[136]

In addition to conferring *imperium* on the higher magistrates, the curiate assembly continued to meet, under the supervision of the *pontifex maximus*, to witness and confirm certain ceremonial acts of private law, such as the *testamentum calatis comitiis* (public testament) and the *adrogatio* or *adoptio per populum* (the solemn adoption of a person not subject to paternal control). When it was summoned to perform these functions the curiate assembly was referred to as *comitia calata*.[137] Irrespective of the purpose for which the *comitia calata* were summoned, the people appear to have had no active role in the proceedings. Their only role was to witness a formal procedure as mere observers. As the *comitia calata* lacked essential characteristics of the ordinary *comitia*, especially the participation of the people, through their vote, in a decision-making process, this assembly resembled a *contio*. The latter term referred to an

---

135 A meeting of an assembly could be interrupted for various reasons, such as the intercession of a tribune, the coming of night before the completion of the proceedings, the breaking of a sudden storm, a person's being struck by an epileptic seizure (*morbus comitialis*) and other occurrences regarded as bad omens.

136 See on this Livy 5. 52; Cicero, *de leg. agr*. 2. 12.

137 The verb *calare*, from which the term *calata* derived, meant 'to convene', 'to summon', and was commonly used by members of the Roman priestly colleges. See Aulus Gellius, *N. A*. 15. 27.

informal, non-voting, gathering of citizens in which the magistrates informed the people of important events or forthcoming laws, elections or trials.

Although the curiate assembly continued to operate down to the early imperial period, by the close of the Republic its functions had become so purely formal that its meetings were no longer attended by the citizens but only by thirty lictors (*lictores curiati*), each representing one *curia.*[138]

The *comitia centuriata*

After the military reforms of the late sixth century BC the word *classis*, which originally signified an army, came to refer to those citizens who could furnish the equipment of a hoplite, or heavy soldier. These were the wealthier members of the community. The rest of the citizens were rated as 'below the class' (*infra classem*) and, although they could be called upon to form lightly armed units, they were not included in the regular infantry. But by the middle of the fourth century BC the need for strengthening Rome's defences compelled the state to draw more and more heavily upon poorer citizens for military service and new classes were formed largely from members of the plebeian class (a development that enhanced the role of the plebeians in Roman political life).

The division of the citizens into classes was based on an assessment (*census*) of the amount of property which each citizen possessed (reflected in the type of armour a citizen was able to equip himself with).[139] According to Livy, in the first class were included those whose property was valued at no less than 100,000 *asses.*[140] Inclusion in the second class required fortune valued at a minimum of 75,000 *asses*. The third and fourth classes were composed of those whose property exceeded the 50,000 and 25,000 *asses* respectively. Finally, in the fifth class were included those who possessed fortune valued at no less than 11,000 *asses.*[141] The citizens

---

[138] Cicero, *de leg agr*. 2. 10. 11. 12.

[139] As has been noted, the taking of the census was carried out first by the consuls and after 443 BC by the censors.

[140] Livy 1. 43. See also Dionysius 4. 16-18.

[141] In earlier times the citizens' classification was probably based on the amount of landed property each citizen possessed measured in *iugera* (one *iugerum* was equivalent to three fifths of an acre). This method of classification was later replaced by one based on the amount of money at which a citizen's property was valued. The monetary unit used in the valuation of property was the *as*, which appeared as a bronze coin towards the close of the fourth century BC. But as the value of the *as* changed during the Republic, the minimum amount of money required for inclusion in each class could not have remained fixed. This

included in the five classes were collectively referred to as *adsidui* or *locupletes*. On the other hand, those whose property fell below the minimum amount required for inclusion in the lowest class were termed *proletarii* or *capite censi* (i.e. those registered simply 'by heads').[142] The classes were subdivided, further, into centuries (*centuriae*), or groups of a hundred men, mainly for recruitment purposes. Half the centuries in each class consisted of men aged seventeen to forty-six (*iuniores*), who formed the regular troops, and half of men aged forty-six to sixty (*seniores*), who formed the reserve troops. The first class was made up of eighty centuries, the second, third and fourth of twenty and the fifth of thirty – thus there were a hundred and seventy centuries in all. To these were later added eighteen centuries of knights (*equites*), situated above the first class, and five supernumerary centuries, two of armourers and smiths (*fabri aerarii*, *fabri tignarii*), two of trumpeters (*tubicines*, *cornicines*) and one of *proletarii* and *capite censi*. Thus the total number of centuries was a hundred and ninety-three. Out of this military organisation emerged the assembly of the centuries (*comitia centuriata*),[143] the chief political assembly of the Roman people during the republican period.[144] In the course of time the centuriate assembly lost its military character, but the timocratic basis of its organisation remained largely unchanged.

The centuriate assembly carried out political, legislative and judicial functions. Of the political functions the most important was the election of the higher magistrates of the state (*magistratus maiores*), i.e. the consuls, the praetors, the censors and, in earlier times, the decemvirs and the military tribunes with consular power.[145] Moreover, in certain exceptional cases, the *comitia centuriata* could appoint those who were to serve as proconsuls and we know of one case in which they nominated a prodictator.[146] Besides electing magistrates, the assembly had a say in other important matters concerning the state, such as the declaration of war and the conclusion of peace or alliances by the senate, the sale of public

---

probably explains the discrepancies between accounts of the system offered by different authors.

142 Cicero, *de re publica* 2. 22; Aulus Gellius, *N. A.* 16. 10; Livy 1. 43; Dionysius 4. 16-18. Dionysius speaks of a sixth class, consisting of one century of *proletarii*.

143 In early times those attending the *comitia centuriata* assembled in military formation and were probably fully armed. The military character of this assembly is also reflected in its description as *exercitus* (the army), *exercitus urbanus* or *exercitus centuriatus*. See Livy 1. 43; Aulus Gellius, *N. A.* 15. 27.

144 Hence its description as *comitiatus maximus*. See Cicero, *de leg*. 3. 4. and 3. 19.

145 Livy 3. 33. 35; 5. 52.

146 Livy 26. 18; 22. 8.

property and the granting of the Roman citizenship or the conferment of various privileges (*privilegia*) on individuals or communities. Within the province of the *comitia centuriata* fell also the enactment of new laws or the abrogation of existing ones. Legislative proposals were submitted to the assembly by the consuls or the praetors by whom it was convened and presided over.[147] Moreover, one of the traditional functions of the assembly was to act as a court of justice hearing appeals against sentences imposed by higher magistrates involving death and other severe punishments (*provocatio ad populum*). From the early years of the Republic, as the judicial powers of the magistrates became more and more restricted by legislation, the criminal jurisdiction of the assembly was more clearly recognised until it became the regular court of justice for the investigation and punishment of the most serious crimes.[148]

The *comitia centuriata* met at the *campus Martius*, a parade and training ground outside the city walls (*pomerium*).[149] On the day of the meeting the auspices were first taken and then a public official (*praeco*, *accensus*) made a verbal proclamation inviting the people to attend. After the auspices had been declared propitious and sacrifices offered, the presiding magistrate opened the proceedings. If the object of the meeting was the election of magistrates, the president announced the names of the candidates and could, if he thought proper, comment upon their comparative merits.[150] After he had finished, any magistrate of equal or higher rank or a tribune could come forth to address the people. Private citizens could also come forward to express their views, provided that they had first obtained permission from the president and the tribunes.[151] After the conclusion of the speeches and if no veto was raised by a tribune the

---

[147] Depending upon the magistrate by whom they had been proposed, laws (*leges*) were referred to as *leges consulares* or *leges praetoriae*.

[148] According to the Law of the Twelve Tables, citizens charged with capital offences could only be tried before the '*comitiatus maximus*', i.e. the assembly of the centuries. XII T. 9. 2. See Bruns, *Fontes* I, p. 34; FIRA I, p. 64. Consider also Cicero, *de leg*. 3. 19.

[149] Livy 6. 20. The practice of holding the meetings of the *comitia centuriata* outside the city walls was justified on the grounds that, according to long - established constitutional principle, no gathering of an armed force could take place within the city of Rome. (And as has been pointed out, originally the centuriate assembly was an army formation of the Roman people.) The *campus Martius* continued to be the place in which this assembly met even after it lost its military character.

[150] Livy 10. 22.

[151] Livy 34. 1; 42. 34.

presiding magistrate called upon the people to separate and prepare for voting.

As was mentioned earlier, the voting in the centuriate assembly was done by centuries. Each century had one vote which was decided by the majority of the individuals by which the century was composed. The assembly's decision on any proposal put before it was determined by the majority of the centuries. Thus the votes of at least ninety-seven centuries were needed for the passing of a proposal (193:2+1 centuries). However, the centuries of the first class together with the eighteen centuries of the *equites*, which made up ninety-eight centuries in all, could outvote the other four classes in the assembly if they all voted in the same way. This was the case notwithstanding the fact that the number of individuals contained in the other four classes outnumbered by far those included in the *equites* and the first class. Moreover, as the equestrian centuries and those of the first class were called upon to cast their votes first, a decision on a question could be reached by these alone, if they all voted in the same way, without the need to proceed further with the voting.[152] The obvious effect of this system was that, in all matters concerning the government of the state, the wealthy had the advantage over the poorer classes. The latter could exert some influence only in those cases where there was disagreement among the members of the upper classes.

The organisation of the centuriate assembly as well as the way in which it operated underwent some important changes in the third century BC. The practice of calling upon the wealthier centuries to cast their vote first was abandoned and the century that was to open the voting was decided by lot (*sortiri*). The century which was thus selected to commence the voting procedure was termed *centuria praerogativa* and its vote carried special weight as it was often followed by the majority of the centuries.[153] Furthermore, under a series of reforms, which Roman tradition attributes to the censor C. Flaminius, centuries were distributed on a tribal basis while the number of the centuries of the first class was reduced from eighty to seventy. As a result of these changes, the centuriate assembly appears to have been in some way combined with the assembly of the tribes. But as the sources provide little and often contradictory information about these developments, no clear picture of the new system can be drawn.

---

[152] Livy 1. 43; 43. 16; Dionysius 4. 20.

[153] Consider, e.g., Livy 5. 18; 10. 22; 26. 22; 27. 6; Cicero, *pro Planc.* 20. Under the new system the influence of the poorer classes increased, for now even a century of the fifth class or that of the *capite censi* might be called upon to vote first. But cases can be found in the sources indicating that this method of voting had not always been followed.

The *comitia tributa*

We saw in chapter 2 that before the close of the regal era the original division of the Roman people into three tribes (*Tities*, *Ramnes*, *Luceres*) was supplanted by the creation of four new territorial tribes (*tribus*), corresponding to the four regions into which the city of Rome had been divided. To these four urban tribes (*tribus urbanae*) were later added a number of rural tribes (*tribus rusticae*). The first rural tribes, sixteen in all, were formed in 495 BC covering the countryside around the city. From the end of the fifth century, as the territory of Rome expanded with the annexation of neighbouring regions, the number of rural tribes was gradually increased to reach a total of thirty one in 241 BC. No further tribes appear to have been added after this year. Roman colonists in newly conquered territories and foreigners granted Roman citizenship were assigned to one or other of the existing tribes. The poorer citizens as well as freedmen (*libertini*) and newly admitted citizens were included in the four urban tribes.[154] The tribes served as the basic administrative units for the registration of the citizens and their property, as required for collecting property taxes, raising military levies and other purposes. The citizens were assigned to the different tribes by the censors during the taking of the census and their allocation was recorded in the *tabulae censoriae* (*libri censorii*), the registers drawn up by the censors during the registration of the citizens. In the early years of the Republic the population of the four urban tribes was more or less proportionate to that of the rural ones. But in later years, as the population of Rome rose as a result of the decline of the free peasantry, those included in the urban tribes came to outnumber by far those enrolled in the rural tribes. As membership in a rural tribe implied wealth and the ownership of landed property, most of the citizens enrolled in these tribes enjoyed a relatively high social status. The social significance of being a member of a rural tribe is manifested by the fact that a citizen's transference from a rural to an urban tribe (*tribu moveri*) was regarded as a form of social downgrading. In the later Republic membership in a tribe became largely hereditary and was no longer determined on the basis of a person's place of residence.

Shortly after the new tribal system was introduced the tribes began to hold informal meetings for the discussion of matters of local or general interest. These meetings began to assume the standing of regular *comitia* in the early fifth century BC. According to Dionysius, the first meeting of the *comitia tributa* as a popular assembly was held in 491 BC, when the tribes were summoned to consider the charges against Cn. Marcius Coriolanus, a

---

[154] See on this Livy 9. 46; Val. Max. 2. 2. 9.

noble accused of siding with Rome's enemies in time of war.[155] This appears to have been an exceptional case, however, as the *comitia tributa* did not begin to operate as a formal assembly, open to all Roman citizens, before the middle of the fifth century BC. From that time the assembly of the tribes was convened mainly for the election of lower state officials, the enactment of laws and the hearing of certain criminal cases. The tribal assembly was originally referred to as *comitia populi tributa*, probably in contradistinction to the meetings of the plebeians (*concilia plebis tributa*), which were also organised on a tribal basis. The assembly of the tribes was probably formed as a response to the need for establishing a more flexible political body to deal with matters which fell outside the province of the assembly of the centuries.

The assembly of the tribes was convened by the highest magistrates of the state, i.e. the consuls and the praetors. Of the political functions assigned to this assembly the most important was the election of the lower magistrates (*magistratus minores*, *magistratus sine imperio*), i.e. the aediles and the quaestors. Other minor officials, such as the *tresviri monetales*,[156] the *tresviri capitales*[157] and the *curatores*,[158] were also elected by the *comitia tributa*.[159] During the later Republic the tribal assembly also elected the tribunes (these were originally chosen by the assembly of the plebeians). Moreover, under the *lex Domitia* of 104 or 103 BC the *comitia tributa* were entrusted with the election of the pontiffs and augurs.[160] Within the province of the *comitia tributa* fell also the voting on legislative proposals submitted to them by higher magistrates. In general, the laws enacted by the assembly of the tribes were less important politically than those enacted by the assembly of the centuries. But as the procedure in the tribal assembly was relatively less complex the senate, in circumstances of emergency, or for reasons of expediency, often asked magistrates to submit

---

155 Dionysius 7. 59.

156 Officials in charge of the minting of coins (masters of the mint).

157 Minor officers exercising police functions in Rome and carrying out the orders of the courts. A *lex Papiria* (late third or early second century BC) provided that these were to be elected by the *comitia tributa* presided over by the *praetor urbanus.*

158 Commissioners entrusted with the administration of public law. *Curatores* were elected to supervise the distribution of public lands (*ager publicus*) among Rome's poorer citizens.

159 See, e.g., Aulus Gellius, *N. A.* 13. 15; Cicero, *de leg. agr.* 2. 7.

160 The *lex Domitia* was repealed in 81 BC by the *lex Cornelia de sacredotiis* of Sulla, but was re-introduced under the *lex Atia* in 63 BC. Under the latter law the tribes were invited to choose one of two candidates nominated by the relevant priestly colleges.

bills to the *comitia tributa*, instead of the *comitia centuriata*. As more and more laws were enacted by the tribal assembly, by the end of the fourth century BC this assembly appears to have superseded the *comitia centuriata* as Rome's main legislative assembly. Finally, the *comitia tributa*, acting as a popular court of justice, heard appeals against pecuniary penalties (*multae*) and other sentences imposed by magistrates (*provocatio ad populum*).[161]

The *comitia tributa* usually met in the lower Forum, within the city walls (*pomerium*). The citizens were given notice of a forthcoming meeting of the tribes by means of a public proclamation (*edictum*) posted in the Forum, and lower officials (*viatores*) were sent around to notify the citizens of the meeting. At the same time the nature of the business for which the meeting was to be held was made known.[162] Proceedings usually began with an announcement by the presiding magistrate of the object of the meeting. If that was the introduction of new legislation, the proposed law was read over by a clerk (*scriba*, *praeco*). In the case of an election, the president announced the names of the candidates. The names of those wishing to address the assembly were then made known (with the exception of the tribunes, no one could speak without permission from the presiding magistrate). After the conclusion of the speeches, the president called upon the people to separate and prepare for voting. Then lots were drawn to determine the tribe that was to cast its vote first (*tribus praerogativa*). As was noted before, voting in the tribal assembly was done by tribes, the vote of each tribe being determined by the majority of its members. The matter at issue was finally decided by the majority of the tribes. But as the rural tribes, to which most of the well-to-do farmers and large landowners belonged, outnumbered the urban ones (notwithstanding the fact that the latter contained far more citizens), it was the wealthier citizens who exercised the most influence in the tribal assembly.

The *concilium plebis*

The *concilum plebis*, the assembly of the plebeians, was accorded legal status in 471 BC under the *lex Publilia Voleronis*. This statute recognised the right of the plebeians to hold meetings to elect their leaders (the *tribuni plebis*) and to discuss matters concerning the interests of their class. One of

---

161 Livy 25. 3; Val. Max. 6. 1. 7. But sentences involving death and other severe punishments, such as the loss of a citizen's freedom or political rights, could only be appealed against before the *comitia centuriata*.

162 Under the *lex Caecilia Didia* of 98 BC no law could be submitted to the assembly unless it was publicly announced (*promulgare legem*) in advance.

the chief functions of the plebeian assembly was the election of the plebeian magistrates (*magistratus plebis*), i.e. the *tribuni plebis* and their assistants, the *aediles plebis*. Moreover, the plebeian assembly issued resolutions, referred to as *plebiscita*,[163] which originally had no general legal effect, applying to the plebeians only. But with the advancement of the plebeian class in Roman political life the *plebiscita* came to be recognised, through a series of enactments, as fully-fledged laws binding on both patricians and plebeians alike. According to Roman tradition, the first such enactment was the *lex Valeria Horatia* of 449 BC. Under this law the resolutions of the plebeian assembly were declared binding on all citizens, subject to their ratification by the senate (*patrum auctoritas*) and/or the assembly of the centuries.[164] The *lex Valeria Horatia* was probably confirmed by the *lex Publilia Philonis* of 339 BC.[165] Finally, the *lex Hortensia de plebiscitis* (287 BC) provided that the resolutions of the plebeian assembly should have the full force of laws without any restrictions.[166] Besides its legislative functions, the *concilium plebis*, acting as a court of justice, heard cases involving violations of the rights of the plebeians.[167] In the jurisdiction of the plebeian assembly fell, moreover, appeals against decisions of the *tribuni plebis* imposing fines and other minor penalties. It remains unclear, however, whether the relevant procedure was understood as being connected with the original *provocatio ad populum*.

The organisation and mode of operation of the *concilium plebis* were similar to those of the *comitia tributa*. Like the assembly of the tribes, the plebeian assembly met in the Roman Forum by tribes (hence its description as *concilium plebis tributum*). The majority within each tribe determined its vote and a simple majority of tribes determined the decision of the assembly as a whole. But whereas the assembly of the tribes was originally convened and presided over by a consul or a praetor, the plebeian assembly was summoned and presided over by a tribune of the plebs. Moreover, it appears that, by contrast with the regular *comitia*, the *concilium plebis* did not follow certain formalities, such as the taking of the auspices (a privilege that belonged exclusively to the patricians).

---

163 From the opening formula *plebi scitum* (resolved by the plebs).

164 Livy 3. 55; Dionysius 11. 45.

165 Under the same law legislative enactments no longer required the formal approval of the senate after they were passed by the people. From that time the senate's approval was given in advance. Consider Livy 8. 12.

166 G. 1. 3; Aulus Gellius, *N. A.* 15. 27. See G. Rotondi, *Leges publicae populi Romani* , Milan 1912, repr. Hildesheim, 1966, 39 ff., 48-61 ff.

167 Livy 8. 12.

Although the formal distinction between the *concilum plebis* and the *comitia tributa* was retained until the close of the Republic, the composition and functions of the two bodies came to be very similar in practice, especially after the middle of the third century BC. The gradual convergence of the tribal and the plebeian assemblies was associated with the elimination of all political distinctions between patricians and plebeians and the rapid increase of the plebeian population as a result of the social and economic changes brought about by Rome's expansion. Moreover, just like the regular *comitia*, the *concilium plebis* was controlled by its richest members. These were the representatives of the new patricio-plebeian nobility that emerged in the closing years of the conflict of the orders. Thus, during the later Republic there were three legislative assemblies in Rome, made up of more or less the same people, whose enactments were binding on the entire citizen body: the *comitia centuriata*, the *comitia tributa* and the *concilium plebis*. Of these the last two were organised in the same way, although they were summoned and presided over by different magistrates.[168]

---

[168] On the Roman assemblies see, H. F. Jolowicz and B. Nicholas, *Historical Introduction to the Study of Roman Law*, 3rd edn, Cambridge 1972, repr. 1978, 17 ff.; W. Kunkel, *Introduction to Roman Legal and Constitutional History*, 2nd edn, Oxford 1973, 9 ff; L. R. Taylor, *Roman Voting Assemblies*, Ann Arbor 1966; *The Voting Districts of the Roman Republic*, Rome 1960; G. Botsford, *The Roman Assemblies from the Origin to the End of the Republic*, New York 1909, repr. 1968; E. S. Staveley, *Greek and Roman Voting and Elections*, London 1972; A. Watson, *Law Making in the Later Roman Republic*, Oxford 1974; A. Lintott, *The Constitution of the Roman Republic*, Oxford 1999, 40 ff; M. Kaser, *Römische Rechtsgeschichte*, Göttingen 1976, 51-52; W. Kunkel/M. Schermaier, *Römische Rechtsgeschichte*, Cologne 2001, 10 ff; J. M. Rainer, *Einführung in das römische Staatsrecht*, Darmstadt 1997, 102 ff; F. Wieacker, *Römische Rechtsgeschichte*, Munich 1988, 388 ff; A. Burdese, *Manuale di diritto pubblico romano*, 3rd edn, Turin 1987, repr. 1994, 81 ff; F. De Martino, *Storia della costituzione romana*, 2nd edn, Naples 1972-75; A. Guarino, *Storia del diritto romano*, Naples 1996, 205 ff; G. Crifò, *Lezioni di storia del diritto romano*, 3rd edn, Bologna 2000, 95 ff.

4 The Archaic Period of Roman Law

Introductory

The formation of the Roman tribes and the *curiae* from the joining together of several clans (*gentes*) in the early archaic period was the first step towards the establishment of a broader political community governed by a common body of norms. Initially, the various *gentes* retained their independence but agreed to place themselves under the command of a common head, the king, who acted as their supreme priest, judge and commander-in-chief in times of war. In the course of time, as the sense of unity among the population grew stronger, the customs of the different *gentes*, which at first may have varied, underwent a gradual change and assimilation and a common body of norms emerged, referred to as *mores maiorum* ('the ways of our ancestors'), regulating the whole community and prescribing the rights of its members. These norms had grown from customs and usages in the community, as well as from cases which had evolved from disputes and which had been brought before the king or the pontiffs for solution. To some of these norms the Romans attributed a divine origin (*fas*) while others were regarded as being of human creation (*ius*), but no clear distinction between the two categories of norms was drawn until the later years of the regal period.[1] Knowledge of the customary law was handed down as tradition in the noble families and was preserved by the college of the pontiffs, who acted as custodians and interpreters of both the sacral and the secular law. With the strengthening of concept of the state, the role of the *gentes* gradually declined and the state took upon itself the task of maintaining domestic peace, acting as a guarantor and enforcer of the norms regulating community life. At the same time, as Roman society continued to grow both in numbers and complexity, the role of custom as the principal source of social regulation began to diminish, for the existing customary norms, often vague and limited in scope, could no longer provide the certainty which a more complex system of social and legal relations required. But the rise of the state and the emergence of legislation by which it was accompanied did not

---

1 On the concepts of *ius* and *fas* see also chapter 1.

eliminate the role of custom. Many of the laws which the state, through its organs, enacted and enforced were based on or sanctioned existing customary norms, and custom continued to play an important part in the interpretation and application of the law.

The Beginnings of Legislation

The laws of the kings

During the early archaic period, when Rome was ruled by kings, it is unlikely that there was anything that could be called legislation (as the term is understood today) for the law was customary and not formally enacted. Limited legislative functions were exercised by the assembly of the *curiae* but, in all probability, its role was limited to approving measures put before it by the king and to authorising departures from established customary norms in particular cases. The power of the king to create law, as well as his position as supreme judge, were closely connected with his role as head of Roman religion. In exercising his judicial functions, the king could introduce new norms which he then applied to the case brought before him for solution.[2] As his decisions were taken to establish precedents, they provided the basis for the development of many of the norms of customary law observed in the administration of justice. However, the king's power to introduce new law was limited by custom and he was expected to consult the senate and seek the approval of the people when dealing with matters of great importance for the state.

Later writers, including the jurist Pomponius, make mention of a series of laws enacted under the kings, referred to as *leges regiae*.[3] According to these writers the laws of the kings were collected and written down by Sextus Papirius, a *pontifex maximus*, in the closing years of the regal era.[4] Some modern commentators have noted that these authors' descriptions are probably based on observations on the law of their own times and therefore are not very reliable. Others have asserted that the *leges regiae* cannot be called 'laws', in a strict sense, as they were mainly

---

2 See Livy 1. 8. 1. ('*iura dedit*'). The early Romans attributed to their kings mystic and supernatural powers and this probably explains their power to create law.

3 D. 1. 2. 2. 2; 1. 2. 2. 36; Dionysius 3. 36. As they were confirmed by the *comitia curiata*, these laws are also referred to as *leges curiatae*.

4 Hence this collection is referred to as *ius Papirianum*.

concerned with matters of a largely religious nature.[5] Nevertheless, the surviving fragments of the *leges regiae* attest to the close connection between *fas* and *ius* that marks the character of archaic law and reflect a system that differed considerably from later Roman law. In this respect they appear to convey a tolerably accurate picture of the nature of the law in the regal era.[6]

The laws of the kings were primarily concerned with religious and family matters and with the punishment of violations of sacral law (*ius sacrum*). Some important rules pertaining to the powers and duties of the head of the family (*pater familias*) are attributed to Romulus, Rome's first king, himself.[7] This king is said to have ordained, among other things, that a *pater familias* could not kill any of his children under the age of three,[8] nor could he sell his wife as a slave.[9] The rule prohibiting a wife from divorcing her husband[10] and the rule providing that a triple sale of a son by his father rendered the son free from paternal control (*patria potestas*)[11] are attributed to the same king. Romulus is said to have introduced, moreover, many of the norms governing the client-patron relationship and prescribing the duties and obligations it entailed.[12] According to a law of king Numa Pompilius, a *pater familias* could not sell a son to slavery after he had given him his permission to marry.[13] Numa is said also to have enacted a law against the crime of murder as distinct from negligent homicide, and to have introduced a rule requiring every citizen to clearly demarcate the bounds of his land.[14] To the same king was ascribed a law which stated that if a pregnant woman died she should not be buried before an attempt was made to save the foetus's life.[15] Other important norms, such as the one which provided that liberated slaves became Roman citizens, as well as the distinction between public prosecutions and private suits are said to have

5 See A Watson, *Roman Law and Comparative Law*, Athens, Georgia 1991, 10; O. Tellegen-Couperus, *A Short History of Roman Law*, London 1990, repr. 1993, 19.

6 For a collection of the *leges regiae* see FIRA I, 4-18; Bruns, *Fontes* I, 1-14.

7 Dionysius 2. 26. 27.

8 Exceptionally, a *pater familias* could dispose of a deformed or abnormal baby immediately after birth, but not before five witnesses testified to the fact and gave their approval. See Dionysius 2. 15.

9 Plutarch, *Romulus* 22.

10 Plutarch, *Romulus* 22.

11 Dionysius 2. 26. 27.

12 Dionysius 2. 9-10.

13 Dionysius 2. 27.

14 Dionysius 2. 74.

15 D. 11. 8. 2. (Marcellus).

originated in the period of the kings. However, many of these early rules seem to have fallen into disuse by the time the Law of the Twelve Tables was introduced, in the middle of the fifth century BC.[16]

Leges and *plebiscita*

Legislation, as the term is generally understood, i.e. the enactment of laws of general application by a competent legislative body, first appeared shortly after the abolition of the Monarchy. The earliest statutes were called *leges* and were enacted either by the *comitia centuriata* on the proposal of a consul or by the *comitia tributa* on the proposal of a consul or a praetor. *Leges* were binding on the whole people, i.e. on both patricians and plebeians alike, as both classes were represented in these assemblies. Another type of statute were the *plebiscita*, the laws enacted by the assembly of the plebeians (*concilium plebis*) on the proposal of a tribune. As was noted in chapter 3, the *plebiscita* were binding only on the plebeians until 287 BC, when they were made binding on the whole people under the *lex Hortensia de plebiscitis*.[17] During the remainder of the republican period most Roman statutes were passed by the *concilium plebis* and its *plebiscita* were frequently referred to as *leges*. The majority of the laws passed during the Republic were concerned with matters relating to the organisation of the Roman state and the definition of the powers and duties of magistrates and other state organs. With respect to private and procedural law, however, these enacted laws were of less importance than the constantly growing body of unenacted law. This unenacted law was not a confused mass of shifting customs, but a steady tradition developed and handed down by specialists, at first the members of the college of the pontiffs and, later, by the jurists.

The Law of the Twelve Tables

We saw in chapter 2 that one of plebeians' principal demands during the struggle of the orders was that the customary law in force should be written down and made public so that it could no longer be applied arbitrarily by

---

16 On the laws of the kings see A. A. Schiller, *Roman Law: Mechanisms of Development*, New York 1978, 14 ff; M. Kaser, *Römische Rechtsgeschichte*, Göttingen 1976, 64; W. Kunkel/M. Schermaier, *Römische Rechtsgeschichte*, Cologne 2001, 34; F. Wieacker, *Römische Rechtsgeschichte*, Munich 1988, 307 ff; A. Guarino, *Storia del diritto romano*, Naples 1996, 134-35; G. Crifò, *Lezioni di storia del diritto romano*, 3rd edn, Bologna 2000, 176-78; F. M. D' Ippolito, *Aspetti di storia costituzionale romana*, Naples 2001, 26 ff.

17 G. 1. 3.

the patrician magistrates who controlled the administration of justice.[18] In 452 BC the two sides agreed to suspend the constitution and a commission of ten patricians (*decemviri legibus scribundis*) was appointed to govern the state and to draft a code of laws.[19] The decemvirs were invested with supreme power (*imperium*) for one year and the powers of the consuls and the tribunes were suspended. In 450 BC the decemvirs produced a collection of laws inscribed on ten tablets, but their work was deemed unsatisfactory. According to Roman tradition, in the same year a second commission of ten men was set up, made up of members of both classes, to complete the codification.[20] In 449 BC two further tablets of laws were added to the existing ten and, after the work was ratified by the people's assembly, it was published under the name *lex duodecim tabularum* and the tablets on which the laws were inscribed were set up in the Forum.[21] The sources tell us that the second commission refused to give up power after completing their work, but they were forced to do so following a popular uprising. Some modern scholars have questioned the historicity of the second decemvirate, adopting the view that the work of the original commission was probably completed by the consuls of the following year.[22]

According to Livy, before the work of codification began, a three-member delegation was sent to Greece to study the legislation of Solon in Athens and the laws of other states.[23] We are also told that the Greek philosopher Hermodorus the Ephesian, then in exile at Rome, contributed significantly to the Decemvirs' work.[24] The second century AD jurist Gaius, in his commentary on the Law of the Twelve Tables, draws attention to certain provisions which he considers to be of Greek origin.[25] Although rules similar to those included in the Twelve Tables can be found

---

18 As A. Watson remarks, 'the law was a secret preserve of the pontiffs and the judges did not regard themselves as bound by the law'. *Roman Law and Comparative Law*, Athens, Georgia 1991, 11; see also, A. Watson, *Rome of the Twelve Tables*, Princeton 1975, 177.

19 Livy 3. 32-33; Dionysius 10. 55-57.

20 Dionysius 10. 58. 4.

21 Dionysius 10. 60; Livy 3. 57; D. 1. 2. 2. 4. (Pomponius). Consider on this L. Wenger, *Die Quellen des römischen Rechts*, Vienna 1953, 56; F. Wieacker, *Römische Rechtsgeschichte* I, Munich 1988, 294 n. 47.

22 See O. Tellegen-Couperus, *A Short History of Roman Law*, London 1990, repr. 1993, 20; but see T. J. Cornell, *The Beginnings of Rome*, London 1995, repr. 1997, 274.

23 Livy 3. 31. 8. and 32. 6. 7.

24 D. 1. 2. 2. 4. (Pomponius).

25 D. 47. 22. 4.

in the laws of Greek cities,[26] most modern scholars believe that it is unlikely that the law of Athens has had a direct impact on the decemviral legislation.[27] The influence of Athenian law has been questioned on the grounds that at that time of the codification the Romans had little contact with states outside Italy.[28] Although it is unlikely that the Decemvirs drew upon Athenian law, the surviving fragments of the Law of the Twelve Tables do reflect a Greek influence. The source of this influence was probably the Greek cities of Southern Italy and Sicily with which the Romans had established contacts from an early period.[29] But, whatever the extent of the Greek influence, the bulk of the rules contained in the Twelve Tables were derived from the existing body of customary norms. As the surviving fragments show, only the most important of these norms were included, whilst the general framework of the customary law was taken for granted.

The original tablets are said to have perished during the sack of Rome by the Gauls in c. 390 BC, but copies of the Law of the Twelve Tables had been made and its text was widely known to later Romans, as testified by Cicero's statement that in his time school-children had to learn it by heart.[30] As we do not possess the complete text of the Twelve Tables, modern reconstructions are based on quotations and indirect references included in the works of later writers. Although the sources differ as to the presentation of the relevant materials, few scholars doubt that when they quote from the code they draw upon the original fifth century document. These fragments, combined with information derived from other sources, give us a reasonably reliable picture of the state of Roman law at the earliest phase of its history.[31]

---

26 These include certain provisions relating to the settling of disputes between neighbours over the boundaries of their lands (the relevant action in Roman law was known as *actio finium regundorum*), the right of forming associations (*collegia*) and restrictions on display at funerals. See Cicero, *de leg.* 2. 23. 59;. 2. 25. 64.

27 Dionysius (10. 57.) and the jurist Pomponius (D. 1. 2. 3. 3-4) tell us that the drafters of the Law of the Twelve Tables took into account Greek laws but do not refer specifically to Athenian law.

28 See A. Watson, *Roman Law and Comparative Law*, Athens, Georgia 1991, 12.

29 Consider on this D. Tamm, *Roman Law and European Legal History*, Copenhagen 1997, 21.

30 *De leg.* 2. 4. 9.

31 Parts of the Law of the Twelve Tables can be found in the writings of Cicero, Aulus Gellius, Macrobius, Livy, Plutarch, Dionysius of Halicarnassus and others. A commentary on the Twelve Tables was written by the jurist Gaius in the second century AD under the title *ad legem duodeci tabularum*, which has been preserved in the Digest of Justinian. The most complete modern

The Law of the Twelve Tables did not amount to a 'code', in the modern sense of the word, for it was not intended to be an all-encompassing statement of the law then in force and many of the areas covered were not dealt with in a systematic and comprehensive way. Moreover, the purpose of its drafters was not so much to reform the law as to fix and make intelligible those controversial rules concerning the rights of citizens and the procedures through which these rights were protected and enforced. Their chief concern was to make the law applicable to all citizens and to remove the arbitrariness in its administration by laying down the circumstances under which rights should be held to have arisen or been lost and specifying the penalties to be imposed when violations of norms occurred. Notwithstanding the fact that important areas of the law, such as those concerned with the structure of the political system and the constitution of the courts, remained under the exclusive control of the patrician nobility, the decemviral legislation had the effect of bringing a variety of norms onto an even platform and placing them before the eyes of the people as one integral body of laws. Citizens could now access publicly available knowledge as to what their rights and duties were and the administration of justice was now based upon a publicly verifiable set of rules and procedures.

The Twelve Tables included provisions dealing with matters of private, public and sacral law. Much emphasis was placed on matters of procedure, for it was in this area that unskilled parties to a dispute, usually members of the plebeian class, could be misled by those conversant with the law. Table I prescribed the way in which a defendant could be summoned by the plaintiff into court[32] and Table II laid down certain rules governing the procedure in court. Table III recognised the right of a

---

reconstruction of the code's text was produced in the early nineteenth century by H. Dirksen under the title *Übersicht der bisherigen Versuche zur Kritik und Herstellung des Textes der Zwölf-Tafel Fragmente*, Leipzig 1824. This furnished the basis for later reconstructions, such as R. Schoell's, *Leges duodecim tabularum reliquiae*, Leipzig 1866. See also FIRA I, Florence 1940-1943, repr. 1968-1969, 23 ff; Bruns, *Fontes* I, Tubingen 1909, repr. Aalen 1969, 15 ff. For an English translation see E. H. Warmington, *Remains of Old Latin* III, Loeb Classical Library 1938, 424 ff; A. C. Johnson, P. R. Coleman-Norton and F. C. Bourne, *Ancient Roman Statutes*, Austin 1961, 9-13. And see M. Crawford (ed.), *Roman Statutes*, London 1996.

32 Table I states: 'If a man is summoned to the court and refuses to go, let witnesses be called and then let the plaintiff arrest him. If he resists or runs away, let the plaintiff seize him by force. If he is hindered by sickness or age, let the plaintiff provide an animal to carry him, but not a covered carriage, unless the plaintiff so chooses'.

creditor to put an insolvent debtor to death or to sell him into slavery (following the condemnation of the debtor by a court of law). The unlimited power of the head of the family (*patria potestas*) over his family members was given legislative recognition under Table IV. This included provisions confirming the customary right of a father to inflict corporeal punishment upon a son, to sell him into slavery or even to put him to death.[33] Table V contained rules dealing with matters of succession and guardianship. It provided, among other things, that if a person died intestate, or if his will was found to be invalid, his property should pass to his nearest agnates (*agnati, sui heredes*) or, in the absence of agnates, to the members of the clan (*gentiles*) to which he belonged. According to another provision, if a man was unable to manage his own affairs, his person and property should be under the power of his agnates or, in default of these, to his *gentiles*. Table VI included provisions regulating the acquisition and transference of private property. It was stated, for example, that a person would acquire ownership upon two years of uninterrupted possession of landed property, or one year in the case of other property.[34] The transference of property by *mancipatio* (a form of transaction involving an imaginary sale and delivery) or *nexum* (a bilateral transaction accomplished like the *mancipatio*) was also recognised together with an early form of contract known as *stipulatio*.[35] Table VII dealt with matters relating to disputes between neighbouring owners and contained provisions prescribing the space to be left between buildings, the width of roads, the right of an owner to gather fruits which had fallen from his tree onto neighbouring property, and some matters relating to the law of land and buildings. Table VIII contained provisions concerning delicts and crimes, as well as the punishments which these entailed. It was stated, for example, that if a person was caught stealing by night, he might lawfully be killed on the spot. If a person was caught stealing by day, he could be killed only if he tried to defend himself with a lethal weapon; but if he did not resist, then the owner of the property could seize him and detain him in bonds. The above applied only if the thief was caught in the act (*fur manifestus*). If

---

[33] If a father sold his son as a slave and the person to whom he was made over set him free, the son returned under the *patria potestas*. But if the process of formal conveyance of the son (*mancipatio*) and release (*emancipatio*) was repeated three times, the son was released from the *patria potestas* and acquired the status of a freeborn Roman citizen (*ingenuus*).

[34] This mode of acquiring property was termed *usucapio*.

[35] This was a verbal contract based on a spoken question (*spondere*? – do you promise on your oath?) followed immediately by a spoken answer (*spondeo* – I promise on my oath). The contract was strictly interpreted on the basis of what was actually said.

he was caught later (*fur nec manifestus*) he was obliged to restore double the value of the property stolen. Moreover, it was recognised that a person who injured another was liable to retaliation (*lex talionis*). The effects of this rule were mitigated as in many cases the injured party could only seek compensation for the injury suffered.[36] In general, the penalties provided for were extremely harsh, although the number of offences punishable by death was limited.[37] Table IX included provisions relating to public law. It made it unconstitutional for a magistrate to propose a law imposing penalties or disabilities upon a particular person only and declared that no one should be put to death except after a formal trial and sentence. It stated, moreover, that only the assembly of the centuries could pass laws affecting the political rights of citizens and that no citizen should be condemned on a capital charge (i.e. a charge involving loss of life, freedom or citizenship) without the right of appeal to the assembly. Table X dealt with sacral law and matters relating to the burial or cremation of the dead.[38] Finally Tables XI and XII contained certain provisions of general character, such as the prohibition of intermarriage between patricians and plebeians (Table XI) and rules relating to the liability of a master of a slave for offences committed by the latter (*noxae deditio*). The provisions of the Twelve Tables are expressed in the form of terse commands and prohibitions with something of a rhythmical cadence that must have facilitated their retention in the memory. But the wording is often abstruse and grammatically ambiguous, and the actual legal principles underlying the various provisions were left unstated as they were probably taken for granted.

The Law of the Twelve Tables marks the beginning of Roman law as we now know it. It is true that the law contained in it was suited to a relatively simple society and included many primitive elements. But the significance of the code lies not so much in its contents as in the fact that it opened up new possibilities. Considered from a political angle, it represents a move away from the arbitrary power held by the ruling patrician class towards the abstract impersonal power exercised by the state

---

36 The amount of compensation fixed for a broken bone was three hundred *asses* if the injured person was a free man, and one hundred and fifty *asses* if he was a slave. In the latter case it was the master of the slave who was considered to be the injured party. For minor assaults the amount of compensation was twenty-five *asses*.

37 Among the capital offences were bribery, libel, slander and sorcery. Death was inflicted by flogging, hanging, burning at the stake and casting from the Tarpeian rock.

38 It contained provisions forbidding burial and cremation within the city, the immoderate wailing or tearing of their faces by women at funerals and the burial of gold ornaments with the dead.

under the rule of law – it is with the Twelve Tables that we see the first recognition of the idea of equality before the law. With respect to law, the code represents not so much an attempt to reform the existing custom as a sign of a change in the way people understood the nature and purpose of law and the role of the lawmaker. Formerly the law was regarded as a revelation made by gods to the ancestors, to sacred kings, to magistrate priests. The impact of the Twelve Tables was that the law came to be seen as being derived, in principle, from the will of the people and as being shaped by social forces. In other words, as the law was now made public, it became less of a religious mystery and was set on a secular basis. With the further recognition of the distinction between religious norms (*fas*) and human positive law (*ius*), the law began to lose its immutable quality and became conventional, human, and therefore subject to change.

The Law of the Twelve Tables furnished the basis for the development of Roman law and legal science in the centuries that followed.[39] This was made possible by the fact that the norms it contained were continuously being modified and extended through interpretation by trained jurists who adapted them to the conditions and needs of their times. Most of the Roman law of the Republic and the Empire was based on the extension and refinement of the provisions of the Law of Twelve Tables.[40]

---

39 Livy (3. 34.) refers to the Law of the Twelve Tables as 'the source of all public and private law' (*fons omnis publici privatique iuris*).

40 On the Law of the Twelve Tables see C. W. Westrup, *Introduction to Early Roman Law* 4, London 1950, 79 ff; P. R. Coleman-Norton, *The Twelve Tables*, Princeton 1950; H. J. Wolff, *Roman Law, An Historical Introduction*, Oklahoma 1951, 54 ff; A. Watson, *Rome of the XII Tables*, Princeton 1975; *The Law of Ancient Romans*, Dallas 1970, 10 ff; H. F. Jolowicz and B. Nicholas, *Historical Introduction to the Study of Roman Law*, 3rd edn, Cambridge 1972, 9 ff, 108 ff; W. Kunkel, *An Introduction to Roman Legal and Constitutional History*, 2nd edn, Oxford 1973, 23 ff; R. A. Bauman, *Lawgivers in Roman Republican Politics*, Munich 1983, 139 ff; T. J. Cornell, *The Beginnings of Rome*, London 1995, repr. 1997, 272 ff; A. A. Schiller, *Roman Law: Mechanisms of Development*, New York 1978, 142 ff; M. Kaser, *Römische Rechtsgeschichte*, Göttingen 1976, 66 ff; W. Kunkel/M. Schermaier, *Römische Rechtsgeschichte*, Cologne 2001, 33 ff; F. Wieacker, *Römische Rechtsgeschichte*, Munich 1988, 287 ff; A. Guarino, *Storia del diritto romano*, Naples 1996, 145 ff; F. M. D' Ippolito, *Aspetti di storia costituzionale romana*, Naples 2001, 48 ff; M. Talamanca (ed.), *Lineamenti di storia del diritto romano*, Milan 1989, 94 ff.

Other important statutes

Besides the Law of the Twelve Tables, a number of important statutes were enacted during the early republican period. As was noted before, most of these statutes were concerned with matters of public law and only a few affected the development of private and procedural law. In the first category belonged, for example, the *lex Valeria Horatia* (449 BC), which recognised the inviolability of the plebeian tribunes; the *lex Canuleia* (445 BC), which permitted intermarriages between patricians and plebeians; the *lex Aemilia* (434 BC), which limited the duration of the censorship to eighteen months; the *lex Publilia Philonis* (339 BC), which removed the early rule according to which legislative enactments of the popular assemblies had to be approved by the senate after their passage; and the *lex Hortensia de plebiscitis* (287 BC) under which the resolutions of the plebeian assembly were made binding on the whole people. Among the most important statutes relating to private law were the *lex Aquilia* (286 BC), which set general rules of liability for damage caused to another person's property, and the *lex Atinia* (third century BC), which excluded stolen things (*res furtivae*) from *usucapio* (the acquisition of ownership through possession of a thing for a prescribed period of time).

The Interpretation

The close connection between religion and law in the archaic period accounts for the special role of the pontiffs as guardians and interpreters of the norms by which early Roman society was governed. For a long period after the founding of the city the pontiffs had a monopoly of legal knowledge and played a key part in the formulation, articulation and application of law.[41] As they alone were acquainted with the technical forms employed in private transactions, it was to them that private citizens went when they needed advice on how to prepare legal documents, such as contracts and wills, aimed at securing certainty in legal relations. The pontiffs also assisted parties at law on matters of legal procedure and drafted the forms which they had to employ in conducting their suits. Moreover, it was upon their opinions that magistrates, judges and litigants relied when faced with difficult questions of law. After the introduction of the Law of the Twelve Tables, the pontiffs continued in their role of giving opinions on questions of law. Apart from the fact that the Twelve Tables did not contain the technical forms that had to be used when litigation took

---

[41] D. 1. 2. 2. 6. (Pomponius).

place, the provisions of the code themselves required interpretation for their application. Thus an important part of the pontiffs' work was occupied in giving practical expression to the code's provisions. In carrying out this task the pontiffs extended or restricted the scope of a legal rule, as the case before them demanded, and, on occasion, they introduced entirely new rules under the cover of interpretation to deal with new situations. An example of lawmaking through interpretation is the way in which the release of a son from his father's control was made possible. A father, in exercise of the absolute power he had over his children, could sell a son to another person for money on the understanding that after he completed his work for that person the son would again return under his father's control. Table IV 3 provided that if a father sold his son three times, the son would be free from paternal authority (*patria potestas*). This provision was intended to protect a son against exploitation by his father. But the code contained no specific rule as to how a father could release a son from his *patria potestas*. However, as time went on, the need arose for some means of emancipating children. Thus the pontiffs seized upon Table IV 3 and, under the pretence of interpretation, introduced the rule that if a father made a fictional three-fold sale of his son to another person the son would be released from *partia potestas* and become *sui iuris* (a person in control of his own affairs).[42] This example shows how a legal provision was utilised to achieve a purpose quite different from that which the legislator had in mind and how, through interpretation, a new norm was created to deal with a new situation. In carrying out the task of interpretation the pontiffs laid the groundwork for the development of Roman legal science.[43]

---

[42] As to daughters, it was recognised that these could be released from *patria potestas* by being sold once and then once freed.

[43] On the role of the pontiffs as interpreters of the law see in general H. F. Jolowicz and B. Nicholas, *Historical Introduction to the Study of Roman Law*, 3rd edn, Cambridge 1972, 88 ff; W. Kunkel, *An Introduction to Roman Legal and Constitutional History*, 2nd edn, Oxford 1973, 95-96; A. A. Schiller, *Roman Law: Mechanisms of Development*, New York 1978, 158 ff; F. Schulz, *History of Roman Legal Science*, Oxford 1967, 6 ff, 15 ff; O. F. Robinson, *The Sources of Roman Law*, London 1997, 42-43; M. Kaser, *Römische Rechtsgeschichte*, Göttingen 1976, 159 ff; W. Kunkel, *Die Römischen Juristen*, Cologne 2001, 45 ff; W. Kunkel/M. Schermaier, *Römische Rechtsgeschichte*, Cologne 2001, 123 ff; F. Wieacker, *Römische Rechtsgeschichte*, Munich 1988, 310 ff; G. Crifò, *Lezioni di storia del diritto romano*, 3rd edn, Bologna 2000, 187 ff; M. Talamanca (ed.), *Lineamenti di storia del diritto romano*, Milan 1989, 292 ff.

The Administration of Justice: Civil Procedure

Introductory

In Roman law the term *iudicia* was used to denote judicial proceedings in general. These were divided into two categories: *iudicia publica* and *iudicia privata*. The former were concerned with wrongful acts affecting the interests of the community as a whole; the object of the latter was the resolution of disputes between private citizens. But in early law the boundary between criminal and civil jurisdiction was not clearly marked and, in contrast to modern law, acts such as theft and robbery were regarded as private wrongs. In general, with respect to private law, the state had no interest beyond that of providing the means for resolving disputes in an orderly and socially acceptable way.

Jurisdictional magistrates and courts

As was observed in chapter 2, during the Monarchy the king acted as a supreme judge, a role closely connected with his position as the community's chief priest. The king's jurisdiction co-existed with that of the head of the family (*pater familias*) who alone, or with the assistance of a family council, decided on matters concerning the affairs of his family. When a case was brought before the king the latter could seek the assistance of an advisory body composed of members of the senate (*consilium*),[44] and, if he thought it proper, could appoint delegates to try the case in his stead. But it is unlikely that the king interfered in private disputes, unless he was appealed to by the parties concerned. In such a case the king stated the applicable norm and determined the method which should be used in obtaining evidence and arriving at the verdict.[45] After the evidence had been obtained the king, or a deputy acting in his name, rendered a decision which was then enforced by the winner of the suit. The later division of legal proceedings into two stages, the first before a magistrate (*in iure*) and the second before a judge (*in iudicio*, *apud iudicem*), probably had its origin in this early practice, although it is not clear how it emerged. After the fall of the Monarchy private disputes were dealt with by the consuls or, according to some scholars, by the pontiffs,

---

44 See, e.g., Dionysius 3. 26. In cases of great importance the king could seek the advice of the senate as a whole.

45 During this period evidence was usually obtained with the help of irrational or supernatural methods, such as ordeal or the taking of the auspices. These methods had their origins in primitive religious beliefs concerning the role of the gods in human affairs.

who determined, on the basis of the applicable law, whether the plaintiff could take legal action and, if so, in what way. After the introduction of the praetorship in 367 BC all private disputes between Roman citizens fell within the jurisdiction of the *praetor urbanus* whilst, from 242 BC, cases involving disputes between foreigners, or between foreigners and Roman citizens were assigned to the *praetor peregrinus*. Besides the praetors, the curule aediles exercised limited jurisdiction over disputes arising from transactions in the market place. In very simple cases the praetor usually decided the matter himself (*actio extraordinaria*). But in most cases, if he decided that legal action was appropriate, he referred the matter to a judge (*iudex*) who conducted the investigation and pronounced the verdict (*actio ordinaria*). Before the trial the praetor instructed the judge as to the point of law involved and laid down the legal principles on the basis of which the case was to be decided. Moreover, after a verdict had been obtained, it fell upon the praetor to ensure that the court's decision was properly implemented. In carrying out his judicial functions the praetor was often aided by an advisory body (*consilium*) consisting of jurists and other experts (*adsessores*, *consiliarii*).

The lay judge who was to conduct the investigation in a civil case (*iudex privatus*, *iudex unus*) was usually nominated by the parties themselves.[46] In case of disagreement he was chosen, with the parties' consent, from the official list of citizens selected to serve as judges in civil and criminal trials which was drawn up every year by the praetor (*album iudicum*).[47] If the dispute was such that it required, in addition to establishing certain facts, certain technical knowledge, the praetor could appoint an expert as a judge (*arbiter*) – in this case the trial was referred to as *arbitrium*.[48] Most civil cases were decided by one judge sitting alone (*iudex unus*). But towards the end of the third century BC two courts were

---

46 It was recognised as a general principle in Roman law that in all cases the person or persons who were to serve as judges should be appointed with the full consent of the parties concerned. See D. 5. 1. 80. (Pomponius).

47 From the part of the *album iudicum* containing the names of those selected to serve as judges in civil trials the plaintiff nominated a *iudex*. If the defendant rejected the plaintiff's choice the matter was determined by lot (*sortitio*). The defendant had the right, within certain limits, to reject the person thus chosen if he was unacceptable to him for some reason (*reiectio iudicis*). Once the parties had reached an agreement, the person chosen was appointed by the praetor as *judex*. Until the later half of the second century BC the *album iudicum* was made up exclusively of members of the senatorial class. From that time members of the equestrian class (*equites*) began to be admitted as *iudices*. See chapters 5 and 6 below.

48 See, e.g., Aulus Gellius, *N. A*. 20. 1. 7; XII T. IX. 3; Cicero, *pro Muren*. 12. 27.

established to deal with cases of a more complex nature, the court of the *centumviri* and that of the *decemviri stlitibus iudicandis*. These courts were made up of several judges who were chosen by lot from the *album iudicum*. Both the plaintiff and the defendant were entitled to challenge one or more judges (*reiectio*) if they had reasons to believe that these would be prejudicial to their case. Moreover a court of at least three judges (*recuperatores*) was set up to deal with private disputes involving foreigners.[49]

Times and places in which justice was administered

During the Monarchy the king exercised his judicial functions in the open, sitting on an ivory chair (*sella curulis*) placed on an elevated platform (*tribunal*).[50] In the republican period the praetor usually heard cases in the *comitium*, the area of the Roman Forum where the *comitia curiata* used to meet, also sitting on a *sella curulis* placed on a *tribunal*.[51] Below the *tribunal* were the seats reserved for the litigants and their representatives. The place in which the praetor performed his judicial functions was also the place in which the *iudices* tried the cases referred to them by the praetor. There were forty days in a year upon which the courts of justice were open and legal disputes could be brought before the praetor – these were referred to as *dies fasti*. *Dies nefasti*, on the other hand, were the days on which neither magistrates nor judges could carry out their judicial functions.[52] Moreover, legal business could not be conducted on days devoted to religious ceremonies (*feriae*) and public games (*ludi*) and, after the passing of the *lex Hortensia* (287 BC), on market days (*nundinae*).

---

49 On the Roman courts see W. Kunkel, *An Introduction to Roman Legal and Constitutional History*, 2nd edn, Oxford 1973, 84 ff; W. Kunkel/M. Schermaier, *Römische Rechtsgeschichte*, Cologne 2001, 106 ff; F. Wieacker, *Römische Rechtsgeschichte*, Munich 1988, 429 ff; R. Monier, *Manuel élémentaire de droit romain*, Aalen 1977, 129 ff. And see chapter 6 below.

50 Livy 1. 8. 3.

51 Varro, *de ling. lat.* 5. 155 (*comitium*). In some cases which did not involve a legal dispute between parties as, for example, in cases of manumission (*manumissio vindicta*), the praetor could carry out his duties in other places outside the *comitium* (see, e.g., G. 1. 20.). In the closing years of the Republic and during the Empire the praetor heard cases in one of the covered porticoes (*basilicae*) which were built in the area surrounding the Forum. See, e.g., Girard, *Textes*, 330 ('*testamenta ...facta in foro vel basilica*').

52 Varro, *de ling. lat.* 6. 29. 30; G. 4. 29. Gaius tells us that, exceptionally, the *legis actio per pignoris capionem* (see following section) could be conducted on a *dies fastus* as the proceedings relating to this action did not take place before the praetor.

Magistrates were allowed to proceed with their judicial activities on the days on which meetings of the popular assemblies were held (*dies comitiales*) as long as this did not prevent them from performing their duties in the assemblies.[53] The Law of the Twelve Tables provided that proceedings had to begin before noon and the decision had to be pronounced by sunset.[54] It remains unclear, however, whether this rule referred to the proceedings before the magistrate (*in iure*) or to the proceedings before the judge (*in iudicio*). Moreover, it seems unlikely that his rule continued to apply after the introduction of the formulary system in the second century BC.

Parties in civil trials

In Roman law the term *actio* signified a person's right to institute proceedings in a court of law.[55] The same word was also used to denote a lawsuit. In a civil case the plaintiff was called *actor* (*qui agit*) or *petitor*; the defendant was referred to as *reus* or *adversarius* (the latter term, however, was often used to describe either party in the proceedings).[56] In actions concerning the division of common property (*actio communi dividundo, actio familiae erciscundae*),[57] either party was at the same time plaintiff and defendant. One should note, moreover, that in the *per formulam* procedure, if the defendant raised an exception (*exceptio*), he was regarded as having the position of a plaintiff with regard to that exception.[58]

The term *iudicia legitima* was used to denote trials in which both litigants were Roman citizens and which took place in the area of Rome before one judge only.[59] By contrast, the term *iudicia imperio continentia* referred to trials in which any one of these requirements was absent (e.g. trials in which one or both parties were foreigners). The former were regulated by statutory law (*lex*), whereas the latter were based upon the *imperium* of a jurisdictional magistrate. Slaves were not allowed to be involved as parties in any trial.[60] In trials concerning a slave's freedom (*causae liberales*) the slave was represented by another person (*adsertor libertatis*) who argued for or defended the right to freedom of the slave

---

53 Varro, *de ling. lat.* 6. 29.
54 XII T. I. 7 and 9.
55 *Inst.* 4. 6. 1. pr.
56 See Festus, '*reus*' in Bruns, *Fontes* II, p. 32.
57 D. 10. 2. 2. 3. (Ulpianus).
58 D. 44. 1. 1. (Ulpianus). On the *per formulam* procedure see chapter 6 below.
59 G. 4. 104. and 109.
60 D. 50. 17. 107. (Gaius).

concerned. Women, children and persons suffering from some form of mental disorder were unable to appear in court alone. Thus, with respect to the *iudicia legitima*, women *sui iuris* (i.e. women who were neither under their father's *patria potestas* nor under the control of a husband) could not take part in any court proceedings without the supervision of their guardians (*auctoritas tutoris*). Children and insane persons were usually represented in court by their tutors or guardians (*tutores*, *curatores*). Under a *lex Hostilia* (an early statute of unknown date), a person who had been taken prisoner in war, or who was absent on an official mission, could be represented by another citizen in a trial involving an allegation of theft committed against the absent person's property (*actio furti*).

It was not required that the parties to a dispute should attend the court proceedings in person. A party was allowed to conduct his case through a representative who, depending on the way in which he was appointed, was referred to as *cognitor* or *procurator*. The *cognitor* was nominated by the party he was to represent in the *in iure* (before the magistrate) phase of the proceedings in a formal way and in the presence of the other party.[61] If the party represented by the *cognitor* was the defendant, the latter had to provide security that he was going to abide by the decision of the court.[62] A *procurator* could be appointed at any time (it was not required that he be nominated before the magistrate), with or without the knowledge of the other party.[63] However, a *procurator* appointed by the defendant was under an obligation to give guarantees that the party he represented would carry out the court's decision.[64] Similarly, a *procurator* representing the plaintiff had to provide security that his acts would be adopted by the party who appointed him (*dominus negotii*) so that the defendant could be sure that the plaintiff would not bring against him a new action for the same object.[65] The representative conducted the case in his own name, not in the name of the person whom he represented.

The *legis actio* procedure

The *legis actio* was the main system of civil procedure during the archaic period. Under this system the relevant forms of procedure in an action at law (*legis actiones*) were regarded as being based on the letter of the law and therefore as being incapable of variation.[66] However, some of the *legis*

---

61 G. 4. 97.
62 G. 4. 101.
63 G. 4. 84.
64 G. 4. 101.
65 G. 4. 98.
66 G. 4. 11.

actiones appear to have emerged from custom,[67] as their origins can be traced to the period before the introduction of the Law of the Twelve Tables. According to Gaius, five categories of *legis actiones* were recognised: the *legis actio sacramento*, the *legis actio per iudicis postulationem*, the *legis actio per condictionem*, the *legis actio per manus iniectionem* and the *legis actio per pignoris captionem*.[68] Of these the first three were employed in order to arrive at a decision on the point in dispute; the last two were used to enforce the execution of the judgement. The *legis actio* procedure was characterised by its rigidity: an action at law had to be formulated according to a prescribed combination of words and gestures. If a party used the wrong *legis actio* or departed, even slightly, from the requisite form, his claim was rejected. Moreover this form of procedure, as it pertained strictly to the Roman *ius civile*, could only be used when both parties to a dispute were Roman citizens.

The *legis actio* procedure was divided into two distinct stages: the first stage (*in iure*) was conducted before a consul (or a pontiff, according to some scholars) and, after the passing of the *leges Liciniae Sextiae* (367 BC), before the praetor; the second stage (*in iudicio, apud iudicem*) took place before a citizen who had been appointed as judge (*iudex*) by the magistrate with the consent of the parties concerned. At the opening stage of the *in iure* phase of the proceedings both parties had to appear before the magistrate. If the defendant refused to do so the plaintiff could bring him before the magistrate by force, unless the defendant could produce a guarantor (*vindex*) who would give assurance that the defendant would appear in court at a fixed later date.[69] At this stage of the proceedings the defendant had three options: (a) he could acknowledge the plaintiff's claim (*confessio in iure*), thus avoiding later condemnation or, (b) he could remain silent, putting forward no defence, in which case he was regarded as having confessed or, (c) he could deny the plaintiff's claim, in which case the procedure *in iure* continued according to the applicable *legis actio* – the form of action that had to be employed by the claimant.[70]

---

67 Such as the *legis actio sacramento* and the *legis actio per manus iniectionem.*

68 G. 4. 12.

69 See XII T. I.

70 For a general look at the *legis actio* procedure see H. F. Jolowicz and B. Nicholas, *Historical Introduction to the Study of Roman Law*, 3rd edn, Cambridge 1972, 175 ff, 192 ff; A. A. Schiller, *Roman Law: Mechanisms of Development*, New York 1978, 188 ff, 213 ff; O. F. Robinson, *The Sources of Roman Law*, London 1997, 80 ff; F. Wieacker, *Römische Rechtsgeschichte*, Munich 1988, 256 ff; A. Guarino, *Diritto privato romano*, Naples 2001, 168 ff; M. Talamanca (ed.), *Lineamenti di storia del diritto romano*, Milan 1989, 132 ff; R. Monier, *Manuel élémentaire de droit romain*, Aalen 1977, 136 ff.

The *legis actiones sacramento, per iudicis postulationem* and *per condictionem*

The *legis actio sacramento* was available in any case for which no other *legis actio* was provided by law.[71] A distinction was drawn between *legis actio sacramento in rem* and *legis actio sacramento in personam.* In the *legis actio sacramento in rem* the plaintiff asserted his ownership of a thing, or his control over a person (e.g. on the basis of *partia potestas*). By a *legis actio sacramento in personam* the plaintiff sought to force the defendant to fulfil an obligation resulting from a transaction or the causing of harm. A common requirement of both was that, at the beginning of the proceedings, the parties had to deposit a certain amount of money with the praetor as a pledge (*sacramentum*). According to a provision of the Law of the Twelve Tables, the amount that had to be deposited was five hundred asses if the value of the object in dispute exceeded one thousand asses, and fifty asses if the object was valued at less than a thousand asses.[72] The judge who tried the case had to decide which of the two pledges, the plaintiff's or the defendant's, was the one supporting a legitimate claim (*sacramentum iustum*). The pledge of the party whose assertion was found to be untrue (*sacramentum iniustum*) was forfeited to the public treasury (*aerarium*) and was used to cover the cost of religious ceremonies. According to Gaius, this amounted to a form of punishment (*poena sacramenti*) inflicted on the party who, without adequate justification, had initiated legal proceedings or defended himself in a court of law.[73] As the word '*sacramentum*' suggests, the *legis actio sacramento* had its origins in sacral law. In the early archaic period the parties to a dispute had to take an oath that their assertions were true; the party whose assertion was found to be untrue was declared an outlaw (*sacer*) and was regarded as being excluded from divine and human protection. In later times the word '*sacramentum*' came to denote a deposit of money in civil suits. The forfeiture of the *sacramentum* was regarded as a form of sacrifice to the

---

Consider also V. Arangio-Ruiz, *Cours de droit romain-Les actions*, Naples 1935, repr. 1980, 5-26; G. Pugliese, II *processo civile romano*, I, *Le legis actiones*, Rome 1962; H. Levy-Bruhl, *Recherches sur les actions de la loi*, Paris 1960; M. Kaser, *Das römische Zivilprozessrecht*, Munich 1996, 25 ff; *Römisches Privatrecht*, Munich 1989, 357 ff; C. A. Cannata, *Profilo istituzionale del processo privato romano* I, *Le legis actiones*, Turin 1980; B. Albanese, *Il processo privato romano delle "legis actiones"*, Palermo 1987.

71 G. 4. 13.

72 G. 4. 14.

73 G. 4. 14.

gods (*piaculum*) aimed at expiating the crime of perjury committed by the party whose assertion was proved to be false.[74]

In a case involving a *legis actio sacramento in rem* the object in dispute or, if that was immovable, a small part of it had to be brought before the praetor.[75] Both the plaintiff and the defendant then asserted their right of ownership over the thing by performing certain symbolic gestures and pronouncing certain words.[76] These formalities marked the beginning the formal contest between the parties (*conserere manum*). A formal dialogue between the parties then followed during which the plaintiff asked the defendant to state the cause (*causa*) upon which his denial of the plaintiff's claim was based (*contravindicatio*). The defendant's claim was then challenged by the plaintiff.[77] At this point the praetor nominated the judge (*iudex*) who was to sit in judgement on the case and, at the same time, designated the party in whose possession the object in dispute was to remain until the conclusion of the trial. The party who was given possession of the thing had to give guarantees that he would make over the thing to his adversary if the latter won the case (*praedes litis et vindiciarum*).[78] If the subject-matter of the case was a person's freedom, the person whose freedom was at stake remained free until the completion of the proceedings. After the nomination of the *iudex*, the praetor called upon those present to act as witnesses to the fact that the procedure had been conducted in a proper manner and that all the formal requirements had been met. At this point the *in iure* phase of the proceedings came to an end (*litis contestatio*).[79] Under a *lex Pinaria*, passed probably in 346 BC, there had to be a thirty days interval between the termination of this phase and the appointment of a *iudex* by the praetor.[80] After the *litis contestatio* the parties could not alter their claims. Very little is known about the way in which the *legis actio sacramento in personam* was conducted but, from the information available to us, it appears that the relevant procedure was in general similar to that of the *legis actio sacramento in rem*.[81]

---

[74] See on this P. Noailles, *Du droit sacre au droit civil*, Paris 1949, 9-15, 72-87, 109-135.

[75] G. 4. 16.

[76] G. 4. 16; Val. Probus 4. 6., in Girard, *Textes* I, 13.

[77] G. 4. 16; Val. Probus 4. 2., in Girard, *Textes* I, 13.

[78] G. 4. 16; ps. Asconius *in Verr.* para 114, in Bruns, *Fontes* II, p. 72.

[79] See Festus, '*contestari litem*', in Bruns, *Fontes* II, p. 5.

[80] G. 4. 15.

[81] See Val. Probus 4. 1., in Girard, *Textes* I, p. 13.

The *legis actio per iudicis postulationem* was concerned with claims arising from verbal contract (*sponsio*)[82] and with disputes relating to the division of an inheritance among co-heirs (*actio familiae erciscundae*). Under a *lex Licinnia* (of unknown date) the scope of this *legis actio* was extended to cover cases involving disputes between co-owners relating to the division of common property (*actio communi dividundo*).[83] This *legis actio* took its name from the formal request (*postulatio*) by which the plaintiff asked the praetor to appoint a *iudex*. When the parties appeared before the praetor, the plaintiff stated the cause of his action (e.g. *ex sponsione*) and called upon the defendant to reply. If the defendant denied the plaintiff's claim, the latter asked the praetor to appoint a *iudex* or an *arbiter* to examine the case and to pass judgement. It seems more likely that the praetor appointed a *iudex* in cases involving actions *ex sponsione* and an *arbiter* in disputes among co-owners. In contrast with the procedure followed in the *legis actio sacramento*, in *the legis actio per iudicis postulationem* the praetor proceeded to the appointment of the *iudex* or *arbiter* immediately following the plaintiff's request (the rule that there had to be a thirty days interval between the *litis contestatio* and the appointment of the *iudex* was not followed in this case).

The *legis actio per condictionem*[84] was introduced after the enactment of the Law of the Twelve Tables at a time when Roman commercial life was at a more advanced stage of development. This *legis actio* was created by two legislative enactments of unknown date, the *lex Silia de condictione* (probably late third century BC) and the *lex Calpurnia de legis actione per condictionem* (probably early second century BC). The former statute covered claims involving a fixed sum of money (*certa pecunia*); the latter made the relevant *legis actio* available for claims involving a specific object (*certa res*).[85] In a *legis actio per condictionem* the plaintiff appeared before the praetor and made a formal statement that the defendant owed him a certain amount of money or an object. He then summoned the defendant to acknowledge or deny his claim. If the defendant denied the plaintiff's claim the latter 'gave notice'[86] to him to

---

82 The earliest form of verbal contract in which an obligation was assumed through an oral answer (*spondeo*: 'I promise') to a question (*spondesne*?: 'do you promise?'). Out of the *sponsio* emerged, in later time, the form of verbal contract known as *stipulatio*.

83 D. 4. 7. 12 (Marcianus).

84 G. 4. 18; *Inst*. 4. 6. 15; Festus, '*condictio*', in Bruns, *Fontes* II, p. 5.

85 G. 4. 19.

86 *Condicere*: 'to give notice'.

appear before the praetor after thirty days in order to have a *iudex* appointed.[87]

Thirty days after the completion of the *in iure* phase of the proceedings, the praetor nominated the *iudex* or *arbiter* who was to try the case. The parties then called upon each other to appear before the judge after three days (*comperendinum diem*).[88] According to a provision of the Law of the Twelve Tables, a trial could be postponed only if a party fell seriously ill (*morbus sonticus*), or if a party was engaged in another trial involving a foreigner (*status dies cum hoste*).[89] In later years additional reasons for the postponement of a trial were introduced.[90]

At the beginning of the trial a statement of the case was made by both parties (*causae coniectio* or *collectio*).[91] This was followed by the presentation of the arguments by which the parties supported their claims (*causam perorare*). Then evidence was adduced, both oral (*testes*) and documentary (*tabulae*, *epistulae*, *codices*, *rationes*). Oral testimony was regarded as particularly important. The Law of the Twelve Tables provided that if a person before whom a transaction *per aes et libram* [92] had taken place refused to appear as a witness, he was to be declared incompetent (*improbus*) to act as a witness in similar transactions in the future as well as to summon others to act as witnesses for him (*intestabilis*).[93] Before they gave evidence, witnesses had to take an oath. Evidence was given only in relation to matters of fact, but how much weight was to be given to the evidence presented was entirely at the judge's discretion. In general, it was assumed that the burden of proof lay with the plaintiff.

After all the evidence had been presented and arguments heard the judge pronounced his verdict (*iudicare*) in the presence of both parties. In many cases, before pronouncing the verdict, the judge sought the opinion of an advisory body (*consilium*) appointed by him. With regard to the *legis actio per iudicis postulationem*, the *legis actio per condictionem* and, probably, the *legis actio sacramento in personam*, the judge's verdict consisted in the condemnation (*condemnatio*) or the exoneration (*absolutio*) of the defendant. By contrast, in the *legis actio sacramento in*

---

87 G. 4. 18.

88 G. 4. 15; Val. Probus 4. 9., in Girard, *Textes* I, p. 13; Festus, '*res comperendinata*', in Bruns, *Fontes* II, p. 32.

89 XII T. II. 2.

90 See Bruns, *Fontes* I, p. 131.

91 Ps. Ascon. 2. 1 para 26, in Bruns, *Fontes* II, p. 71; G. 4. 15.

92 The term *per aes et libram* denoted a legal transaction involving the use of copper and scales (e.g. *mancipatio*, *nexum*) and the performance of certain formal acts in the presence of five Roman citizens acting as witnesses.

93 XII T. VIII 22.

rem, the verdict simply identified the party to whom the thing under dispute should belong. In cases involving an *actio in personam*, the party who lost the case (*iudicatus*) was subject to a *legis actio per manus iniectionem* – one of the two *legis actiones* discussed below.

The *legis actiones per manus iniectionem* and *per pignoris capionem*

The *legis actio per manus iniectionem* was aimed at enforcing the execution of a judgement which had been arrived at following a procedure based on a *legis actio sacramento, per condictionem* or *per iudicis postulationem*. According to a provision of the Law of the Twelve Tables, this *legis actio* could be raised against a defendant who in the *in iure* phase of the proceedings had acknowledged his debt (*confessus*), as well as against a defendant who had been condemned by the *iudex* at the end of the *in iudicio* phase of the proceedings and who had failed to discharge his debt within thirty days after the relevant decision.[94] It could be relied upon, however, only in those cases in which no sureties (*praedes*) had been given by the party who was defeated in the trial. The *legis actio per manus iniectionem* had its origin in the early archaic period, prior to the introduction of the Law of the Twelve Tables.

Thirty days after the defendant's confession, or his condemnation by the *iudex*, the creditor summoned the defendant to appear before the praetor.[95] If the latter refused to do so, the creditor was entitled to bring him before the praetor by force. When both parties appeared before the praetor the creditor laid his hands on the debtor and pronounced this formal phrase: 'inasmuch as you have been sentenced to pay the sum of (e.g.) 1000 denarii and you did not pay, I lay my hands on you for that sum'.[96] Unless someone offered to act as a guarantor (*vindex*) for the debtor, the latter was made over to the creditor who could put him in a private prison. A *vindex* could either pay the debt or challenge the judgement, thus releasing the debtor.[97] If, however, in the trial that followed the creditor's claim was confirmed, the *vindex* could be condemned to pay double the amount owed by the original debtor who, after the intervention of the *vindex*, was in all probability released from the debt.

The Law of the Twelve Tables provided that the creditor had to provide a minimum supply of food to his imprisoned debtor, if the latter

---

94 XII T. III 1; G. 4. 21; *lex Urson.* 61. 1-2, in Bruns, *Fontes* I, p. 123.
95 XII T. III 1-2.
96 G. 4. 21.
97 G. 4. 21.

was unable to cater for himself.[98] The creditor kept the debtor in bonds for sixty days and, during this period, made a public proclamation on three successive market days (*nundinae*) before the praetor demanding payment of the debt.[99] If, at the end of this period, no one came forward to release the debtor by paying the debt, the creditor could use the debtor as a slave, sell him outside the city limits (*trans Tiberim*) or even put him to death. If there was more than one creditor the Law of the Twelve Tables contained a provision which, if literally interpreted, gave them permission to divide the body of the debtor into pieces, each creditor taking a piece proportionate to his claim.[100] Although there is no evidence in the sources that an execution of this kind ever took place, there is no doubt that in the archaic period the treatment of debtors by their creditors was extremely cruel.[101]

The procedure of the *manus iniectio iudicati* was extended by later enactments to cover cases in which there had been no formal condemnation of the debtor (*manus iniectio pro iudicato*: 'as if upon a judgement').[102] Moreover, in certain cases of *manus iniectio* recognised by special laws the debtor could resist arrest by the creditor and defend himself without the intervention of a *vindex* (*manus iniectio pura*).[103]

By a *legis actio per pignoris capionem* a creditor could take a pledge from his debtor's property without having to go through the regular judicial process, provided that he followed a prescribed procedure involving the use of a set form of words (*certa verba*) in the presence of witnesses. The taking of the pledge (*pignoris capio*) could be done at any time, even in the

---

98 XII T. III 3-4.

99 XII T. III 5; Aul. Gell. 20. 1. 46-47 in Bruns, *Fontes* I, p. 21.

100 XII T. III 6; Aul. Gell. 20. 1. 48-52 in Bruns, *Fontes* I, p. 21.

101 The treatment of persons condemned as a result of a *legis actio* appears to have improved in the course of the fourth century BC and the killing of a debtor by a creditor was forbidden.

102 G. 4. 22-24.

103 The so called '*manus iniectio pura*' was neither *manus iniectio iudicati*, i.e. resulting from a condemnatory judgement, nor *manus iniectio pro iudicato*, i.e. resulting from a presumption of condemnation, but was introduced by special enactments, such as the *lex Furia testamentaria* (169 BC) and the *lex Marcia de fenore* (104 BC), for specific claims (e.g. claims against usurers). A *lex Vallia* (of unknown date, probably second century BC) provided that the *manus iniectiones* were to be regarded as 'pure', hence allowing the debtor to resist arrest without the intervention of a *vindex*. Under this law the intervention of a *vindex* remained relevant only in cases of *manus iniectio iudicati* and *manus iniectio depensi* (the latter were based on an action by a guarantor who was not reimbursed by the principal debtor within six months after he paid the principal debtor's debt). See G. 4. 22-25.

absence of the debtor.[104] Only some forms of execution by *pignoris capio* were based on statute, whilst others had been derived from custom.[105] This form of execution, reminiscent of the early practice of self-redress, was of limited application, however, as it was employed mainly to enforce certain claims of a religious or military character. According to the Law of the Twelve Tables, the *legis actio per pignoris capionem* could be used against a person who had acquired an animal for sacrificial purposes but failed to pay the price.[106] Furthermore, by custom the *pignoris capio* was given to soldiers for the enforcement of claims connected with military service, such as the payment of their salary (*aes militare*).[107] Finally, under the *leges censoriae*, the decrees by which the censors assigned the task of collecting public revenues to private contractors (*publicani*), the latter could use the *pignoris capio* in order to enforce the collection of taxes.[108] The person who took something as a pledge was probably not allowed to sell or otherwise dispose of the thing taken, but he could keep it until his demand was met.

Concluding note

As was noted before, the *legis actio* procedure was inflexible and often difficult to apply, especially in later years when lawsuits became more frequent and more complicated. From the middle of the second century BC this form of procedure was gradually superseded by a new and more flexible system, known as the *per formulam* procedure. Nevertheless, the *legis actiones* continued to be used until the later part of the first century BC when they were formally abolished under the *leges Iuliae iudiciorum publicorum et privatorum* (17-16 BC) of Augustus.[109]

The Criminal Law

Introductory remarks

Roman criminal law may be defined as a system of conduct-guiding rules backed by sanctions which were laid down by the organs of the state for

---

104 G. 4. 29.
105 G. 4. 26.
106 G. 4. 28; XII T. XII 1.
107 G. 4. 27.
108 G. 4. 28.
109 After that time the *legis actio* procedure was employed only in certain exceptional cases. On the formulary procedure see chapter 6 below.

the protection of common or collective interests. The enforcement of these rules was guaranteed by the machinery of the state through a system of publicly verifiable procedures. But Roman law provided for the punishment not only of those who committed offences against the state, but also of those who violated rules aimed at the protection of private interests. The former were subject to a public form of criminal trial and the penalties inflicted upon them were similarly of a public nature. The latter were subject to prosecution not by the state but by the injured party according to the procedures of private law and, if condemned, had to pay a penalty to the person or persons harmed. In this respect, the term *delictum* denoted an unlawful act causing damage to a private interest; on the other hand, the term *crimen* signified an unlawful act directed against the state, or the community as a whole. In the category of *delicta privata* fell, for example, offences such as theft (*furtum*), bodily injury (*iniuria*), robbery (*rapina*), defamation of character and damage to another person's property (*damnum iniuria datum*).[110] On the other hand, offences such as treason and murder were classified as *crimina publica* and were subject to prosecution by state organs. The development of Roman criminal law was closely connected with the development of the procedures through which offences were investigated and punished. In other words, it was the public or private nature of the formal process adopted in dealing with different types of unlawful conduct that determined the classification of an offence as a *crimen* or a *delictum* and the forms of punishment that were imposed. It should be noted here, however, that even though in general we may speak of the Roman criminal law as belonging to the domain of public law, the line of demarcation between the spheres of public and private law was far from clear, especially in the archaic period of Roman law. With respect to the archaic period the reader should keep in mind, moreover, that very little can be said with certainty about the nature and operation of the norms relating to wrongdoing and punishment, and early Roman criminal law remains both obscure and subject of much debate among scholars.

Wrongdoing and punishment in the archaic age

Prior to the emergence of the Roman state wrongdoers were usually dealt with by the *familia* or the *gens* concerned and the penalties inflicted (often by the injured person himself or his relatives) were mainly retributive in character. With the gradual development of the state during the regal era

---

[110] The term *obligationes ex delicto* denoted the legal obligations arising from the commission of offences against the individual; the legal actions through which these obligations were enforced were referred to as *actiones poenales*.

the punishment of wrongdoers came to be regulated by a system of customary norms of a largely religious nature. These norms introduced limitations to the right of self-redress and the exercise of private vengeance – a practice that had deep roots in archaic society. At the same time a new type of offence began to emerge which were pursued by the state itself and not a private individual. These crimes were initially comparatively few in number and included treason, sedition, murder, and a few others. With respect to crimes against the state, it fell to the king, or a delegate acting in his name, to order the arrest of the accused, open and conduct the trial and pronounce the sentence. The punishment for such crimes was death, although the methods of inflicting capital punishment varied depending on the nature of the crime. Between private offences and public crimes there were many wrongdoings which were not classified and which were left totally in the hands of the individuals concerned. Thus the field of self-redress remained large and private vengeance continued to be an important factor throughout this period.

Of the public interests requiring protection one of the most important was the maintenance of the state of peace between the community and its gods (*pax deorum, amicitia*). In this respect, the punishment of those who committed certain crimes of a religious nature was primarily expiatory in character: it served to restore the *pax deorum* by eliminating the state of collective impurity brought about by the commission of the offence. The typical sanction imposed for such offences was the *consecratio*, i.e. the assignment of the culprit (*consecratio capitis*) and his property (*consecratio bonorum*) to a deity for purification (*piaculum*). As a result the offender (referred to as *sacer*) was deprived of the protection of the laws and could be put to death by anyone, his killing being regarded as a sacrifice to the deity to which he had been assigned. With respect to less serious offences, the transgressor was required to sacrifice an animal as a means of appeasing the deity. It should be added here that many punishments originally justified on grounds of retribution were ascribed a religious significance. Penalties involving a religious element were imposed, for example, on a son who mistreated his father,[111] on a patron who violated his obligations towards his client,[112] on a *pater familias* who killed his newborn child,[113] on a wife who committed adultery,[114] on a husband who repudiated his wife or sold her into slavery,[115] and on a

[111] In such cases the punishment was imposed by the father himself.

[112] Dionysius 2. 10.

[113] Dionysius 2. 15.

[114] Dionysius 2. 25. 6. According to a law attributed to king Romulus a wife who committed adultery could be lawfully killed by her husband.

[115] Plutarch, *Romulus* 22.

person who removed the fence that marked the boundaries of his land.[116] Of a similar nature were the punishments imposed for murder (*parricidium*),[117] the theft of sacred things (*furtum sacrorum*) or things dedicated to the gods (*res religiosae*), the giving of false testimony (*testimonium falsum*), arson (*incendium*) and certain forms of maleficent magic (*carmen malum, incantare, excantare fruges*).

During the early Republic the religious basis of many criminal offences began to fade away. This is reflected in the Law of the Twelve Tables, notwithstanding the fact that this legislation contained a number of provisions of a clearly religious nature.[118] Under the same legislation the right of self-redress was recognised in certain cases, although the indiscriminate use of private force against acts damaging private interests was restricted. Thus, for a number of offences involving injury to person or property specific pecuniary penalties were provided and the application of retaliatory punishment was made subject to certain conditions.[119] Moreover, in the republican period the number of crimes against the state continued to increase with the addition of offences committed by state officials in the execution of their duties. In this category fell, for example, acts of cowardice while in command of an army, the misappropriation of things belonging to the state (such as war booty or indemnities), the embezzlement of public money (*peculatus*, *furtum publicum*), acts of oppression against allied communities in time of war and the violation of the *sacrosanctitas* of the tribunes of the plebs.

---

116 Dionysius 2. 74.

117 Avenging the killing of a kinsman was regarded as a religious duty. This notion was so deeply rooted that long after murder had been made a crime against the state and subject to public prosecution a kinsman was bound to set such prosecution in motion and, if he failed to do so, he was not allowed to take anything of the deceased person's inheritance.

118 For example, a religious element is evident in the punishment imposed on a patron who wronged his client (XII T. VIII 21.), on witnesses who refused to testify at a trial (XII T. VIII 22.) and on a person who depastured or cut down a neighbour's crop by stealth in the night (XII T. VIII 9.).

119 Thus, fines were provided for offences involving minor bodily injury to a person. On the other hand an offence involving serious bodily harm entailed a more severe penalty. In the latter case the principle of retaliation was given priority and the victim or his nearest relatives were permitted to inflict bodily injury on the culprit. However, the infliction of such a punishment might be excluded if the offender agreed to compensate the victim for the injury he caused. See XII T. VIII 2. 3. 4.

Murder (*parricidium*)

The term *parricidium*, which initially denoted the killing of a *pater familias*, came to signify the voluntary and malicious (*dolo sciens*) killing of any free citizen. A law dealing with the crime of murder was attributed to king Numa Pompilius, who was also said to have introduced, for the first time, the distinction between murder and negligent homicide.[120] Wilful killing was punishable by death, the execution of the offender serving an expiatory purpose. On the other hand, a person who killed another by accident had to atone for the deed by sacrificing a ram before the parents of the person killed. In the archaic period cases of murder were investigated by specially appointed officials, referred to as *quaestores parricidii*.[121] According to Mommsen, the person found guilty of the offence and condemned to death was entitled to put his case before the assembly of the people which acted as the court of final appeal.[122] Some scholars have challenged this view, however, and many Romanists now accept that only the assembly had the authority to impose the sentence of death after a person had been convicted by a *quaestor parricidii*.[123]

Treason (*perduellio*)

High treason (*perduellio*) was recognised as one of the main crimes against the state from a very early period. Within its ambit came a variety of acts regarded as threatening the security of the state, such as assisting an enemy in time of war or inciting an enemy to attack the Roman state, delivering a Roman citizen to an enemy and stirring up an internal rebellion. The person found guilty of treason was punished by death,[124] his killing being regarded as a form of expiatory sacrifice. In the archaic period cases of treason were usually dealt with by special officials, the *duumviri perduellionis*, appointed first by the king and later by the consuls.[125] A person found

---

[120] Festus, '*parricidii* ' in Bruns, Fontes II, p. 21. And see XII T. VIII 24.

[121] XII T. IX 4; D. 1. 2. 2. 23. (Pomponius).

[122] Th. Mommsen, *Römisches Staatsrecht*, 3rd ed., Leipzig 1887, repr. Graz 1952, 163-4; and see A.H.M. Jones, *The Criminal Courts of the Roman Republic and Principate*, Oxford 1972, 1-39.

[123] B. Santalucia, *Diritto e processo penale nell' antica Roma*, Milan 1989, 31-89. Santalucia argues that this procedure was followed in cases involving serious crimes against the state, while minor offences were punished by the magistrates. Consider also J. L. Strachan-Davidson, *Problems of the Roman Criminal Law*, Oxford 1912, repr. Amsterdam 1969, 138-40.

[124] XII T. IX 5.

[125] Consider, e.g., Livy 1. 26.

guilty of treason was entitled to raise an appeal before the assembly of the people. Another type of offence relating to treason was the *proditio*. Within this category of offence came various acts involving disobedience to orders given by a magistrate in pursuance of his duties as a military commander.

The criminal jurisdiction of the magistrates

During the early Republic only magistrates had *iudicatio*, i.e. the power to bring criminal charges against citizens.[126] The tribunes and the quaestors usually dealt with political offences, the aediles prosecuted crimes against public morals and infringements of social legislation and, as was noted before, special magistrates appointed by the consuls, the *quaestores parricidii* and the *duoviri perduellionis*, investigated cases of murder and treason respectively. Furthermore, the pontiffs dealt with cases involving violations of religious norms, such as the neglect of religious duties by ministers of religion. The *praetor urbanus* initially had jurisdiction over matters concerning public peace and security. But after the introduction of the *lex Papiria* (of unknown date, probably mid-third century BC) jurisdiction in cases involving persons belonging to the lower classes and slaves was delegated to the *tresviri capitales* (or *tresviri nocturni*), minor officials whose duties included policing the city at night and arresting nocturnal criminals, preventing the breaking of fires, superintending the state prisons and carrying out executions.[127] The consuls probably seldom exercised their power of bringing criminal charges. A criminal prosecution could be based on a specific statutory enactment, such as the Law of the Twelve Tables, an established customary rule or an order issued by a state organ. Magistrates tried cases according to either laws or customs (*vel legibus vel moribus*), although the former were generally given priority. When a person was charged with an offence that entailed capital punishment, the magistrate would usually convict the accused and then leave the sentence to be decided by the *comitia centuriata*. Minor offences were dealt with by the magistrates in a summary fashion.

---

[126] See J. L. Strachan-Davidson, *Problems of the Roman Criminal Law*, Oxford, 1912, repr. Amsterdam 1969, 96.

[127] D. 1. 2. 2. 30. (Pomponius); Sallust, *Cat.* 55; Aulus Gellius, *N.A.* 3. 3. 15; Val. Max. 5. 4. 7; 6. 1. 10; 8. 4. 2. And see W. Kunkel, *An Introduction to Roman Legal and Constitutional History*, 2nd edn, Oxford 1973, 64. For another perspective see C. Cascione, *Tresviri capitales: storia di una magistratura minore*, Naples 1999.

The institution of the *provocatio ad populum*

The term *provocatio ad populum* denoted the right of a Roman citizen to appeal to the assembly of the people against sentences involving the loss of life or liberty, corporal punishment or the permanent loss of social and political rights imposed by magistrates.[128] During the early archaic period the right of appealing to the *comitia curiata* must have been a prerogative of the patricians; it was probably granted to the plebeians after the establishment of the *comitia centuriata* in the late sixth century BC. According to Roman tradition, the institution of the *provocatio ad populum* received legislative recognition by the *lex Valeria* of 509 BC.[129] This statute probably furnished the basis for the further recognition of the *ius provocationis* as a general right under subsequent legislative enactments, such as the Law of the Twelve Tables,[130] the *lex Valeria Horatia* of 449 BC and the *lex Valeria* of 300 BC. Appeals against capital sentences were submitted to the *comitia centuriata*, whilst appeals against pecuniary penalties to the *comitia tributa*. The *lex Valeria Horatia* is said to have been accompanied by a *plebiscitum*, the *lex Duilia de provocatione* (449 BC), which provided the death penalty for anyone seeking to abolish the tribunate or to create a magistracy whose decisions could not be subject to *provocatio* (*magistratus sine provocatione*).[131] Under the *lex Valeria* of 300 BC magistrates were prohibited from inflicting the death penalty or corporal punishment (flogging) on any citizen who raised an appeal before the people's assembly.[132] The same law, however, seems to have excluded *provocatio* from being raised against punishments imposed by military commanders on soldiers. The recognition of the *ius provocationis* as a general right by the Valerian legislation resulted in the elimination, for all practical purposes, of the distinction between cases tried before the *comitia* directly and cases tried before the *comitia* following an appeal, for *provocatio* was now considered implicit in any prosecution entailing capital punishment. The *lex Valeria* was supplemented by three successive enactments, the *leges Porciae* (first half of the second century BC). Although not much is known about these laws, it is believed that they

---

128 The notion of *provocatio ad populum* appears in the sources for the first time in the case of Horatius in connection with the crime of *perduellio* (in early ages the term *perduellio* was probably used to describe any atrocious crime against the life of a citizen). See Livy 1. 26.

129 Cicero, *de re publica* 2. 31; Livy 2. 8; 3. 55; 10. 9; Val. Max. 4. 1. 1; Dionysius 5. 19; D. 1. 2. 2. 16. (Pomponius).

130 XII T. IX 4.

131 Livy 3. 55.

132 Livy 10. 9.

extended *provocatio* to certain forms of corporal punishment (*verberatio*, *castigatio*) as well as to punishments imposed by military commanders on their soldiers. Moreover, under the same legislation, magistrates who violated the *ius provocationis* were made subject to punishment (probably capital punishment).

The criminal jurisdiction of the *comitia: iudicia populi*

During the early Republic the Roman assemblies operated as courts of justice in cases where an appeal was raised before the people against a sentence imposed by a magistrate. As was noted before, capital offences fell within the province of the *comitia centuriata*, whilst appeals against pecuniary penalties were raised before the *comitia tributa*.[133] The criminal jurisdiction of the assemblies was extended, especially in the period following the introduction of the Law of the Twelve Tables, as a result of the recognition and frequent exercise of the right of *provocatio*. In the course of time, as the judicial powers of the magistrates became more and more restricted by legislation, the judicial functions of the assemblies were more clearly recognised until they became the regular courts (*iudicia populi*) for the investigation and punishment of the most serious crimes.

Only a magistrate could bring a charge against a citizen and summon the assembly before which the case was to be tried. The magistrate who had resolved to impeach a citizen gave public notice of his intention at a *contio*.[134] He named the accused, specified the offence with which he was charged and the form of punishment which it entailed, and set the day on which the trial was to take place (*diem dicere*). The magistrate might include more than one charge in the same accusation but he was not allowed to leave the penalty open. He could, however, alter the form or amount of punishment proposed during the initial stages of the proceedings[135] and could withdraw the charge at any stage of the trial – there were usually three sessions in a trial, held on different days. Besides presiding over the proceedings, the role of the magistrate was both to accuse (*accusare*) and to investigate the facts of the case (*anquirere*). He called upon the accused and his opponents to present their arguments and invited witnesses who gave evidence under oath. But as the normal rules of

133 From as early as the middle of the fifth century BC the magistrates' power of imposing fines was limited by a series of laws (*lex Aternia Tarpeia*, *lex Menenia Sextia*) which set maximum limits as to the fines which magistrates could impose. See Aulus Gellius, *N. A.* 11. 1; Dionysius 10. 50; Cicero, *de re publica* 2. 35.

134 An informal gathering of citizens.

135 See, e.g., Livy 26. 3.

veto remained in force during the trial, a magistrate's decisions could be blocked by another magistrate of the same or higher rank. Thus a trial could be prevented before it began or stopped at any point during the proceedings, or a proposed punishment might be precluded by another magistrate's veto. Nevertheless, the right of veto seems to have been sparingly exercised and was restricted largely to breaches of established rules of procedure.[136]

After the conclusion of the third session an interval of at least three market days (*trinum nundinum*) elapsed before the magistrate passed formal judgement on the accused. If the latter was found guilty, he could raise a *provocatio ad populum.*[137] In such a case further speeches were made and arguments heard and then the magistrate's proposal (*rogatio*) ordering the infliction of punishment on the accused was put to the vote of the people (i.e. the *comitia tributa* , if the penalty was a fine, or the *comitia centuriata*, if he was found guilty of a capital offence). The voting procedure and the associated formalities were not different from those followed when the assembly had to decide on a legislative proposal. But if the vote had to be postponed due to a rainstorm or a similar ill omen, the accused was released, as if he had been found innocent, and could not be charged with the same offence again. An accused charged with a capital offence, especially one of a political nature, was customarily given the option of leaving the community and going into voluntary exile before a final condemnatory sentence was passed. If he took that option a plebiscite was issued declaring that the accused had forfeited all his political rights as a Roman citizen (*aquae et ignis interdictio*).[138] The trial before the *comitia* was the first type of public trial that took place according to a set form of procedure. The relevant judgement was termed *iudicatio* and was

---

[136] Such as the rule which precluded the prosecution of the same person for the same offence twice. Moreover, according to established convention a magistrate who was in office or who was away on official business (*absens rei publicae causa*) could not be prosecuted, and prosecutions of tribunes, whose person was protected as sacrosanct, were deemed illegal.

[137] It should be noted here that there could be no appeal from a decision of a dictator; similarly, in the early Republic, soldiers in the army could not appeal against decisions of their superior officers.

[138] Consider, e.g., Livy 26. 3. 12. The person who was declared an *interdictus* was deprived of the protection of the law and, if he returned to Rome without permission, he might be lawfully killed by anybody. On the legal principles relating to exile see Cicero, *de domo* 78; *pro Caecina* 100; *pro Balbo* 28.

distinguished from the *coercitio*, i.e. the summary punishment imposed by magistrates.[139]

The extraordinary courts: *quaestiones extraordinariae*

Although serious offences fell within the jurisdiction of the *comitia*, from an early period it became common for the *comitia* to set up special tribunals (*quaestiones extraordinariae*) for the investigation of certain crimes, especially crimes of a political nature. One of the main reasons behind this development was that it was often very difficult for a popular assembly to inquire into the complexities of a criminal prosecution and to handle complicated and often inconsistent evidence. Moreover, the business of calling together an assembly was cumbersome and time wasting. In the later Republic special tribunals set up by decree of the senate or by a plebiscite dealt with crimes relating to abuse of power or dereliction of duty by magistrates and provincial governors and other acts regarded as detrimental to interests of the state.[140] Such a special *quaestio* was, for example, the commission set up by the senate in 186 BC to investigate and punish the crimes committed by members of the Bacchanalian societies.[141] In these courts the presiding magistrate, usually a

---

[139] On the *iudicia populi* and the institution of the *provocatio ad populum* see in general H. F. Jolowicz and B. Nicholas, *Historical Introduction to the Study of Roman Law*, Cambridge 1972, 305 ff; A. H. M. Jones, *The Criminal Courts of the Roman Republic and Principate*, Oxford 1972, ch. 1; J. L. Strachan-Davidson, *Problems of the Roman Criminal Law*, Oxford 1912, repr. Amsterdam 1969, 127 ff; W. Kunkel, *Untersuchungen zur Entwicklung des römischen Kriminalverfahrens in vorsullanischer Zeit*, Munich 1962, 9 ff; J. Martin, 'Die Provokation in der klassischen und spaten Republik', (1970) *Hermes* 98, 72; R. A. Bauman, *Crime and Punishment in Ancient Rome*, London and New York 1996, ch. 2; 'The lex Valeria de provocatione of 300 BC', (1973) *Hist.* 22, 34-47; E. Staveley, 'Provocatio during the fifth and fourth centuries BC', (1954) *Hist.* 3, 413; B. Santalucia, *Diritto e processo penale nell' antica Roma*, Milan 1989, ch. 2; V. Giuffrè, *La repressione criminale nell' esperienza romana*, Naples 1998, 24 ff; M. Talamanca (ed.), *Lineamenti di storia del diritto romano*, Milan 1989, 89 ff, 274 ff; A. Burdese, *Manuale di diritto pubblico romano*, 3rd edn, Turin 1987, repr. 1994, 243 ff.

[140] See, e.g., Livy 38. 54; 42. 21. In 123 BC, however, the *lex Sempronia de capite civis* reaffirmed the principle that no citizen could be tried for a capital crime without the formal approval of the assembly. This law seems to have forbidden the setting up of special tribunals by senatorial decree alone and without the sanction of the people.

[141] See Livy 39. 8-19; Cicero, *de legibus* 2. 37; and see *Sc. De Bacchanalibus* in FIRA I, p. 240.

consul or a praetor, was assisted by a *consilium*, or body of assessors, whose role was similar to that of a modern day jury.[142] The decision of the court was determined by the majority of the assessors and, as the court was regarded as representing the people, no appeal against its decisions was permitted. In the changed social and political conditions of the later Republic, the *quaestiones extraordinariae* provided a more efficient way of dealing with criminal cases than the usual procedure before the *comitia*, and the role of the latter in the administration of justice gradually declined. The introduction of these courts was an important step towards the establishment of the permanent court system (*quaestiones perpetuae*), which began to emerge from the middle of the second century BC.[143]

---

142 Until the passing of the *lex Sempronia iudiciaria* in 123 BC the *consilium* was composed exclusively of members of the senatorial class.

143 On the *quaestiones extraordinariae* see H. F. Jolowicz and B. Nicholas, *Historical Introduction to the Study of Roman Law*, Cambridge 1972, 313-14; J. L. Strachan-Davidson, *Problems of the Roman Criminal Law*, Oxford 1912, repr. Amsterdam 1969, 225 ff; B. Santalucia, *Diritto e processo penale nell' antica Roma*, Milan 1989, 56 ff; *Studi di diritto penale romano*, Rome 1994, 181 ff; V. Giuffrè, *La repressione criminale nell' esperienza romana*, Naples 1998, 40 ff; A. Burdese, *Manuale di diritto pubblico Romano*, 3rd edn, Turin 1987, repr. 1994, 249.

5 The Later Republic

The Roman Expansion in the Mediterranean World

In the years following the end of the conflict of the orders Rome concentrated her attention on foreign affairs. Having established herself as the dominant power in Italy, she assumed new responsibilities in world politics, opened up new diplomatic relations and began to pursue the expansion of her territory and influence outside the Italian peninsula. The other great powers of this period were, in the East, the Hellenistic monarchies of Egypt, Syria and Macedonia, which had emerged from the breaking down of the empire of Alexander the Great, and, in the West, the city-state of Carthage, a great maritime power that dominated the western Mediterranean basin.

The city of Carthage, which was situated on the northern coast of Africa, near present-day Tunis, had started off as a Phoenician colony in the ninth century BC. By the end of the fourth century BC she had grown to become the wealthiest and most powerful city in the western Mediterranean world. The Carthagenian empire extended over the northern coast of Africa from the Gulf of Syrtis westward beyond the Strait of Gibraltar, southern Spain, Sardinia and most of Sicily. Carthage was governed by an oligarchy of powerful merchant families and, for her military strength, was relying on her large mercenary army. The contacts between the Carthagenians and the Romans had began in the second half of the fourth century BC when the two states were linked by a number of treaties. At the beginning of the third century BC Carthage offered aid to Rome in her conflict with the Greek cities of southern Italy, Carthage's chief commercial rivals. But, shortly after the subjugation of the Greek city-states and the annexation of all the important ports of southern Italy by Rome, this precarious coalition turned into open rivalry and war between the two powers seemed unavoidable. When the first Punic (Phoenician) War broke out in 264 BC Carthage was much wealthier than Rome and had almost twice as many inhabitants. Rome, on the other hand, had a more dependable citizens' army and a more loyal population. In 241 BC, after twenty-three years of almost continuous fighting, the war ended with victory for Rome. As a result of her victory, Rome acquired her first overseas province, Sicily, and secured her position as a growing international power. The Carthagenians attempted to recover the lost ground in 218 BC. In that year a large expeditionary force led by Hannibal, Carthage's most capable general, was dispatched to attack the Romans in Italy. Despite the initial successes of her armies, Carthage was finally overwhelmed by the Romans in 201 BC and her political and commercial supremacy came to an end. Carthage lost all her possessions outside her home territory, was forced to pay a substantial indemnity and was reduced to the position of a client-state of Rome. As a result of their success in the second Punic War the Romans gained control of Sardinia and southern Spain and established themselves as the undisputed masters of western Mediterranean. Rome's dominant position in the West was secured further after the subjugation of the Celtic tribes of northern Italy in the early years of the second century BC.

Although initially Rome showed no interest in expanding eastwards, antagonisms between eastern powers and, in particular, the ambitions of Syria and Macedonia to restore the empire of Alexander the great at the expense of smaller states in the region, gave her the opportunity to enter the scene of Hellenistic politics, first as a guarantor of the existing balance of power and, subsequently, in pursuit of her own expansionist designs. Among Rome's chief opponents in the East was king Philip V of Macedonia, who had sided with the Carthagenians during the second Punic War. Seizing upon Philip's aggressive policies and claiming to act as protectors of the independence of the Greek city-states the Romans declared war on Macedonia in 200 BC.[1] Philip's defeat in 197 BC put an end to the Macedonian domination over Greece and secured a permanent role for Rome in Greek affairs, although no Greek territory was annexed by the Romans this time. The Romans declared themselves liberators of Greece and soon withdrew their armies from the country, leaving the Greek city-states and leagues free to govern themselves.

In 192 BC Rome found herself at war with king Antioch III of Syria, following the latter's attempt to interfere in Greek affairs. After four years of fighting the king's power was finally broken. Rome renewed her treaties of friendship with the Greek city-states, once more guaranteed their independence, and withdrew. But as Roman power and influence continued to increase, the Romans' attitude towards their allies in the East became more and more domineering. The Roman policy of interfering in other states' internal affairs drove many Greek cities to regard Macedonia's new king, Perseus, as a possible deliverer from the despotism of Rome. To prevent the expansion of Macedonian influence in Greece Rome declared war on Perseus in 171 BC (the third Macedonian war). Following Perseus's

1 This year marks the beginning of the second Macedonian War. The first Macedonian War was fought during and as part of the second Punic war.

defeat in 168 BC the Macedonian kingdom was broken up into four separate republics, each being governed by its own magistrates and a senate composed of representatives elected in the several cities. But in 148 BC, after a short-lived revolt, the republics were dissolved and Macedonia was turned into a Roman province. Finally, after the dissolution of the Achaean confederacy and the sacking of Corinth by the Romans in 146 BC the whole of Greece fell under Roman domination. Unlike Macedonia, however, Greece was not organised as a Roman province. The Greek city-states were compelled to enter into treaties of alliance with Rome and the whole country was placed under the supervision of the governor of Macedonia.[2] The same year marks the end of the third Punic War (149-146 BC) which resulted in the complete destruction of Carthage and the annexation of its territory as part of the Roman province of Africa.

In 133 BC the rich kingdom of Pergamum (situated in the north-west part of Asia Minor) was made over to Rome under the will of its last king, Attalus III. Out of the kingdom of Pergamum the province of Asia was formed in 129 BC. Moreover, following Rome's victory in the war against Iugurtha (112-105 BC), ruler of the north African kingdom of Numidia, further territories were added to the Roman province of Africa. In 88 BC Rome embarked on a series of wars in the East against the king of Pontus Mithridates Eupator who, having declared himself liberator of the Greeks, had started a campaign aiming at driving the Romans out of Asia Minor and Greece.[3] Although for a time Roman power in the East seemed doomed, Mithradates was finally defeated in 63 BC. Rome regained control of Greece and a continuous belt of Roman provinces was created along the coasts of the Black and Mediterranean Seas from northern Asia Minor to Syria and Judaea. Behind these provinces to the east Rome's sphere of interest was safeguarded through a band of client states which formed a buffer zone against the powerful Parthian Empire. This phase of Roman expansion came to an end with the conquest of Gaul by Julius Caesar (58-53 BC) and the annexation of Egypt by Octavian in 30 BC.[4]

---

2 Southern Greece became a Roman province under the name of Achaia in the closing years of the first century BC.

3 The Kingdom of Pontus was situated in the north-east part of Asia Minor.

4 On the Roman expansion see R. M. Errington, *The Dawn of Empire*, London 1971; W. V. Harris, *War and Imperialism in Republican Rome*, 327-70 BC, Oxford 1979; E. Badian, *Roman Imperialism in the Late Republic*, 2nd edn, Oxford 1968; K. Christ, *Krise und Untergang der römischen Republik*, Darmstadt 1979, chs 1 & 2.

The Organisation of Italy and the Provinces

Italy

As was noted in chapter 2, after the whole of Italy came under Roman domination in the early third century BC, some of the towns were annexed whilst others were admitted into alliance with Rome on terms which differed for almost every individual community. At the same time, a large number of new settlements or colonies were established by the Romans throughout the country.

Communities in alliance with Rome (*civitates foederatae, socii Italici*) retained their autonomy. Despite the fact that they were regarded by the Romans as foreigners (*peregrini*), the inhabitants of these communities enjoyed certain rights under Roman law, such as *commercium* (the right to trade with Romans on equal terms and to use the forms of contract available to Roman citizens) and *conubium* (the right to enter into a valid Roman marriage). Every allied community was bound to Rome by a special treaty (*foedus*) which set out the rules governing its relations with Rome. Although these treaties differed from one case to another, they all obliged the allied communities to aid Rome militarily and to surrender control over foreign relations. On the whole Rome respected the treaty rights of her allies, although some cases can be found in the sources in which these rights were encroached upon by Roman officials. But as the Roman power and influence continued to grow, the allies tended to sink into a position of greater inferiority and to be regarded, in effect, as clients at the disposal of their Roman masters. With the gradual Romanisation of Italy the generally disadvantageous position of the allies was felt more keenly and the acquisition of the Roman citizenship became one of the chief demands of the allied communities. Following a revolt of the allies against Rome, which led to the so-called Social War (90-88 BC), this demand was finally met with the passing of the *lex Iulia* in 90 BC and the *lex Plautia Papiria* in 89 BC.

Many formerly independent communities which, as a result of the expansion of Roman territory, had been incorporated into the Roman state were allowed to retain some local autonomy and to continue governing themselves in accordance with their former constitutions. These communities were referred to as *municipia* and their inhabitants as *municipes*.[5] To the category of *municipia sine suffragio* (municipalities

---

5 The term *municipes* was used to denote those who bore the burdens of the Roman citizenship , such as those relating to taxation and military service. And see Festus, '*municium*' in Bruns, *Fontes* II, p. 15.

whose members did not have the right of suffrage) belonged those communities of Roman citizens whose inhabitants had all the obligations but only the private rights of the Roman citizenship. On the other hand, citizens belonging to *municipia cum suffragio* enjoyed all the private and public rights of the Roman citizenship, including the right of voting in the Roman assemblies.[6] The status of the *municipia sine suffragio* was a halfway stage in the process towards the complete amalgamation with Rome of formerly independent communities. This process was completed in the early first century BC, when all the communities in Italy became *municipia cum suffragio* and their inhabitants were granted full Roman citizenship.[7] The municipal system was a distinctly Roman approach to solving the problem of local government in an enlarged city-state. It provided a means of incorporating previously independent communities into the Roman state without the dissolution of their community life or an abrupt break with their previous customs, traditions and culture. For the inhabitants of these communities this system brought the advantages as well as the obligations associated with the Roman citizenship, while allowing them to retain some local autonomy. For Rome it brought an increase of manpower which helped her to meet growing military needs and facilitated the gradual incorporation of foreign populations into the Roman citizen body.

The term *coloniae* was used to denote the new settlements founded by Rome in conquered lands in Italy and elsewhere. Usually, when a new territory was conquered, a part of it became property of the Roman state (*ager publicus*) and was used as a source of public revenue under the administration of the senate; another part was divided among Roman citizens who had chosen to leave Rome and to settle permanently in the conquered country as *coloni* (cultivators of the land). The colonies served several important purposes: they safeguarded Rome's conquests by protecting them against internal uprisings and external invasions,[8] helped to diffuse Roman culture in the conquered lands thus precipitating the assimilation of the local population and provided a much needed outlet for the poorer elements of Rome's rapidly growing population. When the decision had been made to establish a new colony (*coloniam deducere*), a special law was passed based upon a resolution of the senate (*ex senatus*

---

6 The members of these communities were full Roman citizens (*cives Romani optimo iure*). Municipalities of full citizens seem to have enjoyed a lesser degree of autonomy than those of citizens without the right of suffrage.

7 Following the passing of the *lex Iulia* (90 BC) and the *lex Plautia Papiria* (89 BC) mentioned above.

8 Hence colonies were often described as garrisons (*praesidia*), fortifications (*propugnacula*) or watch towers (*speculae*).

consulto) which designated the boundaries of the relevant territory and the way in which it was to be divided among the settlers. This law (*lex coloniae*), which was the foundation charter of the new colony, specified also the obligations of the settlers, especially the number of soldiers which the colony was required to provide. Moreover, two or more commissioners (*curatores*) were appointed to act as leaders of the settlers and to carry out the implementation of the law by which the colony was established. These commissioners remained in office for three or, sometimes, five years, and exercised supreme jurisdiction in the colony.

There were two types of colonies: Latin colonies (*coloniae Latinae*)[9] and Roman colonies (*coloniae civium Romanorum*). The inhabitants of the former enjoyed *commercium* with Rome, but not *conubium* (unless this right had explicitly been granted to them). Latin colonists (*Latini coloniarii*) could acquire full Roman citizenship if they became magistrates in their own towns (*per magistratum*), or if the citizenship was granted to them by law. Sometimes Roman citizens who had been deprived of some of the rights of the citizenship as a form of punishment (*deminutio capitis*) became members of Latin colonies. Each Latin colony had full rights of local self-government, with its own laws, magistrates and a constitution closely modelled upon that of Rome. The Roman colonies were made up of Roman citizens as well as elements of the local population. Their laws were those of Rome and in their external relations they had to follow the policies of their mother city. Of the Roman colonies those situated along the sea coast (*coloniae maritimae*) were regarded as particularly important and were often granted special privileges. As to the old inhabitants of the territory in which a colony was established, these appear to have occupied an inferior position, having been forced to abandon their own laws and institutions and to adopt those of the Romans. In the course of time, especially after the passing of the *lex Iulia* (90 BC) and the *lex Plautia Papiria* (89 BC), the distinction between Roman and Latin colonies, as well as the political differences between the Romans and the inhabitants of the allied communities, disappeared. As a result, the various ethnic elements in Italy became a single nation and a uniform culture developed on the basis of common citizenship.[10]

---

9 These were established largely by Latin citizens, but in some cases Romans and citizens of other allied states were also enrolled.

10 On the organisation of Italy and the spread of the Roman citizenship consider A. N. Sherwin-White, *Roman Citizenship*, 2nd edn, Oxford 1973; E. T. Salmon, *Roman Colonisation*, London 1969; P. A. Brunt, *Italian Manpower*, Oxford 1987; M. Humbert, *Municipium et civitas sine suffragio*, Paris 1978; C. Nicolet, *The World of the Citizen in Republican Rome*, London 1980; H. F. Jolowicz and B. Nicholas, *Historical Introduction to the Study of Roman Law*,

The provinces

The term *provincia* signified a territory or district outside Italy which the Romans had conquered by war.[11] When a country was subjugated a Roman magistrate, usually the one who carried out the conquest, together with a commission of senators (*legati*), were entrusted with the task of organising it as a province.[12] They arranged the terms of peace with the defeated local population, designated the boundaries of the new province and drew up a constitution prescribing the way in which the province was to be governed. Upon the return of the *legati* to Rome these arrangements were put before the assembly for approval in the form of a legislative proposal (*rogatio legis*). The proposal, once it became law (*lex data*, *lex provinciae*), formed the constitutional charter governing the organisation and administration of the province.[13] This law, however, could be modified or amended by subsequent legislation, senatorial decrees or edicts of the provincial governors themselves. The number of troops that were to be stationed in the province, [14] as well as the amount of money that its governor was to receive from the public treasury, were determined by the senate.[15]

Each province comprised a number of communities (*civitates*) enjoying local self-government but having no political bond of unity. A distinction was drawn between three categories of communities: free and federate (*civitates liberae et foederatae*), free and nontributary (*civitates liberae et immunes*) and tributary (*stipendiariae*). To the first category belonged those communities (very few in number) which retained their

---

3rd edn, Cambridge 1972, 58 ff; W. Kunkel, *An Introduction to Roman Legal and Constitutional History*, 2nd edn, Oxford 1973, 35 ff; M. Kaser, *Römische Rechtsgeschichte*, Göttingen 1976, 55 ff, 91 ff; W. Kunkel/M. Schermaier, *Römische Rechtsgeschichte*, Cologne 2001, 50 ff; F. Wieacker, *Römische Rechtsgeschichte*, Munich 1988, 368 ff, 514-15; A. Guarino, *Storia del diritto romano*, Naples 1996, 247; G. Crifò, *Lezioni di storia del diritto romano*, 3rd edn, Bologna 2000, 133 ff; M. Talamanca (ed.), *Lineamenti di storia del diritto romano*, Milan 1989, 259 ff.

11 One should note, however, that a country was not always converted into a province immediately after it was conquered. Macedonia, for example, although fully conquered in 168 BC, did not become a Roman province until 148 BC.

12 See on this Plutarch, *Aem.* 28; Paus. 7. 10. 7; Livy. 33. 43; 45. 16. 17. 18. 30-32.

13 Such laws were, for example, the *lex Rupilia* for Sicily, the *lex Aquillia* for Asia, and the *leges Aemiliae* for Macedonia.

14 These forces could be used in defending the province against external invasion or in putting down a rebellion within, but could not conduct operations outside the boundaries of the province without express orders from the senate.

15 See, e.g., Cicero, *ad Att.* 3. 24; *de leg. agr.* 2. 13; *in Pison.* 35.

independence. These were permanently bound with Rome by treaties of alliance. Into the second category fell a small number of communities to which Rome had granted, by virtue of the provincial charter and without the existence of a bilateral treaty, certain privileges, such as exemption from taxation. These privileges could be revoked by the senate at any time, however. The third group, which was by far the most numerous, furnished most of the taxes imposed upon the province.

A province was governed by a Roman magistrate with *imperium*, usually a consul or a praetor. In the last century of the Republic, under Sulla's *lex Cornelia de provinciis ordinandis* (81 BC), consuls and praetors, after their year in office expired, were required to serve as governors of provinces as pro-magistrates (*proconsules* or *propraetores*) for one more year. It was usually left to the senate to determine which provinces were to be governed by consuls (*provinciae consulares*) and which by praetors (*provinciae praetoriae*). In general, as consular provinces were designated those provinces in which peace was not yet fully established or which remained under the threat of war.[16] The governor of a province was assisted by a *quaestor provinciae* and other officials (*legati*), appointed by the senate but usually nominated by himself.

The governor, by virtue of his *imperium*, acted as commander-in-chief of the troops stationed in the province and regulated all matters relating to the internal administration of the province. Besides his military and administrative duties, he had supreme jurisdiction with respect to matters of both civil and criminal law. He presided as judge over serious cases arising among provincials, and over all cases between provincials and Romans or between Roman citizens living in his province. Cases referred to the governor were heard either in the capital of the province, where the governor had his seat (*praetorium*), or in the principal towns of the province, where conventions (*conventus*) were held at regular intervals.[17] Upon taking up office the governor issued an edict (*edictum provinciale*), usually modelled upon that of his predecessors, setting out the legal

---

[16] But whether a province was to be assigned to an ex-consul or an ex-praetor did not depend, exclusively, on such considerations. See, e.g., Cicero, *ad Att.* 1. 13. 16; *de prov. cons.* 7. 15; Plutarch, *Pomp.* 61.

[17] The word *conventus* was used to denote a gathering of people in a province meeting together to attend a court of justice. The same word referred also to an assembly of Roman citizens living in a province.

principles which he would enforce during his term of office.[18] He also issued *decreta*, orders of an administrative or judicial character.[19]

The task of collecting taxes in the provinces was assigned to private contractors (*publicani*) who formed companies referred to as *societates publicanorum*. Besides the ordinary taxes, such as the property-tax (*tributum*), which they were required to pay on a regular basis, the provincials were often subjected to the arbitrary demands of local Roman officials. They were required, for example, to provide winter shelter for the troops, to equip and maintain ships for war or transport and to provide supplies for the governor's household. As these burdens were usually imposed at the discretion of the governor or local magistrates, they were often used by them as means of intimidation and oppression. An attempt to check the abuses of power by provincial governors and magistrates was made in 149 BC with the passing of the *lex Calpurnia de repetundis*. Under this law, which was confirmed by subsequent enactments, a regular court was instituted (*quaestio perpetua*) to deal with cases of extortion and other abuses committed by provincial magistrates.[20]

---

18 G. 1. 5. 6; Cicero, *ad Att.* 6. 1. 15. The provincial governor's edict was in many respects similar to the edict issued by the praetor in Rome.

19 See, e.g., the *decretum* of the proconsul of Hispaniae Ultimae of 189 BC in FIRA I, no. 51.

20 On the Roman provincial administration see M. Cary and H. H. Scullard, *A History of Rome*, 3rd edn, London 1975, ch. 17; J. Richardson, *Roman Provincial Administration, 227 BC to AD* 117, Basingstoke 1976; A. Lintott, *Imperium Romanum: Politics and Administration*, London & New York 1993, 22 ff; H. F. Jolowicz and B. Nicholas, *Historical Introduction to the Study of Roman Law*, 3rd edn, Cambridge 1972, 66 ff; W. Kunkel, *An Introduction to Roman Legal and Constitutional History*, 2nd edn, Oxford 1973, 39 ff; W. Dahlheim, *Gewalt und Herrschaft. Das provinziale Herrschaftssystem der römischen Republik*, Berlin and New York 1977; M. Kaser, *Römische Rechtsgeschichte*, Göttingen 1976, 93 ff; W. Kunkel/M. Schermaier, *Römische Rechtsgeschichte*, Cologne 2001, 53 ff; F. Wieacker, *Römische Rechtsgeschichte*, Munich 1988, 483, 515 ff; A. Guarino, *Storia del diritto romano*, Naples 1996, 245 ff; G. Crifò, *Lezioni di storia del diritto romano*, 3rd edn, Bologna 2000, 133 ff; M. Talamanca (ed.), *Lineamenti di storia del diritto romano*, Milan 1989, 261 ff.

Social and Economic Conditions

The social classes

As was said in chapter 2, by the close of the third century BC the old patrician aristocracy had been replaced by a new type of nobility, made up of a small number of wealthy patrician and plebeian families, whose members monopolised the highest offices of the state. Since the Roman senate consisted largely of members of leading families who had served as magistrates, this new nobility was referred to as the senatorial class (*ordo senatorius*). In the *ordo senatorius* were included all the descendants of families which had been represented in the senate, whether or not members of the immediate family were senators at a given time. The position which a person occupied within the senatorial class depended largely upon the rank of the state offices which members of his family had held.[21] Despite the divisions that existed within the *ordo senatorius* and the antagonisms that often developed between its members, community of economic and political interests tended to promote solidarity among the senatorial families. The chief source of these families' wealth was landed property, as senators were debarred by custom and law from engaging in trade and industry and were not allowed to enter into contracts with the state for the collection of taxes and other public revenues. Thus, under the *lex Claudia* of 213 BC senators were forbidden to engage in commercial activities other than the selling of the produce of their own estates.[22] Senators who had served as army commanders usually received a large share of the spoils of war and were able to take possession of large tracts of land in the conquered countries. However, the fact that many senators had large financial interests in the provinces did not make for disinterested public administration of the provinces. Senators who served as provincial governors had plenty of opportunities to gain wealth by means that were not honest and, as they had almost unlimited power and were free from the restraint of public opinion, they often yielded to the temptation.

Political and economic developments led to the emergence, during the second century BC, of a new social class in Rome, which became known as the equestrian class (*ordo equester*). The term *equites* originally

---

21 The highest distinction was reserved for those whose ancestors had held the consulship.

22 This law excluded senators from maritime commerce by prohibiting them from owing vessels capable of carrying more than three hundred amphorae (i.e. ships that could be used for carrying out large-scale commercial activities). This law seems to have fallen in abeyance in the closing years of the Republic. See Cicero, *in Verr*. 5. 18.

referred to those citizens who were rich enough to be included into the eighteen centuries of knights (*centuriae equitum*), which constituted the cavalry of the Roman army. As was noted in chapter 3, these citizens made up the prestigious equestrian centuries of the centuriate assembly.[23] After the wars of the mid-republican period, the term *equites* gradually ceased to be associated with military service and came to denote the powerful class of rich merchants and entrepreneurs many of whom made their fortune by exploiting the opportunities brought about by Rome's wars of expansion. An active and very visible minority within the equestrian class acquired their wealth by entering into contracts with the Roman state for the carrying out of various public operations. These included, for example, the construction of public buildings and roads, the operation of publicly owned mines, the provisioning of the Roman army and the collection of taxes and other public revenues. Many equestrians were also active in shipping, especially in the transportation of agricultural products from the provinces to Rome. Traditionally activities such as these were regarded as undignified and therefore unsuitable for members of the senatorial nobility. The *lex Claudia*, mentioned above, greatly facilitated the formation of the equestrian class which, however, was not fully recognised as a distinct social order before the passing of the *lex Sempronia iudiciaria* in 122 BC.[24]

Below the *equites* lay the aristocracy of the various communities in Italy and the provinces, whose members were usually faithful supporters of Rome and had adopted the Roman culture and way of life. Slightly lower down in the social hierarchy were the members of the lower middle class: the small landowners in the country and the artisans and small traders in the cities. Although their economic situation was markedly worse, to the same class belonged also the bulk of the urban and rural proletariat, whose only means of support was what they could get from the state in the form of grants, or from the wealthy families to which many of its members had attached themselves as clients. As Rome's urban proletariat was susceptible to political manipulation and prone to violence, it came to constitute a serious threat to political stability, especially during the last century of the republican era.[25]

---

23 During the Monarchy the *equites* were probably selected by the *comitia curiata* (Dionysius 2. 13.). After the Servian reforms this duty fell upon the king, who was in charge of the census. During the early Republic the *equites* were chosen first by the consuls and, from 443 BC, by the censors.

24 Under this law the equites were given the right of serving as jurors in criminal trials, to the exclusion of senators.

25 On the Roman social classes see M. Gelzer, *The Roman Nobility*, Oxford 1969; C. Nicolet, *L'ordre équestre à l'époque républicaine*, Paris 1974; H. Hill, *The*

Slaves and freedmen

By far the most vulnerable group in society were the slaves (*servi*). In the early republican period the number of slaves in Rome was relatively small and most agricultural works and ordinary trades were carried out by freedmen. But from the early third century BC the slave population began to grow rapidly and, in the later Republic, slave labour had become a predominant factor in economic life. Large numbers of foreign slaves were brought into Italy during the period of the Punic Wars and, as the demand for slave labour continued to grow, more followed in the course of the Roman campaigns in the East.[26] Besides the wars, another source of slaves were the large slave markets of the East, such as the one on the island of Delos in the Aegean.[27] Moreover, as the children of slave families were themselves slaves by birth, the slave population continued to grow and, by the end of the republican age, probably more than one third of the whole population of Italy consisted of slaves.[28] The living conditions of slaves varied considerably, depending upon their personal skills and education as well as their place of work. By and large, the urban slaves were treated better than those living on country estates or working in the mines, and were more frequently released from slavery.[29] In general, however, the vast majority of slaves, especially those working on the large estates, lived in misery and were treated with brutality by their masters. The deep resentment felt by slaves against their Roman masters erupted in a series of large-scale uprisings during the late second and early first centuries BC.

A slave had no personal rights, being regarded in the eyes of the law as a thing (*res*). Thus, if he was killed or injured by another this was dealt with by the law not as a wrong done to the slave but as damage to his

---

Roman Middle Class in the Republican Period, Oxford 1952; G. Alföldy, *The Social History of Rome*, London 1985, chapters 2 and 3.

26 According to the ancient law of nations (*ius gentium*), not only enemy soldiers seized in battle, but even entire populations of conquered territories were subject to enslavement. Consider, e.g., Livy 27. 16; 29. 29; 41. 11. 8; 41. 28. 8; 45. 34. 5.

27 The geographer Strabo of Amasia reports that, on this island, up to ten thousand people could be sold as slaves on one day alone (14. 5. 2.) Most of the slaves sold there were victims of kidnapping by pirates or prisoners captured during wars between eastern states.

28 See on this M. K. Hopkins, *Conquerors and Slaves*, Cambridge 1978, 99-106.

29 Educated urban slaves were often employed as instructors, clerks or physicians. On the estates an educated slave could become estate manager, work supervisor or book-keeper.

master's property.[30] Moreover, if one's slave caused damage to another's property, the master of the slave had to make amends to the person whose property was damaged or to surrender the slave to the authorities for punishment.[31] As to the penalties inflicted upon slaves, these varied considerably depending upon the seriousness of the offence committed and the circumstances of the case. Among the most common and least severe forms of punishment were flogging and the transference of the slave from the city to a country estate where living conditions were much harsher. If a slave had committed a more serious offence he was forced to perform the hardest labours, often in chains, or was confined to an underground cell. Slaves found guilty of grave crimes were usually sentenced to death by crucifixion.[32]

A slave could be released from slavery by his master (*manumissio*) in three different ways: by a formal announcement by the master in public and before a higher magistrate (usually a praetor) that the slave was free (*vindicta*); after the enrolment of a slave as a Roman citizen by the censor, on the master's request (*censu*); and under his master's will (*testamento*).[33] After his liberation a slave was referred to as *libertinus* (freedman) and had, in theory at least, all the rights and obligations of a Roman citizen.[34] In practice, however, freedmen and their descendants were viewed as socially inferior by those with no slaves in their ancestry and were virtually excluded from all the important offices of the state. A large part of Rome's urban proletariat was formed by liberated slaves. Nevertheless, many freedmen succeeded in earning a steady living through their involvement in

---

30 Under the *lex Aquilia* of 286 BC, in such cases the master could bring an action for the damage to his property. See D. 9. 2. 2. (Gaius).

31 G. 4. 75. See also G. 3. 222; *Inst.* 4. 8.

32 When a master was murdered in his own house by one of his servants, or even by an unknown assassin, all the slaves who were in the house at the time of the killing could be put to death.

33 G. 1. 17. A master could free his slave by will directly, or he could instruct his heir to free the slave, sometimes under certain conditions, at a later time (*per fideicommissum*). Besides these legally recognised ways of manumission, there were other informal ways of liberating slaves, e.g., when a master in the presence of his friends declared his slave to be free (*manumissio inter amicos*), or when he expressed such a wish in a letter (*manumissio per epistulam*), or even when he shared his table with his slave (*manumissio per mensam*). Although these ways of manumission provided little security for the slave, the latter, if he could prove that the relevant actions took place, could refuse to return to slavery by appealing to the praetor.

34 In relation to his former master, now termed *patronus*, a liberated slave was referred to as *libertus*. The relationship between a *libertus* and his *patronus* was similar to that between a client and his patron.

trade, industry and the arts, and some even gained access to positions of power, especially in the last century of the Republic and during the early Empire.[35]

Economic conditions

The Roman expansion was accompanied by profound changes in the economic and social life of Rome and Italy. In the course of the second century BC the city of Rome emerged as an important commercial centre which attracted large numbers of merchants and tradesmen from other parts of Italy and overseas and private businesses of all kinds were set up which provided services and manufactured goods.[36] The increase in economic activity during this period is manifested by the development and widespread use of currency[37] and by the establishment of financial institutions in Rome and other Italian cities.[38] Furthermore, sea-trade was

---

35 For a closer look at the position of the *libertini* and slaves see S. Treggiari, *Roman Freedmen during the Late Republic*, Oxford 1969; W. L. Westerman, *The Slave Systems of Greek and Roman Antiquity*, Philadelphia 1955; M. I. Finley (ed.), *Slavery in Classical Antiquity*, Cambridge 1960; M. K. Hopkins, *Conquerors and Slaves*, Cambridge 1978; E. M. Staerman, *Die Blütezeit der Sklavenwirtschaft in der römischen Republik*, Wiesbaden 1969; A. Watson, *Roman Slave Law*, Baltimore 1987; K. Bradley, *Slavery and Society at Rome*, Cambridge 1994, repr. 1997; J. F. Gardner, *Being a Roman Citizen*, London & New York 1993, ch. 2; K. Christ, *Krise und Untergang der römischen Republik*, Darmstadt 1979, 82 ff; J. C. Dumont, *Servus. Rome et l'esclavage sous la République*, Rome 1987.

36 Many of these private businesses were run by freedmen working for themselves or for their patrons.

37 In early times the Romans used, instead of coins, lumps or bars of copper (*aes*) which were not counted but weighed. These bars were called *stipes* or *stips*. The only Roman coin minted before the third century BC was a heavy copper coin called the *as*. In the third century BC, as economic activity increased, the Romans adopted coinage based on a silver standard, common among the Hellenistic states of the East. The basic silver coin was the denarius which was subdivided into four brass sesterces and sixteen bronze asses. For a closer look at the early development of Roman coinage see C. H. V. Sutherland, *Roman Coins*, London 1974; R. A. G. Carson, *Coins of Greece and Rome*, 2nd edn, London 1970; H. Mattingly, *Roman Coins*, 2nd edn, London 1960; M. Crawford, *Coinage and Money under the Roman Republic*, London 1985.

38 In the course of Rome's victorious campaigns in the East large amounts of gold and silver from the wealthy countries of the Hellenistic world were brought to Rome. A part of this capital was invested in various financial enterprises and banking businesses were established, similar to those found in the East, which

facilitated by the establishment of new commercial ports on the coasts of Italy, such as that of Puteoli in the vicinity of Naples.[39]

Notwithstanding the growth of trade and industry, agriculture remained the basis of the Roman economy during the later Republic. In the course of the Roman expansion in Italy and in the years that followed, the economic position of the small independent farmers, traditionally the backbone of Rome's economic system, was temporarily strengthened, as more public land (*ager publicus*) became available for distribution. A part of this land was sold by auction, thus providing a source of funds for the public treasury, and a part was apportioned amongst Rome's poorest citizens and army veterans (*assignatum*), or was used to set up new colonies. The lands given away ceased to be part of the *ager publicus*, coming under the full ownership of the recipients. Large tracts of the *ager publicus* which remained under the control of the state were leased on rent to private individuals.[40] Moreover, citizens who took possession of lands devastated by war were often allowed to remain in possession for an indefinite period of time, paying a sum of money or rendering a portion of the produce to the Roman state in return.[41] Although the state reserved the right to reclaim these lands at any time, lands held in this way could remain in the hands of a family for several generations, as the right of occupancy could be transferred by will. With the administration of the *ager publicus* were concerned the so-called agrarian laws (*leges agrariae*), which began to be introduced from as early as the fifth century BC.[42] Among the most important of these was a *lex Licinia Sextia* (367 BC), which limited the

---

provided all kinds of financial services, including money-lending and money-depositing services.

39 It should be noted here that the Romans themselves were not particularly interested in maritime trade, which remained largely in the hands of the Greeks and the Phoenicians. In the first century BC, however, sea-trade came to a standstill as a result of the organised activity of pirates who, having established their bases in southern Asia Minor, preyed upon the coasts of eastern Mediterranean. This threat was finally removed and sea trade was revived after the Roman general Pompey cleared the sea of the pirates in 67 BC.

40 These were not always citizens of Rome. Sometimes conquered lands belonging to the Roman *ager publicus* remained in the hands of their former owners. The latter, however, were now regarded as mere tenants, entitled to hold the lands for a specified period of time only and having to pay rent to the Roman state.

41 The term *possessio* was used to denote a piece of public land under such occupation (the occupant was referred to as *possesor*). The term *usus* signified the act of occupancy while the word *fructus* denoted the benefit which the state derived from such an arrangement.

42 The first law of this kind was probably the *lex Cassia*, passed in 486 BC. See Livy 2. 41; Dionysius 8. 76.

amount of land which a person could lawfully occupy to a maximum of five hundred *iugera* (about three hundred acres).[43] But in the later Republic this law appears to have fallen in abeyance (although it was never formally repealed) and a small number of wealthy families gradually came to control, through purchase or inheritance, tracts of public land exceeding by far the maximum limits prescribed by this law.

In the years that followed Rome's wars of expansion in the East the peasant population of Italy decreased considerably and the free workers of the land were almost entirely replaced by slave labour.[44] As the production of corn and wheat was no longer profitable, for these were now imported in large quantities from overseas, many small farm-owners in Italy faced bankruptcy. Although some of the most enterprising farmers were able to shift to other products, such as olives and grapes, which could be sold more easily to overseas markets, or turned to cattle-raising, the great majority of the small proprietors could no longer hold their own against the great estate-owners and were forced to abandon their land. Many of them continued to work the soil as tenants or hired labourers, while others left farming altogether and turned into professional soldiers or moved to the cities where they lived on government grants or became clients of wealthy citizens. Gradually, whole districts were turned into cattle-ranches or large estates (*latifundia*), owned by a few wealthy families and worked by slaves or tenants. During the late second century BC thousands of landless and poverty-stricken people from all over Italy flowed into Rome where they joined the growing urban proletariat of the city. The transformation of a large part of the Roman citizenry into what became known as the Roman mob had a profound effect on Roman social and political life and was one of the principal factors of the crisis that led to the weakening and final collapse of the republican system of government.[45]

---

43 Livy 6. 35. The same enactment set the maximum number of cattle that a person was allowed to keep on pastures belonging to the *ager publicus*. It provided, moreover, that not only slaves but also a certain number of free workers had to be employed by the possessor for the cultivation of the land. The same law probably included provisions on how the boundaries of public land were to be drawn, as well as on the issue of rent which the possessor had to pay to the state. See Appian, *B.C.* 1. 7. 8; 1. 100.

44 Plutarch, *Tib. Gracchus* 8.

45 On the decline of the free peasantry see P. A. Brunt, *Italian Manpower*, 225 *BC - AD* 14, Oxford 1971; P. D. A. Garnsey (ed.), *Non-slave Labour in the Greco-Roman World*, Cambridge 1980; J. M. Frayn, *Subsistence Farming in Roman Italy*, London 1979. On the ownership of land among the senatorial nobility see I. Shatzman, *Senatorial Wealth and Roman Politics*, Brussels 1975.

A form of economic activity that appears to have flourished during this period revolved around the contractual undertaking of various public works (*publica*) by private individuals. The word *publicum*, in a broad sense, denoted property belonging to the state (both in Italy and overseas), such as forests and pastures, stone quarries and mines, roads, bridges, aqueducts and all kinds of public buildings. In a narrower sense, the same word meant public revenue. The Roman revenues were derived in part from lands and other forms of property owned by the state and in part from taxes paid by the citizens of Rome or her subjects in Italy and the provinces. Most of these revenues, especially taxes, were not collected directly by the state, due to its lack of the necessary means, but were let on lease to private contractors. The latter undertook, at their own risk and expense, to exploit the state's assets or to collect taxes, and to pay a fixed amount on an annual basis to the Roman state treasury. Those who entered into such contracts with the state were referred to as *publicani*. As the great majority of the *publicani* belonged to the equestrian class, the terms *equites* and *publicani* were treated for all practical purposes as synonymous.[46] In order to minimise the financial and other risks involved in carrying out their work most *publicani* were organised in companies referred to as *societates publicanorum*.[47] Of the several companies competing for the undertaking of a public work the one which would put in the lowest tender for carrying out the work was usually awarded the contract.[48] The wealth and influence of this class of businessmen grew rapidly as Rome expanded in territory and her revenues increased. But as the *publicani* always sought to profit from the excess they collected over the amount they were bound to turn over to the state, they became notorious for their greed and cruelty.[49]

---

46 See, e.g., Cicero, *pro Planc.* 9; Livy 23. 48. 49.

47 Each company was presided over and represented by its chairman, termed *manceps*. Besides the *manceps*, each company had a managing director, the *magister societatis*, who was responsible for the running of the company's affairs and directed its personnel. The members of such a company were referred to as *socii*. See on this Cicero, *ad Att.* 1. 17; *pro Planc.* 13.

48 These contracts were usually drawn up by the censors (hence their description as *leges censoriae*), who were also entrusted with the task of granting the relevant leases. The granting of a lease by the state took place in the open and was decided by public auction. The company's chairman (*manceps*) carried out the bidding and provided guarantees to the state for the proper discharge of the terms and conditions of the contract.

49 On the *publicani* see E. Badian, *Publicans and Sinners: Private Enterprise in the Service of the Roman Republic*, Oxford 1972; P. A. Brunt, 'The Equites in the late Republic', in R. Seager (ed.), *The Crisis of the Roman Republic*, Cambridge 1969, 83 ff.

Cultural development

In addition to creating new administrative problems and transforming economic life, the expansion of Rome brought about profound changes in Roman culture. These changes were the inevitable result of the close contact of Roman Italy with the Greek and Hellenistic civilisation. Rome had been subject to Greek influences from as early as the sixth century BC, both indirectly, through the Etruscans, and directly, through the Greek cities of southern Italy and Sicily. But it was after their expansion in the East that the Romans began to feel the full impact of Greek civilisation. Important channels of Greek culture were the Greeks who came to Rome as ambassadors, teachers, physicians, merchants and artists, as well as the large numbers of educated Greek slaves who were employed in Roman households. The introduction of Greek models had a profound effect on every aspect of the Roman culture, including education, religion, art and science.[50] Knowledge of Greek now became essential for every educated Roman and, as the demand for instruction in Greek language, rhetoric and philosophy increased, schools began to be established under the patronage of prominent men.

Greek philosophical thinking, in particular, attracted many followers among the members of the Roman upper classes, despite the fact that the Romans at first looked upon philosophers with some suspicion and on two occasions (in 173 and 161 BC) fears of the possibly subversive effects of philosophical doctrines on the moral order resulted in the temporary banishment of Greek philosophers. Schools of philosophy offering rules of life, such as Stoicism and Epicureanism,[51] accorded well with the practical tendencies of the Roman character for, unlike the Greek philosophy of earlier periods, what these schools were primarily concerned with was not so much ways of thinking about the world but, rather, ways of teaching people how to live in the world and how to attain success in public and private life through the practice of virtue. The success of these schools, and in particular Stoicism, was also due to the fact that their teaching reflected best the cosmopolitan ideals of the times. The Stoic ideal of a world state based on the brotherhood of men exercised a strong influence on Roman thought and provided one of the foundations upon which the political philosophy of the Empire was built.

---

[50] It was during this period that a national literature emerged in Rome based on Greek standards.

[51] The Stoic philosophy was introduced in Rome by the philosopher Panaetius of Rhodes (185-109 BC) who became a leading member of the circle of influential writers and philosophers gathered around Scipio Aemilianus (the so called 'Scipionic circle').

The reception of Greek civilisation gave a tremendous impulse to Roman cultural development. At the same time, however, the adoption of Greek models had an erosive effect on the long-established moral and religious norms upon which the unity of the Roman society was based, notwithstanding the fact that in many respects the Romans remained faithful to traditional ideals. Greek morals, in particular, were laxer and more sophisticated than those of the Romans and their sudden introduction into this new world of wealth, power and uncertain standards led to moral confusion.[52] The weakening of the old value system, established by a tradition-conscious upper class, ultimately undermined social cohesion and was one of the main factors that precipitated the socio-political crisis that marks the closing years of the republican period.

The Breakdown of the Republic

The organisation of the Roman state underwent no considerable changes during the period of expansion. Rome remained a city-state governed by the new patricio-plebeian aristocracy of wealth and office which had emerged from the socio-political strife of the early republican period. Supreme power was in the hands of the senate, which had evolved from a mere advisory body to the magistrates into an executive body with a wide range of customary powers over foreign policy, finance, legislation and the administration of justice. The Roman successes during the wars of expansion enhanced further the senate's prestige and reinforced its position as the cornerstone of the Roman political system. The magistrates and the assemblies showed themselves ready to follow its lead and, although only popular assemblies had the constitutional right to enact legislation, senatorial resolutions (*senatus consulta*) came to be regarded, for all practical purposes, as having the force of laws. Moreover, while the actual ratification of treaties or declarations of war fell in the province of the *comitia*, the senate usually carried matters so far that there was nothing for the *comitia* to do but give their assent. There seems to have been no political division between the senate and the people, at least until the later part of the second century BC. Political contest took place mainly within the senate, where a number of rival groups of allied families were striving to increase their power and political influence.

However, from as early as the middle of the second century BC it became clear that the existing system of government, which was originally designed for a city-state, was inadequate to meet the organisational and

---

52 Consider Sallust, *Cat.* 10. 2. ff.

administrative needs of a world empire. And as the ideological underpinnings of the Roman political system began to crumble with the weakening of the traditional value system, the ruling senatorial class found it increasingly difficult to achieve satisfactory solutions to the economic, social and political problems brought about by Rome's expansion. The oncoming crisis manifested itself in the intensification and widening of factional political strife within the ruling class. This, combined with growing social unrest, gave to ambitious political and military leaders an opportunity to achieve power by gaining the support of discontented social groups demanding various kinds of reform. At the same time, the maltreatment of Rome's allies and subjects in Italy and the provinces led to the breaking out of dangerous large-scale insurgencies in many parts of the empire. And when internal political conflict erupted into fully-fledged civil war, in the first century BC, the final collapse of the republican political system appeared unavoidable.

By the close of the second century BC Rome's political life came to be dominated by two factions, or interest groups, known as *populares* and *optimates*. The *populares*, who represented, in modern terms, the radical reformers, included a number of senators who had espoused the view that Rome's problems could not be resolved without the introduction of measures designed to improve the position of the lower classes. Among their chief objectives was the restoration of the powers of the people's assembly and its representatives. The *optimates*, on the other hand, whose camp included the large majority of senators, were against any radical changes that were likely to undermine the senate's grip on power. But it would be misleading to describe these groups as distinct political parties, in the modern sense, for their activities revolved not so much around broad political programmes but, rather, around the personal goals and interests of political leaders and their supporters. Thus, it was not unusual even for senators who had sided with the *optimates* to advocate or support reform legislation, although they often did so reluctantly and in terms of their own vested interests.[53]

---

[53] As F. E. Adcock explains, 'A Roman group in politics was not a large body of men of all classes pursuing principles or far-reaching long-range policies (such as, for instance, nationalisation of means of production and exchange), a body of government to whom control of the government is a means to an end, the end being the carrying through of a consistent programme dictated by principles or theories. A Roman political group in the revolutionary age was normally a small group of nobles and their personal adherents pursuing interests of themselves or their leaders to advance careers, to enjoy power and profits, or to meet some immediate crisis by this or that means, sometimes beneficent but not always so'. *Roman Political Ideas and Practice*, 6th edn, Ann Arbor 1975, 61-62.

At the heart of the crisis lay the land question and the deepening divide between the growing masses of the impoverished urban and rural proletariat on the one hand and the small number of wealthy families holding the bulk of the Roman *ager publicus* on the other. An attempt to rectify the situation was made in 133 BC by the leader of the *populares* Tiberius Gracchus, who had been elected tribune of the plebs for that year. Gracchus brought a bill before the assembly which provided that no Roman citizen could hold more that 500 *iugera* (about 300 acres) of Roman public land. The lands that were to be freed after the large landowners returned the tracts of land they held in excess, as well as those lands remaining undistributed, were to be portioned out, in small sections, among Rome's landless citizens. In effect, Gracchus's bill was a restatement, with some modifications, of the *lex Licinia Sextia* of 367 BC which, as was noted before, had in the meantime fallen in abeyance. Although the bill was met with fierce resistance by the great landowners, it was finally passed under the name *lex Sempronia agraria* and a commission was appointed to put it into effect.[54] But the passing of this law became possible only after Tiberius Gracchus had succeeded in removing his fellow-tribune who, having been bought off by the opposition, blocked the bill by exercising his right of veto. When his year in office expired Gracchus stood for re-election, as he feared that if he no longer held the office of tribune – an office that guaranteed the inviolability of the person who held it – he would become an easy prey to the machinations of his political enemies. But this move played in the hands of his opponents, as it violated a long-established constitutional custom prohibiting the re-election of the same person to the tribunate and gave the impression that Gracchus was seeking to enhance his personal power through his control of the assembly. In the violent clashes that took place on the day of the election, in 132 BC, Tiberius Gracchus and many of his supporters were killed by a large group of senators and their followers. The senators justified their action on the grounds that they were defending constitutional order against an armed insurrection headed by Gracchus. Despite Gracchus's death, the commission entrusted with the implementation of his law continued its work until 129 BC, but Gracchus's ultimate goals, especially the curbing of the power of the senatorial aristocracy, were not accomplished. The senate retained its control of the state and a special court was set up to try for treason those who had aided Gracchus in his more radical undertakings.

---

54 The commission, referred to as *tresviri agris iudicandis assignaris*, was composed of Tiberius Gracchus himself, his brother Gaius and Appius Claudius Pulcher.

A second attempt at reforming the system was made ten years later by Tiberius Gracchus's younger brother Gaius, who was elected tribune of the plebs in 123 and 122 BC. One of Gaius's first actions was to introduce legislation designed to protect himself and his supporters against prosecution. As the senatorial court mentioned above had refused to allow those found guilty to appeal to the assembly, a law was now passed establishing the right of appeal from such judicial commissions and providing that only the people's assembly had the right of imposing capital punishment on a Roman citizen. Moreover, in an attempt to secure the support of the powerful equestrian class, Gaius introduced measures which strengthened the position of the *equites* at the expense of the senate. These measures included the *lex Sempronia iudiciaria* of 122 BC by which the right of serving as jurors in criminal trials, which until then belonged exclusively to senators, was transferred to the *equites*. As a result of this and other measures the *equites* were for the first time recognised as forming a distinct order in the state (*ordo equester*) and began to play a more important role in political life. Although Gaius Gracchus's reform programme, and especially his *leges agrariae*, was in general more successful than that of his brother, it failed to achieve its ultimate goals – a failure for which Gaius paid with his life in 121 BC.[55] After Gaius's death most of the measures he had initiated were repealed or drastically modified and the senatorial aristocracy re-established its full control of the state.[56] Although the Gracchi left no immediate successors who could revive or carry further their reform programmes, they left behind a heritage of confrontation in Roman political life which was to lead to more bitter conflicts in the years that followed.[57]

Ten years after Gaius Gracchus's death the senate's control of the state was again called into question after Rome suffered a series of humiliating defeats at the hands of Jugurtha, ruler of the northern African

---

[55] The most important part of Gracchus' s programme, the extension of full citizenship to the Latins and possibly to all the Italians remained unaccomplished.

[56] After the death of Gaius Gracchus several laws were enacted aiming at confirming, revising or modifying the Gracchan legislation.

[57] For a closer look at the Gracchan period see M. Cary and H. H. Scullard, *A History of Rome*, 3rd edn, London 1975, ch. 20; M. Grant, *History of Rome*, London 1978, ch. 10; A. Lintott, *Violence in Republican Rome*, Oxford 1968, ch. 12; D. Stockton, *The Gracchi*, Oxford 1979; H.C. Boren, *The Gracchi*, New York 1968; A.H. Bernstein, *Tiberius Sempronius Gracchus: Tradition and Apostacy* , Ithaca and London 1978; G. Alföldy, *The Social History of Rome*, London 1985, 73 ff; K. Christ, *Krise und Untergang der römischen Republik*, Darmstadt 1979, 117 ff.

kingdom of Numidia, and the invading Germanic tribes of Cimbri and Teutones. These setbacks were attributed to the feebleness and depravity of the senatorial rule and the incompetence of the generals to whom the senate had entrusted the conduct of the military operations. In 107 BC Gaius Marius, the new leader of the *populares* and a man of considerable military ability, was elected consul and was sent to Africa to take command of the army. Marius's success in putting an end to the Jugurthine war (106-105 BC) and his subsequent victory over the Cimbri and Teutones (102-101 BC) greatly increased his popularity and political influence.[58] One of Marius's chief objectives as a consul was the reorganisation of the Roman army whose strength had been undermined by the rapid decline in numbers of the class of small property holders – traditionally the army's main source of recruits. To deal with this problem he resorted to the formation of a long-standing professional army consisting, for the most part, of volunteers drawn from Rome's urban and rural proletariat. As a result of Marius's military reforms, the army became a decisive factor in political life. By contrast with the citizen army of the old type whose members, as citizens in the service of the state, were not supposed to take part in political strife, the new professional army might be expected to give its unified support to a popular commander against any party in the state, and even the state itself. Moreover, as the new professional army could be raised only by a military leader of established reputation, rather than by any magistrate designated by the senate (as it was the case in the past), the senate might be forced to call upon a leader whom it did not trust and whom it could not control. Thus the way was prepared for the military dictatorships of the last century of the Republic which ultimately destroyed oligarchic government and replaced it with a disguised monarchy.[59]

When Marius was elected to the consulship for a sixth time, in 100 BC, he attempted to introduce an agrarian law under which newly conquered territories were to be distributed to poor citizens. In addition to that, he demanded that new colonies be established for his army veterans. But as his proposals were seen as detrimental to the interests of the landowning aristocracy, they were rejected by the majority of senators. The result was a new round of violent conflicts in the streets of Rome between the *optimates* and the *populares*. Finally Marius was forced by the senate to turn against his own party in trying to quell street fighting. With his credibility as a popular leader seriously wounded and still being regarded

---

58 He was re-elected to the consulship for three consecutive years, from 104-102BC, in contravention of long-established constitutional custom.

59 On the organisation of the Roman army during the closing century of the Republic see R. E. Smith, *Service in the Post-Marian Army*, Manchester, 1958.

as an enemy by the oligarchy, Marius was forced to retire from public life.[60]

In 91 BC Rome found herself at war with her allies in Italy who, resentful at the senate's refusal to grant them full Roman citizenship, revolted and set up their own state. The so called 'Italian' or 'Social' War dragged on for more than three years and, for a time, it seemed that it could put an end to Rome's domination over Italy. The war finally ended in 88 BC with military victory for Rome. But this victory became possible only after the unity of Rome's opponents was broken by the granting of the Roman citizenship first to those allied communities who did not take part in the revolt (90 BC)[61] and, shortly after, to all members of allied communities who would lay down the arms and apply for the citizenship within a certain period of time (89 BC).[62] After the end of the Social War all the political communities in Italy received full Roman citizenship. As a result, the distinction between Roman colonies (*coloniae civium Romanorum*) and Latin colonies (*coloniae Latinae*), as well as the political differences between the various races within the same community, were erased.[63]

During the Social War the *populares* and the *optimates* abstained from further conflict, as the very existence of the Roman state came under threat. But shortly after the end of the war the struggle between the two camps began again in all its force. At the centre of the dispute was the question of who was to lead the Roman army in the war against the king of Pontus Mithradates VI, the Eupator, who was threatening Rome's hold over her provinces in the East.[64] The obvious choice, under the constitution, was

---

60 For a closer look at Marius's political career see T.F. Carney, *A Biography of C. Marius*, Chicago 1970.

61 By the *lex Iulia de civitate*.

62 By the *lex Plautia Papiria*. Under this law all Italian allies who would apply to the *praetor urbanus* in Rome for enrolment in the citizens' lists within sixty days would receive the Roman citizenship. Another legislative enactment, introduced by the consul Gnaeus Pompeius Strabo, also in 89 BC, granted the Roman citizenship to all communities in the Cispadane Gaul and Latin rights to the population of Transpadane Gaul, north of the river Po. These laws provided for the creation of a number of new tribes in which the new Roman citizens were to be included. See Velleius 2. 20; Appian, *B.C.* 1. 49. But these enactments were subsequently superseded, on this issue, by the *lex Sulpicia* (88 BC), which stipulated that the new citizens were to be distributed among the existing thirty-five tribes. See Appian, *B.C.* 1. 55. 64.

63 For a closer look at this development see A. N. Sherwin-White, *Roman Citizenship*, 2nd edn, Oxford 1973, ch. 6.

64 By the end of 89 BC many communities in Greece and Asia Minor, embittered by the injustices of Rome's provincial administration, had sided with the king,

one of the two consuls of 88 BC, and the lot fell on Lucius Cornelius Sulla, an aristocrat and ardent supporter of the senate. But following a popular movement in Rome under the leadership of Sulpicius Rufus, a tribune of the plebs, Sulla was stripped of his command by decree of the people's assembly and the conduct of the war was turned over to Marius, the former leader of the *populares*, who had re-surfaced from political oblivion. Enraged by this, Sulla marched with his well-trained and loyal army on Rome and, after a bloody battle with Marius' followers, gained control of the city. Following the restoration of the senatorial party to power and the abrogation of all the new laws introduced by his democratic opponents, Sulla left with his army for Greece to face the invading forces of Mithradates. But not long after his departure Marius, who after Sulla's earlier victory had escaped to Africa, returned to Rome with an army, crushed the resistance of the senate and took control of the state. A long reign of terror followed in the course of which a large number of senators and their supporters were put to death. The massacres finally came to an end with Marius' death in 86 BC.

The *populares*' control of the state ended in 83-82 BC with the return of Sulla who, in the meantime, had defeated both Mithradates and the Roman army which had been sent out by his political enemies to fight him in the East. After crushing the resistance of his opponents in a fierce battle before the gates of Rome and securing control of the city, Sulla was appointed dictator by the senate and was given full power to reorganise the state. During the new round of persecutions that followed (82-79 BC) the enemies of the senate, whose names had been included in Sulla's lists of proscribed persons, were killed by the hundreds and their properties were confiscated. Among Sulla's earliest measures was the introduction of legislation depriving the tribunes of their right to propose laws in the popular assembly and restricting their power of veto. Moreover, the senatorial class was restored to full control of the administration of justice by a law which secured for its members the right of serving as jurors in criminal trials. However, in the years that followed Sulla's abdication (79 BC) and death (78 BC) most of his measures, which were designed to strengthen the position of the senate at the expense of the magistrates and

---

whom they saw as their liberator from the Roman rule. In 88 BC, when at the order of the king a large number of Italians living in the East, including Roman officials and traders, were put to death, the senate declared war on Mithradates and his allies.

the people's assembly, were overturned and, by 70 BC, the *populares* were again the dominant power in Roman politics.[65]

After the end of Sulla's regime the civil warfare between the senate and the forces of the democratic opposition resumed both in Italy and in the provinces. The situation was exacerbated further by the outbreak of a large-scale slave rebellion in Italy (73-71 BC),[66] by the renewed aggression of Mithradates in the East (74 BC) and by the continual raids of pirates who controlled most of the eastern Mediterranean. During these turbulent years there emerged in Rome a new leader, Gnaeus Pompeius Magnus (Pompey the Great), who, like most of the prominent political figures of this period, owed his reputation to his successful conduct of military operations. Despite his aristocratic background, Pompey was elected to the consulship in 70 BC with the backing of the *populares*, to whom he had promised to repeal the Sullan constitution and, in particular, to restore the tribunes to all their former powers. In a series of successful military campaigns Pompey put an end to the activities of the pirates (67 BC) and won a decisive victory over Mithradates and his allies (63 BC).[67] As a result of these successes the Roman possessions in Asia increased with the addition of two new provinces, Syria and Bithynia. After organising the political administration of the new provinces and securing Rome's eastern frontiers by setting up a buffer zone of client states, Pompey returned in triumph to Italy. In the meantime, in Rome the struggle between the *optimates* and the *populares* continued unabated. This period is marked by the conspiracy of L. Sergius Catilina, a former member of the aristocracy, who, with the support of elements of the *populares*, tried to seize control of the state; it is also marked by the political activities of the rhetor and philosopher M. Tullius Cicero, who succeeded in putting an end to the Catilinarian conspiracy.[68]

Upon his return to Rome, and despite fears that he was planning to set up a dictatorship, Pompey disbanded his army and sought to gain from the senate and the people positions of honour in recognition of his achievements. Moreover, he asked the senate to provide land for his army veterans and to ratify the arrangements he had made in the East. But his demands were rejected by the majority of senators. In response Pompey sought to renew his political alliance with the *populares*. Among the most

---

65 For a more detailed account of Sulla's regime see E. Badian, *Sulla: The Deadly Reformer*, Sydney 1970; on Sulla's proscriptions consider F. Hinard, *Les proscriptions de la Rome républicaine*, Rome 1985.

66 The slave rebellion was headed by Spartacus, a Thracian gladiator.

67 The war against the pirates was entrusted to Pompey by the *lex Gabinia* of 67 BC and the war against Mithradates by the *lex Manilia* of 66 BC.

68 Cicero was elected consul in 63 BC.

prominent political figures at that time were Marcus Licinius Crassus, Pompey's co-consul in 70 BC and winner of the war against the slaves (71 BC) and Gaius Julius Caesar, a relative of Marius and then governor of Spain. In 60 BC these and Pompey formed a coalition, known as the First Triumvirate, through which they hoped to further their political goals by increasing their influence in the senate and the people's assemblies. Shortly after the formation of the coalition Pompey's demands were satisfied; Caesar was elected consul for 59 BC and, a year later, was appointed governor (*proconsul*) of Gaul for a period of five years. During the period 58-49 BC Caesar completed the conquest of Gaul after a long and arduous war against the local Celts and invading Germanic tribes. But Caesar's growing popularity and political influence was a cause of concern for both the senate and his two partners in the Triumvirate. The renewal of the Triumvirate in 56 BC only delayed the oncoming crisis, which became unavoidable after the death of Crassus in the war against the Parthians in 53 BC.[69] In the civil war that broke out in 49 BC Pompey joined forces with the senate against Caesar and his supporters but, a year later, his army was defeated in a decisive battle in Greece. Despite Pompey's death,[70] shortly after his defeat, the war between the two camps continued down to 45 BC, when the last remnants of the senatorial forces were destroyed in Spain. Thus Caesar became the undisputed master of Rome but, by contrast with what happened in earlier civil wars, no general persecution or slaughter took place in the wake of his victory.

Caesar's position as supreme leader of Rome was confirmed and secured through his tenure of the highest offices of the state and by means of the special powers and honours conferred upon him by the senate and the people. In 46 BC he was appointed dictator for ten years and, in the following year for life. From 48 BC he held the office of consul continuously and enjoyed the inviolability of the tribunes of the plebs. He also held the position of *pontifex maximus* from 63 BC and in 46 BC was given censorial powers under the title 'prefect of morals' (*praefectus morum*). Moreover, special laws were passed conferring upon him the right to appoint Rome's provincial magistrates, the right to propose half of the candidates for magisterial positions in Rome, the right to cast the first vote in the senate and the right to issue edicts without consulting the senate. At the same time he had full control of the army and supervised the administration of public finances. From this position of supreme power

---

69 The Parthian empire occupied a large area between the Persian gulf and the Caspian Sea, on Rome's eastern borders.

70 For a closer look at Pompey's career see J. Leach, *Pompey the Great*, London 1978.

Caesar embarked upon a series of far-reaching reforms, aiming at reorganising Rome's political and social life. An important part of his programme was concerned with the establishment of a large number of new colonies outside Italy, intended to absorb part of Rome's urban proletariat, and the improvement of the position of the provincials through the conferment upon many of them of the rights of Roman citizenship. Moreover, steps were taken to improve the administration of the provinces and to protect the local populations against abuses committed by Roman provincial magistrates. In order to meet administrative needs in Rome Caesar increased the positions available for certain magistracies, such as the praetorship and the quaestorship. At the same time the senate was considerably enlarged through the appointment as senators of a large number of Caesar's supporters, from both Italy and the provinces. But the concentration of so much power in the hands of one man was received with hostility by many senators who began to see in him not a restorer of the republican order but a usurper and a tyrant. A conspiracy was formed and in 44 BC Caesar was assassinated in the Senate House by a group of senators.[71] After his death his plans for the reorganisation of the Roman state were left unfulfilled.[72]

Contrary to the conspirators' expectations, Caesar's assassination was not followed by the immediate restoration of the senate's control of the state. Instead the position of the senate became even more precarious when it became clear that the people of Rome, aggrieved at Caesar's killing, were unwilling to submit to senatorial rule. The initiative was seized by Caesar's friend Mark Antony, consul for 44 BC, who, joined by Lepidus, Caesar's master of the horse, gained control of events. Antony came to an agreement with the senate under which the latter would ratify Caesar's acts in exchange for the granting of amnesty to the conspirators. However, Antony's claim to being Caesar's successor was challenged by Gaius Octavius, Caesar's grand-nephew and adopted son. It was not long before the rivalry between the two men resulted in a fully-fledged armed conflict. Octavius, who now assumed the name Gaius Julius Caesar Octavianus, with the support of the senate and Caesar's veterans defeated Antony's

---

71 The conspiracy was led by Gaius Crassus, praetor for 44 BC, and Marcus and Decimus Brutus. In all sixty senators were involved in the plot.

72 For a closer look at Caesar's political career and reforms see J.F.C. Fuller, *Julius Caesar, Man, Soldier and Tyrant*, London 1965; M. Gelzer, *Caesar, Politician and Statesman*, Oxford 1968; S. Weinstock, *Divus Julius*, Oxford 1971. See also L.R. Taylor, *Party Politics in the Age of Caesar*, Berkeley and Los Angeles 1949.

forces in a battle in northern Italy.[73] But the senate's plans for resuming control of the state were frustrated when, shortly after, Octavian made his peace with Antony and marched with his army on Rome where he enforced his appointment to the consulship (43 BC). In the same year, at a conference near Bologna, Octavian, Antony and Lepidus formed the Second Triumvirate, a coalition intended to secure for the participants the unlimited powers they needed in order to carry out the reorganisation of the state (*tresviri reipublicae constituendae*). The formation of the Triumvirate was followed by a new reign of terror during which many senators, including Cicero, were put to death. A last stand against the rule of the Triumvirs was made by the senate in Greece, but it ended in failure when the republican army was defeated by the combined forces of Octavian and Antony at Philippi (42 BC).

After their victory at Philippi the two Triumvirs divided the empire among themselves. Antony assumed control of the eastern provinces and Octavian took over most of the West. But not long after the division of the empire, and while the civil war was continuing, the old antagonism between Octavian and Antony began to re-surface. Events took a decisive turn in 37 BC when Octavian disposed of his republican opponents in the field and removed Lepidus, thus becoming the undisputed ruler of the West. The breach between him and Antony widened in 36 BC when the latter, although still married to Octavian's sister Octavia, married the Queen of Egypt Cleopatra and set himself the task of becoming master of the East. Antony's decision to join forces with Cleopatra and to give her certain parts of the empire that had once belonged to Egypt alienated popular sentiment in Rome and many began to suspect that he wanted to establish in the eastern Mediterranean a new independent kingdom. In 32 BC Octavian persuaded the senate to declare war on Egypt and, a year later, his army met the combined forces of Antony and Cleopatra at Actium, an island off the west coast of Greece. The battle ended in victory for Octavian who, in the following year, invaded and conquered Egypt, which became a Roman province under his direct control.[74] After re-establishing the old provinces and client kingdoms in the East, Octavian

---

[73] Among Octavian's supporters in his contest with Antony was Cicero, who in his Philippic Orations mounted a bitter attack against Antony and his followers. But, as subsequent events proved, Cicero and the senate were mistaken in believing that, after Antony was eliminated, Octavian could be manipulated into becoming a mere instrument in the senate's hands.

[74] After the defeat of their army Antony and Cleopatra escaped to Egypt and, when the country fell to Octavian, they committed suicide in Alexandria. For a closer look at Antony's political career see E. Goltz Huzar, *Mark Antony*, London 1978.

returned in triumph to Rome in 29 BC. Early in 27 BC he appeared before the senate and proclaimed his intention to relinquish his special powers and to give the republic back to the senate and the people of Rome. This gesture earned Octavian the reputation of being the restorer of the republic. At the same time it legitimised his *de facto* control of the state as the senate, in return, conferred upon him the title *Augustus*, by which he was henceforth known, and began to bestow upon him a range of powers and titles. In receiving these powers Octavian came to surpass all other magistrates in authority and political influence and came to be designated as *princeps civium Romanorum*, i.e. the first of the Roman citizens. From the word *princeps* arose the term 'Principate', a term which came to describe the new form of government which Octavian established for the empire.[75]

[75] On the crisis of the later Republic see in general S. Gruen, *The Last Generation of the Roman Republic*, Berkeley 1974; A. Lintott, *Violence in Republican Rome*, Oxford 1968; M. Beard & M. Crawford, *Rome in the Late Republic*, Ithaca 1985; P. Brunt, *The Fall of the Roman Republic*, Oxford 1988; R. Syme, *The Roman Revolution*, Oxford 1939; L. Taylor, *Party Politics in the Age of Caesar*, Berkeley 1949; G. Alföldy, *The Social History of Rome*, London 1985, ch. 4; K. Christ, *Krise und Untergang der römischen Republik*, Darmstadt 1979; E. Betti, *La crisi della Repubblica e la genesi del principato in Roma*, Rome 1982.

6 The Pre-Classical Period of Roman Law

Introductory

The Roman law of the archaic period was built around a relatively simple system of rules for a community of farmers and large landowners and its scope of application did not extend beyond the boundaries of the city-state of Rome. Like other primitive systems of law, it was closely bound up with religion and custom and was characterised by its formalism, rigidity and limited field of application. During the later Republic, the expansion of the Roman power in the Mediterranean world and the social and economic changes by which it was accompanied had a profound effect on the character and development of Roman law. By the end of this period the old system of law had partly been abolished or changed in such a way that its scope was extended to meet the needs of a complex and highly sophisticated society. It was in response to changed social, economic and political conditions that Roman law broke through the barrier of formalism, was secularised and internationalised, and from a system that was strictly and often unjustly applied, became a highly developed system marked by its flexibility and adaptability to new and changing conditions. Of great importance for the development of the law were the secular jurists, who appeared on the scene in the second century BC, and the edict of the praetor, through which the notions of equity and good faith were introduced in the application of the law.

Legislation

We saw in chapter 3 that during the republican period there were three legislative assemblies in Rome: the *comitia centuriata*, the *comitia tributa* and the *concilium plebis*. The laws enacted by the *comitia centuriata* were termed *leges centuriatae* and were binding on all Roman citizens. Laws enacted in the *concilium plebis* were called *plebiscita* and, in early times, were binding on the plebeians only. Under the *lex Hortensia* of 287 BC the *plebiscita* were recognised as having the same force as the *leges centuriatae* and as being binding on all citizens. In the years that followed the passing of the *lex Hortensia* the *concilium plebis* gained in importance and tended to become the legislative assembly *par excellence*, whilst the *comitia centuriata* remained the senior elective assembly. As a result, the *plebiscita* gradually replaced the *leges centuriatae* as the main form of legislation and the term *lex* was often used to denote a *plebiscitum*.[1]

A law could be proposed only by a magistrate who had the right to summon the assembly (*ius agendi cum populo*), such as a consul or a praetor. The magistrate's legislative proposal or bill was termed *rogatio legis* and the relevant laws were called *leges rogatae*. The *leges rogatae* were distinguished from the *leges datae*, i.e. the laws which were introduced by magistrates on special occasions after obtaining the permission of the senate. In the category of *leges datae* belonged, for example, the various *leges coloniae* and *leges provinciae* by which new colonies and provinces were founded. According to established constitutional custom, a bill had to be published at least three weeks before it was formally submitted to the assembly so that its contents could be known in advance (*promulgatio, promulgare rogationem*).[2] During this period the citizens, in informal meetings (*contiones*), could discuss the bill and recommend changes, or even its withdrawal, to the magistrate who proposed it. But once the bill had been brought before the assembly it could not be modified in any way; the assembly could either accept it (*iubere rogationem*) or reject it as a whole and in the form in which it was submitted by the magistrate. A bill that was passed (*rogatio lata est*) became a *lex* following a formal announcement of the assembly's decision (*renuntiatio*) by the presiding magistrate. In the earlier years of the Republic a law passed by the assembly could not come into force until it had been approved by the senate (*patrum auctoritas*).[3] By granting the *patrum auctoritas* the senate guaranteed the constitutionality of the statute

---

1 See on this A. Watson, *Law Making in the Roman Republic*, Oxford 1974, ch. 1; H. F. Jolowicz and B. Nicholas, *Historical Introduction to the Study of Roman Law*, 3rd edn, Cambridge 1972, 86-87. On the law-making process consider also A. A. Schiller, *Roman Law: Mechanisms of Development*, New York 1978, 221 ff; O. F. Robinson, *The Sources of Roman Law*, London 1997, 29 ff; O. Tellegen-Couperus, *A Short History of Roman Law*, London and New York 1993, 19 ff, 49-50; W. Kunkel/M. Schermaier, *Römische Rechtsgeschichte*, Cologne 2001, 45 ff; F. Wieacker, *Römische Rechtsgeschichte*, Munich 1988, 400 ff; A. Guarino, *Storia del diritto romano*, Naples 1996, 289 ff; M. Talamanca (ed.), *Lineamenti di storia del diritto romano*, Milan 1989, 226 ff.

2 See A. A. Schiller, ibid, 235 ff.

3 The period between the formal enactment of a law and its coming into force was termed *vacatio legis*.

as required for its subsequent implementation. But after the introduction of the *lex Publilia Philonis*, in 339 BC, the *patrum auctoritas* had to be granted before the bill was submitted to the assembly for voting. From that time laws usually took effect immediately following the formal announcement of the assembly's decision endorsing the magistrate's proposal.[4] After their passing laws were inscribed on tablets of copper or marble and were kept, under the supervision of the *quaestors*, in the state treasury (*aerarium populi romani*).[5]

A law was made up of three parts: (a) the preamble (*praescriptio legis*), which included the name of the magistrate who proposed it (and after whom it was named), the place and time of its enactment, and the name of the century (*centuria*) or tribe (*tribus*) which cast the first vote in the proceedings;[6] (b) the main text of the law (*rogatio*), usually divided into sections; and (c) the ratification of the law (*sanctio*).[7] The *sanctio* specified the penalties that were to be imposed if the law was violated and stated the rules governing the relation between the new statute and earlier and future legislation.[8] A distinction was drawn between 'perfect laws' (*leges perfectae*), 'imperfect laws' or laws without any sanction at all (*leges imperfectae*) and 'less than perfect laws' (*leges minus quam perfectae*). A law was called perfect when infringement of any of its provisions resulted in the nullification of any legal act that took place under it.[9] The infringement of an imperfect law, by contrast, did not affect the validity of

---

4 On the role of the senate see A. Graeber, *Auctoritas patrum*, Berlin & Heidelberg 2001.

5 The state treasury was also known as *aerarium Saturni* because it was located in the temple of Saturn.

6 Sometimes the preamble also included certain words indicating the subject-matter of the relevant law, e.g., *lex Hortensia de plebiscitis* (287 BC), providing that the resolutions of the plebeian assembly were to be binding on all citizens, *lex Sempronia agraria* (133 BC), concerning the distribution of public lands (*ager publicus*), *lex Sempronia de provocatione* (123 BC), confirming the right of citizens convicted of capital offences to appeal to the people's assembly (*ius provocationis*).

7 A. A. Schiller, *Roman Law: Mechanisms of Development*, New York 1978, 236 ff; G. Rotondi, *Leges publicae populi Romani*, Milan 1912, repr. Hildesheim 1966, 148 ff.

8 For example, in the *sanctio* it could be stated that a previous law remained fully or partially in force, despite the introduction of the new law.

9 See, e.g., the *lex Falcidia delegatis* (40 BC), mentioned by Gaius (2. 227.), according to which legacies were not allowed to reduce what remained to the heir below a quarter of the value of the inheritance.

the relevant legal acts.[10] The violation of a less than perfect law did not render the relevant legal act invalid, but the transgressor was liable to punishment. Moreover, laws containing unrelated or superfluous provisions were referred to as *leges saturae*, or *per saturam*, and were forbidden under early law. This prohibition was renewed by the *lex Caecilia Didia* in 98 BC.

As was noted in chapter 4, most of the legislation of the republican period was concerned with matters of public law and only a few statutes were passed directly relating to private law. Of the latter statutes probably the most important were the *lex Atinia* (240 BC), which excluded stolen things (*res furtivae*) from *usucapio* (i.e. the acquisition of ownership through possession of a thing for a certain period of time); the *lex Aquilia* (286 BC), which set general rules of liability for damage caused to another person's property; the *lex Laetoria de minoribus* (second century BC), aimed at protecting persons under twenty-five years of age from fraud; the *lex Voconia* (169 BC), which imposed limitations upon the testamentary capacity of women; and the *lex Falcidia* (40 BC), specifying the amount of legacies which could be bequeathed.

The role of the senate in legislation

During the Republic, the senate did not operate as a legislative body. Its role was confined to ratifying the laws enacted in the assemblies and to giving advice or instructions to the magistrates who were the executives of the state. However, as the power and influence of the senate continued to increase, especially during the period of Rome's expansion, the senate began to play a more active part in the legislative process. In reality the assemblies rarely enacted legislation without the collaboration of the senate which usually decided the matter in all important respects and later obtained the sanction of the people. As was noted earlier, it was customary for the higher magistrates to seek the senate's advice on legislative proposals before they submitted them to the people.[11] The senate's opinion

---

[10] Consider, e.g., the *lex Cincia* of 204 BC, a plebiscite prohibiting the giving of gifts for the carrying out of tasks the performance of which was regarded as a sacred duty. Gifts promised in violation of this law were not void, but the donor could raise an exception (*exceptio legis Cinciae*) if he was sued for payment. The category of *leges imperfectae* was abolished in the post-classical period (439 AD) under an enactment of Emperors Theodosius II and Valentinian III. See C. 1. 14. 5; G. Rotondi, *Leges publicae populi Romani*, Milan 1912, repr. Olms 1966, 153 ff.

[11] Consider C. Nicolet, 'Le sénat et les amendements aux lois a la fin de la République', (1958) 36 *RHD*, 260-75.

took the form of a resolution (*senatus consultum*) which was incorporated by the magistrate in his proposal. In effect, this was legislation promoted by the senate, although a *senatus consultum* could not be put into effect until it was adopted by a magistrate and had technically become part of his proposed law.[12] The influence of the senate on legislation is manifested by the fact that Cicero mentions both the *senatus consulta* and the *leges* as sources of law.[13] During the early Empire the senate assumed most of the legislative powers of the assemblies and, from the middle of the second century AD, the *senatus consulta* came to be recognised as a direct source of law.

The Edicts of the Magistrates

The higher magistrates of the Roman state, such as the consuls, the praetors and the aediles, as well as the provincial governors, had the right of issuing administrative regulations or edicts (*edicta*) within their field of competence (*ius edicendi*). Initially an edict consisted in a verbal announcement before a public meeting (*contio*) by which a magistrate notified the citizens of the rules by which he intended to be guided in carrying out his duties. In later times the magistrates' edicts were written on wooden tablets and were set up in the Forum (the market-place) for everyone to see. Of the edicts of the magistrates the most important from the point of view of private law were the edicts of the praetors (the *praetor urbanus* and the *praetor peregrinus*) and, to a lesser extent, those of the aediles (*aediles curules*). It is important to note, however, that the magistrates were not regarded as lawmakers (the enactment of legislation fell in the province of the assemblies). The chief function of their edicts was to give effect to the law by laying down the rules and procedures that had to be followed in the administration of justice. Thus the praetor's role was to ensure that a legal dispute between private individuals was properly formulated according to law and, after that, that a judge was appointed to arbitrate in the dispute as it was formulated. In his edict, which he issued upon taking up office, the praetor stated the rules of procedure which he intended to follow during his year in office and defined the circumstances in which he would exercise his power to grant an action in law. This edict was known as the perpetual edict (*edictum perpetuum*), since it was to remain in force for the whole year, in contrast with the temporary edict

---

12 A *senatus consultum*, like a magisterial decree, could be vetoed by a tribune or a higher magistrate.

13 Cicero, *Topica* 5. 28.

(*edictum repentinum*), which was issued by the praetor on special occasions.[14]

Initially the praetors' edicts were based upon the much older procedure that applied under the highly formalised system of the *legis actiones*. Under this system, when a party brought a suit against another he was obliged to make his claim according to a prescribed form, derived directly from the letter of the law, and to this form it was necessary for the plaintiff to adhere strictly. But from the third century BC, as Roman society continued to grow both in numbers and complexity, this system was recognised as inadequate. Cases were now increasingly arising where a right should clearly have been recognised but no legal action was available under the existing *ius civile*. At the same time, with the expansion of commercial activities and the ever-increasing influx of foreigners into Rome, the need arose for the introduction of a more flexible system of procedure under which disputes between foreigners and between foreigners and Roman citizens could be resolved. Until that time a foreigner living in Rome could not take part in legal transactions and if aggrieved by another the *ius civile* supplied no remedy. In response to this need the office of the *praetor peregrinus* was created in c. 242 BC. In carrying out his judicial functions the *praetor peregrinus* enjoyed much greater liberty than the *praetor urbanus*, his colleague who dealt exclusively with disputes between citizens. Out of the edict of the *praetor peregrinus* emerged, in the course of time, a body of rules based largely on common sense, expediency and fairness, which became known as *ius gentium*.[15] But the development of the *ius gentium* was not without its effect on the *ius civile* administered by the *praetor urbanus* who, finding the rules of the *ius gentium* more adaptable to the needs of society, began to incorporate them into his own edict. He did this by relying upon the discretionary power vested in him which enabled him to go beyond the strict letter of the law and admit or reject an action, if he considered this to be fair and equitable, even where this was not in accordance with the *ius civile*.[16] Thus, although the praetor was not empowered to make new laws, when he was extending the existing forms of action or was introducing new ones in order to deal with new

---

[14] Cicero, *in Verr*. 3. 14. 36.

[15] On the concept of *ius gentium* see M. Kaser, *Römische Rechtsgeschichte*, Göttingen 1976, 134 ff; *Das römische Privatrecht*, Munich 1971, 202 ff; A. A. Schiller, *Roman Law: Mechanisms of Development*, New York 1978, 528-29. See also chapter 1.

[16] For example, a praetor could state in his edict: 'if there is an allegation of fraud (*dolus malus*) and no other action is available, then, if good cause is shown and no more than a year has elapsed since the plaintiff was in a position to sue, I shall grant an action'.

circumstances, he was in effect creating new legal rights.[17] In preparing his edict the praetor acted on his own responsibility but, since he might not be an expert in law, he often sought the advice of jurists. Thus the praetorian edict at any given time represented the consensus of opinion of the best-qualified legal minds of the past and present. Normally a praetor would adopt the greater part of his predecessor's *edictum perpetuum*, and that part of the *edictum perpetuum* which was carried on from year to year was referred to as *edictum tralaticium*. In this way the praetor changed the character of Roman law. For all practical purposes he created a vast body of law which extended and corrected the existing *ius civile* and filled the gaps in it. This body of law became known as *ius praetorium* or *ius honorarium* (because it proceeded from the holders of offices – *honores*).[18]

A turning-point in the development of the *ius praetorium* was the passing of the *lex Aebutia* (c. 125 BC), which recognised the right of the praetor to introduce new forms of action in order to deal with claims not covered by the existing system of *legis actiones*. The relevant procedure became known as the formulary or *per formulam* procedure (the *formula* was the written document by which the praetor authorised the judge in a civil trial to condemn the defendant if certain facts were proved or, if they were not proved, to absolve him). The praetor's edict contained model *formulae* for each of the forms of action promised, although new forms of action could be granted by the praetor at any time after the publication of his edict. These were usually included in the edict which was published by his successor in the following year. In this way the *formulae* used in given types of cases became relatively fixed and the number of these established *formulae* was constantly being increased by the introduction of new *formulae*.

---

17 It is important to note at this point that, by contrast with modern law, which places the emphasis on rights, Roman law placed the emphasis on remedies, on the forms of action rather than on the causes of action.

18 According to the jurist Papinian, the role of the *ius honorarium* was to assist (*adiuvandi*), supplement (*supplendi*) and correct (*corrigendi*) the existing *ius civile* as found in the various statutory enactments and the interpretations of the jurists. See D. 1. 1. 7. 1; *Inst.*1. 2. 7. On the development of *ius honorarium* see in general A. A. Schiller, *Roman Law: Mechanisms of Development*, New York 1978, 422 ff, 531 ff; O. F. Robinson, *The Sources of Roman Law*, London 1997, 39 ff; W. Kunkel, *An Introduction to Roman Legal and Constitutional History*, 2nd edn, Oxford 1973, ch. 6; M. Kaser, *Römische Rechtsgeschichte*, Göttingen 1976, 142 ff; *Das römische Privatrecht*, Munich 1971, 205 ff; W. Kunkel/M. Schermaier, *Römische Rechtsgeschichte*, Cologne 2001, 102 ff; F. Wieacker, *Römische Rechtsgeschichte*, Munich 1988, 470 ff; A. Guarino, *Storia del diritto romano*, Naples 1996, 300 ff.

In the history of Roman law the praetor occupies a position between the legislature and the jurists. He may be described as the keeper of the common sense of the Roman people, for it fell upon him to decide in what cases the principles of natural justice (*naturalis aequitas*) were to be given priority over the strict letter of the law.[19] In the closing years of the Republic the *ius honorarium* stood out as a source of law distinct from the *ius civile*, and the number of the established *formulae* was so great that, according to Cicero, there seems to have been a *formula* for every possible occasion. Cicero reports, moreover, that in his time the *ius honorarium* was studied, along with the Law of the Twelve Tables, by those who wanted to become lawyers.[20] In the course of time, however, it came to be expected that the praetor should not change the edict but abide by the remedies and procedures that had been developed by his predecessors.[21] Thus praetorian initiatives became increasingly rare and, by the middle of the first century BC, the content of the edict became crystallised. As a result, the work of the praetor as a creator of law came to an end, although the edict continued to apply as law during the imperial period. In about 130 AD it was codified by the jurist Salvius Julianus by order of Emperor Hadrian and, from that time, it could only be altered by law.[22]

Legal Science

We saw in chapter 4 that during the archaic period knowledge of the law and the rules governing legal procedure was confined to the college of the pontiffs, whose members were drawn exclusively from the patrician class. After the introduction of the Law of the Twelve Tables (c. 450 BC) and the establishment of the system of *legis actiones* the authoritative interpretation of statutory law and the conduct of the actions at law remained within the province of the pontiffs, who continued in their role of giving opinions to magistrates and litigants on questions of law.[23]

---

19 The *ius praetorium* comes quite close to *equity*, the separate body of norms that supplemented the common law of England from the Middle Ages onwards.

20 Cicero, *pro Rosc. com.* 8.

21 This expectation was reflected in the *lex Cornelia de edictis* of 67 BC which provided that the praetor had to administer the law according to his *edictum perpetuum*.

22 This codified edict did not survive in its original form. Modern reconstructions are based on commentaries and interpretations of jurists of the classical period as well as on a few fragments that have been included in the Digest of Justinian. See chapter 8.

23 D. 1. 2. 2. 6. (Pomponius).

According to Roman tradition, the pontiffs' monopoly of legal knowledge was ended in c. 304 BC when Gnaeus Flavius, secretary (*scriba*) to Appius Claudius,[24] published a manuscript containing the legal *formulae* and ritual words that were employed when litigation took place. This publication, which became known as *ius civile Flavianum*, was shortly afterwards followed by the publication of the calendar of days (*dies fasti* and *dies nefasti*) on which it was permitted or forbidden, according to religious practice, to bring an action at law.[25] In 300 BC, under the *lex Ogulnia de auguribus*, the plebeians were admitted to the college of the pontiffs and in 253 BC the first plebeian *pontifex maximus*, Tiberius Coruncanius, began to discuss cases and to give legal advice in public (*publice profiteri*) in such a way that the knowledge he imparted became common to all.[26] Finally, in about 200 BC, Sextus Aelius Paetus Catus, consul in 198 BC, published his *tripertita*, a work in three parts, containing the text of the Law of the Twelve Tables, a commentary on it and a list of the legal forms employed in the *legis actio* procedure.[27] The *ius Aelianum*, as this work became known, and the earlier *ius Flavianum*, played an important part in the process of secularisation of the law and the subsequent development of Roman legal science.[28]

By the early first century BC secular jurists, the *jurisprudentes* (those possessing the knowledge of the law) or *iurisconsulti* (those who were consulted on matters relating to law) had supplanted the pontiffs, the original interpreters of the law. With few exceptions these jurists were members of Rome's wealthy upper classes and were actively involved in politics. Like the pontiffs, they received no remuneration for their work as they considered it their duty to impart instruction in law and to assist the citizens who came to them with their legal problems. Although legal science did not become a profession through which one could earn a living, it provided an outlet for wealthy and educated citizens who sought to distinguish themselves in social and political life. Because of the respect and honour which they gained through their activities, jurists, especially some of those who did not enjoy inherited power and prestige as members of noble Roman families, were able to increase their influence among their fellow citizens and, by widening the circle of their friends and dependants,

24 A prominent patrician who was appointed censor in 312 BC.

25 Livy 9. 46; Cicero, *ad Att.* 6. 1; D. 1. 2. 2. 7. (Pomponius).

26 D. 1. 2. 2. 35 and 38. (Pomponius). See F. D' Ippolito, *I giuristi e la città*, Naples 1978, 29 ff.

27 See Cicero, *Brut.* 20; D. 1. 2. 2. 7. and 38. (Pomponius). And see D' Ippolito, idid, 53 ff.

28 Both these works were lost in the course of antiquity, however.

to win their way to public office.[29] But from the late first century BC, as interest in politics began to decline in the settled political conditions of the early Empire, jurists tended to withdraw from political life and dedicate themselves exclusively to the practice and study of the law. It is important to note, at this point, that the contributions of the jurists are not evenly distributed over the whole field of law; private law and civil procedure dominate very clearly, whereas many areas of public law never became the object of the same intensive analysis and constructive development.[30]

The activities of the jurists of the late republican period were, in general, similar to those of the pontiffs. They consisted in giving advice on questions of law to private citizens, magistrates and judges (*respondere*); providing assistance to litigants on matters of legal procedure and preparing the forms necessary for filing a suit (*agere*); and drafting legal documents, such as contracts and wills, aimed at safeguarding a person's interests in legal transactions by protecting him against certain eventualities (*cavere*).[31] As magistrates and judges were not necessarily expert lawyers, they relied upon the opinions (*responsa*) of jurists when carrying out their tasks relating to the administration of justice. Thus it was customary for the praetor to construct his *edictum perpetuum* with the help of jurists who, either as individual advisers or as members of his *consilium*, advised him on matters relating to the structure of his edict and the forms of action or remedies that should be granted under certain circumstances. Indeed, much of the *ius praetorium*, or *ius honorarium*, was the work of the jurists who provided guidance to the magistrates in charge of the administration of justice. Similarly, judges often relied upon the advice of

---

29 See W. Kunkel, *Introduction to Roman Legal and Constitutional History*, 2nd edn, Oxford 1973, 96. And see Cicero, *pro Murena* 4. 9; *de off.* 2. 19. 65.

30 On the jurists of the Republic see in general R. A. Baumann, Lawyers in Roman Republican Politics. A Study of Roman Jurists n their Political Setting, 316-82 BC, Munich 1983; H. F. Jolowicz and B. Nicholas, Historical Introduction to the Study of Roman Law, 3rd edn, Cambridge 1972, 88 ff; F. Schulz, History of Roman Legal Science, Oxford 1953, 6ff, 40 ff; O. F. Robinson, The Sources of Roman Law, London 1997, 42 ff; A. Watson, Law Making in the Later Roman Republic, Oxford 1974, chs 7, 9-11; O. Tellegen-Couperus, A Short History of Roman Law, London & New York 1993, 60-62; M. Kaser, Römische Rechtsgeschichte, Göttingen 1976, 159 ff, 164 ff; W. Kunkel, Die Römischen Juristen, Cologne 2001, ch. 1; W. Kunkel/M. Schermaier, Römische Rechtsgeschichte, Cologne 2001, 123 ff; F. Wieacker, Römische Rechtsgeschichte, Munich 1988, 531 ff; A. Guarino, Storia del diritto romano, Naples 1996, 317 ff; G. Crifò, Lezioni di storia del diritto romano, 3rd edn, Bologna 2000, 199 ff.

31 See Cicero, *de orat.* 1. 48. 212; *Topica* 17. 65-66. See also Varro, *de r. r.* 2. 3. 5; D. 4. 4. 3. 1. (Ulpianus); Aulus Gellius, *N. A.* 14. 2; D. 31. 47. (Proculus).

jurists in dealing with difficult legal and procedural issues and, as the settling of disputes was an extremely technical process, the role of the jurists in litigation became increasingly important. It is important to note, however, that the jurists very rarely argued cases in the courts of law – this was left to advocates (*oratores*). Although trained in law, advocates often relied on the help of jurists in difficult cases to ensure that their clients' claims were properly stated according to the prescribed *formulae*. Moreover, an advocate would normally seek a jurist's advice when he intended to request the granting of a new form of action from a magistrate (at the *in iure* stage of the proceedings), and when he pleaded the case before the judge (*apud iudicem*).

The jurists were also entrusted with the task of educating those who wished to enter the practice of law. Legal education in Rome had a largely practical orientation; there was no theoretical or academic legal training and there were no educational institutions in which law was formally taught.[32] Upon completion of his basic education, a young man would join the household of a jurist as an apprentice and would live with him and his family for several years. He would follow his master about his daily business, observing him giving legal advice, drafting legal documents and assisting clients in legal proceedings.[33] Moreover, students were often invited to discuss difficult points of law and to formulate arguments for or against the solutions put forward by the jurists (*disputatio fori*).

As time went by, the jurists began to combine the teaching of law (*docere*) with writing (*scribere*) commentaries or treatises on different branches of the law. Furthermore, juristic opinions began to be collected into books and, gradually, a large body of legal literature came into existence. The emergence of legal writing in Rome was largely the result of the influence of the Greek culture and science on the Roman higher classes to which most jurists belonged. As they became familiar with Greek philosophical thought, and the intellectual methods and tools which Greek science had created, the jurists began to develop a systematic approach to the study of law. Thus, in dealing with legal issues, they began to utilise the dialectic method developed by Greek philosophers and rhetoricians. This was a form of logical analysis that differentiated between the various juridical concepts and, at the same time, subsumed those concepts sharing similar characteristics under common headings. By employing this method the jurists sought to logically relate and categorise the various institutions of Roman law as parts of an all-embracing logical scheme. At the same

---

32 Systematic instruction by professional law teachers was not introduced until the later Empire.

33 See Cicero, *de orat.* 1. 43. 191; *Brutus* 89. 306; Aulus Gellius, *N. A.* 13. 13. 1.

time, the jurists became aware of the logical syllogism and learned to construct legal concepts in a deductive manner. Moreover, familiarity with Greek philosophical ethics enabled the Roman jurists to become aware of the sociological function of law and, as a result, they began to lay more emphasis on arguments based on equity and other general guiding principles. Indeed, the greatest achievement of the jurists was their ability to look behind the accidental elements of a case and to define the essential legal problem it posed as a *quaestio iuris*. It is important to note here, however, that, notwithstanding the influence of Greek philosophy, the approach of the jurists remained essentially casuistic and practical. The jurists did not seek to construct systems of abstract theories nor did they regard arriving at flawless logical conclusions as an overriding consideration. What they were primarily concerned with was exercising mature judgement and practical wisdom in dealing with questions arising from individual cases, while taking into account the solutions offered by other jurists in similar cases in the past. It was this combination of practical aims with an interest in systematic analysis that ultimately gave Roman jurisprudence its most characteristic features: its pragmatism and flexibility as well as its clarity and intellectual superiority to the old, formalistic approach to the rules of the *ius civile*.

Probably the most prominent jurist of the republican era was Quintus Mucius Scaevola, who served as *pontifex maximus* and consul in 95 BC. Scaevola is said to have been the first jurist who set out the institutions of the *ius civile* in a systematic way.[34] Unlike earlier jurists, he did not confine himself to the discussion of isolated cases or questions of law. Instead, by applying the dialectic method, he sought to identify and categorise the different kinds (*genera*) of legal relationships with which the various rules of law were concerned. Thus he was able to define, in clear outline, legal institutions such as guardianship, possession, legacy, sale, partnership etc. Scaevola's approach was an important step forward as, for the first time, by the side of collections of precedents and isolated legal rules, there appeared a scheme of law conceived as a logically connected whole. Scaevola's main works included a commentary on the *ius civile* in eighteen books (*libri duodeviginti de iure civili*), and a *liber singularis*, containing definitions and classifications of legal concepts. To him is also attributed the introduction of standard legal clauses and presumptions, such as the *cautio Muciana* (a promise given by a legatee that he would return the legacy if he acted against the condition which was attached to the legacy)[35] and the *praesumptio Muciana* (the presumption that everything a married woman

---

[34] D. 1. 2. 2. 41 (Pomponius).

[35] D. 35. 1. 73. And see M. Kaser, *Das römische Privatrecht*, Munich 1971, 254.

possessed had been given to her by her husband, until the contrary was proved). Moreover, as governor of the province of Asia, Scaevola drew up a provincial edict (*edictum provinciale*) which was used as a model by other provincial governors. Scaevola's work remained influential for a long time and commentaries were still being written on it as late as the second century AD.[36]

Other distinguished jurists of the pre-classical period include Manius Manilius, consul in 149 BC, whose work *venalium vendendorum leges* ('conditions of sale for things capable of being sold'), consisting largely of model formulas relating to contracts of sale, is mentioned by Cicero and other writers;[37] the two Catos, M. Porcius Cato Censorius, consul in 195 BC and censor in 184 BC, whose work *de agricultura* (On Agriculture) comprised forms and precedents for the drawing up of agrarian contracts, and his son, M. Porcius Cato Licinianus, author of a celebrated treatise on the *ius civile* (*de iuris disciplina*);[38] M. Junius Brutus, praetor in 142 BC, who wrote a number of books on the *ius civile*;[39] Gaius Aquilius Gallus, praetor in 66 BC, who introduced the *formulae* connected with the action for fraud (*actio doli*)[40] and the *stipulatio Aquiliana*;[41] C. Trebatius Testa, a friend of Cicero's, whose work on the *ius civile* was highly regarded by the classical jurists;[42] P. Alfenus Varus, consul in 39 BC, who produced an extensive work (*Digesta*) in forty books;[43] Servius Sulpicius Rufus, consul in 51 BC, whose writings included an important commentary on the praetorian edict;[44] and P. Rutilius Rufus, consul in 105 BC, who devised the bankruptcy procedure described by Gaius (*actio Rutiliana*).[45] Unfortunately, only a few scattered and fragmentary traces of the works of these jurists have been preserved through the writings of jurists of the classical period.[46]

---

36 But only a few fragments of Scaevola's works have come down to us, largely through the Digest of Justinian.

37 Cicero, *de orat.* 1. 246; Varro, *De r.r.* 2. 5. 11; D. 1. 2. 2. 39. (Pomponius).

38 D. 1. 2. 2. 38. (Pomponius).

39 Cicero, *pro Cluent.* 141; *de orat.* 2. 142. 224; D. 1. 2. 2. 39. (Pomponius).

40 D. 4. 3. 1. 1. (Ulpianus).

41 D. 46. 4. 18. (Florentinus); *Inst.* 3. 29. 2.

42 D. 1. 2. 2. 45. (Pomponius); *Inst.* 2. 25. pr.

43 D. 1. 2. 2. 44. (Pomponius).

44 According to Cicero, Servius was the first jurist to apply the dialectic method in the study of legal problems (*Brut.* 152 ff.). And see D. 1. 2. 2. 43. (Pomponius).

45 G. 4. 35.

46 For a reconstruction of the works of the pre-classical jurists see O. Lenel, *Palingenesia iuris civilis*, 2 vols, Leipzig 1889, repr. Graz 1960. See also F. Bremer, *Iurisprudentiae ante-hadrianae quae supersunt*, I, Leipzig 1896.

Custom

In the years that followed the introduction of the Law of the Twelve Tables, custom (*consuetudo*) ceased to operate as an autonomous source of law. However, it continued to play a part in the formulation of the norms of positive law as found in the *leges*, the *edicta* of the magistrates and the interpretations of the jurists.[47] Thus, a great deal of the forms of action devised by the praetors in order to deal with situations not covered by the existing *ius civile* reflected customary norms approved and observed by the people for a long time (*opinio necessitatis*).[48] The primary duty of the praetor in a legal dispute was to determine whether the title upon which a party based his claim was valid and, in doing so, the praetor was guided by current public opinion and the general sentiment as to what was right and proper in the circumstances. Similar considerations informed the jurists when formulating their *responsa*.

The Administration of Justice: Civil Procedure

The courts

As was explained in chapter 4, most civil cases were decided by one judge sitting alone (*iudex unus*), who was appointed by the praetor with the consent of the parties concerned. From the third century BC new courts began to be established made up of several judges to deal with cases of a more complex nature. The members of these courts were selected by lot (*sortitio*) from the *album iudicum*, although both the plaintiff and the defendant had the right to challenge one or more of the judges so chosen (*reiectio*).

The court of the centumviri

The centumviral court was instituted in the second half of the third century BC. It consisted of 105 members, three from each of the thirty-five tribes

---

[47] As stated by the jurist Paul 'custom is the best interpreter of statutes'. See D. 1.3. 37. On the role of custom see A. A. Schiller, *Roman Law: Mechanisms of Development*, New York 1978, 253 ff, 560 ff; O. F. Robinson, *The Sources of Roman Law*, London 1997, 28-9; M. Kaser, *Das römische Privatrecht*, Munich 1971, 196; F. Wieacker, *Römische Rechtsgeschichte*, Munich 1988,499 ff; G. Crifò, *Lezioni di storia del diritto romano*, 3rd edn, Bologna 2000, 172 ff.

[48] Cicero, *de invent*. 2. 22. 67; D. 1. 3. 32. 1. (Julianus); D. 1. 3. 35. (Hermogenianus).

(*tribus*) into which the territory of Rome was divided. The court exercised its jurisdiction in the name of the Roman people either as a single body (*collegium*) or divided into sections (*consilia*) which heard cases separately. During the Republic it was presided over by ex-quaestors. In the imperial period it consisted of a panel of 180 persons and was normally divided into four sections presided over by the *decemviri*.[49] We are unable to state with certainty what sort of cases fell in the jurisdiction of this court. On the basis of the scanty evidence available it appears that it dealt with cases concerning inheritances valued at no less than 100,000 sesterces, with disputes about guardianship and the ownership of land and with certain criminal cases. The regular form of procedure before the centumviral court was that of the *legis actio sacramento*, even after this type of procedure was abolished by Augustus in 17 BC.[50] According to Gaius, when the court sat in judgement (*centumvirale iudicium*) a spear (*hasta*) was set upright before the judges as a symbol of the court's authority to settle disputes.[51] Trials before the centumviral court attracted a great deal of attention and, according to Pliny, this court was the most exciting forum for a forensic orator. Eminent lawyers, including Q. Mucius Scaevola and L. Licinius Crassus, delivered some of their most splendid speeches before this court (acting as advocates, rather than jurists). The centumviral court was finally abolished in the third century AD.

The decemviri stlitibus iudicandis

This court was composed of ten members and had jurisdiction over disputes concerning a person's status as a free man (*liberales causae*).[52] After the enactment of the *leges Iuliae iudiciorum* of Augustus in 17 BC the *decemviri* served as chairmen of the different sections of the centumviral court.[53]

---

[49] Cicero, *de leg. agr.* 2. 17; Pliny, *Epp.* 6. 33. 3; Quintilian 4. 1. 57; 5. 2. 1; 11. 1. 78; 12. 5. 6; Val. Max. 7. 8. 1; Aulus Gellius, *N. A.* 16. 10.

[50] G. 4. 16. 31. 95.

[51] G. 4. 16.

[52] During the Republic the *decemviri stlitibus iudicandis* were originally minor judicial magistrates, members of the *vigintisexviri*, a body comprising 26 magistrates with different functions.

[53] On the decemviral court see D. 1. 2. 2. 29 (Pomponius); Cicero, *pro Caec.* 33. 97; *de domo* 29. 78; Suetonius, *div. Aug.* 36; Cassius Dio 54. 26.

The recuperatores

The term *recuperatores* originally referred to a mixed body of commissioners appointed under treaties between Rome and foreign states for the purpose of trying cases involving disputes between foreign merchants.[54] Later a court consisting of three or, sometimes, five members was established in Rome, which dealt with disputes between Roman citizens and foreigners under the supervision of the *praetor peregrinus*.[55] As the relevant procedure was simpler and more flexible than that followed by the ordinary courts,[56] disputes between Roman citizens also were often submitted to this court by mutual consent of the parties (especially when a speedy decision was desired). In the first century AD the jurisdiction of the *recuperatores* was extended to cover cases concerning the state treasury (*aerarium*).[57] The court of the *recuperatores* is not mentioned in postclassical law.

Actions at law and their classification

As was noted in chapter 4, the term *actio* referred to a person's right of instituting proceedings in a court of law for the purpose of obtaining what was due to him.[58] In a narrower sense the same term was used to denote a lawsuit.[59] One should keep in mind that, unlike modern law, Roman law drew no clear distinction between rights and the legal means by which rights were protected or enforced.

Actions were classified in a number of ways. When considered in reference to the object of the relevant claim, actions were divided into actions relating to things (*actiones in rem*) and actions relating to persons (*actiones in personam*).[60] An *actio in rem* was brought in order to establish

---

54 See Festus, '*reciperatio*' in Bruns, *Fontes* II, 30.

55 The *recuperatores* were private citizens acting as judges (*iudices*) in the second stage of the trial. Until the close of the Republic only persons of thirty years or older could serve as judges. In the Augustan age, under the *leges Iuliae iudiciorum*, the minimum age was fixed to twenty-five. See FIRA I, no. 68 & no. 44; comp. Suetonius, *div. Aug.* 32. 3.

56 Disputes brought before this court were resolved on the basis of the *ius gentium*, the flexible body of law built upon the edicts of the *praetor peregrinus*, according to the *per formulam* procedure.

57 Suetonius, *Nero* 17.

58 See *Inst.* 4. 6 pr.; D. 44. 7. 51. (Celsus).

59 The word *actio* was derived from the verb *agere*: initiating (proceedings in a court of law). And see G. 1. 8: '*ius quod ad actiones pertinet*'.

60 G. 4. 1. 2. 3.

the plaintiff's claim to some corporeal object (*res*) as opposed to a claim of the defendant, or to compel the defendant to acknowledge some property right, e.g. a servitude (*servitus*), which the plaintiff claimed to have. According to Gaius, the *actiones in rem* were also referred to as *vindicationes* (vindications).[61] Unlike modern law, which views real actions as being aimed at the person who violated the plaintiff's right to property, the *actiones in rem* were aimed at the thing or property right claimed rather than at another person. An *actio in personam,* on the other hand, was brought by the plaintiff in order to compel the defendant to perform a contractual or delictual obligation. Of the personal actions, those aimed at compelling the defendant to give or to do something (*dare facere oportere*) were termed *condictiones*.[62] When considered in reference to their sources, actions were divided into actions based on the *ius civile* (*actiones civiles*) and actions based on the praetorian edict (*actiones honorariae*). A further division of actions was that between temporary actions (*actiones temporales*), i.e. actions which could be brought only within a fixed period of time, and perpetual actions (*actiones perpetuae*), i.e. actions which could be brought without limit of time.[63] *Actiones temporales* were, for example, the *actiones aediliciae* (i.e. actions introduced by the aedilician edict), which had to be brought within a period of six months, and the *actiones praetoriae* (i.e. actions originating in the praetorian edict), which had to be brought within a year (*actiones annales*). A further category of actions were the *actiones arbitrariae*. These were actions with respect to which the judge, if he reached the conclusion that the plaintiff was right, could ask the defendant to restore (*restituere*) the object claimed to the plaintiff. If the defendant complied, he was absolved; if not, the judge could condemn him to pay a sum of money – a result which was worse for the defendant than the immediate fulfilment of the judge's order (he might be condemned to pay a higher amount and, in some cases, could be branded as an *infamis*). The term *actiones famosae* referred to actions in which the condemnation of the defendant entailed infamy (*infamia*), i.e. the diminution of his social standing accompanied by certain civil disabilities.[64] Actions that could be brought by any Roman citizen as relating to the protection of general public interests (*ius populi*) were called

---

61 G. 4. 5; and see *Inst.* 4. 6. 15.

62 G. 4. 5.

63 Under the formulary system, however, a temporary action was transformed into a perpetual one upon completion of the *in iure* phase of the lawsuit. See D. 27. 7. 8. 1. (Paulus). In the post-classical period it was recognised that perpetual actions were extinguished after thirty or, in certain exceptional cases, forty years from the time the plaintiff could institute legal proceedings.

64 G. 4. 182.

actiones populares.[65] These actions were of a penal character and, if the defendant was condemned, the penalty was usually paid to the plaintiff. In some cases, however, the penalty was paid to the state or was divided between the state and the accuser. Finally, Roman law also recognised certain preliminary actions (*actiones praeiudiciales*) which, unlike the ordinary actions, were not directly associated with specific claims. A preliminary action was concerned with establishing or clarifying certain matters upon which an ordinary action depended.[66]

The formulary system

As we saw in chapter 4, in the *legis actio* procedure claims had to be made in accordance with certain forms (*legis actiones*) derived directly from the law. If, in making his claim, a plaintiff used the wrong *legis actio*, or departed from the prescribed form, his claim was rejected. Because of the extremely formalistic nature of this system a legal remedy was sometimes denied, even though a right should clearly have been recognised in the circumstances. This is illustrated by a case, mentioned by Gaius, in which a man who sued another for having chopped down his vines was denied a remedy because in his claim he used the word '*vites*' (vines) instead of the word '*arbores*' (trees), as prescribed by the Law of the Twelve Tables.[67] Another problem with the *legis actio* procedure was that, as it pertained strictly to the *ius civile*, it could be used only when both parties to a dispute were Roman citizens.[68] But as economic life became more complex and the number of foreigners (*peregrini*) living in Rome continued to increase, especially during the period of Rome's expansion, it became obvious that this system was inadequate to meet the needs of social and commercial life. Thus, a new and more flexible system was developed, known as the formulary (*per formulam*) procedure, which gradually replaced the *legis actio* procedure, although the latter continued to be used in certain exceptional cases for a long time.

The *per formulam* procedure was probably first introduced by the *praetor peregrinus* as a way of dealing with disputes involving foreigners.

---

65 D. 47. 23. 1. (Paulus). To this category belonged, e.g., the *actio legis plaetoriae* (an action brought against a person who exploited a minor), the *actio de albo corrupto* (an action brought against a person who damaged or falsified the tablet (*album*) on which the praetorian edict was inscribed) and others.

66 G. 4. 44. On the classification of actions see M. Kaser, *Das römische Zivilprozessrecht*, Munich 1996, 326 ff; R. Monier, *Manuel élémentaire de droit romain*, Aalen 1977, 181 ff.

67 G. 4. 11.

68 According to the principle of the personality of the laws. See chapter 1.

Its application was subsequently extended to cases in which both parties to a dispute were Roman citizens by the *lex Aebutia*, passed in the first half of the second century BC.[69] The reform of civil procedure was completed by the *leges Iuliae iudiciorum publicorum et privatorum* of Augustus in 17-16 BC.[70] By one of these laws the *legis actio* procedure was abolished except in cases which fell in the jurisdiction of the centumviral court and in certain cases involving a threat of damage to another person's property (*damnum infectum*).[71] Under the new system, the praetor was given the freedom to go beyond the strict letter of the law and accept or refuse a claim, even where this did not accord with the *ius civile*, on the grounds of what he considered to be right and equitable. He did this not by introducing new legal rights (as was pointed out earlier, the magistrates had no legislative powers) but by granting the claimant an action and promising that if the facts upon which his claim was based were proved to be true in the subsequent trial he would grant a remedy. But, as in Roman law a right was regarded as a legal right only if it could be enforced by a recognised process of law, by introducing new remedies the praetor was in effect creating new legal rights.

Once the praetor had decided to grant an action to a claimant, he nominated the judge (*iudex*) who was to try the case and instructed him to condemn the defendant if certain facts were proved or, if not, to absolve

---

69 On the formulary system see in general A. A. Schiller, *Roman Law: Mechanisms of Development*, New York 1978, 435 ff; H. F. Jolowicz and B. Nicholas, *Historical Introduction to the Study of Roman Law*, 3rd edn, Cambridge 1972, 199 ff; O. F. Robinson, *The Sources of Roman Law*, London 1997, 84 ff; W. Kunkel, *An Introduction to Roman Legal and Constitutional History*, 2nd edn, Oxford 1973, ch. 6; B. Nicholas, *An Introduction to Roman Law*, Oxford 1991, 19 ff; D. Johnston, *Roman Law in Context*, Cambridge 1999, 112 ff; M. Kaser, *Römische Rechtsgeschichte*, Göttingen 1976, 140 ff; M. Kaser, *Das römische Zivilprozessrecht*, Munich 1996, 151 ff; W. Kunkel/M. Schermaier, *Römische Rechtsgeschichte*, Cologne 2001, 110 ff; F. Wieacker, *Römische Rechtsgeschichte*, Munich 1988, 447 ff; R. Monier, *Manuel élémentaire de droit romain*, Aalen 1977, 150 ff, 157 ff; A. Guarino, *Diritto privato romano*, Naples 2001, 183 ff; *Storia del diritto romano*, Naples 1996, 305 ff; D. Mantovani, *Le formule nel processo privato*, Como 1992; G. Pugliese, II, *processo formulare*, Milan 1963; C. A. Cannata, *Profilo istituzionale del processo privato romano II, Il processo formulare*, Turin 1982.

70 G. 4. 30.

71 The term *damnum infectum* referred to a damage threatening a person's property having to do with the defective state of a neighbouring property. The owner of the threatened property had against his neighbour an *actio damni infecti*. See G. 4. 31.

him. The praetor's instruction to the judge was set out in a written form and was called *formula.* The various forms of action based on these *formulae* were included in the praetorian edict (*edictum perpetuum*) and were termed *actiones honorariae*, i.e. actions derived from the *ius honorarium.* As was noted before, these were distinguished from the *actiones civiles*, i.e. the actions derived directly from the *ius civile*. The principal forms of action through which the praetor carried out his functions were the *actiones utiles* and the *actiones in factum*. The *actiones utiles* were actions created by the praetor through a modification of an existing *formula* in order to deal with a situation not covered by the original *formula*. To the category of *actiones utiles* belonged the *actiones fictitiae*, i.e. actions adapted to situations not covered by an existing *formula* by the use of a fiction in the original *formula*. In other words, here the praetor fictitiously presumed the existence of certain facts which according to law had to be present if an action at law was to be granted. For example, if the parties to a dispute were not citizens of Rome, certain actions could be made available to them through the addition to the relevant *formula* of the phrase 'as if they were Roman citizens'.[72] An *actio fictitia* was the famous *actio Publiciana*, named after the praetor Publicius who introduced it at the beginning of the first century BC. By this action the owner of a thing who had lost possession of it could reclaim his property, even though he did not yet have a title, if he could prove that he had acquired the thing under conditions which put him in the position of becoming its owner by *usucapio* (i.e. by remaining in undisputed possession of the thing for a certain period of time). This action was an *actio fictitia* in that the completion of the period of *usucapio*[73] was fictitiously presumed.[74] The *actiones in factum* were new actions granted by the praetor to deal with claims not covered by any of the already existing *formulae*. When such an action was granted the actual facts of the case were incorporated into a new *formula* (*formula in factum concepta*).

An important category of actions that needs to be mentioned here were the so-called *actiones bonae fidei*, actions whose *formulae* included the clause *ex fide bona* (in good faith) as a further condition. In *bona fidei* actions the judge was free to decide the matter (for example, to determine the form and amount of compensation which the defendant had to pay to the plaintiff) on the basis of the principle of good faith. He could inquire

---

72 As, e.g., in the action for theft (*actio furti*).

73 In classical law, the period of *usucapio* was two years for land and one year formoveables.

74 G. 4. 36; D. 6. 2. 1. (Ulpianus). And see M. Kaser, *Das römische Privatrecht*, Munich 1971, 438 ff; *Das römische Zivilprozessrecht*, Munich 1996, 106-7, 238-9, 326 ff; A. Guarino, *Diritto privato romano*, Naples 2001, 196.

into the true intentions of the parties and could take into account any equitable defences (even if these were not expressly pleaded), as the *formula* in these cases instructed the judge to ascertain what the defendant ought to do or give *ex bona fide* and to condemn accordingly. Actions arising from real or consensual contracts, such as *emptio venditio* (sale), *locatio conductio* (hire), *mandatum* (mandate) and *societas* (partnership), were actions *bonae fidei*. By contrast, the term *actiones stricti iuris* was used to denote actions the *formulae* of which did not include the clause *ex fide bona*. In actions *stricti iuris* the relevant *formula* had to be strictly construed and the judge could not take into consideration anything not contained in it. Actions based on unilateral contracts, such as the *stipulatio*,[75] where the promisor was bound to the very thing he had promised, belonged to this category of actions.[76]

The structure of the *formula*

As was noted above, the *formula* was the written document by which the praetor nominated the private judge (*iudex privatus*) who was to try the case and authorised him to condemn the defendant if certain facts were proved or, if these facts were not proved, to absolve him. The instructions to the judge contained in this document were carefully worded and adapted to the circumstances of the particular case. By contrast with the *legis actio* procedure, in which the relevant *legis actio* was selected by the plaintiff at his own risk, in the *per formulam* procedure the *formula* was issued by the magistrate at the request of the party concerned. A distinction was drawn between two types of *formulae*: *formulae in ius conceptae* and *formulae in factum conceptae*. The former were employed when the judge was called upon to determine the legal consequences of a factual situation already established – when he was required to decide, for example, if the plaintiff had suffered a legally recognised harm, or to determine the amount of compensation to which the plaintiff was entitled. A *formula in factum concepta*, on the other hand, was issued when the judge was called upon to decide whether the facts upon which the plaintiff's claim was based were true or not, as well as the legal significance of these facts.[77] A *formula in*

[75] G. 3. 92-93; *Inst*. 3. 15 pr.

[76] When fraud was committed in the context of such a contract, initially the victim had no remedy against the defrauder, except on the basis that the fraud had induced a mistake on his part. In the first century BC, however, the action for fraud (*actio doli*) was introduced for the compensation for any loss sustained; at the same time the *exceptio doli* was given to prevent any action based on the contract by the defrauder. See D. 4. 3. 1. pr. (Ulpianus).

[77] G. 4. 47.

factum concepta was incorporated into the praetor's edict in the form of an announcement that an action would be granted in certain cases not covered by the existing law.

According to Gaius, a *formula* consisted of four parts: the *demonstratio*, the *intentio*, the *adiudicatio* and the *condemnatio* (although the presence of all four elements was not always necessary).[78] The *demonstratio* was the part of the formula setting out the factual situation upon which the plaintiff's claim was based. This part of the *formula* always began with the word '*quod*': inasmuch (e.g. 'inasmuch as the plaintiff sold a horse to the defendant...').[79] The *intentio* was the part of the *formula* in which the plaintiff's claim was stated.[80] It began with the phrase '*si paret*' or '*quidquid paret*': 'if it appears', 'whatever it appears'. Depending upon whether the object of the claim was clearly identified or not, an *intentio* could be certain (*certa*) or uncertain (*incerta*). For example, an *intentio certa* would read as follows: 'If it appears that the defendant ought to pay the plaintiff the sum of 1000 sestercii...' On the other hand, an *intentio incerta* would be worded in this way: 'whatever it appears that the defendant ought to pay to the plaintiff...' In actions relating to person (*actiones in personam*) the *intentio* contained the names of both the plaintiff and the defendant; in those relating to property (*actiones in rem*) only the name of the plaintiff was included. The *adiudicatio* was the part of the *formula* in which the judge was authorised to transfer the object that constituted the subject-matter of the dispute to one of the litigants. This was an essential part of *formulae* relating to actions concerned, e.g., with the division of common property, or the division of property among co-heirs.[81] Finally, the *condemnatio* was the part of the *formula* in which the judge was given authority to condemn or absolve the defendant.[82] The *condemnatio* specified the amount of money which the defendant had to pay to the plaintiff, if the former was condemned, or authorised the judge to fix that amount at his discretion.[83] A *formula* always included an *intentio* and a *condemnatio*. Exceptionally, actions concerned with preliminary matters upon which a subsequent lawsuit depended (*actiones praeiudiciales*) did not include a *condemnatio*, but only an *intentio*. For example, a patron who wanted to sue his freedman for failing to carry out his duties could bring a preliminary action whose aim was to determine whether the defendant was in fact a freedman. Such an action was not

78 G. 4. 39. 44.
79 G. 4. 40.
80 G. 4. 41.
81 G. 4. 42.
82 G. 4. 43.
83 G. 4. 49. 50.

concerned with the condemnation of the defendant but with simply providing an answer to the question raised.[84] Besides the four parts mentioned by Gaius, a *formula* always contained a nomination of a judge and, sometimes, one or more defences and counter-defences raised by the defendant and the plaintiff respectively.[85]

Suppose that in a case brought before the praetor the defendant had promised by *stipulatio*, a verbal contract, to pay the plaintiff 3,000 denarii, but he failed to do so. In such a case the plaintiff could bring against the defendant an action known as *condictio certae pecuniae*. The *formula* for this action, as found in the praetorian edict, ran as follows:

> Let X be the judge. If it appears that the defendant ought to pay to the plaintiff 3,000 denarii, let the judge condemn the defendant; if this does not appear, let the judge absolve him.

In this case the judge was asked simply to examine whether the plaintiff's claim was true or not. The defendant could oppose the plaintiff's claim as a matter of fact by denying that he had promised to pay to the plaintiff 3,000 denarii. Or the defendant could admit the existence of the promise but claim that he was no longer bound by it due to the presence of an exceptional circumstance. He might argue, for example, that the plaintiff, at a later time, had informally agreed to absolve him of the debt. Although, under the *ius civile*, such an informal agreement could not negate the initial promise, the praetor could grant the defendant a plea in bar of the plaintiff's action (*exceptio pacti*).[86] The defendant's defence (*exceptio*) would in such a case be included in the *formula* as a further condition.[87] Thus the *formula* would be worded as follows:

> Let X be the judge. If it appears that the defendant ought to pay to the plaintiff 3,000 denarii and if there was no agreement between the plaintiff and the defendant that absolved the latter from the debt, let the judge

---

84 G. 4. 44.

85 On the parts of the *formula* see H. F. Jolowicz and B. Nicholas, *Historical Introduction to the Study of Roman Law*, 3rd edn, Cambridge 1972, 203-208; M. Kaser, *Das römische Zivilprozessrecht*, Munich 1996, 310 ff; A. Guarino, *Diritto privato romano*, Naples 2001, 197 ff; R. Monier, *Manuel élémentaire de droit romain*, Aalen 1977, 176 ff.

86 The term *exceptio* was used to denote a defence raised by the defendant against the plaintiff's claim and which, if successful, would preclude the defendant's condemnation by rendering the plaintiff's claim ineffective.

87 An exception was inserted in the formula between the *intentio* and the *condemnatio* and began with the words '*si...non*' (unless).

condemn the defendant; if this does not appear, let the judge absolve the defendant.

Depending upon their period of operation, exceptions were divided into peremptory or perpetual and dilatory or temporary.[88] A peremptory (*peremptoria*) exception could be raised without limit of time (*exceptio perpetua*). The party who, due to some mistake, failed to raise such an exception when the relevant *formula* was being prepared, could seek the insertion of his exception in the *formula* at a later time.[89] Dilatory or temporary defences, on the other hand, could be raised only within a limited period of time or under certain circumstances.[90] For example, a defendant might raise a dilatory (*dilatoria*) exception in order to bar the plaintiff's action on the grounds that the action was brought prematurely, i.e. before the passing of the prescribed period of time (*dilatoria ex tempore*);[91] or on the grounds that the person who brought the action was legally incapable of doing so, e.g. because the action had been brought by a representative who had not been appointed according to law (*dilatoria ex persona*).[92] In such a case the plaintiff could, before the conclusion of the *in iure* phase of the proceedings, withdraw his action and bring it again later, i.e. after the prescribed period of time had passed, or after the impediment relating to the capacity of his representative had been removed. If the plaintiff did not withdraw his action, a dilatory exception, like a peremptory exception, if accepted, resulted in the rejection of his claim.[93] Exceptions were divided, further, into *exceptiones civiles* and *exceptiones honorariae*. The former were based on the *ius civile*;[94] the latter were granted by the praetor under certain circumstances and were included in the *edictum perpetuum*.[95] Of the *exceptiones honorariae* probably the most important was the *exceptio doli*, based on the claim that the plaintiff had acted fraudulently (*dolo*).[96] The term *exceptiones utiles*

---

88 G. 4. 120.

89 G. 4. 125.

90 G. 4. 116. 119. 121-2.

91 G. 4. 122.

92 G. 4. 124.

93 G. 4. 123.

94 Such an exception was provided, e.g., under the *lex Laetoria* (192-1 BC). This law aimed at protecting persons under twenty-five years of age (*minores*) who had been defrauded in a transaction. Although the transaction may have been *prima facie* valid, the person defrauded could bar the plaintiff's action for payment by raising an *exceptio legis Laetoriae*.

95 G. 4. 118.

96 D. 4. 3. 1. pr; 4. 3. 1. 2. (Ulpianus).

referred to exceptions which had been formulated by the praetor on the basis of other exceptions found in the *edictum perpetuum*. *Exceptiones in factum*, on the other hand, were new exceptions granted by the praetor in response to claims not covered by any of the exceptions already recognised.[97]

Now, when an exception was raised the plaintiff could deny the facts giving rise to the defendant's defence, or raise his own counter-defence against it. For example, he might deny the defendant's claim that the plaintiff had promised not to bring an action against him by asserting that this promise had subsequently been revoked, or was limited to a given period of time. The plaintiff's counter-exception, termed *replicatio*, was also inserted into the relevant *formula* as a further condition.[98] To the plaintiff's *replicatio* the defendant might again respond by raising a further *exceptio*, now called *dublicatio* , and so on until each party's case was fully stated.[99] All the exceptions and counter-exceptions were inserted into the relevant *formula*.[100] However, the use of *exceptiones* appears to have become less frequent as a result of the proliferation of the *actiones bonae fidei*, i.e. actions in relation to which good faith was explicitly taken into consideration.[101]

---

97 A further division of exceptions, probably introduced during the classical period, was that between personal exceptions (*personae cohaerentes*) and non-personal ones (*rei cohaerentes*). The former could be raised only by the defendant himself. See D. 44. 1. 7. pr. (Paulus). The latter could be raised by the defendant or any other person acting on his behalf. Such an exception was, for example, the *exceptio doli*. See D. 44. 1. 7. 1. (Paulus); D. 44. 4. 4. 27. (Ulpianus).

98 G. 4. 126; D. 44. 1. 2. 1. (Ulpianus).

99 G. 4. 127-8.

100 Besides the *exceptio*, another type of clause or proviso sometimes included in the *formula* was the *praescriptio*. The aim of the latter was to give a more precise description of the claim upon which the relevant action was based. As its name suggests, a *praescriptio* was placed at the beginning of the *formula*, before the *intentio*, and was introduced by the words '*ea res agatur*' ('let the action be...'). See G. 4. 133. Initially *praescriptiones* could be granted in favour of both the plaintiff (*pro actore*) and the defendant (*pro reo*), but in the time of Gaius (second century AD) it appears that the *praescriptiones pro reo* had disappeared, having been replaced by exceptions. For example, a *praescriptio pro actore* could be inserted in the *formula* in a case where the plaintiff, by his action, demanded payment of part only of a debt. In such a case a *praescriptio* could be included in the *formula* stating: 'let the action be (*ea res agatur*) only for what is already due'. See G. 4. 131.

101 On the *exceptiones* see M. Kaser, *Das römische Zivilprozessrecht*, Munich 1996, 256 ff; 320; *Römische Rechtsgeschichte*, Göttingen 1976, 141 ff; A.

As was noted before, the *formulae* for actions *bonae fidei* included the clause *ex fide bona* (in good faith) as a further condition. Take for example a case in which the plaintiff claimed that, by a contract of sale (*emptio venditio*), he sold the defendant a horse and that the defendant did not pay the price. In such a case the plaintiff could be granted an action (*actio venditi*) based on the following *formula*:

> Let X be the judge. Inasmuch as the plaintiff has sold the defendant a horse, which matter is the subject of this action, whatever it appears that the defendant in good faith ought to give to or do for the plaintiff, let the judge condemn the defendant to give or do; if it does not appear, let the judge absolve him.

Actiones bonae fidei were the actions relating to real contracts (except the *mutuum*)[102] and to consensual contracts, i.e. contracts based on mere agreement (sale, hire, partnership and mandate). Whereas all other contracts required observance of certain formalities (set words, writing or delivery of a thing), consensual contracts were binding as soon as the parties agreed on the essential elements of their contract.[103] Contracts in which the obligations of the parties were determined according to the requirements of good faith began to play an important part in economic life during the later republican period.

The formulary procedure

Like the *legis actio* procedure, the procedure *per formulam* was divided into two stages: before the magistrate (*in iure*) and before the judge (*in iudicio, apud iudicem*).

The proceedings *in iure*

Preliminary stage

Before formal proceedings began the plaintiff announced his intention to bring an action against the defendant (*editio actionis*). By this

---

Guarino, *Diritto privato romano*, Naples 2001, 208 ff; H. F. Jolowicz and B. Nicholas, *Historical Introduction to the Study of Roman Law*, 3rd edn, Cambridge 1972, 206-208.

102 *Mutuum* was a loan for consumption of money or other things which could be weighed, numbered or measured (*res fungibiles*), such as wine, oil, corn, silver or gold.

103 *Inst*. 3. 22. 1.

announcement, which was done extrajudicially and informally, the plaintiff notified the defendant of his claim, as well as the type of action he intended to bring, thus giving him an opportunity to settle the matter before it came to trial. The next step was the summoning of the defendant by the plaintiff to appear before the praetor (*in ius vocatio*). The provisions of the Law of the Twelve Tables concerning the summoning of the defendant continued to apply under the formulary system. Thus, if the defendant refused to appear, or attempted to escape, the plaintiff had the right to bring him before the praetor by force. Moreover, the praetor, in order to force the defendant to come forth, could issue a *missio in possessionem*, a coercive measure by which the plaintiff was authorised to enter into possession of the defendant's property. In addition to that, the praetor could grant the plaintiff an *actio in factum* by which the defendant who failed to appear could be compelled to pay the plaintiff a sum of money.[104] But a defendant did not have to appear in person before the praetor if he could find another person who would act as his guarantor (*vindex*).[105] The *vindex* gave assurance that the defendant would appear before the court at a fixed later date. If the defendant failed to come forth, however, the *vindex* was liable to the plaintiff who could bring against him a praetorian *actio in factum*. In some cases the plaintiff could not summon the defendant without first obtaining permission by the praetor. For example, the praetor's permission was required for the summoning by a freedman (*libertinus*) of his patron or his patron's closest relatives.[106] If the procedure before the praetor could not be concluded within the same day, the defendant had to promise that he would appear again before the magistrate at a fixed later date (*se certo die sisti*). This promise, termed *vadimonium*, was sometimes strengthened by an oath or a real security. The amount given as a security, which could not exceed half the value of the object in dispute, could be claimed by the plaintiff if the defendant did not keep his promise.[107]

The main procedure

When both parties appeared before the praetor, the plaintiff reiterated his claim (*editio actionis*) and asked the praetor to grant him permission to bring an action against the defendant (*postulatio actionis*). The defendant could respond in one of the following ways:

---

[104] G. 4. 46. and 183.

[105] But a proposed *vindex* would not be acceptable to the magistrate unless he was wealthy enough to guarantee the eventual payment of the defendant's debt, if the latter was condemned by the judge.

[106] G. 4. 183; D. 2. 4. 4. 1. (Ulpianus).

[107] G. 4. 184-186.

(i) He could acknowledge the plaintiff's claim (*confessio in iure*). Such an acknowledgment resulted in the termination of the proceedings since, with respect to its consequences, it was regarded as amounting to a condemnation by a judge.[108] This rule, already established under the Law of the Twelve Tables,[109] applied where the plaintiff's claim involved payment by the defendant of a fixed sum of money (*aes confessum*). If, however, the plaintiff's claim did not specify the debt, immediate execution was impossible and proceedings continued now based upon an *actio confessoria*. The purpose of this action was the determination of the amount of money which the defendant who had already admitted his liability ought to pay to the plaintiff.

(ii) The defendant could deny that he was liable. In such a case the praetor would consider if, on the basis of the available evidence, a *prima facie* case could be made out and, if he thought that the plaintiff's claim lacked sufficient grounds of support, he refused to grant an action (*denegatio actionis*).[110] If, on the other hand, he concluded that the plaintiff's claim was well-founded, he granted an action and issued the *formula* on the basis of which the case was submitted to the judge for further examination.

(iii) Often the defendant did not deny the plaintiff's claim but put forward one or more defences against it and asked the praetor to insert these (*adiunctiones*) into the relevant *formula* in the form of exceptions (*postulatio exceptionis*).[111] The plaintiff could, in turn, raise one or more counter-defences of his own (*replicationes*) by which he sought to deny the defendant's exceptions.

(iv) Finally, the defendant could simply refrain from replying to the plaintiff's claim. The consequences of a defendant's passive stance varied depending upon whether the action sought was an action relating to property (*in rem*), or an action relating to person (*in personam*). With respect to the former, the rule that applied was that a person was not obliged to defend a thing if he did not wish to do

---

[108] D. 42. 2. 1.(Paulus).

[109] XII T. III 1.

[110] D. 50. 17. 102. 1. See on this A. Metro, *La denegatio actionis*, Milan 1972.

[111] In the *per formulam* procedure, if the defendant raised an exception, he was regarded as having the position of a plaintiff with regard to that exception. See D. 44. 1. 1. (Ulpianus).

so.[112] In such a case the plaintiff would normally be given possession of the thing he claimed (*res indefensa*). With respect to an *actio in personam*, on the other hand, the plaintiff might be given permission to lay hands on the defendant who refused to defend himself (*indefensus*) and imprison him[113] or enter into possession of his property (following the issuing of a *missio in possessionem*).

After hearing the claims of both parties and considering the available evidence the praetor, at his discretion, could grant an action where, according to the letter of the law, no action seemed available, or refuse to grant an action where, according to the letter of the law, an action appeared possible. A plaintiff who was denied an action, however, could bring the matter again before another praetor, or ask a tribune to exercise his veto (*intercessio*) against the praetor's decision. If the praetor concluded that the plaintiff's claim was well-founded he granted him permission to bring an action against the defendant (*dabat actionem*) and, often with the help of his *consilium*, prepared the relevant *formula*. The *formula* was usually selected from the list of *formulae* included in the *edictum perpetuum*. If no appropriate *formula* for the plaintiff's action could be found in the edict, the praetor could adapt a *formula* designed to cover cases of a similar nature (*actio utilis*, *actio fictitia*), or draw up a *formula* for a new action (*actio in factum*).[114] The *formula* was then given to the plaintiff (*iudicium dare*) who, in the presence of the praetor, notified its contents to the defendant. With the announcement of the *formula* and its acceptance by the defendant (*iudicium accipere*)[115] the *in iure* phase of the proceedings came to a close.

Litis contestatio

The point at which all the elements of the *formula* had been finalised and the parties agreed to surrender their dispute to the judge was termed *litis contestatio*. At this point the parties were presumed to have agreed to accept and abide by the decision of the judge. Moreover, this was probably the point at which the praetor formally granted the person who had been nominated judge the authority to sit in judgement of the case and

---

[112] D. 50. 17. 156. pr. (Ulpianus).

[113] '*Duci iubere*'. See Girard, *Textes* I, p. 454; FIRA II, p. 310.

[114] It is important to remember that in preparing the *formula* the praetor was concerned with giving effect to the real intentions of the parties. Thus, although initially the *formula* was prepared by the praetor himself, in later years this was done in consultation with the parties concerned.

[115] G. 4. 90. and 114.

pronounce a verdict (*iudicare iubere*).[116] An important consequence of the *litis contestatio* was that the judge could take into consideration the parties' claims as they had been formulated at the time of the *litis contestatio*. As a general rule, subsequent events did not affect the nature of the case or the basis upon which it was dealt with by the judge. Moreover, the death of the plaintiff following the *litis contestatio* did not necessarily result in the extinction of his claim. In such a case the relevant action could be transferred to the plaintiff's heirs, even though this would have been impossible before the *litis contestatio* because of the personal nature of the relevant claim. A further consequence of the *litis contestatio* was that actions which could be brought only within certain time limits (*actiones temporales*) became *actiones perpetuae*, i.e. actions that could be brought without limit of time. The rule that events taking place after the *litis contestatio* did not affect the nature of the original claims was subject to certain exceptions. It was recognised, for example, that if the object in dispute was accidentally destroyed or damaged the defendant was no longer liable. Moreover, with respect to actions relating to property (*actiones in rem*), it was recognised that the defendant who lost the case had to return, together with the property claimed, the fruits he collected, or should have collected from the property, to the plaintiff.[117]

After the *litis contestatio* the plaintiff's claim was said to have been 'consumed' (*consumitur*), and this meant that the plaintiff could not bring an action against the defendant again for the same claim. At this point, however, one should consider the distinction the Romans drew between *iudicia legitima* and *iudicia imperio continentia*.[118] The term *iudicia legitima* was used to denote trials which took place within the city of Rome, or within a mile from it, before one judge (*iudex unus*), and in which both parties were Roman citizens.[119] A trial in which any one of these elements was missing was called *iudicium imperio continens*.[120] By contrast with the *iudicia legitima*, which were regulated by statutory law, the *iudicia imperio continentia* depended upon the *imperium* of a jurisdictional magistrate. Now, with respect to *actiones in personam* based on the *ius civile* (*actiones in ius conceptae*), which were tried by a *iudicium legitimum*, the plaintiff was automatically precluded from

---

116 See *lex Rubria*, XX, 15-17 in Bruns, *Fontes* I, p. 98.

117 On the effects of the litis contestatio see H. J. Wolff, Die litis contestatio im römischen Zivilprocess, Karlsruhe 1968. And see M. Kaser, Das römische Zivilprozessrecht, Munich 1996, 285 ff, 295 ff; R. Monier, Manuel élémentaire de droit romain, Aalen 1977, 163-5.

118 G. 4. 103.

119 G. 4. 104 and 109.

120 G. 4. 105.

bringing the same action twice against the defendant.[121] On the other hand, with respect to *actiones in rem, actiones in personam* based on the *ius praetorium, actiones in factum* and other actions tried by a *iudicium imperio continens* the bringing of the same action twice was precluded only if the defendant raised an exception based on the fact that the case has already been tried and decided upon (*exceptio rei iudicatae*); or on the fact that in the first trial a decision had not been rendered but the point of *litis contestatio* had been reached (*exceptio rei in iudicium deductae*).[122] The relevant exception was inserted, upon the defendant's request, in the praetor's *formula*.

Finally, another important implication of the *litis contestatio* was that the plaintiff's claim was substituted for a claim for pecuniary compensation, as the condemnation of the defendant under the formulary system always entailed the payment of a sum of money to the plaintiff. At the same time it was recognised that the plaintiff's claim, now regarded as being based on the *ius civile*, was transferable and indefeasible.[123]

The proceedings *apud iudicem* or *in iudicio*

In the *in iudicio* or *apud iudicem* phase of the proceedings a judge (*iudex unus, iudex privatus*), or a panel of judges, often assisted by persons learned in the law, tried the case with a view to arriving at a verdict either accepting or rejecting the plaintiff's claim as expressed in the *formula* issued by the praetor.[124] This phase of the proceedings was governed by the principle that all the arguments and procedural acts had to be conducted orally before the judge. But the judge did not himself direct the parties as to which questions should be raised. The proceedings were not formally recorded, although private records could be taken by the litigants. The arguments were primarily concerned with facts: the plaintiff sought to prove the facts upon which the validity of his claim depended; the defendant denied the factual basis of his adversary's claim, or accepted it but asserted that the law upon which the claim was based was inapplicable, or that there were good reasons for recognising an exception. Moreover, arguments sometimes focused on the interpretation of the law or the

---

[121] G. 4. 107; 3. 180-81; see also Gaius, *Fragm. Augustodun.* 106 in FIRA II, p. 227 ('*in legitimo iudicio ipso iure actio consumitur*').

[122] G. 3. 181; 4. 106 and 107.

[123] The Roman jurists referred to this as 'renewal' (*novatio*) of the relevant action. See *Fragm. Vat.* 263 in FIRA II, pp. 519-20; D. 46. 2. 1 pr.

[124] Judges played an important part in the development of private law, as their decisions were often taken into consideration by the praetor in modifying existing *formulae* or in creating new ones.

formula relating to the plaintiff's action. A party could argue, for example, that the law governing the issue should be given a broader meaning than the one usually adopted, or that the purpose of the law was different from that assumed by his adversary.

A litigant could argue his case by himself or through an advocate (*patronus*, *advocatus*),[125] who advised his client before and during the trial and pleaded for him in court.[126] Although in principle any Roman citizen could serve as an advocate, this task was usually performed by senators or members of the equestrian class. The advocates were persons trained in the art of rhetoric which began to be taught in Rome from the second century BC. An important aspect of the relevant instruction was devoted to the selection of the arguments which had to be employed in dealing with a particular legal question, and the courts provided an excellent stage for the display of a person's skills as an orator and powers of persuasion. Forensic speaking reached its highest point of development during the later republican age when success at the law courts had become a key which opened the door to a successful political career.[127] Often advocates referred to previous cases taken to lend support to their arguments. And as the focus of their arguments was often the interpretation of the praetorian *formula* and the question of whether the remedy it granted was justifiable in the circumstances, their views were often taken into account by the praetor in modifying existing *formulae* or in developing new ones. In this way the advocates played a part in the development of the *ius praetorium*.

On the appointed day both the plaintiff and the defendant appeared before the judge who, before the trial commenced, swore that his judgement on the case would be impartial. The parties then stated their claims[128] and evidence was adduced, both oral and documentary.[129] Witnesses (*testes*) were required to take an oath before giving their testimony. If a witness was unable to appear in person, his testimony could be read in court after it was taken down in writing (*testimonia per tabellam*

---

[125] Consider, e.g., Cicero, *pro Cluent.* 40; *pro Sull.* 29.

[126] During the Republic advocates did not receive any remuneration for their services, although sometimes they were given gifts or small symbolic payments.

[127] See G. Kennedy, *The Art of Rhetoric in the Roman World* (300 BC-AD 300), Princeton 1972; J. A. Crook, *Legal Advocacy in the Roman World*, London 1995, M. C. Alexander, *Forensic Advocacy in the Late Roman Republic*, Toronto 1977; J. M. Kelly, *Roman Litigation*, Oxford 1956; *Studies in the Civil Judicature of the Roman Republic*, Oxford 1976 .

[128] It is not clear if this practice was followed in the context of the formulary procedure, however.

[129] By contrast with the *in iure* phase of the proceedings, the proceedings *in iudicio* could go ahead even in the absence (*contumacia*) of one of the parties.

dare). The written evidence included letters (*epistolae*), memoranda (*libelli*), written declarations (*cautiones*), private account books (*tabulae accepti et expensi*), wills and other documents. When these documents were produced they were sealed up in the presence of witnesses (*obsignatores*) and were delivered to the judge who opened them in court. The evidence included, moreover, the results of inspections carried out by experts and state officials. A confession before the judge (*confessio in iudicio*) was also relevant as evidence, although its value was determined by the judge at his discretion.[130] In the absence of direct evidence, the court sometimes relied upon presumptions (*praesumptiones*) when the existence of certain facts could be logically inferred from other facts already established.[131] These presumptions were defeasible, however, and could be refuted by further evidence. As a general rule, it fell upon the plaintiff to prove the facts upon which his claim was based, although the judge was not always bound by this rule.

After all the evidence had been presented and the arguments heard the judge pronounced (*pronuntiatio*) his verdict (*sententia*), usually in the presence of the parties or their representatives.[132] When deciding on a case a judge was often assisted by a panel of experts (*consilium*) whose opinions, however, were not binding on him. If the judge thought that the case remained unresolved (*sibi non liquere*), he could defer issuing a decision until further evidence was obtained.[133] According to the Law of the Twelve Tables, the trial had to be concluded within one day.[134] It is unlikely, however, that this rule applied under the formulary system. The *lex Iulia iudiciorum privatorum* (17 BC) provided that, with respect to the *iudicia legitima*, the trial expired eighteen months after the *litis contestatio*, if no decision had in the meantime been reached.[135] On the other hand, with respect to the *iudicia imperio continentia*, a trial came to an end with the

---

[130] See Cicero, *pro Caec.* 9. 24.

[131] For example, the child of a married woman was presumed to be a legitimate child. See D. 1. 6. 6. (Ulpianus).

[132] D. 42. 1. 47. pr. (Paulus). Under the Law of the Twelve Tables, if one of the parties was absent, the judge had to wait until noon before he pronounced his verdict. The relevant provision probably continued to apply in the context of the formulary procedure. There is some uncertainty, however, as to whether this provision pertained to the decision of the praetor in the *in iure phase* of the proceedings, or that of the judge in the *apud iudicem* phase of the proceedings.

[133] In such a case the judge was required to swear that, in the light of the available evidence, he was unable to reach a decision. See D. 4. 8. 13. 4. (Ulpianus); D. 42. 1. 36. (Paulus); Aulus Gellius, *N. A.* 14. 2. 25; Cicero, *pro Caec.* 4.

[134] XII T. I 7-9.

[135] G. 4. 104.

expiry of the *imperium* of the jurisdictional magistrate who had instituted the proceedings.[136]

As has been noted, in deciding a case the judge was bound by the conditions of the *formula* upon which the relevant lawsuit was based. If the plaintiff had claimed that the defendant owed him something, the judge's verdict had to include a condemnation (*condemnatio*) or, if the claim proved unfounded, an acquittal (*absolutio*). In the former case the defendant had to pay the plaintiff a certain sum of money (*condemnatio pecuniaria*), often determined by the judge in the light of considerations of good faith and equity. When the judge decided on a divisory action (*actio communi dividundo*), the verdict had to include an adjudgment (*adiudicatio*). In some cases the *adiudicatio* could be accompanied by a *condemnatio pecuniaria*, if that was necessary for the fair division of the common property. A plaintiff who in the *intentio* (i.e. the part of the *formula* containing his claim) had asked for more than he was entitled (*plus petere*) would lose his case.[137] If he had asked for less (*minus petere*) he was only entitled to what he had asked for. In the latter case the plaintiff could sue again for the remainder of the debt. The relevant action could not be granted by the same praetor, however, as it could be blocked by an *exceptio litis dividuae*.[138] In general, the judge's decision generated an obligation for the party who lost the case to execute it (*iudicatum facere oportere*).[139] Moreover, a decision by which an object was adjudged to one of the parties or, in a divisory action, to more than one persons (*adiudicatio*), created new ownership rights on the property or share adjudged to the party or parties concerned. Finally, certain decisions entailed for the party condemned a diminution of his estimation among his fellow-citizens (*infamia*). This occurred when the person condemned had

---

[136] G. 4. 105.

[137] According to Gaius, a plaintiff might have asked more than he was entitled in relation to the object (*re*), the time (*tempore*), the place (*loco*) and the cause (*causa*) of the relevant action. In a *pluris petitio re* the plaintiff claimed a bigger amount than was owed to him; in a *pluris petitio tempore* he asked for payment of a debt before the payment was actually due; in a *pluris petitio loco* he demanded that payment be made to him at a place different from that originally agreed; and in a *pluris petitio causa* he claimed a certain thing although the defendant was entitled to choose between two or more things. In all the above cases the plaintiff lost his case definitely. See G. 4. 53; *Inst.* 4. 6. 33. In some exceptional cases the praetor could grant the plaintiff a *restitutio in integrum*, a special remedy aimed at reinstating the parties in their former legal position. See Girard, *Textes* I, p. 285.

[138] G. 4. 56 and 122.

[139] G. 3. 180.

committed an act involving personal turpitude, such as, for example, theft (*furtum*) or wilful fraud (*dolus malus*).[140]

During the republican period the judge's decision was final and therefore not subject to appeal. The right of appeal (*appellatio*) against decisions arrived at through the *per formulam* procedure was introduced by Emperor Augustus in the early years of the Empire.[141] This right was first introduced in connection with the *extra ordinem* procedure[142] and was associated with the power of the emperor to block by veto (*intercessio*) official acts of other magistrates. Appeals were addressed to the emperor and were decided either by the emperor himself or, more often, by state officials acting in his name.[143] The purpose of an appeal was either the reversal of a decision or merely its modification. Furthermore, a decision could be declared invalid if some important condition relating to the legality of the relevant process had not been met as, for example, where the decision had been issued by a judge who did not meet the prescribed age. The validity of a decision could be challenged by the party who lost the case, but if his challenge was rejected he had to pay double the amount specified in the original judgement (*revocatio in duplum*).[144]

The execution of judicial decisions under the formulary system

As we saw in chapter 4, with respect to personal actions (*actiones in personam*), the execution of a decision under the *legis actio* procedure often involved the use of physical force by the party who won the case against the defendant (*manus iniectio iudicati*). Although this form of execution did not disappear after the introduction of the formulary system, it was gradually replaced by forms of execution aimed at the property rather than the person of the party condemned. Thus, the *manus iniectio* was superseded by the *actio iudicati*, brought by the plaintiff against the defendant who failed to pay the debt within thirty days from his condemnation by the judge (in the *in iudicio* phase) or his acknowledgment of the debt before the praetor (in the *in iure* phase). The *actio iudicati* was instituted in the same way as any other action: it was raised before the

---

140 Among the legal consequences of a person's being declared an *infamis* was that he became incapable of holding public office (*turpi iudicio damnati omni honore ac dignitate privantur*). See Cicero, *pro Cluent.* 42; *pro Sull.* 31. 32.

141 Suetonius, *div. Aug.* 33. 3.

142 The new form of civil procedure that was developed during the early Empire See chapter 8 below.

143 Appeals by Roman citizens were usually heard by the *praetor urbanus*; those raised by provincials were heard by ex-consuls. See Suetonius, *div. Aug.* 33. 3.

144 See, Girard, *Textes* I, p. 345.

praetor (*in iure*) and, if the defendant contested the validity of the judicial decision by which he had been condemned or claimed that he had already paid his debt, the case was referred to a private judge for trial (*apud iudicem*). Before the trial the defendant had to provide security that, if he lost the case, the debt would be paid (*satisdatio iudicatum solvi*).[145] But if the defendant against whom an *actio iudicati* was brought lost his case, he was condemned to pay double the amount specified in the previous judgement.

Now, if the defendant was condemned at a trial for an *actio iudicati* or if, before the trial ended, he admitted his debt, the execution of the judge's decision could be carried out against the defendant's person or his property. In the former case the execution was conducted in the same way as in the *legis actio* procedure: the praetor issued an order (*decretum*) by which the plaintiff was authorised to seize and imprison the defendant (*duci iubere*).[146] This form of execution was governed by the provisions of the Law of the Twelve Tables relating to the *manus iniectio iudicati*, [147] although the provisions under which a creditor was permitted to kill his debtor or to sell him as a slave no longer applied. An execution against the debtor's property involved the selling of the property or, under certain conditions, its surrender by the debtor to his creditor or creditors. In the former case the debtor's property was sold as a whole. This method of execution, known as *venditio bonorum*, was introduced before 118 BC by the praetor Publius Rutilius,[148] and was probably modelled on a similar procedure followed by the quaestors in enforcing the payment of debts to the public treasury (*aerarium*).

In the procedure of the *venditio bonorum* the praetor, or the provincial governor, upon the creditor's request, issued an order (*decretum*) authorising the creditor to enter into possession of the debtor's property (*missio in bona*). Moreover the praetor appointed a *curator bonorum*, i.e. the person by whom the property of the insolvent debtor was to be administered. By appointing a *curator bonorum* the praetor sought to preserve the property by preventing the debtor from disposing of it before the execution procedure was completed (*rei servandae causa*). At the same time it was announced publicly that the property of the insolvent debtor was to be sold (*proscriptio*). Creditors had to come forward and announce their claims within thirty days from this announcement.[149] After the thirty-

---

145 G. 4. 25.

146 See Ulpianus, *disp*. 3. 7., in Girard, *Textes* I, p. 454; also in FIRA II, p. 310.

147 Discussed in chapter 4.

148 G. 4. 35.

149 Or within fifteen days in the case the debtor died. See G. 3. 78-79.

day period had passed the debtor was pronounced *infamis* (dishonest). At the same time the praetor invited the creditors to nominate from among themselves a receiver (*magister bonorum*) who would organise the sale of the debtor's property. The property was then sold at a public auction conducted by the *magister bonorum* under the supervision of the praetor.[150] The property was made over to the highest bidder (*bonorum emptor*) who, however, did not acquire full ownership before the completion of the period of usucaption (*usucapio*).[151] The buyer of the property could be granted an *interdictum possessorium* [152] for entering into possession of the property, as well as other actions for the payment to him of debts originally due to the insolvent debtor (*actio Rutiliana, actio Serviana*).[153] It should be added here that the insolvent debtor whose property was sold through a *venditio bonorum* was not released from his obligations towards his creditors. A year after the *venditio bonorum* the creditors could initiate a new sale of any property which the debtor had in the meantime acquired, if their claims were not fully covered by the proceeds of the earlier sale. The debtor, however, could in some cases rely on a *beneficium competentiae*, a special remedy that entitled the debtor to pay his creditors only as far as his means permitted.

Because of the grave consequences which a *venditio bonorum* entailed for the debtor, certain categories of persons could not be subjected to it. These included members of the senatorial class and persons who, in the eyes of the law, were incapable of regulating their own affairs, provided that they had no guardian. If a person belonging to one of these categories became insolvent his property was placed by the praetor under the control of an administrator (*curator distrahendorum bonorum gratia*).[154] The latter conducted the sale of the insolvent person's property by individual items (not as a whole) until enough money was obtained to satisfy the creditor's claims. This method of execution, termed *bonorum distractio*, did not result in *infamia* for the insolvent person. Finally, under a *lex Iulia*, introduced in the time of Augustus, it was recognised that a person who became insolvent without his fault could seek permission by the praetor or the provincial governor to surrender the whole of his property to his creditors (*cessio bonorum*) in order to avoid the consequences (especially the *infamia*) which an execution by a *venditio*

---

[150] G. 3. 79.

[151] According to the Law of the Twelve Tables this was one year for moveable property and two years for houses or lands. See G. 3. 80.

[152] G. 4. 145.

[153] G. 4. 35.

[154] D. 27. 10. 5. (Gaius).

bonorum entailed.[155] If the debtor's request was accepted, he was entitled to a *beneficium competentiae*, i.e., he was required to pay only as much as his means permitted and without being deprived of the necessary means of subsistence.[156] The property (or part thereof) surrendered was sold at a public auction and the proceeds were divided among the creditors.

Other forms of praetorian remedies

Besides actions and exceptions, the praetor, by virtue of his *imperium*, could issue other legal remedies aimed at protecting certain recognised interests. These remedies fell into one of four categories: *stipulationes praetoriae*, *missiones in possessionem*, *restitutiones in integrum* and *interdicta*.

Stipulationes praetoriae

In certain cases the praetor could order one or both litigants to assume by *stipulatio* (a verbal solemn promise) the obligation to do or refrain from doing something. The giving of such a promise was imposed on a litigant for the purpose of ensuring his cooperation during the proceedings, or of ascertaining that he would abide by the judge's decision.[157] Moreover, a praetorian *stipulatio* could be ordered at the request (*postulatio*) of a person for the purpose of guaranteeing that an action would be made available to that person in certain circumstances.[158] In general, the praetorian stipulations were divided into *stipulationes iudiciales*, i.e. stipulations aimed at ensuring the normal progress of a trial,[159] *stipulationes cautionales*, i.e. stipulations by which a person was promised an action,[160] and *stipulationes communes*, i.e. stipulations relating to both the above purposes.[161] In all these cases an ordinary action could be brought against the party who failed to fulfil the promise he gave.

---

155 G. 3. 78.

156 D. 42. 3. 4 pr (Ulpianus).

157 G. 4. 91.

158 For example, a guardian (*curator*) could be to promise that his administration of the property of the person under his protection will not diminish the property's value. See G. 1. 199.

159 D. 46. 5. 1. (Ulpianus).

160 D. 46. 5. 2. (Ulpianus).

161 D. 46. 5. 3. (Ulpianus). On the *stipulationes praetoriae* see M. Kaser, *Das römische Zivilprozessrecht*, Munich 1996, 429 ff; A. Guarino, *Diritto privato romano*, Naples 2001, 238-9; R. Monier, *Manuel élémentaire de droit romain*, Aalen 1977, 186 ff.

Moreover, the praetor could order a *missio in possessionem* against the party upon whom a *stipulatio* was imposed if he refused to abide by the praetor's order.

Missiones in possessionem

A *missio in possessionem* was an order by which the praetor granted authority to the claimant to take temporary possession of his adversary's property (in whole or in a part).[162] Such an order could be issued for the purpose of ensuring the normal progress of judicial proceedings, or of securing a creditor's claim over his debtor's property, or of inducing a debtor to provide security, if he refused to do so voluntarily. In most cases the claimant was given simple custody of the property in order to ensure that the property would remain intact and be used exclusively for the satisfaction of the creditors' claims. In certain cases, however, the claimant was given real possession of the property, including the right to dispose of it. An order by which a claimant was given possession of the entire property was referred to as *missio in bona*.

Restitutiones in integrum

A *restitutio in integrum* was a special remedy granted by the praetor at the request of a person who had suffered an unjust loss as a result of the strict application of the law and was aimed at reinstating the parties in their former legal position.[163] In the context of a trial, a *restitutio in integrum* returned the parties to the legal position which they had prior to the *litis contestatio*. This remedy was granted by a praetorian decree (*decretum*) after an examination by the praetor of the circumstances that gave rise to the claimant's request (*causa cognita*). For example, under the *lex Plaetoria de minoribus* (192-1 BC), a *restitutio in integrum* could be granted to a person under twenty-five years of age (*minor*) who had entered into a transaction under conditions detrimental to his own interests. The remedy reversed the legal effects of such a transaction, despite the fact that the transaction remained valid under the *ius civile*. The circumstances in which the praetor was prepared to grant a *restitutio in integrum* were set out in the *edictum perpetuum*.

---

[162] See Kaser, ibid, 427 ff; Guarino, ibid, 239-40.
[163] See Kaser, ibid, 421 ff; Guarino, ibid, 237-8.

Interdicta

The *interdicta* were summary orders (*decreta*) by which the praetor prohibited a person from doing or continuing to do something, or ordered him to carry out certain act.[164] An *interdictum* was issued at the request of the person or persons concerned, following an examination by the praetor of the circumstances of the case, and was usually based upon a *formula* included in the praetorian edict. The praetor could issue such an order for the purpose of protecting a public interest,[165] an interest of a religious nature,[166] or a private interest.[167] For example, the praetor could issue an *interdictum* forbidding a person to disturb the possession of property which the claimant had acquired in a lawful manner. Moreover, a person could request an *interdictum* when some wrong had been done or was likely to be done to him, in order to redress or prevent that wrong at the earliest possible time, without having to go through the ordinary judicial proceedings. One should note, however, that an *interdictum* was effective only when the person against whom it was issued agreed to comply with the relevant order. If he did not, the claimant could resort to the normal trial procedure in order to confirm or defend his right.[168]

In general, *interdicta* were divided into *restitutoria*, *exhibitoria* and *prohibitoria*.[169] The *interdicta restitutoria* were aimed at the restoration (*restitutas*) of a legal situation that had been disrupted by a person's actions. For example, the actual possessor of a property who had been forcibly ejected from it could apply for an *interdictum* ordering the return of possession to him until any questions as to the rights of the parties concerned had been answered by a court of law. By an *interdictum exhibitorium* the praetor ordered the defendant to produce (*exhibeas*) a person (e.g. a child) or a thing (e.g. a testament) held by him in a court of law. However, no obligation was imposed upon the defendant at this stage to return the person or thing to the claimant. By an *interdictum prohibitorium* a defendant was prohibited from doing something, e.g. from hindering the claimant in the exercise of a property right. For instance, if the value of a house was likely to be substantially diminished by some act

---

[164] G. 4. 139-140. *Inst.* 4. 15. pr.

[165] Such an order was, e.g., the *interdictum de locis publicis*. See D. 43. 8. 1. (Paulus).

[166] E.g., the *interdictum ne quid in loco sacro fiat*. See D. 43. 6. 1. (Ulpianus).

[167] E.g., the *interdictum de arboribus caedendis*. See D. 43. 27. 1. pr. and 7. (Ulpianus).

[168] On the *interdicta* see M. Kaser, *Das römische Zivilprozessrecht*, Munich 1996, 408 ff, 416 ff; A. Guarino, *Diritto privato romano*, Naples 2001, 235-7.

[169] G. 4. 140. 142.

of the person in possession of that house, a person claiming a right over the house could request the issuing of an *interdictum prohibitorium* forbidding such an act. Furthermore, a distinction was drawn between *interdicta simplicia* and *interdicta duplicia*.[170] With respect to the former the relevant order was addressed to one of the parties to a dispute. With respect to the latter, either party was at the same time defendant and plaintiff. In this category belonged, for example, the *interdicta uti possidetis* and *utrubi*, concerned with the maintenance of an existing possessory situation.[171]

As was noted above, an *interdictum* could be issued in order to prevent any damage from being suffered by either of the parties in a suit until their respective claims were decided by a court of law (the *interdictum* did not in itself determine whose claim was to prevail). In some cases, however, an application for an *interdictum* resulted in a preliminary lawsuit, as the praetor could refuse granting the claimant's request until he heard the claim of his adversary as well. After an *interdictum* had been issued, questions might arise as to whether the praetor's order had been duly carried out and this could result in a separate lawsuit. If the person to whom the *interdictum* was addressed did not comply with it, the legal proceedings that followed could take one of two forms: *per sponsionem* and *per formulam arbitrariam*. The *per sponsionem* procedure was the only one followed in relation to *interdicta prohibitoria*, whether *simplicia* or *duplicia*. With respect to the *interdicta restitutoria* and *exhibitoria*, either the *per sponsionem* or the *per formulam arbitrariam* procedure could be followed.[172] Both forms of procedure began with the summoning by the claimant of the person to whom the *interdictum* had been addressed to appear before the praetor.

Proceedings per sponsionem

When both parties appeared before the praetor, the party on whose initiative the *interdictum* had been issued called upon his adversary to undertake by *sponsio*[173] that he was going to pay him a sum of money as a penalty (*poena*) if, in the trial that was to follow, he was condemned by the judge. The party against whom the *interdictum* had been issued could also ask the claimant to promise, by *restipulatio*, that he was going to pay him the same amount of money if it was established that his non-compliance

---

170 G. 4. 156-160; *Inst.* 4. 15. 7.

171 G. 4. 139. 143.

172 G. 4. 141.

173 This was a verbal promise expressed in the form of a question and answer using the solemn verb *spondere* (*spondesne*? – *spondeo*: do you solemnly promise? – I do solemnly promise). See G. 4. 93.

with the *interdictum* was legally justified. In a case involving an *interdictum duplex* each party had to promise to pay a penalty if condemned. The amount of money specified was forfeited by the party who lost the case. In a trial regarding an *interdictum* the judge had to decide, as a preliminary matter, whether the *interdictum* had been issued according to law. With respect to the *interdicta prohibitoria*, the party on whose initiative the *interdictum* had been issued, if he won in the trial regarding the *sponsiones*, was granted a special action, known as *iudicium secutorium* or *cascellianum*.[174] The aim of this action was to compel the party against whom the *interdictum* had been issued to carry out the relevant order. With respect to the *interdicta restitutoria* and *exhibitoria*, the relevant action was termed *iudicium de re restituenda vel exhibenda*.[175]

The procedure per formulam arbitrariam

In relation to the *interdicta restitutoria* and *exhibitoria* the party against whom an *interdictum* had been issued was entitled, until the completion of the proceedings *in iure*, to ask for the appointment of an arbitrator (*arbiter*).[176] If the defendant lost the case, the *arbiter* called upon him to return or produce the person or thing under dispute. If the defendant did so, he was absolved.[177] But if he refused to comply, he was condemned to pay a sum of money equal to the value of the object he had been ordered to return or produce.[178]

Criminal Law and Procedure

Introductory

As we saw in chapter 4, in the early republican period the prosecution and punishment of criminal offences fell within the jurisdiction of the magistrates and the *comitia*. The term *coercitio* referred to the magistrates' power of enforcing obedience to their orders and of punishing offences by certain coercive or punitive measures. Acts of magisterial *coercitio* were preceded by no formal procedure and the punishments imposed were determined by the magistrates at their discretion. However, the magistrates'

---

174 G. 4. 169.
175 G. 4. 165.
176 G. 4. 164-165.
177 Hence this procedure was referred to as one 'without penalty or risk': '*sine poena, sine periculo*'. See G. 4. 141.
178 G. 4. 163.

power to punish was subject to limitations imposed by custom and public opinion. Moreover, with respect to serious offences, the magistrates' power to punish was limited by various legislative enactments establishing the right of citizens to submit themselves to the judgement of the *comitia* (*provocatio ad populum, ius provocationis*). When a citizen could appeal to the *comitia* against a sentence imposed upon him by a magistrate, the original sentence would always be appealed against and in time it became a mere preliminary to the real trial before the *comitia*. However, as only a magistrate had the right of bringing a charge against a citizen (as well as of summoning the assembly), it was necessary for an accuser to appeal to a magistrate in order that a formal accusation might be lodged against a person suspected of a crime. By the time of the Punic Wars we find that the magistrates still possessed the right to inflict minor penalties on their own responsibility, but that charges involving the penalty of death or loss of citizenship were tried in the *comitia centuriata*, and other charges of a relatively serious nature in the *comitia tributa*. Besides the *comitia*, the senate sometimes exercised the functions of criminal jurisdiction, although it could not inflict punishment on any citizen without the intervention of a magistrate, or the right of an appeal to the *comitia*. From the second century BC special tribunals (*quaestiones extraordinariae*) began to be set up under the authority of the people or the senate to deal with certain criminal offences. These included various offences relating to abuse of power or dereliction of duty by state officials and other offences of a largely political nature. In all these cases consuls or praetors were assigned to conduct the investigation and preside over the court proceedings.

However, in the changed social and political conditions of the later Republic the existing system of criminal justice was no longer adequate. The concentration of large numbers of impoverished citizens in Rome during this period was accompanied by a rapid increase in crime, especially violent crime. As there was no regular police force in Rome, the detection of criminals was usually left to the injured parties or common informers, and this made the prosecution of offenders very difficult. Moreover, the business of calling together the *comitia* for the purpose of conducting a criminal investigation was cumbersome and time-consuming and, as the rules governing the trial process were not adequately defined, the relevant procedure often resulted in inconsistent verdicts. At the same time, as the number of offences, especially those of a political nature, increased, the practice of setting up extraordinary tribunals became increasingly inconvenient and inefficient.[179] In response to these problems two measures were introduced: first, besides the *praetor urbanus*, responsibility for the prosecution and punishment of offences against public order, especially those committed by slaves, foreigners and citizens from the lower classes of society, was assigned to the *tresviri capitales*, low-ranking magistrates elected by the *comitia tributa*;[180] secondly, permanent courts of justice, the *quaestiones perpetuae*, began to be established for the investigation and punishment of offences of a serious nature, especially offences threatening the security of the state. It was only with the establishment of these permanent courts that a closer regulation of criminal procedure was effected.[181]

The emergence of the permanent court system

The first permanent court in Rome was introduced as a response to the need of revising the method of prosecuting the offence of extortion (*crimen repetundarum*) – an offence frequently committed by provincial magistrates against the people of their provinces. In 149 BC, under the *lex Calpurnia*, a law proposed by the tribune L. Calpurnius Piso, the task of investigating charges of extortion was assigned to a permanent tribunal (*quaestio de repetundis*) made up exclusively of members of the senatorial class.[182] The jurors (*iudices*) were selected by a designated magistrate from a standing list (*album*) and the issue was determined by a majority vote. The procedure that applied was that of the *legis actio sacramento*[183] followed in civil suits, and the penalty imposed was simple restitution.[184]

---

179 Those who suffered most as a result of the inadequacy of the existing system of criminal justice were the foreigners and the members of allied communities in Italy (*socii*). See e.g. the case of M. Popilius Laenas in Livy 42. 7-10. 21-22.

180 See Cicero, *de legibus* 3. 6; Sall., *Cat.* 55; Aulus Gellius, *N. A.* 3. 3. 15; Livy 39. 14. 10; Pliny, *N. H.* 21. 8; Val. Max. 5. 4. 7; 6. 1. 10; 8. 4. 2; Varro 50. 50. 5. 81; D. 1. 2. 2. 30. And see W. Kunkel, *An Introduction to Roman Legal and Constitutional History*, 2nd edn, Oxford 1973, 64 ff.

181 In the provinces criminal justice was administered through a system of courts similar to those operating in Rome.

182 See on this Cicero, *Brut.* 27. 106; *de off.* 2. 21. 75; II *in Verr.* 3. 84. 195; 4. 25. 56.

183 Discussed in chapter 4.

184 In later years the person found guilty of extortion was condemned to pay twice the value of the illegally appropriated property; other penalties that could be imposed included the expulsion of the offender from the senate and his being declared an *infamis*. On the nature of the *quaestio de repetundis* see W. Kunkel, *Kleine Schriften*, Weimar 1974, 49-50; A. H. M. Jones, *The Criminal Courts of the Roman Republic and Principate*, Oxford 1972, 48-9; H. F. Jolowicz and B.

As in private actions, proceedings were initiated by the injured party and the relevant claim pertained to the return of the property by the person by whom it had been illegally appropriated (*pecuniae repetere*). No appeal from this court to the *comitia* was allowed, nor could its decisions be suspended by tribunician veto.

As the *quaestio de repetundis* was controlled by the senate, juries often decided in favour of members of the senatorial nobility brought before them for investigation. A reorganisation of the court took place during the tribuneship of Gaius Gracchus with the passing, in 123 or 122 BC, of the *lex Acilia de repetundis*, introduced by Gracchus's colleague M. Acilius Glabrio. Under this enactment the senatorial juries were abolished and the right of serving as jurors in the court of the *repetundae* was transferred from the senate to the equestrian class. From that time it became the normal practice that the juries of this court were drawn by the *praetor peregrinus* from an album of 450 jurors who had not held any magistracy up to quaestor or tribune of the plebs and who were not members of senatorial families.[185] As was noted in chapter 5, as a result of this and other measures introduced by Gracchus, the equestrian class began to play an important role in Roman political life. But the opening up of the court system to the *equites*, at the expense of the senate, did not eliminate the influence of factional politics on the administration of justice. It simply allowed a class whose political role was largely neglected in the past to begin to play a part in what was until then regarded as an 'in-house' affair.

The *quaestio de repetundis*, Rome's first standing court, provided the model for the creation of other permanent courts in the years that followed. These courts had the status of *iudicia publica*, i.e. courts operating on the basis of a publicly verifiable procedure. Thus, by the close of the second century BC, four permanent courts had been established: for extortion in the provinces (*de repetundis*), for high treason (*de maiestate*), for electoral corruption (*de ambitu*) and for embezzlement of public funds (*de*

Nicholas, *Historical Introduction to the Study of Roman Law*, 3rd edn, Cambridge 1972, 308; J. S. Richardson, 'The purpose of the lex Calpurnia de repetundis', (1987) 77 *JRS*, 1-12; R. A. Bauman, *Crime and Punishment in Ancient Rome*, London & New York 1996, 22-23; A. M. Riggsby, *Crime and Community in Ciceronian Rome*, Austin 1999, ch. 5; A. Lintott, *Judicial Reform and Land Reform in the Roman Republic*, Cambridge 1992, ch. 2; B. Santalucia, *Diritto e processo penale nell' antica Roma*, Milan 1989, 65 ff; V. Giuffré, *La repressione criminale nell' esperienza romana*, Naples 1998, 42 ff.

185 Velleius, 2. 6. 3; 2. 13. 2; 2. 32. 3; Tacitus, *Ann.* 12. 60; Diod. Sic. 35. 25; Appian., *B.C.* 1. 22. 2; Cicero, I *in Verr.* 51.

peculatu),[186] all manned by jurors drawn from the equestrian class. Each court was created by a separate legislative enactment which also prescribed the relevant offence, the penalties imposed upon those found guilty and the rules of procedure governing its operation (these rules could be modified by subsequent legislation). In general, the permanent courts were governed by rules similar to those governing the extraordinary courts and, like the latter, were regarded as operating under the authority of the people. It should be noted here that the supreme jurisdiction of the *comitia* remained unaffected in principle. The *comitia* could be called together, like before, to hear certain cases or to set up special tribunals for the investigation of offences falling outside the jurisdiction of the existing permanent courts.

An attempt to restore the senatorial class to its former position was made in 106 BC, when the consul Q. Servilius Caepio carried a law (*lex Servilia Caepionis*) altering the composition of the courts to the advantage of the senate.[187] But Caepio's legislation was short-lived, for in c.101 BC Cn. Servilius Glaucia, a tribune of the plebs, passed a law (*lex Servilia Glauciae*) putting the courts back under the exclusive control of the *equites*.[188] Under the same enactment certain changes to the rules governing criminal procedure were introduced, such as the division of the trial, in cases of extortion, into two parts (*comperendinatio*). Another important legislative enactment of the same period was the *lex Appuleia de maiestate*, passed between 103 and 100 BC by L. Appuleius Saturninus, a tribune of the plebs. This law defined the crime of treason (*crimen maiestatis*) and established a permanent court for it composed of a jury drawn from the equestrian class.[189]

As we saw in chapter 5, in the period following the conclusion of the Social War (88 BC) factional political strife intensified. For more than five years Rome was in a state of chaos, the formal rules and procedures of Roman justice were suspended and thousands perished in a bloodbath of political executions carried out without formal charges or trials. A measure

---

186 The crime of *peculatus* was distinguished from the theft of private property, termed *furtum*. The punishment for embezzlement of public funds was normally a fine which usually amounted to four times the value of the stolen property. Similar to *peculatus* was the *sacrilegium*, the theft of sacred objects (*res religiosae*). The latter offence entailed the death penalty, but the culprit was allowed to go into exile before the sentence was pronounced, in which case he became subject to an *aquae et ignis interdictio*.

187 Cicero, *de invent*. 1. 92; Tacitus, *Ann*. 12. 60.

188 Cicero, *pro Scauro* in Asconius 21; *Brut*. 224.

189 Cicero, *de invent*. 2. 17. 18; *de orat*. 2. 48. 199. An extraordinary court entrusted with the investigation of charges of treason had been established by the *lex Mamilia* of 109 BC.

of political stability was attained, although only temporarily, following the rise to power of L. Cornelius Sulla in 83 BC. During his dictatorship Sulla embarked on a series of reforms aimed at strengthening the position of the senate and at re-establishing order by repressing popular discontent. As part of his programme he restored the law-courts to the senate.[190] At the same time he increased the number of senators from three hundred to six hundred by enrolling in the senate friendly equestrians, soldiers and distinguished members of Italian communities.[191] Moreover, he reorganised the administration of justice by remodelling the existing permanent courts and establishing a number of new ones.

Under a *lex Cornelia de repetundis* the court of *repetundae* was retained. Furthermore, the *quaestio de maiestate*, which had been instituted by Saturninus in c. 103 BC, was recognised as the principal court for high treason by the *lex Cornelia de maiestate* of 81 BC. Before the introduction of the latter law the tribunes could still convene the *comitia* to hear charges of treason. Sulla precluded this option by restricting the powers of the tribunes. At the same time he broadened the definition of the *crimen maiestatis* to encompass any act done by a Roman citizen which impaired the safety and dignity of the Roman state. Under this crime came wrongdoings which in earlier times were treated as *perduellio* or *proditio*, such as sedition, unlawful attacks against magistrates, desertion and the like.[192] The *crimen maiestatis* entailed capital punishment, although the person charged with the offence was usually allowed to go into exile before the sentence was pronounced (in such a case he became subject to an *aqua et ignis interdictio*). In the closing years of the first century BC two further statutes on the crime of *maiestas* were enacted, the *lex Iulia maiestatis* of Julius Caesar in 46 BC and the *lex Iulia maiestatis* of Augustus in 8 BC, upon which a number of later imperial laws were based.[193]

Moreover, the court dealing with charges of electoral corruption (*de ambitu*) was retained, although under Sulla's own *lex Cornelia de ambitu*

---

[190] But this arrangement lasted for only about ten years.

[191] Appian, *B. C.* 1. 100; Dionysius 5. 77. See also Cicero, I *in Verr.* 37; Velleius 2. 32; Tacitus, *Ann.* 11. 22.

[192] And see Cicero, *in Pison.* 50. Moreover, under an earlier statute, the *lex Varia* of 92 BC, treason was committed by those who 'by help and advice' (*ope et consilio*) induced an allied state to take up arms against Rome. On the *lex Varia* see Appian, *B.C.* 1. 37; Val. Max. 8. 6. 4; Cicero, *Brut.* 304.

[193] Cicero, *Phil.* 1. 21-3; D. 48. 4; C. 9. 8. And see R. A. Bauman, *The Crimen Maiestatis in the Roman Republic and Augustan Principate*, Johannesburg 1970.

heavier penalties for this crime were introduced.[194] As to homicide, a court for hearing cases of poisoning (*quaestio de veneficis*) seems to have been established before the time of Sulla.[195] A court dealing with cases of assassination (*quaestio de sicariis*) had been introduced as early as 142 BC, but it appears to have operated only as a *quaestio extraordinaria*. Trials for parricide (*parricidium*) were usually held before the *comitia*. All three forms of homicide now came under Sulla's *lex Cornelia de sicariis et veneficis* of 81 BC, which also provided for the punishment of those who attempted to procure the unlawful conviction of a person under this enactment.[196] Moreover, under Sulla's *lex Cornelia de iniuriis* a permanent court was set up to deal with cases of assault and housebreaking.[197] Sulla also established a *quaestio de falsis*, a new permanent court dealing with cases involving forgery of official documents, wills and the counterfeiting of money.[198] Thus, after Sulla's reorganisation of the court system, there were seven standing courts in Rome: for extortion (*repetundae*), treason (*maiestas*), electoral corruption (*ambitus*), murder and poisoning (*de sicariis et veneficis*), embezzlement of public funds (*peculatus*), assault and housebreaking (*de iniuriis*) and fraud (*de falsis*). Besides these courts, a number of other statutory courts were established in later years, such as the *quaestio de vi* for crimes of violence,[199] the *quaestio de plagiariis* for

---

194 A series of laws aimed at the repression of corrupt electoral practices were introduced during the second and first centuries BC, such as the *lex Cornelia Baebia* (181 BC), the *lex Cornelia Fulvia* (159 BC), the *lex Maria* (119 BC), the *lex Acilia Calpurnia* (67 BC), the *lex Tullia* (63 BC), the *lex Licinia* (55 BC) and the *lex Pompeia* (52 BC). The last law on *ambitus* was the *lex Iulia de ambitu* passed by Augustus in 18 BC.

195 In an inscription attributed to C. Claudius Pulcher, consul in 92 BC, reference is made to his office of *iudex quaestionis veneficis*. See H. Dessau, *Inscriptiones Latinae Selectae*, Berlin 1892-1916, 45.

196 Cicero, *pro Cluent*. 148-9. 151. 154; D. 48. 8. 1. (Marcianus); C. 9. 16.

197 These included beating (*pulsare*), striking (*verberare*) and housebreaking (*domum introire*) and other forms of wrongful conduct. *Iniuria* was of course also a delict and the two procedures, the criminal and delictual, operated side by side. See Cicero, *pro Caec*. 12. 35; D. 3. 3. 42. 1. (Paulus); D. 47. 10. 5. pr. (Ulpianus).

198 By the *lex Cornelia testamentaria* or *de falsis*. See Cicero, II *in Verr*. 1. 108; D. 48. 10. 1. (Marcianus).

199 This court was established under the *lex Lutatia de vi* in 78 BC ; this law was supplemented by the *lex Plautia de vi*, passed around 63 BC. There were two kinds of violent crime, the *vis publica* and the *vis privata*. The former covered various forms of seditious conduct that fell outside the scope of the *crimen maiestatis*, as well as the organisation and arming of gangs for the purpose of obstructing the activities of state organs. The punishment for such offences was

kidnapping, treating a free man as a slave and inciting a slave to leave his master,[200] the *quaestio de sodaliciis* for electoral conspiracy,[201] and the *quaestio de adulteriis*, for adultery and the seduction of respectable unmarried women.[202]

As a result of Sulla's reforms criminal offences were defined more clearly and similar wrongdoings were subsumed under general offence categories for purposes of procedural convenience and efficiency. Furthermore, criminal liability was now imposed for certain types of wrongful conduct, such as assault and fraud, traditionally regarded as falling in the sphere of private law. Sulla's reforms furnished the basis for the subsequent development of Roman criminal law and some of the laws he enacted, such as the *lex Cornelia de falsis* and the *lex Cornelia de sicariis et veneficis* were still in force in the time of Justinian.[203]

---

banishment. The *vis privata*, on the other hand, covered acts of violence against individuals and, like theft, it was considered a private offence (*delictum*). The distinction between the two forms of violent crime was confirmed by two laws of Augustus, the *lex Iulia de vi publica* and the *lex Iulia de vi privata*. See D. 48. 6 and 7; C. 9. 12.

200 Created under the *lex Fabia de plagiariis* (of unknown date, probably first century BC). D. 48. 15; C. 9. 20.

201 Created under the *lex Licinia de sodaliciis* of Crassus in 55 BC. See Cicero, *pro Planc*. 36-41; *ad fam*. 8. 2. 1; *ad Att*. 4. 15. 9; Dio Cass. 39. 37. 1.

202 Established under Augustus' *lex Iulia de adulteriis* of 18 BC. The penalty for this offence was the banishment of the adulteress and confiscation of part (one-third) of her property. D. 48. 5; C. 9. 9.

203 On the system of the *quaestiones perpetuae* see in general T. Mommsen, *Römisches Strafrecht*, Leipzig 1899, repr. Darmstadt 1955; E. S. Gruen, *Roman Politics and the Criminal Courts, 149-78 BC*, Cambridge. Mass. 1968; J. A. C. Thomas, 'The development of Roman criminal law', (1963) 79 *LQR*, 224-37; A. H. M. Jones, *The Criminal Courts of the Roman Republic and Principate*, Oxford 1972, ch. 2; H. F. Jolowicz and B. Nicholas, *Historical Introduction to the Study of Roman Law*, Cambridge 1972, ch. 18; B. Santalucia, *Diritto e processo penale nell' antica Roma*, Milan 1989, ch. 5; *Studi di diritto penale romano*, Rome 1994, 185 ff, 205 ff, 238 ff; O. F. Robinson, *The Criminal Law of Ancient Rome*, London 1995, 1-6; R. A. Bauman, *Crime and Punishment in Ancient Rome*, London and New York 1996, 21 ff; W. Kunkel, *Kleine Schriften*, Weimar 1974, 56 ff; M. C. Alexander, *Trials in the Late Roman Republic, 149 BC to 50 BC*, Toronto 1990; V. Giuffrè, *La repressione criminale nell' esperienza romana*, Naples 1998, chapters 3 & 4; A. Burdese, *Manuale di diritto pubblico romano*, 3rd edn, Turin 1987, repr. 1994, 249 ff.

Criminal procedure in the standing courts

As has been noted, each permanent court was established by a separate legislative enactment which also prescribed the rules of procedure governing its operation. These rules were from time to time modified by subsequent legislation. Every case submitted to a standing court was tried before a judicial magistrate, usually a praetor or a *iudex quaestionis* (normally an aedile or ex-aedile),[204] and a panel of jurors (*iudices*) referred to as *consilium*. The magistrate was in charge of the proceedings while the jury's task was to decide on the question of guilt or innocence after hearing the pleadings and considering the evidence. The praetors were assigned to the different courts by lot,[205] after the senate decided which courts should be presided over by a praetor. Usually praetors were assigned to the courts dealing with offences of a political nature, such as extortion, electoral corruption, conspiracy against the state, treason and embezzlement. Aediles were usually assigned, also by lot, to cases involving murder, violence and fraud. The presiding magistrate had to swear that he would abide by the statute by which the court had been established and could be liable to punishment if found guilty of corruption.

After the passing of the *lex Acilia de repetundis* (122 BC), the persons who were to serve as jurors in criminal trials were chosen by the praetor at the beginning of each year.[206] Those included in the annual list of jurors (*album iudicum, iudices selecti*) were persons between the ages of thirty and sixty, living in Rome or the surrounding area, who had not held any magistracy up to the position of quaestor or tribune of the plebs. Senators and their closest relatives were excluded as were those who had been found guilty of offences affecting their status as Roman citizens. The praetor was required to make the list of jurors publicly known and to swear an oath that only the best men had been chosen.[207] As was said earlier, under Sulla jury service was transferred from the *equites* to the senators. The *lex Aurelia* of 70 BC provided that jurors were to be drawn equally

---

[204] After the passing of the *lex Calpurnia* (149 BC), by which the court of*repetundae* was established, the duty of presiding over the relevant proceedings fell upon the *praetor peregrinus*, as most of the claimants were foreigners. But in later years, as the number of cases increased and new standing courts were created, the number of praetors was increased to eight and of these six presided over the courts. Consider on this Cicero, *pro Cluent*. 55. 89. 79. 94. 147. 148; *Brut*. 264; *pro Balbo* 23. 52; *de nat. deorum* 3. 30. 74.

[205] Cicero, I *in Verr*. 8. 21; *pro Mur*. 20. 42.

[206] Under the *lex Acilia* the album consisted of 450 persons, but in later years the number of jurors was increased (probably to 900).

[207] See FIRA I, 7. 11. 12-18.

from senators, *equites* and the *tribuni aerarii* (the latter probably also belonged to the equestrian class). Under the *lex Pompeia*, passed by Pompeius in his second consulship (55 BC), the jurors continued to be chosen from the three groups named in the *lex Aurelia*, but the only richest men within each group were eligible. The *tribuni aerarii* were excluded by a *lex Iulia* of Caesar, passed in 46 BC. Finally, Augustus restored the three classes of the Aurelian law, and added a fourth representing the lower classes of the community.

Prosecutions were initiated by private indictment. Initially only the party directly aggrieved or his closest relatives were entitled to bring an indictment,[208] but in later years almost every citizen of good repute had the right to bring an indictment and conduct a prosecution.[209] However, as accusers were often motivated by the prospect of personal gain, the indictment procedure was often abused and, despite the possibility of a suit of slander against false accusers, some people even made a profession out of accusing rich fellow-citizens. The first step in a criminal prosecution was the *postulatio*, an application on the part of the citizen concerned to the praetor, or the *iudex quaestionis*, in charge of the court dealing with the alleged crime for permission to bring charges.[210] This was an essential preliminary, as it was possible that the applicant was precluded by law from bringing charges against any person, or against the particular person whom he intended to prosecute. If two or more persons applied at the same time for leave to bring an indictment against the same person the question of who was to be given priority was decided by a panel of jurors after the arguments of all the parties seeking permission to prosecute had been considered (*divinatio*). When this was decided the accuser formally and in writing stated the name of the accused and the crime with which he was charged (*nominis et criminis delatio*) in the presence of the accused.[211] The document containing the accusation (*inscriptio*) was then signed by the accuser and by all those willing to support his claim (*subscriptores*). Moreover, the accuser had to take an oath that he did not bring a false accusation out of malice (*calumnia*) or in collusion with the accused (*praevaricatio*).[212] The presiding magistrate then formally accepted the

[208] This seems to have been the rule under the *lex Acilia*.

[209] Women and minors could only bring an indictment when personally harmed. Freedmen and sons could not bring charges against their patrons and parents respectively.

[210] Cicero, *div. in Caec.* 64; *Inst.* 4. 18. 1.

[211] D. 48. 2. 3. pr. (Paulus).

[212] *Calumnia* (*crimen calumniae*) was committed when a person bought charges against another knowing that the latter was innocent. False accusers were liable to severe penalties that entailed infamy and exclusion from public office.

indictment (*nominis receptio*) and, from that moment, the person against whom the charge was brought became technically a defendant (*reus*). This was followed by the fixing of the day on which the trial was to begin, if that was not determined by the law by which the relevant court had been established. The accuser was given a reasonable time to prepare his case (*inquisitio*) – in most cases the minimum seems to have been ten days but in certain cases where evidence had to be gathered from overseas a longer period could be allowed.[213] The accuser might also ask for up to forty-eight witnesses to be summoned by the praetor, although the latter was free to summon as many as he thought fit (*testimonium denuntiare*).[214] The next step was the selection of the jurors who were to hear the charges against the accused and to pass judgement. Under the *lex Acilia* the jury had to be empanelled and the advocates appointed immediately after the *nominis delatio*. But this exposed the jurors to the dangers of intimidation and corruption and for that reason, after the judicial reforms of Sulla, juries were empanelled after the *inquisitio* and shortly before the day on which the trial was to begin. Consisting of several dozen members, in individual cases up to seventy-five, the jury was chosen for each case by lot (*iudicum sortitio*) from the relevant *album iudicum*.[215] After the required number of jurors had been selected in this way both parties were given the opportunity to disallow a certain number of jurors whom they suspected of being biased against them (*iudicum reiectio*).[216] After the *iudicum reiectio* the presiding magistrate replaced the disqualified jurors by drawing more names from the *album iudicum* (*iudicum subsortitio*).[217] After their selection the jurors were sworn in.

During the trial it was the accuser and the accused who dominated the scene, with their advocates and witnesses engaged in what were often very

---

Praevaricatio referred to the collusion between the accuser and the accused in a criminal trial for the purpose of obtaining the latter's acquittal. A person found guilty of *prevaricatio* was severely punished and branded with infamy. See Cicero, *ad fam*. 8. 8. 3.

213 Cicero, *ad Q.F*. 2. 13. 2; *in Vat*., 14.

214 See FIRA I, 7. 11. 30-35.

215 But this was not the only method of selecting jurors in criminal cases. For a closer look at the different methods of appointing *iudices* see A. H. M. Jones, *The Criminal Courts of the Roman Republic and Principate*, Oxford 1972, 66 ff.

216 Roman legal procedure was governed by the principle that a person could not be appointed as a juror without the consent of the parties concerned. The rules governing the *iudicum reiectio* were settled by the *lex Vatinia* of 59 BC. See Cicero, *pro Cluent.* 43; II *in Verr*. 2. 77.

217 Cicero, *pro Cluent*., 33 35; I *in Verr*. 16. 30.

rancorous cross-examinations.[218] The jurors listened in silence and were forbidden to speak to each other, while the presiding magistrate was responsible for the orderly progress of the proceedings. The trial began with the accuser delivering a speech in which he detailed the charges and set out his arguments. The accused's reply then followed. The accused stood in a particularly strong position, as he was entitled to as many as six advocates and was allowed twice the total speaking time allocated to the prosecution. The accuser then introduced his evidence, to be followed by that of the defendant. The evidence could be oral by witnesses (*testes*), documentary, or mixed. Witnesses testified under oath and were examined by their own side and cross-examined by the other. Witnesses for the defence were often invited to speak not only about facts but also about the accused's character.[219] In the category of documentary evidence fell records of various kinds, such as account books (*tabulae accepti et expensi*), letters (*epistolae*), written notices (*libelli*) and, in some cases, the account books of those entrusted with the collection of public revenues (*publicani, tabulae publicanorum*). The prosecuting party was entitled to enforce, if necessary, the production of certain documents. Following their delivery, these materials were sealed up (*obsignatae*) in front of witnesses (*obsignatores*) and handed over to the presiding magistrate who alone could reveal their contents in court. The written evidence also included the statements of witnesses who, for various reasons (ill health, old age, absence from Rome etc.) were unable to appear in court in person,[220] as well as certain public statements relating to the case issued by state organs (*testimonia publica*).

After all the evidence had been presented and the closing speeches delivered the presiding magistrate convened the jury (*mittere iudices in consilium*) and put the question of guilt or innocence of the accused to the vote. In early times the vote was open but, following the enactment of the *lex Cassia* in 137 BC, the outcome of the trial was determined by secret

---

218 If the accuser failed to appear in court on the day of the trial his case was dismissed. The absence of the accused did not stop the proceedings, although, in such a case it was required (under a law of Augustus) that his condemnation be unanimous. See Cassius Dio 54. 3.

219 Witnesses who testified to the good character of the accused were referred toas *laudatores*. Character evidence carried special weight and the absence of *laudatores* was regarded as in itself damning.

220 These statements were taken down in writing (*testimonia per tabellam dare*) in the presence of witnesses (*signatores*) whose signature attested their authenticity.

ballot (*per tabellas*).[221] Each juror was given a small wax covered tablet marked on one side 'A' (*absolvo*) and on the other 'C' (*condemno*). He then erased one or the other and cast the tablet into an urn (*sitella*). Jurors had also the third choice of 'NL' (*not liquet*: not proven) if they were unable to reach a decision.[222] The outcome of the case was determined by the majority of the votes. If there was a majority of 'C's the accused was pronounced guilty by the presiding magistrate; if the 'A's were in the majority, or if there was an equality of votes, he was pronounced not guilty. If the majority of the jurors voted '*non liquet*' the presiding magistrate announced that a more thorough investigation into the case was necessary and fixed a day for a new hearing (*ampliatio*).[223]

The procedure that was followed in trials for extortion (*de rebus repetundis*) was somewhat different from the one described above. After the enactment of the *lex Servilia Glauciae* (c. 101 BC) criminal proceedings in cases of this nature were divided into two distinct parts (*comperendinatio*).[224] In the first part (*actio prima*) the prosecution and the defence presented their cases before the court and witnesses on both sides were called upon to testify. In the second part (*actio secunda*), which began after a day's interval, a second hearing took place during which the parties had the opportunity to comment on the evidence presented and to supply additional information. After the conclusion of this hearing the jury was invited to give their verdict which now took the form of 'guilty' or 'innocent' only (the 'not proven' option was not available in such cases).

The punishments imposed by the standing courts were set down in the statutes governing these courts at different times and followed automatically upon conviction (neither the presiding magistrate nor the jury had any discretion as to the penalty).[225] In general, they were of two kinds: capital punishments and monetary penalties.[226] Although during the later Republic many crimes falling within the jurisdiction of the standing courts were punishable by death (*poena mortis*), this penalty very rarely applied

---

[221] Under a *lex Cornelia* of Sulla the defendant was given the right to choose whether the jury's vote should be open or secret. But this provision appears to have been of limited application. See Cicero, *pro Cluent*. 20. 27.

[222] In such a case jurors probably had to erase both 'A' and 'C' and scratch in the letters 'NL'. Just to erase 'A' and 'C' counted as no vote. See Cicero, *pro Cluent*. 28. 76.

[223] See FIRA I, 7. 11. 46-8.

[224] Cicero, II *in Verr*. 1. 26.

[225] Cicero, *de invent*. 2. 59; *pro Sulla* 63.

[226] The term *poena capitalis* (or *poena capitis*) did not refer only to the death penalty but to any penalty involving the loss of a citizen's *caput*, i.e. his personal freedom or rights as a Roman citizen.

in practice as the accused was usually allowed to leave the city before the sentence was pronounced.[227] In these cases an *aquae et ignis interdictio* was pronounced by the senate or a high magistrate after the culprit's departure. In practice, this entailed banishment accompanied by the loss of citizenship and property.[228] If the person subject to an *aquae et ignis interdictio* returned without permission he was deprived of legal protection and, in theory at least, could be put to death by anyone. If an accused was found guilty of extortion, embezzlement and similar offences the usual penalty was restitution. Sometimes, depending on the statute under which the charge was brought, the culprit could be forced to return double or more the amount of property he had illegally appropriated. The precise amount of compensation was determined by the jury after a verdict of guilty had been returned (*litis aestimatio*). Imprisonment was not recognised as a penalty under the standing court system.[229] Irrespective of the gravity of the punishment imposed, no appeal against a verdict or sentence was possible, although it is likely that tribunician *intercessio* could be raised against the presiding magistrate's actions during the preliminary phase of the proceedings.[230] However, the *comitia* reserved the right to grant pardon to a convicted person by a legislative act.[231]

Concluding note

Although the introduction of the standing court system made for the more efficient administration of the criminal law, the system was not free from problems. Proceedings were expensive and cumbersome and, as cases often had to be heard more than once, trials could drag on for a long time. It is true that (unlike the earlier *iudicia populi*) a jury of less than a hundred members could follow complicated evidence and assess the parties' credibility better than a crowd of thousands. However, as the presiding magistrate did not provide any assistance by directing the jury or by summing up at the end, jurors were often as amenable to emotional pleas as

---

227 The death penalty was probably more often carried out where an accused was found guilty of the murder of his parents (*parricidium*). This penalty was also frequently inflicted on slaves and members of the lower classes who had been condemned for a capital offence by the police court of the *tresviri capitales*.

228 Where the culprit's property was confiscated the accuser was entitled to a share of the property.

229 Condemnation to forced labour became a regular penalty for slaves and members of the lower classes during the Empire. See chapter 8 below.

230 Cicero, *in Vat.* 14. 33.

231 Cicero, *pro Sulla* 22. 63-64; *Phil.* 2. 23. 56; Caesar, *B. C.* 3. 1; Suet., *Caes.* 41; Cassius Dio 43. 27; 45. 47.

the people in the *iudicia populi*. A further problem was that, as laws often overlapped in the offences with which they dealt, a person could find himself charged with the same type of offence twice – especially if the prosecution was politically motivated. From the early years of the Augustan era a new type of legal procedure, known as *cognitio extra ordinem*, became more and more important while the jury courts, although still in existence in the second century AD, gradually faded into the background. Under the new system the private juror disappeared and the guilt or innocence of the accused, as well as the sentence, was determined by the emperor, or by a state official acting as a delegate of the emperor.[232]

---

[232] See chapter 8 below.

7 The Principate

The Coming of the Empire

Augustus and the transformation of the Roman constitution

As we saw in chapter 5, after his victory at Actium (31 BC) and the subjugation of Egypt Octavian became the sole master of Rome. But the Roman world was still in a state of confusion, and it was necessary for him to restore order and set up some form of government which could ensure permanent security. Octavian saw that a return to the republican system of government was out of the question, for that system could no longer meet the organisational needs of the vast empire with its diverse populations and cultures, nor could it guarantee the political stability needed for efficient administration and the defence of the state. At the same time, however, he was aware that an attempt to establish an absolute monarchy would offend republican sensitivities and might lead to further unrest. The main demand of the times was a return to the security which only a fully-functioning system of law could provide. But the whole administration of law was so bound up with the republican regime and its ruling class that security without the upholding of the republican institutions was all but impossible. On the basis of this quite realistic appraisal of the situation Octavian, by masterful manipulations, effected the transformation of the Roman system of government into a system that was republican in form and semblage, but monarchical as far as actual executive power was concerned. The prerogatives of the senate were restored and the right of citizens to participate in the government through their vote in the assemblies was maintained. At the same time Octavian won the support of the powerful equestrian class by allowing them a greater degree of participation in the administration of public affairs. In return, Octavian's special position as the warrantor of the constitutional order was recognised by the senate and the people, and special laws were passed giving him all the essential powers which were important to him.[1] It was through the gradual acquisition of these powers that Octavian came to surpass all other Romans in authority and so he came to be designated as *princeps*, i.e. the first of the Roman

---

1 For an interesting account of the attitude of the Roman upper classes towards Augustus's regime see R. Syme, *The Augustan Aristocracy*, Oxford 1986.

citizens (*princeps civium Romanorum*).[2] Octavian was invested with all the powers and titles which, under the republican constitution, pertained to the highest magistrates of the state. What was new, however, was that these powers were no longer subject to the limitations traditionally imposed on magisterial authority, such as those arising from the principles of collegiality and annuality. Thus, although the prince, like the magistrates, was recognised as part of a constitutional order that defined and legitimised his position, the concentration of so much power in the hands of one man precipitated the decline of the principles by which that order was buttressed and led to the emergence of a regime that was in essence a monarchy dressed in republican forms. The monarchical character of the new system became more apparent under Octavian's successors, but the system was heavily encumbered by its contradictions between facade and reality and it was to be a long time before the naked exercise of imperial power to the fullest extent became possible.

In 27 BC the senate granted Octavian the title '*Augustus*', by which he was henceforth known. This title, which had never been given to a Roman citizen before, had a religious significance and marked out its bearer as one who by divine help brought prosperity to the state (it was derived from the word *augere,* meaning 'to increase'). It is also connected with the word '*auctoritas*', denoting prestige, moral authority and social influence. The term '*potestas*' referred to the legal powers regularly associated with a particular magistracy. Although equal to the other magistrates in terms of *potestas*, Augustus was deemed superior to all in terms of *auctoritas*. Subsequent emperors regarded their *auctoritas* as the ultimate source of their acts in the legislative, judicial and administrative fields (*ex auctoritate nostra*). As was noted above, Octavian also bore the title *princeps*, a term that simply meant 'the first citizen of the state'.[3] This should be distinguished from the title '*princeps senatus*' which Octavian held from 28 BC and which indicated his position as the first member of the senate. Another title of Augustus was that of *imperator*, conferred upon him by the army and the senate and denoting his supreme military command. From this is derived the term emperor, commonly used to describe Augustus and his successors. In 23 BC the senate issued a decree granting Augustus tribunician power (*tribunicia potestas*) for life, despite the fact that he was precluded from formally holding the office of tribune

---

2 From the word *princeps* arose the term 'principate', a term by which the new system of government became known.

3 The title *princeps*, however, was not included among the titles of the emperors in official records.

because he was a descendant of a patrician clan (the *gens Iulia*).[4] Thus, although he enjoyed personal inviolability (*sacrosanctitas*) and could veto acts of other magistrates, as he was not a tribune his own acts were not subject to tribunician veto (*intercessio*). By virtue of his tribunician power Augustus could convene the senate (*ius agendi cum senatu*) and the assemblies of the people (*ius agendi cum populo*) and propose laws to them. One of Augustus's most important powers was the proconsular power (*imperium proconsulare*) over the frontier provinces, conferred upon him for life by vote of the senate in 23 BC.[5] The provinces placed under him (*provinciae imperatoriae*), Spain, Gaul and Syria, were those with the largest contingents of the Roman army, and that gave him practical control over military matters and foreign relations. Augustus administered these provinces through representatives (*legati Augusti pro praetore*) appointed by him for an indefinite period. These were answerable to him only (not to the senate) and could be removed at his discretion. The *imperium proconsulare* of the prince differed in some important respects from that of the ordinary and extraordinary proconsuls appointed under the Republic: a) it was universal, extending without restriction over all parts of the empire (hence its description as *imperium proconsulare infinitum*); b) it was not limited in time but perpetual, requiring no renewal; c) it remained in force both within and outside the city of Rome (*pomerium*). The proconsular power of the prince was referred to as *imperium proconsulare maius* to indicate its superiority over the ordinary *imperium* of the proconsuls who governed the senatorial provinces. In 19 BC Augustus received the consular power (*imperium consulare*, *consularis potestas*) for life, without, however, formally assuming the office of consul.[6] In 29, 19 and 12 BC he was vested with censorial powers on occasion of forthcoming *lectiones senatus*, and in 22 BC he was entrusted with the *cura annonae*, whereby he became responsible for the provisioning of Rome with foodstuffs and the regulation of prices. From 12 BC, as holder of the position of *pontifex maximus*, he exercised general supervision over the religious affairs of the state.[7] Upon his death in 14 AD Augustus was elevated to the position of *divus*, a term denoting the deification of the deceased emperor.

---

4 Cassius Dio 42. 20; 51. 19; 53. 32.

5 Cassius Dio 53. 32.

6 Cassius Dio 54. 10.

7 Suetonius, *div. Aug*. 31. 1.

The problem of succession

The fact that Augustus did not hold any one office but rather a combination of offices and powers granted to him at different times by law meant that a successor could not automatically take office. The situation allowed the possibility that, upon the death of the emperor, his powers might fall back into the senate which had granted them. But, in the circumstances, placing the government of the state in the hands of the senate seemed impossible. At the same time, however, it was obvious that unless some provision for a successor was made the stability of the empire could be at risk. Being aware that he could not legally name a successor, Augustus sought to resolve this problem by elevating to positions of power certain persons whom he regarded as suitable to succeed him expecting that, upon his death, the senate would recognise the successor he had chosen. When he died, in 14 AD, the sole survivor of this group of contemplated successors was his adopted stepson, Tiberius, whom he had made his colleague in the *imperium proconsulare* and the *tribunicia potestas*, and the senate and the people had no choice but proclaim Tiberius emperor. This idea of 'adoptive emperorship' provided the answer to the problem of succession, but in later years, as the republican element in the constitution faded away, the army began to play a decisive role in the selection of emperors.

The consolidation of the Principate

For nearly a century and a half after the establishment of the Principate the Roman empire continued to expand territorially and to develop politically along the lines set by Augustus. Externally, it expanded until it included all the countries within the natural boundaries outlined by its founder: Thrace, the Rhine regions, Britain, Armenia and Mauretania.[8] During the same period the Roman world enjoyed an unprecedented degree of peace and prosperity and the Greco-Roman civilisation continued to spread throughout Rome's provinces. In Gaul, Spain, Southern Germany and Britain in the place of earlier rural settlements new cities emerged, built upon Greek and Roman models, which were almost as cultured as Rome herself. Moreover, from the early years of the Principate Roman citizenship began to spread in the provinces. As a result, the political differences

8 See M. Cary and H. Schullard, *A History of Rome*, 3rd edn, London 1975, 331-450.

between Italy and the provinces were gradually disappearing and the concept of empire was being strengthened.[9]

The new system of government inaugurated by Augustus was consolidated and developed further under his successors: the Julio-Claudians (Tiberius 14-37 AD, Caligula 37-41 AD, Claudius 41-54 AD and Nero 54-68 AD), the Flavians (Vespasian 69-79 AD, Titus 79-81 AD and Domitian 81-96 AD), and the Antonines (Nerva 96-98 AD, Trajan 98-117 AD, Hadrian 117-138 AD, Antoninus Pius 138-161 AD, and Marcus Aurelius 161-180 AD). In spite of the contradictions inherent in the elective theory upon which it was based and its dynastic practice, this system made possible for more than two hundred years political stability and the peaceful development of Roman civilisation. Its success was due to the fact that it served the needs of the times and had the support of large sections of the population which profited from its existence and maintenance. In the course of time, however, the absolutism inherent in the imperial office became more and more obvious. The extent to which the government of the empire came to depend upon the personal qualities of the ruling emperors is manifested, in a frightening way, by the short and disastrous reigns of insane or incompetent rulers, such as Caligula, Nero and Commodus. Notwithstanding the impact of imperial personalities on the way the empire was run, imperial administration at all times depended as much on the bureaucracy, the army and factions in the governing establishment as it did on the emperors themselves. Thus, as long as Roman power was unimpaired and internal peace prevailed, the bureaucracy and the army were able to mitigate the negative consequences of a bad reign for at least some time. But, from the closing years of the second century AD, as a deep social and economic crisis began to set in and the frontiers of the empire came under threat, the ideological underpinnings of the Principate began to fall apart and a military monarchy emerged in all its brutality.[10]

---

9 Under Emperor Claudius (41-54 AD) provincials were for the first time admitted as members of the senate and, by the end of the first century AD, the office of emperor itself was opened to persons of Roman descent whose families lived in the provinces.

10 On the transformation of the Roman constitution under Augustus and his successors see R. Syme, *The Roman Revolution*, Oxford 1939; K. Raaflaub and M. Tohler (eds), *Between Republic and Empire: Interpretations of Augustus and his Principate*, Berkeley 1990; F. E. Adcock, *Roman Political Ideas and Practice*, Ann Arbor 1975, ch. 6; M. Cary and H. Scullard, *A History of Rome*, 3rd edn, London, 1975, 283 ff; C. Wirszubski, *Libertas as a Political Idea at Rome during the Late Republic and Early Principate*, Cambridge 1968; Z. Yavetz, *Plebs and Princeps*, Oxford 1969; A. Magdelain, *Auctoritas Principis*,

The Imperial Government

The emperor

As has been noted, under the Augustan constitution the powers of the emperor were those exercised by the higher magistrates of the Republic, now combined and concentrated in one person. In the course of the Principate the powers and responsibilities of the emperor were gradually extended, although their legal basis remained largely unchanged. A great deal of the emperor's power hinged upon his *tribunicia potestas*, which gave him the right to veto actions of other state organs (*intercessio*) and the right to summon and submit proposals to the senate and the assembly of the people. The *imperium proconsulare maius* gave the emperor supreme power in all the provinces and made him commander-in-chief of the armies of the state. As head of the state's administrative apparatus, the emperor appointed the members of the imperial civil service and nominated delegates who carried out various governmental tasks in his name. He also directed foreign policy and decided on matters of war and peace, subject only to formal ratification by the senate.

During the earliest period of the Principate the emperor does not appear to have had direct legislative power. His legislative proposals acquired the force of law only after they had received the formal approval of the senate. In the course of time, however, as the senate fell under the complete control of the emperor, its approval became a mere formality and the emperor's proposals came to be regarded as rules of law in their own

---

Paris 1947; H. F. Jolowicz and B. Nicholas, *Historical Introduction to the Study of Roman Law*, 3rd edn, Cambridge 1972, 321 ff; W. Kunkel, *An Introduction to Roman Legal and Constitutional History*, 2nd edn, Oxford 1973, 48 ff; D. Shotter, *Augustus Caesar*, London and New York 1992; C. Wells, *The Roman Empire*, 2nd edn, London 1992, 49 ff; A. H. M. Jones, *Augustus*, London 1970; 'The Imperium of Augustus', in *Studies in Roman Government and Law*, Oxford 1960, 1-17; D. Kienast, *Augustus: Prinzeps und Monarch*, Darmstadt 1982; F. Millar, *The Emperor in the Roman World* , New York 1977; A. H. M. Jones, *Studies in Roman Government and Law*, Oxford 1960; F. Jacques & J. Scheid, *Rom und das Reich in der Hohen Kaiserzeit*, Stuttgart and Leipzig 1998, ch. 1; A. Guarino, *Storia del diritto romano*, Naples 1996, 333 ff, 396 ff; E. Betti, *La crisi della repubblica e la genesi del principato in Roma*, Rome 1982, 527 ff. And see *Res Gestae Divi Augusti*, an account of Augustus's achievements written by Augustus himself and preserved in an inscription found in Ankara, Turkey (hence it is also known as *Monumentum Ancyranum*). For a translation see P. A. Brunt and J. M. Moore, *Res Gestae*, Oxford 1967. And see J. Gagé, *Res gestae divi Augusti*, Paris 1977.

right.[11] Not only did the emperor legislate through controlled decrees of the senate, but he acquired independent legislative authority and directly created new rules of law in a number of ways. Of general character were the *edicta*, issued by the emperor in exercise of his *ius edicendi* and containing rules laid down for both private citizens and state officials, and the *mandata*, instructions addressed by the emperor to officials subject to his orders. Moreover, the emperor issued judicial decisions (*decreta*) in exercise of his jurisdiction in civil and criminal matters, and responses (*rescripta*) to petitions of his subordinates or persons under his authority. All the above forms of imperial enactments, collectively referred to as *constitutiones principis*, were regarded as establishing rules of law and remained in force in perpetuity unless revoked by subsequent legislation. According to Gaius and Ulpian, the *constitutiones principis* derived their binding force from the sovereign power (*imperium*) conferred upon the emperor by the people and the senate through the *lex de imperio*.[12] The custom of granting the emperor the power of *imperium* by statute had its origins in the *lex curiata de imperio* by which the higher magistrates of the Republic received their *imperium*. However, with the decline and eventual disappearance of the popular assemblies and the further strengthening of imperial authority in the second century AD the notion that the emperor's *imperium* stemmed from the will of the people became devoid of all substance.[13]

The imperial civil service

In order to manage the wide-ranging responsibilities which his office entailed the emperor needed assistants answerable directly to him. This

---

11 The term *oratio principis* came to denote an imperial law promulgated in the senate. See chapter 8.

12 D. 1. 4. 1. pr. (Ulpianus); G. 1. 5. And see *lex de imperio Vespasiani* (69-70 AD) in FIRA I, p. 154. On the *constitutiones principis* as a source of law see chapter 8.

13 Hence Ulpian's statement that the emperor is not bound by the laws (*'princepslegibus solutus est'*). D. 1. 3. 31. And see D. 1. 4. 1. pr. On the constitutional position of the *princeps* see H. F. Jolowicz and B. Nicholas, *Historical Introduction to the Study of Roman Law*, 3rd edn, Cambridge 1972, 324-5; M. Kaser, *Römische Rechtsgeschichte*, Göttingen 1976, 103, 105; W. Kunkel/M. Schermaier, *Römische Rechtsgeschichte*, Cologne 2001, 63 ff, 90 ff; A. Guarino, *Storia del diritto romano*, Naples 1996, 396 ff; F. M. D' Ippolito, *Aspetti di storia costituzionale romana*, Naples 2001, 107 ff; F. Jacques & J. Scheid, *Rom und das Reich in der Hohen Kaiserzeit*, Stuttgart and Leipzig 1998, 37 ff.

need led to the development of the imperial civil service, a trained group of professionals entrusted with the various tasks of government. Since wealthy Roman families traditionally placed the administration of their property in the hands of their own freedmen, the natural place for the emperor to seek assistants was from among his own household staff. Thus, the early emperors began to use a growing number of freedmen to fill government positions, although certain posts were reserved for senators and members of the equestrian class. This practice continued until the second century AD, when it was established that the most important posts formerly held by freedmen were to be filled by equestrians. The new imperial officials gradually took over most of the duties of the old republican magistrates, although the latter continued to exist, at least in name, throughout the imperial era. The imperial magistrates differed from those of the Republic in at least three important respects: a) they were chosen by the emperor himself without the involvement of the senate or the popular assemblies, and reported directly to him; b) they were appointed for an indefinite period of time, although the emperor could dismiss them at any time at his pleasure; c) they had no *imperium* or *potestas* as their authority was derived directly from the emperor who could approve, reverse or modify their decisions as he thought fit.[14]

The praefectus praetorio

The office of the *praefectus praetorio* was created by Augustus in 2 BC. Initially its holders acted as commanders of the special military units which served as the emperor's personal body-guard (*praetoriani, cohors praetoria*).[15] Besides guarding his person, the *praetoriae cohortes* were relied upon by the emperor to keep the senate in check and to suppress any popular uprising threatening his rule. But, as the presence of regular troops within the city limits of Rome conflicted with a long-established

---

14 For a closer look at the development of the imperial civil service see A. H. M. Jones, 'The Roman Civil Service', in *Studies in Roman Government and Law*, Oxford 1960, 153-75; M. Kaser, *Römische Rechtsgeschichte*, Göttingen 1976, 113-4; W. Kunkel/M. Schermaier, *Römische Rechtsgeschichte*, Cologne 2001, 87 ff; F. Jacques & J. Scheid, *Rom und das Reich in der Hohen Kaiserzeit*, Stuttgart and Leipzig 1998, 108 ff; A. Guarino, *Storia del diritto romano*, Naples 1996, 379 ff; G. Crifò, *Lezioni di storia del diritto romano*, 3rd edn, Bologna 2000, 275 ff; M. Talamanca (ed.), *Lineamenti di storia del diritto romano*, Milan 1989, 475 ff.

15 Military units of this type were formed for the first time during the turbulent period of the later Republic; but these consisted of soldiers selected from the ordinary troops and never constituted a separate branch of the army.

constitutional custom, initially only three of the nine (or ten) praetorian cohorts were stationed in Rome (the rest were dispersed in neighbouring towns in Italy). However, from the time of Tiberius (14-37 AD) these units were all based in Rome, where they were stationed at a permanent and strongly fortified camp (*castra praetoria*).[16] The emperors, being aware of the power of the praetorians, often gave them gifts and extended their privileges in order to secure their allegiance.

In the course of time the office of the *praefectus praetorio*, which was held initially by two, then by three or, occasionally, four individuals, increased in importance and its holders came to exercise great power and political influence. Gradually their military command was extended over all the troops stationed in Italy and, from the time of Commodus (180-192 AD), they began to carry out, in addition to their military duties, important administrative and judicial functions. As regards their judicial duties, these officials tried cases and heard appeals relating to both civil and criminal matters. Their jurisdiction extended all over Italy (with the exception of a hundred mile zone around Rome) and the provinces. As they exercised their judicial functions in the name of the emperor, no appeal was allowed against their decisions.[17] Among the holders of the office of the *praefectus praetorio* were some of the prominent jurists of the Empire, such as Papinian, Paul and Ulpian. The *praefecti praetorio* probably observed the principle of collegiality (like the higher magistrates of the republican period).

The praefectus urbi

The office of the *praefectus urbi* was introduced in 26 BC by Augustus and became a permanent office during the reign of Tiberius.[18] The *praefectus urbi* was appointed by the emperor for an indefinite period and was responsible for the maintenance of peace and order within the city of Rome (*custodia urbi*).[19] He was invested with broad powers for the suppression of offences against public order and all the police forces and their officers

---

16 Tacitus, *Ann.* 4. 1-5; *Hist.* 2. 93; 3. 84; Suetonius, *div. Aug.* 49; *Tib.* 37; Cassius Dio 52. 24; 57. 19.

17 On the duties of the praetorian prefect see D. 1. 11. (Arcadius Charisius).

18 In accordance with established custom, only senators who had in the past held the position of consul (*consulares*) could serve as *praefecti urbi*. On the development of the *praefectura urbana* see Cassius Dio 49. 16; 51. 3; 52. 21; 54. 6. 19; Tacitus, *Ann.* 6. 11; 14. 41; Suetonius, *div. Aug.* 37.

19 For a general look at the administration of Rome during this period see O. F. Robinson, *Ancient Rome: City Planning and Administration*, London and New York 1992.

acted under his commands.[20] His jurisdiction extended over the city of Rome and the surrounding area up to a distance of a hundred miles from the city. In the course of time the *praefectus urbi* became the supreme judge in civil and criminal cases, with the exception of those cases which by the emperor's orders were assigned to the senate, and heard appeals sent up from lower courts in Rome, Italy and the provinces. The jurists Ulpian and Paulus, who lived in the early third century AD, wrote extensive treatises on the powers and functions of the *praefectus urbi* which are quoted in the Digest of Justinian.[21]

The praefectus annonae

An extraordinary magistrate bearing the title of *praefectus annonae* appeared as early as the middle of the fifth century BC. He was responsible for the supply of Rome with sufficient amounts of corn and other provisions in times of scarcity. In the closing years of the Republic the need for securing a steady supply of provisions necessitated the creation of a permanent magistracy to carry out this task. In 6 AD, by order of Augustus, a magistrate bearing the title of *praefectus annonae* was appointed for an indefinite period to oversee the supply of provisions to the market in Rome and to regulate the prices. The person who held this office was chosen from the equestrian order and was regarded as occupying a very dignified position. In addition to the aforementioned duties, the *praefectus annonae* exercised general civil and criminal jurisdiction in matters connected with the supply and trade of foodstuffs, although his decisions might be appealed against before the emperor. The office of the *praefectus annonae* continued to exist until the fall of the Empire, but in later years it appears to have had lost much of its earlier prestige.[22]

The praefectus vigilum

The *praefectus vigilum* was the head of the seven *cohortes vigilum*, units consisting mainly of freedmen (*libertini*), whose chief task was to police the city by night. In addition to their police duties they were responsible for the prevention and extinction of fires (which occurred frequently in ancient Rome). Each cohort was responsible for two of the fourteen districts

---

20 Moreover, the *praefectus urbi* acted as commander of the *urbanae cohortes*, a sort of militia or national guard entrusted with the defence of Rome.

21 D. 1. 12.

22 On the *praefectus annonae* see Livy 4. 12; Cicero, *ad Att*. 4. 1; Tacitus, *Ann*. 1. 7.; 11. 31; Pliny, *Panegyr*. 29; Suetonius, *div. Aug*. 37; Cassius Dio 52. 24; 54. 1. 17; 55. 26. 31. And see A. J. B. Sirks, *Food for Rome*, Amsterdam 1991.

(*regiones*) into which the city had been divided. The *praefectus vigilum* had *coercitio*, the power of taking coercive measures in order to enforce obedience to his orders of inflicting punishment for minor offences against public order. The penalties imposed by a magistrate in exercise of his *coercitio* were determined by the magistrate himself at his discretion and were not subject to appeal. The *praefectus vigilum* was chosen from the equestrian class and, in the exercise of his duties, was subordinate to the *praefectus urbi*.[23]

The procuratores

In Roman law *procurator* was a technical term referring to a legal agent entrusted with the management of property. Thus, the term *procurator Caesaris* was originally used to denote an official who managed property belonging to the emperor. But since no clear distinction between imperial property and state property was drawn, imperial *procuratores* were in reality public officials. In time there developed a whole hierarchy of *procuratores*, the most important of whom were drawn from the equestrian class. *Procuratores* were usually entrusted with the administration of fiscal matters and those employed at Rome were headed by the *procurator a rationibus*, who was in effect the empire's minister of finance. Others were responsible for the collection of taxes in the provinces, the management of state revenues, the supervision of public buildings and factories, and other tasks. *Procuratores* were also used as governors of certain provinces not assigned to imperial or senatorial *legati*.[24]

The consilium principis

In carrying out his duties the emperor was assisted by a body of advisers referred to as *consilium principis*. This was initially composed of close friends of the emperor (*amici*, *comites*), including senators and higher magistrates. The *consilium* assisted the emperor in preparing legislative proposals and administrative orders and in carrying out judicial inquiries.[25] But the opinions of the *consilium* were of an advisory character only and were not binding on the emperor. In the course of the Principate the *consilium principis* underwent considerable changes with respect to its

---

23 On the *praefectus vigilum* see D. 15; Suetonius, *div. Aug*. 30; Cass. Dio 54. 4.

24 On the *procurators* see H. G. Pflaum, *Les procurateurs équestres sous le haut-empire romain*, Paris 1950; P. C. Weaver, 'Freedmen procurators in the imperial administration', 14 *Historia* (1965), 460-9.

25 See Cassius Dio 53. 21; Suetonius, *div. Aug*., 35.

constitution and sphere of responsibilities. Under Emperor Hadrian (117-138 AD) it became a permanent organ composed of the highest officers of the state and its members (*consiliarii*)[26] began to receive regular remuneration for their services. From the time of Caracalla (211-217 AD) eminent jurists began to be appointed as members of the *consilium principis*. By the middle of the third century AD this body had become the most important element of the imperial administration, having assumed most of the functions which once pertained to the senate, and during the reign of Diocletian (284-305 AD) it was recognised, under the name *consistorium principis*, as an independent department of the imperial government.[27]

The scrinia

The administrative apparatus of imperial Rome included a complex network of offices (*scrinia*)[28] manned, at a lower level, by slaves (*servi Caesaris*) and, at a higher level, by freedmen (*libertini*). The use of freedmen and slaves in the *scrinia* may be explained on the grounds that Augustus and his successors were in need of persons upon whom they had direct control in order to carry out the functions of government efficiently. In the second century AD Emperor Hadrian restricted the role of freedmen in the *scrinia* and began to use free born Roman citizens, largely members of the equestrian class, at the higher levels of the administration.

The various *scrinia* were named by reference to the different tasks assigned to them. Thus the *scrinium a rationibus* was concerned with matters relating to public finance. The *scrinium a libellis* (or *libellorum*) dealt with various kinds of petitions (*libelli*) addressed to the emperor. There were two divisions of this office, one handling petitions written in Greek (*scrinium a libellis graecis*) and the other dealing with petitions written in Latin (*scrinium a libellis latinis*). The *scrinium ab epistulis* responded to petitions addressed to the emperor by public officials and provincial magistrates. The investigation of judicial disputes referred to the emperor was carried out by the *scrinium a cognitionibus*. During the reign of Emperor Hadrian a new office was created, the *scrinium a memoria*, which continued to operate until the close of the imperial era. This carried

---

[26] The title *consiliarii* was held by the members of this body from the time of Emperor Marcus Aurelius (161-180 AD).

[27] On the development of the *consilium principis* see J. A. Crook, *Consilium Principis: Imperial Councils and Counsellors from Augustus to Diocletian*, Cambridge 1955.

[28] In a narrow sense the word *scrinia* was used to denote the boxes in which official records were kept.

out all the secretarial work associated with the decisions, letters, orders and decrees issued by the emperor. The *scrinia* were headed by officials, referred to as *magistri*, or *comites*, who, during the later Empire, were supervised by the *magister officiorum*. The personnel of the various offices received regular salaries as well as special bonuses and gifts.

The fiscus

Augustus created in the provinces new revenue offices (*fisci*) which were independent of Rome's central state treasury (*aerarium populi romani*). These offices were managed by freedmen and their revenues, which were derived largely from the rental of state lands, mines and other sources, were used to cover the cost of provincial administration. Under Augustus' successors, and probably during the reign of Claudius (41-54 AD), these provincial *fisci* were integrated to create the *fiscus Caesaris*, which became the main state treasury and gradually absorbed the earlier *aerarium populi romani*. State revenues derived from taxation and other sources both in Italy and the provinces were deposited in the *fiscus Caesaris* and were used to cover the cost of public works and services and to pay the salaries of state officials and soldiers. Although the *fiscus* was not regarded as personal property of the emperor, it was controlled and administered by him through specially appointed officials, the *procuratores a rationibus* or *fisci*. In the course of time the *fiscus* assumed a special legal personality and, from the late second century AD, it began to be represented in the courts when disputes arose between the *fiscus* and private individuals concerning debts. Distinct from the *fiscus* was the personal property of the emperor, referred to as *patrimonium Caesaris*, which was administered by officials known as *procuratores patrimonii*. Upon the emperor's death, the *patrimonium Caesaris* went to his heirs according to the rules governing testamentary succession. The *fiscus*, by contrast, was transferred to his successor to the throne.[29]

---

[29] On the development of the imperial *fiscus* see P. A. Brunt, 'The fiscus and its development' and 'Remarks on the imperial fiscus', in *Roman Imperial Themes*, Oxford 1990, chapters 7 and 16. See also A. H. M. Jones, 'The aerarium and the fiscus', in *Studies in Roman Government and Law*, Oxford 1960, ch. 6; F. Millar, 'The fiscus in the first two centuries', 53 *JRS* (1963), 29-42.

The Republican Elements of the Constitution

The Assemblies of the People

During the early Principate the people's assemblies continued to operate, but their political role was greatly diminished and their acts came to amount to little more than mere ratifications of the emperor's wishes. As a result of the transference of the magisterial elections to the senate and the replacement of popular legislation by senatorial decrees, by the end of the first century AD the popular assemblies had become dead institutions and ceased to play any part in political life.

The comitia curiata

The *comitia curiata*, Rome's oldest assembly, continued to function in a shadowy form as a gathering of thirty lictors (*lictores*) representing the thirty *curiae* into which the *populus Romanus* was in early times divided. Before them, and under the supervision of the *pontifex maximus*, took place the *adrogatio per populum*, the formal procedure through which a person *sui iuris* and his descendants passed by adoption into another family. This procedure was later on superseded by the *adrogatio per rescriptum principis*, by which adoption was effected by a rescript of the emperor without further formalities.[30] Finally, it seems more likely that, during the Principate, the *lex de imperio*, the special law by which the emperors were granted their *imperium*, was enacted by the *comitia centuriata* and not by the *comitia curiata*.

The comitia centuriata and the comitia tributa

After the fall of the Republic the *comitia* continued to exercise their legislative functions probably until the close of the first century AD. Augustus submitted several legislative proposals to them in accordance with ancient forms, and his example was followed by some of his successors. Among the most important statutes enacted by the *comitia* during this period were the *lex Iulia de maritandis ordinibus*[31] and the *leges Iuliae iudiciorum publicorum et privatorum*[32] of Augustus, and the

---

[30] However, the practice of *adrogatio per populum* was not formally abolished until the time of Diocletian, in the late third century AD. On the *comitia curiata* see Suetonius, *div. Aug.* 65; Tacitus, *Ann.* 12. 26. 41; *Hist.* 1. 15; Cassius Dio 69. 20.

[31] Dealing with several issues connected with marriage.

[32] Dealing with matters of legal procedure in civil and criminal cases.

lex Claudia of Emperor Claudius.[33] Gradually, however, popular legislation was superseded by the decrees of the emperor and the resolutions of the senate. The last law passed by the *comitia* was a *lex agraria* enacted under Emperor Nerva (96-98 AD), a law mentioned in the Digest in an extract of the jurist Callistratus.[34] Moreover, the *comitia* were still summoned to elect magistrates as late as the second century AD, but now the choice of the candidates rested largely with the emperor. In the time of Augustus the emperor proposed the persons whom he desired to be elected to the consulship and half of the number of candidates for the other magistracies, whilst the remaining places were, in principle, open to free competition.[35] There were two ways in which the emperor could nominate a candidate: by simply expressing his support for a person (such an informal recommendation was termed *suffragatio* and was not regarded as binding), and by *commendatio*, a binding recommendation of a candidate. Under Augustus and his successor, Tiberius, a further system was introduced, the *destinatio*, applying to the election of the consuls and praetors. Under this system, a body composed of senators and *equites* proposed to the assembly the candidates for these two offices.[36] This system does not appear to have lasted for a long period, however. Finally, from the time of Tiberius it became customary for the emperor to nominate the consuls and a number of the lower magistrates, while the rest were chosen by the senate. The role of the *comitia* was limited to the mere confirmation of the candidates selected following the formal announcement of their names (*renuntiatio*) by the senate.[37] In the course of the second century AD the role of the *comitia* in the election of magistrates continued to decline and, by the end of the third century AD, they had ceased to exist as political institutions.[38]

---

[33] Abolishing the guardianship of the next relatives over women. See G. 1. 157. 171.

[34] D. 47. 21. 3. 1.

[35] A similar practice had been followed by Julius Caesar. See Suetonius, *Caes.* 41; *div. Aug.* 40. 56; *Vitell.* 11; Tacitus, *Hist.* 1. 77; Cassius Dio 53. 21; 55. 34; Appian, *B.C.* 1. 103.

[36] The procedure of *destinatio* is known from a statute preserved on a bronze tablet found in 1948 in Magliano, near the Roman colony of Heba in Etruria (*tabula Hebana*, 19 AD). For a translation of the *Tabula Hebana* see J. H. Oliver & R. E. A. Palmer, 75 *American Journal of Philology* (1954), 225.

[37] Tacitus, *Ann.* 1. 15. 81; Cassius Dio 58. 20. An attempt was made under Emperor Caligula to restore the election of magistrates to the *comitia* but it was met with failure. See on this Suetonius, *Cal.* 16; Cassius Dio 52. 30; 59. 20; D. 48. 14. 1. pr. (Modestinus).

[38] Ammian. Marcell. 14. 6. 6. On the decline of the popular assemblies during the Principate see F. Jacques & J. Scheid, *Rom und das Reich in der Hohen Kaiserzeit*, Stuttgart and Leipzig 1998, 54 ff; A. Guarino, *Storia del diritto*

The Senate

In contrast with the people's assemblies, during the early years of the Principate the power of the senate appears to have increased. Its members retained all their privileges, and political power was, in theory at least, shared between it and the emperor. All the powers and titles of the emperor were formally bestowed upon him by vote of the senate and, before the establishment of the *consilium principis*, the senate acted as the emperor's advisory body. In reality, however, the senate had lost much of its earlier authority, for its members were now chosen by the emperor himself who also controlled its legislative functions through the exercise of his veto (*intercessio*). Augustus reduced the number of senators from nine hundred to six hundred by expelling those persons whom he regarded as unworthy of holding the position of senator; at the same time he appointed a number of new members from among his closest friends and supporters.[39] The right of emperors to revise the composition of the senate (*lectio senatus*), admitting new members and excluding those whom they deemed undesirable, was connected with their *censoria potestas* and their role as upholders of the laws and morals of the community (*cura legum et morum*).[40] Moreover, the emperor could admit new members into the senate indirectly, by conferring the title of ex-magistrates on persons who had not in the past held a magistracy or who had served as magistrates of a rank lower than that which was conferred upon them (*adlectio*). In the course of the first and second centuries AD the composition of the senate underwent a considerable change as more and more Roman citizens from the provinces were admitted to it, whilst the number of senators belonging to Roman and Italian families continued to decline.[41]

The emperor, by virtue of his position as *princeps senatus*, could summon the senate at any time (*ius agendi cum senatu*) and, even when not presiding, put before it proposals for deliberation. As was noted before, the election of magistrates was arranged between the emperor and the senate, while the *comitia* were simply called upon to confirm the list of candidates put before them – a list which they could neither reject nor modify. Although the senate assumed the legislative functions of the assemblies and, in the course of time, its resolutions (*senatus consulta*) came to be

---

romano, Naples 1996, 390 ff; M. Talamanca (ed.), *Lineamenti di storia del diritto romano*, Milan 1989, 403 ff.

39 Suetonius, *div. Aug.* 35. 1; Cassius Dio 54. 13. 14.

40 Suetonius, *div. Aug.* 27. 5; *Vesp.* 9; Cassius Dio 54. 13. 14; 55. 3; Tacitus, *Ann.* 4. 42.

41 Consider here, e.g., the *senatus consultum Claudianum* (48 AD), in Bruns *Fontes* I, no. 52; also in FIRA I, no. 43.

regarded as having the force of laws,[42] the legislative activity of the senate was largely under the control of the emperor. In the first century AD the procedure leading to the enactment of a *senatus consultum* was initiated by the emperor himself, or a magistrate acting in his name, through a speech containing the emperor's legislative proposal (*oratio principis in senatu*). From the second century AD the emperor's proposals were approved by the senate as a matter of course and, in most cases, without discussion.[43] In addition to its legislative functions, the senate had jurisdiction over criminal cases involving offences of a political nature, such as offences committed by senators, state officials and provincial magistrates. Moreover, questions of foreign policy, such as the declaration of war or the conclusion of peace, although usually decided by the emperor in his capacity as supreme military commander, were occasionally assigned to the senate.[44] Finally, during this period the senate continued to administer the public treasury (*aerarium*), to govern the senatorial provinces through proconsuls and to carry out, with the help of members of the priestly colleges, certain functions of a religious character.[45]

The Magistrature

The tribunes

During the Principate the tribunes retained their rights of *intercessio* and *auxilium*. However, their authority was greatly diminished as a result of the

---

[42] G. 1. 4.

[43] See chapter 8.

[44] See, e.g., Cassius Dio 60. 23; 68. 9.

[45] Under certain circumstances, the senate could also issue a special decree publicly stigmatising an emperor whose conduct was deemed disgraceful (*damnatio memoriae*). This could be done during the emperor's lifetime or posthumously. On the powers and functions of the senate during the Principate see R. J. A. Talbert, *The Senate of Imperial Rome*, Princeton 1984; M. Kaser, *Römische Rechtsgeschichte*, Göttingen 1976, 107 ff; W. Kunkel/M. Schermaier, *Römische Rechtsgeschichte*, Cologne 2001, 69 ff; F. Jacques & J. Scheid, *Rom und das Reich in der Hohen Kaiserzeit*, Stuttgart and Leipzig 1998, 72 ff; A. Chastagnol, *Le Sénat romain à l'époque impériale*, Paris 1992; A. Guarino, *Storia del diritto romano*, Naples 1996, 392; G. Crifò, *Lezioni di storia del diritto romano*, 3rd edn, Bologna 2000, 296 ff; M. Talamanca (ed.), *Lineamenti di storia del diritto romano*, Milan 1989, 387 ff; A. Burdese, *Manuale di diritto pubblico romano*, 3rd edn, Turin 1987, repr. 1994, 168 ff. On the composition of the senate see D. McAlindon, 'Entry to the Senate in the Early Empire', 47 *JRS* (1957), 191-7; M. Hammond, 'Composition of the Senate, AD 68-235', 47 *JRS* (1957), 74-81.

disappearance of the *concilium plebis* as an independent political assembly and, in practice, none of their powers could be effectively exercised without the emperor's consent.[46] In the first century AD the tribunes occasionally summoned and presided over meetings of the senate and, together with the praetors and the aediles, were entrusted with the general superintendence of the fourteen districts into which the city of Rome had been divided. During this period the tribunes were chosen by the senate, usually with the approval of the emperor, from among those who had held the office of quaestor.[47] As has been noted, an important basis of the emperor's sovereign power was the *triunicia potestas* with which he was vested for life and against which no *intercessio* could be raised either by a tribune or by any other magistrate.

The consuls

In the period under consideration the consulship retained much of its earlier prestige but was now under the control of the emperor who conferred it upon whom he pleased or assumed it in person (despite the fact that he already possessed the *imperium consulare*) whenever he thought fit.[48] Moreover, whereas during the Republic the office of consul was normally held by two persons in the course of one year, it now became common practice to appoint several pairs of consuls during one year, the number varying according to the number of persons on whom the emperor wished to bestow the title. Under normal circumstances, the consuls remained in office for a period of two months (thus there were twelve consuls in all in each year).[49] The two consuls who took office at the beginning of the year (*consules ordinarii*) gave their name to the year and were held in higher honour than those who followed (the latter were

---

46 Cassius Dio 57. 15; 59. 24; 60. 16. 28; Suetonius, *Caes.* 79; *Tib.* 23; Tacitus, *Ann.* 1. 13; 6. 12; 13. 28; *Hist.* 2. 91; 4. 9.

47 As the tribunate had lost its earlier prestige, very few were interested in holding the office. This necessitated the passing of a law which provided that the tribunes were to be chosen by lot out of those who had held the quaestorship and who had not yet reached the age of forty. Suetonius, *div Aug.* 40; Cassius Dio 54. 26. 30.

48 Under Augustus and his successors the title of consul was often granted to certain individuals as a mark of personal distinction and as a reward for their services to the state (*ornamenta consularia*). This practice was extended to the praetorship and other high offices of the state (hence the terms *ornamenta praetoria, ornamenta aedilitia* and *ornamenta quaestoria*).

49 Cassius Dio 58. 20.

referred to as *consules suffecti*, or *consules minores*).[50] The consuls retained the right of summoning and presiding over the senate and the *comitia centuriata*, and occasionally acted as judges in civil cases. Within their jurisdiction fell, in particular, cases involving the question of whether a person was a slave or a free man (*causae liberales*) and cases concerning the protection of minors.[51] Despite the fact that the consuls were divested of much of their earlier power, the office remained, down to the closing years of the Empire, one of the most prestigious offices of the state. The governors of the senatorial provinces as well as some of the imperatorial ones, and the highest imperial officials were usually chosen from among those who had held the office of consul.

The praetors

During the Principate the praetors continued to exercise their usual judicial functions in the context of the formulary system. However, with the gradual replacement of the formulary system by the new system of the *cognitio extra ordinem*, their role in the administration of justice diminished as more and more cases came within the jurisdiction of imperial officials. During this period the number of praetors was increased, initially to twelve and later to eighteen.[52] Of these the *praetor urbanus* and the *praetor peregrinus* exercised general jurisdiction, whilst the jurisdiction of the rest was limited to certain matters only. Thus, in the Augustan era the management of the public treasury (*aerarium*) was entrusted to two praetors, referred to as *praetores aerarii*; from the time of Claudius a special praetor was appointed to deal with cases concerning trust estates (*praetor de fideicommissis*); under Nerva a special praetor was entrusted with the resolution of disputes that arose between private individuals and the imperial exchequer (*praetor fiscalis*); and in the time of the Antonine emperors the appointment of guardians and the resolution of disputes which arose between guardians were consigned to a special praetor known as *praetor tutelarius*. The office of *praetor peregrinus* disappeared after the Roman citizenship was granted to all the free inhabitants of the empire in the early third century AD. By contrast, the office of the *praetor*

---

50 In the later years of the Empire the *consules suffecti* probably disappeared, although the sources speak of a new category of consuls, the *consules honorarii*, as distinct from the *consules ordinarii*. C. 10. 31. 66; *Nov*. 81. 1.

51 Tacitus, *Ann*. 4. 19; 13. 4; Pliny, *Epp*. 9. 13;. Cassius Dio 69. 7.

52 Velleius 2. 89; Tacitus, *Ann*. 1. 14; 2. 32; Cassius Dio 53. 32; 56. 25; 58. 20; 59. 20; 60. 10; D. 1. 2. 2. 32. (Pomponius).

urbanus continued to exist until the end of the Western Roman Empire in the middle of the fifth century AD.[53]

The aediles

The aediles, whose number had been increased to six by Julius Caesar, continued to exist as independent magistrates during the first two centuries of the Principate. However, most of their original duties were taken over by imperial officials. As was noted before, the task of ensuring the regular supply of Rome with corn and other provisions was assigned to the *praefectus annonae*, and the aediles' police duties were transferred to the *praefectus urbi* and the *praefectus vigilum*. Within the aediles sphere of responsibilities remained only the inspection of streets, baths and other public places and the enforcement of sanitary regulations. The aedileship finally disappeared in the third century AD.

The quaestors

The number of the quaestors, which had been increased to forty by Julius Caesar, was reduced by Augustus to twenty, as it was in the time of Sulla.[54] In the Augustan era the duties of the *quaestores urbani* pertaining to the administration of the public treasury (*aerarium*) were transferred to the two *praetores aerarii* and an imperial magistrate who bore the title *praefectus aerarii*. Two of the quaestors were assigned to the emperor and were referred to as *quaestores principis*, whilst the rest served under the consuls (*quaestores consulis*) and the provincial governors (*quaestores provinciarum*). The office of quaestor retained some significance as it was regarded as an important first step by those who wished to attain a high magistracy or to join the imperial civil service.

The censors

During the later Republic the office of censor was stripped of most of its powers and, by the middle of the first century BC, it appears to have fallen into disuse. As was noted before, in the early years of the Principate Augustus took upon himself the supervision of public morals (*cura morum*) and the drawing up of the list of senators (*lectio senatus*), tasks originally entrusted to the censors. In 48 AD Emperor Claudius assumed the title of

---

53 The office of *praetor urbanus*, as well that of the *praetor tutelarius*, remained in existence in the Eastern Roman Empire for a much longer period.

54 Tacitus, *Ann.* 11. 22.

censor, as did Vespasian in 74 AD. From the time of Domitian (81-96 AD) it became customary for the emperors to exercise censorial powers for life and the censorship ceased to exist as an independent office.[55]

The Administration of Italy and the Provinces

During the Principate the administrative organisation of Italy and the provinces remained largely as it was during the later Republic, although gradually it became more centralised. In the first century AD Italy retained its privileged position in relation to the rest of the empire. Its inhabitants enjoyed all the rights of the Roman citizenship and Italian lands were exempted from taxation (*stipendium, tributum soli*) as being subject to *dominium ex iure Quiritium*, i.e. ownership according to the rules of the Roman *ius civile*. In the course of time, however, the centre of the empire's economic life shifted from Italy to the provinces and, by the middle of the second century AD, the position of Italy was not different from that of the rest of the empire.[56]

The administrative organisation of Italy

Augustus divided Italy into eleven administrative districts (*regiones Italiae*) for the purpose of facilitating the management of state lands (*ager publicus*) and the conduct of the *census* (the registration of the citizens and their property). This arrangement remained in place until 120 AD, when Emperor Hadrian divided Italy into four districts headed by jurisdictional magistrates of consular rank (*consulares iuridici*). The latter were appointed by the emperor and exercised both administrative and judicial functions. Moreover, from the early second century AD permanent commissioners began to be appointed by the emperor to supervise the financial administration of towns and communities in Italy. These officials (*curatores rei publicae civitatis*) had jurisdiction over matters relating to the management of municipal finances and supervised transactions concerning municipal property. Other administrative tasks were assigned to minor imperial officials, such as the *curatores viarum*, responsible for the

---

[55] The censorship appeared again, for a brief period, during the reign of Decius (249-251 AD).

[56] On the administration of Italy and the provinces during the Principate sec A. Lintott, *Imperium Romanum: Politics and Administration*, London & New York 1993, chapters 7-9; R. Thomsen, *The Italic Regions from Augustus to the Lombard Invasion*, Rome 1966; F. Jacques & J. Scheid, *Rom und das Reich in der Hohen Kaiserzeit*, Stuttgart and Leipzig 1998, 173 ff.

maintenance of public roads, the *praefecti alimentorum*, charged with the distribution of provisions among the poor, and *procuratores*, concerned with the management of taxes and other revenues. In 211 AD all four districts into which Italy had been divided were placed under the supervision of an imperial magistrate bearing the title of *corrector*. From the time of Aurelian (270-275 AD) the *corrector* of Italy became a permanent official now referred to as *corrector utriusque Italiae*. As was noted before, criminal jurisdiction throughout Italy was exercised by the *praefectus praetorio*, with the exception of Rome and the surrounding area which came under the jurisdiction of the *praefectus urbi*.

The provinces

In the early years of the Principate the number of Roman provinces was increased. This was partly due to the introduction of a new system of territorial division and partly due to the further expansion of Roman territory following the conquest of new lands (such as Britain, the Rhine and Danube regions, and parts of Mesopotamia and Arabia). Moreover, measures were introduced aimed at improving the situation of the provincials: the process of bringing to justice provincial magistrates accused of extortion was simplified; provincial taxation was reorganised and a permanent civil service was formed for the conduct of the census and the collection of taxes; the development of new urban centres was encouraged; new roads were built; banditry and piracy were suppressed; trade and commerce were facilitated. These measures reflected a policy of enlightened imperialism directed towards the welfare of Rome's subject populations.

We saw earlier that Augustus, as holder of the proconsular power (*imperium proconsulare*), exercised direct control over the frontier provinces in which the bulk of the Roman army was stationed. The rest were placed under the control of the senate. This led to the eventual division of the Roman provinces into two categories: imperial provinces (*provinciae principis*) and senatorial provinces (*provinciae senatus*). Outside these two classes of provinces but really within the empire, Augustus and his successors allowed some client kingdoms to exist.[57] These enjoyed internal self-government and paid no taxes to Rome, but their foreign relations were under the control of the emperor and they were bound to aid Rome militarily.

---

[57] Client kingdoms were, for example, Thrace, Mauretania, Pontus, Galatia, Cappadocia and Lesser Armenia.

The senatorial provinces

The provinces placed under the control of the senate were usually (although not always) those in which conditions of peace and security prevailed and which, therefore, did not require the presence of large armies. The governors of these provinces (*proconsules*) were chosen from among those who had held the office of consul (for the provinces of Asia and Africa), or praetor (for the remaining provinces), and their appointment was for one year. An ex-magistrate was eligible for the proconsulship five years after his term in office expired. Although the appointment of governors was regulated by the senate, emperors often interfered in the selection process in order to secure the appointment of their preferred candidates.[58] Moreover, it was not unusual for an emperor to by-pass the senate and interfere directly in the affairs of a senatorial province.

As holder of the *imperium proconsulare*, the governor exercised general jurisdiction in civil and criminal matters and supervised the political and financial administration of his province. In carrying out his duties he was assisted by deputies termed *legati pro praetore*. The latter were appointed by the governor, with the approval of the senate or the emperor, and performed certain judicial functions as delegates of the governor (*iurisdictio mandata*).[59] With respect to matters relating to the financial administration of the province, such as the collection of taxes, the governor was aided by quaestors (*quaestores provinciales*) whose duties were similar to those of the *aediles curules* in Rome. In the senatorial provinces the emperor was represented by a *procurator*. This official was entrusted with the management of the emperor's property in the province, and was responsible for the collection of the taxes payable to the imperial treasury (*fiscus*).

The imperial provinces

The imperial provinces included all the frontier provinces which required the constant presence of legionary garrisons. These provinces and their armies were under the direct control of the emperor and were governed by military officers termed *legati Augusti pro praetore*. The latter were appointed by the emperor from the senatorial class and exercised, as his representatives, all the powers pertaining to his *imperium proconsulare*. Some of the smaller imperial provinces or parts of provinces (such as, e.g.,

---

58 According to the *lex Pompeia* of 52 BC. On the *proconsules* see Cassius Dio 52. 23; 53. 13; Suetonius, *div. Aug.* 47; Tacitus, *Ann.* 16. 18.

59 D. 1. 16. 5. (Papinianus) and 6. (Ulpianus). C. 1. 35. 1.

Judaea) were governed by officials (*praefecti*, *procuratores*) chosen from the equestrian class. The governors of the imperial provinces were usually appointed for a five-year term. They were accompanied by lictors and were assisted by lower officials, such as the *legati legionum* in military matters, and the *legati iuridici* in matters relating to the administration of justice. The revenues of the imperial provinces were collected by imperial *procuratores* and the proceeds were paid into the imperial treasury (*fiscus*). Under extraordinary circumstances the government of a province, whether senatorial or imperial, was entrusted to an imperial *procurator*, instead of a *proconsul* or *legatus*. Moreover, on certain occasions the emperor and the senate conjointly granted supreme control over a number of provinces to one person.[60]

The administration of Egypt

Although it belonged to the imperial provinces, Egypt had its own organisation since the late first century BC (when it was conquered by Octavian). From that time it was regarded as a private estate of the emperor rather than as part of the dominions of the Roman people. The special significance, political, economic and military, which Egypt had for the emperor is manifested by the fact that its governor was not permitted to leave his post before the arrival of his successor.[61] Moreover senators and eminent members of the equestrian class were prohibited from entering the province without the emperor's permission.[62]

Egypt was governed by a representative of the emperor, usually a member of the equestrian class,[63] who bore the title *praefectus Alexandriae et Aegypti*. He was appointed by the emperor himself for an indefinite period (although usually this did not exceed five years), and his powers were similar to those of the proconsuls.[64] In the eyes of the Egyptians, however, the position of the *praefectus Aegypti* was no different from that of a king.[65] In carrying out his duties the *praefectus Aegypti* was assisted by a large number of officials, some of whose offices had been in existence

---

60 For example, Augustus on two occasions placed all the Eastern provinces under the command of Agrippa, and under Tiberius the whole of the East was committed to Germanicus. See Tacitus, *Ann.* 2. 43; 15. 25.

61 D. 1. 17. 1. (Ulpianus).

62 Tacitus, *Ann.* 2. 59; Cassius Dio 51. 17; 53. 12.

63 Tacitus, *Hist.* 1. 11.

64 D. 1. 17. 1. (Ulpianus). On the *praefectus Aegypti* see O. W. Reinmuth, *The Prefect of Egypt from Alexander to Diocletian*, Wiesbaden 1935, repr. Aalen 1963.

65 Tacitus, *Hist.* 1. 11; Strabo, *Geogr.* 17. 1. 12.

since the Ptolemaic period. The most important of these was the *iuridicus Aegypti*, a magistrate with competence in matters relating to the administration of justice.[66] During the Principate the Greek cities in Egypt (Alexandria, Naucratis, Ptolemais) retained, in principle, a limited degree of autonomy. As to the Egyptian inhabitants of the country, although these were free, they lacked citizenship and had no political rights (*peregrini dediticii*).[67]

Provincial administration and local government

The internal administration of a province was in the hands of its governor[68] who, by virtue of his *imperium*, issued decrees binding throughout the province (*ius edicendi*), tried cases and heard appeals against judicial decisions of local magistrates. In criminal cases he had the right to impose any punishment he thought fit, including the death penalty (*ius gladii*). During the Principate governors were more closely supervised by the central government, usually through imperial procurators, and could be more quickly and certainly brought to justice if they abused their power.[69] Besides the check on power exercised by Rome, there was also a control in the province itself. In the capital city of every province[70] assemblies (*concilia*) were held once a year composed of representatives of the various communities in the province. The original purpose of these gatherings was the carrying out of certain religious ceremonies associated with the cult of the emperor. In addition to that, the assemblies discussed various matters concerning the administration of the province, assessed actions of the governor and provincial magistrates and submitted petitions to the emperor. Petitions containing accusations of corruption might result in the criminal

---

66 Strabo, *Geogr*. 17. 1. 12.

67 On the administration of Egypt during the early Empire see P. A. Brunt, 'The administration of Roman Egypt', 65 *JRS* (1975), 124-47; N. Lewis, *Life in Egypt under Roman Rule*, Oxford 1983; A. K. Bowman, *Egypt After the Pharaohs 332 BC - AD 642*, London 1986, repr. Oxford 1990; H. Idris Bell, *Egypt from Alexander the Great to the Arab Conquest*, Oxford 1948; E. Seidl, *Rechtsgeschichte Ägyptens als römischer Provinz - Die Behauptung des ägyptischen Rechts neben dem römischen*, S. Augustin 1973.

68 From the second century AD the governor of a province, whether senatorial or imperial, was referred to as *praeses provinciae*, while the term *dux* denoted the military commander of a province. D. 1. 18. 1. (Macer).

69 Governors accused of corruption were tried in Rome by a court made up of members of the senate, with leading senators or provincial representatives acting as prosecutors.

70 With the exception of Egypt.

prosecution of the governor at Rome. The *concilia* maintained contact with the governor through envoys. The communication between the governor and the provincial population was facilitated, further, by the judicial gatherings (*conventus*) which were held by the governor in the larger towns of the province during his annual tour of the province.

The period of the Principate is marked by the progressive Romanisation of the provinces, especially those of the West. This process, which was actively promoted by the imperial government, was precipitated by the establishment of new colonies (*coloniae*) and towns (*municipia*), both Roman and Latin, throughout the empire. In the provinces, especially those of the East, there existed also many cities and towns whose inhabitants were foreigners (*civitates peregrinorum*). Some of these communities were allowed to administer their own affairs without direct interference by the Roman authorities (*civitates liberae*). The status of a *civitas libera* was granted by a special law (*lex data*), often as a reward for a city's support to Rome in times of war or for various political purposes. Other provincial communities (*civitates immunes*) enjoyed special privileges, such as exemption from taxation or other burdens regularly imposed upon the inhabitants of the province. One should note here, however, that *libertas* did not necessarily imply *immunitas*, as a community might be a *civitas libera* and yet heavily taxed.[71] In a similar manner, a community might have enjoyed *immunitas* without being a *civitas libera*. Furthermore, a provincial community might enjoy certain privileges by virtue of a special treaty (*foedus*) concluded between it and Rome (i.e., a treaty distinct from the law regulating the government of the province as a whole). Such communities were referred to as *civitates foederatae*. Sometimes the status of *colonia* was granted by the emperor as a privilege to an existing *municipium* or *civitas peregrinorum*, and was accompanied by the granting of the Roman citizenship to its inhabitants. Moreover, from the late second century AD some *civitates peregrinorum* were granted by the emperor the *ius Italicum*, i.e., the status which Italian communities had during the Republic. The *ius Italicum* entailed certain privileges, such as exemption from land tax and the ability to acquire ownership over land according to the Roman *ius civile* (*dominium ex iure Quiritium*).

The various provincial communities (*coloniae*, *municipia*, *civitates peregrinorum*) had their own assemblies, magistrates and town councils. The latter were modelled on the Roman senate and consisted usually of a hundred members, termed *decuriones* or *senatores,* representing the local aristocracy (*ordo decurionum*). The *decuriones* were selected, in part, from among those who had served as magistrates in the past and, in part, from

---

[71] See, e.g., Tacitus, *Ann.* 12. 62. 63.

persons of a high standing in the community. Within the competence of the local councils fell all matters involving the interests of the community and their resolutions (*decreta*) were binding upon the local magistrates. With the progressive decline of the democratic institutions during the imperial era the *ordo decurionum* gradually came to assume the most important functions of the local assemblies.[72] The administration of a city was usually headed by four magistrates (*quattuorviri*), two *duoviri iuri dicundo* and two *duoviri aediles*. The *duoviri iure dicundo* were elected annually by the local assembly and their functions were similar to those of the consuls and praetors in Rome. They summoned and presided over the municipal council and the assembly of the people, administered the community's finances and conducted the census (*duoviri censoria potestate*), and exercised general jurisdiction in civil and criminal matters. Each of them had the right of veto (*intercessio*) against acts of the other. The duties of the *duoviri aediles* were similar to those of the Roman aediles. Within their competence fell, among other things, the maintenance of public order, the management of public roads and buildings, the supervision of market transactions and the organisation of public games and festivals. In most cities there were also *quaestores*, usually two in number, who served as treasurers of the community. In the *civitates peregrinorum* private disputes were resolved according to each city's own system of laws. In the course of time, however, the continual interference of the Roman authorities into the affairs of the provincial communities and, more importantly, the heavy taxation imposed upon them by the imperial government, led to the decline of their institutions and the gradual erosion of their autonomy.[73]

Property rights and taxation in the provinces

In the provinces the whole of the land was regarded, in theory at least, as belonging by right of conquest to the Roman state (*dominium populi Romani*, or *dominium Caesaris*). In practice, however, private lands were seldom confiscated by the state and remained in the hands of their owners on payment of a land tax. Nevertheless, with the exception of those territories belonging to communities which had been granted the *ius Italicum*, provincial lands could not be the subject of private ownership

---

[72] The popular assemblies ceased to play any political role in the third century AD.

[73] On the development of local government during the Empire see F.F. Abbott and A.C. Johnson, *Municipal Administration in the Roman Empire*, New York 1926; J. S. Reid, *The Municipalities of the Roman Empire*, Cambridge 1913; W. T. Arnold, *The Roman System of Provincial Administration to the Accession of Constantine the Great*, Oxford 1914.

according to the rules of the Roman *ius civile* (*dominium ex iure Quiritium*). Land belonging to a community as a whole, on the other hand, was usually seized by the Romans and was disposed of in various ways: a part was sold and the proceeds were deposited into the Roman public treasury (*aerarium*); a part was let to tenants who were required to pay a fixed rent to the Roman state; and a part was left in the hands of the community to which it originally belonged, although it became subject to taxation.

In the provinces land tax was imposed upon all lands not granted the privileged status of Italian soil (*ius Italicum*). In the imperial provinces this tax was a fixed proportion of the annual yield, whereas in the senatorial ones it was a sum fixed annually for each community.[74] Besides the land tax, provincials were usually required to pay a property tax (*tributum capitis*) which was calculated for each individual according to the amount of property (other than landed property) which he possessed. A provincial census was regularly conducted for the purpose of ascertaining the taxable property available.[75] In addition to the revenues derived from land and personal taxation, revenues were raised from several other sources. These included the duties levied on exports and imports, the profits realised from mines and salt works, the five per cent tax on the value of emancipated slaves and the five per cent inheritance tax. But besides the regular taxes provincials were often liable to extraordinary exactions and levies. Thus, they might be required to provide shelter for the troops, to equip and maintain fleets for war or transport and to provide supplies for the household of the governor. These additional burdens were usually determined by the provincial governor at his discretion and often proved more onerous to the local population than the regular taxes. During the Principate the practice of employing tax farmers (*publicani*) for the collection of direct taxes (i.e. land and personal taxes) continued in some senatorial provinces. But in the imperial ones the *publicani* were replaced by *procuratores* appointed by the emperor. Indirect taxes, on the other hand, continued to be collected by *publicani*, now under the supervision of imperial procurators.[76] By the third century AD tax farming was everywhere superseded by the system of direct collection of taxes by *procuratores*.

---

74 The land-tax paid by provincials was referred to as *stipendium* in the senatorial provinces and *tributum* in the imperial ones. See G. 2. 21. Consider on this F. Grelle, *Stipendium vel tributum, L' imposizione fondiaria nelle dottrine giuridiche del 2 et 3 secolo*, Naples 1963.

75 Cassius Dio 53. 22; Pliny, *Epp*. 10. 112.

76 See on this P. A. Brunt, 'Publicani in the Principate' in *Roman Imperial Themes*, Oxford 1990, 354-432.

The Roman citizenship

Roman citizenship was that status whereby a person enjoyed the rights and was subject to the duties of the Roman *ius civile*. In the republican period, as Rome's power and influence grew, Roman citizenship became highly valued, was sought after by many and was granted sparingly. It was conferred, mainly as a reward for faithful service to Rome, sometimes on individuals and occasionally on whole communities by a special law enacted either by the *comitia centuriata* or the *comitia tributa*. In the last century of the Republic the people occasionally delegated the power to grant the citizenship to some of their favourite leaders, such as Marius and Pompey. Sulla and Caesar, when they were at the height of their power, appear to have exercised it freely and in most cases without challenge. But by that time Roman citizenship had become less valuable as a result of its bestowal on all the free inhabitants of Italy in the course of the Social War (91-87 BC).

From the early years of the Principate the citizenship was granted with increasing frequency to individuals or whole communities, often following the concession of the *ius Latii* (the intermediate legal status between citizen and foreigner given to members of Latin colonies). By granting the Roman citizenship to more and more inhabitants of the empire the emperors sought to secure the loyalty of the provincial upper classes and, at the same time, to establish islands of Roman civilisation in the provinces.[77] Persons who did not belong to organised communities (*peregrini dediticii*) and who thus lacked citizenship (*nullius civitatis*) could also acquire Roman citizenship but only after they had formally been admitted as citizens of another state.[78] Those persons to whom citizenship was granted were not required to abandon the citizenship which they had previously held.[79] Thus newly admitted Roman citizens were not released from their civic duties towards the communities to which they originally belonged.[80] The gradual extension of the citizenship precipitated the process of Romanisation of the provinces, especially those of the West, the

---

77 Consider, e.g., the edicts of Augustus regarding the citizens of Cyrene (7-6 BC) in FIRA I, no. 68; and see F. de Visscher, *Les édits d'Auguste découverts à Cyrène*, Louvain and Paris 1940.

78 See, e.g., Pliny, *Epist.* 10. 6. 1. (It remains unclear, however, if this applied throughout the empire or only in the province of Egypt.)

79 Abandoning one's former citizenship seems to have been a condition for holding the Roman citizenship during the Republic. See Cicero, *pro Balbo* 11. 28.

80 See, e.g., the edict of Cyrene in FIRA I, no. 68. 3. 56-58.

decline of the old concept of the city-state and the gradual levelling of the inhabitants of the empire with respect to their legal and political rights.[81]

The constitutio Antoniniana

The process of Romanisation of the empire was completed in 212 AD when Emperor Caracalla issued an edict, the *constitutio Antoniniana*, by which he bestowed Roman citizenship upon all the free inhabitants of the empire who were members of organised communities.[82] According to Dio Cassius, one of the main reasons behind the introduction of this measure was the emperor's desire to increase the numbers of those who had to pay inheritance tax (*vicesima hereditatum*)[83] and the tax levied upon the emancipation of slaves (*vicesima libertatis* or *vicessima manumissionum*)[84] – taxes which only Roman citizens were required to pay.[85] It has also been suggested that the enactment of this law may also have been motivated by Caracalla's desire to mitigate public reaction to the assassination, ordered by him, of his brother Geta and the influential jurist and *praefectus praetorio* Papinian. But, whatever the emperor's motives may have been, the enactment of the *constitutio Antoniniana* can be seen as the final step in the long process of Romanisation of the empire and the realisation of political and legal unity within its borders. This process towards universalisation was precipitated by the dissemination of common values and, in particular, by the influence of Stoic philosophical ideas on the political theory of the empire. This transition from the concept of the city-state to that of a world state is reflected in the writings of Roman jurists of

---

81 On the extension of the Roman citizenship during the Republic and the Principate see A. N. Sherwin-White, *The Roman Citizenship*, 2nd edn, Oxford 1973; A. Lintott, *Imperium Romanum: Politics and Administration*, London & New York 1993, ch. 10.

82 D. 1. 5. 17. (Ulpianus); And see L. Mitteis and U. Wilcken, *Grundzüge und Chrestomathie der Papyruskunde* I, Leipzig 1912, 55-56; FIRA I, no. 88. Consider also C. Sasse, *Die Constitutio Antoniniana*, Wiesbaden 1958; M. Kaser, *Römische Rechtsgeschichte*, Göttingen 1976, 116-7; W. Kunkel/M. Schermaier, *Römische Rechtsgeschichte*, Cologne 2001, 80-1, 99-100; G. Crifò, *Lezioni di storia del diritto romano*, 3rd edn, Bologna 2000, 485 ff; M. Talamanca (ed.), *Lineamenti di storia del diritto romano*, Milan 1989, 520 ff.

83 From the time of Augustus Roman citizens had to pay five per cent tax on testamentary and intestate successions. The collection of this tax was assigned to special officers termed *procuratores hereditatium*.

84 Upon the manumission of a slave the slave's master paid a tax equal to five per cent of the slave's value.

85 Cassius Dio 78. 9.

the classical period who speak of Rome as 'our common country' (*communis patria*).[86]

With the enactment of the *constitutio Antoniniana* Roman law was extended to the whole empire. Although the government was slow in enforcing this change, local differences gradually disappeared and the law of the empire became uniform. However, in this process of universalisation of the law, Roman law was in many ways adapted to and influenced by local laws and customs. As a result, the common law that finally emerged was in reality a mixture of Roman law and local systems and thus very different in character from the Roman law of the pre-classical and early classical periods.

Social and Economic Conditions

The social classes

The senatorial class

During the Principate the term *ordo senatorius* referred to a small and exclusive social class consisting of elements of the old particio-plebeian nobility as well as of many *homines novi* (persons who had been elevated to the position of senator by the emperor) and their families. Officeholding and the possession of a considerable amount of fortune remained the two basic prerequisites for admission to the senate,[87] and membership of the *ordo senatorius* continued to be hereditary.[88] The prospective senator was required to fill one of the minor city magistracies (*vigintivirate*) after completing a term of military service as a tribune in a legion, and then, at the age of twenty-five, to become a candidate for the quaestorship, the office which entailed immediate admission to the senate. From the quaestorship the senatorial career led through the ordinary magistracies, the aedileship or tribunate and the praetorship, to the consulship. However, all the important positions of the *cursus honorum* were now subject to the direct or indirect influence of the emperor, who could use recommendations to the quaestorship, praetorship and consulship to

---

[86] D. 48. 22. 18. (19.) (Callistratus) and 50. 1. 33. (Modestinus).

[87] Membership of the *ordo senatorius* came to presuppose the possession of property valued at no less than one million sesterces. See Cassius Dio 54. 17. 26. 30; Tacitus, *Ann.* 1. 75; 2. 37.

[88] The senatorial order included the senators and their agnate descendants up to and including the third generation.

appoint as senators men who did not meet the normal requirements for enrolment.

The members of the senatorial order enjoyed many privileges,[89] and it was from their ranks that the highest officers of the state were chosen. At the same time, however, senators were subject to certain restrictions: they were required to reside in Rome, they could not engage in commercial activities, they were not allowed to conduct marriages with freed slaves (*libertini*) and, from the time of Trajan (98-117 AD), they were required to invest part of their patrimony in Italian lands. With the rapid decline in numbers of the old patricio-plebeian aristocracy[90] and the gradual shift of the economic and political centre of the empire from Italy to the provinces the composition of the senatorial class gradually changed. Already from the first century AD the recruitment of new senators from Italian families became more and more infrequent and provincial *novi homines* were admitted into the senate in ever increasing numbers. But the progressive provincialisation and de-Romanisation of the senate had little effect on the spirit of solidarity that always characterised the *ordo senatorius*, whose members strove to retain or expand their privileges, prestige and political influence, at times even against the imperial power.[91]

The equestrian class

As we saw in chapter 5, the emergence of the *ordo equester* as a distinct social class was precipitated by the judicial legislation of C. Gracchus in 122 BC, which gave the *equites* the right to serve as jurors in criminal trials. During the last century of the Republic the *equites* established themselves as Rome's capitalist nobility whose wealth was derived largely from business, industry, commerce and the financial management of state resources. Through their engagement in these activities they acquired considerable wealth and administrative skills and, from the early years of the Principate, they began to play an important part in the administration of the empire. But the loose structure of the equestrian order, its heterogenous composition and the varying economic circumstances of its members did

---

89 The sons of senators, in particular, were permitted to attend the meetings of the senate and enjoyed special rights and immunities in relation to both civil and military matters. Cassius Dio 52. 31; 53. 15; 54. 26; D. 1. 9. 5-10; D. 23. 2. 44; D. 50. 1. 22. 5; Tacitus, *Hist.* 2. 86.

90 Partly as a result of imperial persecution and partly because of late marriages and fewer children in the senatorial families.

91 On the position of the *ordo senatorius* during the early Empire see G. Alföldy, *The Social History of Rome*, London 1985, 115 ff. And see R. Syme, *The Augustan Aristocracy*, Oxford 1986.

not permit the *equites* to form a social group as closely-knit as the *ordo senatorius*. Moreover, by contrast with the senatorial order, membership of the equestrian order was not in principle hereditary, as admission depended not so much on blood ties as on the personal success of the individual.[92] In the course of time an increasing number of citizens from Italian and provincial communities were admitted into the equestrian class.

The career of an equestrian followed a fixed pattern of salaried positions: after a lengthy spell as a junior army officer, an equestrian was eligible for a procuratorship, i.e. a post in the civil service, usually the administration of public finances;[93] after filling several procuratorships, he might finally attain one of the highest offices in the imperial administration, such as that of the *praefectus vigilum*, the *praefectus annonae*, the *praefectus Aegypti* and the *praefectus praetorio*. Moreover, *equites* often served as members of the *consilium principis* and occasionally were appointed as governors of small provinces. In time the equestrian order was integrated into the political structure of the Principate, and emperors regularly chose new senators from among the most eminent equestrians, including many from the provinces. The latter sought to adopt the values and manners of the Roman aristocracy, but their loyalties were often divided between Rome and their native countries and their presence in positions of high responsibility was bitterly resented by members of the traditional Roman nobility. The resultant tension was but one more element in the delicate social fabric which emperors sought, ultimately without success, to hold together.[94]

The urban middle class

A notable feature of the early imperial period was the rapid growth of urban life in the provinces and the emergence of a prosperous middle class

---

92 The equestrian order was open to all free-born citizens who possessed property valued at no less than four hundred thousand sesterces. Admission to the order was controlled by the emperor who also had the right to elevate *equites* whose property exceeded in value the one million sesterces to the rank of senator.

93 From the time of Hadrian (117-138 AD) the most important offices of the imperial chancery (*scrinia*) were placed under the management of officers drawn from the equestrian class.

94 On the role of the *equites* during the Principate see G. Alföldy, *The Social History of Rome*, London 1985, 122 ff; T. P. Wiseman, 'The definition of "Eques Romanus" in the late Republic and early Empire'. 19 *Historia* (1970), 67-83; P. A. Brunt, 'Princeps and equites', 73 *JRS* (1983), 42-75; H. G. Pflaum, *Les carrières procuratoriennes équestres sous le Haut-Empire romain*, I-IV, Paris 1960-1961.

composed largely of land-owners, merchants, bankers, and private contractors. This class furnished the members of the municipal senates (*decuriones, ordo decurionum*) who, after their election, became citizens of Rome. In addition to their normal duties pertaining to local government, city management and the administration of justice, the *decuriones* were expected to make regular contributions to all kinds of local causes, such as public games and festivals, the building and maintenance of schools, temples, baths, libraries, etc. In return for such expenses, which were often considerable, a *decurio* received various privileges and honorific titles from the community and could anticipate admission into the *ordo equester* or even into the *ordo senatorius*. This Romanised class safeguarded Rome's political control over the conquered territories and facilitated the diffusion of Roman culture in the provinces.[95] Of particular importance also was the role which wealthy freedmen played in the social and economic life of Italian and provincial communities. Much of the actual conduct of business was in their hands and, although they had no part in political life, they came to constitute a 'second order' in society alongside the *ordo decurionum* (as did the *ordo equester* alongside the *ordo senatorius* in the imperial society at large). This class is sometimes referred to as *ordo Augustalium*, as it furnished the members of the *Augustales*, the body who cared for the imperial cult throughout the empire. From the second century AD the heavy taxation that was imposed by the emperors on the provincials to cover the ever increasing cost of government led to the gradual decline of the urban middle class which finally disappeared during the crisis of the third century AD.

The lower classes

As has been noted in chapter 5, in the later years of the Republic the term *plebs* gradually lost its original meaning and, by the time of Augustus, it came to refer not to a politically distinct social group but to the lower classes of the population in general – those whose means were small and whose position in society was humble. As Roman citizens, the members of the *plebs* enjoyed a social advantage over slaves, freedmen and foreigners but, with the decline of the popular assemblies, they ceased to play a part in the political process. Although many of them were involved in the operation of small businesses, the majority were unable to earn a steady living as they lacked the essential capital to compete with foreign entrepreneurs and in the labour market the availability of cheap slave

---

[95] On the *ordo decurionum* see G. Alföldy, *The Social History of Rome*, London 1985, 126 ff.

labour made employment difficult. In general, the urban proletariat (*plebs urbana*) enjoyed a better social position than the masses of the rural population (*plebs rustica*), as its members had better prospects for employment, more scope for participation in public life, and were regularly provided with food supplies (in Rome often by the emperor who, as *defensor plebis*, assumed responsibility for their physical needs, and in other cities by wealthy citizens). During the imperial era large numbers of poverty-stricken Roman citizens and foreigners continued to place themselves under the protection of wealthy men as clients. A client was expected to be at his patron's beck and call at all hours of the day and to escort him about the city. In return for his services the client received daily gifts of food, money or clothes and occasional favours. By far the largest class in society was that of the small farmers and peasants. The basic complaint of the peasantry during this period was exploitation. Significantly, the manner in which the peasantry was exploited followed much the same pattern as that of the urban clientship: essentially the peasant had been reduced to the position of a rural client. Instead of being a small independent land holder living a free life in his rural community, the peasant had become almost everywhere in the empire the tenant of an absentee landlord and, as such, was subject to the same kind of humiliating servitude and social degradation as the urban clients. The social relationship implicit in the system of clientship, that is, the complete dependence of the poor upon the rich, was a fact of life everywhere in the Roman world.

From the second century AD a new social distinction began to emerge between two broad social groups, the *honestiores* ('honourable') and the *humiliores* ('humble'). The former constituted the aristocracy of the empire and included senators, equestrians, civil servants, soldiers and the members of the provincial town councils (*decuriones*). All the rest belonged to the class of the *humiliores*. The *humiliores* had a distinctly inferior standing in the eyes of the law and were subject to heavier penalties, including crucifixion and forced labour in the state mines; they had little chance of securing any kind of state job and were forced to experience all the discomforts of city life without enjoying any of its benefits.[96]

---

[96] See on this P. Garnsey, *Social Status and Legal Privilege in the Roman Empire*, Oxford 1970.

The freedmen

The freedmen (*libertini*) were former slaves who had been granted freedom through the formal process of manumission. In the later Republic manumission had become so common a practice that, at the beginning of the Augustan era, the number of freedmen and their offspring exceeded by far that of the free-born Roman citizens. This was seen as a social problem by the Roman aristocracy and, under Augustus, measures were introduced aimed at reducing the number of freedmen. These included the introduction of a tax on manumitted slaves, the curtailment of manumission by will and the prohibition of manumission by persons under the age of twenty. Manumission did not result in complete freedom for the former slave. Besides the permanent stigma of being an ex-slave, strict rules governed relations between freedmen and their former masters (*patroni*). Above all, a *libertinus* owed allegiance to his *patronus* and had no legal rights over him. Thus it is not surprising that the great majority of freedmen continued in the same jobs which they had before they were freed in their masters' households. In spite of their inferior status, a minority of freedmen succeeded in acquiring considerable wealth, especially in the provinces, and came to play an important part in the empire's economic life.[97] Of particular importance was the role of the freedmen who belonged to the imperial household. During the earlier part of the imperial era these imperial freedmen served at every level of the official bureaucracy and many of them were elevated to positions of power.[98]

The slaves

During the later Republic and early Principate slaves constituted a significant segment of the population and served many different functions in economic life. Large numbers of them worked as domestic servants and as land labourers on the plantations, and skilled slaves were employed in various trades and industries. The treatment of slaves varied considerably depending upon such factors as geographical location, personal skills,

---

97 On the role of freedmen in trade and commerce see A. Kirschenbaum, *Sons, Slaves and Freedmen in Roman Commerce*, Hebrew U. and Catholic U. of America Press 1987; P. Garnsey, 'Independent Freedmen and the Economy of Roman Italy under the Principate', *Klio* 63 (1981), 359.

98 Pliny, *Paneg*. 88. 16. On the role of the imperial freedmen consider P. R. C. Weaver, *Familia Caesaris: a Social Study of the Emperor's Freedmen and Slaves*, Cambridge 1972; H. Chantraine, *Freigelassene und Sklaven im Dienst der römischen Kaiser*, Wiesbaden 1967.

attitudes of owners and political conditions.[99] The slave revolts of the later Republic attest to the widespread discontent among the slave population at the time, but from the first century AD the situation of slaves gradually improved as a result of the promulgation of humanitarian legislation by emperors.[100] The *lex Petronia* (of unknown date, probably second half of the first century AD), prohibiting owners from forcing their slaves to fight with wild beast without a magistrate's permission, was probably the earliest legislative enactment aimed at the protection of slaves. Moreover, under a law of Hadrian, also adopted by Antoninus Pius, a master was forbidden to put a slave to death unless the latter was condemned by a court of justice.[101] A special category of slaves were those who belonged to the imperial household. Most of these slaves performed menial household tasks, but some rose to subordinate positions in the provincial administration and a few became unofficial advisers to the emperor himself.[102] But, following the administrative reforms of Hadrian, the role of slaves in the administration was curtailed and by the third century AD slaves were no longer employed as members of the imperial bureaucracy.

The army

Under Augustus and his successors the principle of maintaining at all times a large standing army was fully recognised. Although the emperor retained the right of ordering a conscription and every Roman citizen was still liable to military service, in practice voluntary enlistment supplied most of the recruits. The legionaries were drawn mainly from Italy and the Roman population of the provinces. Besides the regular army of citizens, a

---

[99] For a general look at the condition of slaves in ancient Rome see W. L. Westerman, *The Slave Systems of Greek and Roman Antiquity*, Philadelphia, 1955; M. I. Finley, *Ancient Slavery and Modern Ideology*, London and New York 1980; K. R. Bradley, *Slaves and Masters in the Roman Empire: a Study in Social Control*, Oxford 1987; K. Hopkins, *Conquerors and Slaves: Sociological Studies in Roman History* I, Cambridge 1978; K. R. Bradley, *Slavery and Society at Rome*, Cambridge 1997, repr. 1997; Z. Yavetz, *Slaves and Slavery in Ancient Rome*, London 1988.

[100] The introduction of such legislation to some extent reflects the influence of Stoic ethical teaching on the attitudes of the Roman governing classes. See, e.g., Seneca, *Epist. Moral.* 31. 11. And see W. Westermann, *The Slave Systems of Greek and Roman Antiquity*, Philadelphia 1955, 113-7.

[101] Consider D. 18. 1. 42. (Marcianus); D. 48. 8. 11. 1. 2. (Modestinus); G. 1. 52. 53; Suetonius, *Claud.* 25.

[102] See P. R. C. Weaver, *Familia Caesaris: a Social Study of the Emperor's Freedmen and Slaves*, Cambridge 1972; H. Chantraine, *Freigelassene und Sklaven im Dienst der romischen Kaiser*, Wiesbaden 1967.

significant segment of the armed forces was formed by auxiliaries, troops recruited from the non Roman population of the provinces. The higher officers were drawn from the senatorial and equestrian orders and the higher classes of the provincial communities.[103] From the early years of the Principate the emperor, as commander-in-chief of the army, was alone responsible for all matters relating to the organisation and maintenance of the armed forces. He appointed the legates who commanded the legions stationed in the imperial provinces and the officers in charge of the auxiliary troops, decided on the distribution of troops in the provinces and their tasks, and made arrangements for the payment of army officers and soldiers. In the course of the second century AD the army became a separate and powerful order in the state and, by the beginning of the third century AD, as the political institutions of the Principate declined, imperial power came to depend almost entirely upon the support of the army.

Economic conditions

The conditions of internal peace and security that prevailed during the early imperial era promoted economic development and led to high levels of prosperity throughout the empire. This prosperity was based largely on agriculture and stock-raising (the principal sources of wealth in Italy and the western provinces). Next to agriculture in importance were industry and commerce. International trade was facilitated by the expansion of the Roman road network, the security of transport, the establishment of a currency system for a whole empire and the opening up of new markets in Italy and the provinces. In the second century AD regular commercial contacts had been established with lands as distant as India, China, Arabia, central and southern Africa and the Scandinavian regions. These lands supplied articles of luxury, such as gold, ivory, precious stones, silk, amber and spices. But by far more important was the trade conducted within the empire itself, between different provinces and cities. Grain and other agricultural products made up the bulk of the trade, but manufactured articles played an increasing part, as did the necessary raw materials for every kind of industry. In the West, Italy was the chief centre of industry, supplying manufactured goods (such as pottery, metal and glass articles and clothes) to markets from Britain to the Danube regions. In the East many cities, such as Alexandria, Ephesus, Corinth and Antioch, remained thriving industrial and commercial centres.[104]

---

[103] For a closer look see G. R. Watson, *The Roman Soldier*, London 1969.

[104] On the development of trade and industry see P. Garnsey and R. Saller, *The Roman Empire: Economy, Society and Culture*, London 1987; R. Duncan-

However, already from the second century AD, the first signs of economic decline appeared, first in Italy and later in other parts of the empire. The Italian economy was based on the export of agricultural products (such as wine and olive oil) and manufactured goods to the provinces. But as more and more Italians migrated to Spain, Gaul and the eastern provinces and these provinces began to produce and export such goods in large quantities, export markets were lost, trade declined and agriculture and industry in Italy ceased to develop. A further factor that precipitated economic decline was the re-emergence of the large-scale ownership of land and the gradual disappearance of the small independent farmers, both in Italy and the provinces. As fewer countries were now conquered, the supply of cheap slave labour dwindled and the great landlords began to give up large-scale farming preferring instead to let their lands to tenants. A tenant would be given a piece of land, usually for a period of five years, and would pay the rent on an annual basis. Many small farmers, unable or unwilling to run the risks which small-scale farming involved, were glad to give up their lands and become tenants. The spread of the tenant system and the change from systematic farming to the more primitive methods practised by the small tenants resulted in the gradual decline of agriculture. As the population of the cities and towns depended upon the produce of land, the fall in agricultural production led to a deterioration of living conditions in the urban centres. At the same time, as the cities became more and more dependent upon the land workers, the rift between city and country widened and the peasantry became more and more oppressed. Besides the usual peasant complaint about their economic exploitation by the land-holding nobility, the peasantry felt totally alienated from the culture and society of the urban centres and a smouldering resentment of the city was added by the peasants to the lengthening list of tensions within the empire.

Economic conditions deteriorated further as a result of the ever-increasing taxation imposed on the population by the imperial government. The situation became critical in the third century AD when, under the threat of internal unrest and external invasion, the government raised its demands to new heights. The emperors sought to meet the cost of government in part by imposing more taxes on the urban population of the provinces and in part by introducing a system of compulsory public labour and extraordinary contributions of money or supplies. In the cities the wealthier classes from which the holders of municipal offices were drawn

---

Jones, *The Economy of the Roman Empire. Quantitative Studies*, Cambridge 1982; F. de Martino, *Storia economica di Roma antica* II. *L' impero*, Florence 1979.

were made responsible for the payment to the state of the taxes and, if they were unable to collect the amount that was demanded, they had to pay it out of their own fortune. As a result, the holding of public office came to be regarded as a burden, rather than as a privilege, and service in the municipal administration became compulsory for those with the requisite property qualifications. At the same time, as the revenues of the state dwindled, the emperors resorted to the continuous debasement of the coinage in order to meet the cost of government. Those most affected by the resulting high inflation were the members of the urban middle class and the municipal councils in the provinces whose income was all but wiped out.

The Crisis of the Third Century

By the close of the second century AD the signs of the oncoming crisis had become clear: a weakening of the imperial authority and the political institutions of the Principate, a rapid deterioration of economic conditions, social unrest and the emergence of new external threats on the empire's frontiers. With the virtual abandonment of the principle of diarchy (the double rule of the emperor and the senate)[105] and the gradual militarisation of the administration, the emperors came to depend entirely upon the support of the legions, and the army, once the servant of the empire, now became its master. In order to meet the ever-increasing demands of the army the imperial government imposed heavy taxes on the population and devalued the currency, precipitating the collapse of the empire's economic system. At the same time, with the proliferation of military usurpers, the empire was torn by civil wars and was left undefended against external enemies. From 235 AD disorder reigned as different armies, one after another, made and unmade emperors at will and used their own strength to plunder without restraint the lands of the empire.[106] As a result of the continuous military mutinies and struggles between different pretenders of the throne the state's defences were weakened and the frontier of the

[105] This took place during the reign of Emperor Septimius Severus (193-211 AD). An attempt to restore the senate to its previous position was made by Emperor Alexander Severus (222-235 AD), but ended in failure in the face of strong opposition by the army. By that time the most important government posts were held by members of a militarised equestrian class and the senate itself had come to consist largely of former army commanders and favourites of the emperors.

[106] Of the twenty-three emperors who ruled from 235 to 285 AD only two died a natural death. The rest were assassinated by their own troops or were killed in military campaigns.

empire was invaded at almost every point. On the Rhine and Danube frontiers Germanic tribes repeatedly crossed into Roman territory and in the East the Persians, under the Sassanid dynasty, rose up again and began to raid deep into the Roman provinces.[107] In the wake of the devastation caused by war and plunder commerce and industry declined, trade came to a standstill, once flourishing urban centres decayed and widespread epidemics ravaged the population.

The political, social and economic crisis was accompanied by profound changes in the cultural and religious life of the empire. Deep psychological changes were occurring and the age was marked by spiritual unrest and a widespread interest in supernatural faith. There was a growing demand for some cure for the ills of life, a cure which neither the established state religion nor the dominant philosophies of the day were able to offer. The weakness of the imperial authority, the corruption of the ruling classes, the insecurity of life and property gave rise to a general feeling that the world was growing old and that some terrible catastrophe was impending. The pessimism that prevailed throughout the Roman world is reflected in both the Christian and pagan literature of this period. It was during this period that oriental mystery religions poured into Rome and other parts of the empire and attracted large numbers of followers from all classes of society. These cults were designed to play upon human emotions; their aim was to bring an awareness of sin, a desire for salvation through the purification of the soul and a promise of eternal life in a future world. In a more articulate form the same attitudes found expression in philosophy. The philosophical schools of this period[108] returned to the religious and metaphysical aspects of previous philosophies and attempts were made to combine Greco-Roman and eastern thought. During the same period scientific curiosity and the standards of art and literature declined and this decline continued in the centuries that followed.[109]

---

[107] Under the threat of barbarian attacks some provinces, left unprotected by the central government, declared their independence from Rome. Gaul, for example, became independent for nearly ten years during this period.

[108] Among the most influential of these schools was Neoplatonism, founded by the philosopher Plotinus (204-270 AD).

[109] For a closer look at this period see M. Cary and H. Schullard, *A History of Rome*, 3rd edn, London 1975, 507 ff; R. MacMullen, *Roman Government's Response to Crisis, AD 235-337*, New Haven 1976; F. Millar, *The Roman Empire and its Neighbours*, 2nd edn, London 1981, ch. 13; M. I. Rostovtzeff, *Social and Economic History of the Roman Empire*, 2nd edn, Oxford 1957, ch. 10; G. Alföldy, *The Social History of Rome*, London, 1985, ch. 6; A. H. M. Jones, *The Later Roman Empire 284-602*, I, Oxford 1964, 21 ff.

Some comments on the causes of the decline of the empire in the third century

The crisis of the third century was the result of the influence of a complex set of interconnected factors. Some of these factors had their origins in conditions already present in earlier ages, especially in the flaws in the system of government established by Augustus and his successors: reliance of emperors on the army to maintain control of the state; creation of a vast administrative apparatus which, in the long run, could not be supported by the resources of the empire; and perpetuation of a class structure that failed to give the producing classes rewards equal to the burdens imposed upon them. Furthermore, in a state where all real power was concentrated in the hands of the ruler and his officials public spirit decreased and servility and lack of enterprise took the place of active participation in public affairs. As a consequence, the ideal which had meant so much to the early Romans – the strong and free citizen who threw himself into the service of his city and state – was all but destroyed by the imperial system. Among the chief causes of the economic decline were the disruption of agriculture, trade and industry by foreign and civil wars, lack of economic equilibrium, rapid inflation combined with coin deterioration and low and declining productivity. The peasant classes, in particular, upon which the empire's economy ultimately depended, were no longer able to bear the burden of taxation and to support such numerous classes as the soldiers, urban proletariat, state officials and estate holders with their numerous retinues. At the same time, as the urban middle class was crushed by high taxation and gradually merged with the oppressed peasantry, cities became less prosperous and the basis of the economy shifted back to an agrarian pattern. These and possibly other controversial or unknown facts of social change inexorably eroded the resources of the empire.

Towards the end of the third century the army was eventually controlled, external threats checked and the political unity of the empire restored. However, politically, economically and culturally the Roman world that emerged from the crisis of the third century was very different from that of the republican and early imperial periods. The civilisation and forms of social and cultural life which had been characteristic of the ancient Greco-Roman world had been irreversibly broken down, and the coming of the Middle Ages was at hand.

8 The Classical Period of Roman Law

Introductory

During the Principate Roman law reached its highest point of development. This was largely due to the influence of the jurists, through whose achievements the genius of the Romans for law found its full scope. The role of the jurists grew in importance after Augustus granted to specially qualified jurists the right of speaking with imperial authority (*ius respondendi*), thus giving them for the first time a constitutional position. Gradually the most distinguished jurists were drawn into the imperial circle and, from the time of Hadrian (117-138 AD), they exercised their chief functions as members of the administrative apparatus of the emperor. During the same period important changes were taking place in the field of legislation. With the concentration of more and more power in the hands of the emperor, decrees emanating from the imperial chancery (*constitutiones principum*) became the principal source of law. The growth of imperial legislative authority was gradual and the first emperors generally achieved their legislative ends through action of the assemblies and the senate. But by the end of the first century AD the assemblies had ceased to play a part in the legislative process. Although its role in legislation was now fully recognised, the senate lost much of its earlier independence as a constitutional body and, in time, senatorial legislation tended to become a mere instrument in the emperor's hands. The *ius praetorium*, the body of law derived from the edicts of the praetors, continued to exist, but praetorian initiatives now became increasingly rare. About 130 AD the content of the *edictum perpetuum* was fixed once and for all, and from that time the *ius praetorium* ceased to operate as an independent source of law.

Sources of Law

Custom

Although classical jurists did not count custom (*usus*, *mos*, *consuetudo*) among the formal sources of law,[1] custom continued to play a part as a basis of the law that applied in the provinces. The local systems of law, both written and customary, which applied in the provinces prior to the Roman conquest remained in force in the form of custom and continued to govern the social and economic life of provincial communities save insofar as they might prove embarrassing to Roman rule. References to customary law, as it applied in the provinces, can thus be found in a number of imperial constitutions, as well as in the juristic literature of this period.[2] As far as Roman law itself was concerned, custom continued to exert an indirect influence on both lawmaking and the application of the law through the interpretations of the jurists, who regarded certain long-established norms as so traditional as not to need any specific legal authority.[3] After the extension of Roman law in the provinces, following the granting of the Roman citizenship to all the free inhabitants of the empire by the *constitutio Antoniniana* (212 AD), many of the earlier local laws continued to apply in the form of custom if sanctioned by imperial legislation.[4]

---

1 G. 1. 2; D. 1. 1. 7. (Papinianus); D. 1. 2. 3. 12. (Pomponius).

2 See, e.g., the *rescriptum* of Emperors Septimius Severus and Caracalla of 199 AD in L. Mitteis and U. Wilcken, *Grundzüge und Chrestomathie der Papyruskunde* , Leipzig 1912, 374; FIRA I, 84 & 85. Ulpian speaks of custom as a direct source of law in the provinces in those cases involving disputes which cannot be resolved on the basis of an existing written law. See D. 1. 3. 33.

3 According to the jurist Julian, rules derived from custom ought to be relied upon in those cases not covered by written law, or where the relevant statute has been repealed by salient agreement of the people through desuetude (D. 1. 3. 32.). It is not clear, however, if this view reflects the classical approach, as the relevant passage might have been inserted by post-classical writers.

4 On the role of custom as a source of law see H. F. Jolowicz and B. Nicholas, *Historical Introduction to the Study of Roman Law*, 3rd edn, Cambridge 1972, 353-5; J. A. C. Thomas, 'Custom and Roman Law', 31 *TR* (1963), 39-53; O. F. Robinson, *The Sources of Roman Law*, London and New York 1997, 28-29; A. A. Schiller, *An American Experience in Roman Law*, Göttingen 1971, 41 ff; *Roman Law: Mechanisms of Development*, New York 1978, 560 ff.

The *leges*

As has been noted, the assemblies of the people continued to meet to elect magistrates and to pass laws until the close of the first century AD. However, the laws they enacted were all part of imperial policy and expressed the emperor's will. In the early years of the Principate Augustus used the popular assemblies to put through a series of important laws concerning the administration of justice (*leges Iuliae iudiciorum publicorum et privatorum*),[5] matters relating to marriage and divorce (*lex Iulia de maritandis ordinibus, lex Papia Poppaea*),[6] the criminalisation of adultery (*lex Iulia de adulteriis coercendis*),[7] the penal repression of

---

5 These laws were enacted in 17 BC and completed the transition from the *legis actiones* to the formulary procedure.

6 The *lex Iulia de maritandis ordinibus* was passed in 18 BC and was supplemented by the *lex Papia Poppaea* in 9 AD. The aim of both laws was to promote marriage and the procreation of children and to check the decline of traditional family values. The earlier statute introduced several prohibitions on marriage (it prohibited marriages between members of the senatorial class and their former slaves and between free-born men and women convicted of adultery). At the same time various privileges were granted to married people who had children, whereas severe social and economic disadvantages were imposed on unmarried and childless persons. The later law excluded unmarried men aged between twenty-five and sixty and unmarried women aged between twenty and fifty from succession under a will. Both laws came to be referred to as *leges Iulia et Papia Poppaea*. See Bruns, *Fontes* I, no. 23, 115 ff. And see J. F. Gardner, *Family and Familia in Roman Law and Life*, Oxford 1998, 47 ff; M. Kaser, *Das römische Privatrecht*, Munich 1971, 318 ff; A. Guarino, *Diritto privato romano*, Naples 2001, 566 ff.

7 Under this law, enacted in 18 BC , adultery (*adulterium*) was made a public crime (but only when it was committed by a married woman). The father of the adulteress was permitted to kill her and her partner if he caught them in his or her husband's house. A husband whose wife had committed adultery had to divorce her, for otherwise he could be found guilty of match-making (*lenocidium*). He (or the woman's father) could also bring an accusation against her before a court of law within two months after the divorce. Thereafter and for four months any citizen could bring a criminal charge. The punishment of a woman found guilty of adultery was banishment, accompanied by confiscation of one-third of her property and loss of part of her dowry. Under the same enactment the illicit intercourse with an unmarried woman or a widow (*stuprum*) was also made subject to criminal prosecution. See Bruns, *Fontes* I, no. 21; D. 48. 5. 13-14; D. 48. 5. 30. 1. (Ulpianus); D. 23. 2. 44. (Paulus). And see P. E. Corbett, *The Roman Law of Marriage*, Oxford 1930, repr. 1969, 133 ff; J. F. Gardner, *Women in Roman Law and Society*, London 1986, 117 ff; *Family and Familia in Roman Law and Life*, Oxford 1998, 121-2; M. Kaser,

electoral corruption (*lex Iulia de ambitu*)[8] and the operation of the senate (*lex Iulia de senato habendo*).[9] Other important legislative enactments of this period included the *lex Fufia Caninia* (2 BC) and the *lex Aelia Sentia* (4 AD), both introducing restrictions on testamentary manumission, and the *lex Claudia*, a law passed on the proposal of Emperor Claudius, abolishing the guardianship of the next relatives (*tutela legitima*) over women.[10] The last known *lex* was an agrarian law passed in the time of Emperor Nerva (96-98 AD).[11]

The edicts of the magistrates

After the establishment of the Principate the praetors and other law-dispensing magistrates continued to exercise their traditional judicial functions. However, the productive strength of the *ius honorarium* as an independent source of law gradually diminished as magisterial initiatives became increasingly rare. Whatever changes were made in the edicts largely embraced measures which had been introduced by other law-making agencies (such as *leges* or *senatus consulta*). By the end of the first century AD, the praetorian edict, as well as the edicts of the aediles and the provincial governors, had become solidified and immutable.[12] This state of affairs was formally recognised during the reign of Hadrian by the codification of the praetorian edict – a task assigned by the emperor to the jurist Salvius Julianus. Although very little can be said with certainty about the way in which the work of codification was carried out, it is believed

---

Das römische Privatrecht, Munich 1971, 319, 323, 326 ff; A. Guarino, *Diritto privato romano*, Naples 2001, 572 ff.

8 The aim of this law, which was passed in 18 BC, was to combat bribery in elections.

9 This law was enacted in 10 BC and contained provisions regulating the voting procedure in the senate.

10 G. 1. 157. For a closer look see J. F. Gardner, *Women in Roman Law and Society*, London and Sydney 1986, 14-20.

11 On the role of popular legislation during the Principate see H. F. Jolowicz and B. Nicholas, *Historical Introduction to the Study of Roman Law*, 3rd edn, Cambridge 1972, 355-6; W. Kunkel, *An Introduction to Roman Legal and Constitutional History*, 2nd edn, Oxford 1973, 125; A. A. Schiller, *Roman Law: Mechanisms of Development*, New York 1978, 225-6; W. Kunkel/M. Schermaier, *Römische Rechtsgeschichte*, Cologne 2001, 165; A. Guarino, *Storia del diritto romano*, Naples 1996, 428.

12 However, there is evidence in the sources that the provincial governors continued to issue special edicts (*edicta repentina*) in certain exceptional cases. See, e.g., the edict of the governor of Egypt Tiberius Iulius Alexander of 68 AD in FIRA I, no. 58.

that the edicts of both the *praetor urbanus* and the *praetor peregrinus*, as well as that of the curule aediles, provided the basis for this compilation. The codified edict was formally ratified by a *senatus consultum* around 130 AD.[13] From that time magistrates were expected to accept and administer the edict as it stood, without modifications, and if further changes were needed these were to be made by imperial enactment.[14] In the years that followed the codification of the edict the praetors no longer had control over the content of their edicts and their role was reduced to that of subordinate officials without any law-making powers.

Imperial constitutions

In the early years of the Principate the emperor achieved his legislative ends indirectly, through controlled decrees of the senate and enactments of the people's assemblies. But as imperial power continued to grow at the expense of the old republican institutions the emperor acquired independent legislative authority and began to create new legal rules directly in a number of ways. According to Roman jurists, the direct law-making power of the emperor was justified on the basis that, as the emperor received his power from the Roman people through the *lex de imperio*, his enactments rested ultimately on the popular will. By the early second century AD the enactments of the emperors (*consitutiones principum*) came to be recognised as a distinct source of law, alongside the *leges* and the *senatus consulta*, and as having full statutory force (*legis vigorem*).[15]

There were four types of imperial constitutions: *decreta*, *edicta*, *rescripta* and *mandata*.[16] The *decreta* were judicial decisions issued by the

---

13 See D. *const. Tanta*, 18.

14 The text of the codified edict has not been preserved in its original form. Modern reconstructions are based on commentaries and interpretations of later jurists, especially those of Pomponius, Gaius, Ulpian and Paul. See O. Lenel, *Das Edictum perpetuum*, 3rd edn, Leipzig 1927, repr. Aalen 1956. On the codification of the edict see H. F. Jolowicz and B. Nicholas, *Historical Introduction to the Study of Roman Law*, 3rd edn, Cambridge 1972, 356 ff; A. A. Schiller, *Roman Law: Mechanisms of Development*, New York 1978, 429 ff; M. Kaser, *Römische Rechtsgeschichte*, Göttingen 1976, 148-9, 153-4; A. Guarino, *Storia del diritto romano*, Naples 1996, 439 ff; G. Crifò, *Lezioni di storia del diritto romano*, 3rd edn, Bologna 2000, 325 ff.

15 G. 1. 5; *Inst.* 1. 2. 6; D. 1. 4. 1. pr. (Ulpianus).

16 See H.F. Jolowicz and B. Nicholas, *Historical Introduction to the Study of Roman Law*, 3rd edn, Cambridge 1972, 365 ff; W. Kunkel, *An Introduction to Roman Legal and Constitutional History*, 2nd edn, Oxford 1973, 127 ff; A. A.

emperor as a judge of first instance or on appeal in exercise of his jurisdiction in civil and criminal matters.[17] Cases referred to the emperor were decided according to the existing law, but the emperor (like the praetor and other jurisdictional magistrates) allowed himself a considerable degree of freedom in the interpretation of the applicable rules and sometimes introduced new legal principles. Thus, in criminal cases he had a free hand in the definition of offences, the choice of penalty and the mode and amount of punishment. Although his decisions were not always made in the formal context of a trial, they were usually regarded as actual statements of the law binding in all future cases. Considering the amount of time the emperor had to devote to other matters (as well as his lack of expertise in legal issues) it is more likely that, in many cases, the imperial decisions came not from the emperor himself but from his advisers in the *consilium principis* which, from the second century AD, included many learned jurists.[18]

The emperor, as holder of magisterial *imperium*, issued edicts (*edicta*) by which he made known his orders and intentions to his subjects. The imperial edicts were similar in form to those of the republican magistrates. Unlike the magistrates, however, the emperor possessed almost unlimited powers and remained in office for life. Thus, his edicts carried much more weight and were usually broader in scope than those of the magistrates, embracing the whole business of the state. Moreover, they remained valid in perpetuity, unless they fell into disuse or were formally rescinded by subsequent legislation. Imperial edicts were often aimed at

---

Schiller, *Roman Law: Mechanisms of Development*, New York 1978, 480 ff; O. F. Robinson, *The Sources of Roman Law*, London and New York 1997, 34-39; M. Kaser, *Römische Rechtsgeschichte*, Göttingen 1976, 149 ff; W. Kunkel/M. Schermaier, *Römische Rechtsgeschichte*, Cologne 2001, 167 ff; A. Guarino, *Storia del diritto romano*, Naples 1996, 448-50; M. Talamanca (ed.), *Lineamenti di storia del diritto romano*, Milan 1989, 409 ff, 417 ff; G. Crifò, *Lezioni di storia del diritto romano*, 3rd edn, Bologna 2000, 312 ff.

17 The appellate jurisdiction of the emperor was explained on the grounds that, since the emperor received his powers from the people and hence acted in their name, an appeal to him was the exercise of the age-old citizen's right of appeal from the decision of a magistrate to the judgement of the people in the assembly.

18 There has been dispute as to whether a formal judicial organ distinct from the *consilium principis* had been established to deal with cases referred to the emperor. See on this J. A. Crook, *Consilium principis,* Cambridge 1955; W. Kunkel, 'Die Funktion des Konsiliums in der magistratischen Strafjustiz und im Kaisergericht', *SZ* 84 (1967) 218-44 and SZ 85 (1968), 253-329; *An Introduction to Roman Legal and Constitutional History*, 2nd edn, Oxford 1973, 110, 130.

modifying existing rules of law or at introducing new ones. Within their scope fell matters pertaining to both public and private law, such as the constitution of the courts and the administration of justice, the organisation and administration of the provinces, and the granting of the Roman citizenship. To the category of imperial edicts belonged, for example, the *consitutio Antoniniana* of Emperor Caracalla (212 AD), by which the Roman citizenship was bestowed upon all the free inhabitants of the empire.[19]

The *rescripta*, or correspondence, were written answers given by the emperor to questions addressed to him by state officials and private citizens seeking advice on matters subject to judicial determination. When the emperor's answer to a petition or inquiry was given in a separate letter it was referred to as *epistula*. The *epistulae* were prepared by the imperial *scrinium ab epistulis* and were usually addressed to state organs in Rome or in the provinces.[20] The term *subscriptiones*, on the other hand, was used to denote answers to petitions, usually from private citizens, endorsed on the application itself.[21] The *rescripta* were initially of an advisory character, much like the *responsa prudentium*; they simply stated what the law was, and what the correct decision would be, if the facts, as stated in the relevant application, were proven.[22] If the judge trying the case felt that the facts had been proven, he was bound by the imperial decision contained in the rescript. In the course of time, as it became customary for judges to

---

19 Consider also Augustus's edict restricting the torture of slaves in D. 48. 18. 8. pr. (Paulus); and see the edict of Emperor Claudius concerning the release of slaves abandoned by their owners because of grave bodily weakness in D. 40. 8. 2. (Modestinus).

20 See, e.g., L. Mitteis and U. Wilcken, *Grundzüge und Chrestomathie der Papyruskunde*, Leipzig 1912, 373; also in Bruns, *Fontes* I, no. 196; FIRA I, no. 78.

21 W. Kunkel, *An Introduction to Roman Legal and Constitutional History* , 2nd edn, Oxford 1973, 128-9; see also W. Williams, 'The *libellus* procedure and the Severan papyri', 64 *JRS* (1974), 86-103.

22 Among the examples of *rescripta* that can be found in the Code of Justinian are the following: 'The Emperors Diocletian and Maximian to Aurelius. The opinion which has prevailed is that a partnership can validly be established in which one partner contributes money and the other labour' (C. 4. 37. 1.); 'The Emperor Alexander to Aurelius Maro, soldier. If your father sold the house under compulsion, the transaction will not be upheld as valid, since it was not carried out in good faith; for a purchase in bad faith is invalid. If therefore you bring an action in your own name, the provincial governor will intervene, especially since you declare that you are ready to refund the buyer the price that was paid'. (C. 4. 44. 1.) See also C. 9. 9. 2; 7. 61. 1; D. 48. 15. 6 pr. (Callistratus). Consider also Pliny, *Ep*. 10.

petition the emperors for decisions on difficult questions of law, the importance of the rescripts increased and, by the middle of the second century AD, they had become an important factor in the development of private law. It should be added here that the authors of the imperial rescripts were, in most cases, the jurists who served as members of the *consilium principis*.[23]

The *mandata* were instructions on administrative and judicial matters given by the emperor to imperial officials in Rome and the provinces, and were always binding on the official to whom they were addressed. They pertained to matters such as public works, the conduct of magistrates while in office, court procedure and the administration of justice.[24] Those addressed to provincial governors were binding only in the province for which they had been issued and continued in force for as long as their recipient remained in office. Based on the emperor's *imperium proconsulare*, the *mandata* were at first personal and internal, but as imperial administration evolved, they developed to become more official and public. Moreover, although they were initially binding only for as long as the emperor and the official to whom they were addressed remained in office, they were often renewed by the next emperor and thus they could retain their validity for a long period of time. In this way a substantial body of law was built up which formed a new source of norms of general application which was of particular importance for the development of certain branches of the law, such as the law of *fideicomissa*, and the law that applied in the provinces.[25] In the course of time various compilations of imperial *mandata* were produced, which became known as *libri mandatorum*.[26]

---

23 Among them were the famous jurists Celsus, Papinian and Paul. See M. Kaser, *Römische Rechtsgeschichte*, Göttingen 1976, 179-80, 188; T. Honoré, *Emperors and Lawyers*, Oxford 1994, ch. 2.

24 An example of an imperial instruction of this kind is the *mandatum* of Emperor Trajan stating that soldiers could make valid wills without being bound by the formalities that had to be observed by ordinary citizens. See D. 29. 1. 1. (Ulpianus). Consider also D. 1. 18. 3. (Paulus); 48. 3. 6. 1. (Marcianus). And see V. Marotta, *Mandata Principum*, Turin 1991.

25 Gaius and other classical jurists did not include the *mandata* among the imperial constitutions but mention them as a special category of imperial enactments. See G. 1. 5. And see C. 1. 15; Consider on this N. van der Wal and J. H. A. Lokin, *Historiae iuris graeco-romani delineatio. Les sources du droit byzantin de* 300 *a* 1453, Groningen 1985, 10 ff.

26 Based on such a collection of imperial mandates is the *Gnomon* of the *Idios Logos*, a work dating from the second half of the second century AD. This work, which has partially been preserved in a papyrus, contains instructions concerned with the financial administration of Egypt; a number of provisions

The acts of an emperor were rescinded (*rescissio actorum*) if, after his death, he was subjected, by senatorial decree, to a *damnatio memoriae* – a disgrace inflicted upon the memory of an emperor whose conduct was stigmatised as morally reprehensible. The emperor's acts were restored if the *damnatio memoriae* was subsequently repealed.

The resolutions of the senate

During the republican period the senate had, in theory, no law-making powers. Its resolutions (*senatus consulta*) were regarded as being of an advisory character only and had no legal effect unless they were incorporated into a statute or the edict of a magistrate. But by the close of the Republic the senatorial resolutions had, in practice, already acquired the force of law. In the course of the first century AD they continued to grow in importance and, by the middle of the second century AD, they came to be recognised as a distinct source of law.[27] This meant that senatorial resolutions now effected changes in the law directly, without magisterial sanction. The growth of the senate's legislative authority was precipitated by the decline of the people's assemblies and the assumption by the senate of their constitutional and legislative functions, as well as by the fact that magistrates came to rely increasingly on the senate's guidance in formulating their edicts.[28]

As has already been noted, the emperor often created and moulded the law through action of the senate – by pushing through resolutions that conformed to his political agenda.[29] The emperor's proposal concerning the introduction of a *senatus consultum* took the form of a speech (*oratio*

---

dealing with matters of private law are also included. See FIRA I, no. 99. Consider also P. R. Swarney, *The Ptolemaic and Roman Idiologos*, Yale 1965; E. Seidl, *Rechtsgeschichte Ägyptens als römischer Provinz*, Verl. H. Richarz 1973, 13 ff.

27 G. 1. 4.

28 On the development of the senatorial legislation see H. F. Jolowicz and B. Nicholas, *Historical Introduction to the Study of Roman Law*, 3rd edn, Cambridge 1972, 363-5; A. A. Schiller, *Roman Law: Mechanisms of Development*, New York 1978, 456 ff; O. F. Robinson, *The Sources of Roman Law*, London and New York 1997, 32-4; M. Kaser, *Römische Rechtsgeschichte*, Göttingen 1976, 133-4; W. Kunkel/M. Schermaier, *Römische Rechtsgeschichte*, Cologne 2001, 165-7; A. Guarino, *Storia del diritto romano*, Naples 1996, 428 ff; G. Crifò, *Lezioni di storia del diritto romano*, 3rd edn, Bologna 2000, 297 ff; 322 ff.

29 *Senatus consulta* were usually named after the magistrate or emperor whose proposal occasioned the relevant resolution.

principis) made before the senate by himself or by an official acting in his name. The senators were then called upon to express their views and a vote was taken. But as the emperor's influence in the senate was great, his proposal was always accepted. This procedure was observed throughout the first century AD, alongside the other form of proposing *senatus consulta*, i.e. through a question put to the senate by a high magistrate. In the course of time, as the senate gradually surrendered to the emperor and his bureaucracy all active participation in government, its role as a legislative organ declined and the *senatus consulta* increasingly became little more than mere declarations of the emperor's will. In the second century AD the senate enjoyed only the passive function of registering its approval of decrees drafted by the emperor and read to it by its representative. As the emperor's proposal or *oratio* and not the *consultum* was now regarded as the essential element in the proceedings, it became customary for lawyers to cite these *orationes* rather than the senatorial decrees based on them.[30] Thus, by the end of the second century AD the term *oratio principis* came to refer to an imperial law promulgated in the senate, whilst that of *senatus consultum* applied only to earlier senatorial resolutions.

In the first two centuries of the Principate a large number of *senatus consulta* were issued by which significant changes were effected in the areas of both public and private law. One of the earliest senatorial decrees of this period was the *senatus consultum Silanianum* of 10 AD, aimed at putting an end to the frequent killing of masters by their slaves.[31] Other important senatorial resolutions of this period included the *senatus consultum Vellaeanum* of 46 AD, forbidding women to assume liability for debts of others, including those of their husbands;[32] the *senatus consultum Libonianum* (16 AD), imposing the penalties of the *lex Cornelia de falsis* for the forging of testaments;[33] the *senatus consultum Trebellianum* (c. 56 AD) and the *senatus consultum Pegasianum* (73 AD), concerning the

---

30 See M. Kaser, *Römische Rechtsgeschichte*, Göttingen 1976, 133.

31 It provided that when a master of slaves was killed and the identity of the urderer or murderers remained unknown, all slaves who lived with him had to be tortured and eventually put to death. A slave who revealed the identity of the killer was to be declared free by order of the praetor. See Tacitus, *Ann.* 14. 42-45.

32 D. 16. 1. 2. 1. (Ulpianus). The relevant transaction remained valid unless the woman who was sued by the creditor raised the *exceptio senatus consulti Valleiani*. She could also demand the return of the sum she had paid in fulfilment of her obligation. And see Bruns, *Fontes* I, no. 50.

33 D. 48. 10.

acceptance of inheritances subject to *fideicommissa*;[34] the *senatus consultum Iuventianum* (129 AD) concerning, among other things, claims of the Roman public treasury (*aerarium populi Romani*) against private individuals for the recovery of vacant inheritances;[35] the *senatus consultum Macedonianum* (second half of the first century AD), forbidding loans to sons who remained subject to *partia potestas*;[36] and the *senatus consultum Tertullianum*, passed in the time of Hadrian, which gave mothers the legal right of succession to their children's inheritance.[37]

Classical Legal Science

Introductory

As we have already seen, in the later republican period there emerged in Rome a group of jurists who practised in private law without being members of the pontifical college. The main focus of their activities was the giving of opinions (*responsa*) on questions of law to magistrates, judges and parties at law. They were also engaged in drafting legal documents, such as contracts and wills, and in guiding litigants on matters of procedure. Of particular importance was their contribution to the development of the *ius honorarium* through the assistance which they gave to the praetors in drafting their edicts, and to judges in interpreting and applying the praetorian *formulae*. In formulating their *responsa* the jurists were guided by their knowledge of legal decisions and juristic opinions of the past. From this knowledge they would generalise and then apply the generalisation to the particular case. This process was probably often unconscious, but in the last century of the Republic we find certain jurists writing systematic treatises on various aspects of the law embodying such generalisations or abstractions. In this way the jurists enlarged the scope of Roman law in a significant fashion and created a systematic rendering of the rules and principles employed in the application of the law.[38]

---

34 On the first of these see G. 2. 253; Bruns, *Fontes* I, no. 55. On the second see G. 2. 254. And see M. Kaser, *Das römische Privatrecht*, Munich 1971, 759 ff.

35 See Bruns, *Fontes* I, no. 60.

36 Such transactions were not void but the son could raise against the lender's claim an *exceptio senatus consulti Macedoniani*. See D. 14. 6. 1. (Ulpianus); C. 4. 28. See also Bruns, *Fontes* I, no. 57.

37 Priority was given, however, to the children's children and their father. See D. 38. 17. Consider on this S. Dixon, *The Roman Mother*, London and Sydney 1988, 52-55.

38 On the rise of the republican jurists see chapter 6.

By the close of the Republic the independent development of the *ius honorarium* had come to an end, as it was felt that the praetor should not change the edict but abide by the remedies and procedures that had evolved in the past. From that time, the further elaboration of the *ius honorarium* lay in the hands of the jurists. And since the jurists in their interpretations never treated the *ius honorarium* in isolation from the *ius civile*, a gradual amalgamation of the two bodies of law began to take place. Thus, in time the old distinction between *ius civile* and *ius honorarium* disappeared and the whole body of legal materials incorporated in the juristic literature of the imperial period, whether derived from the *ius civile* or the *ius honorarium*, came to be regarded as a single body of law, referred to as '*ius*' or the jurists' law.

The *ius publice respondendi*

In the closing years of the Republic the number of jurists practising in Rome greatly increased and, as in principle the opinions they gave all carried the same weight, it was difficult to tell with certainty which opinions should be relied upon. As a result, the practice of law was thrown into a state of confusion, which was exacerbated further by the large number of complex and often controversial statutes passed during this period. In response to this problem and in order to establish a certain indirect control over the jurists Augustus issued an ordinance by which he conferred upon the most distinguished jurists the right to publicly give *responsa* in the name of the emperor, i.e. the right of speaking with imperial authority (*ius publice respondendi ex auctoritate principis*).[39] Initially the *ius publice respondendi* was granted only to jurists belonging to the senatorial class, but from the time of Tiberius jurists belonging to the

39 D. 1. 2. 2. 49. (Pomponius). See on this F. Wieacker, 'Respondere ex auctoritate principis', in J. A. Ankum, J. E. Spruit and F. B. J. Wubbe (eds), *Satura Roberto Feenstra Oblata* , Fribourg 1985, 71 ff; B. W. Frier, *The Rise of the Roman Jurists*, Princeton 1985, 223; R. A. Bauman, *Lawyers and Politics in the Early Roman Empire*, Munich 1989, 10 ff; F. Schulz, *History of Roman Legal Science*, Oxford 1967, 112 ff; A. A. Schiller, *Roman Law: Mechanisms of Development*, New York 1978, 297 ff; M. Kaser, *Römische Rechtsgeschichte*, Göttingen 1976, 178 ff; W. Kunkel/M. Schermaier, *Römische Rechtsgeschichte*, Cologne 2001, 141 ff; A. Guarino, *Storia del diritto romano*, Naples 1996, 425 ff; M. Talamanca (ed.), *Lineamenti di storia del diritto romano*, Milan 1989, 439; G. Crifò, *Lezioni di storia del diritto romano*, 3rd edn, Bologna 2000, 366 ff.

equestrian class were also given this privilege.[40] In this way the important role of consultant on legal matters was confined to a relatively small circle of specially qualified experts of high social standing.[41] Jurists without this imperial licence were allowed to continue giving legal advice and judges were not in principle bound by the opinions of the jurists upon whom the *ius respondendi* had been conferred. In practice, however, it was very difficult for a judge to ignore the advice of a jurist whose *responsa* were backed by the authority of the emperor.[42] In the early second century AD Emperor Hadrian issued a *rescriptum* by which he conferred upon the opinions of the jurists enjoying the *ius respondendi* the full force of law, as long as these opinions were in harmony with each other. If there was not unanimity among the jurists, the judge was free to choose the opinion that best suited the case at hand.[43] The emperor intended to make it clear beyond doubt that, where the authorised jurists agreed, their unanimous opinion had to be followed as binding. At the same time, however, Hadrian abandoned the practice of granting the *ius respondendi* to individual jurists. From that time opinions were given in the form of imperial rescripts, issued under the emperor's own direct authority. By the close of the second century AD the imperial edicts had become the chief source of legislation, corresponding to the *leges* and the edicts of the praetors of the republican period, while the *responsa prudentium* had been superseded by the rescripts of the emperors on legal and judicial matters.

The work of the jurists

The granting of the *ius publice respondendi* to leading jurists by Augustus and his successors gave fresh impetus to legal science. The development of

---

[40] The first jurist of equestrian origin who was granted the *ius publice respondendi* was Massurius Sabinus. D. 1. 2. 2. 48. (Pomponius). The granting of the *ius respondendi* to persons not belonging to the senatorial aristocracy became more frequent from the time of Hadrian. D. 1. 2. 2. 49. (Pomponius).

[41] The jurists who had been granted the *ius publice respondendi* were referred to as *iurisconsulti* or *iurisprudentes*, although the same terms were sometimes also used to describe any prominent jurist irrespective of whether he enjoyed this privilege or not. The term *iurisperiti*, on the other hand, was used to denote less important jurists, especially jurists practising in the provinces. Such lesser jurists were particularly active in Egypt and other Roman provinces in the East. See, e.g., Bruns, *Fontes* I, no. 119.

[42] Modern scholars disagree as to whether the opinions of jurists with the *ius respondendi* were binding on judges. See O. Tellegen-Couperus, *A Short History of Roman Law*, London and New York 1993, 95-96.

[43] G. 1. 7.

jurisprudence in the early imperial period was precipitated also by the shift in emphasis from politics to administration, the broadening of the scope of Roman law through the gradual extension of the Roman citizenship in the provinces, the proliferation of legal transactions that resulted from the growth of trade and commerce, and the increased demand for legal education. The jurists now became professional lawyers in the true sense, i.e. men fully committed to the vocation of law. Besides their usual advisory activities and their involvement in the resolution of legal disputes, many leading jurists took a direct part in governmental tasks and assisted the emperors in the development and organisation of the various branches of the imperial administration. Thus it is not surprising that many jurists came to occupy prominent posts in the imperial civil service, from various magisterial positions right up to the prefecture of the praetorian guard.

Like their predecessors of the republican period, the jurists of the Principate were engaged in various activities relating to the practice of law and the administration of justice. They gave opinions on questions of law to magistrates, imperial officials and judges (*respondere*); assisted citizens in formalising transactions and in drafting legal documents (*cavere*); advised litigants on the appropriate legal forms that had to be used by them in expressing their claims and on how to argue their cases in court,[44] and sometimes argued cases as advocates themselves (*agere*).[45] Furthermore, the jurists were engaged in the systematic exposition and teaching of the law. In carrying out this task they gave opinions when their students raised questions for discussion based on hypothetical cases. These opinions were almost equal in terms of influence to those given on questions arising from actual cases and, in an indirect way, helped to develop Roman law in new directions. As has already been noted, leading jurists exercised a considerable influence on the development of the law as members of the emperor's *consilium* and as holders of high offices in the imperial administration.

An important aspect of the jurists' work was legal writing. The majority of juristic works were of a casuistic and practical nature: they grew out of legal practice and were written primarily for legal practitioners. It was only in their expository works, such as elementary textbooks and

44 However, they no longer drew up new *formulae* for use in the *per formulam* procedure for, as was noted before, by the end of the Republic the content of the praetorian edict had been fixed.

45 Although the forensic speeches of jurists have not been preserved, information about the way in which they argued cases is derived from various historical sources, such as the *Controversiae* of Seneca the Elder, the *De Institutione Oratoria* of Quintilian and the works of Pliny the Younger (see, e.g. Pliny, *Epist.* 4. 9.).

manuals, that the jurists adopted a more theoretical approach to the study of law. Depending upon their subject-matter and scope, the literary works of the classical jurists have been classified as follows:

(i) *Responsa, quaestiones, disputationes, epistulae* – collections of opinions or replies delivered by jurists in exercise of the *ius respondendi*. Works of this type were written for practitioners and usually consisted of two parts: the first part contained juristic opinions concerned with the praetorian edict (*ad edictum*), whilst the opinions included in the second part were connected with *leges*, *senatus consulta* and *constitutiones principis*. The adaptation of the original *responsa* for publication sometimes necessitated the further elaboration of the position adopted, especially when the opinions of other jurists were being argued against. Some of these works, especially the *quaestiones* and the *disputationes*, dealt with problems that arose out of actual cases discussed by the jurists in their capacity as teachers. Others, such as the *epistulae*, contained legal opinions given in writing by jurists to judicial magistrates, judges, private citizens or other jurists. Sometimes responses relating to one theme were collected in one book.[46]

(ii) *Regulae, definitiones, sententiae* – short statements of the law, originally issued in connection with specific cases, but later reformulated and expressed in the form of general rules. They were couched in easy to memorise terms as they were intended for the use of legal practitioners and, possibly, students.[47]

(iii) General works on the *ius civile*. Some of these works became known as *libri ad Sabinum* or *ex Sabino*, because they were modelled on the relevant work of the famous jurist Massurius Sabinius (*Libri* III *iuris civilis*). Others were based on the earlier work of the jurist Q. Mucius Scaevola (first century BC) in which the materials were arranged in a way different from that adopted by Sabinus.

(iv) Commentaries on the *ius praetorium* (or *ius honorarium*), referred to as *libri ad edictum*. In these works the edicts of the magistrates were examined and commented upon in connection with those aspects of the *ius civile* which they were aiming to supplement or correct.

(v) *Digesta* – comprehensive treatises on the law dealing with both the *ius civile* and the *ius honorarium*.

---

46 Such as, e.g., the *liber singularis* of Modestinus dealing with the institution of *manumissio*.

47 See P. Stein, *Regulae Iuris*, Aberdeen 1966.

(vi) *Institutiones* or *enchiridia* – introductory or expository textbooks written primarily for beginners and students. A work of this type was the Institutes of Gaius.

The jurists also produced commentaries on individual *leges* or *senstus consulta*, commentaries on the works of earlier jurists and other kinds of monographs. The areas of the law, the legal institutions and the specific legislative enactments which were the subject-matter of the jurists' works were subjected to detailed analysis, usually backed by discussion of actual or hypothetical problems. Hypothetical problems, in particular, were often relied upon as a means of testing the limitations of a particular legal rule, principle or concept. Of the juristic literature of the classical period the Institutes of Gaius is the only work that has survived in its original form. Our knowledge of the rest is derived for the most part from fragments that have been included in the Digest of Justinian and other post-classical compilations of law.[48]

The law-schools

According to Pomponius, during the early Principate period Roman jurisprudence was dominated by two rival schools (*sectae*) of jurists, known as the Proculians and the Sabinians.[49] Although during this period

48 In the Digest each extract is preceded by an *inscriptio*, which includes the name of the jurist from whose work it is taken. These extracts, as well as references by one jurist to another, have made it possible for modern scholars to obtain a good idea of the nature and structure of the original works. The dating of the individual works has been deduced largely on the basis of information found in the surviving fragments, such as references to emperors, legislative enactments or events whose dates are known from other sources. For a reconstruction of the juristic literature of the classical period see O. Lenel, *Palingenesia iuris civilis*, 2 vols, Leipzig 1889, repr. Graz 1960. On the work of the classical jurists see in general H. F. Jolowicz and B. Nicholas, *Historical Introduction to the Study of Roman Law*, 3rd edn, Cambridge 1972, 374 ff; W. Kunkel, *An Introduction to Roman Legal and Constitutional History*, 2nd edn, Oxford 1973, 105 ff; A. A. Schiller, *Roman Law: Mechanisms of Development*, New York 1978, 383 ff; F. Schulz, *History of Roman Legal Science*, Oxford 1967, 141 ff; M. Kaser, *Römische Rechtsgeschichte*, Göttingen 1976, 182 ff; W. Kunkel/M. Schermaier, *Römische Rechtsgeschichte*, Cologne 2001, 154-5, 160 ff; A. Guarino, *Storia del diritto romano*, Naples 1996, 465 ff; G. Crifò, *Lezioni di storia del diritto romano*, 3rd edn, Bologna 2000, 386 ff.

49 D. 1. 2. 2. 47. The school of the Sabinians derived its name from Massurius Sabinus who lived in the time of Tiberius. That of the Proculians was named after Proculus, who lived in the time of Nero.

there were numerous private schools (*stationes*) in Rome where law was being taught,[50] it appears that these two schools played a special part in Roman legal life. It is not clear, however, what Pomponius meant by the term '*sectae*' and it is impossible to determine with certainty what the basis of the rivalry between the two schools was. According to some scholars, these schools were not regular teaching institutions; they were probably closer in character to aristocratic clubs or unions formed by lawyers for the discussion of legal and political issues under the guidance of leading jurists. Others have suggested that the two schools espoused different philosophical theories: the Sabinians were adherents of Stoicism, while the Proculians followed the principles of Aristotelian (peripatetic) philosophy. The examples known to us, however, do not show the alleged conservatism of the Sabinians or the reformatory spirit attributed to the Proculians, and it appears that, in reality, there were no deep-rooted philosophical or political differences that separated the two schools. Notwithstanding the political affiliations of their founders, the schools appear to have differed only with respect to the techniques and methods which they adopted in dealing with questions of law rather than in their general attitudes or principles. In general, it is believed that, when dealing with legal problems, the Sabinians preferred to adhere to the letter of the law, while the Proculians endeavoured to discover the purpose of the relevant enactment and then to decide according to its spirit.[51]

Pomponius relates that the school of the Proculeans was formed around Marcus Antistius Labeo, whilst that of the Sabinians was founded by Ateius Capito.[52] Both lived in the time of Augustus and were for a time

---

50 See Aulus Gellius, *N. A.* 13. 13.

51 On the origins and character of the law-schools see in general O. F. Robinson, *The Sources of Roman Law*, London 1997, 116; W. Kunkel, *An Introduction to Roman Legal and Constitutional History*, 2nd edn, Oxford 1973, 114; H. E. Dirksen, *Beiträge zur Kunde des römischen Rechts. Erste Abhandlung: Über die Schulen der römischen Juristen*, Leipzig 1825; F. Schulz, *History of Roman Legal Science*, Oxford 1967, 119 ff; H. F. Jolowicz and B. Nicholas, *Historical Introduction to the Study of Roman Law*, 3rd edn, Camridge 1972, 378-80; A. A. Schiller, *Roman Law: Mechanisms of Development*, New York 1978, 327-30; G. L. Falchi, *Le controversie tra Sabiniani e Proculiani*, Milan 1981; R. Bauman, *Lawyers and Politics in the Early Roman Empire*, Munich 1989, 44 ff; M. Kaser, *Römische Rechtsgeschichte*, Göttingen 1976, 186 ff; W. Kunkel/M. Schermaier, *Römische Rechtsgeschichte*, Cologne 2001, 150 ff; A. Guarino, *Storia del diritto romano*, Naples 1996, 463 ff; M. Talamanca (ed.), *Lineamenti di storia del diritto romano*, Milan 1989, 440-2; G. Crifò, *Lezioni di storia del diritto romano*, 3rd edn, Bologna 2000, 346 ff.

52 D. 1. 2. 2. 52. (Pomponius); Pliny, *Ep.* 7. 24; Tacitus, *Ann.* 3. 75. It should be noted here, however, that the original founder of the school of the Proculians

political rivals. A staunch supporter of the republican political system and opponent of the Augustan regime, Labeo held the office of praetor but refused the position of consul when it was offered to him by Augustus.[53] He was the author of a number of influential works, including an extensive commentary on the Law of the Twelve Tables, commentaries on the edicts of the *praetor urbanus* and the *praetor peregrinus*, and several collections of *responsa* and *epistulae*. At the time of his death his writings amounted to 400 volumes.[54] Capito is said to have been a keen supporter of Augustus by whom he was elevated to the position of consul.[55] His works were relatively few in number and included a collection of *quaestiones* relating to matters of public law, a book *de officio senatorio*, collections of *epistulae* and a number of books on the *ius pontificum*. But neither Labeo nor Capito established regular schools themselves, nor did they give regular tuition in the form of connected lectures; they taught law as the earlier republican jurists did, i.e. by giving answers to legal questions in the presence of students with whom they sometimes discussed problems that emerged out of actual or hypothetical cases. The schools of the Proculians and the Sabinians continued to operate well into the second century AD. Among the most distinguished members of the Proculian school were the two Nervas, Pegasus and the Celsi; to the school of the Sabinians belonged the jurists Cassius Longinus, Iavolenus, Salvius Iulianus and Gaius.

Other leading jurists of the Principate period

Massurius Sabinus

Massurius Sabinus, after whom the Sabinian school was named, lived in the times of Tiberius and Nero.[56] Although he was of humble origin and was not admitted to the equestrian class until later in life, Tiberius granted him the *ius pulice respondendi* in recognition of his exceptional knowledge and outstanding ability as a lawyer.[57] His chief work, a systematic treatise on the *ius civile* in three books, exercised a strong influence on Roman legal thought and was subjected to extensive commentary by later jurists in

---

was Labeo's teacher Trebatius, a pupil of Q. Mucius Rufus; the school of the Sabinians was established by Capito's teacher Ofilius, who studied under Servius Sulpicius.

53 D. 1. 2. 2. 47. (Pomponius). Compare with Tacitus, *Ann.* 3. 75; Aulus Gellius, *N. A.* 13. 12.

54 D. 1. 2. 2. 47.

55 Tacitus, *Ann.* 3. 75.

56 G. 2. 218.

57 D. 1. 2. 2. 48; 1. 2. 2. 49-50. (Pomponius).

works known as '*ad Sabinum*'. In this work Sabinus adopted a division of the *ius civile* into four parts: law of succession, law of persons, law of obligations and law of things.[58] Other works attributed to Sabinus included a commentary on the edict of the *praetor urbanus*, a collection of *responsa*, a monograph on theft (*de furtis*) and a commentary on the *lex Iulia de iudiciis privatis*.[59]

Proculus

Very little is known about the jurist Proculus, from whom the Proculian school derived its name. All that is known about him comes from citations by later classical jurists included in Justinian's Digest. It appears that he had achieved success in political life (he was probably elected to the praetorship) and that his works, of which only a collection of *epistolae* is known, were highly regarded by other jurists.

Gaius Cassius Longinus

C. Cassius Longinus belonged to a leading plebeian family and lived in the times of Claudius, Nero and Vespasian. He was a student of Sabinus whom he later succeeded as head of the Sabinian school.[60] He attained the urban praetorship and the consulship (30 AD), and served as governor of Asia and Syria several times between the years 40 and 49 AD. Mercifulness does not appear to have been one of his virtues, as his name is associated with the persecution of slaves during the reign of Nero.[61] However, his reputation for legal knowledge was unparalleled and his works were highly regarded by his contemporaries. His chief work, an extensive treatise on the *ius civile*, is known to us mainly from references and fragments included in the writings of later jurists.

Iavolenus Priscus

Iavolenus was born about 60 AD and was still alive in the time of Hadrian. He headed the Sabinian (or Cassian) school and was a member of the *consilium principis* during the reign of Trajan. He also held the position

---

58 Although no direct reference to Sabinus's work is found in the Digest, its structure and general nature has been made out from information derived from the works of other classical jurists that are based on it. For a closer look see R. Astolfi, *I libri tres iuris civilis di Sabino*, Padua 1983.

59 Aulus Gellius, *N. A*. 14. 2. 1.

60 D. 4. 8. 19. 2. (Paulus). This school was later called *schola Cassiana*.

61 Tacitus, *Ann*. 14. 42. 45.

of consul in 86 AD and served as governor of Germany, Syria and Africa. His main works included a collection of *epistulae* in fourteen books, commentaries on the works of earlier jurists (*libri ex Cassio*, *ex Plautio*), and a collection of texts from Labeo's posthumous work *posteriores*.[62] Fragments of these have been included in the Digest of Justinian.

Publius Iuventius Celsus (filius)

Celsus lived in the early second century AD and succeeded his father (P. Iuventius Celsus the Elder – a less known jurist) in the leadership of the school of the Proculians. He held the praetorship and the consulship, was a member of the *consilium principis* under Hadrian, and served as governor of Thrace. Fragments of his main work *Digesta*, which consisted of thirty-nine books, can be found in the Digest. He also published collections of *epistulae*, *quaestiones* and commentaries. To Celsus is attributed the classical definition of law as 'the art of good and equitable'.[63]

Salvius Julianus

Julian, the last known head of the Sabinian (or Cassian) school and probably the greatest jurist of the second century AD, was born in Hadrumentum in the province of Africa.[64] Like other eminent jurists of this period, he had a brilliant political career. He occupied the highest offices of the state during the reigns of Hadrian, Antoninus Pius and Marcus Aurelius, including those of tribune, praetor, consul, pontifex and governor of Germany, Spain and Africa. He was also a member of the now permanent *consilium principis*. As we saw earlier, Julian was assigned by Emperor Hadrian the important task of consolidating the praetorian edict – a task which he completed in about 130 AD. Another important work of his was the *Digesta*, a collection of *responsa* in ninety books. The *Digesta* appears to have exercised a strong influence on the legal thinking of the classical period, as manifested by the numerous references to it by later jurists and the large number of fragments included in the Digest of Justinian.

---

62 See B. Eckhard, *Iavoleni Epistulae* , Berlin 1978; U. Manthe, *Die Libri ex Cassio des Iavolenus Priscus*, Berlin 1982.

63 '*Ius est ars boni et aequi*' – D. 1. 1. 1. pr. (Ulpianus). And see Pliny, *Ep*. 6. 5; D. 28. 1. 27.

64 Much of what we know about his life comes from an inscription found near Tunis in northern Africa. See *Coprus Inscriptionum Latinarum*, Berlin 1863, 8. 24094.

Sextus Pomponius

Pomponius, a contemporary of Julian, is the author of several works, including three treatises on the *ius civile* written in the form of commentaries on earlier juristic writings (*ad Quinum Mucium, ad Plautium, ad Sabinum*), an extensive commentary on the praetorian edict, collections of *epistulae* and several monographs on various individual subjects (*stipulationes, senatusconsulta*, etc.). He is also the author of the *liber singularis enchiridii*, a work containing an outline of Roman legal and constitutional history from the period of the kings down to his own day. The relevant fragment has been preserved in its entirety in the Digest of Justinian, under the title '*de origine iuris*' ('on the origin of law') and, notwithstanding its gaps and inconsistencies, constitutes one of our primary sources of information on the historical development of Roman law.[65] Pomponius appears to have been better known as an antiquarian rather than as a lawyer, although some of his doctrinal writings are referred to by other jurists and numerous fragments have been included in the Digest. There is no evidence that he ever held public office and, as no *responsa* of his are mentioned, it is not known whether he had been given the *ius publice respondendi*.

Gaius

Although Gaius is regarded as one of the most influential jurists of the classical period,[66] almost nothing is known about his personal life – not even his family name (Gaius is only a *praenomen*, or first name). Evidence from his own work suggests that he lived during the reigns of Hadrian (117-138 AD), Antoninus Pius (138-161 AD) and Marcus Aurelius (161-180 AD), and that he completed his Institutes after 161 AD.[67] His style of writing and his knowledge of the laws and customs that applied in the eastern provinces suggested to some modern scholars that he was a provincial, probably from Asia, although this cannot be established with certainty.[68] But there is no doubt that he was a Roman citizen, as manifested by the fact that he draws a distinction between 'customs obtaining among foreigners (*apud peregrinos*) and our (Roman) customs

65 D. 1. 2. 2.

66 He is one of the five leading jurists mentioned in the Law of Citations of emperor Theodosius II (426 AD); in the Institutes of Justinian is referred to as '*Gaius noster*' ('our Gaius') (*const. Omnem* 1, *Inst.* 4. 18. 5.).

67 See D. 34. 5. 7. pr; G. 1. 7.

68 For a closer look see W. Kunkel, *Die Römischen Juristen*, Cologne 2001, 190 ff.

(*apud nos*)'.[69] The fact that he refers to the leaders of the Sabinian school as 'our teachers' indicates that he had studied law at Rome. It is believed that Gaius was engaged in the public teaching of law (*ius publice docens*), but he had not been accepted as a member of the select group of jurists to whom the *ius respondendi* had been granted, as his opinions are not cited by subsequent jurists. Probably he was one of the many lesser jurists outside this group, rescued from oblivion by the later recognition and influence of his Institutes.[70]

Gaius's works included a commentary on the Law of the Twelve Tables in six books, commentaries on the *edictum provinciale*, the aedilician edict and the edict of the *praetor urbanus*, and a number of treatises and monographs on various *leges*, *senatus consulta* and imperial constitutions. Of his works one has survived almost intact, the Institutes (*institutionum commentarii quattor*), written about 161 AD. Until 1816, when Gaius's text was discovered in the cathedral library at Verona,[71] only fragments of the juristic literature of this period survived in later collections, especially in the Digest of Justinian and other compilations of the post-classical era. Although the manuscript found at Verona dates from the fifth or early sixth century AD (i.e. more than three centuries after Gaius's time), it is generally believed that it accords with Gaius's original text. This view was confirmed further after the discovery in 1933 in Egypt of fragments of another manuscript, dating probably from the late fourth century AD, which largely matches the text found at Verona. About one tenth of the manuscript's content is lost or is totally illegible, but some of the missing parts have been reconstructed on the basis of extracts included in later compilations. A great deal of what we know about the Roman law of the principate period, including important information about the formulary system and the system of the *legis actiones* which preceded it, is derived from Gaius's Institutes. One should keep in mind, however, that Roman law, especially during the first century of the principate, was continually changing and thus the picture that Gaius gives us of certain

---

69 G. 1. 193. See also G. 1. 55; 3. 134; 4. 37. Consider on this A.M. Honoré, *Gaius*, Oxford 1962, 75 ff.

70 According to one theory, the works attributed to Gaius were in fact written by Gaius Cassius Longinus and were re-edited by another jurist in the time of Marcus Aurelius. See A. M. Honore, *Gaius*, Oxford 1962, 12 ff. Most modern scholars do not accept this view, however.

71 The discovery was made by the German historian B. G. Niebuhr who detected the text of the Institutes underneath a text of St Jerome written on the same parchment in the seventh or eighth century AD. (These manuscripts in which more than one texts are written one on top of the other are referred to as palimpsests).

matters may not always represent accurately the state of the law under the early emperors.

In the Institutes Gaius adopts a division of the entire body of law into three parts: the law of persons (*ius quod ad personas pertinet*), the law of property and obligations (*ius quod ad res pertinet*) and the law of actions (*ius quod ad actiones pertinet*).[72] The law of persons (Book 1) is defined as that part of the law which deals with the legal status of persons and their capacity to have rights and assume obligations. In its sphere fall matters relating to liberty and slavery (*status libertatis*), citizenship (*status civitatis*), family (*status familiae*), marriage and guardianship. The law of property (Books 2 and 3) contains the rules governing inheritable and moveable property (including servitudes), testate and intestate succession, contract and delict. Finally, the law of actions (Book 4) pertains to the various ways in which legal claims could be formulated and legal rights could be pursued and protected. This division of the subject was followed by the compilers of Justinian's Institutes and has been adopted with various modifications in modern codes and treatises on civil law.[73]

Aemilius Papinianus

Generally regarded as the greatest of the classical jurists, Papinian lived during the reigns of Marcus Aurelius, Commodus, and Septimius Severus (late second/early third century AD).[74] Besides being a member of the *consilium principis*, he was *assessor* to the *praefectus praetorio*,[75] head of the imperial *scrinium a libellis* and, from 203 AD, he held the office of *praefectus praetorio*. In 212 AD he was murdered by order of Emperor Caracalla because he refused to devise a justification for the killing by Caracalla of his brother and co-regent Geta. Among Papinian's most important works were thirty-seven books of *quaestiones* and nineteen books of *responsa*, which also contained references to *responsa* of earlier jurists as well as to judicial decisions issued by the emperor and the prefects. He also produced a collection of *definitiones* in two books and a

---

72 G. 1. 8. This classification of the law had probably been followed by Roman jurists well before Gaius's time.

73 On the later influence of Gaius's system see the Introduction in P. B. H. Birks and G. MacLeod (trs), *The Institutes of Justinian*, London 1987. Modern translations of Gaius's Institutes include Francis de Zulueta, *The Institutes of Gaius*, New York 1946, Oxford 1985; W. M. Gordon and O. F. Robinson, *The Institutes of Gaius*, London 1988.

74 Papinian was a relative and close friend of Emperor Septimius Severus. See *Hist. Aug.*, *Carac.* 8. 2.

75 Under Emperor Marcus Aurelius. See D. 22. 1. 3. 3. (Papinianus).

monograph on adultery. Numerous fragments of these works have been preserved in the Digest and other post-classical compilations of Roman law. Papinian's works are admirable examples of creative legal reasoning, reflecting an independent mind and a profound understanding of the principles governing the application of the law. Subsequent writers, including the compilers of Justinian's Digest, attribute special importance to his works and often refer with admiration to his exceptional qualities as a lawyer.[76]

Julius Paulus

Paul was a member of the *consilium principis* during the reigns of Septimius Severus and Caracalla (together with Papinian and Ulpian) and held the office of *praefectus praetorio* under Alexander Severus. He produced a large number of works, including a treatise on the *ius civile* in sixteen books (*ad Sabinum*), twenty-three books of *responsa*, an extensive commentary on the praetorian edict in eighty books, commentaries on various *leges*, *senatus consulta* and the works of earlier jurists (Julian, Scaevola, Papinian), two collections of *decreta* and numerous monographs on various subjects relating to both public and private law. A collection of extracts from Paul's works, known as *Pauli sententiae*, was widely used during the later imperial period.[77] Materials from this collection have been included in various post-classical compilations, such as the Vatican Fragments, the *Consultatio*, the *Collatio* and the *lex Romana Visigothorum*. About one-sixth of the Digest of Justinian is made up of extracts drawn from Paul's works.[78]

Domitius Ulpianus

Ulpian was of Phoenician origin and was born in the city of Tyre about 170 AD.[79] Most of his legal works were produced during the reign of Caracalla (211-217 AD). Like Papinian and Paul, he held several positions in the imperial administration, including those of the *praefectus annonae* and *praefectus praetorio*. He also served as head of the imperial *scrinium a libellis*. But his political influence made him unpopular among the members of the powerful praetorian guard by whom he was finally

---

76 See C. 6. 42. 30; 7. 45. 14; *Const. Omnem* 1.

77 Consider on this E. Levy, *Pauli Sententiae: a Palingenesia of the Opening Titles*, Cornel U.P. 1945.

78 See FIRA II, pp. 317-417 and pp. 419-32.

79 D. 50. 15. 1 pr. (Ulpianus).

assassinated in 223 AD (or 228 AD). Ulpian was a most voluminous writer. His contribution to juristic literature included fifty-one books on the *ius civile* (*ad Sabinum libri LI*), eighty-three books on the edict (*ad edictum libri LXXXIII*), two books of *responsa*, a legal manual for beginners in two books (*institutiones*), collections of *regulae* and *definitiones*, and several monographs on individual statutes, state offices (e.g., proconsuls, consuls, urban prefect) and matters of legal procedure. Although his work lacks the originality of other jurists, it is characterised by its remarkable lucidity and attention to detail. Nearly half of Justinian's Digest (about 42 per cent) consists of materials derived from Ulpian's writings.[80]

Herennius Modestinus

Probably the last of the great jurists of the classical period, Modestinus was a student of Ulpian[81] and held the position of *praefectus vigilum* between 226 and 244 AD.[82] He produced nine books of *differentiae* (controversial questions), *responsa* in nineteen books, a collection of *regulae* and a treatise on exceptions from guardianship (*de excusationibus*). Modestinus is one of the five prominent jurists whose works were considered authoritative under the Law of Citations of 426 AD.[83]

Some comments on the character of Roman jurisprudence

The most characteristic feature of classical Roman jurisprudence was its predominantly technical, strictly legal, nature. The jurists were men who dedicated themselves exclusively or essentially to the interpretation of the extant source material and the application of legal rules and principles in individual cases. Although they sometimes played a part in the law-making process as advisers or draftsmen, they did not consider it part of their tasks to analyse the law from ethical, historical or other more general points of view, nor were they interested in the laws and customs of other nations, save insofar as these could be incorporated into the conceptual framework of their own legal system. Notwithstanding their open-mindedness towards the phenomena of social and economic life, they did not observe and comment on the law from the outside, as a philosopher, moralist or sociologist would do. Of course, as members of the educated upper classes,

---

80 For a closer look at Ulpian's contribution to jurisprudence see T. Honoré, *Ulpian*, Oxford 1982.

81 D. 47. 2. 52. 20. (Ulpianus).

82 See *Lis fullonum* in Bruns, *Fontes* I, no. 188; FIRA III, no. 165.

83 See chapter 10.

the jurists came into contact with the intellectual and ideological movements of their times and both their tasks and habits of reasoning were to some extent influenced by them. Thus, it is not surprising that they were familiar with Stoic philosophy and its notions of natural law and natural justice and that they held, essentially, such humane and enlightened views as were common stock among the ruling classes of the empire. However, there is little evidence in their work to suggest that they took a direct interest in constructing all-embracing philosophical theories of law or that they consciously and systematically put into use philosophical and ethical principles and precepts in their treatment of the law. They were practical lawyers who were primarily concerned with the application of the law as it stood through the exercise of mature judgement and practical wisdom in each case that came before them, while taking into account the position taken by earlier jurists in similar cases. In general, their attitude towards the law was conservative: they endeavoured to preserve the system within which they worked, while at the same time developing it by exploring new ways of putting its institutions to satisfactory practical use. In this way they created a system and a science by means of which they managed to develop the law according to the needs of a complex and growing society.

In carrying out the work of interpretation the jurists sought to arrive at the contents of the law by means of logical deduction from extant sources, utilising methods borrowed from Greek rhetoric and philosophical logic;[84] they also relied upon intuitive insight into the problems that arose out of various factual situations – insight based on their familiarity with previously decided cases and earlier juristic opinions. The jurists were fully aware of the problems arising from the fact that the tenor and the intended meaning of a legal text did not always coincide and of the significance of the linguistic context as a tool by means of which texts are understood more thoroughly than if examined in isolation. In their interpretations they usually proceeded from consideration of the letter (*verba*) of the relevant law (statute, edict, imperial constitution, senatorial resolution) and continued with an inquiry into the intention, purpose or 'spirit' of the law (*sententia*). Depending upon whether a legal rule had been expressed in broad or narrow terms, they sought to make more concrete through a restrictive construction or expand through an extensive construction the scope of the relevant provision. In dealing with problems relating to silence of or ambiguity in the law they often relied upon the methods of comparing and analogy and utilised such general concepts as

84 Such as the method of arguing from opposites (*argumentum a contrario*) or that of arguing from a minor premise towards a conclusion (*argumentum a minori ad maius*). See also chapter 6.

aequitas, *utilitas* and *humanitas*.[85] Of particular importance in the work of interpretation was the concept of *aequitas*, which was often relied upon to correct or expand existing rules of law so that they could better meet the needs of social and commercial life.[86] It is important to note, however, that the jurists never formulated a systematic theory of legal interpretation which had the characteristics of a coherent and closed system but confined themselves to the establishment of catalogues of intellectual tools and general interpretative maxims.

A unique quality of the jurists was their ability to look beyond the accidental elements of the individual case, the *species facti*, and to define the relevant legal problem as a *quaestio iuris* – i.e. as a question of justice that had to be answered in the light of certain general principles. Indeed the development of Roman legal science in the classical period involved the ever-broader formulation of general principles of law and their systematisation. This process of abstraction and simplification is natural enough, and is indeed inevitable if the law is to consist in anything more than a collection of particular rules; but it carries with it the danger that a rule, once formulated, tends to dominate legal life rather than to accommodate itself to it. The legal genius of the Roman jurists was shown in their ability not only to erect abstract propositions by way of analysis of their law, but also to make their abstractions sufficiently flexible to be synthesised into new principles when subsequent experience showed that changes in the law were desirable.[87]

---

85 They recognised, for example, that if a legal provision is open to more than one interpretation, the most moderate interpretation should be adopted ('*in re dubia benigniorem interpretationem sequi*'). See D. 50. 17. 192. 1; 28. 4. 3. (Marcellus). On the concept of *utilitas* see D. 9. 2. 51. 2. (Iulianus); 46. 3. 95. 7. (Papinianus). See also chapter 1.

86 The importance which the jurists attributed to the concept of *aequitas* is reflected in the definition of *ius* , attributed to the jurist Celsus, as 'the art of discovering that which is good and equitable' ('*ius est ars boni et aequi*'). See D. 1. 1. 1 pr. (Ulpianus); 4. 1. 7. (Marcellus); 50. 17. 183. (Marcellus). And see chapter 1.

87 On the development of classical legal science see W. Kunkel, *An Introduction to Roman Legal and Constitutional History*, 2nd edn, Oxford 1973, 95 ff; *Die Römischen Juristen*, Cologne 2001, ch. 3; H. F. Jolowicz and B. Nicholas, *Historical Introduction to the Study of Roman Law*, 3rd edn, Cambridge 1972, 359 ff., 374 ff; T. Honoré, *Emperors and Lawyers*, London 1981; G. Fassò, *Storia della filosofia del diritto*, I, 3rd edn, Bologna 1974, 125 ff; A. Brimo, *Les grands courants de la philosophie du droit et de l'état*, Paris 1978, 27 ff; O. F. Robinson, *The Sources of Roman Law*, London and New York 1997, 10-13 and 42-48; H. J. Wolff, *Roman Law, An Historical Introduction*, U. of Oklahoma Press, 1951, 103 ff; F. Schulz, *History of Roman Legal Science*,

The Administration of Justice: Civil Procedure

The formulary system

As we saw in chapter 6, in the later Republic the *per formulam* procedure gradually replaced the earlier system of the *legis actiones* and finally became the main form of civil procedure in Rome (after the enactment of the *lex Iulia iudiciorum privatorum* in 17 BC).[88] As has been explained, the procedure by *formula* consisted of two distinct phases. The first phase (*in iure*) took place before the praetor who decided on the admissibility of the plaintiff's claim, i.e. determined whether or not the plaintiff should be granted an action. If the praetor was satisfied that the plaintiff had an arguable case, the appropriate *formula* was drawn up nominating the judge (*iudex*) by whom the case would be heard, stating the matter in dispute, defining the scope of the action and prescribing the consequences of the judge's decision. The second phase of the proceedings took place before the judge (*apud iudicem*) who listened to the pleadings, assessed the evidence and rendered a judgement according to the *formula* agreed upon in the *in iure* phase. During the early imperial era proceedings under the formulary system were basically the same as they had been during the Republic. The only change that occurred had to do with the operation of the praetorian edict. As was noted earlier, from the closing years of the Republic the productive strength of the praetorian edict as a source of law began to weaken as praetorian initiatives became increasingly rare. This trend continued during the Principate and, as the praetor's ability to introduce new legal remedies was curtailed, whatever changes were made in the edict were now based on measures which had been initiated by other law-making agencies (i.e. *leges* or *senatus consulta*). The making of law administratively by the praetor was finally brought to an end during the reign of Hadrian, when the content of the edict was fixed once and for all following its codification by the jurist Julian.[89] From then on if further changes were needed they were made by imperial enactment. Although no longer an independent source of law, the *ius praetorium* continued to play

---

Oxford 1967, 99 ff; O. Tellegen-Couperus, *A Short History of Roman Law*, London and New York 1993, 94 ff; M. Kaser, *Römische Rechtsgeschichte*, Göttingen 1976, 170 ff; W. Kunkel/M. Schermaier, *Römische Rechtsgeschichte*, Cologne 2001, 140 ff; A. Guarino, *Storia del diritto romano*, Naples 1996, 458 ff.

88 G. 4. 30.

89 In the late second century AD the term *edictum perpetuum* no longer referred to the edict issued by the praetor at the beginning of his year in office but came to denote the body of the praetorian edict as codified by Julian.

a part in the administration of private law well after the formulary system had fallen into abeyance in the third century AD.

The *cognitio extra ordinem*

From the early years of the Principate period a new type of legal procedure, known as *cognitio extra ordinem* or *cognitio extraordinaria*, began to be used alongside the *per formulam* procedure. The *cognitio* procedure was used to settle private disputes, but was also employed in criminal cases and in disputes between private citizens and state organs. Under the new system magistrates and imperial officials acting on behalf of the emperor used their administrative authority to cut through the formalities that had to be observed in regular court proceedings. In Rome and Italy the magistrates concerned were the special praetors (such as the *praetor de liberalibus causis*, the *praetor tutelarius* and the *praetor fireicommissarius*), the consuls, and various imperial officials (such as the *praefectus praetorio*, the *praefectus urbi* and the *procuratores fisci*). In the provinces justice was administered by the governors (*praesides*) and other high-ranking provincial magistrates. Often these magistrates exercised their judicial functions through delegates. However, unlike the *iudices* appointed by the praetor under the formulary system who were private citizens chosen by the parties, these delegates were lower state officials (*iudices dati* or *pedanei*) appointed by their superiors.[90] As in the *cognitio extra ordinem* proceedings were based largely on written communications, the magistrates were assisted by secretaries (*scribae*) and, like the judicial magistrates of the Republic, they often relied on the advice of panels of experts (*consilia*).

The *cognitio extra ordinem* was based on the idea that the administration of justice is primarily a function of the state and probably originated in the early practice which allowed magistrates to try certain cases directly and on their own initiative.[91] It was first introduced in the provinces during the later republican period and was usually employed in criminal cases, in cases involving private disputes between foreigners and in cases involving disputes between Romans when not enough Roman citizens were available who could serve as judges. Such cases were dealt with by the provincial governor either directly or through a delegate (*iudex pedaneus*) without observing the rules governing the ordinary *per formulam* procedure. From the time of Augustus the *cognitio extra ordinem*

---

[90] See, e.g., A. S. Hunt and C. C. Edgar, *Select Papyri* II, London 1963, no. 262 (P. Thead. 15) and No. 293 (P. Ryl. 114).

[91] By contrast, under the formulary system, proceedings were initiated by the parties concerned who also dominated the scene in the trial that followed.

was the only form of procedure used in the imperial provinces, where the administration of justice was entrusted to imperial officials who acted as representatives of the emperor (*legati Augusti pro praetore*). In the senatorial provinces it became the regular form of procedure during the second century AD. By the end of the third century AD it had entirely superseded the *per formulam* procedure throughout the empire.[92] The adoption of the *cognitio* procedure as the main form of procedure was in part due to its greater simplicity and in part due to the fact that, in accordance with imperial ideas, it facilitated the centralisation of state authority by transferring to state organs power which had been in the past vested in lay judges.[93]

In the *cognitio extra ordinem* there was no division of the proceedings into two distinct phases (*in iure* and *apud iudicem*) nor a *formula*, and the term *litis contestatio* came to denote simply the moment at which the trial began before the magistrate.[94] The summons was now issued by the plaintiff to the defendant with the backing of the jurisdictional magistrate (*denuntiatio ex auctoritate*), or by the magistrate himself on the plaintiff's request.[95] If the defendant failed to appear in court the judge could condemn him by default (*contumacia*).[96] By contrast, under the formulary system it was up to the plaintiff to ensure that the defendant appeared before the magistrate and a judgement by default was impossible since there could be no trial without the agreement of both parties. Under the new system the term *praescriptio* (or *exceptio*) came to signify any defence raised by the defendant against the plaintiff's claim. As to the means of evidence, these were the same as under the formulary system, although now written evidence carried much more weight than oral testimony. All the relevant evidence was assessed freely by the magistrate in charge, but the burden of production was born by the litigating parties.

---

92 The *per formulam* procedure was formally abolished in 342 AD. Consider C. 2. 57. 1. See also C. 3. 3. 3.

93 On the emergence of the *cognitio* procedure see H. F. Jolowicz and B. Nicholas, *Historical Introduction to the Study of Roman Law*, 3rd edn, Cambridge 1972, 397-8; M. Kaser, *Römische Rechtsgeschichte*, Göttingen 1976, 126, 150, 154-5; *Das römische Zivilprozessrecht*, Munich 1996, 451 ff; W. Kunkel/M. Schermaier, *Römische Rechtsgeschichte*, Cologne 2001, 171 ff; A. Guarino, *Storia del diritto romano*, Naples 1996, 444 ff; M. Talamanca (ed.), *Lineamenti di storia del diritto romano*, Milan 1989, 423 ff.

94 See M. Kaser, *Das römische Zivilprozessrecht*, Munich 1996, 490-1.

95 The summons of the defendant by the magistrate could be made either by a letter (*evocatio litteris*) or, if the defendant's domicile was unknown, by a public announcement (*evocatio edicto*). See D. 5. 3. 20. 6d. (Ulpianus).

96 See, e.g., FIRA III, no. 169.

The magistrate's decision had to be given in writing and announced in the presence of the parties concerned.[97] Unlike the formulary system, under which the judgement of the *iudex* was regarded as final, in the *cognitio extra ordinem* the party who lost the case could appeal from the original decision of the magistrate to have his case brought before the emperor or a higher magistrate.[98] A more detailed description of the *cognitio* procedure, as it applied during the later imperial period, is given in chapter 10 below.

Criminal Law and Procedure

The Criminal Trial

In the last century of the Republic offences of a serious nature fell within the jurisdiction of the standing courts (*quaestiones perpetuae*); less serious offences were dealt with in a summary fashion by lower magistrates, the *tresviri capitales*. During the early years of the Principate the criminal jurisdiction of the *tresviri capitales* was taken over by imperial officials, the *vigiles*, acting under the supervision of the *praefectus vigilum*.[99] The *quaestiones perpetuae* continued to function following the reorganisation of the standing court system by the *lex Iulia iudiciorum publicorum* of Augustus in 17 BC. This law dealt with matters concerning the composition of the standing courts, the rights of the parties and their advocates and the conduct of the trial. Under the same enactment the participation of the *equites* as jurors in criminal trials was warranted and increased, and the minimum age for jury service was lowered from thirty to twenty-five. Moreover, about 18 BC two new tribunals were added to the existing ones: the *quaestio de adulteriis*, created under Augustus's *lex Iulia de adulteriis*,[100] and the *quaestio de annona*, established by the *lex Iulia de annona*. Within the jurisdiction of the first court fell cases involving adultery (*adulterium*), extra-marital relationships involving women of a high social standing and procurement.[101] The second dealt with accusations

---

[97] As the decision was regarded as binding only upon those present. See *Pauli Sententiae receptae*, 5, 5a, in Girard, *Textes* I, p. 345.

[98] For example, there might be an appeal from the *iudex pedaneus* to the higher magistrate who appointed him. Appeals to the emperor were not allowed except in cases involving matters of special importance.

[99] Offences falling in the jurisdiction of the *praefectus vigilum* included arson, robbery, burglary and theft, although the most serious cases were dealt with by the *praefectus urbi*. See D. 1. 15; C. 1. 45.

[100] Suetonius, *div. Aug*. 34. 1; Cassius Dio 54. 30. 4.

[101] D. 48. 5; C. 9. 9.

against merchants engaged in unfair market practices relating to the transportation and sale of foodstuffs.[102] Further changes in the system of the *quaestiones perpetuae* were introduced by a number of senatorial resolutions issued during this period.

Although the system of the *quaestiones perpetuae* on the whole guaranteed a relatively well-balanced handling of criminal cases, it had several deficiencies which were not adequately addressed by the Augustan legislation and subsequent senatorial resolutions. As the crimes that fell within the jurisdiction of the standing courts were rather narrowly defined, offences which did not correspond to the prescribed definitions could not be dealt with by these courts. A further shortcoming of the system had to do with the fact that, as the courts sat only in Rome, it was impracticable to bring all citizens accused of serious crimes to the capital for trial. Moreover, the penalties imposed for offences tried by the standing courts were often considered to be too mild and therefore disproportionate to the gravity of the offences committed. In addition to that, proceedings in the jury-courts were expensive and laborious and, since cases not infrequently had to be heard more than once, trials could drag on for a very long time.[103] Thus, from the early years of the Principate the system of the *quaestiones perpetuae* began to lose ground and the so-called extraordinary criminal procedure (*cognitio extra ordinem*) became more and more important. During this period new crimes emerged which fell outside the scope of the statutes by which the standing courts had been established. Many of these crimes were offences which in the past were treated as private delicts; others were offences of a special nature (such as certain offences committed by slaves or foreigners) which lacked precise statutory definitions. These new crimes were dealt with by imperial tribunals following the *extra ordinem* procedure.[104] As more and more offences came within the jurisdiction of the extraordinary courts, the *quaestiones perpetuae* faded into the background and finally disappeared in the closing years of the second century AD.[105] Under the new system the emperor and

---

[102] D. 48. 12.

[103] In the time of Septimius Severus the *quaestio de adulteriis* alone had over 3000 undecided cases.

[104] The offences that fell in the jurisdiction of the extraordinary courts were referred to as *crimina extraordinaria*.

[105] For a closer look at the development of the criminal justice system during the Principate see B. Santalucia, *Diritto e processo penale nell'anctica Roma*, Milan 1989, ch. 6; *Studi di diritto penale romano*, Rome 1994, 211 ff, 223 ff; A. H. M. Jones, *The Criminal Courts of the Roman Republic and Principate*, Oxford 1972, chapter 3; R. A. Bauman, *Crime and Punishment in Ancient Rome*, London 1996, ch. 5; O. F. Robinson, *The Criminal Law of Ancient*

imperial officials used their administrative powers to decide criminal cases directly either in the first instance or on appeal.[106] Besides the extraordinary court of the emperor, the courts of the *praefectus urbi* and the *praefectus vigilum* (for offences committed within the city limits of Rome),[107] the court of the *praefectus praetorio* (for offences committed in Italy),[108] and the court of the *praefectus annonae*,[109] the senate also developed into a court of justice dealing with offences committed by senators and members of the upper classes.[110] Moreover, criminal jurisdiction was assigned by decree of the senate or imperial constitution to the consuls and praetors who decided cases *extra ordinem* with the help of a body of advisers (*consilium*). In the senatorial provinces criminal justice was administered by the governors, whilst in the imperial ones it was administered by imperial officials acting as representatives of the emperor (*legati Augusti*). The *legati*, in their capacity as military commanders, had the power to impose on offenders all kinds of punishment, including the death penalty (*ius gladii*). Governors of senatorial provinces, on the other hand, could not impose the death penalty on Roman citizens unless the latter were given the opportunity to have their case heard by a court in Rome. But as the number of Roman citizens living in the provinces steadily increased, this practice appears to have been abandoned and the *ius gladii* was gradually granted to all provincial governors. In conducting a trial a governor commonly followed the *extra ordinem* procedure and, like the emperor in Rome, was assisted by a body of advisers (*consilium*). A possible exception to the finality of a provincial governor's decision lay

---

Rome, London 1995, 6 ff; W. Kunkel, *An Introduction to Roman Legal and Constitutional History*, 2nd edn, Oxford 1973, 69 ff; V. Giuffrè, *La repressione criminale nell' esperienza romana*, Naples 1998, chapters 4 & 5. And see I. Buti, "La 'cognitio extra ordinem' da Augusto a Diocleziano", in H. Temporini and W. Haase (eds), *Aufstieg und Niedergang der römischen Welt* II, Berlin and New York 1982, 29-59.

106 Augustus is said to have devoted much of his time to hearing cases *extra ordinem* (see, e.g., Cassius Dio 55. 7. 2; 56. 24. 7; Suetonius, *div. Aug.* 33. 1. and 2; 51. 2.). In the post-Augustan period this task was usually carried out by imperial officials acting as representatives of the emperor.

107 The *praefectus urbi* had criminal jurisdiction in Rome from the beginning of the Principate and, by the end of the second century, within a hundred miles of the city. See D. 1. 12. 1. pr. and 4; Cassius Dio 52. 21. 1-2; Tacitus, *Ann.* 6. 10-11.

108 Outside the hundred-mile radius of Rome.

109 This official had jurisdiction over offences connected with the food supply of Rome. See D. 48. 12. And see chapter 7.

110 Tacitus, *Ann.* 3. 49-51 and 68; 4. 15; 13. 10. and 32; 14. 15; 14. 28. and 40. Pliny, *Ep.* 2. 11. 4; 4. 9. 17; Suetonius, *Tib.* 30; Cassius Dio 52. 43.

with the emperor who could receive any appeal, even an appeal from a person who was not in theory entitled to raise one.

We saw in chapter 6 that the regular jury-courts were not allowed to deal with crime inquisitorially, i.e., they were not allowed to start a criminal investigation on their own initiative and to make use of any means at their disposal in order to arrive at a verdict. Proceedings were initiated by a private citizen – not a state organ – who assumed the role of the accuser by filing a charge against the alleged offender with the magistrate who presided over the relevant standing court. The new system of the *cognitio extra ordinem*, however, had a predominantly inquisitorial character. Although the victim of a crime was still allowed to act as an accuser, criminal prosecutions were now started by the state, and the magistrate in charge took a much more active part in the trial process than the president of a regular jury-court.[111] In a trial *extra ordinem* there were at first no limitations placed upon the magistrate in arriving at his knowledge (*cognitio*) of the crime, and the outcome depended largely upon the peculiarities of the individual case. By contrast with the system of the *quaestiones perpetuae* in which the guilt or innocence of the accused was determined by the jury, both the verdict and the sentence were now determined by the magistrate at his discretion. As there were no fixed penalties, the magistrate was free to impose any penalty he thought fit by considering, among other things, the circumstances of the offence, the personal condition of the offender and the social class to which he belonged. In the course of time, however, a system of norms emerged based on imperial mandates and rescripts,[112] as well as on juristic opinions, that fixed in a more definite way the scope of the relevant offences and matters relating to criminal procedure and punishment. As to the ancient institution of the *provocatio ad populum*, with the disappearance of the *comitia* in the early Principate period and the establishment of imperial control over the criminal justice system, this turned into the *appellatio ad imperatorem*.[113] The latter term was used to denote an appeal addressed to the emperor or a higher court against a sentence pronounced by a lower court or magistrate.[114]

[111] The *inquisitio* (investigation, inquiry) was carried out by lower officials under the supervision of the prosecuting magistrate. It must be added here that a criminal investigation was usually triggered by a complaint put forward by the injured party or a private informer.

[112] See, e.g., C. 4. 19-21.

[113] See A. H. M. Jones, *Studies in Roman Government and Law*, Oxford 1960, 191.

[114] D. 49. 2. 1; 49. 3. 1. (Ulpianus). See also D. 49. 3. 2. (Venuleius Saturninus); 49. 3. 3. (Modestinus).

The senatorial cognitio extra ordinem

During the Republic the senate did not have independent criminal jurisdiction. Its role in the administration of justice was limited to setting up, under certain circumstances, temporary courts of inquiry (*quaestiones extraordinariae*) and to introducing, in times of emergency, whatever measures were deemed necessary for the security of the state. From the early years of the Principate period, however, the senate began to operate as a court of justice in its own right (*cognitio senatus*). Within its jurisdiction fell offences involving a threat or injury to the Roman state and offences involving abuse of power perpetrated by senators and, sometimes, *equites*.[115] In the time of Tiberius the jurisdiction of the senate was extended over a wide range of crimes, including adultery, murder and forgery, committed by senators or members of the *ordo senatorius*.[116] This practice continued until the later part of the second century AD, although not without exceptions. The rules of procedure under which cases were tried by the senate were similar to those governing the ordinary courts, although many of the formalities associated with the regular trial process were dispensed with. Proceedings were initiated by an application by the person concerned for leave to bring an accusation (*postulatio*) and the formal announcement of the charge and the name of the accuser (*delatio*). The magistrate to whom the application was made then formally registered the name of the accused (*nominis receptio*) and the day was fixed on which the trial was to begin. On the appointed day the senate was convoked and the trial began under the supervision of a higher magistrate, usually a consul. After all the evidence had been presented and the arguments of the parties heard the senators decided, by vote, on the question of guilt or innocence of the accused as well as on the form and amount of punishment that was to be imposed if the accused was found guilty. The judicial functions of the senate were curtailed during the reign of Commodus (180-192 AD) and by the early third century AD the senate had ceased to operate as a court of justice.

---

115 Tacitus, *Ann.* 1. 73; 1. 74; 2. 27 ff; 3. 12-14. 38. 66-70; 4. 15. 31; 4. 18-21. 28. 34-35; 6. 8. 14; 11. 4; 12. 22. 52. 59. 65; 13. 30. 33. 43. 52; 14. 18.28. 40. 46; 16. 8-9; Pliny, *Ep.* 2. 11; 3. 9; 4. 9; Suetonius, *Tib.* 30.

116 Tacitus, *Ann.* 3. 12-14. 22-23; 4. 22. 42; 6. 47-48; 13. 44; 14. 40.

Punishments imposed under the system of the *cognitio extra ordinem*

With respect to offences that fell within the jurisdiction of the standing courts, the range of penalties that could be imposed was rather limited and, in most cases, a person found guilty of a crime was given the opportunity to avoid punishment by leaving the city before the sentence of the court was pronounced (*aqua et ignis interdictio*).[117] During the Empire the number of penalties available to the judge in trials *extra ordinem* was much greater. In determining the form and amount of punishment to be imposed the judge took into account not only the gravity of the offence and the circumstances in which it was committed but also the social class to which the offender belonged.[118] Thus, depending on whether the offender belonged to the *honestiores*, i.e. the upper classes,[119] or to the *humiliores*, i.e. the lower classes, different penalties could be imposed for the same offence.[120] Among the most common punishments imposed upon members of the upper classes were expulsion (*relegatio*), involving the exclusion of the wrongdoer from residence in a specified territory (normally Italy and one's own province),[121] and deportation (*deportatio*), usually to an island or oasis. The latter punishment was of a more serious nature and was accompanied by the loss of property and citizenship, though not of personal freedom.[122] Other penalties included expulsion from the *ordo* to which the offender belonged, exclusion from civic offices[123] and prohibition from pleading in the courts of law.[124] When capital punishment (*poena capitis*) was imposed upon a member of the nobility, death was usually inflicted by decapitation.[125] A form of punishment reserved for members of the lower classes was condemnation to forced labour in the

---

[117] See chapter 6.

[118] See, e.g., D. 48. 13. 7(6). (Ulpianus); 48. 19. 16. 1-8. (Claudius Saturninus).

[119] The *ordo senatorius* and the *ordo equester* in Rome and the *ordo decurionum* and the *ordo Augustalium* in the provinces.

[120] This class distinction in relation to criminal penalties became established in the second century AD. Consider on this P. Garnsey, *Social Status and Legal Privilege in the Roman Empire*, Oxford 1970; R. Rilinger, *Humiliores-Honestiores*, Munich 1988.

[121] The *relegatio* was a mild form of exile (*exilium*) as it did not entail loss of personal freedom or citizenship and was imposed for a specified period only. D. 48. 22. 4. 7. 14. 18.

[122] *Deportatio* could only be imposed by the emperor or the *praefectus urbi*. D. 48. 19. 2. 1; 48. 22. 6. 14. And see Tacitus, *Ann.* 3. 68-69; 4. 21. 30.

[123] D. 48. 22. 7. 20-22. (Ulpianus); 48. 7. 1. (Marcianus).

[124] D. 48. 19. 9. (Ulpianus).

[125] D. 48. 19. 8. 1. (Ulpianus).

mines (*ad metalla*) – the sentence might be for a fixed term or for life, and in the latter case it was accompanied by loss of liberty.[126] Besides the mines there was also hard labour on public works (*in opus publicum*) or in public games (*ad ludos*) which was usually imposed for a fixed term and did not entail loss of personal freedom.[127] *Humiliores* were liable to exacerbated forms of the death penalty, such as crucifixion, impalement and burning at the stake.[128] Other punishments included condemnation to become a gladiator or to fight with wild beasts (*dare ad bestias, condemnare ad bestias*), flogging and flagellation, the total or partial confiscation of the offender's property (*ademptio bonorum, confiscatio, publicatio bonorum*), and various pecuniary fines (*multae*) which were paid to the state.[129] Imprisonment (*carcer*) was used as a way of assuring that a person would appear for trial, but it was not regarded as a legal penalty.[130] As to the aims of punishment, these included general deterrence, rehabilitation, retribution and the satisfaction of the victim's family.[131]

Categories of offences

Crimen repetundarum and concussio

In the Principate period the crime of extortion (*crimen repetundarum*) was extended to include cases involving abuse of power by any person entrusted with public office.[132] A person found guilty of such an offence was now subject to *deportatio* and could be compelled to pay four times

---

[126] D. 48. 19. 8. 4. (Ulpianus); 48. 19. 36. (Hermogenianus).

[127] D. 48. 19. 8. 11. (Ulpianus).

[128] D. 48. 19. 9. 11; 8. 2. (Ulpianus); 28. pr. 11-12. and 15. (Callistratus); 38. 1. (Paulus).

[129] D. 48. 19. 7; 28. 3. (Callistratus); 48. 1. 2. (Paulus).

[130] D. 48. 3. 2. pr. (Papinianus); 3. 3. (Ulpianus). On the forms of punishment imposed see B. Santalucia, *Diritto e processo penale nell'anctica Roma*, Milan 1989, 114 ff; *Studi di diritto penale romano*, Rome 1994, 239 ff; R. A. Bauman, *Crime and Punishment in Ancient Rome*, London and New York 1996, 142 ff.

[131] D. 48. 19. 20. (Paulus); D. 48. 19. 28. 15. (Callistratus); D. 48. 19. 16. 10; (Claudius Saturninus); 48. 19. 38. 5. (Paulus); 50. 16. 131. (Ulpianus). See on this C. Gioffredi, *I principi del diritto penale romano*, Turin 1970, 41 ff.

[132] The *crimen repetundarum* was regulated by the *lex Iulia* of Caesar (59 BC) which remained the basis of the penal repression of extortion until the time of Justinian. See D. 48. 11. 1 pr. (Marcianus). And see O. F. Robinson, *The Criminal Law of Ancient Rome*, London 1995, 81-82; B. Santalucia, *Diritto e processo penale nell' antica Roma*, Milan 1989, 118-9; V. Giuffrè, *La repressione criminale nell' esperienza romana*, Naples 1998, 109-10.

the value of the extorted property. Related to the *crimen repetundarum* was the *concussio*, an offence involving the extortion of property by means of intimidation and abuse of authority by a magistrate or by a person who falsely assumed an official role.[133] If committed by a person belonging to the lower classes (*humiliores*) the *concussio* entailed severe penalties, including the *poena capitalis*.

Ambitus and crimen maiestatis

After the *comitia* ceased to play a part in the political process, having been deprived of their legislative and electoral functions, the offence of *ambitus*, concerned with electoral corruption, was redefined so as to cover cases involving corruption of judicial organs as well as buying office or promotion within the imperial civil service.[134] The scope of the *crimen maiestatis* (treason) was also broadened to cover, among other things, acts threatening the safety and dignity of the emperor or his family.[135] A refusal to take an oath in the name of the emperor and, in later years, the profession of Christianity, were treated under the *crimen maiestatis*.

Peculatus and sacrilegium

Peculatus, the misappropriation of property belonging to the state, and *sacrilegium*, the theft of things used for religious purposes (*res religiosae*) continued to be regarded as serious offences, although the scope of the latter offence was extended in the later Empire to cover acts against the sanctity of imperial orders or enactments. A person convicted of such an offence was now subject to *relegatio*, if he was a member of the nobility, or to *deportatio* or the death penalty if he belonged to the lower social classes.[136]

---

[133] D. 47. 13; C. 12. 61.

[134] The offence of *ambitus* was the subject of *lex Iulia ambitus* of Augustus enacted in 18 BC. D. 48. 14. (Modestinus); C. 9. 26. See Robinson, *The Criminal Law of Ancient Rome*, London 1995, 84-86; B. Santalucia, *Diritto e processo penale nell' antica Roma*, Milan 1989, 119.

[135] D. 48. 4; C. 9. 8. And see Robinson, ibid, 74 ff; Santalucia, ibid, 118; R. A.Bauman, *The Crimen Maiestatis in the Roman Republic and Augustan Principate*, Johannesburg 1970, Part 3.

[136] D. 48. 13; C. 9. 28. 29. And see Robinson, ibid, 83-4; Santalucia, ibid, 93-4, 122.

Calumnia, praevaricatio, tergiversatio

The offence of *calumnia* – wilfully bringing a false accusation against another – which had already been recognised during the Republic, was now broadened to include any ill-considered accusation, not only accusations motivated by malice.[137] A person found guilty of such an offence was subject to the punishment which the offence he falsely accused another of committing entailed. The offence of *praevaricatio*, concerned with cases in which an accuser was induced by corrupt motives to conduct his case in such a manner as to secure the acquittal of the accused, was similarly redefined.[138] The punishment for the crime of *tergiversatio*, committed when an accuser, without proper justification, abandoned the accusation, was extended by the *senatus consultum Turpillianum* (61 AD) to include infamy and a heavy fine.[139]

Vis publica and vis privata

The scope of the offence of *vis publica* was broadened to include various acts of violence against public interests, such as the disruption of proceedings in a court of law, the senate or other state bodies, the exercise of pressure on judges or judicial magistrates, the disruption of public ceremonies and funerals etc. To the same category belonged also various forms of abuse of power and grave breaches of official duty committed by state officials. Moreover, certain cases of *vis privata* involving violence against individuals or the use of arms were now subject to prosecution by state organs, in addition to the private action taken by the individual concerned. Those found guilty of violent crimes were subject to *deportatio* and the confiscation of their property.[140]

---

137 The *lex Remmia* of 80 BC provided that a person charged with *calumnia* had to be tried by the same court before which he had prosecuted an innocent person. D. 3. 6; C. 9. 46. See Santalucia, ibid, 122.

138 D. 48. 16. 1. 6. (Marcianus); C. 9. 9. 10; 9. 42. 2. 1. See also Tacitus, *Ann.* 14. 41; Pliny, *Ep.* 3. 9. 29-33. *Praevaricatio* included also a collusion between an advocate and the adversary of his client to the detriment of the latter. D. 47. 15. And see Santalucia, ibid, 122-3.

139 D. 48. 16. For a closer look at the development of procedural offences in Roman criminal law see Robinson, *The Criminal Law of Ancient Rome*, London 1995, 99-103.

140 The relevant offences were prescribed by the *lex Iulia de vi publica* and the *lex Iulia de vi privata* of Augustus. See D. 48. 6; C. 9. 12. For a closer look see B. Santalucia, *Diritto e processo penale nell' antica Roma*, Milan 1989, 121-2.

Homicidium

During the Empire the term *homicidium* was used to describe the intentional killing of any free citizen. Inducing another to commit murder, assisting another in the commission of the crime and participation in armed bands of murderers were also treated under this offence.[141] Moreover, from the middle of the second century AD the killing of a slave by his master came to be regarded as *homicidium*. The requisite guilty intention was inferred from the act of killing, although the lack of premeditation on the offender's part might reduce the level of liability for homicide.[142] The offender's motive, however, was irrelevant. Infants or lunatics could not be punished as murderers since they could not form a murderous intent. The punishment imposed for homicide depended upon the circumstances of the individual case and the social status of the offender.

Falsum

The offence of forgery was the subject of the Sulla's *lex Cornelia de falsis* (81 BC), by which the relevant *quaestio perpetua* was established. During the Empire Sulla's statute remained in force but was extended, through senatorial resolutions (*SC Geminianum, SC Libonianum, SC Licinianum*), juristic interpretation and the practice of the courts, to cover certain acts that fell outside the scope of the original offence definition. These included the fraudulent manipulation of seals, the forging of imperial enactments, the assumption of a false name or title, giving false evidence in a court of law and withholding or withdrawing evidence, and the suborning judges or jurors.[143]

In addition to the above-mentioned offences, a number of wrongdoings previously falling in the category of *delicta privata* came to be classified as crimes. These included, for example, stealing in public places, breaking and entering, cattle stealing, the taking of things belonging to an inheritance before it was passed to the lawful heir (*expilatio*), the violation of tombs, the removal of border marks and various forms of fraudulent behaviour.

---

141 D. 48. 8. For a closer look at the crime of *homicidium* see Robinson, *The Criminal Law of Ancient Rome*, London 1995, 41 ff.

142 In general greater attention was now paid to the subjective or guilt element in crime.

143 D. 48. 10; C. 9. 22. 23. 24. On the offence of *falsum* see B. Santalucia, *Dirittoe processo penale nell' antica Roma*, Milan 1989, 120-1.

Principles of criminal liability and punishment

As has been noted, in the context of the *cognitio extra ordinem* the judge had considerable freedom in conducting the investigation and in determining the nature and gravity of the offence and the form of punishment to be imposed. Offenders might be treated differently, depending upon the circumstances in which the crime was committed, but also upon the offender's age, sex, state of mind and social and legal status. The idea of equality before the law played no part in Roman criminal law. There were, however, some general norms pertaining to the conditions of criminal liability and punishment – norms developed by the jurists and established through imperial enactments and the practice of the courts.[144] Some of these norms were concerned with procedural matters whilst others pertained to the requirements of criminal responsibility, such as conduct, intent and defences. Thus, it was recognised that criminal punishment should only be imposed by a competent judicial organ acting in accordance with a pre-existing law;[145] and should there be genuine uncertainty as to which of two (or more) statutes applied, the milder one (i.e. the one entailing the less severe penalty) should be given priority.[146] It was held, moreover, that persons accused of crimes should be duly notified of the charges and given the opportunity to defend themselves in a court of law;[147] and a person should not be punished as a criminal before the final decision of the court had been pronounced nor should he be tried for the same offence twice;[148] the descendants or heirs of a convicted criminal should not be stigmatised for the latter's crime, for criminal responsibility was seen as personal and as such its consequences should be borne by the offender only.[149] It was accepted, further, that criminal liability and punishment presupposed an overt act – a person should not be punished for thoughts alone.[150] Moreover, for the commission of a crime a guilty

---

144 Some of these norms had their origins in the archaic and pre-classical periods. On the conditions of criminal liability see O. F. Robinson, *The Criminal Law of Ancient Rome*, London 1995, 16 ff; A. Lebigre, *Quelques aspects de la responsabilité pénale en droit romain classique*, Paris 1967; R. A. Bauman, *Crime and Punishment in Ancient Rome*, London and New York 1996; A. Burdese (ed.), *Idee vecchie e nuove sul diritto criminale romano*, Padua 1988; C. Gioffredi, *I principi del diritto penale romano*, Turin 1970.

145 D. 50. 16. 131. (Ulpianus).

146 D. 48. 19. 32. (Ulpianus).

147 D. 48. 2. 3. (Paulus) and 7. (Ulpianus); 48. 19. 5. (Ulpianus).

148 D. 48. 19. 2. 2. (Ulpianus).

149 D. 48. 19. 20. (Paulus) and 26. Callistratus).

150 D. 48. 19. 18. (Ulpianus).

intention (*dolus*) was normally required, although in some cases recklessness might be sufficient. Children under the age of seven were excluded from criminal liability as being incapable of forming a guilty intention.[151] Lunatics were also exempted from punishment on similar grounds, although they might be kept under restraint if they posed a threat to public safety.[152] A person was not criminally liable if he caused a prohibited harm by accident.[153] However, mistake or ignorance as to the law, in contrast to mistake of fact, did not preclude culpability, for citizens were under a duty to know the law.[154] Certain categories of persons, such as minors (under the age of twenty-five), women and country dwellers, were treated with leniency if found guilty of certain offences or when they caused harm due to ignorance of the law.[155] Roman law also recognised a number of general defences and mitigating pleas which negated or reduced culpability for a criminal act, such as self-defence,[156] superior orders,[157] loss of self-control,[158] duress and necessity.[159] It was acknowledged, moreover, that offenders should not be subjected to excessive or unnecessary punishment, especially when they were weak in body or mind.[160]

---

[151] Children up to puberty were presumed incapable of forming a criminal intent, although this presumption could be rebutted. D. 9. 2. 5. 2. (Ulpianus); 48. 8. 12. (Modestinus); 29. 5. 14; Maecianus); 21. 1. 23. 2 (Ulpianus); 47. 12. 3. 1. (Ulpianus); 48. 6. 3. 1. (Marcianus); 48. 10. 22. pr. (Paulus); C. 9. 47. 7.

[152] D. 21. 1. 23. 2. (Ulpianus); 29. 5. 3. 11. (Ulpianus); 48. 4. 7. 3. (Modestinus); 1. 18. 13. 1. (Ulpianus); 1. 18. 14. (Macer).

[153] D. 48. 19. 11. 2. (Marcianus); C. 9. 16. 4 (5).

[154] D. 39. 4. 16. 5. (Marcianus); C. 9. 16. 1.

[155] D. 2. 1. 7. 4. (Ulpianus); 22. 6. 9. pr. (Paulus); 48. 5. 39. 2. (Papinianus); 4. 4. 37. 1. (Tryphoninus).

[156] D. 48. 8. 9. (Ulpianus); 9. 2. 45. 4. (Paulus); 48. 8. 1. 4. (Marcianus).

[157] D. 48. 10. 5. (Julianus); 50. 17. 4. (Ulpianus); 9. 2. 37. pr. (Javolenus); 44. 7. 20. (Alfenus).

[158] This might be caused by justified anger or drunkenness. D. 48. 8. 1. 5. (Marcianus); 48. 5. 39(38). 8. (Papinianus); 48. 3. 12. pr. (Callistratus); 49. 16. 6. 7. (Arrius Menander).

[159] D. 19. 2. 13. 7. (Ulpianus). Consider also Tacitus, *Ann.* 11. 36; Cassius Dio 60. 22.

[160] D. 48. 19. 8. 3. (Ulpianus); 48. 3. 14. 4. (Herennius Modestinus); 48. 19. 3. (Ulpianus); 48. 19. 22. (Modestinus); 48. 19. 38. 12. (Paulus). See also Cicero, *de off.* 1. 25. 89.

9 The Dominate

The Reorganisation of the Imperial System

The assassination of Emperor Alexander Severus in 235 AD marks the beginning of a long period of crisis during which the Roman empire came close to disintegration. In the wake of the devastation caused by civil wars and foreign invasions, imperial unity was shattered, agriculture, commerce and industry declined and the economic and political foundations of ancient civilised life were badly shaken. But amidst the chaos a feeling was gathering strength, especially among the upper classes of the population, that they must, by some means or other, defend Roman civilisation, save the cities from destruction and restore the unity of the state. In the later part of the third century a succession of capable emperors[1] began the work of restoring the crumbling empire. Eventually, discipline in the army was restored, external enemies were repelled and imperial unity was re-established. The work of these so called 'soldier emperors' paved the way for the systematic changes of structure which were to take place during the reigns of Diocletian and Constantine the Great in the late third and early fourth centuries AD.

With Diocletian (284-305 AD) begins a new period in Roman history, known as the 'Dominate' (*dominatus*). During this period the autocratic tendencies that had grown ever stronger during the later Principate era prevailed and the emperor was openly recognised as the sole ruler (*dominus*) of the Roman world. At the same time Diocletian gave the empire a bureaucratic organisation better suited to the needs and conditions of the times. The relative success of the extensive programme of reforms initiated by Diocletian was largely due to the same conditions which had helped Augustus to succeed about three hundred years earlier: after nearly half a century of anarchy and civil war the Roman world was thirsting for peace and stability and the chance to return to a more settled life. Diocletian was quick to realise the temper of the times and to make use of it. Like Augustus, he brought together what had grown up in the confusion

---

[1] Such as Decius (249-251 AD), Claudius Gothicus (268-270 AD), Aurelian (270-275 AD) and Probus (276-282 AD).

of the age, made it into a system and gave it the permanence of a constitutional form.[2]

The reforms of Diocletian

As was noted in chapter 7, the empire in the third century had been dogged by three interconnected problems: the weakness of the imperial authority, the inadequacy of the empire's administrative structure and the decline of the economy. Politically, the emperor was in the hands of the army, which had become the real master of the empire. Administratively, the government was incapable of ruling the empire efficiently and of defending its frontiers against foreign enemies. Economically, the continuous increases in taxation had led to the devaluation of the currency with disastrous consequences. The character of Diocletian's regime is reflected in the solutions which he devised for these problems.

The remedy for the first weakness was the strengthening of the authority of the emperor, by giving the imperial ideology a new form and content. The emperor was now elevated to the position of an absolute monarch and had himself portrayed as being closer to the divine realm than any Roman *princeps* in the past. He assumed the dignity and attributes of the oriental god-kings and was set apart by a framework of complicated ceremonial and court etiquette accompanied by tremendous pomp. As the system assumed the characteristics of an Eastern despotism, the remaining republican institutions became mere shadows of their former selves or were entirely abandoned. This orientalisation of the imperial office had been going on throughout the third century and Diocletian's arrangements simply completed the transformation.

Diocletinan's answer to the empire's administrative problem was the introduction of the system of the 'tetrarchy'. Recognising that the empire could not be governed efficiently by a single ruler, or from a single administrative centre, he devised a system by which imperial rule was divided whilst, at the same time, the principle of imperial unity remained unaffected. In 285 AD he appointed Maximian, one of his ablest generals, as Caesar and co-ruler. In 286 AD Maximian was promoted to Augustus and was made ruler of the West, while Diocletian himself took over the rule of the East. In 293 AD each Augustus appointed as his assistant and

---

2 For a closer look at this part of Roman history see in general A. H. M. Jones, *The Later Roman Empire*, Oxford 1964; M. Cary and H. H. Scullard, *A History of Rome*, 3rd edn, London 1975, 507 ff; A. Cameron, *The Later Roman Empire*, London 1993; P. Brown, *The World of Late Antiquity*, London 1971; R. Collins, *Early Medieval Europe 300-1000*, London 1991; T. D. Barnes, *The New Empire of Diocletian and Constantine*, Cambridge Mass., 1982.

successor a Caesar and the four ruled jointly, each having control over one quarter of the empire. From Nicomedia, his capital city, Diocletian ruled over Asia, Egypt and Thrace, while his Caesar, Galerius, governed the Balkan peninsula. Maximian, whose seat of government was at Mediolanum (Milan), had control over Italy, Africa and Spain, while his Caesar, Constantius Chlorus, ruled over Britain and Gaul.[3] This proliferation of the imperial summit was designed not only to facilitate the administration of the empire but also to discourage attempts at usurpation by establishing a stable succession mechanism.[4] Under the new system the provinces were made much smaller in size and their number was increased, mainly to ensure closer supervision of administration. The provinces were grouped into new districts, the dioceses, while neighbouring dioceses were joined into larger units called prefectures. There were four prefectures altogether (Gaul, Italy, Illyricum and the Orient) divided into twelve dioceses[5] and over a hundred provinces. Each prefecture was ruled by a praetorian prefect, the highest civil official of the empire. Subordinate to the prefects were the chiefs of dioceses, or vicars, and the provincial governors, while the whole organisation centred in the persons of the Augusti and Caesars. As has been noted, the system of tetrarchy was not seen as introducing a division of the empire but, rather, as introducing a division of the rule over an undivided empire. Thus legislation was always promulgated in the names of all four rulers, coins were minted by all in common and sacrifices and other ceremonies of homage were carried out before the busts of all four.

The Tetrarchs sought to remedy the economic ills besetting the empire by introducing measures calculated to strengthen the role of the state in economic life. State control over the productive resources of the empire was extended until, by the fourth century, nearly all forms of economic activity important to the state came to be regulated by the government.[6] To raise the revenues needed for the maintenance of the

---

3 Although Rome was no longer the administrative capital of the empire, it continued to enjoy a privileged status and its citizens were catered for by the state.

4 As the success of the system of tetrarchy depended largely upon the concord among the rulers, the four hastened to demonstrate their mutual amity by all possible means.

5 The number of dioceses was soon increased to thirteen and later again to fifteen by further subdivisions of Italy and Greece.

6 This form of 'command' economy did not come into being as a set plan nor was it inspired by any theories about state ownership of the means of production. It was the result of reforms initiated by Diocletian in response to practical necessities and carried to conclusion by his successors.

military establishment, the enlarged bureaucracy and imperial court the state intervened more and more in economic matters, taking a direct share in the production of food, textiles and military supplies. State factories were set up and the internal and external commerce of the empire was regulated by the state. Realising that economic instability was due in part to the depreciation of the coinage, Diocletian attempted to introduce a new, stable gold and silver currency, but his devaluation of the copper coins then in circulation caused more inflation which was further accentuated by production shortages. The Tetrarchs' response, the famous Edict of Prices (*edictum de pretiis*) of 301 AD, was a systematic attempt at a price regulation by the state, and thus also at state planning in the economic sector, but its effects were short-lived. Diocletian's reorganisation of the tax system, on the other hand, was to prove of lasting importance. In order to protect the state against future inflation a new type of land tax was introduced (*annona*) which was levied in kind. Besides this, various monetary taxes were imposed in accordance with fairly specified criteria and the system of compulsory public labour and extraordinary contributions that had been introduced during the late Principate period was developed further. To provide sufficient labour for the state factories and farms, and to prevent men from escaping from the various taxes and extraordinary requisitions a rigid hereditary caste system was developed: every man was now bound to the trade to which he was born and membership in the associations of tradesmen, businessmen and craftsmen (*corpora*) became hereditary. During this period the wealth and power of the great land-owners continued to increase as more and more land was concentrated in their hands and individuals and village communities, anxious to avoid the heavy burden of taxation and exactions by the state, continued to place themselves under their patronage becoming their tenants. These changes did not affect all the provinces of the empire equally, however. In the Greek-speaking eastern provinces the system of centrally controlled economy achieved a measure of success and the conditions of internal peace which now prevailed facilitated economic development. In the West, on the other hand, the system largely failed and the feudalistic tendencies continued to grow stronger as a result of the inability of the central government to exercise control over the great land-owners.[7]

---

7 On the reforms of Diocletian see S. Williams, *Diocletian and the Roman Recovery*, London 1985, 61 ff; R. MacMullen, *Roman Government's Response to Crisis*, New Haven 1976; W. Kunkel, *An Introduction to Roman Legal and Constitutional History*, 2nd edn, Oxford 1973, 137-143; A. H. M. Jones, *The Later Roman Empire*, Oxford 1964, ch. 2; S. Corcoran, *The Empire of the Tetrarchs*, Oxford 1996; F. M. D' Ippolito, *Aspetti di storia costituzionale*

The reign of Constantine the Great

As has been said, the system of the tetrarchy was designed to resolve the problem of succession by putting an end to the flood of pretenders – one of the chief causes of the anarchy and civil war that dogged the empire in the third century. However, this arrangement did not last very long. Shortly after Diocletian's abdication in 305 AD the system of the tetrarchy broke down in hopeless confusion and a new round of civil wars began between the claimants to the throne. In 312 AD, after six years of war, Constantine, the son of Constantius Chlorus, defeated his chief opponent, Maxentius, thereby becoming the sole emperor of the West . In the following year Licinius became emperor of the East. But in 323 AD war broke out between the two Augusti. In 324 AD Licinius was finally defeated and Constantine made himself ruler of the whole empire. The new emperor restored the unity of the state and completed the work of Diocletian giving the organisation of the empire the basic form which it retained until the fall of the empire in the West and its transition to the Byzantine empire in the East.

Administratively and militarily, the measures of Constantine, like those of Diocletian, were calculated to facilitate internal control and to strengthen the empire's defences. The greatly enlarged bureaucratic apparatus was further centralised in the imperial consistory, made up of the highest financial and administrative officials of the imperial court. The notion that the emperor was the chief magistrate of the Roman people was abandoned once and for all and, with the introduction of the principle of hereditary succession to the throne, the transformation of the imperial government into an absolute monarchy was now complete. Constantine made full use of his autocratic power to develop further the totalitarian regime whose foundations had been laid by Diocletian and earlier emperors. He regimented the occupations of practically all classes of the population and continued Diocletian's work aimed at stabilising the monetary system. At the same time he gave special attention to the administration of justice and sought to secure greater protection for the members of the lower classes. The army remained an important basis of imperial power but its influence was limited as a result of Constantine's military reforms.[8] Among the most important events of Constantine's reign

---

romana, Naples 2001, 111 ff; A. Guarino, *Storia del diritto romano*, Naples 1996, 495 ff.

8 The real fighting force now consisted of four mobile mercenary armies in which the Germanic element became increasingly prominent. The principle of universal obligation to military service was in theory retained, but in practice it

were the recognition of Christianity and the transference of the imperial capital from Rome to Constantinople.[9]

The rise of Christianity

During the Principate period Christians were largely tolerated and by the early third century they had become an accepted part of the imperial society. There were times at which Christians were persecuted, but these persecutions never took the form of a large and organised attempt to stamp out the Christian religion.[10] These measures were directed not so much against Christian religion as such, but against practices which manifested a disregard for the established institutions of the Roman state. As strict monotheists, Christians refused to worship the empire's gods, and especially the emperor, as the state demanded. In the eyes of many Romans this amounted to opposition to the national worship and the Christians appeared to be members of a secret society which was plotting against the integrity of the state. The hostility towards the Christians escalated as a result of the crisis of the third century and the first systematic persecutions of Christians were carried out during the reign of Decius (249-251 AD). Further measures were taken by Valerian (257 AD), including large-scale confiscations of Church property. These measures were justified on the grounds that the Christians posed a threat to the old pagan culture upon which the unity of the state depended. In the years that followed the death of Valerian state persecution of Christians ceased but a new round of persecutions began during the reign of Diocletian. Diocletian felt that the unity of the empire could not be realised without unity in religion and that this necessitated the eradication of Christianity and a return to the old religious practices. Thus between 302 and 305 AD he issued four edicts

---

was replaced by a special tax the proceeds of which were used to maintain the mercenary troops.

9 For a closer look at the reign of Constantine see T. D. Barnes, *Constantine and Eusebius*, Cambridge, Mass. 1981; R. MacMullen, *Constantine*, New York 1969; T. D. Barnes, *The New Empire of Diocletian and Constantine*, Cambridge, Mass., 1982; A. H. M. Jones, *The Later Roman Empire*, Oxford 1964, ch. 3; H. Kraft (ed.), *Konstantin der Grosse*, Darmstadt 1974.

10 When Nero, in 64 AD, accused the Christians of burning Rome, he did so in order to divert attention from himself. Under Domitian there were some trials of Christians and Trajan outlawed Christianity, but no organised persecution occurred (see, e.g., the *rescriptum* of Trajan replying to a question by Pliny the Younger in Pliny, *Ep.* 10. 96-97). Persecutions of Christians, such as those which took place in Lugdunum (Gaul) in the time of Marcus Aurelius, were largely localised.

which revived the state's persecution of the Christian Church. Under these laws all Christian officials were to lose their positions, Christian churches and sacred books were to be destroyed, the members of the clergy were to be imprisoned and Christians who refused to make offerings to the Roman gods were to be put to death as enemies of the state. But the persecution of Christians initiated by Diocletian did not produce the desired effect and, as citizens and officials alike connived to protect their Christian neighbours from arrest and punishment, the relevant laws gradually fell into abeyance and persecutions slackened or ceased. Finally, in 311 AD, Galerius, the Augustus of the East, issued an edict granting the Christians the right to worship their God and to rebuild their churches, provided that they did not offend public order.

In 313 AD Constantine and Licinius issued the famous Edict of Milan by which Christians were granted unrestricted freedom of worship and confiscated Church properties were restored.[11] Constantine himself did not immediately convert to Christianity (he was baptised Christian only at the end of his life) but Christians of his day were so pleased with the new turn of events that they did not object to the pagan practices which the emperor continued. Although under Constantine Christianity did not become the exclusive religion of the state, it enjoyed imperial preference and the emperor became a lavish patron of the Church, supporting it with generous gifts and privileges.[12] It remains unclear whether Constantine's attitude towards Christianity was the result of genuine religious conviction or political calculation. Whatever the emperor's motives may have been, it is doubtful whether Christianity ever would have triumphed as the dominant religion of the empire if it had not had some imperial patron, such as Constantine, to enhance its popularity and power. Convinced that the unity of the Church was a condition for the survival of the empire, Constantine used his imperial prestige and power to settle the theological disputes which were now arising among the Church leaders. Thus, in 325 AD he called a meeting of bishops and Church officials from all parts of the empire at the city of Nicea in Asia Minor to deal with the Arian controversy.[13] The Council of Nicea and others that followed in the fourth

---

11 Lactant., *de mort. pers.* 48. 2-12. See also G. Hanel, *Corpus Legum ab imperatoribus Romanis ante Iustinianum Latarum*, Leipzig 1857, repr. Aalen 1965, 186ff.

12 Clerics were exempted from personal services in 313 AD and from taxation in 319 AD.

13 Early in the fourth century Arius, bishop of Alexandria, argued that Christ was a created being – a position that contradicted the concept of the Trinity upon which Christian doctrine was founded. Arian's doctrine attracted many followers and threatened to destroy the unity of the Church. At Nicea the Arian

century confirmed the position of the emperor as the head of the Christian Church.[14] At the same time the Church found in these councils a means of reaching agreement on disputed points of religious doctrine.[15] Finally, in 380 AD Emperor Theodosius I issued the Edict of Thessalonica by which Christianity was recognised as the official religion of the state.[16] With the spreading of Christianity and its recognition as state religion Christian doctrine began to exercise a strong influence on the development of Roman law. At the same time the first disputes began to emerge between secular and Church authorities as to the bounds of their respective jurisdictions.[17]

In the period following the council of Nicea the Church appeared as a unified society embracing all Christian congregations of the empire, and Church and state became increasingly intertwined. At the same time the Church found in the political organisation of the Roman state, as it existed after the reforms of Diocletian and Constantine, a model upon which to fashion its own system of administration. The first Christian churches had been established in some of the major cities of the empire, such as Rome, Antioch, Alexandria, Carthage and Corinth. From these centres branch

---

position was declared heretical and a statement of the articles of faith was proclaimed (Nicene Creed).

14 On the rise of Christianity see in general A. Alföldi, *The Conversion of Constantine and Pagan Rome*, Oxford 1969; N. H. Baynes, *Constantine the Great and the Christian Church*, Oxford 1969; R. MacMullen, *Christianizing the Roman Empire. AD 100-400*, New Haven 1984; *Constantine*, New York 1969, ch. 6; A. H. M. Jones, *Constantine and the Conversion of Europe*, Toronto 1978; W. H. C. Frend, *The Rise of Christianity*, Philadelphia 1984; M. Sordi, *I Cristiani e l' Impero Romano*, Milan 1984.

15 Proceedings in the church councils resembled closely those of the Roman senate. The meeting was presided over by the emperor or his representative; attending bishops were entitled to express their views on the matter under consideration and to cast their vote; following their formal sanctioning by the emperor the decisions of the councils became legally binding upon all the parties concerned.

16 C. Th. 16. 1. 2. And see N. Q. King, *The Emperor Theodosius and the Establishment of Christianity*, London 1961.

17 Before the recognition of Christianity as the preferred religion Christians would usually submit legal disputes among themselves to the arbitration of bishops rather than to the regular courts. Constantine sanctioned the jurisdiction of Church organs in civil cases but Arcadius (383-408 AD) restricted it to cases voluntarily submitted by litigating parties to the bishops' judgement. Bishops do not appear to have had direct jurisdiction in criminal matters but, as the right of sanctuary was accorded to churches, they were often able to guarantee the safety of persons seeking their protection. Moreover, the emperors often sought the assistance of bishops in implementing legislation of a humanitarian character. On the jurisdiction of the ecclesiastical courts see chapter 10.

churches were sent out to other towns. The faithful in each town chose from among themselves a bishop, or overseer, who was then consecrated by the bishops of the larger cities in the province. The latter, because of the size of their congregations, assumed a position of supremacy over the bishops of the smaller towns and thus a hierarchy was developed within the Church which corresponded in its general divisions to the administrative hierarchy of the Roman state. At the top of this hierarchy was the emperor who was represented, in the West, by the bishops of Rome and Carthage and, in the East, by those of Constantinople, Antioch, Jerusalem and Alexandria. Below them were the bishops of the provincial capitals under whose authority came the bishops of the smaller towns in their provinces and the lower clergy.[18] But as the power and influence of the Church increased, rivalries began to emerge between certain episcopal sees within the Church structure, especially between those of Rome and Constantinople.[19] Despite attempts at reconciliation, concord was not established and the divisions within the Church organisation persisted throughout the later imperial period and in the centuries that followed.

The founding of Constantinople

Shortly after his victory over Licinius, Constantine decided to establish a new capital city on the old site of Byzantium in the East. The choice of Byzantium as the location for the new city indicates that the empire's political centre of gravity had shifted to the East. It was also probably motivated by Constantine's desire to break with the pagan past and to centre the empire in a new Christian foundation. Construction of the new city, called Constantine's city or Constantinople, began in 324 AD and was completed in 336 AD. The city was strategically located midway between the important Danubian and eastern frontiers on the crossroads between Europe and Asia Minor, and had a much better commercial situation than

---

[18] In the fourth century the bishops who led the oldest and largest Christian cities (Rome, Constantinople, Jerusalem, Alexandria and Antioch) were called patriarchs, whilst the bishops of the large cities in the provinces were termed metropolitans. The areas over which the patriarchs and metropolitans exercised their ecclesiastical authority corresponded in general terms with the prefectures, dioceses and provinces in which the empire had been divided for administrative purposes. In the Catholic church of today aspects of this form of organisation and the related terminology still exist.

[19] Just as the bishops of Rome had enjoyed a position of ecclesiastical pre-eminence because Rome had been the capital of the empire, so now the bishop of Constantinople claimed to enjoy a similar position because he was bishop of New Rome.

Rome. This location not only provided Constantinople with immense economic vitality, but also made it an effective political and administrative centre. In time Constantinople came to be regarded as a second Rome. It was given all the privileges of Rome, such as the *ius italicum*,[20] and had its own senate[21] which was presided over by the *praefectus urbi*. Rome kept its rank as a capital city, although the emperors seldom resided there during this period.[22]

Government and Civil Administration during the Later Empire

The emperor

With the transformation of the government into an absolute monarchy, all the sovereignty of the Roman people was held to be transferred to the emperor, whose right to rule was now based on the divine will revealed in his election by a human agency.[23] The emperor was no longer the 'first' Roman citizen but a divine monarch (*dominus et deus*: 'lord and god') presiding over a highly centralised administration which effectively regulated the social and economic life of each subject. He was the sole authority in all spheres of government, administrative, military, legislative, judicial. He appointed the members of the imperial civil service at his discretion, controlled the state's finances, imposed taxes and decided on matters of foreign policy. As the sole fount of laws, he was also their final interpreter. His person and everything in any way associated with him were attributed a sacred character – hence the terms *sacra constitutio* (imperial constitution), *sacrum consistorium* (imperial council), *sacrum palatium* (imperial palace), etc. Because his acts were regarded as divinely inspired, those who questioned or disobeyed his orders were guilty of sacrilege. In the rare cases in which he appeared in public an elaborate code of court ceremonial and etiquette was observed based on Hellenistic and Persian

---

[20] C. Th. 14. 13. 1. (Valentinian I and Valens).

[21] The senate of Constantinople was instituted in 361 AD.

[22] When Constantinople was founded Milan had replaced Rome as the imperial centre in the West. On the establishment and development of Constantinople in the fourth century see G. Dagron, *Naissance d'une capitale*, Paris 1974; R. MacMullen, *Constantine*, New York 1969, ch. 8.

[23] An emperor was either appointed by another emperor or elected by high military and civilian officials. After his election he was crowned before the soldiers and the populace who saluted him as *Imperator* and *Augustus*.

models.[24] This court ceremonial was designed to emphasise the divine nature of imperial authority and was aimed at inducing people's loyalty by taking advantage of the attraction which mysticism and supernatural faith exercised on the masses.[25] After Constantine's conversion to Christianity the imperial cult was adapted to the demands of a stringent monotheism. The emperor was now regarded as governing in the name of God (*Deo auctore*) and as being divinely inspired and protected.[26]

The imperial council

The emperor was assisted by a permanent body of advisers, the *sacrum consistorium*,[27] which had developed out of the earlier *consilium principis* as this was organised by Emperor Hadrian in the second century AD. The *sacrum consistorium* consisted of the highest officials of the imperial administration and functioned as a privy council of the emperor in legislative, judicial and administrative matters. Its members included the heads of the four main government departments, i.e. the chief of the imperial offices (*magister officiorum*), the minister of finance (*comes sacrarum largitionum*), the minister in charge of the administration of the imperial lands (*comes rerum privatarum*) and the minister of justice (*quaestor sacri palatii*), as well as the chamberlain of the imperial household (*praepositus sacri cubiculi*)[28] and a number of full-time councillors termed *comites consistoriani*. The jurists who served as

---

24 His subjects were required to kneel and kiss the hem of the emperor's robe (*proskynesis* or *adoratio purpurae*, the eastern ceremony of genuflection addressed to divinity), and the nimbus, the gleaming disc of light about the emperor's head, the globe and sceptre, now became permanent parts of the imperial tradition.

25 The observance of the court ceremonial and the maintenance of order in the imperial palace was entrusted to a body of officials referred to as *silentiarii*.

26 On the position of the emperor during the later imperial period see H. F. Jolowicz and B. Nicholas, *Historical Introduction to the Study of Roman Law*, 3rd edn, Cambridge 1972, 421-3; A. Alföldi, *Die monarchische Repräsentation im römischen Kaiserreiche*, Darmstadt 1970; F. Millar, *The Emperor in the Roman World* , New York 1977; A. H. M. Jones, *The Later Roman Empire*, Oxford 1964, 321 ff; M. Kaser, *Römische Rechtsgeschichte*, Göttingen 1976, 206-7; W. Kunkel/M. Schermaier, *Römische Rechtsgeschichte*, Cologne 2001, 181; A. Guarino, *Storia del diritto romano*, Naples 1996, 515-7, 525; M. Talamanca (ed.), *Lineamenti di storia del diritto romano*, Milan 1989, 561 ff; A. Burdese, *Manuale di diritto pubblico romano*, Turin 1987, repr. 1994, 219.

27 So called because its members had to stand (*consistere*) in the presence of the emperor.

28 Although not as a regular member.

members of the imperial council exercised a strong influence on imperial legislation, the chief source of law during the later imperial period. Besides its advisory functions, the *sacrum consistorium* sometimes operated as an imperial court of justice, usually dealing with appeals from decisions of lower courts.

The imperial court

With the concentration of all power in the hands of the emperor, the imperial court (*comitatus*) began to play a prominent role in the affairs of the state. It consisted of a large number of officials (*comites*) and was headed by the chamberlain of the imperial household (*praepositus sacri cubiculi*) who often participated in the deliberations of the imperial council (*sacrum consistorium*). As the *praepositus* and the *comites* who formed the imperial retinue were in daily contact with the emperor, they became the most influential persons during the later imperial period.

The *scrinia*

As under the Principate, various tasks of the imperial administration were carried out by offices or cabinets (*sacra scrinia*), each being headed by a *magister*. The *scrinium epistularum*, based on the earlier *scrinium ab epistulis*, responded to letters sent to the emperor by public officials and was headed by the *magister epistularum*. The *scrinium libellorum*, which was a continuation of the *scrinium a libellis* of the early imperial period, handled various petitions (*libelli*) addressed to the emperor by state officials and private citizens. The *scrinium dispositionum* dealt with private matters of the emperor, including the organisation of his personal correspondence. Finally, the *scrinium memoriae*, which was first introduced in the time of Hadrian, was responsible for the drafting of official documents, such as those containing appointments and orders issued by the emperor. All the above offices operated under the general superintendence of the head of the imperial offices (*magister officiorum*).

The imperial officials

The administrative reforms initiated by Diocletian and completed by Constantine were aimed at removing heavy concentrations of power from the hands of state officials and army commanders, thus minimising the risk of internal revolt. This was achieved, in part, through the strict separation of civil and military authority. Employment in the civil branch of the administration, now referred to as *militia*, was distinguished from service in the army, which was termed *militia armata*. The members of the civil service were drawn, to a large extent, from the ranks of former army officers. The internal organisation of the civil service was in many respects similar to that of the army and the privileges granted to soldiers upon retirement were gradually extended to civil servants. The career of public officials up to the position of *magister* was regulated by law while above that level officials were nominated by the emperor at his discretion. The members of the civil service received regular remuneration, often in kind (*annona*), as well as gifts (*sportulae*) from the citizens.

One of the most important civil functionaries of the later imperial period was the *quaestor sacri palatii*, the officer in charge of the administration of justice. The *quaestor*, usually a distinguished jurist, was the emperor's adviser on legal matters and played an important part in the preparation of imperial legislation. From the fourth century AD he presided over the imperial council (*sacrum consistorium*), when the latter met in the absence of the emperor. Among the highest offices of the state was also that of the master of the offices (*magister officiorum*), created in 320 AD. As was noted above, the *magister officiorum* exercised general superintendence over the secretarial bureaus of the palace (*scrinia*). He also supervised the imperial intelligence service (*agentes in rebus*, *curiosi*), the imperial bodyguard and the public post system. As master of the ceremonies, he exercised control over all personal attendants of the emperor and regulated imperial audiences. Moreover, he exercised considerable influence on matters of foreign policy. Another important office that should be mentioned here was that of the *comes sacrarum largitionum*, the officer in charge of the financial administration of the state. This officer managed the state treasury (*fiscus*), supervised the collection and disbursement of taxes paid in money and controlled the operation of mines, mints and state factories. Moreover, he had jurisdiction over matters relating to taxation, his decisions being final and not subject to appeal before the emperor. With financial matters was also concerned the *comes rerum privatarum* (or *comes rei privatae*). This official was entrusted with the administration of the private property of the emperor and the management of the imperial lands (*res privata principis*). The *res privata principis* was distinguished from the *patrimonium Caesaris*, the crown property, which already from the time of Septimius Severus (193-211 AD) had come to be regarded as the public property of the emperor. During the later Empire the *patrimonium Caesaris* was administered by a special official termed *comes sacri patrimonii*.[29]

---

[29] The distinction between *res privata principis* and *patrimonium Caesaris* was not always observed, however.

Besides the imperial officers mentioned above, the praetorian prefects (*praefecti praetorio*) continued to play a significant part in the administration of the empire. Under Diocletian their number was increased to four – with one prefect being assigned to each member of the tetrarchy. In the time of Constantine, however, the praetorian prefects were divested of their military authority (following the disbandment of the praetorian guard) and became purely civilian officials entrusted with the civil administration of each of the four prefectures into which the empire had been divided. Within the province of the *praefecti praetorio* fell, among other things, the collection and distribution of taxes in kind and matters relating to the administration of justice. The prefects acted as supreme judges in their territory and their decisions could not be appealed against before the emperor. Subordinate to the prefects were the heads of the dioceses (*vicarii*) and the provincial governors.

The cities of Rome and Constantinople were each administered by an urban prefect (*praefectus urbi*) who, being responsible for the maintenance of peace, was armed with broad powers for the suppression and punishment of offences against public order. Most of the powers which once appertained to the praetors and aediles were now concentrated in his hands and all police magistrates were acting under his commands. He had general jurisdiction in both criminal and civil cases and, with the assistance of a board of assessors, he decided on appeals sent up from lower courts. Within his jurisdiction fell, moreover, cases involving accusations against persons belonging to the senatorial class. Besides his judicial and police functions, the urban prefect convoked and presided over meetings of the senate and published the imperial laws in the city. He was also responsible for the regular supply of the city with provisions, having under his command the *praefectus annonae*. The *praefectus urbi* carried out his duties under the supervision of a *vicarius in urbe* who acted as a representative of the *praefectus praetorio*.[30]

---

[30] On the imperial civil service see W. Kunkel, *An Introduction to Roman Legal and Constitutional History*, 2nd edn, Oxford 1973, 141-2; H. F. Jolowicz and B. Nicholas, *Historical Introduction to the Study of Roman Law*, 3rd edn, Cambridge 1972, 423 ff; A. H. M. Jones, *The Later Roman Empire*, Oxford 1964, chapters 11, 12 and 16; A. Cameron, *The Later Roman Empire*, London 1993, 39-41; M. Kaser, *Römische Rechtsgeschichte*, Göttingen 1976, 208 ff; E. Stein, *Untersuchungen über das Officium der Prätorianerpräfektur seit Diokletian*, Amsterdam 1962; J. Harries, 'The Roman imperial quaestor from Constantine to Theodosius II', 78 *JRS* (1988), 148-72; A. Giardina, *Aspetti della burocrazia nel Basso Impero*, Rome 1977; J. Harries, *Law and Empire in Late Antiquity*, Cambridge 1999, 38 ff; R. Delmaire, *Les Institutions du Bas-Èmpire romain, de Constantin à Justinien*, I, *Les Institutions palatines*, 1995;

The old magistrature

Of the old republican magistrates the consuls, praetors and quaestors continued to exist, although very little remained of their former powers. The consulship was divested of all executive functions and came to be regarded as a purely honorary office. The main function of the consuls, who were now nominated by the emperor at his discretion, was to give their name to the current year. Two consuls were appointed annually, one in Rome and the other in Constantinople, until 541 AD, when the consulship was abolished by Emperor Justinian. The praetors and quaestors were chosen from the ranks of the senators on the recommendation of the urban prefect. Eligibility for these magistracies was determined by the *censuales*, officials responsible for calculating the taxes imposed on senators and the preparation of taxation lists. After the disappearance of the jury-courts in the time of Septimius Severus the praetors were divested of their judicial functions and their role was limited to organising public games and festivals.[31]

The senate

Although as a constitutional body the senate at Rome had lost all its authority since the beginning of the third century, it continued to exist during the Dominate and, after the founding of Constantinople, a similar senate was established there in the middle of the fourth century. The two senates functioned mainly as municipal councils, although the actual administration of Rome and Constantinople was in the hands of the urban prefects and their subordinates. Occasionally the senate was called upon to

---

F. De Martino, *Storia della costituzione romana* V, Naples 1975, 253 ff, 373 ff; A. Burdese, *Manuale di diritto pubblico romano*, Turin 1987, repr. 1994, 222 ff; A. Guarino, *Storia del diritto romano*, Naples 1996, 527 ff; M. Talamanca (ed.), *Lineamenti di storia del diritto romano*, Milan 1989, 564 ff. An important source of information about the organisation of the empire under the Dominate is the so-called *Notitia dignitatum* ('List of Offices'), dating from the early fifth century AD. It is a handbook of all the officials, both of high and of low status, in the imperial and provincial administration. O. Seeck (ed.), *Notitia Dignitatum*, Berlin 1876 (Eng. trans. W. Fairley, Philadelphia 1899); and see R. Goodburn and R. Bartholomew, (eds.), *Aspects of the Notitia Dignitatum*, Oxford 1976; J. H. Ward, 'The Notitia Dignitatum', 33 *Latomus* (1974), 397-434; G. Clemente, *La 'Notitia Dignitatum'*, Cagliari 1968.

31 The holding of the praetorship was now regarded as a burden (*munus*) as it involved an obligation on the part of the magistrate to cover the cost of these events.

give its advice to the emperor on current affairs or to carry out certain ceremonial tasks (such as the inauguration of a new emperor). Moreover, it made recommendations for the praetorship and the quaestorship, discussed with imperial officials matters of taxation concerning the senatorial class and sometimes participated in drafting imperial legislation. However, it no longer operated as a regular court of justice having jurisdiction over its own members; charges brought against senators were now tried before the urban prefect or a provincial governor.[32] The senate of Constantinople was dominated by the emperor's favourites, imperial officials and even representatives of the city trades, whilst in that of Rome it was the representatives of the old senatorial families and landed proprietors who set the tone. Although the senate no longer possessed political power, the position of senator entailed great prestige and its holders enjoyed many privileges, including exemption from certain taxes and financial obligations in the municipalities where their estates were situated. Moreover, senators enjoyed certain legal privileges and, as a rule, demeaning forms of punishment or torture were not employed against them. In return for these privileges they had to pay a landed property tax (*collatio glebalis*), to make special contributions to the state (*aurum oblaticium*) and to bear the costs of public games and festivals held in Rome and Constantinople.[33]

The Administration of the Provinces

In order to facilitate the administration of the empire and to minimise the risk of internal revolt Diocletian increased the number of the provinces to a hundred and twenty (including Italy). The governors of the various provinces were divided into three categories depending on their rank. The highest among them were the *proconsules* who ruled the provinces of Africa, Asia and Achaia. Below them in terms of authority were the *correctores* and the *praesides*. The provinces were grouped into fourteen

---

[32] However senators were often appointed as judges and it appears that the senate of Constantinople did function as a special court of justice from time to time.

[33] On the role of the senate during the late imperial era see H. F. Jolowicz and B. Nicholas, *Historical Introduction to the Study of Roman Law*, 3rd edn, Cambridge 1972, 431-2; W. Kunkel, *An Introduction to Roman Legal and Constitutional History*, 2nd edn, Oxford 1973, 138; A. H. M. Jones, *The Later Roman Empire*, Oxford 1964, 331-3; M. Kaser, *Römische Rechtsgeschichte*, Göttingen 1976, 212; A. Burdese, *Manuale di diritto pubblico romano*, Turin 1987, repr. 1994, 221. And see A. Chastagnol, *Le Sénat romain à l'époque impériale*, Paris 1994, chapters 14-18.

greater administrative units, called dioceses,[34] with each diocese (*dioecesis*) being headed by a vicar (*vicarius*).[35] Neighbouring dioceses were joined into a larger unit called prefecture (*praefectura*), of which there were four: Gaul, Italy, Illyricum and the Orient. From the time of Constantine the Illyrian prefecture was at times merged with the prefecture of Italy, but from the end of the fourth century AD it acquired a separate status and, together with the prefecture of the Orient, made up the Roman Empire of the East; Italy and Gaul constituted the Empire of the West. Each prefecture was headed by a *praefectus praetorio*. Of these the most important was the prefect of the Orient who, from 334 AD, bore the title of *comes orientis*. The provincial governors, vicars and praetorian prefects were purely civilian officials;[36] military command was entrusted to officers called *duces* whose authority extended over more than one province.[37]

The provincial governors exercised administrative as well as judicial functions (hence they were sometimes referred to as *iudices*). In carrying out their administrative duties the governors were aided by bureaus whose members, called *cohortales*, were usually appointed by the emperor. In some provinces there were also provincial councils made up of great land-owners (*possessores*) and former members of the provincial city councils (*honorati*). Among the main functions of these bodies were the publication of imperial laws and the issuing of decrees (*decreta*) which, after their approval by the emperor, were binding within the province. In 368 AD Emperors Valentinian I and Valens introduced the office of the *defensor civitatis* or *defensor plebis*. This officer was entrusted with the protection of the lower classes of the population against abuses committed by great land-owners and state officials. The *defensor* supervised all provincial magistrates, advised the governors on administrative matters and exercised jurisdiction over minor disputes between citizens. He had the right to report directly to the emperor, bypassing the provincial governor. The *defensores* were chosen from among former magistrates and other persons of influence, initially by the *praefectus praetorio* and later by local councils with the participation of bishops and local clerics.[38] The institution of the *defensor civitatis* proved largely unsuccessful, however, as many of those who held the office often committed abuses themselves or were

---

34 The three provinces governed by proconsuls were excluded.

35 The office of *vicarius* was abolished during the reign of Justinian.

36 With the exception of the prefect of the Orient.

37 However, from the time of Justinian both civil authority and military command were again entrusted to the same person, especially in the frontier provinces.

38 See C. 1. 55. 8. (Honorius and Theodosius II). The *defensores* were initially appointed for a indefinite period but in later yeas their term in office was limited to five years and, from the time of Justinian, to two years.

manipulated through bribery or intimidation. In the fifth century AD the office lost its initial prestige and became an additional burden imposed upon members of the municipal councils.

Social and Economic Conditions

Social structure

The development of the imperial society during the Dominate period was a direct continuation of the process of change that had began as early as the second century AD.[39] Although after the extension of the Roman citizenship to all the free inhabitants of the empire in the early third century the distinction between Roman citizens and foreigners lost its earlier social significance, divisions in society grew even deeper and the gap between the *honestiores* (honourable) and the *humiliores* (humble) continued to widen. To the class of the *honestiores* belonged imperial and municipal senators, state functionaries and administrative personnel, soldiers and, from the early fourth century AD, the higher members of the Church hierarchy. The class of the *humiliores* comprised free craft workers, small farmers with some land of their own, free land workers, a relatively small proportion of freedmen and some slaves in numbers varying greatly from region to region. To these were now added new groups, such as displaced persons and fugitives who had lost their means of subsistence as a result of foreign invasions or state persecution, war prisoners who had been assigned to the great landlords as labourers, and monks and hermits whose numbers had considerably increased, especially in the eastern provinces of the empire. As has already been noted, a person's legal status as well as his treatment by those responsible for enforcing the law were largely determined by reference to the class to which he belonged. Thus the *honestiores* were not subject to grave or degrading forms of punishment, were exempt from torture in judicial investigations and had the right of appealing to the emperor against sentences imposed upon them by judicial magistrates.

Authors of the fourth century speak of a distinction between the *potentiores* or *potentes* (the 'more powerful') and the *humiliores* or

[39] On the later Roman society see in general J. Cagé, *Les classes sociales dans l'Empire Romain*, Paris 1964; G. Alföldy, *The Social History of Rome*, London 1984, 186 ff; A. H. M. Jones, *The Later Roman Empire*, Oxford 1964; A. Chastagnol, *L'evolution politique, sociale et économique du monde romain de Dioclétien à Julien. La mise en place du régime du Bas-Empire (284-363)*, Paris 1982, 265 ff.

tenuiores or *plebs*.[40] For the most part the *potentiores* belonged to the senatorial aristocracy – the wealthiest class in society – out of whose ranks the senior officials of the imperial administration were chosen.[41] Members of the senatorial class bore the title of *clarissimus*, acquired by inheritance, by imperial grant or by the attainment of certain important offices. The great increase in the number of the imperial officials was accompanied by the creation of different status groupings within the *clarissimi*, such as the *spectabiles* ('respectable') and the *illustres* ('illustrious'). The title of *illustris* was given to some of the highest officers of the state, such as the *praefecti praetorio*, the *praefecti urbi*, the *comes sacrarum largitionum* and the *quaestor sacri palatii*. In the sixth century AD these state functionaries were referred to as *gloriosi* ('glorious'). The titles Caesar and *nobilissimus* ('most noble') were reserved for members of the imperial household. To the *potentiores* belonged also many leading *equites*, a great part of the officer corps and a large number of senior imperial officials (*officiales*).[42] During the early years of the Dominate period the position of the *equites* was temporarily strengthened as a result of the administrative reforms of Diocletian, who used *equites* in many posts of the imperial administration. However, from the time of Constantine, as the number of senatorial positions in the government continued to increase, the leading groups of the equestrian class were gradually incorporated into the senatorial order and, in the fifth century, the *ordo equester* ceased to exist as a distinct social order.[43]

In the provinces of the East, where urban life continued, the great land-owners, referred to as *possessores*, lived in the cities, while in the West they resided in their country estates. For the cultivation of their lands they used tenants (*coloni*) and slaves over whom they exercised powers of jurisdiction similar to those exercised by the procurators on the imperial estates. The immunities which the great land-owners enjoyed, such as exemption from municipal taxes and other burdens, tended to give an almost manorial character to their position. They frequently defied the organs of the imperial government, formed private armies, refused to pay taxes and, sometimes, even imposed taxes and other exactions themselves

40 Anon., *De reb. bell.* 2. 3.

41 As in earlier periods, senators invested their money in great estates widely scattered over the provinces and in palatial townhouses in the cities.

42 Like the senators, these were divided into different status groupings under the titles of *perfectissimi* and *egregii*.

43 On the character of the senatorial class during the later imperial period see M. Arnheim, *The Senatorial Aristocracy in the Late Roman Empire*, Oxford 1972; J. Matthews, *Western Aristocracies and Imperial Court, AD 364-425*, Oxford 1975.

within the districts under their control. Such was their power that whole village communities, anxious to avoid the burdens imposed upon them by the local authorities, often placed themselves under their patronage (*patrocinium vicorum*) becoming their tenants. A number of imperial enactments of this period were concerned with abuses of power on the part of *possessores*. Complaints by local authorities to imperial officials often fell on deaf ears, however, as these officials were themselves *possessores* and usually sided with their own class.[44] The power of the state was thus nullified by its chief servants and, in time, the land-owning aristocracy became the real inheritors of the empire.

As was noted in chapter 7, during the crisis of the third century the situation of the urban middle class worsened and city life declined. Nevertheless, many cities and several smaller towns continued to exist, especially in the Greek-speaking eastern provinces where cities such as Alexandria, Antioch and Ephesus remained important commercial and cultural centres. In the cities there were still magistrates and the municipal councils (*curiae*) continued to operate. But during the later Empire the burdens imposed upon the members of the municipal councils (*curiales*, *decuriones*) by the imperial government made their position untenable. Besides being responsible for the keeping of public order and the defence and provisioning of the city, the *curiales* were expected to finance public games and festivals, to contribute to the construction and maintenance of public buildings and to collect all the taxes in their community, being personally liable for the total amount owed to the state and with their own property standing surety. As eligible citizens sought by every means to escape responsibility, service on the municipal councils was made compulsory and hereditary.[45] Moreover, the *curiales* were obliged to reside in their own town and could not leave their community or sell their estates without the permission of the provincial governor.[46] In essence, the *curiales* became unpaid civil servants and their freedom was greatly restricted. Looked upon with hostility by their fellow citizens and faced with financial ruin many *curiales* sought to escape their responsibilities by fleeing their towns. Others joined the army or, with the connivance of corrupt officials, sought to acquire privileged status that would enable them to avoid the demands placed upon them by the state. A number of measures

---

44 As was mentioned before, the institution of the *defensor civitatis,* which was aimed at putting a check on the abuses of the *possessores*, proved largely unsuccessful.

45 Thus the son of a *decurio* became a member of the *ordo decurionum* when he reached the age of eighteen. See C.Th. 12. 1. 7. (Constantine).

46 If they were absent from their town for more than five years their property was subject to confiscation.

were introduced by the imperial government aimed at stemming such practices and at putting an end to the depopulation of the local *curiae*, but these were met with little success.[47] By the end of the fourth century the urban middle class which supplied the members of the town councils was bankrupt and the class as a whole was facing extinction, especially in the more backward western provinces.

Under government control were also various groups of persons engaged in occupations which were regarded as being of vital importance to the state, such as mariners (*navicularii*), bakers (*pistores*) and butchers (*suarii*). These were required to join together in associations (*corpora*) which operated under the supervision of state organs (the urban prefects in Rome and Constantinople and the provincial governors and local magistrates in the municipalities). The members of the *corpora* (*corporati*) were required to provide products or services to the state or their municipalities and the government made their corporations responsible for carrying out the relevant orders. To ensure that the needs of the state were met membership in the *corpora* was made compulsory and hereditary and measures were introduced aimed at preventing *corporati* from evading their obligations by changing their occupation, enrolling in the army or becoming tenants of senatorial landholders.[48] As the needs of the state continued to grow the obligations imposed upon the members of the *corpora* (*corporati*) became heavier.

During the later Empire the general situation of the peasantry continued to worsen. Driven to desperation by the growing demands of the state and the great land-owners many farmers abandoned their lands and lived as brigands. As the abandonment of the land by farmers naturally threatened state revenues in kind, the government stepped in and institutionalised the system of *colonatus*. Like the *curiales* and the *corporati*, the *coloni* were now prohibited from entering public service or another occupation and their status became permanent and hereditary.[49]

---

47 See, e.g., C.Th. 12. 1. 6; 12. 1. 22; 12. 1. 27; 12. 1. 186; C. 5. 5. 3.

48 See, e.g., C. Th. 14. 7. 1. (Arcadius and Honorius). Similar restrictions were imposed upon members of the army and their families. For example, the sons of soldiers or army veterans (*veterani*) were required to choose between joining the army or serving as members of the municipal councils. See A. H. M. Jones, 'The Caste System in the Later Roman Empire', in P. Brunt (ed.), *The Roman Economy. Studies in Ancient Economic and Administrative History*, Oxford 1974, 396.

49 For more on the institution of the colonate see A. H. M. Jones, *The Later Roman Empire*, Oxford 1964, 795 ff; 'The Roman colonate', in P. Brunt (ed.), *The Roman Economy. Studies in Ancient Economic and Administrative History*, Oxford 1974, 293.

Although in the eyes of the law the *coloni* were free citizens, they were not allowed to leave the estates where they had been working and, when an estate was sold, they passed from one land-owner to another.[50] According to a law of Constantine a fugitive *colonus* was to be returned by force to the estate which he had left and the person who had offered him shelter had to pay compensation to the state for any loss of tax incurred.[51] Although a number of imperial edicts were issued during this period defining the rights and duties of the *coloni*, as time went on the condition of the *coloni* became closer to servitude – a halfway between free men and slaves.[52] But not all farmers were reduced to the status of *coloni*. In some parts of the empire, especially in the more prosperous eastern provinces, small land-holders continued to exist.[53] In an effort to deal with the problems of desertion and depopulation of the land the government began to impose on free farmers the obligation to cultivate, besides their own land, neighbouring lands abandoned by their owners (*agri deserti*) and to pay the relevant taxes to the state (*adiectio sterilium*).[54]

Economic conditions

The administrative and military reforms of the late third and early fourth centuries greatly increased state expenditure, and the immediate problem that confronted the government was how to raise the revenues needed to finance the ever growing bureaucracy and military establishment. The devaluation of the currency in the third century and the high inflation by which it was accompanied had caused havoc with government salaries (which were largely fixed) and prices. In order to stabilise the currency and combat inflation, Diocletian attempted to institute coinage reform by issuing improved gold and silver coins. Because of the shortage of gold and

---

50 C.Th. 13. 10. 3. Although the *coloni* had the right to contract a legal marriage, under a law of 380 AD they were prohibited from marrying outside their class. See C.Th. 10. 20. 10.

51 C.Th. 5. 17. 1. But a fugitive *colonus* who managed to avoid capture for thirty years (or twenty in the case of women) did not have to return to the estate where he was born. See C.Th. 5. 18. 1.

52 Much closer to slavery was the situation of a special class of *coloni* called *coloni adscripticii*.

53 Many of these, faced with increasing oppression by government agents, placed themselves under the protection of senatorial landowners (*potentiores*, *possessores*) who acted as their patrons (*patroni*).

54 A number of imperial enactments issued under Constantine and subsequent emperors were concerned with the regulation of the system of *adiectio sterilium*. See, e.g., C.Th. 11. 1. 4; C. 11. 59. 2; 1. 34. 2.

silver needed to issue sufficient amounts of coins, however, extensive use was made of billon coins of small denominations. As the value of these small coins kept falling, prices continued to rise at an appalling rate. In an attempt to deal with this problem Diocletian issued in 301 AD his famous edict of prices (*edictum de pretiis rerum venalium*) which set maximum prices over a wide range of goods and services and prescribed the penalties to be imposed on profiteers.[55] However, this law proved largely ineffective due to the absence both of an adequate mechanism for enforcement and of parallel regulation of supply. Diocletian's currency reform was carried further by Constantine who issued a new gold coin of a fixed weight, the *solidus*, which was to become the money of international exchange until the eighth century. But government officials, whose job was to determine the relation between the *solidus* and the inflated billon coinage did so at rates advantageous to themselves and the state, and the population at large, which very rarely used the gold coins, benefited little from the currency reform. Diocletian's and Constantine's attempts at fixing the cost of living show the government's concern and also its failure to bring economic life into harmony with harsh reality. This failure was largely due to the fact that the relevant measures were imposed from above without sufficient understanding of or control over the general conditions which were in fact causing the problems.

Faced with the complete disorganisation of public finances caused by inflation and economic decline, Diocletian revised drastically the system of taxation. Realising the inadequacy of the taxes which the government collected in cash, he resorted to the regularisation and expansion of the taxes in kind (*annona*) which had been introduced, as extraordinary taxes, during the late Principate period. The new system of taxation avoided the vicissitudes of monetary debasement and price fluctuations, as now government officials and the troops were paid largely in agrarian products and other commodities. At the same time it enabled the government to formulate a regular budget based on the agricultural produce of the empire, and some check was placed on the extraordinary requisitions which had become such a burden during the third century. The assessment of the land tax (*indictio*) was carried out at first every five years and, after 312 AD, every fifteen years, and was based on a division of productive land into units called *iugera* (hence the tax paid on landed property was referred to

[55] For a complete edition of the text of this law see M. Giacchero, *Edictum Diocletiani et Collegarum de pretiis rerum venalium*, 2 vols, Genoa 1974. See also J. Reynold in C. M. Roueche, *Aphrodisias in Late Antiquity*, London 1989, no. 231; H. Blümner, *Der Maximaltarif des Diokletian*, Berlin 1958; S. Lauffer, *Diokletians Preisedikt*, Berlin 1971.

as *iugatio terrena*). The *iugatio terrena* was distinguished from the *capitatio humana*, a sort of poll-tax paid by agricultural workers,[56] and the *capitatio animalium*, a tax paid per head of cattle. The *capitatio* was assessed on the basis of the *caput*, a unit of human labour equivalent to the *iugum*. The total tax was based on both the *iugatio* and the *capitatio* and, as was said before, was paid in kind (*in natura*). Besides the levies in kind there were other taxes which were collected in cash. Thus traders and craftsmen who were exempted from the *annona* paid a tax called *chrysargyrum.* A tax known as *aurum oblaticium* was paid by members of the senatorial order. The *aurum coronarium*, a nominally voluntary but really compulsory contribution, was paid by municipal councillors every five years to enable the government to distribute largesse to officials and troops. From the time of Constantine a special levy, the *collatio glebalis* or *follis senatoria*, was imposed on senatorial lands and a tax termed *aurum lustralis collatio* was paid every five years by urban merchants and corporations.[57] Besides the regular taxes the government made its subjects perform various public services (*munera*), such as running the public post system and furnishing shelter and supplies to troops and state officials. In exacting these charges and collecting taxes and revenues in kind government officials practised extortions which often were more onerous to citizens than the taxes themselves.[58]

The economic policies of Diocletian and Constantine ultimately failed to restore balance in the economy: price regulation and currency reform were ineffective in stimulating production and in curbing inflation; tax collection remained unsatisfactory owing to continuing corruption; trade and industry declined, as the state, once the biggest customer, now

---

56 As these belonged to the landless peasantry, this tax was also called *capitatio plebeia*. From the *capitatio humana* was exempted the urban population (*plebs urbana*). See C.Th. 13. 10. 2.

57 On the system of taxation that applied during the later empire see T. D. Barnes, *The New Empire of Diocletian and Constantine*, Cambridge, Mass. and London 1982, 226 ff; S. Williams, *Diocletian and the Roman Recovery*, London 1985, 115 ff; A. H. M. Jones, *The Later Roman Empire*, Oxford 1964, 462 ff; 'Over-Taxation and the Decline of the Roman Empire', in P. Brunt (ed.), *The Roman Economy. Studies in Ancient Economic and Administrative History*, Oxford 1974, 82; W. Goffart, *Caput and Colonate: Towards a History of Late Roman Taxation*, Toronto 1974.

58 On the Roman economy during the late Empire see in general C. E. King (ed.), *Imperial Revenue, Expenditure and Monetary Policy in the Fourth Century* AD, Oxford 1980; M. Hendy, *Studies in the Byzantine Monetary Economy c.* 300-1450, Cambridge 1985; A. H. M. Jones, *The Later Roman Empire*, Oxford 1964, 411 ff and 712 ff.

became a large producer itself. The heavy burden of taxation imposed upon the peasantry, the backbone of the empire's economic system, forced farmers to abandon their lands or to become tenants of senatorial landlords. The urban middle class, weighed down by the financial demands imposed on it, was in distress and, as towns declined, the country villas became centres of economic life, especially in the western provinces. Generally speaking, economic conditions throughout the empire grew steadily worse, especially from the latter part of the fourth century. But it would be a mistake to regard the Dominate as a period of uninterrupted and universal economic decline, as there were important differences in the levels of prosperity maintained in various provinces. Thus, while the West was sinking into primitive conditions, in the Greek-speaking eastern provinces the system of state-controlled economy achieved a measure of success and private enterprise continued to flourish in spheres in which the state was uninterested. In many eastern cities, such as Constantinople, Alexandria and Antioch, manufactured goods were produced on a large scale, and Egyptian agriculture showed signs of recovery. At the same time trade within or between provinces was resumed or became more active and commerce with Persia, India and the Far East continued. The political division of the empire into a western and an eastern part at the end of the fourth century reflected the new economic reality which determined the destinies of the two halves of the empire during the closing years of this period and in the centuries that followed.

The Demise of the Western Empire

After Constantine's death in 337 AD imperial unity was for some time maintained under his son, Constantius II, and his successor, Julian. But in 364 AD Valentinian I again divided the administration of the empire, giving the rule of the eastern half to his brother Valens. In 378 AD Valens was killed in battle trying to repel an invasion by the Visigoths and was succeeded by Theodosius who, after defeating several rebellious officers in the West, became sole ruler of the empire in 394 AD. Theodosius succeeded in keeping the Visigoths in check and was able to maintain the unity of the empire, but the difficulties besetting the government (economic decay, depopulation, corruption, decline of the urban centres, growth of the power of the great landlords) increased rather than diminished during his reign. A staunch supporter of Christianity, he took drastic measures to eliminate both paganism and Christian heresies and asserted the right of the emperor to exercise authority in Church matters. Theodosius died in 395 AD having divided the empire between his two sons Arcadius, who was given the rule of the East, and Honorius, who was made Augustus of the West. Although during their reign imperial unity was in theory preserved, in reality the empire had been split into two independent states and this division now became permanent. But by the end of the fourth century the Western empire could no longer be defended as successive invasions by the Goths, Vandals, Franks and other Germanic tribes had reduced the imperial authority to a shadow of its former self. By the beginning of the fifth century Spain, Gaul and Britain had been lost, and in 410 AD Rome herself was sacked by the Goths, although the invaders finally withdrew from Italy. In the years that followed true power in the West was in the hands of the German generals who now commanded the barbarised Roman armies. One puppet emperor succeeded another until 476 AD when the last of them, Romulus Augustulus, was overthrown by the German troops which had placed him on the throne. This date is traditionally regarded as marking the end of the Roman empire in the West.

The Survival of the Empire in the East

While the Western Roman empire was being replaced by Germanic kingdoms, the empire in the East was able to survive the crisis with its institutions and frontiers intact. The emperors at Constantinople succeeded in maintaining their territory in Asia Minor against the restored power of Persia and were able to resist the infiltration of the Germans and the decentralising influence of the great landlords. The survival of the empire in the East was largely due to its greater material resources, the strength of its more developed urban society, and the greater homogeneity and loyalty of its population. Nevertheless, the empire was clearly on the defensive, being constantly threatened by barbarian incursions and internal conflicts.

In 527 AD a talented new ruler, Justinian, came to power over the eastern part of the Roman world. From the time he ascended the throne at Constantinople Justinian directed all his energies to fulfilling his ultimate ambition: the restoration of the Roman empire to its ancient grandeur. To this end he inaugurated a programme centred upon three goals: the western provinces were to be reconquered and imperial rule re-established throughout the Mediterranean basin; religious orthodoxy was to be enforced; and Roman law was to be codified and used as a consolidating force. Following the conclusion of a peace treaty with the Persian empire in the East, Justinian turned his attention to the Vandals who were established in northern Africa. In 533 AD a landing in Africa was effected, the Vandals were defeated and Africa was restored to its former position as a province of the Roman empire. The invasion of Sicily in 535 AD marked the beginning of the reconquest of Italy. After a bitter struggle which lasted more than two decades the Ostrogothic kingdom was overthrown and Rome, the old capital of the empire, was recaptured. In 554 AD Justinian's ambitions took him to the far western Mediterranean where the southern portion of Spain was wrested from the Visigoths and added to the empire. Within the empire, Justinian sought to protect his subjects against oppression by initiating a series of administrative reforms, and measures were introduced aimed at stimulating commerce and industry. But in his effort to restore religious orthodoxy within the Christian Church, the unity of which was being threatened by various schisms, he ran into insurmountable difficulties.[59]

Justinian accomplished his reconquest of the West at a very high price: the exhaustion of the empire's resources in money and manpower. Moreover, the centralising forces so manifest in Justinian's programme failed to overcome the centrifugal tendencies in the West. A few years after his death in 568 AD, most of the West was again lost and imperial authority was reduced to a few strongholds in Italy and Spain. The loss of the western provinces transferred the empire's centre of gravity from the Latin to the Greek element and precipitated the transformation of the Eastern empire into an essentially Greek state – the Byzantine empire.

---

[59] Justinian demanded religious conformity of his subjects and steadily persecuted the followers of any other creed than the orthodox Catholic. Although he succeeded in stamping out what was left of paganism, his attempt to put an end to the strongly-rooted Monophysite heresy was met with failure (this failure is not unrelated to the fact that his wife, Theodora, was a member and ardent supporter of the Monophysite sect). Moreover, the religious differences between the Eastern and the Western Churches persisted throughout his reign and in the years that followed. On Justinian's reign see A. H. M. Jones, *The Later Roman Empire*, Oxford 1964, ch. 9; T. Honoré, *Tribonian*, London 1978, ch. 1; J. Moorhead, *Justinian*, London and New York 1994; R. Browning, *Justinian and Theodora*, London 1987.

10 The Post-Classical Period of Roman Law

Introductory

In the later imperial era the old divisions of the law into carefully defined categories faded away along with many of the ancient traditions of Rome. As has already been noted, the distinction between *ius civile* and *ius honorarium* disappeared partly as a result of the abandonment of popular legislation and the making of law administratively by the praetors, and partly as a result of the jurists' attitude of treating both bodies of law as belonging to a single category. The body of law that emerged from the combination of these two sources came to be regarded as a single source of law, termed *ius* or 'jurists law'. This was distinguished from the body of rules emanating from imperial legislation, referred to as *lex*. But as the making of law in the authoritarian and bureaucratic state of this period became more and more strongly centralised, jurisprudence ceased to be the driving force it had been in the past, having been annihilated at its source by the absolutism of the imperial system, and earlier juristic works came to be regarded as a body of finally settled doctrine. At the same time great efforts were made by the emperors to bring some order into the vast and chaotic mass of laws claiming validity in the empire, and these eventually led to the introduction of legal codes in which the various imperial enactments were arranged in an orderly fashion. Moreover, with the obliteration of the distinction between *civis* and *peregrinus* following the enactment of the *constitutio Antoniniana* in the early third century the old distinction between *ius civile* and *ius gentium* disappeared: in theory every free man in the empire was now a citizen governed by the same 'Roman law'. In actual fact, however, local systems of law remained in force in the form of custom. Roman law began to infiltrate these systems and, at the same time, to be infiltrated by them and, in the course of time, a system of law emerged which had undergone a process of vulgarisation. Yet the fundamental standards of Roman law continued to determine law making and the administration of justice throughout the later imperial era. The end of this period is marked by the enactment of what was to be the final statement of Roman law, the *Corpus Iuris Civilis* of Emperor Justinian.

Imperial Legislation

With the transformation of the Roman government into an absolute monarchy, all positive legislation, in the sense of formal law making, emanated directly from the emperor. Depending on their scope and reach, imperial enactments fell into two broad categories: the edicts or *leges generales*, and the *rescripta*. The term *leges generales* (or *edicta imperatorum*) was used to denote enactments of the emperor containing legal norms of general application. Imperial edicts were regarded as being based on the right of the emperor to issue generally binding orders (*ius edicendi*) – a right which, in theory, he had inherited from the higher magistrates of the republican period. But unlike the edicts of the magistrates, whose application was limited in time, those of the emperor remained in force for an indefinite period unless they were rescinded by subsequent imperial legislation. Imperial edicts were usually drafted by the minister of justice, often with the help of legal experts, and prior to their publication were discussed in the imperial council (*sacrum consistorium*). An edict was expressed in the form of a letter addressed either to an imperial official, by whom it was then published, or directly to the people, or the group of people concerned. After the division of the empire, imperial edicts were regarded as binding in both parts of the empire, even if they had been promulgated by one of the emperors only, although an emperor could ordain that a law issued by him was to apply only within the part of the empire over which he ruled.[1] An example of an imperial enactment of this type was the famous Edict of Prices (*edictum de pretiis*) of Diocletian, issued in 301 AD.[2] Similar to the *leges generales* were the *pragmaticae sanctiones*, edicts issued by the emperor in response to petitions. These were usually concerned with matters of public administration, such as the granting of special privileges to certain groups of persons or the operation of administrative organs.[3] The term *pragmaticae sanctiones* referred also to the pronouncements by which the emperors of the eastern and western parts of the empire confirmed the validity of each other's edicts in their domain.

---

1 From 439 AD the provisions contained in the Theodosian Code, the first official compilation of imperial laws, applied in both the western and the eastern parts of the empire.

2 See chapter 9.

3 An example of such an enactment is the *sanctio pragmatica pro petitione Vigilii* by which Emperor Justinian, in response to a request by Vigilius, bishop of Rome, addressed a number of problems relating to the application of the law in Italy after its liberation from the Goths. By the same enactment Justinian introduced his legislation into Italy. And see C. 1. 23. 7. 2. (Zeno).

The *rescripta*, also referred to as *leges speciales*, were answers of the emperor to questions of law which had arisen in actual cases and which were submitted to him by private citizens or state officials.[4] In contrast with the *leges generales*, and unlike the position usually adopted during the Principate, they were not regarded as being generally binding. Thus, in 315 AD Emperor Constantine ordained that a *rescriptum* that deviated from an established *lex generalis* was invalid.[5] And according to a decree issued by Arcadius in 398 AD, a *rescriptum* was to be considered binding only in the individual case for which it had been issued.[6] However, in 426 AD, Emperors Theodosius II and Valentinian III returned to the earlier position and decreed that, as it constituted a declaration of a general principle in an individual case, a *rescriptum* could, under certain conditions, be regarded as generally binding.[7] This view seems to have prevailed during the fifth and sixth centuries. Another type of imperial constitution, similar to the *rescriptum*, was the *adnotatio*, a decision of the emperor in response to a petition addressed to him written in the margin of the petition.[8] As both the *rescriptum* and the *adnotatio* served similar purposes, the distinction between the two gradually disappeared. As to the *mandata*[9] and the *decreta*,[10] these continued to be issued during this period, although not as often as during the Principate (the *mandata* were to a large extent superseded by the *leges generales*, while the *decreta* were replaced by the *rescripta*). The language of the majority of the imperial enactments of this period was Latin, but from the fifth century the number of those issued in Greek gradually increased.[11]

---

4 The importance of the *rescripta* increased in this period as a result of the development of the procedure *per rescriptum*. In the context of this procedure the emperor, or an official acting in his name, decided on a case on the basis of a written report submitted to him by the parties concerned, on the understanding that the facts stated in the report were accurate. Legal disputes in the provinces were transmitted in this way to the emperor who gave his decision in a rescript addressed to the judge who then notified the decision to the litigants.

5 C.Th. 1. 2. 2. & 3.

6 C.Th. 1. 2. 11.

7 C. 1. 14. 3.

8 Originally the *adnotatio* seems to have been a written instruction by the emperor for the drafting of a rescript by the imperial chancery *a libellis*.

9 As was noted in chapter 8, these were instructions on judicial or administrative matters issued by the emperor and addressed to provincial governors and other state officials. See, e.g., C. 1. 50. 2. (Theodosius II and Valentinian III).

10 Decisions of the emperor in civil or criminal cases.

11 Moreover, from the end of the fourth century, judges were allowed to issue their decisions in Greek. See C. 7. 45. 12. (Arcadius & Honorius). On forms of imperial law-making see in general H. F. Jolowicz and B. Nicholas, *Historical*

Early compilations of imperial legislation

Collections of imperial constitutions began to be produced as early as the second century AD. These included various *libri mandatorum*[12] and compilations of *rescripta* and *decreta*. We know, for example, of a collection of thirteen rescripts of Septimius Severus published in 200 AD and a collection of *decreta* produced by the jurist Paul in the closing years of the Principate.[13] By the end of the third century the confusion in the practice of law caused by the ever-growing and chaotic mass of imperial constitutions gave rise to an urgent need for them to be collected together in an orderly fashion. This led to the publication, probably in 291 AD, of the *Codex Gregorianus*, a compilation of imperial enactments, mostly rescripts, from the time of Hadrian up to that of Diocletian.[14] This collection was followed in c. 295 AD by the *Codex Hermogenianus*, a compilation of constitutions issued during the reign of Diocletian.[15] A second edition of this work, containing constitutions of both Diocletian and Constantine, appears to have been published around 314 AD. The Gregorian and Hermogenian Codes were private collections and, as such, had no legislative force. The fact that their authors had access to the imperial archives, from which they reproduced a large number of constitutions in their original form, suggests that they held important state positions and that they must have carried out their work under official supervision. As neither of the above-mentioned collections has survived, modern reconstructions are based on extracts included in the Code of

---

Introduction to the Study of Roman Law, 3rd edn, Cambridge 1972, 460 ff; W. Kunkel, *An Introduction to Roman Legal and Constitutional History*, 2nd edn, Oxford 1973, 154-6; M. Kaser, *Römische Rechtsgeschichte*, Göttingen 1976, 223 ff; W. Kunkel/M. Schermaier, *Römische Rechtsgeschichte*, Cologne 2001, 198 ff; A. Guarino, *Storia del diritto romano*, Naples 1996, 538 ff; M. Talamanca (ed.), *Lineamenti di storia del diritto romano*, Milan 1989, 593 ff. See also T. Honoré, *Emperors and Lawyers*, Oxford 1994, ch. 2; J. Harries, *Law and Empire in Late Antiquity*, Cambridge 1999, 19 ff.

12 See chapter 8.

13 We also know, through Justinian's Digest, of an early collection of rescripts, mainly of Marcus Aurelius and Lucius Verus, that was part of Papirius Justus's *libri XX constitutionum*, a work that appeared in the late second century AD.

14 The Gregorian Code was arranged into books and titles probably along the lines of the praetorian edict.

15 The author of this work, Hermogenianus, appears to have been one of the later jurists mentioned in the Digest of Justinian.

Justinian, the *Fragmenta Vaticana*, the *Collatio* and other post-classical compilations of law.[16]

The Theodosian Code

In 429 AD Emperors Theodosius II (Eastern emperor, 408-450 AD) and Valentinian III (Western emperor, 423-455 AD) entrusted a specially appointed committee with the task of updating and systematising the whole body of law (including the 'jurists law') and of producing a code that would meet the need for legal certainty in all areas of legal practice. But this task proved too difficult to accomplish and in 435 AD another committee was set up for the purpose of collecting together, in a systematic way, all the imperial laws in force, starting with those issued in the time of Constantine. The work of codification was completed in 438 AD and the collection was published under the name *Codex Theodosianus*. Unlike the Gregorian and Hermogenian Codes, the Theodosian Code was an official compilation of the law which applied equally in both parts of the empire. The Code came into force on 15 February 438 AD in the East, and on 1 January 439 AD in the West. From then on, only constitutions contained in it were to be relied upon in the courts. The Theodosian Code, in the form in which it was published, was little more than an extension and continuation of the Gregorian and Hermogenian Codes upon which it was modelled and which continued to be used in the practice of law. Moreover, the Code did not affect the application of the Law of Citations of 426 AD which laid down the rules prescribing the weight of authority that was to be accorded to the works of the classical jurists.

The Theodosian Code includes over 3000 constitutions from the time of Constantine (c. 312 AD) to 438 AD. The material is arranged in sixteen books thematically, according to subject, and subdivided into titles with the constitutions in chronological order. The majority of the constitutions included in the Code are concerned with public rather than with private law. Private law is the subject of the first five books; books 6-8 are concerned with matters of constitutional and administrative law; criminal law is the focus of book 9; books 10-11 contain the law relating to public revenue; books 12-14 lay down the rules governing municipalities and

---

[16] For a reconstruction of the Gregorian and Hermogenian Codes see P. Krüger, *Collectio librorum iuris anteiustiniani* III, Berlin 1878-1927; FIRA II, pp. 653-665. And see M. Kaser, *Römische Rechtsgeschichte*, Göttingen 1976, 228; M. Talamanca (ed.), *Lineamenti di storia del diritto romano*, Milan 1989, 611-3; A. Cenderelli, *Ricerche sul 'Codex Hermogenianus'*, Milan 1965; D. Liebs, *Hermogenians Epitomae*, Göttingen 1964, 23 ff.

corporations; book 15 includes provisions pertaining to public works and games; and book 16 contains provisions on ecclesiastical matters. The Theodosian Code effected a measure of uniformity in the administration of the law throughout the empire and served as an important vehicle for the propagation of Roman law by furnishing a model for later codifications. Most of its contents, as well as a number of imperial constitutions issued after its enactment (*novellae*), have been preserved through later collections, especially the Code of Justinian and the *Lex Romana Visigothorum*. Moreover, extensive fragments of its original text have come down to us through two manuscripts, one dating from the fifth and the other from the sixth century.[17]

The influence of Christianity on post-classical law

In the years following the recognition of Christianity in the early fourth century Christian doctrine began to exercise an ever-increasing influence on the development of Roman law, largely through imperial legislation. Thus, under the influence of Christian ideas, measures were introduced aimed at the protection of the socially and economically disadvantaged,

---

[17] A number of reconstructions of the Theodosian Code have been produced since the sixteenth century. Of the earliest editions the most important is that of Gothofredus (*Codex Theodosianus, cum perpetuis commentariis*), published in Lyons in 1665. Other editions of the Code were published by Hanel (Bonn 1837) and Th. Mommsen (Berlin 1905). Mommsen's edition (*Theodosiani libri XVI cum constitutionibus Sirmondianis*) is the one most widely used. For an English translation see C. Pharr (ed.) *The Theodosian Code and Novels and the Sirmondian Constitutions*, Princeton 1952. On the history and character of the Theodosian Code see H. F. Jolowicz and B. Nicholas, *Historical Introduction to the Study of Roman Law*, 3rd edn, Cambridge 1972, 463 ff; A. A. Schiller, *Roman Law: Mechanisms of Development*, New York 1978, 56 ff; O. F. Robinson, *The Sources of Roman Law*, London 1997, 19-20, 61-2; M. Kaser, *Römische Rechtsgeschichte*, Göttingen 1976, 231-2; W. Kunkel/M. Schermaier, *Römische Rechtsgeschichte*, Cologne 2001, 202 ff; A. Guarino, *Storia del diritto romano*, Naples 1996, 560 ff; M. Talamanca (ed.), *Lineamenti di storia del diritto romano*, Milan 1989, 613 ff. Consider also T. Honoré, *Law in the Crisis of Empire*, Oxford 1998, chapters 5-7; 'The Making of the Theodosian Code', *SZ* 103, rom. Abt. (1986), 133-222; J. Harries, *Law and Empire in Late Antiquity*, Cambridge 1999, 59 ff; J. Harries and I. Wood (eds) *The Theodosian Code: Studies in the Imperial Law of Late Antiquity*, London 1993; J. F. Matthews, *Laying Down the Law, A Study of the Theodosian Code*, New Haven and London 2000; F. de Marini Avonzo, *La politica legislativa di Valentiniano III e Theodosio II*, Turin 1975; G.G. Archi, *Teodosio II e la sua codificazione*, Naples 1976.

and certain cruel forms of punishment, such as crucifixion and gladiatorial combat, were abolished. At the same time, however, a number of new offences were introduced, such as offences relating to the suppression of heretical cults and practices. With respect to private law, the impact of Christianity is particularly noticeable in the sphere of the law of marriage and family relations. Thus, in the light of Christian principles pertaining to the sanctity of marriage, attempts were made to restrict the practice of divorce and severe penalties were imposed on those who divorced without proper justification.[18]

Custom

After the enactment of the *constitutio Antoniniana* (212 AD) by which Roman citizenship was extended to all the free inhabitants of the empire, in theory Roman law became the common law of the realm and, as a result, the earlier distinction between *ius civile* and *ius gentium* faded away. This enactment extended the notion of what was considered 'Roman' to cover a multitude of ethnically and locally divergent cultures and legal systems in different stages of development. In actual fact, however, local systems of law did not disappear but continued to apply in some measure in the form of custom.[19] During the Dominate the role of custom as a supplementary source of law was further recognised. According to the jurist Hermogenian, an established customary norm had the same force as written law because it was based upon the tacit consent of the citizens (*'tacita civium conventio'*).[20] The same principle was endorsed by imperial legislation, on the condition that a customary norm did not contradict a written law and had a logical basis.[21] The centralisation of law-making activity seems to have contributed, in an indirect way, to the enlargement of the role of custom as a source of law during this period. As all laws now emanated immediately from the emperor and his bureaucracy, who were often unfamiliar with conditions obtaining in the provinces, many imperial

---

18 According to a law of Emperor Constantine, a wife who divorced her husband without good reason was to be punished by deportation and loss of her dowry. A husband who did the same was not allowed to marry again. If he did remarry, his former wife could seize the new wife's dowry. These penalties did not affect the validity of the divorce, however. See C.Th. 3. 16. 1. On Constantine's family legislation see J. Evans Grubbs, *Law and Family in Late Antiquity. The Emperor Constantine's Marriage Legislation*, Oxford 1995.

19 See chapter 8.

20 D. 1. 3. 35. See also D. 1. 3. 32. 1. (Julianus).

21 C. 8. 52. (53.) 2 (Constantine).

enactments were at variance with local practices and conceptions of justice. Changing local customs that were generally and regularly observed was not easy and implementing imperial legislation in the provinces sometimes proved to be an impossible task.[22]

The growing influence of custom is not unrelated to the so-called 'vulgarisation' of Roman law that marks the development of the law during the later imperial era. We saw earlier that, prior to the promulgation of the *constitutio Antoniniana*, communities in the provinces were permitted to carry on observing their own systems of law insofar as these were not incompatible with the Roman rule. When the Roman citizenship was extended to all the inhabitants of the empire, provincial communities were required to adopt and apply a system of law whose rules and procedures were largely alien to them. As the inhabitants of these communities were often reluctant to abandon the norms by which they had been governed in the past, Roman law was in the course of time infiltrated by elements of local systems and many of the traditional institutions of Roman law were transformed or fell into abeyance. At the same time, local conceptions of justice and legal practices underwent a considerable degree of change under the influence of Roman law. As a result, the law which in fact applied in the provinces was an amalgam of simplified Roman law and local custom, varying from area to area, which shared little of the sophistication of the Roman law of the classical period. Elements of this 'vulgarised' Roman law, or 'Romanised' customary law (*vulgarrecht*), are clearly visible in imperial constitutions, legal codes and documents of the post-classical period.[23]

---

22 For example, the institution of *abdicatio* (pertaining to the right of the head of a family to renounce a child) continued to be followed in practice during the later imperial period, despite the fact that it had been abolished by a *rescriptum* of Diocletian (C. 8. 46. (47.) 6.). In a similar way, polygamy continued to be practised in some communities in the East, although such a practice was prohibited under Roman law (C. 5. 5. 2.).

23 For example, under the influence of Greek and Hellenistic law, which adopted a much narrower conception of paternal authority than Roman law, Constantine introduced restrictions to the traditional Roman institution of *patria potestas* by recognising that, under certain circumstances, persons *in potestate* could have proprietary rights (thus, it was accepted that property which a mother had bequeathed to a child should belong to the child, even if the latter remained under the *potestas* of his father – see C. 6. 60. 1.). The scope of the *patria potestas* was restricted further by later emperors. Other examples of changes in the law that resulted from the influence of custom include the abandonment of certain formalities relating to the making of binding agreements, and the blurring of the distinction between ownership and possession. For more examples see E. Levy, *West Roman Vulgar Law, the Law of Property*,

The Jurists' Law

As has already been observed, in the later imperial era Roman jurisprudence was no longer a living source of law and the place of the responses of the jurists had been taken by the letters of the emperors on legal and judicial matters. The juristic works of the classical period were now regarded as a body of finally settled doctrine which could be applied in a case at any time. This body of law, which was taken to incorporate legal rules and principles established by the former agencies of legislation (*leges*, *senatus consulta*, *ius honorarium*), was termed *ius*, in contradistinction with the law contained in the enactments of the emperors, referred to as *lex*. However, the application of *ius* was beset by serious difficulties. The classical jurists had left a vast body of literature containing an extensive range of opinions which often reflected conflicting viewpoints. The situation was exacerbated further by the fact that, at a time when legal texts circulated only in manuscript copies, there were many works which were attributed to classical jurists but which in actual fact had not been written by them. Judges, whose decisions were expected to be based upon established authority, often found themselves confronted with the problem of having to choose between two or more conflicting sources, all regarded as being equally authoritative. This situation created a great deal of confusion as to the state of the law and invited abuse, as advocates often sought to confuse or deceive unskilled judges by producing captious quotations from what they alleged to be classical texts. What was urgently needed was a way of finding which works formed part of the authoritative classical literature and which approach was to be adopted if the authorities conflicted in their opinions.[24]

The emperors tried to deal with these problems through a series of legislative enactments prescribing which juristic works should be relied upon by the courts and what weight should be accorded to different

---

Philadelphia 1951, 22-23, 64- 66. On the influence of the *vulgarrecht* see W. Kunkel, *An Introduction to Roman Legal and Constitutional History*, 2nd edn, Oxford 1973, 150-2; H. F. Jolowicz and B. Nicholas, *Historical Introduction to the Study of Roman Law*, 3rd edn, Cambridge 1972, 473 ff; J. Harries, *Law and Empire in Late Antiquity*, Cambridge 1999, 31 ff; M. Kaser, *Römische Rechtsgeschichte*, Göttingen 1976, 232 ff; W. Kunkel/M. Schermaier, *Römische Rechtsgeschichte*, Cologne 2001, 193 ff; A. Guarino, *Storia del diritto romano*, Naples 1996, 537-8; M. Talamanca (ed.), *Lineamenti di storia del diritto romano*, Milan 1989, 600 ff.

24 As was noted in chapter 8, in an attempt to deal with this problem Emperor Hadrian had issued a *rescriptum* which declared that the unanimous view of the privileged jurists had the full force of law. G. 1. 7.

sources. Thus, a law issued by Emperor Constantine in 321 AD deprived of validity the comments of Paul and Ulpian on the works of Papinian, thus making the latter jurist supreme.[25] In 328 AD another enactment of Constantine confirmed the authority of the works of Paul, and especially the *sententiae*, a collection of pronouncements and rules attributed to this jurist.[26] By far more comprehensive was an edict issued in 426 AD by Theodosius II and Valentinian III, which became known as the Law of Citations.[27] By this statute the imperial government sought to fix once and for all the degree of authority that was to be accorded to the classical texts. Thus, it was proclaimed that the opinions contained in the writings of the four leading jurists of the late classical period, namely Papinian, Ulpian, Paul and Modestinus, as well as those of Gaius, should be regarded as binding. If the authorities adduced on a legal question were divided, the judge was to adopt the view of the majority, while in the case of a tie, priority was to be given to the opinion which had the support of Papinian. If the opinions adduced were equal in number on each side and no relevant utterance of Papinian could be found, then it was left to the judge to determine at his discretion which of the solutions proposed was to be preferred. The same law also provided that opinions of other jurists quoted by the five principal jurists might also be relied upon, provided that their authenticity could be verified. This meant that if any of the five principal jurists quoted with approval the opinion of a jurist outside the five then he made that opinion his own, and it was so to be taken on the condition that the accuracy of the quotation was confirmed through a comparison of manuscripts. The Law of Citations achieved a measure of uniformity and predictability in the administration of justice. However, the mechanical treatment of legal authorities which it adopted provides a clear indication of the low level to which jurisprudence had sunk and shows the preponderance of dogmatism over creative legal thinking that marks the character of post-classical law.

---

[25] C.Th. 1. 4. 1.

[26] C.Th. 1. 4. 2. It is now believed that the work known as *Pauli sententiae* was not written by Paul himself but by an unknown author on the basis of Paul's works.

[27] C.Th. 1. 4. 3. On the Law of Citations see this H. F. Jolowicz and B. Nicholas, *Historical Introduction to the Study of Roman Law*, 3rd edn, Cambridge 1972, 451-3; M. Kaser, *Römische Rechtsgeschichte*, Göttingen 1976, 230-1; W. Kunkel/M. Schermaier, *Römische Rechtsgeschichte*, Cologne 2001, 200 ff; A. Guarino, *Storia del diritto romano*, Naples 1996, 542-3; M. Talamanca (ed.), *Lineamenti di storia del diritto romano*, Milan 1989, 606.

Post-classical compilations of *ius*

The difficulties surrounding the application of *ius* were compounded by the fact that the manuscripts containing the works of the classical jurists were few and not easily accessible to legal practitioners, especially to those working in the provinces. Furthermore, as a result of the general decline in the standards of jurisprudence and the 'vulgarisation' of legal thinking, lawyers found it increasingly difficult to handle and comprehend the language of the classical texts. In response to these problems a new type of juristic literature began to emerge consisting largely of compilations of assorted extracts from the works of the classical jurists. The purpose of these compilations was to make the classical works easier to understand and to facilitate their application by adapting them to the needs of the times. The authors of these works chose from the original texts those parts which appeared to them to be of interest to contemporary readers, whilst other parts were reproduced in summary form or were altogether omitted if they were thought to be useless or superfluous. Occasionally passages were replaced by others of the authors' own making or entirely new passages were added to the original texts. As a result of these changes classical texts were often distorted to such an extent that they no longer represented the views of their original authors, reflecting, instead, the 'vulgarised' legal thinking of the post-classical period.

Among the most important of the post-classical compilations of law is the so-called 'Vatican Fragments' (*Fragmenta Vaticana*), discovered in the Vatican library in 1821. This collection, which is probably the remains of a handbook for practitioners, contains extracts from the works of the jurists Papinian, Paul and Ulpian; it also includes a number of imperial constitutions (*rescripta*) dating from the period 205-372 AD and reproduced from the Gregorian and Hermogenian Codes.[28] The texts are arranged under titles according to subject, each title being preceded by a note indicating the name of the jurist from whose work the materials have been taken or, if the text is a rescript, the name of the emperor who issued it. Among the subjects dealt with at some length are sale, usufruct, dowry, gift and legal representation. This collection, although incomplete, is of great value for the study of Roman law as it contains materials that have not be included in other compilations or that can be found only in a greatly abbreviated form.[29]

---

[28] It is believed that the work was completed between 318 and 324 AD and that the three imperial constitutions of 330, 337 and 372 were added later.

[29] For the text see FIRA II, pp. 461-540. A critical edition of this work was produced by Th. Mommsen in 1860 – see P. Krüger, Th. Mommsen & G.

Another work of the same period, currently known as the *Collatio Legum Mosaicarum et Romanarum* (or *Collatio*),[30] dates from the early fourth century AD. The purpose of this work appears to have been to compare some selected Roman norms, chiefly of penal character, with related norms of the Mosaic law in order to show that Roman law, in its basic principles, corresponded with, or possibly was based upon Mosaic law. Like the Vatican Fragments, it is divided into titles, each beginning with passages taken from the Old Testament and followed by extracts from the works of the jurists Paul, Ulpian, Papinian, Modestinus and Gaius, and various imperial constitutions from the Gregorian and Hermogenian Codes.[31] The author of this work remains unknown, although the attempted comparison of Roman and Mosaic law suggests that he was probably of Jewish origin.

Two further collections of this period should also be mentioned here: the *Sententiae* of Paul and the *Regulae* of Ulpian. The first of these works, entitled *Pauli sententiarum ad filium libri V* but usually referred to as *Pauli Sententiae*, consists largely of brief pronouncements and rules attributed to the third century jurist Paul. It deals with a broad range of topics relating to both private and criminal law and appears to have been used as a handbook by legal practitioners.[32] But there is no evidence that Paul himself ever composed a work under this title and it is now assumed that the *Pauli Sententiae* was produced by an unknown author in the latter half of the third century AD on the basis of Paul's writings. This collection appears to have been very influential during the later Empire, as manifested by the fact that it is cited repeatedly in the imperial legislation of this period.[33] Although the original text of the *Pauli Sententiae* has not survived, it has been reconstructed on the basis of extracts included in various post-classical compilations, such as the Digest of Justinian, the *Lex Romana*

Studemund, *Collectio librorum iuris anteiustiniani* III, Berlin 1927. See also B. Kübler & E. Seckel, *Iurisprudentiae anteiustinianae reliquias in usum maxime academicum compositas a* P. E. Huschke, 6th edn, Leipzig 1927.

30 'A Comparison of Roman and Mosaic Law'. The original title of this work, as found in the surviving manuscript, is *Lex dei quam praecipit dominus ad Moysen* (the divine law which the Lord gave to Moses).

31 See FIRA II, pp. 541-89. The *Collatio* was first edited in the sixteenth century but more materials were added later based on two manuscripts discovered in the nineteenth century. The standard modern edition is that of Th. Mommsen included in his *Collectio librorum iuris anteiustiniani* III, Berlin 1927; see also B. Kübler & E. Seckel, *Iurisprudentiae anteiustinianae reliquias in usum maxime academicum compositas a* P. E. Huschke, 6th edn, Leipzig 1927.

32 See F. Schulz, *History of Roman Legal Science*, Oxford 1967, 176.

33 C.Th. 1. 4. 2. (Constantine); 1. 4. 3. (Law of Citations).

Visigothorum and the above-mentioned *Collatio*.[34] The *Regulae Ulpiani*, also known as *tituli ex corpore Ulpiani*, is believed to be an abridgment of Ulpian's work *liber singularis regularum*, hence it is also referred to as *Ulpiani Epitome*.[35] It was composed probably in the early fourth century AD and, like the *Pauli Sententiae*, it appears to have been intended mainly for practitioners. This work has come down to us, although in a fragmentary form, through a manuscript dating from the tenth or eleventh century.[36]

Reference should also be made here to the *Consultatio Veteris Cuiusdam Iurisconsulti* (or *Consultatio*),[37] a work dating from the end of the fifth century AD and first edited by Cujas (*Jacobus Cujacius*) in 1577.[38] This work, which was probably designed for instructional purposes, consists of a number of legal questions with the answers to them. It is based on Paul's *Sententiae* and materials drawn from the Gregorian, Hermogenian and Theodosian Codes.[39]

From the eastern part of the empire have survived two important collections: the Syrio-Roman book of law and the *Scholia Sinaitica*. The first of these works was written in Greek by an unknown author and was published in the late fifth century AD, probably in Constantinople. It appears to have been intended for use in legal education. The original Greek text has not survived – we possess only translations of it in Syrian, Armenian and Arabic, dating from the eighth century. In the past it was believed that the law contained in this work was a mixture of Roman and Greek law. The current view, however, is that the law reproduced in the Syrio-Roman book is largely Roman in character.[40] The work known as *Scholia Sinaitica* was written in Greek, probably between 438 and 529 AD,

---

34 See FIRA II, pp. 317-417, 419-432.

35 Some modern scholars proposed that this work was based on the Institutes of Gaius and other classical works, but this view has been called into question. See H. L. W. Nelson, *Überlieferung Aufbau und Stil von Gai Institutiones*, Leiden 1981, 80-96.

36 The *Ulpiani Epitome* was first published in 1549 but both its opening and concluding passages are missing. See FIRA II, pp. 261-301. See also F. Schulz, *Die Epitome Ulpiani des Codex Vaticanus Reginae 1128*, Bonn 1926.

37 'Consultation with an Ancient Jurisconsult'.

38 Cujas, who taught at the University of Bourges, was a leading member of the humanist movement of the 16th and 17th centuries. See chapter 11 below.

39 See FIRA II, pp. 591-613.

40 FIRA II, pp. 751-98. See also K.G. Bruns & E. Sachau, *Syrisch-Römisches Rechtsbuch*, Leipzig 1880, repr. Aalen 1961; P. E. Pieler, *Byzantinische Rechtsliteratur* in H. Hunger, *Die hochsprachliche profane Literatur der Byzantiner*, Bd. 2, Munich 1978, 393 ff.

and was discovered in 1880 at the monastery of St Catherine of Sinai. It is a commentary on the work of Ulpian *libri ad Sabinum* and was probably written at the law-school of Beirut where it was used for instructional purposes. This work is important because it gives us a clear picture of the way in which law was taught at the law-schools of the East in the pre-Justinianic period as well as of the way in which the classical texts were approached by the post-classical commentators.[41]

Post-classical jurists and law-schools

As was said in chapter 8, in the time of Hadrian the practice of granting the *ius publice respondendi* to individual jurists came to an end. From that time leading jurists were drawn more and more into the imperial circle and, by the end of the third century, they had been incorporated into the administrative machinery of the emperor. By that time jurisprudence had ceased to exist as an independent source of law as it was inconsistent with the autocratic power of the emperor, now openly acknowledged to be the sole fount of laws. Besides playing a part in the formulation of legislation as members of the imperial bureaucracy, the jurists of the later Empire were concerned with making the works of the classical jurists more accessible to legal practitioners and judicial magistrates through the production of new copies, collections and summaries of the classical works. At the same time, increased emphasis was placed on the study of the classical sources and their adaptation to the needs and conditions of the times.[42] Of great importance for the preservation of the classical tradition were the law-schools of the empire whose influence appears to have increased significantly in the period following the reorganisation of the Roman state by Diocletian and Constantine.

The earliest law-schools of the empire were established in Rome and in Beirut in the early third century AD.[43] The purpose of these schools was

---

[41] FIRA II, pp. 635-52; P. E. Pieler, *Byzantinische Rechtsliteratur* in H. Hunger, *Die hochsprachliche profane Literatur der Byzantiner*, Bd. 2, Munich 1978, 391 ff; N. van der Wal & J. H. A. Lokin, *Historiae iuris graeco-romani delineatio. Les sources du droit byzantin de* 300 *a* 1453, Groningen 1985, 20-24.

[42] In the years following the granting of Roman citizenship to all the free inhabitants of the empire by the *constitutio Antoniniana* (212 AD) knowledge of Roman law became necessary for those engaged in the practice of law, especially in the provinces where the newly admitted citizens were required to conduct their affairs according to a system of law about which they knew very little.

[43] Greg., *orat. paneg. ad Orig*. 5. 62.

to train those wishing to practise law as advocates or to join the imperial civil service. As the administrative needs of the empire increased, following the reorganisation of the government by Diocletian and Constantine, a number of new law-schools were established in places such as Alexandria, Caesaria, Athens and Constantinople[44] in the East, and Carthage and Augustodunum in the West. At first private institutions, the law-schools gradually came under government control and a number of measures were introduced aiming at promoting or facilitating legal education. For example, a constitution of Emperors Diocletian and Maximian exempted students who were studying at the law-school of Beirut from compulsory services in their hometown.[45] In the course of time, professional lawyers trained in the law-schools (*causidici*, *advocati*) replaced the earlier orators (*oratores*) whose training in law was usually only elementary. This was confirmed by an edict of Emperor Leo I, issued in 460 AD, according to which only persons who had undertaken formal legal training at one of the recognised law-schools of the empire were allowed to serve as advocates in the courts of law.[46]

Legal education in the law-schools was based largely on the study of the extant works of the classical jurists and collections of imperial constitutions. In the schools of the East legal instruction was given in Greek, although knowledge of Latin was necessary for the study of the classical texts. As to the method of instruction adopted, this was similar to that followed in the schools of rhetoric: the literary works of the classical period and imperial constitutions, as found in various compilations of law, were discussed and explained step by step and, when possible, compared to or contrasted with parallel texts. On this basis general legal principles were formulated and then applied to resolve specific problems of law emerging from actual cases. The teaching was done by professional law-teachers, not by practitioners, and the courses offered were fitted into a fixed curriculum. At the end of their studies, which lasted up to five years, students were awarded a certificate which entitled them to serve as advocates in the courts or to join the imperial civil service. The quality of the legal education offered varied from time to time and from place to place. During the late third and early fourth centuries scholarly interest in classical law remained alive in the West, where the law-school of Rome became an important centre of legal learning. However, from the middle of the fourth century, as the political centre of the empire shifted to the East, legal culture in the West took a sharp downward trend. The decline of legal

---

44 The law-school of Constantinople was founded in 425 AD. See C.Th. 14. 9. 3.

45 C. 10. 50. 1.

46 C. 2. 7. 11.

learning in the western part of the empire was precipitated further by the worsening social and economic conditions, political instability and the threat of barbarian invasions. In the Greek-speaking East, by contrast, the conditions of economic and political stability that generally prevailed facilitated the growth of legal studies. At the two main centres of legal learning, Beirut and Constantinople, the study of the classical works gave rise to a new type of scientific jurisprudence which provided the basis for the great codification of Roman law by Emperor Justinian in the sixth century.[47]

Among the most distinguished of the east-Roman law professors, the 'teachers of the universe', as they were admiringly called, were Cyrillus, Patricius, Eudoxius, Leontius, Amblichus and Demosthenes.[48] It is known that these men produced several works of various kinds, such as commentaries on imperial constitutions and works of classical jurists, summaries (*indices*), annotations and collections of rules on particular legal questions. As was noted before, these works were concerned not so much with developing new legal doctrine but with helping students and legal practitioners to gain a sound knowledge and understanding of the classical sources. In the eyes of the east-Roman law professors the works of the classical jurists constituted a valuable heritage which had to be studied and preserved. This 'classicism' of the post-classical legal science, combined with Greek modes of thought and methods of instruction, did succeed in getting back genuine familiarity with the whole of the classical achievement. The new insight into the workings of the classical law had a considerable impact on the technique of imperial legislation, as manifested by the fact that the imperial laws of the late fifth and sixth centuries were superior, both in clarity and style, to those of the early post-classical age. Despite its lack of originality and its tendency towards simplification, post-classical jurisprudence succeeded in drawing attention to the perennial validity of the classical system and facilitated its adaptation to the

---

47 This revival of legal studies appears to have been confined in the two places mentioned, whilst in the other law-schools of the empire the standards of legal education must have been rather low. This is manifested by the fact that only the names of professors of these two law-schools are still known. This view seems to be confirmed, moreover, by an enactment of Justinian ordering the closure of the law-schools of Alexandria and Caesaria on the grounds that those who taught were poorly educated and were conveying to their students a false knowledge. (see *const. Omnem* 7: '*imperitos homines devagare et doctrinam discipulis adulterinam tradere*'.)

48 Among the teachers of the law-school of Beirut was probably Sabinus, one of the authors of the *Scholia Sinaitica,* one of the post-classical collections mentioned before.

conditions of the times. It was largely due to the work of the post-classical scholars that the spirit of classical jurisprudence was preserved and found its way into the codification of Justinian and, through it, into modern law.[49]

The Administration of Justice

During the later Empire the administration of justice was in the hands of imperial officials, who tried cases directly according to the procedure of the *cognitio extra ordinem.*[50] In Rome and Constantinople the judges of first instance were the *praefecti urbi*; in the provinces the normal court of first instance was that of the provincial governor. Lower municipal magistrates continued to exercise limited jurisdiction over disputes involving small amounts of money and petty crimes. Alongside these there existed, in the later Dominate period, the *defensor civitatis*, a special magistrate entrusted with the protection of members of the lower classes against abuses of power committed by great landowners (*potentiores, possessores*). The *defensor* had jurisdiction in both civil and criminal matters and his court was designed to deal speedily and efficiently with all kinds of cases, although his decisions were subject to appeal before the provincial governor. Under Constantine bishops too were allowed to act as judges in private disputes but, in later years, it was established that they could only hear cases which had been submitted to them by agreement of both parties concerned. The higher magistrates often carried out their judicial functions through delegates (*iudices dati* or *pedanei*). The latter were usually low-ranking officers and their decisions could be appealed against to the magistrates who appointed them. As judicial magistrates were not always experts in law, they often relied on the advice of panels of

---

49 On the character of post-classical jurisprudence see in general H. F. Jolowicz & B. Nicholas, *Historical Introduction to the Study of Roman Law*, 3rd edn, Cambridge 1972, 451-460; W. Kunkel, *An Introduction to Roman Legal and Constitutional History*, 2nd edn, Oxford 1973, 146 ff; F. Schulz, *History of Roman Legal Science*, Oxford 1967, 267 ff; M. Kaser, *Römische Rechtsgeschichte*, Göttingen 1976, 225 ff, 237 ff; W. Kunkel/M. Schermaier, *Römische Rechtsgeschichte*, Cologne 2001, 189 ff, 195 ff; A. Guarino, *Storia del diritto romano*, Naples 1996, 543 ff; M. Talamanca (ed.), *Lineamenti di storia del diritto romano*, Milan 1989, 604 ff; D. Liebs, *Die Jurisprudenz im spätantiken Italien (260-640 n. Chr.)*, Berlin 1987.

50 On the court system during the later Empire see in general H. F. Jolowicz & B. Nicholas, *Historical Introduction to the Study of Roman Law*, 3rd edn, Cambridge 1972, 445 ff; M. Kaser, *Das römische Zivilprozessrecht*, Munich 1996, 517 ff.

adsessores, persons who had studied law at the law-schools and who usually belonged to the legal profession. Moreover, as the *extra ordinem* procedure was based largely on written communications, the magistrates were assisted by secretaries (*scribae*).

The decisions of jurisdictional magistrates could be appealed against before higher officials in the administrative hierarchy. An appeal could be made, for instance, from a decision of a provincial governor either to the *vicarius* of the diocese or to the *praefectus praetorio* of the prefecture to which the relevant province belonged. A further appeal from the *vicarius* to the emperor was possible, but the decisions of the *praefectus praetorio* were not subject to appeal, as the latter was considered to administer justice on behalf of the emperor.[51] Under certain exceptional circumstances the *praefecti praetorio* and the *vicarii* could deal with cases as judges of first instance, especially when a case involved a matter of great importance for the state. The emperor, as head of the state, could in principle exercise jurisdiction, both as a judge of first instance and on appeal, in all kinds of cases, whether of a civil or criminal nature; in practice, however, he rarely tried cases in person, as the nature of the imperial office during this period did not permit close contact between him and his subjects (cases submitted to him were usually referred to the *praefectus praetorio* or to the minister of justice).

Besides the regular courts there existed also a large number of special courts which dealt with cases of a particular type or with matters concerning certain categories of persons. Most of these courts operated under the old Roman principle according to which a magistrate had administrative jurisdiction over matters arising out of his departmental duties as well as a disciplinary jurisdiction over his subordinates. A court of this type was, for example, the court of the *rationalis*, the magistrate who represented the public treasury in a diocese, which tried cases involving disputes relating to taxation and other fiscal issues. A decision of the court of the *rationalis* could be appealed against to the *comes sacrarum largitionum*, the minister in charge of state finances. Cases involving disputes over crown property were dealt with by the *comes rei privatae* (or *comes rerum privatarum*), the official entrusted with the administration of the private property of the emperor and the management of imperial lands. At Rome and Constantinople, the *praefecti annonnae* had jurisdiction over matters connected with trade practices and the supply and administration of foodstuffs. Within the jurisdiction of the *praefectus urbi* fell cases involving violations of public order in the city and breaches of building

---

51 An appeal to the emperor from the decision of the urban prefect was allowed under certain conditions.

regulations. Moreover, the *praefectus urbi* was the exclusive judge in cases involving members of the senatorial order, if the latter lived in Rome or Constantinople, whilst those living in the provinces came under the jurisdiction of the provincial governors.[52] In the later Dominate period decisions of provincial governors in such cases were subject to review by the emperor or the urban or praetorian prefects. Imperial civil servants came under the jurisdiction of the heads of their departments or the master of the offices (*magister officiorum*), who also dealt with cases involving servants and subordinate employees of the imperial household (*silentiarii*, *castrensiani*). From the middle of the fourth century members of the clergy involved in civil disputes or accused of criminal offences could submit their cases to ecclesiastical courts for trial (*privilegium fori*).[53]

Civil Procedure

As we saw in chapter 8, from the early years of the Principate a new form of legal procedure, the *cognitio extra ordinem* or *cognitio extraordinaria*, began to be used concurrently with the *per formulam* procedure. Under the new system imperial officials, acting as representatives of the emperor, tried cases directly, without having to go through the formalities of the *per formulam* procedure. By the end of the third century the latter procedure had entirely been superseded by the *cognitio extra ordinem* and, in 342 AD, was formally abolished by an edict of emperors Constantius and Constans.[54] The *cognitio extra ordinem* was the chief form of civil procedure during the Dominate period and continued to apply under the legislation of Justinian and in the years that followed. Moreover, the same procedure was adopted by the ecclesiastical courts which began to be set up by the Church during this period. A description of the main stages of the *cognitio extra ordinem*, as it was applied during the post-classical

---

52 Until the time of Constantine members of the senatorial class, no matter where they lived, were deemed to be domiciled at Rome or Constantinople and therefore were regarded as coming within the jurisdiction of the prefects of the two capitals.

53 Initially only bishops appear to have enjoyed this privilege, while lower members of the clergy were tried by the ordinary courts. In the early fifth century this privilege was extended to all the clergy, although in the East it continued to be confined only to bishops until the time of Justinian. C. Th. 16. 2. 41; *Nov.* 123. 21.

54 C. 2. 57. 1.

period and under the Justinianic legislation, is given in the following paragraphs.[55]

The summons

The first step in a civil action was the submission by the plaintiff or his representative of a letter to the judicial magistrate setting out in a summary form the factual and legal basis of his claim and asking the magistrate to notify the defendant of the claim (*postulatio simplex*).[56] Following a preliminary assessment of the plaintiff's claim, the magistrate then served upon the defendant a summons accompanied by the plaintiff's statement. This form of summons was termed *litis denuntiatio* and was considered to be issued by the plaintiff to the defendant with the backing of the magistrate (*denuntiatio ex auctoritate*). The term *libellus contradictories* referred to the defendant's written reply to the plaintiff's claim.[57] By this the defendant assumed the obligation to appear before the court, usually within four months, to contest the plaintiff's claim. If the defendant failed to appear following three monthly summons (*trina denuntiatione*) the magistrate could prosecute him for insubordination or order that he be brought before him by force. If the defendant could not be found he was tried *in absentia* and was condemned.[58]

From the middle of the fifth century the *litis denuntiatio* was replaced by a new method of summoning the defendant. This method, which was the one recognised by the legislation of Justinian, was based upon a written complaint (*libellus conventionis*) addressed no longer to the defendant, as under the earlier system, but to the court.[59] In his statement the plaintiff outlined the facts upon which his claim was based and asked the court to summon the defendant (*postulatio simplex*). If the plaintiff's application was accepted, the court, through a clerk (*exsecutor litium*), served upon the

---

55 On the procedure of the *cognitio extra ordinem* during the later imperial period see H. F. Jolowicz and B. Nicholas, *Historical Introduction to the Study of Roman Law*, 3rd edn, Cambridge 1972, 439 ff; J. Harries, *Law and Empire in Late Antiquity*, Cambridge 1999, ch. 5; R. Monier, *Manuel élémentaire de droit romain*, Aalen 1977, 188 ff; 192 ff; D. Simon, *Untersuchungen zum Justinianischen Zivilprozess*, Munich, 1969; V. Zilletti, *Studi sul processo civile giustinianeo*, Milan 1965; R. Orestano, *L' appello civile in diritto romano*, Turin 1953, repr. 1966.

56 See, e.g., FIRA III, no.173 (338 AD); Bruns, *Fontes* I, no. 103 (361-363 AD).

57 See on this C.Th. 2. 14. 1; also in C. 2. 14. 3. (Arcadius and Honorius).

58 D. 2. 5. 2. 1. (Paulus); see also *Pauli sententiae receptae* (P.S.), 5. 5a. 6. In Girard, *Textes* I, p. 345.

59 *Inst*. 4. 6. 24. (Theophilus).

defendant a summons and at the same time notified him of the plaintiff's claim. The defendant was required to respond in writing (*libellus contradictorius*) within ten or, from the time of Justinian, twenty days.[60] Moreover, he was required to give the court officer (and not the plaintiff, as in the *per formulam* procedure) security (*cautio iudicatum sisti*), by nominating a guarantor (*fideiussor in iudicio sistendi causa*), that he would appear in court and that he would bear the court costs if he was condemned.[61] A defendant who failed to give this guarantee, if he belonged to the class of the *humiliores*, was held in prison by the *exsecutor* until the end of the trial. If he belonged to the class of *illustres*, by contrast, he was relieved from the obligation to give security – a formal promise under oath was deemed sufficient.[62] The party who failed to appear before the court on the appointed day (*contumacia, eremodicium*) would lose his case.[63]

The trial

On the day of the trial the parties appeared before the judge who, as was noted earlier, might be one of several officials (e.g., a *praefectus urbi*), or a judge to whom a judicial magistrate had assigned the case (*iudex delegatus, iudex pedaneus, iudex datus*).[64] Before proceedings began both parties and their advocates (*advocati*)[65] were sworn in.[66] The parties, supported by their advocates, then presented their claims and the facts upon which they were based, as set out in the *libellus conventionis* and the *libellus contradictorius*. In the *cognitio extra ordinem* the term *exceptio* or *praescriptio* was used to denote any defence put forward by the defendant in order to counter the plaintiff's claim. It should be noted here, however, that not all defences had to be raised at this stage, but only defences relating to preliminary matters and certain dilatory exceptions. The term *litis contestatio* denoted the point at which the parties had concluded the

60 See, e.g., FIRA III, no. 177 (427 AD).

61 *Inst*. 4. 11. 2.

62 C. 12. 1. 17. pr. (Zeno).

63 C. 3. 1. 13. 2-2b (530 AD); *Nov*. 112. 3. (541 AD).

64 Higher state officials, such as provincial governors, often delegated their jurisdiction to specially appointed representatives, especially in cases of minor importance (*negotia humiliora*).

65 The advocates were persons who had received formal legal education law at the law-schools and served as legal advisers in a professional capacity (their fees were regulated by law). An advocate was attached to one particular court and had to follow the rules of the order or association to which he belonged.

66 Both parties and their advocates had to swear that the claim and the defence to it were not malicious or based on false declarations.

presentation of their claims before the judge,[67] although they were more or less free to modify them in the course of the trial. Thus, if the plaintiff's claim was deemed excessive (*pluris petitio*), this did not necessarily result in the loss of the case for him (in contrast with the position adopted under the formulary system); the plaintiff was in such a case permitted to modify his claim. Under the legislation of Justinian, the trial had to be completed within three years from the *litis contestatio*.[68]

In the next phase of the proceedings evidence was adduced and the parties presented their arguments, usually through their advocates. Both oral testimony and documentary evidence were considered, although the latter was regarded as carrying much more weight.[69] To the category of documentary evidence belonged various public records (*instrumenta publica*), such as documents kept by a public authority (*insinuatio actis*) or documents drawn up by a public organ at the request of the party concerned (*apud acta*), and various private records. The latter included documents drafted by public notaries (*tabelliones*)[70] (these documents were termed *instrumenta publice confecta*), written declarations (*cautiones*), letters (*chirographa*) and other records. In general, private records carried little evidentiary weight unless they had been signed by three credible witnesses who testified to their authenticity (*instrumentum quasi publice confectum*). Witnesses were summoned by the court and were often required to give surety for their appearance. They were interrogated by the presiding judge and their answers were recorded.[71] Of the various means of evidence the confession (*confessio in iure*) carried special weight, although it did not necessarily result in the termination of the trial.[72] A further means of evidence was the oath, although its value was assessed by the

---

67 C. 3. 9. 1. (Septimius Severus). It should be noted here, however, that in the context of the *cognitio extra ordinem* the *litis contestatio* did not produce the effects it produced under the formulary system as the legal consequences attached to it in the *per formulam* procedure were now associated with the final judgement itself.

68 C. 3. 1. 13.

69 C. 4. 20. 1.

70 The *tabelliones* exercised their profession in public places or in offices (*stationes*) with the assistance of clerks (*scribae, notarii*). They carried out their activities under government supervision and were subject to punishment if they were found guilty of fraud or involvement in illicit transactions. See C. 4. 21. 17. (528 AD).

71 In general, the testimony of witnesses was assessed according to the social status of the witness. Oral testimony by a single witness carried no weight at all. See C. 4. 20. 4. (Carus, Carinus and Numerian).

72 See, e.g., FIRA III, no. 178.

judge at his discretion. An oath might be taken by one of the parties to a trial upon order of the judge (*iusiurandum iudiciale*), or might be imposed upon one party by the other with the judge's consent (*iusiurandum in iure* or *necessarium*).

The presiding judge played an active part in the proceedings and had a considerable degree of freedom in assessing the evidence. At the same time, however, as a state official, he was bound by the instructions of his superiors. In addition to that, he was expected to follow certain evidentiary rules, such as those relating to legal presumptions (*praesumptiones*). With respect to the latter, it was recognised that a fact had to be deemed proved, despite the absence of direct evidence, if its existence could be inferred from other facts established by the available evidence.[73] Presumptions were defeasible, however, as the conclusions arrived at on this basis could be disproved by counter-evidence.

The decision

A distinction was drawn between two kinds of decisions, preliminary decisions (*interlocutiones*) and final judgements (*sententiae definitivae*). Decisions were set down in writing,[74] were formally recorded and were publicly announced.[75] They were rendered in Latin or, from the end of the fourth century, in either Latin or Greek.[76] After the judge's final verdict (*sententia definitiva*) had been pronounced, the party who lost the case was usually condemned to cover the court costs.[77] Moreover, if the defendant was absolved, the judge could render a decision against the plaintiff if, in the course of the trial, it was proved that he was indebted to the defendant.[78] After the publication of the decision, the plaintiff was barred from bringing another action against the defendant concerning the same object (*de eadem re*), according to the principle that the same matter could not be litigated twice.[79] Against such an action the defendant could raise an *exceptio rei iudicatae* – a defence based on the claim that the same matter had definitely been decided on in a previous trial.

---

73 See, e.g., D. 34. 3. 28. 3. (Scaevola); 34. 5. 9. 4. (Tryphoninus).
74 C.Th. 4. 17. 1. and C. 7. 44. 3. 1. (Valentinian, Valens and Gratian).
75 C. 7. 44. 2. pr; D. 42. 1. 47. (Paulus).
76 C. 7. 45. 12. (Arcadius and Honorius).
77 C. 7. 51. 5. (Zeno), and *Bas*. 9. 3. 69; C. 3. 1. 13. 6 (Justinian); Inst. 4. 16. 1.
78 C. 7. 45. 14.
79 D. 50. 17. 57. (Gaius).

Forms of appeal

Under the system of the *cognitio extra ordinem* the party who lost the case could appeal against the judge's decision (such an appeal was not possible under the formulary system). An appeal from a lower to a higher court, or from a *iudex pedaneus* to the magistrate who had appointed him, was termed *appellatio* or *provocatio*.[80] An appeal addressed to the emperor was termed *supplicatio* and was permitted only in cases of exceptional importance.[81]

The appeal process began with the submission by the party concerned of a notice of appeal (*libellus appellationis*) to the court which had issued the decision. Such a notice had to be given within two (*biduum*) or three (*triduum*) days[82] (under the legislation of Justinian, within ten days)[83] from the time the decision was published. In Rome and Constantinople appeals were usually heard by the *praefectus urbi*. Appeals against decisions of local courts were dealt with by the governor of the province (*praeses provinciae*) in which the court was situated. As was noted before, appeals against decisions of provincial governors were addressed to the *vicarius* or to the *praefectus praetorio* of the relevant diocese or prefecture, while appeals against decisions of the *vicarii* and the *praefecti urbi* were heard by the emperor. The decisions of the *praefectus praetorio* could not be appealed against, as in judicial matters the praetorian prefect was regarded as acting in the name of the emperor.[84] Until the time of Justinian, both interlocutory and final decisions could be appealed against.[85] As this could cause long delays in resolving cases, however, Justinian ruled that there could be no more than two appeals concerning the same case.[86] Moreover, appeals against interlocutory decisions were no longer permitted. The appellate court either confirmed the decision of the lower court (in which

---

80 C. 7. 62. 19. (Constantine); C. 7. 62. 32. (Theodosius and Valentinian).

81 C. 7. 70. 1. (Justinian).

82 D. 49. 1. 5. 4. (Marcianus).

83 *Nov*. 23. 1.

84 C. 7. 62. 19. pr. (Constantine); D. 1. 11. 1. 1. (Arcadius Charisius).

85 D. 49. 5. 2. (Scaevola). Under Constantine grave penalties were imposed (forced labour at the mines for the *humiliores* and two years exile accompanied by the confiscation of half of their property for members of the upper classes) on those who sought to delay the resolution of a case by raising unfounded or unnecessary appeals. See C.Th. 1. 5. 3. Justinian adopted a less rigid approach, leaving it to the judge to determine the appropriate punishment, usually a fine, at his discretion (a similar approach seems to have been adopted under Diocletian). See C. 7. 62. 6. 4.

86 C. 7. 70. 1; *Nov*. 82. 5.

case the appellant incurred certain penalties) or, if the appeal was accepted, quashed or altered that decision. In dealing with an appeal the higher court could consider additional evidence and assess new defences. A petition addressed to the emperor (*supplicatio*) was an extraordinary form of appeal usually raised against decisions of the *praefectus praetorio* which, as was said before, could not be appealed against in the regular manner. If the emperor accepted the appellant's plea, the case was returned to the *praefectus praetorio* for retrial.

The execution of judgement

By contrast with the position adopted under the formulary system, in the *cognitio extra ordinem* the judge could order the defendant to return the property claimed to the party who won the case, and the latter could rely on the coercive power of the court to ensure that this was done (*manu militari*).[87] Where the judgement was for money, the execution could be carried out against the debtor's person or property. However, the execution of judgement could not proceed before the passing of two months (four, under Justinian) from the announcement of the decision or, if there was an appeal, from the time the decision was made final (*a die confirmationis sententiae*).[88]

If the execution was carried out against the debtor's person, the latter was usually confined in a public prison – confinement in a private prison, as was the case in earlier ages, was now clearly forbidden.[89] This method of execution was, however, relatively rare as, in most cases, the execution was carried out against the debtor's property. In the latter case property belonging to the debtor was seized by court officials (*excecutores*) to be kept as a pledge (*pignus in iudicati causa captum*) and, if the debtor did not comply with the court's decision within two months, it was sold off for the benefit of the creditor.[90] Movables were sold first, then immovable property; if these were not sufficient to cover the debt, then any credits which the debtor may have had were taken in execution and sold.[91] Each piece of property was sold separately and what was left after the payment of the debt was returned to the debtor. Where there were several creditors

---

[87] D. 6. 1. 68. (Ulpianus).

[88] C.Th. 4. 19. 1. pr.; C. 7. 54. 3. 3; C. 7. 54. 2.

[89] C. Th. 9. 11. 1. (Valentinian, Theodosius and Arcadius); C. 9. 5. 2. (Justinian). In practice, however, powerful landowners (*potentiores*), taking advantage of the difficulties of the imperial government in implementing the relevant legislation, often kept their debtors in private prisons.

[90] D. 42. 1. 15. pr. and 2. 4. (Ulpianus).

[91] D. 42. 1. 15. 2. (Ulpianus).

the entire property of the insolvent debtor was sold, item by item (*distractio bonorum*), at an auction organised by the person appointed as administrator of the debtor's estate (*curator bonorum*). To avoid the infamy which the compulsory sale of his property entailed, the insolvent debtor could seek the permission of the court to surrender his property to the creditors (*cessio bonorum*).[92]

The procedure *per rescriptum*

Instead of following the usual method for bringing a suit, i.e. by a *libellus conventionis*, the plaintiff could petition the emperor for a decision on his case. In his application (*preces*), which had to be submitted in writing (*libellus principi oblatus*), the plaintiff set out the factual basis of the dispute. The relevant department of the imperial chancery (*scrinium libellorum*) examined the case and drafted the decision which was then submitted to the emperor for approval by the *quaestor sacri palatii*. In his answer (*rescriptum*) the emperor laid down the solution to the case according to the applicable law, on the understanding that the allegations as to the factual situation contained in the plaintiff's petition were true.[93] Provided that the facts as stated in the petition were not disproved, the judge, who was usually nominated by the same *rescriptum*, was bound by the imperial decision. Some restrictions on the use of the *per rescriptum* procedure were introduced by Justinian in order to prevent abuses of the system.[94]

Arbitration and the ecclesiastical courts

Roman law recognised arbitration (*arbitrium*) as an extra-judicial method for resolving legal disputes. This was based upon a formal agreement (*compromissum*) between the parties to submit their dispute to an arbitrator (*arbiter*) for resolution. The person who was to act as an arbitrator was chosen by the parties themselves and the scope of his authority was prescribed in the *compromissum*. The formal agreement by which the person nominated as an arbitrator assumed the task of handling the dispute was termed *receptum arbitri*. The person who had thus undertaken the role of arbitrator was under an obligation to carry out his duties and might be compelled by the praetor to do so, unless good reasons were obtained for

---

92 D. 42. 3; C. 7. 71.

93 C. 1. 23. 7. pr. (Zeno).

94 *Nov*. 113. 1. and 114.

releasing him from this obligation.[95] The decision of the arbitrator (*pronuntiatio arbitri*) was not binding unless the parties had undertaken, through mutual consent, to abide by the decision. Such an agreement, which was included in the *compromissum*, usually provided for some form of penalty (*poena compromissi*) to be imposed on the party who failed to abide by the arbitrator's decision.[96] Under the legislation of Justinian, the decision of the arbitrator was binding if it had been signed by both parties, or if neither party expressed his disapproval of the decision to the arbitrator or the other party within ten days from the announcement of the decision.[97]

The institution of the arbitration furnished the basis for the development, in the later imperial period, of the jurisdiction of the ecclesiastical courts over private disputes. The early Christians, following the exhortation of apostle Paul not to submit their disputes to the secular courts,[98] often resorted to arbitration proceedings before local bishops. After the recognition of Christianity in the early fourth century, Emperor Constantine confirmed and expanded the jurisdiction of local church authorities over private disputes (*episcopalis audientia*), proclaiming their decisions to be legally binding.[99] As was noted earlier, Constantine also ruled that a dispute might be submitted to an ecclesiastical court at the initiative of one of the parties concerned.[100] But by the end of the fourth century the consent of both parties was recognised as a necessary condition for a case to come under ecclesiastical jurisdiction.[101] Although decisions of ecclesiastical courts could not be appealed against, this form of procedure became very popular because proceedings were simpler, faster and less costly than those followed by the regular courts.[102]

---

95 D. 4. 8. 15. (Ulpianus).

96 D. 4. 8. 27. 7. (Ulpianus).

97 C. 2. 55. 5. pr. and 1. (Justinian). On the institution of arbitration see M. Kaser, *Das römische Zivilprozessrecht*, Munich 1996, 639 ff. And see J. Harries, *Law and Empire in Late Antiquity*, Cambridge 1999, 175 ff.

98 1 *Cor*. 6, 1-6.

99 C.Th. 1. 27. 1.

100 *Const. Sirmondiana*, 1. (333 AD). There are some doubts, however, as to the authenticity of this enactment.

101 C. 1. 4. 7; C.Th. 16. 11. 1. (Arcadius and Honorius).

102 On the *episcopalis audientia* see M. Kaser, *Das römische Zivilprozessrecht*, Munich 1996, 641 ff; K. H. Ziegler, *Das private Schiedsgericht im antiken römischen Recht*, Munich 1971; G. Vismara, *Episcopalis audientia*, Milan 1937. See also J. Harries, *Law and Empire in Late Antiquity*, Cambridge 1999, ch. 10.

Criminal Law and Procedure

By the early third century the *cognitio extra ordinem* had become the regular form of procedure for criminal trials, having superseded the earlier system of the *quaestiones perpetuae*. Criminal proceedings were usually initiated by public prosecution (*inquisitio*), whilst indictments brought by private citizens, although still possible,[103] became increasingly rare because of the risks involved.[104] (A person who made an unfounded accusation against another was subject to severe punishment.)[105] A charge, once it was accepted by the court, was put into writing (*inscriptio*, *libellus accusationis*); the relevant document was then signed by both the accuser and the accused and was entered in the court register.[106] After he was arrested, an accused might languish in prison for months, waiting until his trial could take place.[107] During the trial the judge had considerable discretion over the control of the proceedings; at the same time, however, he was bound by various rules relating to evidence.[108] The principle that prevailed was that an accused could not be convicted if there was uncertainty as to whether he had committed the crime he was charged with. Thus judges sometimes made use of torture on an accused and even on witnesses (especially if these belonged to the class of the *humiliores*) in order to extract the evidence needed or, best of all, a confession. A person convicted of a crime was entitled to appeal against the court's decision. However, the right of appeal was sometimes restricted in order to prevent delays in the administration of justice, especially when the culprit was found guilty of certain serious crimes, such as murder or adultery, or when he had admitted his guilt.[109]

During the period under consideration existing offence categories were redefined and extended and a large number of new offences were created by imperial legislation. Many of these offences were concerned

---

103 See C.Th. 9. 3. 1. and C. 9. 4. 1.

104 It should be noted here that a criminal investigation was usually triggered by an individual complaint either by the injured party or by a private informer.

105 Consider, e.g., C. 9. 39. 2. 3; C.Th. 10. 10. 2.

106 A criminal prosecution for a serious offence could not be initiated by an oral accusation alone. C.Th. 9. 1. 5. and C. 9. 2. 17. pr.

107 Because there were so many prisoners on remand, some attempts were made to improve prison conditions and to limit the period for which prisoners could be held in prison before their case came up for trial. Consider, e.g., C.Th. 9. 1. 7 and 18; C.Th. 9. 3. 6. and C. 9. 4. 5; C. 9. 4. 6; C.Th. 9. 3. 1 and C. 9. 4. 1.

108 See e.g., C.Th. 9. 1. 14 and C. 9. 2. 13; C.Th. 9. 1. 19. and C. 9. 2. 17. See also C.Th. 1. 16. 9.

109 Consider, e.g., C.Th. 11. 36. 1; 11. 36. 4; 9. 40. 4. and C. 9. 47. 18.

with the repression of various forms of abuse of power and dereliction of duty perpetrated by imperial officials and municipal magistrates. For example, the *crimen repetundarum* (crime of extortion) was extended so as to include all kinds of breaches of duty committed by state officials.[110] The definitions of *ambitus* (corruption) and the *crimen maiestatis* (treason) were similarly broadened[111] and more severe penalties were introduced for the offence of *peculatus* (the misappropriation of state property), including deportation and, in some cases, the death penalty.[112] Moreover, under the crime of *sacrilegium* were now treated various offences involving neglect or violation of imperial enactments.[113] The concept of *vis* (violence) was also extended to cover various kinds of abuses committed by private citizens or state officials and the penalties imposed on offenders became more severe (they included deportation, confiscation of the culprit's property and, under Constantine, the death penalty). Certain wrongdoings involving violence, such as castration,[114] circumcision[115] and the exposure of babies incurred severe penalties, and those found guilty of crimes such as adultery, abduction, incest[116] and pederasty were now liable to capital punishment.[117] Moreover, after the recognition of Christianity as state religion, acts of opposition to the official religious doctrine, such as professing heretical views or refusing to observe religious holidays, were punished as crimes,[118] and various disabilities were imposed on renegades, pagans and Jews.[119] As criminal offences were also punished certain forbidden marriages, such as marriage between a Roman and a foreigner,[120]

---

110 See D. 48. 11. 1. pr. (Marcianus).

111 *Ambitus* now covered any attempt to climb faster or hold a rank longer in the imperial civil service contrary to established regulations. See C.Th. 9. 26 passim. Within the scope of *maiestas* now fell offences such as coining or maintaining a private prison. See C.Th. 9. 11. 1; 9. 21. 9. and C. 9. 24. 3.

112 C. 9. 28.

113 As was note earlier, imperial decrees were regarded as deriving their authority from the divine will. Consider on this C. 9. 29.

114 C. 4. 42; *Nov*. 142.

115 C.Th. 16. 9. 1 and 2; and see C. 1. 10. 1; C.Th. 16. 8. 26.

116 The scope of incest was extended to include the union between uncles and nephews as well as that between cousins.

117 C.Th. 11. 36. 4; C. 9. 9. 29. 4; *Nov*. 117. 5. Severe penalties, including deportation, were also imposed on those found guilty of *lenocinium* (procuring adultery or other forms of sexual misconduct).

118 Consider C.Th. 16. 2. 31. and C. 1. 3. 10.

119 C.Th. 16. 10. 4. and C. 1. 11. 1. and 9; C.Th. 16. 9. 1. and C. 1. 10. 1; C.Th. 9. 7. 5. and C. 1. 9. 6; C.Th. 16. 5. 1. and C. 1. 5. 1; 1. 5. 20.

120 C.Th. 3. 14. 1.

between a Christian and a Jew[121] and between a freedman and his female patron (or the daughter or former wife of his male patron).

The penalties that a judge could impose were prescribed by law and, as was noted earlier, varied according to the social status of the offender. Among the most frequently imposed punishments were death, deportation, forced labour in the mines, confiscation of property, corporal punishment (usually imposed on members of the lower classes and slaves) and various monetary penalties.[122] Certain forms of punishment available in earlier times were modified or abolished. For example, the *aqua et ignis interdictio* was replaced by the *deportatio* and, under the influence of Christianity, death by crucifixion and gladiatorial combat were abolished.[123] But other cruel forms of punishment, such as mutilation and burning at the stake, were retained and in fact were more widely used than before. In general, the criminal law of the post-classical period was brutal and often inefficient. Little attention was paid in practice to the requirements of liability and the rules governing criminal procedure and, as imperial legislation on criminal matters was fragmentary and often inconsistent, the arbitrary exercise of power by those in charge of the administration of justice seems to have increased.[124]

The Germanic Codes of Roman Law

As we saw in chapter 9, by the end of the fifth century the western provinces of the empire had fallen into the hands of various Germanic tribes and a host of new kingdoms had arisen in the West. Despite the fact that large numbers of Germans had settled in the lands of the former Roman empire of the West, the majority of the population remained Roman. In most of the newly established kingdoms Germans and Romans lived side by side as separate peoples, each governed by its own laws and

---

[121] C.Th. 9. 7. 5; 3. 7. 2.

[122] The various penalties which normally entailed a loss of personal dignity for the offender were now referred to under the general term *poenae existimationis*.

[123] C.Th. 9. 40. 8.

[124] On the development of Roman criminal law and procedure during the post-classical period see O. F. Robinson, *The Criminal Law of Ancient Rome*, London 1995, 11-14; J. Harries, *Law and Empire in Late Antiquity*, Cambridge 1999, chapters 6-7; A. Burdese, *Diritto pubblico romano*, 3rd edn,Turin 1987, repr. 1994, 267-9; B. Santalucia, *Diritto e processo penale nell' antica Roma*, Milan 1989, ch. 7; V. Giuffrè, La repressione criminale nell' esperienza romana, Naples 1998, chapters 7-8; M. Talamanca (ed.), *Lineamenti di storia del diritto romano*, Milan 1989, 580 ff.

customs. In general, the Germanic kings did not attempt to impose their own systems of law upon the Romans, nor did they adopt Roman law for their own subjects.[125] Thus, in the West the once universal system of Roman law was replaced by what may be described as a conglomeration of legal systems: the Roman part of the population and the clergy continued to be governed by Roman law (*leges romanae*), whilst the Germanic tribes were observing their own systems of law (*leges barbarorum*). The principle that now prevailed was that of the personality of the laws: the law applicable to a person was determined not by the territory in which he lived but by the national group to which he belonged. However, the confusion surrounding the state of the law that resulted from the deterioration of the Roman culture in the West made the administration of Roman law very difficult for the courts and lawyers of this period. To deal with this problem some German kings considered it necessary to lay down, alongside their own Germanic laws, codes of Roman law for their Roman subjects. Of these codes the most important were the *Lex Romana Visigothorum*, the *Lex Romana Burgundionum* and the *Edictum Theoderici*. Although the law contained in these compilations was only a crude version of the classical system, their importance for the study of Roman law is great. Besides providing a picture of the state of the law and society at the beginning of the Middle Ages, they preserved for us a number of Roman legal texts which cannot be found in any of the surviving Roman sources.[126]

The *Lex Romana Visigothorum*

The *Lex Romana Visigothorum*, also known as the Breviary of Alaric (*Breviarium Alarici*), was issued in 506 by the king of the Visigoths Alaric II for his Roman subjects. It contains materials from the Gregorian, Hermogenian and Theodosian Codes, a number of post-Theodosian constitutions, an abbreviated version of Gaius's Institutes (*Epitome Gai*),

---

[125] At the same time many of them, although in reality independent, regarded themselves as governing under the authority of the Roman emperors of the East and, in this way, a fiction of unity between West and East was maintained.

[126] On the Germanic codes see in general H. F. Jolowicz and B. Nicholas, *Historical Introduction to the Study of Roman Law*, 3rd edn, Cambridge 1972,466-8; W. Kunkel, *An Introduction to Roman Legal and Constitutional History*, 2nd edn, Oxford 1973, 159-62; M. Kaser, *Römische Rechtsgeschichte*, Göttingen 1976, 235 ff; W. Kunkel/M. Schermaier, *Römische Rechtsgeschichte*, Cologne 2001, 204 ff; A. Guarino, *Storia del diritto romano*, Naples 1996, 563 ff; M. Talamanca (ed.), *Lineamenti di storia del diritto romano*, Milan 1989, 623 ff.

fragments from the *Sententiae* of Paul and a short *responsum* of Papinian as a conclusion. The various passages appear largely unaltered but many of them are accompanied by interpretations, i.e. summaries or paraphrases of the original texts aimed at facilitating their understanding and application.[127] As the *Lex Romana Visigothorum* was intended to replace all other sources of law, it was proclaimed that imperial constitutions and juristic opinions not included in it had no binding force in the courts of law.[128] But in the middle of the seventh century, with the shift from the system of personal laws to a territorial system, it was replaced by another lawbook, known as *Codex Legis Visigothorum* (or *Lex Visigothorum Recesvindiana*), which was to apply to both the Roman and Gothic subjects of the Visigothic kingdom in Spain.[129] In France, however, the *Lex Romana Visigothorum* continued to be used for almost five hundred years after its enactment (even though no longer as an official code) and contributed to the preservation of the knowledge of Roman law and its later reception in that part of western Europe.[130]

The *Lex Romana Burgundionum*

The Roman Law of the Burgundians (*Lex Romana Burgundionum*) was drafted during the reign of the Burgundian king Gundobad and was enacted by his son Sigismund in 517 AD for use by the Roman inhabitants of his kingdom. Like the Visigothic Code of Roman law mentioned above, it draws on the Gregorian, Hermogenian and Theodosian Codes, an abbreviated version of the Institutes of Gaius and the *Sententiae* of Paul. But, unlike the former compilation, it contains no extracts from the original Roman sources; instead, the materials are incorporated into a set of newly formulated rules which are systematically arranged and distributed over

---

[127] These interpretations were clearly influenced by the *Vulgarrecht* and were probably derived from earlier sources.

[128] The surviving copy of the Visigothic Code of Roman law is addressed to a count (*comes*) named Timotheus and is officially certified by one Anianus, presumably a royal secretary. The aims of the code are proclaimed to be 'the correction of what seems unfair in the laws; the clearing up of the complexities which are present either in the written Roman laws or in the unwritten principles of ancient law; the removal of all abstrusiveness and the gathering within a single book of selected extracts from the works of earlier jurists'.

[129] This new code was in part based upon the *Lex Romana Visigothorum*.

[130] For a modern reconstruction of the Visigothic Code of Roman law see G. Hänel, *Lex Romana Visigothorum*, Lipsiae 1849, repr. 1962. See also FIRA II, 667 ff. (appendices only). And see R. Lambertini, *La codificazione di Alarico II*, Turin 1991.

forty-seven titles.[131] As a source of information on the Roman system the Burgundian lawbook is inferior to the *Lex Romana Visigothorum* for, besides lacking direct references to the original Roman sources, both its contents and structure reflect a stronger Germanic influence. The *Lex Romana Burgundionum* fell into abeyance soon after the Burgundian kingdom was taken over by the Franks in the middle of the sixth century, and does not appear to have had any notable influence on legal developments during the Middle Ages.[132]

The *Edictum Theodorici*

The *Edictum Theodorici* was issued in the second half of the fifth century and is probably the earliest of the Germanic compilations of Roman law. In the past it was believed that it was the work of the king of the Ostrogoths Theodoric the Great (493-526 AD) and that it had been issued for the Roman subjects of the Ostrogothic kingdom of northern Italy. The current view, however, is that it was enacted by king Theodoric II (453-466 AD), ruler of the Visigothic kingdom of southern France, and applied to both Romans and Visigoths alike. The *Edictum Theodorici* is made up of 154 titles and contains extracts from the *Sententiae* of Paul, the Gregorian, Hermogenian and Theodosian Codes and some post-Theodosian constitutions.[133]

The Codification of Justinian

Introductory

The Roman imperial government had always been inefficient in systematising the enormous legal repository which centuries of imperial edicts and juristic opinions had created. The Theodosian Code (438 AD), the first official codification of the law, was from the outset incomplete, for it ignored that important part of Roman law built upon the commentaries of the classical jurists. Although the Law of Citations (426 AD), concerning the authority of juristic works, remained in force, it did not achieve legal certainty, as these works were great in number, contained

[131] The order of the topics is the same as in the *Lex Condobada*, an earlier compilation issued for the Germanic part of the population.

[132] For a modern reconstruction of the *Lex Romana Burgundionum* see R. L. De Salis, MGH, *Leges* I. 2, Hanover 1892; and see FIRA II, 711 ff.

[133] See F. Bluhme (ed.), MGH, *Leges* I. 5, Hanover 1875-1889; FIRA II, 681 ff. Consider also G. Vismara, *Edictum Theodorici*, Milan 1967.

a tremendous amount of cases and problems and abounded in disputes and contradictions.[134] Moreover, in the years following the enactment of the Theodosian Code, a large number of new imperial laws were issued and many the constitutions contained in the Code became obsolete. Under these conditions legal practitioners and state officials often found it very difficult to discover just what the current state of the law was. What was urgently needed was a comprehensive and authoritative statement of the law, making clear the changes brought about by post-Theodosian legislation and removing the uncertainty surrounding the content and authority of juristic works. Producing such a statement was among the first tasks which Justinian set himself when he became emperor in 527 AD. At the same time, he resolved to centralise and thereby control the teaching and interpretation of the law and to improve the quality of legal education. Accordingly, commissions consisting of jurists and imperial officials were assigned the task of reading thousands of legal works stretching back over hundreds of years of legal development with these goals: (a) the collection and editing with a view to their current applicability of all imperial laws which had been promulgated up to that time; (b) the gathering together and bringing into harmony the opinions of the Roman jurists; and (c) the creation of a standard textbook which would clearly and systematically introduce the first principles of the law to students. The key figure in this undertaking was Tribonian, head of the imperial chanceries (*quaestor sacri palatii*) and, from 530 AD, minister of justice (*magister officiorum*).[135] Of great importance was also the contribution of Theophilus, professor (*antecessor*) at the law-school of Constantinople, and Dorotheus and Anatolius, who taught law at the law-school of Beirut.

---

[134] The revival of interest in the works of classical jurisprudence in the law-schools of the East in a way contributed to the confusion that beset the practice of law in the post-classical period. As W. Kunkel has remarked, 'Unlike those elementary works which contained a fairly manageable number of...principles and decisions which could be used when needed even by lawyers of low intellectual standing, the later classical writings contained an infinite abundance of cases and problems and, above all, innumerable disputes and contradictions. It is thus easily credible that the reanimation of classical law in the eastern Empire, though it might raise the level of judicial activity, was none the less bound to exacerbate the difficulties of the practitioners ... and to make especially urgent a legislative limitation and simplification of the whole body of inherited legal material'. *An Introduction to Roman Legal and Constitutional History*, 2nd edn, Oxford 1973, 162.

[135] See Procop., *Anecd.* 13. 12. and 20. 16-17. On the life and work of Tribonian see T. Honore, *Tribonian*, London 1978.

The Code

The old Code

On 13 February 528 AD Justinian, by means of an imperial constitution known as *Constitutio Haec*, assigned to a ten-member commission composed of high officials and advocates, including Tribonian and the jurist Theophilus, the task of consolidating into a single code all the imperial enactments still valid. The commissioners drafted, in accordance with their instructions, a code drawing from the Gregorian, Hermogenian and Theodosian Codes and from constitutions issued between 438 and 529, omitting all obsolete laws and also changing some so as to bring them up to date. The constitutions were classified according to subject-matter and were arranged in chronological order under separate titles. On 7 April 529 the work was published under the name *Codex Iustinianus* and was given the force of law as from 16 April 529 (*Constitutio Summa*). The *Codex Iustinianus* replaced the earlier codes, and imperial enactments not included in it were forbidden to be quoted in the courts of law (with a few exceptions). However, the mass of new legislation issued by Justinian after 529 soon rendered the Code obsolete and, in 534 AD, it was superseded by a revised edition. All that has come down to us from Justinian's first Code, referred to as *Codex vetus* (the old Code), is an index found on a fragment of papyrus in Egypt in the early nineteenth century.[136]

The second Code

At the beginning of 534 AD Justinian informed the senate of Constantinople that he had commissioned Tribonian, Dorotheus and three advocates to prepare a revised edition of the Code. The revised Code was to incorporate, under appropriate titles, the large number of imperial enactments that had been issued subsequent to the first Code, including the 'Fifty Decisions' (*quinquaginta decisiones*), a series of ordinances issued by Justinian for the purpose of settling certain controversial questions arising from the works of the classical jurists.[137] As with the first Code, the

---

136 *P. Oxy*. XV 1814. See B. P. Grenfell, A. S. Hunt, *The Oxyrhynchus Papyri*, London 1898. And see P. E. Pieler, *Byzantinische Rechtsliteratur* in H. Hunger, *Die hochsprachliche profane Literatur der Byzantiner*, Bd. 2, Munich 1978, 412 ff. Consider also P. de Francisi, 'Frammento di un indice del primo Codice Giustinianeo', 3 *Aegyptus* (1922), 68-79; P. Krüger, 'Neue juristische Funde aus Agypten', 43 *SZ* (1922), 560-3.

137 The Fifty Decisions were published as a single collection on 17 November 530 AD. No copy of the original collection has been preserved.

commission was instructed to omit all obsolete matter and to remove unnecessary repetitions and contradictions. The new Code was published under the name *Codex repetitae praelectionis* on 16 November 534 and came into force on 29 December 534 (*constitutio Cordi*). It was divided into twelve books which were in turn subdivided into titles according to subject with imperial enactments in chronological order under each title. The first book is concerned with jurisdiction and ecclesiastical matters; books two to eight deal with private law; book nine pertains to criminal law; and books ten to twelve cover matters of administrative law. The oldest of the approximately 4000 imperial enactments included in the Code date from the time of Hadrian (early second century AD), whilst the majority (approximately 1200 constitutions) originate from the reign of Diocletian (late third/early fourth century AD). About 400 of Justinian's own enactments are included. Each constitution is headed by the name of the emperor who had issued it and the names of the persons to whom it was addressed. The vast majority of the constitutions are written in Latin, but some of those issued by Justinian appear in Greek. As with the first Code, the new Code was to be the sole authority with respect to all imperial legislation that had been issued up to the date of its publication.[138] Shortly after its coming into force several copies of the Code were produced which, despite Justinian's prohibition, included commentaries and summaries by jurists of the time. Parts of one of these later manuscripts has come down to us through a palimpsest dating from the sixth or early seventh century. The text of the Code underwent considerable alterations in the hands of medieval commentators but, under the influence of the humanist movement, it was partly restored during the sixteenth and seventeenth centuries.[139]

The Digest or Pandects

After the publication of the first Code Justinian turned his attention to the goal of systematising that part of the law derived from the works of the classical jurists (*ius*). In the course of their work on the *Codex* the compilers encountered many questions on points of law upon which the classical authorities differed and which could not be settled under the Law

[138] Although it was provided that further enactments may be introduced in the future if any should be required.

[139] Modern scholars usually rely on the complete edition (*editio maior*) of the *Codex Iustinianus* published last century by P. Krüger (Berlin 1877). For the *editio stereotypa* (*minor*) see P. Krüger, *Codex Iustinianus*, in *Corpus Iuris Civilis* II, 11th edn, Berlin 1954, repr. Dublin and Zurich 1970. See also T. Honoré, *Tribonian*, London 1978, 212 ff.

of Citations. A condensation and simplification of the whole body of juridical literature was urgently needed and, as a preparatory step, Justinian issued the series of enactments known as 'Fifty Decisions' (*quinquaginta decisiones*), mentioned above. Following on from the Fifty Decisions, on 15 December 530 AD Justinian issued the *Constitutio Deo Auctore* by which he entrusted Tribonian with the task of setting up a commission to carry out the work of collecting, reviewing and presenting in an abridged form the whole mass of Roman law contained in the writings of the classical jurists. Tribonian formed a sixteen-member body consisting of Constantinus, a high imperial official, Theophilus and Cratinus, professors at the law school of Constantinople, Dorotheus and Anatolius, professors at the law school of Beirut, and eleven leading advocates. Like the compilers of the *Codex*, the members of Tribonian's commission were given wide discretionary powers. It rested with them to determine which juristic writings were to be included and which were to be omitted as superfluous, imperfect or obsolete; they could shorten the relevant texts, eliminate contradictions and correct and bring the matter up to date taking into consideration current legal practice and changes in the law brought about by imperial legislation. All the juristic works were to be considered (i.e. not only those of the five jurists mentioned in the Law of Citations) on their own merits and no special weight was to be given to opinions of any jurist because of his personal reputation or earlier influence.[140] Although the material relied upon stretched back over hundreds of years of legal development, the compilation, which was to be in the form of an anthology of the writings of the classical jurists with exact references, was to be a correct statement of the law at the time of its publication and the only authority in the future for jurisprudential works (and the imperial laws included in them).

Although the commission was given up to ten years to finish its work, remarkably, the compilation was completed in only three years. This was largely due to the dedication of Tribonian and the great interest which Justinian himself took in the project as well as the fact that the members of the commission, being well-versed in the classical authorities, were able to identify the most important fragments within a relatively short period of time. The work was published under the name *Digesta* or *Pandectae*[141] on 16 December 533 by means of the *Constitutio Tanta* (in Latin) or *Dedoken*

---

140 Justinian stipulated, however, that the commission was to avoid inserting matter already incorporated in the *Codex* and always indicate from which work of which jurist a fragment was taken.

141 *Digesta* (from *digerere*) means 'that which has been arranged or systematised'; *Pandecta* (from the Greek phrase '*pan dehesthe*') means 'an all embracing work' or 'encyclopaedia'.

(in Greek) and came into force on 30 December 533. From that date only juristic writings included in it were regarded as legally binding; references to the original works were now deemed superfluous and the publication of commentaries of a critical nature upon the Digest was prohibited. In the introductory constitution it is stated that the commissioners read nearly 2000 books containing 3,000,000 lines and that these were reduced to 150,000 lines; it is added, moreover, that 'many things and of highest importance' were changed in the process.[142] The Digest is divided into 50 books which (with the exception of books 30, 31 and 32) are subdivided into titles (*tituli*); each title is in turn subdivided into separate fragments (*fragmenta*), sections containing the text relevant to the topic indicated in the superscription of the title, the quoted jurist's name and the title and section of the work from which the quote was taken. Most of these fragments were further divided by later editors into paragraphs.[143] The Digest contains extracts from the works of thirty-nine jurists (mainly jurists to whom the emperors had given the *ius publice respondendi*); the earliest of these were Quintus Mucius Scaevola, Alfenus and Aelius Gallus, who lived in the later republican period. The vast majority of the fragments are derived from the writings of jurists of the classical era (100

---

142 There is some doubt as to whether these remarks should be understood literally (in reality the juristic works relied upon do not appear to have exceeded the 1625).

143 Indicating first the number of the relevant book and then those of the title, fragment and paragraph is the generally accepted method of making references to the Digest. It should be added here that the *constitutio Tanta* or *Dedoken*, by which the Digest was formally introduced, provided for a division of the materials into seven parts (paras 2-8). The first part, entitled '*Prota*' (Books 1-4), contains general rules relating to the administration of justice (public officials, jurisdiction, the treatment of certain categories of persons etc); the second part (Books 5-11) is entitled *De iudiciis* and deals with real actions and judicial proceedings; contracts and personal actions is the subject-matter of the third part, entitled *De rebus* (Books 12-19); the fourth part (Books 20-27) bears the title *Umbilicus Pandectarum* and is concerned, among other things, with matters of marriage, guardianship, the rights of mortgagees etc; in part five (Books 28-36) various rules relating to wills, legacies and testamentary trusts are included under the heading *De testamentis*; these are followed in part 6 (Books 37-44) by rules governing the acquisition of ownership and possession of property, intestate succession, interdicts, exceptions etc; finally, part seven (Books 45-50) covers matters such as obligations and civil injuries, local government, public works, appeals, criminal offences (included in Books 47 and 48 entitled '*libri terribiles*'), the meaning of legal terms and maxims of the law. This division, which was introduced mainly for educational purposes, is of historical significance only.

AD-250 AD), especially Ulpian, whose opinions make up approximately one-third of the entire Digest, Paul, Papinian, Pomponius, Julianus and Gaius.[144] The extensive use of some of the latter jurists' writings is not unrelated to the fact that these writings were the most recent and most widely used and therefore the best preserved.

Considering the enormity of the task and the time in which it was accomplished, questions have arisen as to the method followed by the compilers of the Digest in carrying out their work. How was it possible that they themselves actually read through the entire body of juristic writings, selected materials, abridged and made changes to the texts in such a short period of time? An answer to this question was given by the German legal historian Friedrich Bluhme in the early nineteenth century and his theory is still accepted by most scholars today.[145] According to Bluhme, the way in which the fragments are grouped and ordered under each title suggests that the various juristic writings were divided into three sections (or 'masses', as Bluhme calls them), and that each section was the subject of the work of a separate sub-committee. One group of fragments, referred to by Bluhme as the 'Sabinian mass', consists of extracts from the commentaries of Ulpian, Paul and others on the *ius civile* arranged according to the system devised originally by the classical jurist Sabinus in his work *Libri tres iuris civilis*. The second group, which is known as the 'edictal mass', is made up of commentaries of classical authors on the *edictum perpetuum* (*ad edictum*) and other closely related texts. This group of works is concerned mainly with the *ius honorarium* as distinct from the rest of the *ius civile*, which is considered in the Sabinian mass. The third group, which Bluhme calls the 'Papinian mass', contains juristic opinions (*quaestiones, responsa, epistulae*) of Paul, Ulpian and Papinian, as well as extracts from similar works of other jurists. Bluhme also distinguished a smaller fourth category, referred to as the 'post-Papinian' or 'appendix mass', consisting of fragments from works of various kinds not included in the first three groups. After the different sub-committees completed their work on each group of juristic materials their members met to piece together and consolidate the selected fragments into a coherent whole.[146]

---

144 Only three jurists of the post-classical period are included.

145 F. Bluhme 'Die Ordnung der Fragmente in den Pandektentiteln', *Zeitschrift für geschichtliche Rechtswissenschaft* 4 (1820), 257-472; also in *Labeo* 6 (1960), 50 ff, 235 ff, 368 ff.

146 A different hypothesis as to how the Digest was constructed has been put forward by H. Peters. Peters proposed that in the law schools of the East there existed a work on the *ius* (a 'pre-Digest'), put together for instructional purposes, and that this work was relied upon as a model by the compilers of Justinian's Digest. This theory, although it attracted some attention in the past,

In ordering the preparation of the Digest Justinian was concerned with preserving the substance of classical Roman law and, at the same time, with formulating a workable body of law adapted to the conditions and needs of his own time. Achieving both these objectives, however, was an almost impossible undertaking. In abridging, harmonising and bringing up to date the various juristic writings the compilers of the Digest made various changes (additions, suppressions, substitutions) in the texts which sometimes distorted their original meaning and misrepresented the intentions of the classical authors. These changes later became known as 'interpolations' (*interpolationes* or '*emblemata Triboniani*'). It is also very likely that the texts had to some extent already been changed in the period that preceded the Justinianic codification. This may have been due to errors during the copying of the original manuscripts, to modifications made during the re-editing of the works by post-classical compilers and also to the insertion of marginal or interlinear notes into the texts.[147] This has been known, of course, for many centuries and, from the beginning of the twentieth century, numerous studies have been conducted aimed at identifying the 'interpolations' and at discovering what the classical jurists actually wrote (largely through a linguistic analysis of the texts). However, the emphasis placed by some scholars on the need to restore the juristic texts to their original, classical form has led to much exaggeration as to the nature of the work done by the compilers of the Digest and the extent to which they altered the texts. At present a much more careful approach to the matter is followed, as scholars came to realise that it would have been hardly possible for the compilers to have effected all the changes attributed to them in the short time in which they completed their work. In general, it is accepted that the texts relied upon by the compilers were largely the same as they were in classical times; at the same time it is recognised that, as the texts had been re-written and had been handed down in more than one tier or edition, the compilers may have incorporated changes that would have inevitably been made to the original works in the intervening

---

is considered to lack sufficient grounds of support. See H. Peters, 'Die oströmischen Digestenkommentare und die Entstehung der Digesten', *BerSachGW* (1913), 65. (A similar thesis has been propounded by G. Hofmann in *Die Kompilation der Digesten*, Vienna 1900.) For more on the construction of the Digest consider T. Honoré, *Tribonian*, London 1978, ch. 5; T. Honoré and A. Rodger, 'How the Digest Commissioners Worked', *SZ* 87 (1970), 246; D. Mantovani, *Digesto e Masse Bluhmiane*, Milan 1987; D. Osler, 'The Compilation of Justinian's Digest', *SZ* 102 (1985), 129-84.

147 The use of 'interpolations' as a method of reconciling and updating earlier legal materials had been introduced well before the time of Justinian (a similar method was used, e.g., by the compilers of the Theodosian Code).

three hundred years. Moreover, there is no doubt that a number of modifications were made by the compilers themselves under the influences of the day and in their attempt to eliminate contradictions and to bring the matter up to date.[148] A text is likely to be regarded as altered where it appears to deviate from the same text as it has come down to us via another reliable source (such as the Vatican Fragments or the Institutes of Gaius). Moreover, texts dealing with legal concepts which are known to have been obsolete in Justinian's times may be presumed to have been interpolated as they had to be brought up to date.[149]

The earliest surviving copy of the Digest dates from the sixth century (c. 550 AD) and was probably one of the approximately eighty copies produced in Constantinople for use by various government departments. A note on the relevant manuscript suggests that it was in Italy in the ninth or tenth century and it is known to have been in Pisa in the late eleventh century. In 1406, when Pisa was captured by the Florentines, it was taken to Florence where it has been kept ever since (hence it has become known as *Littera Florentina* or *Codex Florentinus*).[150] This manuscript provided the basis for most of the later editions of the Digest.[151] Several other manuscript copies of the Digest date from the Middle Ages and, more specifically, from the period associated with the revival of Roman legal

---

148 It must be remembered that in the eastern Roman empire, over which Justinian reigned, Greek influences were particularly strong and his codification was influenced by local conditions. In addition to that, Christianity had become the official religion of the empire and changes had to be made in the legal texts to ensure that the law accorded with certain aspects of Christian religious doctrine.

149 See on this H. F. Jolowicz and B. Nicholas, *Historical Introduction to the Study of Roman Law*, 3rd edn, Cambridge 1972, 486 ff; O. F. Robinson, *The Sources of Roman Law*, London and New York 1997, 105 ff; O. Tellegen-Couperus, *A Short History of Roman Law* , London and New York 1993, 143; M. Kaser, *Römische Rechtsgeschichte*, Göttingen 1976, 248-9, 257 ff. Consider also M. Kaser, *Zur Methodologie der römischen Rechtsquellenforschung*, Vienna, Cologne and Graz 1972; A. Watson, '*Prolegomena* to establishing pre-Justinianic texts', 62 *TR* (1994), 113-125.

150 Originally it was referred to as *Littera Pisana*.

151 For a photographic copy of this manuscript see A. Corbino and B. Santalucia (eds), *Justiniani augusti Pandectarum Codex Florentinus*, Florence 1988. Among the most important early editions of the Digest are those of Gothofredus (1583) and Spangenberg (1776-1791). The most complete edition is that of T. Mommsen and P. Krüger, under the title *Digesta Iustiniani Augusti*, Berlin 1868-1870, repr. 1962-1963. For a shorter version of this see T. Mommsen and P. Krüger, *Iustiniani Digesta* in *Corpus Iuris Civilis* I (pars 2a), 16th edn, Berlin 1954, repr. Dublin and Zurich 1973. For an English translation see A. Watson, *The Digest of Justinian*, Philadelphia 1985.

studies in the West (11th - 14th centuries).[152] Parts of the Digest have also come down to us in Greek through the *Basilica*, a Byzantine compilation published in the tenth century during the reign of Emperor Leo the Wise.[153]

The Institutes

As an authoritative statement of the law, the Digest was intended to be used not only by legal practitioners and state officials but also by those engaged in the study of law. However, even before it was published, it became obvious that the work was far too long and complex for students to use, especially for those in their first year of their studies. What was needed was an introductory textbook which would allow students to grasp the basic principles of the law before passing on to the more detailed and more complex aspects of legal practice.[154] It was with this idea in mind that Justinian ordered, in 533 AD, the preparation of a new official legal textbook for use in the empire's law schools. The task was entrusted to a three-member commission consisting of Tribonian, Theophilus and Dorotheus. The commissioners were instructed to produce a book that was to reflect the law of their own time, leaving out obsolete matter but including, where necessary, some mention of the earlier law. The work was to be based on the Institutes of Gaius and other introductory legal works of the classical period. The completed work was confirmed on 21 November 533 AD under the name *Institutiones* or *Elementa* (*Constitutio Imperatoriam maiestatem*) and came into force as an imperial statute, together with the Digest, on 30 December 533 AD (*Constitutio Tanta* or *Dedoken*).[155]

With respect to both content and structure, the Institutes borrowed much from the Institutes of Gaius (about two-thirds of the entire work consists of materials taken from Gaius's Institutes), as well as from another work attributed to Gaius called 'Law in Daily Life' (*res cottidianae*); the commissioners drew also on institutional works of other authors, such as Ulpian, Paul, Marcian and Florentinus, and on various classical

[152] Medieval scholars of the school of the Glossators introduced a division of the Digest into three parts: *Digestum Vetus* (books 1-24), *Infortiatum* (books 24-38) and *Digestum Novum* (books 39-50). See chapter 11.

[153] The compilers of the *Basilica* relied on various works based on Justinian's legislation, including an important abridgment of the Digest produced by an unknown author. On the *Basilica* see chapter 11.

[154] The Institutes of Gaius, which had been used for centuries as an introductory textbook by law students, was now regarded as obsolete in many respects.

[155] The work was carried out by Theophilus and Dorotheus, each producing two of the four books of the Institutes, under the supervision of Tribonian.

commentaries. Moreover, the Institutes incorporated many of Justinian's own enactments and legal reforms. The authors of the Institutes retained Gaius's division of the law into three parts (the law of persons, the law of things and the law of actions) as well as his division of the material into four books (but, unlike Gaius's Institutes, the books are subdivided into titles).[156] Book one is concerned with the law of persons (except for an introductory preface on jurisprudential matters and the sources of law), books two, three and part of book four deal with the law of things, with the law of actions taking up the remainder of book four. In book four Gaius's discussion of the *legis actio* and the *per formulam* procedure has been replaced by a brief description of the *cognitio extra ordinem* (the procedure used in the post-classical period) followed by two titles on the duties of a judge (*de officio iudicis*) and on criminal law (*de publicis iudiciis*). Unlike the Digest, where the material is presented as a collection of extracts, the authors of the Institutes adopted a narrative style, sacrificing citations and attributions but producing a blended, continuous essay under each title to increase readability. However, the method of composition appears to have been similar to that followed by the compilers of the Digest, as the provenance of the individual passages is discoverable, although the process of creating the impression of a continuous text would have involved a different management of the extracts than that required in the preparation of the Digest.

Of the numerous manuscript copies of the Institutes which were produced in Justinian's time none has survived (with the exception of a few fragments dating from the sixth century). The work has come down to us mainly through various manuscript copies dating from the eleventh century or later.[157] These, combined with the text of Gaius's Institutes discovered in 1816, furnished the basis for most of the modern reconstructions of the Institutes.[158]

---

156 The standard way of making references to the Institutes is to indicate the number of the relevant book first followed by the numbers of the title and paragraph.

157 The earliest printed edition of the Institutes appeared in 1468 but the first scholarly edition was produced by Cujas in 1585.

158 The definitive modern edition of the Institutes is P. Krüger's *Iustiniani Institutiones*, *Corpus Iuris Civilis* I (pars 1a), Berlin 1872. For English translations see J. A. C., Thomas, *The Institutes of Justinian*, Cape Town 1975; P. B. H. Birks and G. MacLeod, *Justinian's Institutes*, New York 1987.

The Novels

In the years following the publication of the second edition of the Code (534 AD) Justinian's legislative activity continued unabated as political and social developments necessitated changes in the law not foreseen by earlier legislation. Over one hundred and fifty 'Novels' (*Novellae constitutiones*), as the new imperial laws came to be referred to, were issued, the majority before Tribonian's death in 546 AD. Although most of them pertained to administrative and ecclesiastical law, Justinian also introduced important innovations in certain areas of private law, such as family law and the law of intestate succession. The majority of these laws were issued in Greek, the language of business in the eastern part of the empire, some in Greek and Latin, and some only in Latin, especially those which were addressed to the western provinces of the empire or contained supplementary provisions to earlier enactments that had been composed in Latin. Although they were intended to be officially collected and published as part of a new edition of the Code,[159] this never happened. What is known of them comes mainly from three later compilations based upon a few private and unofficial collections produced during and after Justinian's reign.

Of the three compilations of Novels that have come down to us the earliest one is the *Epitome novellarum Iuliani*, an abridged version of a collection of 124 constitutions from the period 535-555 AD composed during the reign of Justinian by Julian, a professor (*antecessor*) at the law school of Constantinople. It was probably intended for use in recently reconquered Italy, as indicated by the fact that the constitutions it contains were translated from Greek into Latin.[160] The second collection, also written in Latin, contains 134 constitutions issued during the period 535-536 AD. It is uncertain when it was originally produced – it may have been made in the sixth century but the oldest manuscript copies date from the late eleventh or early twelfth century. This collection is known as the *Authenticum* (or *liber Authenticorum*), a name given to it by the Glossator Irnerius (11th century) who regarded it as an official collection of Novels promulgated by Justinian for use in Italy after its reconquest. However, the prevalent view today is that Irnerius was mistaken and that the collection, which contains only the Latin Novels in their original text and the Greek ones in a faulty Latin translation, was prepared mainly as a teaching aid for

---

[159] See *constitutio Cordi* 4.

[160] The oldest manuscript copies date from the late seventh or early eighth centuries. For a modern reconstruction of Julian's collection see G. Hänel, *Iuliani Epitome Latina Novellarum Iustiniani*, Lipsiae 1873.

use in the law schools of the East.[161] The most complete collection of Novels is the *Collectio Graeca*, a compilation of 168 constitutions issued in Greek by Justinian and his successors Justin II (565-578 AD) and Tiberius II (578-582 AD).[162] It was published after 575 AD, probably during the reign of Tiberius II, and has come down to us through two manuscripts dating from the thirteen and fourteenth centuries. One of these manuscripts, which is kept in Venice, contains thirteen additional Novels (two of these can also be found in the other manuscript) which are referred to as *Edicta Iustiniani*. This collection, which was used by the compilers of the *Basilica*, does not appear to have been known in western Europe until the fifteenth century – it was introduced there by Byzantine scholars who fled to Italy after the fall of Constantinople to the Ottoman Turks in 1453 and was brought to light by the humanist scholars of the fifteenth and sixteenth centuries.[163]

The *Corpus Iuris Civilis*

The Code (*Codex repetitae praelectionis*), the Digest, the Institutes and the Novels make up the bulk of Justinian's legislative work. All four compilations together constitute what is known as *Corpus Iuris Civilis*. The latter term did not originate in Justinian's time,[164] however, but was first introduced in 1583 by Dionysius Godofredus (1549-1622), author of

---

[161] For a modern edition of this collection see G. E. Heimach, *Authenticum, Novellarum constitutionum Iustiniani versio vulgata*, I-II, Lipsiae 1846-1851. And see P. E. Pieler, *Byzantinische Rechtsliteratur*, in H. Hunger, *Die hochsprachliche profane Literatur der Byzantiner*, Bd. 2, Munich 1978, 409 ff, 425 ff; N. van der Wal and J. H. A. Lokin, *Historiae iuris graeco-romani delineatio. Les sources du droit byzantin de* 300 a *1453*, Groningen 1985, 37-38.

[162] Four constitutions of Justin II and three of Tiberius II have been included in this collection which also contains some further texts which are not imperial constitutions at all but decrees of *praefecti praetorio*.

[163] The *Collectio Graeca* (together with the *Edicta* and other constitutions of Justinian) provided the basis for the modern standard edition of the Novels prepared by R. Scholl and G. Kroll in 1895 (in this the Novels are divided into chapters and paragraphs). See *Novellae, Corpus Iuris Civilis* III, 10th edn, Berlin 1972. For the Novels that have survived in various papyri and inscriptions see M. Amelotti and L. Migliardi Zingale, *Le costituzioni Giustinianee nei papiri e nelle epigrafi* , Milan 1985.

[164] In the Code Justinian refers to his work as pertaining to the 'whole body oflaw' ('*in omni...corpore iuris*'). C. 5. 13. 1. pr.

the first scholarly edition of Justinian's work, in contradistinction to the codification of the canon law (referred to as *Corpus Iuris Canonici*).[165]

Some comments on the character of the Justinianic codification

The outstanding feature of Justinian's reign is its focus on the idea of unity – unity in territory, in religion, in law. In this respect, the compilations of law made under his authority should be viewed as interconnected parts of an organic whole. Through the codification of the law Justinian sought to produce, on the basis of the legal inheritance of the past, a complete and authoritative statement of the law of his own day that would replace all former statements of law in both juridical literature and legislation. In this way he hoped to make the law uniform throughout the empire and, at the same time, to preserve the best of classical jurisprudence, displacing the diffuse mass of legal materials that had caused so much confusion in the past. The tendency towards a return to the classical sources that characterises Justinian's legislative work reflects his ambition to restore the empire to its former greatness. It is also connected with the revival of legal learning in the law schools of the East, where the works of the classical Roman jurists were studied and held in respect.

Justinian's intention to produce a living system of law based on classical foundations is particularly evident in the Digest, the largest and perhaps most important part of his codification. But having been completed in such haste and involving such a massive reduction of the classical texts, the work was in many respects imperfect and, contrary to Justinian's instructions, reproduced contradictions and repetitions which were exacerbated by the mutilation and alteration of the original texts. As a result, the law it contained was neither the authentic law of the classical period nor an accurate statement of the law of Justinian's own day, but a layered amalgam which ignored many of the post-classical changes. As such it was in many respects alien to current conditions and practices and thus very difficult to use in practice as a source of law. It should therefore come as no surprise that, despite Justinian's orders to the contrary, his compilations were translated into Greek, abbreviated, commented upon and continuously modified for use in the Byzantine East.[166] In the West, where Germanic kingdoms had overrun the empire, Justinian's legislative work was in the course of time largely forgotten. It was to take nearly five centuries before it was re-discovered and made the object first of academic

---

[165] A.A. Schiller, *Roman Law: Mechanisms of Development*, New York 1978, 29.
[166] See chapter 11.

study and, subsequently, of far-reaching reception, i.e. a reintegration as valid law in large parts of western Europe.

With the codification of Justinian comes to an end the first period of the history of Roman law. Although he failed to achieve his cherished goal of rebuilding the old Roman empire, Justinian did succeed in collecting together and preserving for the future the bulk of the Roman legal heritage – an immense body of imperial laws and juristic literature stretching back over hundreds of years of legal development. Whatever its limitations, the *Corpus Iuris Civilis* is one of the greatest monuments of legal activity the world has known. It was of tremendous importance in later western Europe where it supplied the common ground upon which the civil law systems of most Continental European countries were built. As a historical source, it provides a comprehensive picture of the way in which Roman law and legal thinking evolved from the first century BC up to the sixth century AD and says a great deal about the state of the law and society during the early Byzantine era. [167]

---

[167] On the codification of Justinian see in general H. F. Jolowicz and B. Nicholas, *Historical Introduction to the Study of Roman Law*, 3rd edn, Cambridge 1972, ch. 29; W. Kunkel, *An Introduction to Roman Legal and Constitutional History*, 2nd edn, Oxford 1973, ch. 11; A. A. Schiller, *Roman Law: Mechanisms of Development*, New York 1978, 29 ff; O. Tellegen-Couperus, *A Short History of Roman Law*, London & New York 1993, 140 ff; O. F. Robinson, *The Sources of Roman Law*, London 1997, 57-60; M. Kaser, *Römische Rechtsgeschichte*, Göttingen 1976, 243 ff; W. Kunkel/M. Schermaier, *Römische Rechtsgeschichte*, Cologne 2001, 209 ff; A. Guarino, *Storia del diritto romano*, Naples 1996, 570 ff; M. Talamanca (ed.), *Lineamenti di storia del diritto romano*, Milan 1989, ch. 5. See also T. Honoré, *Tribonian*, London 1978.

11 The History of Roman Law after Justinian

The Legislation of Justinian in the East: Byzantine Law

The historical framework of Byzantine law

We saw in chapter 9 that by the end of the fourth century the Roman empire had in effect been split into two independent states (even though contemporaries did not regard this as a formal division). After a long period marked by economic and cultural decay, foreign invasions and internal strife the Roman empire of the West finally came to an end in 476 AD, when the last Western emperor was overthrown by his German mercenaries. The loss of the western provinces transferred the centre of gravity in the empire from the Latin to the Greek element and accelerated the transformation of the Roman empire of the East into the medieval Byzantine empire. Byzantium inherited from Rome a great deal of her political, social and cultural institutions; Roman law remained in force as a living system, and the concept of *imperium Romanum*, now in the form of *imperium Christianum*, furnished the basis of Byzantine political theory. Though the elements of continuity between the Byzantine world and the world of antiquity are clear and undeniable, so too are the differences. Byzantine civilisation was a new cultural synthesis based on the classical traditions of antiquity but combined with important new elements introduced by the upheavals of the later imperial era and by the rise of Christianity. Justinian, more than any other ruler, was responsible for establishing the finished forms and setting the tone of the Byzantine society. The distinctive features of the emerging Byzantine culture are clearly manifest in his political, religious and artistic programme. His legislation too, despite its classical leanings, naturally shows traces of Greek and eastern influences.

As has been noted earlier, Justinian's reconquest of the West proved ephemeral and exhausted the empire economically and militarily contributing further to the weakness arising from sectarian and cultural diversity. After his death the empire quickly lost its briefly regained strength and internal disruptions, economic decay and foreign invasions threatened the very existence of the Byzantine state. As the empire's defences crumbled, Spain fell again to the Visigoths and another Germanic tribe, the Lombards, moved into Italy from the North conquering most of the peninsula. At the same time Persian armies were advancing through the eastern provinces and the Slavs and Avars were overrunning the Balkans. Only in 627 had Heraclius, a capable emperor, succeeded in stemming the Persian tide and in expelling the Slavic assaults. Then came the Moslem conquests, beginning about 630 AD, in which Egypt, Syria and a large part of Asia Minor fell to the Arabs. But as the imperial boundaries receded, retrenchment produced a comparative strengthening of the state and the Byzantine empire acquired the homogeneity which the policies of Justinian had failed to produce. This was due to the fact that the new borders corresponded more nearly with ethnic and religious lines, for the inhabitants of the empire were now largely Greek-speaking and Orthodox Christian. It was during these years that the empire fully entered its Byzantine period, Greek in speech, deeply orientalised with Christianity engrained in its thought and ethos.

The Arab threat was held in check and the empire entered a period of recovery in the early eighth century during the reign of Leo III the Isaurian (717-740). Leo strengthened imperial authority, reorganised the government and the law and introduced measures aimed at stimulating commerce and industry. However, the considerable benefits which the empire derived from his rule were, to some extent, cancelled out by the great iconoclastic controversy – the quarrel over the admissibility of images in religious art – which was initiated by him and which consumed Byzantine society for more than a century. The recovery from the crisis of the seventh century and the resultant consolidation in the eighth century produced a strengthened empire which was to attain new heights during the Macedonian dynasty (867-1057). During this period the internal organisation of the Byzantine state was strong enough for the emperors to be able to embark upon a programme of territorial expansion. By the early eleventh century the empire had been cleared of foreign enemies and its boundaries stretched from the Danube to Crete and from Southern Italy to Syria. The peace and prosperity that followed served as a powerful stimulus to art, literature and educational activity both in the capital and the provinces.

Yet, within half a century after the death of Basil II (976-1025), the last of the great Macedonian emperors, both the Macedonian dynasty and the prosperity which it had created had disappeared. The cause of the decline was a remarkable confluence of internal ills which exhausted the body of the empire as it was being attacked from the outside by powerful new foes (such as the Seljuk Turks and the Normans). Probably the most virulent of these illnesses was the strife between the military establishment and the imperial bureaucracy. The successes of the Byzantine military machine in the tenth and eleventh centuries bred a great arrogance in the military class and an ambition to overthrow the hegemony of the bureaucrats within the government. Basil II was able to hold these ambitions in check through military action and persecution; but he was succeeded by weak rulers who were unable to control the army, and the prolonged struggle between the generals and civil officials undermined the empire's strength at a critical period. At the same time, a growing economic crisis caused by a decline in state revenues (largely due to the abandonment of arable land in the provinces) compounded the empire's difficulties. In spite of a limited recovery under Alexius I Comnenus (1081-1118), the ills of Byzantium so weakened the empire that by the end of the twelfth century the end was virtually inevitable and, in 1204, Constantinople fell to the forces of the Fourth Crusade. Although the capital was recaptured by the Byzantines and the empire was restored about half a century later (1261), the political splintering of the Byzantine world which resulted from the Latin conquest hastened the final collapse.

During the fourteenth and fifteenth centuries, the age of the Palaeologan emperors (1261-1453), dynastic competition, social struggles and religious strife ravaged the empire and played into the hands of the Ottoman Turks who continued to expand their territory at the expense of Byzantium. In spite of the civil wars and military disasters, the Palaeologan period witnessed a last great flowering of literary and artistic activity, accompanied by a revival of interest in classical studies. The end came in the spring of 1453. After a heroic but hopeless defence, Constantinople fell into the hands of the Turks, who had already overrun most of the empire's narrow footholds in the Balkans and Asia Minor. During this period a large number of Byzantine scholars migrated to western Europe, especially to Italy, carrying with them important records of the Greco-Roman inheritance in art, philosophy, literature and law. A great deal of the classical knowledge, which had been preserved by Byzantium, was thus transmitted to the West and gave a fresh impetus to the progress of the so-called Italian Renaissance.

The sources of law

The enactments of the emperors remained the chief source of law during the Byzantine era. Until the twelfth century Byzantine imperial legislation was similar in form to the imperial legislation of the Dominate period[1] and enactments of a general character (*leges generales*, *edicta*) continued to be issued after the manner of the edicts of the Roman emperors.[2] A general law was preceded by a preamble (*praefatio*), in which reference was made to the position of the emperor as God's representative on earth, supreme lawgiver and protector of his people; this was followed by the description of the situation which the law aimed to rectify (*narratio*), the main text of the law (*dispositio*), and the conclusion; the latter contained the penalties (*sanctiones*) which the violation of the law entailed and prescribed the scope of the law and the manner of its publication. Similar to the earlier *mandata* were the *diatyposes*, internal directions given by the emperor to officials in his service (especially to provincial authorities). The earlier *rescripta* were replaced by the *lyses*, answers given by the emperors to inquiries of officials on matters of administrative law, and the *semeoses*, responses of the emperors to petitions concerning matters of civil or ecclesiastical law. From the twelfth century the term *chrysovoullos logos* was used to denote an imperial enactment of a general character, whilst the *lyses* and the *semeoses* were replaced by the *prostagmata* or *orismoi*. The majority of the imperial laws were concerned with public administration and matters of socio-economic policy. Moreover, a number of laws were enacted which introduced innovations in the fields of criminal and family law. In general, Byzantine imperial legislation was 'humanitarian' in character, aiming to protect those whom it considered weak against those whom it considered strong,[3] and greatly influenced by Christian ethical principles. At the same time it continued the move away from formalism, although this move was accompanied by a decline in technique.

During the Byzantine era custom continued to play a part as a secondary source of law. Despite the general reluctance of Justinian and

---

1 From the early sixth century imperial laws were no longer issued in Latin, but in Greek. However, Latin continued to play a part in public administration as well as in the teaching of law until the twelfth century.

2 The last imperial law expressly referred to as an edict was issued by Emperor Manuel I Comnenus in 1166. See Zepos I. and Zepos P., *Ius Graecoromanum* (IGR) I, Athens 1931, repr. Aalen 1962, Coll. IV, Nov. LXX.

3 'Humanity', as conceived by Greek philosophers and construed in the light of Christian religious doctrine, was traditionally regarded as a fundamental principle from which all the duties of the imperial office were derived. It furnished an important basis of the legislative activity of the emperor, whose chief aims were supposed to be the accomplishment of justice and the protection of his subjects. It also served as a restraining force, in the light of the fact that the emperor's actions were always kept within certain limits by public opinion.

subsequent emperors to recognise the validity of customary law,[4] numerous customary norms found their way into various imperial enactments and official compilations of the law. Some of these norms had their origin in Greek and Hellenistic institutions of much earlier ages; others were formed in later years, especially after the twelfth century, and reflect the influence of trade practices introduced into Byzantium by the Venetians and other western powers.[5]

Byzantine law during the period 534-867

In the years following the publication of Justinian's law-books Byzantine legal science flourished, especially at the two outstanding places of legal learning, the law schools of Constantinople and Beirut.[6] As was noted in chapter 10, Justinian had forbidden all commentary on his legislation under the threat of punishment, proclaiming that the right to interpret the law pertained only to the emperor.[7] He had allowed only the composition of summaries of contents (*indices*) and literal (*kata podas*) translations of the Latin texts into Greek. The purpose of this prohibition was, as Justinian himself stated, to protect his legislation from the uncertainty which could arise from disputes as to the meaning of the legal norms it contained.[8] But, even before his death, this prohibition appears to have fallen into abeyance and manuscripts began to circulate containing summaries, commentaries and interpretations of Justinian's texts, as well as treatises on individual topics. Most of these works were composed by jurists who taught at the law schools of the East. Among the most distinguished of these law professors (*antecessores*) were Theophilus of the school of Constantinople, and Dorotheus and Anatolius of the school of Beirut. Other notable jurists of the same period were Thalelaeus, Cobidas, Stephanus and Julian. Theophilus produced a Greek paraphrase of Justinian's Institutes based on an earlier version of Gaius's Institutes different to some extent from that

---

4 For custom was seen as a factor likely to undermine legal unity.

5 For a closer look at the sources of Byzantine law see N. van der Wal and J. H. A. Lokin, *Historiae iuris graeco-romani delineatio. Les sources du droit byzantin de* 300 *a* 1453, Groningen 1985; J. Karayannopoulos and G. Weiss, *Quellenkunde zur Geschichte von Byzanz* (324-1453), Wiesbaden 1982; see also H. J. Scheltema, *Byzantine Law*, in *The Cambridge Medieval History*, IV, II, Cambridge 1967, 55-77.

6 Justinian allowed only these two schools, as well as the law school of Rome, to carry on under the new programme of legal education introduced by him (*const. Omnem* 7).

7 *Const. Tanta* or *Dedoken* 21; *const. Deo auctore* 12.

8 *Const. Tanta* or *Dedoken* 21.

used by Justinian's drafters. Theophilus's paraphrase played an important part in the development of Byzantine law and was the first work on Roman law in Greek that was published in Western Europe (1533).[9] It has come down to us through various manuscripts accompanied by comments of other contemporary jurists. Fragments of other juristic works of the same period have survived in the form of commentaries incorporated in later Byzantine compilations. These include a commentary on the Digest by Stephanus, a professor of the law school of Beirut, an extensive interpretation of the Code by Thaleleaus, who also taught at Beirut, a translation of and commentary on the Code by Anatolius and an abridgment of the same work by Stephanus. Abridgments of Justinian's Novels were produced by Julian, a professor at the law school of Constantinople, and other jurists. In the course of time the works of the Byzantine scholars largely replaced the original texts of Justinian's codification (whose Latin language made their use very difficult in the Greek-speaking East) and came to be relied upon as the chief sources of legal materials by later Byzantine compilers and commentators.

In the years following the death of Justinian Byzantine jurisprudence entered a period of decline, accompanied by a sharp fall in the standards of legal education. As the old law-schools fell into decay, the teaching of law was taken up by teachers of a new kind, who were members of professional associations of advocates. Unlike the earlier *antecessores*, who were dedicated to the theoretical study of the Justinianic codification, these new teachers were primarily concerned with the legal practice of their own day and its needs. Their teaching was based chiefly on Greek translations of the Institutes and on summaries of the Novels, the part of Justinian's legislative work most relevant to current legal practice, whilst very little attention was paid to the Code and the Digest. A tendency towards simplification and the ironing out of all legal subtleties is visible in the surviving works of this period. These include two abridgments of the Novels by Athanasius and Theodorus of Hermopolis, a summary of the Digest by an unknown author (referred to in later Byzantine sources as Enantiophanes) and three monographs on special subjects. Theodorus of Hermopolis also produced a summary of Justinian's Code known from a number of quotations included in the *Basilica*.

By the middle of the seventh century the production of legal works had ceased and the legislative and juristic texts of the sixth century, which had become scarce and difficult to understand, had largely fallen out of use. Moreover, the disruption of official communications between the

---

9 See C. Ferrini, *Institutionum Graeca Paraphrasis Theophilo vulgo tributa*, 2 vols, Milan & Berlin 1884, 1897.

capital and the provinces by war undermined the government's ability to ensure the uniform application of the law throughout the empire. As a result, local custom began to play an important role as a source of social regulation. Under these conditions lawyers and imperial officials found it increasingly difficult to discover what the state of the law was. What was urgently needed was the introduction of a new legislative work which would adapt the Roman law of Justinian to usages actually observed by the inhabitants of the empire and which would set out, in a simple and systematic way, the applicable law. These were the objectives of the compilers of the *Ecloga Legum*, the new legal code enacted in the first half of the eighth century.

The *Ecloga Legum*[10] was published in 741 under the authority of Emperor Leo III the Isaurian and his son and co-Emperor Constantine V.[11] It is written in Greek and consists of a preface and eighteen titles dealing with the law of marriage, succession, tutelage, contracts and crimes.[12] In the preamble it is stated that the code is based on a selection of laws derived from the Institutes, the Digest, the Code and the Novels of Justinian, modified in the direction of greater 'humanity'. As this suggests, the purpose of the *Ecloga* was not to replace the codification of Justinian, but to make the law contained therein more understandable, both in language and in spirit, to those involved in the administration of justice (especially in the provinces where the texts of Justinian were no longer available). It appears, however, that its drafters relied not on the original texts of the Justinianic codification but on Greek translations, abridgments and commentaries by which Justinian's texts had in the meantime been replaced. Moreover, the *Ecloga* incorporated a number of legislative enactments issued by emperors of the post-Justinianic era and introduced important innovations reflecting Greek and oriental influences. In general the work is characterised by its simplicity and by the special emphasis it lays on Christian and humanitarian principles (especially in the sphere of criminal law and the law governing family life).[13] Although the *Ecloga* was

---

10 *Ecloga Legum*: Selection of the Laws.

11 The work was prepared by a three-member commission headed by the quaestor Nicetas.

12 Most of the surviving manuscripts include an appendix containing materials on civil and criminal law taken from various sources. It is believed that the appendix, in its original form, dates from the late eighth century.

13 In criminal law the influence of these principles is reflected in the restrictions imposed on the application of the death penalty. At the same time, the recognition of the penalty of mutilation, which was introduced as a form of punishment for crimes which in the past entailed the death penalty, reflects the strong influence of oriental practices on Byzantine criminal law. For a closer

abrogated by the Macedonian emperors in the ninth century (in pursuance of their policy of reversing the reforms introduced by the Isaurians), some of its provisions continued to apply in practice, especially in the provinces and among neighbouring peoples in the Balkans and Asia Minor.[14]

From the age of the Isaurian emperors date also three unofficial compilations dealing with special branches of the law: the Military Code, the Rural or Farmers' Code and the Rhodian Maritime Code. The Military Code consists largely of penal provisions aimed at securing discipline in the army. The Rural Code is believed to have originated in the provinces and was probably based on the legislation of Justinian and other early sources. It contains provisions of a punitive character intended to protect small farmers and tenants against exploitation.[15] The Rhodian Maritime Code is a collection of rules of the customary law of the sea that applied in the East between the sixth and eighth centuries. This compilation was widely used throughout the Mediterranean during the Middle Ages and furnished the basis for the further development of the law governing maritime trade.[16]

Byzantine law during the period 867-1204

The accession to the throne of Basil I the Macedonian (867-886) marks the beginning of the most creative period in the history of Byzantine law after Justinian. What characterises the legislation of this period is a renewed emphasis on the Justinianic codification as the basis of the Byzantine legal system. The return to the Roman law of Justinian was connected with the general revival of interest in the classical tradition and reflects the imperial desire to strengthen the image of the Byzantine state as a direct heir of the ancient *imperium Romanum*. Among the chief objectives of the legislative programme of the Macedonian emperors was the restoration of the

---

look at the character and contents of the Isaurian lawbook see L. Burgmann, *Ecloga. Das Gesetzbuch Leons III und Konstantinos V*, Frankfurt 1983.

14 Translations of the *Ecloga* have survived in Slavic, Armenian and Arabic.

15 In the seventh century the concentration of land in the hands of a few feudal lords had resulted in the gradual breaking down of the small-scale land ownership and the deterioration of the living conditions of the rural population. One of the objectives of the Isaurian emperors was to curb the power of the great landlords and to reorganise rural economy to the advantage of peasant communities.

16 On the Rhodian Maritime Code see W. Ashburner, *The Rhodian Sea-Law*, Oxford, 1909, repr. 1976; K. M. T. Atkinson, 'Rome and the Rhodian Sea-Law', *Iura* 25 (1974), 46-98; R. Zeno, *Storia del diritto marittimo italiano nel Mediterraneo*, Milan 1946, 96-113.

substance of Justinianic Roman law. To this end many of the changes to the law effected by the Isaurian legislation were to be removed and the precedence of written law over custom was to be re-established. At the same time the legal system was to be brought up to date with the elimination of matters which had become obsolete.

The first in a series of legislative works aimed at the general revision of the law was the *Eisagoge*, also known as *Epanagoge*, published under the authority of Basil I and his sons Leo and Alexander about 885. It contained a selection of laws drawn from Greek translations of Justinian's codification and consisted of forty titles and a preamble. In the preamble the *Ecloga* of the Isaurians was contemptuously discredited and abrogated as far as necessary.[17] A revised edition of the *Eisagoge*, known as *Prochiron*, was published in the early tenth century by Emperor Leo VI the Wise.[18] It was made up of extracts from Greek translations and abridgments of Justinian's legislation, fragments from the *Ecloga* and enactments of the Macedonian emperors amending and complementing the law. As in the *Eisagoge*, the materials are divided into forty titles preceded by a preamble. Neither the *Prohiron* nor the *Eisagoge* appear to have been given the force of law, however; their purpose was simply to present, in a readily accessible form, those parts of the Justinianic legislation which were actually applicable.

As announced in its preamble, the *Eisagoge* was intended to serve as an introduction to a new, all-embracing code of law, originally known as 'Revision of the Ancient Laws' (*Repurgatio veterum legum*). Work on this project began under Emperor Basil I and was completed during the reign of his son, Leo VI the Wise, early in the tenth century. The original title of the new law-book appears to have been *Basilica nomima* (Imperial law), but in later years (from the eleventh century) it came to be referred to as *Basilica*. As stated in the preamble, the aim of this work was to gather together, update and bring into harmony the laws contained in the codification of Justinian. In it materials from the Code, Digest, Institutes and Novels are combined into one body of work and, although the sequence of the titles is somewhat different from that in Justinian's books, the contents are largely the same.[19] The vast majority of the extracts were drawn not from the original Latin text of Justinian's codification but from Greek translations

17 Although the criminal law of the *Ecloga* was for the most part retained.

18 Modern scholars disagree as to the date of publication of the *Prochiron*. According to some, this compilation was composed during the reign of Basil I (probably between 870 and 879), i.e. before the publication of the *Eisagoge*.

19 No legislative enactment issued in the period between Justinian and Basil I was included, although some of the provisions on Criminal law reflect the influence of the *Ecloga*.

and abridgments of later century jurists.[20] Only with respect to the Novels was the original Greek text used (probably taken from the *Collectio Graeca*, a collection of 168 constitutions published during the reign of Tiberius II in the late sixth century). Moreover, the text of the *Basilica* is accompanied by a large number of annotations (scholia), including interpretations, examples, explanations and references of various kinds; some of these comments are taken from the works of sixth century jurists (old scholia),[21] whilst others are derived from juristic works of the post-Macedonian period (new scholia).[22] The materials are arranged into sixty books divided into titles, paragraphs and themes. The whole work is made up of six volumes. The *Basilica* was not intended to replace the codification of Justinian, the validity of which as the ultimate source of law was never called into question, but only to adapt it to the conditions and needs of the times. Hence the new Code was not given the force of law until the reign of Manuel I Comnenus in the late twelfth century. By that time, however, both the *Basilica* and the Justinianic codification appear to have been superseded in the practice of law by abridgments and other elementary legal manuals which lawyers found easier to use. Only about two-thirds of the *Basilica* have come down to us through various manuscripts. The contents of the missing parts are known to us through later works, such as the *Tipoukeitos*, a legal repertory published in the late eleventh century. The *Basilica* is a monumental work, second only to the codification of Justinian in importance, and constitutes one of our chief sources of information on the Byzantine law and jurisprudence of the Justinianic and post-Justinianic periods.[23]

---

20 Among the chief works relied upon by the compilers of the *Basilica* was an abridgment of the Digest by an unknown author (referred to as Enantiophanes), a commentary on the Code by Thalelaeus and Theophilus's paraphrase of the Institutes.

21 These include Cyrill, Stephanus and the unknown author referred to as Enantiophanes.

22 According to some modern scholars most of both old and the new comments were added to the *Basilica* in the eleventh century at the law school of Constantinople. Also included in the *Basilica*, probably in the twelfth century, was the Rhodian Maritime Code mentioned earlier.

23 For the standard modern edition of the *Basilica* see G. E. Heimbach, *Basilicorum libri* 60, 1-6, Leipzig 1833-1850 (with prolegomena, 1870); and see H. J. Scheltema, D. Holwerda, N. van der Wal, *Basilicorum libri* 60, Groningen 1953-1988. Consider also P. Zepos, *Die byzantinische Jurisprudenz zwischen Iustinian und den Basiliken*, in *Ber. zum* IX *Intern. Byz-Kongr.*, V, I, Munich 1958, 1-27.

In the years following the publication of the *Basilica* Leo VI issued a number of new laws (*novellae constitutiones*) of which a collection of 113 has been preserved together with four individual enactments. The majority of these were concerned with administrative and ecclesiastical issues, whilst only a few dealt with matters of private law. Some of Leo's novels were aimed at removing apparent contradictions between written law and established customary norms. From the closing years of Leo's reign date also the *Eparchiakon Biblion*, an official compilation of rules governing the operation of the various associations of businessmen, tradesmen and craftsmen of Constantinople (*corpora*). Besides the official collections of law, a number of private works, largely legal abridgments or epitomes, were composed by jurists for practical use or for instructional purposes. Probably the most notable amongst these are two works known as *Epitome Legum*, composed in 913,[24] and *Synopsis Basilicorum Maior* (late tenth century). The *Epitome* contains materials drawn from the codification of Justinian, the *Basilica* and the *Prochiron*, as well as a number of constitutions of Leo VI. The *Synopsis Basilicorum Maior* is a collection of brief abstracts from the *Basilica* arranged in alphabetical order (most of the manuscript copies of this work are accompanied by an appendix containing materials from imperial laws of the tenth and later centuries and other sources).[25] Three other works may also be mentioned in this connection: the *Experientia Romani* or *Peira* (c. 1050), a collection, under 75 titles, of juristic decisions drawn largely from the writings of Eustathius Romanus, a judge at Constantinople; the *Tipoukeitos*, a repertory on the *Basilica* composed by Patzes, a judge, in the late eleventh century; and the *Synopsis Legum*, (c. 1070), a collection of laws from the codification of Justinian and the *Basilica* prepared by the jurist and philosopher Michael Psellus and dedicated to his pupil, the Emperor Michael VII Ducas.

The revival of literary activity in the post-Macedonian period was facilitated by the establishment, about 1045, of a new law-school at Constantinople by Emperor Constantine IX Monomachus (1042-1055).[26]

---

24 During the reign of Constantine VII Porphyrogenitus. A revised edition of the same work was published in 920.

25 On the basis of the *Synopsis Maior* and another work written by Michael Attaliates in c. 1073 (known as *Opusculum de iure* or Poihma nomikon) a lesser abridgment of the *Basilica* known as *Synopsis Basilicorum Minor* was composed about the middle of the thirteenth century.

26 As was noted earlier, in the years following the death of Justinian legal learning took a sharp downward trend. How long the old law-schools of Constantinople and Beirut remained open we do not know for sure, but it appears that they had fallen into decline and probably closed by the end of the sixth century. About the middle of the ninth century Caesar Bardas, uncle of Emperor Michael III,

The buraeucratisation of the imperial administration in the eleventh century increased the government's need for well-educated officials. In part because of this need and in part because of the inadequacy of the current system of legal education (advocates had to teach themselves or learn from private tutors) Constantine founded a school of law and laid down the conditions under which the professors and students should work. The constitution of the school specifically stated that no person could practise law until he had finished the prescribed courses and received testimony to his competence from the professors.[27] Admission to the school was open to capacity and students did not have to pay fees. The head of the school, who bore the title *nomophylax*,[28] as well as the professors (*magistri*) were appointed and paid by the emperor. Until the end of the eleventh century the teaching of law was based directly on the texts of the Justinianic codification, the contents of which were studied and explained step by step. In the twelfth century, however, the Justinianic codification appears to have been superseded in the study of law by various abridgments and commentaries. The law-school of Constantinople probably remained open until the capture of the city by the Latins in 1204.

Byzantine law during the period 1204-1453

In the course of the thirteenth century legal culture in the East took a sharp downward trend, which was precipitated by the confusion caused by the political disintegration of the Byzantine world in the years following the Latin conquest of Constantinople. After the re-taking of Constantinople by the Byzantines, in 1261, the emperors of the Palaeologan dynasty set themselves the task of reorganising the administration of justice, largely

---

established a university in the capital in which law was taught, but we know little about the quality of the legal instruction offered. Whatever its contribution to legal learning, Bardas's university was dissolved in the tenth century and legal instruction continued be given by private teachers, usually members of professional bodies of advocates or notaries.

27 On Constantinus's enactment by which the school was founded see E. Follieri, *Sulla novella promulgata da Costantino* IX *Monomaco per la restaurazione della Facoltà giuridica a Costantinopoli*, in *Studi Voltera* II, Milan 1971, 647 ff; see also P. Speck, *Die kaiserliche Universität von Konstantinopel*, Munich 1974.

28 The position of *nomophylax* was regarded as one of the highest offices of the state and its holders were admitted to the senate. The first *nomophylax* of the law-school was John Xiphilinus, a distinguished judge who later became Partiarch of Constantinople.

through a reform of the court system.[29] But no serious effort was made to improve the quality of legal education which, after the dissolution of the law-school of Constantinople, was at a low ebb – legal instruction was now given in private, largely by practitioners, and was haphazard, unsystematic and based on fragmentary legal sources. The lawyers of this period paid little attention to the codification of Justinian, whose texts had become extremely difficult to find, using instead contemporary Greek summaries and adaptations. The most notable amongst these was the *Hexabiblos*, a manual of the whole law in six books compiled in about 1345 by Constantine Harmenopoulos, a judge at Thessalonica, and intended for the use of judges and court officials. It contains materials drawn from the *Prochiron*, the *Basilica*, the *Peira* and other sources, arranged into titles and paragraphs.[30] The text is accompanied by a large number of annotations, mostly of Harmenopoulos himself. After the fall of Byzantium the *Hexabiblos* continued to be used, especially by the ecclesiastical courts, throughout the Ottoman period and contributed significantly to the preservation of the Roman law tradition in the Balkans.[31] In Greece it was recognised as an official source of law after its liberation in the early nineteenth century and remained in force until a modern civil code was enacted in 1946.[32]

During the later Byzantine epoch the Church played an increasingly important part in the administration of justice. We saw earlier that since the fourth century the ecclesiastical courts had rights of jurisdiction in cases involving clerics as well as in civil disputes submitted to them by the parties concerned. By the end of the twelfth century the competence of these courts had been extended to a variety of civil cases, including all

---

29 The reform of the court system was the subject of a series of laws issued by Emperors Andronicus II (1282-1328) and Andronicus III (1328-1341). The earliest of these laws provided for the establishment of a High Court consisting of twelve judges in Constantinople. But the reform programme of the Palaeologi was met with limited success. For the relevant legislative enactments see I. Zepos and P. Zepos, *Ius Graecoromanum* I, Athens 1931, repr. Aalen 1962, Coll. V., Nov. XLI-XLIII.

30 Private law is dealt with in Books 1-5 and is divided into five parts: general principles, law of property, law of obligations, family law and law of succession – a division similar to that adopted by modern civil law systems – whilst Book 6 is concerned with criminal law. For the text see G. E. Heimbach, *C. Harmenopuli, Manuale Legum sive Hexabiblos*, Lipsiae 1851, repr. Aalen 1969.

31 The Hexabiblos also found its way into the West, where it was published in 1540.

32 The modern Civil Code of Greece was modelled on the German Civil Code which also has its roots in Roman law.

matrimonial cases and cases concerning charitable bequests. The tendency towards widening the jurisdiction of the Church courts grew considerably after the interlude of the Latin conquest (1204-1261). As the ecclesiastical law became closely allied with the civil law, the distinction between civil and ecclesiastical jurisdictions became more and more blurred. This development is not unrelated to the general weakening of the Byzantine state, following the political disintegration of the empire in the thirteenth century, and the parallel enlargement of the role of the Church in civil administration (for it was upon the Church organisation that the emperors now increasingly relied in their effort to maintain imperial unity). As the importance of canon law increased, there appeared during this period, along with the various condensations of Roman law, a number of compilations combining both canon and civil law, known as *Nomocanons* or *Syntagmata*.[33] Works of this kind were produced by Theodorus Bestos (11th century), Theodorus Balsamon (12th century), John Zonaras (12th century), Mathaeus Blastaris (14th century), Constantine Harmenopulos (14th century) and other jurists. They continued to be produced and to be relied upon by the ecclesiastical courts throughout the Ottoman period and played an important part in the preservation of the Greco-Roman legal tradition in countries formerly within the orbit of Byzantine civilisation.

The Later History of Roman Law in the West

The historical background

As we saw in chapter 9, the fifth century AD is marked by the complete breakdown of the Roman state in the West. During this period of disintegration the process of infiltration of the western provinces by Germanic barbarians, first as legionaries and later as settlers, became greatly accelerated until whole nations migrated into Roman territory, power passing from Roman officials to Germanic kings. South-western Gaul and Spain fell under the control of the Visigoths in 412 AD; about the same time the Burgundians moved into south eastern Gaul, while the Ripuarian Franks and the Alamani established themselves in northern Gaul; the Vandals invaded northern Africa where they established their own kingdom in 429 AD; the Angles and Saxons moved into England in about 430 AD; the Italian peninsula, largely isolated by the establishment of the

[33] Among the earliest work of this kind was the *Nomocanon* produced about the middle of the sixth century by John of Antioch, who later became Patriarch of Constantinople.

Visigoths in the northwest and the Vandals in the south, became an easy prey to another Germanic people, the Ostrogoths, in 488 AD. About ten years earlier, in 476 AD, the last West-Roman emperor, Romulus Augustulus, had been deposed by his Germanic mercenaries, led by Odoacer, and the imperial insignia were returned to Constantinople. In the sixth century Justinian succeeded in reconquering Africa (533 AD), Italy and even a part of Visigothic Spain (c. 554 AD), but his conquests proved short-lived. A few years after his death in 565 AD Spain fell again to the Visigoths and Italy was overrun by another Germanic tribe, the Lombards, who gradually extended their dominion over most of the country. About half a century earlier, in 507, Clovis, king of the Salian Franks, subdued the Visigoths of southwestern Gaul and added their territory to his Frankish kingdom. In 531 the Franks seized the remaining Visigothic possessions in Gaul and, three years later, they overthrew the Burgundians, bringing all of Gaul under Frankish rule.

With the disintegration of the Roman empire Europe moved slowly but surely into what is generally known as the Middle Ages. During this period of transition the civilisation and forms of social and cultural life which had been characteristic of the Greco-Roman world gradually broke down. Urban life, which had been the ideal of the Greeks and which the Romans had introduced throughout the Mediterranean basin, declined and many towns disappeared altogether giving way to forms of habitation built around fortified manors and small village communities. Although some of the great urban centres in Italy and Gaul continued to exhibit signs of commercial activity, trade and industry decayed and economic life reverted to an agricultural and pastoral type geared to maintaining local self-sufficiency. At the same time, as centralised authority everywhere disintegrated, political conditions moved towards the decentralised localism associated with the feudal system, and the economically self-sufficient manor became the principal economic and administrative unit. Moreover, as a result of the confusion caused by the Germanic invasions and the decay of the cities, which had been for centuries the centres for learning and the propagation of ideas, general culture in the West declined sharply and illiteracy became widespread. Nevertheless, vestiges of the classical civilisation remained alive throughout this period and, in the course of time, their fusion with the crude culture of the Germanic peoples and the learning of Christianity produced a new cultural synthesis. Of great importance for the development of medieval civilisation was the fact that most of western Europe passed to peoples already Christianised or soon to become so and that the Church, chiefly through the monasteries, was able to become the guardian of the remnants of ancient culture.

By the end of the sixth century the great Germanic migrations into western Europe were over. But of all the Germanic kingdoms established in the lands of the former Roman empire of the West only that of the Franks was destined to endure, whilst most of the others disappeared after a brief existence.[34] The first great Frankish dynasty was that of the Merovingians, founded by Clovis (481-511). Under Clovis the Merovingian rule was transformed from the leadership of a loosely organised tribe of Germans to a strong kingship extending over the whole of Gaul. But in the years following Clovis's death the development of the Frankish kingdom was hindered by the political division of the land and the disunity of his successors who continuously intrigued and fought against each other for power.[35] Under these circumstances royal authority weakened and the kings came to rely upon an increasingly independent group of nobles for sustenance, advice and support in war, which they repaid with grants of land, offices and privileges. Notwithstanding the feebleness of Clovis's successors, the Frankish kingdom, aided by the Catholic Church, not only survived as a single realm but even expanded its territory. Of the nobles in the court the most powerful was an official styled *maior domus*, or mayor of the palace. From the middle of the seventh century, as royal authority declined, the mayors of the palace in the respective courts became the real rulers of the kingdom. In 681 Pippin II of Heristal, mayor of the palace of Austrasia (one of the three provinces into which the Frankish domain had been divided), made himself mayor of all the united Frankish kingdom. After Pippin's death his illegitimate son Charles Martel (714-741), who had succeeded his father in the office of mayor of the palace, gained control of the realm and, although he did not take the royal title himself, became the founder of a new line of rulers known as the Carolingians. Charles' grip on power was secured further after he defeated the Arabs, who had already overrun Spain, at the battle of Poitiers (732), thus stemming their further advance into western Europe. His son Pippin the Short, who became mayor

---

[34] The Vandal kingdom in northern Africa and the Ostrogothic state in Italy were overthrown by the forces of the Eastern Roman empire in the first half of the sixth century. The Visigoths, expelled from southern Gaul by the Franks in 507, established themselves in Spain but their state met a violent end when it was conquered by the Arabs in the early eighth century. In Britain the Angles and Saxons were divided into many petty kingdoms incessantly warring upon each other. The Lombard kingdom in Italy lasted until the late eighth century when it was incorporated into the Frankish empire. Various other Gemanic tribes were assimilated by native populations.

[35] The Frankish territory was divided into three nearly autonomous provinces, the Austrasia (north-eastern Gaul and the Rhineland), Neustria (north of the Loire River and the west of Mause) and Burgundy.

of the palace after his father's death, deposed the Merovingian for whom he ruled and, with the backing of the Church, assumed the title of the king of the Franks in 751. To secure the support of the Church, which he needed in order to legitimise his rule, Pippin offered the Pope his protection against the Lombards, who were then threatening Rome, and ceded to him the Exarchate of Ravenna (in northern Italy) which he took by conquest from the Lombards after the latter had driven out the last remnants of the Byzantine garrisons. By the time of his death, in 768, the borders of the Frankish kingdom had been extended into the Lowlands, Lombardy and the Pyrenees.

The greatest monarch in the Carolingian line was Pippin's son Charles, known to history as Charlemagne (768-814), who became sole ruler of the Franks on the death of his brother Carloman in 771. After a long series of wars Charlemagne put an end to the Lombard kingdom in northern Italy making himself its ruler (774), subdued the Saxons adding a large tract of territory in Germany to the Frankish realm, strengthened his suzerainty over Bavaria and the area which would later become Austria and repulsed the Arabs beyond the Pyrenees gaining control of Barcelona. Like his predecessors, he followed a policy of close cooperation with the Church. He confirmed the grant of territory in Italy which had been previously presented to the Pope by his father and made it part of his policy to spread the Christian faith in the newly conquered lands. The partnership between the Carolingians and the Papacy culminated in Charlemagne's coronation by Pope Leo III as Emperor in Rome on 25 December 800.[36] In internal affairs Charlemagne did much to promote centralised rule. He exercised general supervision over the Church using the Church organisation as a vehicle for extending his authority, held the nobles in check (although he often sought their advice in matters of state policy), and ensured closer supervision of the administration by appointing counts and margraves to govern the various parts of his realm. Moreover, he ordered the unwritten laws of the various tribes to be written down, and earlier codes, such as the Salic Code of the Franks (*Lex Salica*), to be edited authoritatively. Although the legal traditions of each locality were fully respected, Charlemagne, by virtue of his position as head of the empire, issued edicts, known as capitularies, applicable to all his subjects. These statutes were not merely statements of popular customs promulgated by a ruling chief; they were the decrees of a sovereign ruler whose will was the source of law, according to the well-known doctrine of Roman law.

[36] Although this act deeply disturbed the Byzantines, as it was taken to violate the principle of one empire, Emperor Michael I Rangabe was finally forced to concede the imperial title to Charlemagne.

Charlemagne's reign also witnessed a revival of learning and artistic and literary activity. In monasteries and palace schools classical texts were once again studied, theological problems pondered, books collected and ancient manuscripts copied. In contrast with these achievements, however, in the economic sphere little progress was made as the feudal and manorialising tendencies of the landlord class increasingly escaped from the control of the central government.

The establishment of a Western empire by Charlemagne was one of the most important events in the rise of a new society in western Europe. Just as the reign of Justinian had precipitated the emergence of Byzantine civilisation, so the achievements of Charlemagne helped to mould the civilisation of western Europe which began to take shape in his time. But in the years following Charlemagne's death the unity of the Frankish empire was broken and political authority everywhere tended to disintegrate. During the ninth and tenth centuries new invaders – Norse Vikings, Saracens, Magyars and Slavs – threatened Europe from all sides and Charlemagne's successors, weakened by continuous dynastic struggles, were unable to check their advance. In the wake of the devastation caused by war and plundering economic conditions worsened, living standards remained at a low level and learning was stifled. The permanent threat of invasion and the inability of the kings to protect and assert their authority over the local communities of their realms strengthened the centrifugal tendencies in the West and feudalism, with its politically divisive and economically retarding influences, became widespread.[37] As the influence

---

37 The feudal system had it roots in later Roman times, but some of its defining characteristics were derived from Germanic traditions, such as the custom of Germanic kings and nobles of granting privileges, land or office to persons close to them who were then obligated to serve them loyally in the government and in time of war. Gradually a hierarchical system emerged: at the top was the king and below him, as vassals and subvassals, were the nobles (dukes, counts, barons and knights), while the base consisted of the peasants who provided a livelihood for all by tilling the land. Each vassal had full control over his own territory in return for definite and well-recognised obligations of a personal and military character due to his overlord. This gave the vassal his much-needed protection, while it provided his overlord with the power and prestige he desired. As medieval kings were not powerful enough to assert their authority over the local communities of their realms, feudal lords acquired a considerable degree of independence and fiefs came to be regarded, economically and politically, as nearly autonomous units. Decentralisation was supreme and remained so until feudalism gave way in the face of the rising tide of nationalism and royal power. On the origins and character of the feudal system see D. Herlihy, *The History of Feudalism*, New York 1970; F. L. Ganshof,

of central authority diminished real power passed into the hands of feudal lords, who came to enjoy essential sovereignty in their own domains, being virtually immune from royal interference. Moreover, the weakness of central authority led to the rise of the power of the Church, which adapted itself to the feudal system by building up vast landholdings and by extending its influence through its own vassals and serfs. As Church officials became feudal lords themselves the division of power between Church and state (the former was supposed to be supreme in matters of faith and morals, the latter in temporal affairs) became difficult to maintain in practice and thus the foundations were laid for the contest between secular and ecclesiastical authorities that was to take place during the later Middle Ages.

In the eleventh century Europe entered a period of political, economic and cultural transformation. The decentralising tendencies which had led to political fragmentation and the expansion of feudalism gradually receded as political authority grew progressively stronger with the rise of powerful new monarchies. The Holy Roman Empire of the German nation, which had been established in the middle of the tenth century by Otto the Great (936-973), asserted its authority throughout the domains of the Carolingian Empire, with the exception of France, and expanded its territories to the east; the kingdom of France, under a new line of rulers initiated by Hugh Capet (987-996), was consolidating itself; well organised Norman kingdoms were being formed in southern Italy and in England; in Spain Arab power declined and, by the close of the eleventh century, Christian rule had been extended beyond the centre of the Iberian peninsula. At the same time the government of the Church was centralised at Rome and, strengthened by a series of reforms initiated by Pope Gregory VII (1073-1085), was soon able to enter into a contest for supremacy with the empire itself. Improved political conditions and the gradual return of order facilitated economic growth and gave medieval thought and culture a more favourable environment for development.

One of the most important developments which stimulated the economic and cultural revival of the eleventh and twelfth centuries was the rise of towns and the emergence of a new urban civilisation. Potent factors in urban growth were the rapid expansion of trade and the increase in popularity of fairs, i.e. organised occasions for commercial exchange. During the crusades the Mediterranean had been reopened as a major West European trading route and new trading possibilities were recognised and exploited. First to profit from this were the Italian coastal cities, such as

---

Feudalism, 3rd edn, London 1964; M. Bloch, *Feudal Society*, 2nd edn, London 1962.

Venice, Genoa and Pisa, which gained in strength, independence and prosperity. The increasing number, size and power of commercial cities naturally led to the growth of the urban middle class and the expansion of its political influence. This new urban class was a powerful force generating new currents in medieval Europe, as opposed to the inertia of the old agrarian feudal order. The latter was characterised by localism, uniformity and repetition, which made it inherently stagnant and custom-bound; by contrast, the urban movement, based upon diversity, novelty and a dynamic and more tolerant outlook on life promoted the introduction of novel social, economic, political and legal elements into medieval life and stimulated cultural endeavours. Townspeople, through their struggle for greater economic and political freedom, redirected the political evolution of Europe, speeding up the decline of feudalism and paving the way for the rise of nation states.

The new upward trend of culture manifested itself in a significant increase in literary and artistic output and educational activity, and a revival of classical studies. Side by side with the traditional forms of education, centred around monasteries and churches, secular education emerged as a vital force in the intellectual development of the European society. Unlike the ecclesiastical schools, where teaching concentrated mainly on dialectic and theology, secular schools focused also on practical subjects, such as medicine and law. It was in connection with the study of law that one of the most significant cultural developments occurred – the establishment of the first medieval universities. The organisation and administration of the medieval universities varied considerably, but there was a common element, namely they were organised like the guilds under a corporate form of control. In the early medieval schools, such as the famous law-school of Bologna, teachers and mature students organised themselves into closely knit communities in order to be able to pursue their scholarly interests free from outside interference. From the thirteenth century onwards an increasing number of universities were established throughout Europe and, by the close of the Middle Ages, more than seventy were in existence.

The eleventh and twelfth centuries are marked also by the long struggle for supremacy between the empire and the papacy. This struggle became known as the 'investiture contest' because it revolved around the right of secular authorities to participate in the choice of bishops and other churchmen and to invest them not only with their secular but also their spiritual authority. Pope Gregory VII (1073-1085) rejected the concept of the papacy as a bishopric of the emperor, demanding supreme authority in all Church affairs and asserting the supremacy of the Church over the state. Drawing upon the writings of early Church fathers, such as St Augustine, he contended that a ruler, whether a king or an emperor, was subject to the universal power of the Church and could only hold office as long as he performed his duties in accordance with Christian principles. The supporters of monarchical authority countered with the theory of the divine right of kings, arguing that while a king should rule justly and for the benefit of his subjects, for his failures he was answerable to God alone and not to priests. Gregory's theories and policies led to conflict with Emperor Henry IV (1056-1106) and war between the papal and the imperial parties raged sporadically throughout Europe until 1122. In that year a compromise was reached by means of a Concordat signed in the German city of Worms. The Concordat of Worms stipulated that the emperor should abandon the right of investing his bishops with the symbols of their spiritual authority and recognised the Church as a separate, autonomous body vested with jurisdiction over a defined constituency and governed by a distinct body of law, the canon law. At the same time recognition was given to non-ecclesiastical political entities and secular legal orders. The Concordat of Worms was a compromise which reflected a gain for the papacy. It was not until monarchs became powerful in fact, towards the close of the Medieval era, that they were able to effectively challenge the supremacy of the Church.

The period between the thirteenth and the fifteenth centuries witnessed the gradual transition of European civilisation from medievalism to the modern age. The most important factors in the institutional background of the decline of the medieval order was the emergence of strong nationalistic monarchies, the growth of towns and of the urban middle class and the decline of the Roman Catholic Church. In the years following the death of Emperor Frederick II (1250) the medieval concept of emperorship was undermined and Germany became, and for centuries remained, a collection of more or less independent principalities, duchies and bishoprics. Not until the rise of Prussia in the seventeenth century was there created a power which ultimately was able to unify the German states. In France feudal institutions were gradually abandoned and the country moved in the direction of a centralised state under the authority of the king. During the reigns of Louis IX (1226-1270) and his grandson Philip IV 'the Fair' (1285-1314) the power of the feudal lords was curbed, the administration was centralised and the jurisdiction of the king's courts was extended over the entire country. Philip became the first European monarch who was able to defy the Roman Catholic Church and, after his victory over Pope Boniface VIII (1294-1303), the papacy could never again safely contest the power of the French monarchy. In England, as in France, centralised political authority grew stronger. In Italy, after the decline of the German imperial influence, city states such as Venice, Genoa, Florence and Milan grew to independence and established themselves as leading financial, commercial and cultural centres. Finally, in the closing phase of the Middle Ages the power of the papacy, which had raised its pretensions to the highest level under Pope Innocent III (1198-1216), declined sharply following the triumph of nationalism and of nationalistic political theory over medieval theocratic unity. By the end of the fifteenth century the institutional basis of medievalism, namely a dominant agricultural economy, feudal politics and a universal and omnipotent Church was breaking down and, with the coming of the Renaissance, the dawn of the modern age was at hand.

Roman law in the early Middle Ages

In the years following the collapse of the Roman empire in the West (476 AD) the once universal system of Roman law was replaced by what may be described as a plurality of legal systems. The Germanic tribes which settled in Italy and the western provinces lived according to their own laws and customs, whilst the Roman part of the population and the clergy continued to be governed by Roman law. This in effect amounted to a return to the principle of the personality of the laws which prevailed in early antiquity (before the third century AD), according to which the law applicable to a person was determined not by the territory in which he lived but by the national group to which he belonged. This arrangement was necessitated by the fact that in the regions under Germanic rule the vast majority of the population remained Roman, and the law of the conquerors was too rudimentary to replace the more refined Roman system. Added to that was the fact that the Germanic kings (with the exception of those of the Vandals), although in reality independent, considered themselves to be governing under the authority of the Roman emperors of the East. In this way a fiction of legal unity between East and West was maintained and Roman law was regarded as continuing, although in the course of time the effective control exercised by the Eastern emperors became more and more shadowy. However, the general deterioration of the Roman culture in the West and the confusion caused by the application of the principle of the personality of the laws made the administration of Roman law a task beyond the powers of the courts and lawyers of this period. As we saw in chapter 10, in response to this problem some Germanic kings ordered the compilation of codes containing the personal Roman law under which many of their subjects lived, as well as the writing down of the laws by which the Germanic part of the population was governed. In the Visigothic kingdom of Gaul the law that applied to the Romans was set out in the *Lex Romana Visigothorum*, issued by King Alaric II in 506 AD. Other important compilations of this period were the *Edictum Theodorici*, enacted by the King of the Visigoths Theodoric II about the middle of the fifth century and applying to both Romans and Visigoths, and the *Lex Romana Burgundionum*, promulgated in the early sixth century by Gundobad, King of the Burgundians, for his Roman subjects.

After the conquest of Italy by the forces of the Byzantium, Justinian's legislation was introduced in that country by a special enactment, the *sanctio pragmatica pro petitione Vigilii*, issued by Justinian at the request of Pope Vigilius on 14 August 554.[38] But shortly after Justinian's death the Lombards moved into Italy and occupied most of the peninsula. Under Byzantine rule remained Rome, the area around Ravenna, the southern part of Italy and Sicily. In the territories under their control the Lombards followed the custom of reducing their own customs to law, allowing their Roman subjects to continue living according to their own system. The majority of the Romans were governed by the Roman law of Justinian, whilst a smaller part of the Roman population followed pre-Justinianic (Theodosian) Roman law.[39] The prevalent view among modern scholars is that of the legislation of Justinian only the Code, the Institutes and the Novels of the *Epitome Iuliani* gained practical significance. The Digest appears to have played no part as a source of law and remained virtually unknown for many centuries. In the areas under Byzantine control the Roman law of Justinian continued to apply until the middle of the eleventh century, when the last of the Byzantine possessions in southern Italy were lost to the Normans.[40] In these areas were also introduced the *Ecloga Legum* of the Isaurians, and the *Prochiron* and the *Eisagoge* (*Epanagoge*) of the Macedonian emperors. These furnished the basis for a number of compilations that appeared in Italy during this period, such as the *Prochiron Legum*, also known as *Prochiron Calabriae*, composed in southern Italy about the end of the tenth century.[41] But it cannot be said with certainty whether the *Basilica* had ever been used as a source of law in Italy.[42]

---

38 Nov. App. VII, 1 in R. Schoell and G. Kroll, *Novellae, Corpus Iuris Civilis* III, Berlin 1972, 799.

39 The Lombards never issued a code of law for their Roman subjects.

40 The Byzantine rule in central Italy came to an end in the middle of the eighth century with the capture of Ravenna by the Lombards. Sicily was lost to the Arabs in the ninth century, but parts of it were temporarily re-taken by the Byzantines early in the eleventh century.

41 This compilation contained materials from the *Prochiron* and the *Ecloga Legum*, as well as a number of constitutions of Emperor Leo VI the Wise.

42 On the application of Byzantine law in Italy see F. Brandileone, *Il diritto bizantino nell' Italia dall VIII al XII secolo*, 1886, repr. Naples 1987.

As in Italy, so in Gaul and Spain Roman law was preserved, even though in a vulgarised form, through the application of the principle of the personality of the laws, but also through the medium of the Church whose law was imbued with the principles and detailed rules of Roman law.[43] Moreover, Roman law, either directly or through canon law, exercised an influence on the various codes of Germanic law which appeared in the West during the early Middle Ages, although this influence varied greatly from region to region and from time to time. Among the most important of the Germanic codes were the *Codex Euricinianus*, enacted about 480 AD by the King of the Visigoths Euric and drafted with the help of Roman jurists;[44] the Salic Code (*Pactus legis Salicae*) of the Franks, composed in the early sixth century;[45] the *Lex Ribuaria*, promulgated in the late sixth century for the Franks of the lower and middle Rhine region;[46] and the *Lex Burgundionum*, issued in the early sixth century for the inhabitants of the Burgundian kingdom.[47] Of the above codes, the Visigothic and Burgundian codes reflect a stronger Roman influence than the Salic and Ripuarian codes.[48]

In the course of time, as the fusion of the Roman and Germanic elements of the population progressed, the division of people according to their national origin tended to break down and the system of personality of the laws was gradually superseded by the conception of law as being bound up with a given territory or locality. As a result, Roman law as a distinct system of law applicable within a certain section of the population fell into abeyance in most parts of western Europe. A considerable degree of integration of the Roman and Germanic elements took place first in the Visigothic territory in Spain, where the *Lex Romana Visigothorum* of

---

43 During the Middle Ages the ecclesiastical courts had rights of jurisdiction over matrimonial cases, matters of succession to personal property and certain aspects of the criminal law. These courts consistently upheld the authority of the Justinianic legislation in cases which fell within their sphere of competence.

44 See A. D'Ors, *El codigo de Eurico*, Rome and Madrid 1960; see also R. Collins, *Early Medieval Spain: unity and diversity, 400-1000*, London 1983, 27-30.

45 On the origins and contents of this code see H. Brunner, *Deutsche Rechtsgeschichte* I, 2nd edn, Leipzig 1906, repr. Berlin 1961, 428 ff.

46 See T. J. Rivers, *Laws of the Salian and Ripuarian Franks*, New York 1986.

47 Like the Visigothic code, the Burgundian code was prepared with the help of Roman jurists. On the Burgundian law see F. Beyerle, 'Zur Textgestalt und Textgeschichte der lex Burgundionum', *ZSS, Germ* LXXI (1954) 23.

48 Other codes reflecting a Roman influence include the Lombard Edict (643), the Alammanic Code (c. 720), the Bavarian Code (c. 750), the Frisian Code (c. 750) and the Saxon Code (c. 800).

Alaric ceased to have any force and in its place a new code, the *Lex Visigothorum*,[49] which was applicable to all the inhabitants of the Visigothic kingdom, was introduced in 654.[50] In the course of the ninth century the shift from the principle of personality to that of territoriality was precipitated further by the development of the feudal system. As has been noted before, the predominant feature of feudalism was an estate or territory dominated by a great lord (duke, count, baron or marquis), who was often the vassal of an emperor or king. Since the domain of a great lord constituted, economically and politically, a quasi-independent unit, the area that was controlled by a particular lord was decisive as to what law was to be applied. But the intermixture of races meant that the laws which were recognised in a territorial unit could no longer be those of a particular race. Instead, all persons living within a given territory were governed by a common body of customary norms, the latter varying from place to place and from time to time. In this way the diversity of laws persisted no longer as an intermixture of personal laws, but as a variety of local customs. Everywhere, however, the customary law that applied was a combination of elements of Roman law and Germanic customary law.

By the end of the tenth century vulgarised versions of Roman law had become so intermingled with Germanic customary law that historians tend to describe the laws of this period as either 'Romanised customary laws' or as 'Germanised Roman laws'. Moreover, Roman law exercised a strong influence on the legislation (capitularies) of the Frankish emperors, as well as on the development of the law of the Roman Catholic Church. Thus, throughout western Europe, Roman law continued to live and to serve both as a strand of continuity and as a latent universalising factor in what was to become known as the civil law tradition. Yet, in comparison with classical Roman law, the overall picture of early medieval law is one of progressive deterioration. The study of law was based on nothing but abstracts and ill-arranged extracts from older works[51] and, as the surviving literature from this period shows, legal thinking was characterised by a complete lack of originality.[52] It was not until the eleventh century that Roman law was

---

49 Also known as *Liber Iudiciorum*: Book of Judicial Actions.

50 The *Lex Visigothorum* follows the structure of the Theodosian Code. It is based on early legislation (especially on a revised edition of Euric's Code issued by King Leovigild) and laws issued by the current monarch (King Reccesuinth). Alaric's code continued to be used in southern France, especially in the territory of the Burgundians, and in some countries north of the Alps.

51 The study of Roman law was part of a rudimentary education controlled largely by the clergy.

52 See P. Vinogradoff, *Roman Law in Medieval Europe*, New York 1909, repr. 2001, ch. 1.

rediscovered as a distinct system and made the object first of academic study and then of a reintegration as valid law in large parts of continental Europe.

The revival of Roman law

As was noted before, from the early eleventh century improved political and economic conditions gave medieval Europe a more favourable environment for cultural development. At the same time, the growth of trade, commerce and industry and the increasing secularism and worldliness of urban business life led to a renewed interest in law. The legal revival began in northern Italy. Among the earliest centres of legal learning was the law-school of Pavia, where both Roman law and the customary and feudal law of the Lombard kingdom were being taught and developed.[53] The study of Lombard law was based primarily upon the *Liber Papiensis*, a work composed probably in the early years of the eleventh century.[54] This compilation contained materials going back to the Edict of Rothari, the basic statement of Lombard Law, which was published in 643 AD.[55] The chief source for the study of Roman law was the *Lex Romana Visigothorum*. By the end of the eleventh century the *antiqui*, the jurists concerned with the study of ancient Germanic sources, had been superseded by the *moderni*, who were interested primarily in the synthesis of Roman law and Lombard customary law. While the *antiqui* regarded Roman law as a system subordinate and supplementary to Lombard law, the *moderni* sought to rely on Roman law as a basis for the improvement and development of native law. But the Lombard capital of Pavia was not the only Italian city where law was being studied and legal works were being produced. At Ravenna, the former centre of the Byzantine Exarchate in Italy, there existed in the eleventh century an important school of law where Justinian's texts were known and studied.[56] In Southern Italy too,

---

53 After the annexation of the Lombard kingdom by the Frankish empire during the reign of Charlemagne Lombard law continued to apply in northern Italy. At Pavia, the centre of Lombard Italy, a school of Lombard law was established probably as early as the ninth century.

54 Other important works of the same period were the *Lombarda* or *Lex Langobarda* and the *Expositio ad Librum Papiensem*, combining materials drawn from Lombard and Roman sources, especially the Institutes, the Code and the Novels of Justinian.

55 On the Edict of Rothari see M. Lupoi, *The Origins of the European Legal Order*, Cambridge 2000, 109 ff.

56 Moreover, Roman law continued to be taught at Rome for centuries after Justinian's time.

which remained for centuries under Byzantine rule, Roman legal learning was preserved through the influence of the Byzantine law.[57]

Towards the end of the eleventh century Roman law studies experienced a remarkable resurgence. It is difficult to assign a single reason for this development, although some writers place central importance on the discovery in Pisa, late in the eleventh century, of a manuscript containing the full text of Justinian's Digest, which had remained largely unknown throughout the early Middle Ages.[58] The rediscovery of the Digest came at a time when there was a great need for a legal system that could meet the requirements of the rapidly changing social and commercial life. The Roman law of Justinian, because of the authority it possessed as a legacy of the ancient *imperium Romanum* and because it was in book form written in Latin, the *lingua franca* of western Europe, offered a hope for a unified law that could in time replace the multitude of local customs. As compared with the prevailing customary law, the works of Justinian comprised a developed and highly sophisticated legal system whose rational character and conceptually powerful structure made it adaptable to almost any situation or problem, irrespective of time or place. The revival of interest in Roman law had been fostered also by the conflict between the empire and the papacy, which was from the outset a conflict of political theories for which the rival parties sought justification and support in the precepts of the law. Roman law attracted the attention of secular scholars seeking to find intellectual grounds for refuting the papal doctrine of the final supremacy of the Church in temporal affairs. At the same time emperors gave it a ready welcome because its doctrine of a universal law, founded on a grand imperial despotism, provided the best

---

57 As was noted earlier Byzantine legislation was based upon the codification of Justinian. After the Norman conquest of Southern Italy in the late eleventh century Byzantine Roman law continued to apply in that region according to the principle of territoriality of the law.

58 As was noted in chapter 10, this manuscript, originally known as *Littera Pisana*, was probably written in Constantinople or in southern Italy in the late sixth century. How it ended up in Pisa and the circumstances surrounding its discovery remain a mystery. After the capture of Pisa by the Florentines in 1406 the manuscript was transferred to Florence – hence it became known as *Littera Florentina* or *Codex Florentinus*. It is the only manuscript of the Digest which survives to this day. A second manuscript, now lost, seems to have been found about the same time. This is referred to as *Codex Secundus* and is believed to have furnished the basis for all the copies made at Bologna. See O. F. Robinson, T. D. Fergus and W. M. Gordon, *European Legal History*, London 1994, 42-43; P. Stein, *Roman Law in European History*, Cambridge 1999, 43-45; E. Spagnesi (ed.), *Le Pandette di Giustiniano. Storia e fortuna della 'littera florentina'*, Florence 1983.

ideological means to support the theory that the emperor stood at the pinnacle of the feudal system.[59]

The Glossators

The principal centre of Roman law studies in Italy was the newly founded (c. 1084) University of Bologna, the first modern European university where law was a major subject. By the close of the thirteenth century a number of similar schools had been established at Mantua, Piacenza, Modena, Parma and other cities of northern and central Italy, as well as in southern France. Of the early teachers of Bologna the most influential was Irnerius, a grammarian, who about 1088 began lecturing on the Digest and other parts of Justinian's codification.[60] Irnerius's fame attracted students from all parts of Europe and, by the middle of the twelfth century, about ten thousand students were studying at Bologna. The jurists of Bologna set themselves the task of presenting as clear and complete a statement of Roman law as possible through a painstaking study of Justinian's texts (instead of the vulgarised versions of Roman law contained in the various Germanic compilations usually relied upon in the past). Their object was to re-establish Roman law as a science, as a systematic body of principles and not simply as a tool for practitioners. But the ancient texts were unwieldy, for they contained an immense body of often ill-arranged materials and dealt with a multitude of institutions and problems that were no longer known. The first thing which therefore had to be done was to accurately reconstruct and explain the texts.

---

[59] The supporters of the papacy argued that, as spiritual power was superior to secular power, the Pope was supreme ruler of all Christendom, and temporal affairs were subject to the final control of the Church. Scholars supporting the papal party were encouraged to search the ancient texts for legal authority that could support this claim and to develop a science of law on this basis. Opponents of the papal views did the same. Relying upon the despotic principle of Roman law, they argued that the power of the state was absolute and could override the opposition of any group within the state. Roman law was thus taken to uphold secular absolutism, a view utterly at variance with the papal claims to primacy. Through the interpretation of Roman political and legal principles a new political theory was developed in the course of time which hinged upon the idea of a secular and independent sovereignty founded on law.

[60] The law-school of Bologna owed its rise and early fame to Irnerius and for that reason this jurist came to be regarded as the founder of the school, although he does not appear to have been the first teacher there – the first public course of law at Bologna was delivered in 1075 by the Pavian jurist Pepo (Joseph), who was probably a teacher of Irnerius. On the study of law at Bologna see P. Stein, *Roman Law in European History*, Cambridge 1999, 52-54.

The work of interpretation, which was closely connected with the Bolognese jurists' methods of teaching, was carried out by means of short notes (*glossae*) explaining difficult terms or phrases in a text and providing the necessary cross-references and reconciliations without which the text was unusable. These notes were written either in the space between the lines of the original text (*glossae interlineares*), or in the margin of the text (*glossae marginales*). The extended glosses of a single jurist formed a connected commentary on a particular legal topic and, through the continuous glossing of the texts, whole collections or apparatuses of glosses emerged dealing with individual parts or the whole of Justinian's codification. By employing the general pattern of scholastic reasoning, the Glossators (*Glossatores*), as the jurists of Bologna became known, sought to expose the conceptual and logical background of the various passages under consideration and to ascertain the consistency and validity of the principles underlying the legal material upon which they commented. They did this by comparing different passages from various parts of Justinian's work dealing with the same or similar issues, explaining away the inconsistencies and harmonising what appeared to be contradictory statements.[61] These successive processes corresponded to the medieval progression in the curriculum of the *trivium* from grammar and rhetoric to logic or dialectic – the content of Justinian's works had first to be understood, and so explanatory notes were used; then the consistency of the texts had to be established through the application of the dialectical method.[62] On the basis of this explanatory work various forms of juristic literature were developed. These included synopses or summaries of contents of particular parts or the whole of Justinian's work (*summae*);[63] works explanatory of conceptual distinctions arising from the texts

---

61 This method was by no means new – it had been relied upon by earlier medieval scholars and was similar to that used by the jurists of the law-schools of Constantinople and Beirut during the later imperial era. On the method of interpretation adopted by the jurists of Bologna see O. F. Robinson, T. D. Fergus and W. M. Gordon, *European Legal History*, London, 1994, 44 ff.

62 Logic was the most important element of medieval education. Based primarily on Aristotle's *Organon*, it became the dominant technique of medieval scholasticism. (Scholasticim, as a system of philosophy, was based on the belief that reality exists in the world of abstract ideas, generally independent of the external sensual world. Its chief assumption was that truth could be arrived at if pursued according to the norms of sound argumentation. From this point of view avoidance of logical fallacies, rather than observation of commonplace nature, was the only path to wisdom.)

63 The *summae* were similar to the *indices* composed by the jurists of the law-schools of the East during the late imperial period.

(*distinctiones*);[64] collections of conflicting juristic interpretations (*dissensiones dominorum*);[65] compilations of unresolved problems arising either from the texts or from actual cases (*quaestiones*); anthologies of opinions on various legal questions connected with actual cases (*consilia*); cases constructed to exemplify or illustrate difficult points of law (*casus*); collections of noteworthy points (*notabilia*) and of statements of broad legal principles drawn from the texts (*brocarda*); and various treatises on particular legal topics, such as the law of actions and legal procedure.

The interpretation and analysis of Justinian's legislative works was the exclusive preoccupation of the Bolognese jurists until the late thirteenth century. Among the successors of Irnerius, the most notable were Bulgarus, Martinus Gosia, Jacobus and Ugo (these became known as the "four doctors of Bologna"), Azo, Vacarius, Rogerius, Placentinus, John Bassianus, Odofredus and Accursius. Late in the twelfth century Rogerius, probably together with Placentinus, founded the law-school of Montpellier, in France, which became an important centre of legal learning. Vacarius, a Lombard, went to England around the middle of the twelfth century and began teaching civil law at Canterbury.[66] Azo became famous for his influential work on Justinian's Code (*Summa Codicis* or *Summa Aurea*).[67] The greatest of the late Glossators was Franciscus Accursius, a pupil of Azo's, who dominated the law-school of Bologna during the first half of the thirteenth century. Around the middle of the thirteenth century Accursius produced his famous *Glossa Ordinaria*, an extensive collection or *apparatus* of glosses of earlier jurists covering the whole of Justinian's codification, supplemented by his own annotations. The *Glossa Ordinaria* both summarised and made obsolete the whole mass of glossatorial writings of the preceding generations of jurists.[68] It represented the

---

64 These consisted of a series of divisions of a general concept into subcategories which were carefully defined and explained until all the implications of the concept had been elucidated.

65 The term *domini* referred to medieval jurists.

66 In 1149 Vacarius composed his *Liber pauperum*, a collection of texts from the Code and the Digest of Justinian accompanied by explanatory notes. The aim of this work was to introduce the Roman law of Justinian to the poorer students in England.

67 The importance of Azo's *Summa Codicis* was reflected in the popular saying: '*Chi non ha Azo, non vada a palazzo*', which meant that in some places a man could not admitted as an advocate unless he possessed a copy of Azo's *Summa*.

68 For subsequent practitioners and jurists the object of study was not so much the texts of Justinian themselves as the *Glossa Ordinaria* of Accursius. The importance of Accursius' gloss was manifested in the popular saying: '*Quod non adgnovit glossa, non adgnoscit curia*', which meant that a rule unknown to the

culmination of the work of the Glossators and gained rapid acceptance in Italy as the standard commentary on Justinian's texts, providing guidance for those engaged in the teaching and practice of law. With the publication of Accursius' great gloss the contribution of the school of the Glossators to the revival of Roman law came to an end, although their methods continued to be applied in the teaching of law at Bologna and elsewhere for a long time.

What characterises the Glossators' approach to Roman law is its lack of historical perspective. Neither the fact that Justinian's codification had been compiled more than five hundred years before their own time, nor the fact that it was made up of extracts of a still earlier date meant much to them. Instead, they looked upon it as if it embodied the law of their own age, paying little attention to the fact that the law actually in force was very different from the system contained in Justinian's texts. This attitude was reinforced by the theory that the Holy Roman Empire was a successor to the ancient Roman Empire – a theory which the Glossators tended to support. It was also associated with the fact that the Glossators' interest in law was chiefly academic and their learning was to a large extent remote from practical affairs.[69] Being true medieval men, the Glossators regarded Justinian's texts in much the same way as theologians regarded the Bible, or contemporary scholars viewed the works of Aristotle. Just as Aristotle was treated as being infallible and his statements as being applicable to all circumstances, so the texts of Justinian were regarded by the Glossators as sacred and as the repository of all wisdom. Nevertheless, the Glossators did succeed in getting back genuine familiarity with the whole of Justinian's codification and their work prepared the ground for the practical application of the legal doctrines contained in it. Their new insight into the workings of Roman law led to the development of a true science of law which was to have a lasting influence on the legal thinking of succeeding centuries.[70]

Glossa Ordinaria was not recognised by a court either. On Accursius' gloss see O. F. Robinson, T. D. Fergus and W. M. Gordon, *European Legal History*, London 1994, 50-52.

69 The general attitude of the Glossators was not affected by the fact that their teachings exercised an influence on the statutory law of Italian cities and entered the practice of law through their graduates who were appointed to the royal councils or served as judges in local courts.

70 On the history and contribution of the school of the Glossators see P. Vinogradoff, *Roman Law in Medieval Europe*, Oxford 1929, repr. New Jersey 2001, 32 ff; J. A. Clarence Smith, *Medieval Law Teachers and Writers*, Ottawa 1975; R. L. Benson and G. Constable (eds), *Renaissance and Renewal in the Twelfth Century*, Oxford 1982; D. Tamm, *Roman Law and European Legal*

The Commentators

By the close of the thirteenth century the attention of the jurists had shifted from the purely dialectical analysis of Justinian's texts to problems arising from the application of the customary and statute law and the conflicts of law that emerged in the course of inter-city commerce. The enthusiasm for the study of the ancient texts, which in the twelfth century had carried so many students and scholars to Bologna, had now waned and the place of the Glossators was taken by a new kind of jurists, known as Post-glossators (*post-glossatores*), or Commentators (*commentatores*).[71] The new school, the chief centres of which were the universities of Pavia, Perugia, Padua and Pisa, reached its peak in the fourteenth century and continued into the fifteenth and sixteenth centuries. Unlike the Glossators, the Commentators were concerned not with the exegesis of Justinian's texts in isolation, but with constructing a complete legal system by adapting the Roman law of Justinian to the needs and conditions of their own time. The positive law that applied in Italy at that time was a mixture of Roman law, Germanic customary law, canon law and the statute law of the Empire and the various self-governing Italian cities. The Commentators set themselves the task of integrating these bodies of law into a coherent and unitary system. In carrying out this task they abandoned the excessive literalism of the early Glossators and, by applying the methods of rational inquiry and speculative dialectic, sought to bring to light the general principles of law and, on this basis, to formulate a general theory of law. Since the Commentators were mainly concerned with the development of contemporary law, they tended to pay little attention to the primary sources of Roman law and the synthesis that occurred was between the non-Roman elements and the Roman law of Justinian as expounded by the Glossators. On this body of law systematic treatises and commentaries were written, especially in areas of the law where there was a need for the development of new principles for legal practice. The Commentators succeeded both in adapting Roman law to the needs of their own time and in giving the contemporary law a scientific basis through the theoretical elaboration of Roman legal concepts

---

History, Copenhagen 1997, 203-6; P. Stein, *Roman Law in European History*, Cambridge 1999, 45 ff; E. Cortese, *Il rinascimento giuridico medievale*, Rome 1992; M. Kaser, *Römische Rechtsgeschichte*, Göttingen 1976, 274 ff; W. Kunkel/M. Schermaier, *Römische Rechtsgeschichte*, Cologne 2001, 230 ff.

71 But it is not easy to determine where the late Glossators ended and the early Commentators began, for both seem to have relied on similar methods (on commentary rather than gloss) in the study and teaching of law. See O. F. Robinson, T. D. Fergus and W. M. Gordon, *European Legal History*, London 1994, 59-69.

and principles. Of particular importance was their contribution to the development of commercial law, criminal law and the theory of conflict of laws.

Among the most influential of the Commentators were Bartolus de Saxoferrato (1314-1354) and his pupil Baldus de Ubaldis (1327-1400). Bartolus took his doctorate at Bologna and lectured at Pisa and Perugia. He enjoyed great fame among his contemporaries and his writings came to dominate the universities and the courts for centuries.[72] Like Accursius' Great Gloss, Bartolus' commentary on the whole of Justinian's codification was acknowledged as a work of authority and was extensively used by legal practitioners and jurists throughout western Europe. In Portugal his writings were declared to have the force of law in 1446; during the same period in Italy, under the doctrine of *communis opinio doctorum* (according to which the solution supported by most juristic authorities should be upheld by the courts), the opinions of Bartolus were regarded as having the same weight as the Law of Citations had accorded to the works of Papinian.[73] Baldus taught at Bologna, Perugia and Pavia. He was best known for his opinions (*consilia*), concerned with the solution of problems arising from actual cases, especially cases involving a conflict between Roman law and local laws and customs.

The thousands of students from all over Europe who had studied at Bologna and other Italian universities carried back to their own countries the new legal learning based on the revived Roman law. Throughout western Europe, in France, Spain, the Netherlands, Germany and Poland, universities were established where scholars trained in the methods of the Glossators and the Commentators taught the civil law on the basis of the texts of Justinian. Their students formed a new class of professional lawyers whose members came to occupy the most important positions in both the administrative and judicial branches of government. Whilst prior to the twelfth century justice was administered by untrained jurors and on the basis of local legal sources, justice now was administered by professional judges appointed by a sovereign who could apply Roman law

---

72 The extent of Bartolus' influence is expressed in the saying: '*nemo jurista nisi Bartolista*': one cannot be a jurist unless one is a follower of Bartolus. On the contribution of Bartolus and the Commentators see P. Stein, *Roman Law in European History*, Cambridge 1999, 71-74; D. Tamm, *Roman Law and European Legal History*, Copenhagen 1997, 206-8; F. Wieacker, *A History of Private Law in Europe*, Oxford 1995, 55 ff; M. Kaser, *Römische Rechtsgeschichte*, Göttingen 1976, 276 ff; W. Kunkel/M. Schermaier, *Römische Rechtsgeschichte*, Cologne 2001, 232 ff.

73 Moreover, special chairs were established for the study of Bartolus' work at Padua (1544) and at Ferrara (1613).

if local sources, either customary or statutory, were found lacking. Through the activities of university-trained judges and jurists Roman law, as expounded by the Glossators and the Commentators, entered the legal life of Continental Europe and became the basis of a common body of law, a common legal language and a common legal science (*ius commune*) – a development known as the 'Reception' of Roman law. Aided by the expansion of economic activity and by the idea of the Holy Roman Empire, the *ius commune* gradually infiltrated or displaced local laws and customs and became international, a body of law that transcended territorial and political boundaries. The unity achieved by the reception of Roman law was fostered further by the development of canon law – the universal law of the Western Church.

The development of canon law

During the fifth century the weakness of imperial authority in the West led to the strengthening of the Church and its acquisition of greater political power. As the Roman system of administration everywhere disintegrated, the Church took over many of the functions of the civil government and, since there was nobody left in Rome who could wield greater power, the bishop of Rome rose to a position of supreme authority. In the course of time the Roman Catholic Church evolved into a grand international organisation, united and disciplined, thoroughly centralised, with an elaborate administrative structure and a comprehensive system of law courts and officials. In its early formative period the institutionalised Church borrowed freely from the structure, general concepts and detailed rules of Roman law, and sought to formulate laws to regulate its constitution and to govern the conduct of its members as precisely and as carefully as did the Roman emperors. It was through the Church, therefore, that a great deal of Roman legal and political institutions were preserved and disseminated. But the growth of the Church and the continued use of Roman law were interconnected: the Church organisation was shaped by Roman law and, at the same time, the development of Roman law in the West was affected by the medium, i.e. the Church, through which it was transmitted. Out of the interaction between Roman law and Christian ideas there emerged the law of the Church, or canon law. Until the revival of Roman law in the eleventh and twelfth centuries, the Church law was the most important universalising factor in the diverse and localised legal systems of western Europe.

In the early Middle Ages, under the system of the personality of the laws, clerics were governed by Roman law, and Roman law compilations were produced for them, such as the *Lex Romana canonice compta*, published in Italy in the ninth century. During the same period the Church continued to develop its own special law. The chief sources of Church law were the decretals of the Popes, the canons of the Church councils and various patristic writings concerned with matters of administrative policy and Church doctrine. From the fourth century a number of compilations of Church law appeared in the West, of which the most important were the *Dionysiana*[74] and the *Hispana*, compiled in the early sixth and early seventh centuries respectively. Early in the ninth century an extended version of the *Dionysiana*, known as the *Hadriana*,[75] was declared by Charlemagne to be the chief code of Church law that applied throughout his empire. In the ninth century there appeared also a collection of both fictitious and genuine canons which became known as the *False Decretals*. The aim of this work was apparently to strengthen the claims of the Pope to temporal power.[76] Its legal importance lies in the fact that both the spurious and the genuine materials it contained were utilised by later canonists in their development of the canon law system. The earlier collections of Church law were composed, for the most part, of Apostolic and conciliar canons; in the later ones the Papal Decretals – the acts through which the Popes, as heads of the Church, exercised their legislative, administrative and judicial powers – made up the bulk of the material. Elements of Church law were incorporated into the various legal codes promulgated by Germanic kings in the West and into the legislation of the Carolingian and Holy Roman Empires. Moreover, during the early Middle Ages the Church claimed and acquired jurisdiction for its own courts (either exclusive or concurrent with that of secular authorities) over certain categories of persons and areas of the law. Within the jurisdiction of ecclesiastical courts fell, for example, matrimonial causes and disputes relating to hereditary succession. Throughout the Middle Ages the limits of the jurisdiction which belonged to the Church tribunals was a matter of constant dispute between Church and secular authorities. Eventually the ecclesiastical courts were everywhere deprived of their civil jurisdiction but by then many of the rules and procedures which they had applied had been adopted by the secular civil courts themselves.

As we have seen, the eleventh and twelfth centuries witnessed the revival of legal studies in western Europe. During the same period canon law also became the object of systematic study. The task of the canonists

---

74 This collection was compiled in Rome by Dionysius Exiguus, a monk, on the basis of Apostolic and conciliar canons.

75 From Pope Hadrian I to whom this work is attributed.

76 It included the so-called 'Donation of Constantine', a forged document which alleged that Emperor Constantine had handed over to the Pope considerable secular power.

was to gather together and bring into harmony the mass of canons contained in earlier canonical collections, eliminating contradictions and bringing the matter up to date where this was necessary.[77] Their ultimate aim was to develop, expand and systematise canon law as an independent body of law and not merely as a set of rules for ecclesiastics. The work that succeeded in transforming canon law into a complete system was the *Decretum* or *Concordia discordantium canonum*, composed by Gratian, a Bolognese monk, about the middle of the twelfth century. The *Decterum Gratiani*, as this work became known, was both a code of and a treatise on canon law. It presented in a systematic way and without inconsistencies and contradictions the rules governing priesthood, ecclesiastical jurisdiction, Church property, marriage and the sacraments and services of the Church. Gratian's method of arranging the materials was similar to that followed by the drafters of Justinian's Institutes. Although it was published as an unofficial private work, Gratian's *Decretum* soon came to be recognised as an authoritative statement of the canon law as it stood in Gratian's time. Like the codification of Justinian, it became the object of systematic study in the universities, and students could obtain their degree either in civil law or in canon law, or they might qualify as bachelors of both civil and canon law. Moreover, Gratian's *Decretum* played an important part in the contest for supremacy between the empire and the papacy. Just as the supporters of the empire sought to buttress the doctrine of the supremacy of the state over the Church by utilising principles derived from Justinian's texts, so the supporters of the papacy relied on the *Decretum* and earlier patristic writings to defend the hegemony of the Church and to justify the papal claims to temporal power. In later years a number of compilations supplementary to Gratian's work were issued by the Popes themselves, such as the *Extra*, or the decretals of Gregory IX, published in 1234; the *Liber Sextus*, published by Boniface VIII in 1298; and the *Clementinae*, issued by Clement V in 1317. In 1501 a private collection of decretals not included in earlier compilations was published under the title *Extravagantes*. All the above works were republished in 1580 by Pope Gregory XIII as parts of an official collection comprising the entire body of canon law, the *Corpus Iuris Canonici*, which became the ecclesiastical equivalent of Justinian's *Corpus Iuris Civilis*. Like Roman law, canon law played an important part in the development of the civil law tradition. Its influence is particularly noticeable in the areas of the law of marriage, the law of succession and the law of obligations. Moreover,

---

77 No less than forty compilations of Church law were made in the two centuries following the appearance of the *False Decretals* and several attempts had been made to gather together the canons in a systematic way.

canon law has had a considerable influence in the fields of criminal law and the law of procedure.[78]

Commercial law

As has been noted earlier, from the twelfth century onwards there occurred a large-scale expansion of economic activity. Once small towns developed into major commercial and industrial centres, maritime and overland trade was stimulated, and new forms of business enterprise were introduced. Since the existing systems of law were no longer adequate to meet the needs of commercial life, in many cities informal tribunals were established by guilds and merchants' associations which heard cases by summary process and in accordance with rules that were practical, fair and based upon the usages actually observed by businessmen in their dealings with one another. These rules came to be recognised and applied by secular and ecclesiastical authorities as customary law and, in the course of time, they evolved into a body of internationally recognised law, the Law Merchant. This common commercial law of Europe, like Roman law and canon law, played an important part as a further universalising factor in the development of what we now think of as the civil law tradition.[79]

The reception of Roman law

We have seen that Roman law, as interpreted by the Glossators and the Commentators, entered, through university-trained lawyers, the legal institutions and practices of the various European territories and came to be accepted as part of the law of the land. Besides the work of the jurists, both the expansion of economic activity and the idea of the continued Roman empire played a part in the process known as the 'Reception' of Roman law – the process through which Roman law became the basis of a common body of law (*ius commune*) that came to apply in most of continental Europe. Like the Latin language and the universal Church, the *ius commune* served as an important universalising factor in the West at a time

---

78 On the development of canon law see O. F. Robinson, T. D. Fergus and W. M. Gordon, *European Legal History*, London 1994,72 ff; P. Stein, *Roman Law in European History*, Cambridge 1999, 49-52; J. A. Brundage, *Medieval Canon Law*, London and New York 1995; F. Wieacker, *A History of Private Law in Europe*, Oxford 1995, 47-54.

79 For a closer look at the development of the Law Merchant see O.F. Robinson, T. D. Fergus and W. M. Gordon, *European Legal History*, London 1994, 90 ff; D. Tamm, *Roman Law and European Legal History*, Copenhagen 1997, 228-30.

when there were no centralised states and no unified legal systems, but a multitude of overlapping and often competing jurisdictions and sources of law (local customs and statutes, feudal, imperial and ecclesiastical law). But the course of the reception was complex and characterised by a lack of uniformity, for the way in which Roman law was received in different parts of Europe was affected to a great extent by local conditions, and the actual degree of Roman law infiltration varied from region to region. Thus, in parts of southern Europe, where Roman law was already part of the applicable customary law, the process of the reception may be described as a resurgence, refinement and enlargement of Roman law. This was the case, for example, in Italy, where the influence of Roman law had remained strong, and in southern France, where the customary law that applied was already heavily Romanised. In northern Europe, on the other hand, where very little of Roman law had survived, the process of the reception was prolonged and, in some regions, at its closing stages much more sweeping. The common law of Europe that gradually emerged towards the close of the Middle Ages was the result of a fusion between the Roman law of Justinian, as explained by medieval scholars, the canon law of the Church and Germanic customary law. The dominant element in this mixture was Roman law, although Roman law itself underwent considerable change under the influence of local custom, statutory law and the canon law of the Church.[80]

The reception of Roman law in France

In the period between the sixth and the ninth centuries three bodies of law applied in France: under the system of the personality of the laws, the Germanic sections of the population were governed by their own laws and customs, whilst the Roman inhabitants of the country continued to live according to Roman law; at the same time everyone in France, irrespective

80 In England Roman law, although it was known and taught from as early as the twelfth century, had little effect on the development of English law. The reason for this lay in the early establishment of a strong government and the development of a national system of law fashioned by the King's courts – the common law; the reception of Roman law in England was also prevented by the rise of a legal profession trained in the national law and having a common interest with the courts in preserving and promoting the common law to the exclusion of the Roman law. Some elements of Roman law were introduced through the ecclesiastical and admiralty courts, and through the Court of the Chancery which owed its origin to the increasing rigidity displayed by the common law. See P. Stein, *Roman Law in European History*, Cambridge, 1999, 87-88.

of ethnic origin, was bound by the laws promulgated by the Frankish monarchs. In the course of the ninth century the personal system of laws began to disintegrate (as the fusion of the different races made its application virtually impossible) giving way to a territorial system. The shift from the system of personality to that of territoriality coincided in time with the expansion and consolidation of the feudal institutions in France. Whilst the territory of every feudal lord was governed by its own customs, in general the customary law that applied in an area tended to be that of the predominant ethnic group. And since the Roman element was dominant in the south of France and the Germanic element was dominant in the north, the whole country came to be divided into two broad regions: the country of the written law (*pays de droit ecrit*) in the south, where Roman law, as modified by local customs, prevailed; and the country of customary law (*pays de coutumes*) in the north, in which a variety of local customs of Germanic origin were in force. In both zones the law in force also included elements derived from royal, feudal, and canonical sources.[81]

In the south of France, the land of written law, notwithstanding local differences, Roman law was in effect the common law of the region. After the revival of Roman law in the late eleventh and twelfth centuries and the spread of its study from Bologna to Montpellier and other parts of France, the Roman law of Justinian was rapidly received in southern France and came to be accepted as the living law of the land.[82] In the northern regions of France, the country of customary law, a multitude of Germanic customs were in force. Some of these customs applied over a wider area (*coutume generale*), whilst others were confined to a particular town or locality (*coutumes locales*).[83] In this part of France Roman law was regarded as a supplementary system, invoked where the customary law was silent or ambiguous. Moreover, in certain areas of the law, such as the law of contracts and the law of obligations, the Roman system had been adopted as being superior to customary law and as being better suited for dealing with many of the new problems that emerged as a result of the expansion of economic activity.

---

81 Thus, matters that fell in the jurisdiction of the ecclesiastical courts, such as marriage, were governed by canon law.

82 In the early twelfth century a summary of Justinian's Code, known as *Lo Codi*, and based on the work of the Glossators was produced in southern France. The study of Roman law in that country was given a fresh impetus by the establishment in the thirteenth century of new law schools at Toulouse and at Orleans. In these schools and the many others that sprang up in the years that followed the civil law was taught on the basis of Justinian's texts.

83 There were sixty general customs and three hundred special or local customs.

From the beginning of the thirteenth century the customs of many of the more important and larger regions of northern France began to be put into writing and a number of collections of customary law appeared, written in the vernacular but modelled on Roman law compilations.[84] The purpose of these works was to gather together and to present in a clear form the rules of customary law that applied in one or more regions so that these rules could more easily be proved in the courts of law. Some of these compilations were private whilst others were issued under the authority of various feudal lords (*chartes de coutumes*). In order to reduce the confusion caused by the multiplicity of customs King Charles VII ordered the compilation of the customs of all regions of France in his Ordinance of Montils-les-Tours in 1453. Although the direction proved largely ineffectual, it was repeated by subsequent monarchs and, by the end of the sixteenth century, most of the customary law had been reduced to writing. The consolidation of customary law through its official publication precluded the wholesale reception of Roman law in northern France, although elements of Roman legal doctrine entered the fixed body of customary law by way of interpretation.[85] Moreover, Roman law continued to apply in areas of private law on which customary law was silent. It was this interaction of Roman and customary sources that gave the law that applied in northern France its distinctive character.

Although the publication of the customs removed much of the confusion caused by local differences, legal unity was by no means achieved. In addition to the differences between northern and southern France, considerable regional differences persisted even within each of the main territorial divisions. It was not until the introduction of the Napoleonic Code in 1804 that legal unity was finally established in France.[86]

---

84 Some of these works, such as the *Les Livres de Jostice et de Plet* (The Books of Justice and Pleading), composed about 1260, reflect a strong influence of Roman law; in others, such as the *Coutumes de Beauvaisis* (the customs of the county of Clermont in Beauvaisis), written in the late thirteenth century, the impact of Roman law is much less noticeable.

85 The tendency towards the reception of Roman law had been resisted by the French monarchs for political reasons having to do with their opposition to the Holy Roman Empire's claims to universal domination.

86 On the reception of Roman law in France see O. F. Robinson, T. D. Fergus and W. M. Gordon, *European Legal History*, London 1994, 113 ff.

The reception of Roman law in Germany

During the early Middle Ages the law that applied in Germany was customary law which, as a result of the shift from the system of personality to that of territoriality of the laws, tended to vary from area to area. Some of the customs applied over a whole region, whilst others were confined to a single city, village community or manor. After the establishment of the Holy Roman Empire in the tenth century imperial law (concerned almost exclusively with constitutional matters) came to play a part as an additional source of law. Although the Holy Roman Emperors regarded themselves as successors to the Roman emperors and imperial legislation was influenced by the idea of a universal empire, initially no attempt was made to make Roman law applicable to all German regions as a form of common law that could replace local customs. In the twelfth and thirteenth centuries Germans who had studied at the law-schools of Italy and France introduced some knowledge of Roman law into Germany; but its effect on the applicable customary laws was limited as Roman law scholars were largely ignorant or contemptuous of the local laws, which they regarded as primitive in both form and substance and as unworthy of the serious attention of the learned.

In the thirteenth and fourteenth centuries there appeared a number of compilations containing the customary laws observed in certain regions of Germany. The most important of these were the *Sachsenspiegel*, or the Mirror of the Saxons, composed around 1225 by Eike von Repgow and containing the territorial customary law observed in parts of northern Germany; the *Deutschenspiegel*, or Mirror of the Germans, published about 1260 in southern Germany; and the *Schwabenspiegel*, or Mirror of the Swabians, a collection of the customs of Swabia, published in the late thirteenth century.[87] These works were aimed at providing a basis for developing a common customary law for Germany, but the centrifugal tendencies that prevailed were far too strong to be overcome by them. The weakness of the imperial power, which was exacerbated by the political splintering of the Holy Roman Empire in the late thirteenth century, and the multitude and diversity of the local customs made impossible the formulation of a native common law for the whole of Germany based upon Germanic sources. A further obstacle to the attainment of legal unity was the fact that there was no organised professional class of lawyers interested in developing a common body of law. The administration of the law was in the hands of lay judges, the *schöffen*, whose task was to declare what the

---

87 Both the Mirror of the Germans and the Mirror of the Swabians reflect some influence of Roman law.

law was on a particular issue in court by reference to the customary law that applied in each district. But the pronouncements of the *schöffen,* concerned only with particular cases and reflecting the personal views of laymen not necessarily guided by generally established rule or principle, added to the uncertainty surrounding the application of customary law.

In the fifteenth century the problems caused by the fragmented nature of the law in Germany became intolerable as commercial transactions between the different territories that formed the German confederation continued to proliferate. Local custom was no longer adequate to meet the needs of a rapidly changing society and the weakness of the imperial government made the unification of the customary law by legislative action alone unthinkable. But if a common body of law could not be developed on the basis of Germanic sources, there was another system, namely Roman law, that offered a readily available alternative. The acceptance of the Roman law in Germany was facilitated by the idea that the Holy Roman Empire of the German nation was a continuation of the ancient Roman empire. In this respect, Roman law was viewed not as a foreign system of law, but as a system that continued to apply within the Empire as its common law.[88] This idea found support in the newly established German universities, where the teaching of law was based exclusively on Roman and canonical sources, whilst Germanic customary law was almost completely ignored. Like the jurists of other countries, German jurists regarded Roman law as superior to the native law and as being in force both as written law (*ius scriptum*) by virtue of the imperial tradition, and as written reason (*ratio scripta*) by virtue of its inherent value.

At a practical level the reception of Roman law in Germany was facilitated by the establishment in 1495 of the Imperial Chamber Court (*Reichskammergericht*) by a legislative act of Emperor Maximilian (1493-1519). This act was aimed at the centralisation of the German system of judicial administration and was part of Maximilian's broader political programme intended to restore the power of the monarchy and to secure legal and political unity. The new imperial court was directed to decide cases 'according to the imperial and common law and also according to just, equitable and reasonable ordinances and customs'. Since the personnel of the court was composed at first as to half, and later wholly, of *Doctores iuris*, i.e. jurists trained in Roman law, the term 'common law' was naturally interpreted as meaning Roman law. The significance of the 1495 legislation was that it formally acknowledged Roman law as positive law in Germany. Although under it judges were required to apply Roman law only where a

---

[88] On the influence of this idea see H. Krause, *Kaiserrecht und Rezeption*, Heidelberg 1952; J. P. Dawson, *The Oracles of the Law*, Ann Arbor 1968, 183.

relevant custom or statutory provision could not be proved, in practice the difficulty in proving an overriding German rule meant that Roman law became the basic law throughout Germany. The example of the Imperial Chamber Court was followed by the territorial courts of appeal founded by local princes in Austria, Saxony, Bavaria, Brandenburg and other German states. At the same time the courts in which lay judges still sat came to rely increasingly on the advice of learned jurists (city advocates, state officials and university professors) for information and guidance concerning local as well as Roman law. In the course of time the role of the lay judges diminished and the administration of justice came to be dominated by professional lawyers who had been trained in Roman and canon law at the universities.[89]

By the end of the sixteenth century Roman law had become firmly established as the common law of Germany. Germanic law had to a large extent been rejected in favour of the more advanced Roman system and German jurisprudence had become essentially Roman jurisprudence. The Roman law that was received was the Roman law of Justinian as interpreted and modified by the Glossators and the Commentators. This body of law was further modified by German jurists to fit the conditions of the times and, in this way, a Germanic element was introduced into what remained a basically Roman structure. Moreover, in some parts of Germany, such as Saxony, Germanic customary law survived, and certain institutions of Germanic origin were retained in the legislation of local princes and of cities. The process of moulding into one system the Roman and Germanic law, carried out by legal practitioners and jurists from the sixteenth to the eighteenth century, led to the development of a new approach to the analysis and interpretation of the Justinianic Roman law, referred to as *usus modernus Pandectarum*.[90] This approach continued to be followed in Germany, subject to local variations, until the introduction of the German Civil Code in 1900.[91]

---

89 By the end of the sixteenth century it had become common practice for judges to seek the advice of university professors on difficult questions of law arising from actual cases. The opinion rendered was regarded as binding on the court that had requested it. This practice (*Aktenversendung*), which continued until the nineteenth century, resulted in the accumulation of an extensive body of legal doctrine that applied throughout Germany. See J. P. Dawson, *The Oracles of the Law*, Ann Arbor 1968, 231.

90 The term *usus modernus Pandectarum* meant "modern application of the Pandects (or Digest)". In practice it referred to the entire *Corpus Iuris Civilis*.

91 For a closer look on the reception of Roman law in Germany see F. Wieacker, *A History of Private Law in Europe*, Oxford 1995, chapters 6-7; W. Kunkel, 'The reception of Roman law in Germany: an interpretation', in G. Strauss (ed.),

From the sixteenth century to the introduction of the first European civil codes

The Humanist movement

We have seen that with the rise of the school of the Commentators in the fourteenth century scholarly attention shifted from the dialectical examination of Justinian's texts to the consideration of the adaptability of Roman law to the needs and conditions of medieval life. But as the Commentators were primarily interested in developing contemporary law, they tended to disregard the historical framework and the primary sources of Roman law. From the fifteenth century the increased interest in the cultural inheritance of classical antiquity, associated with the rise of humanistic scholarship, led to the development of a new approach to the study of Roman law. Scholarly attention now turned to the consideration of Roman law as a historical phenomenon and special emphasis was placed on the importance of the techniques of history and philology for its proper understanding and interpretation. The methods used by the Commentators in the study of Justinian's texts had led to the formulation of theories which, from the Humanists' point of view, were utterly unwarranted when the texts were studied in their proper historical context; such theories had therefore to be rejected in favour of interpretations based upon the true historical sense of the texts. The chief aim of the Humanist scholars was thus the rediscovery of Roman law as it was in Roman times through the application of the historical method instead of the scholastic method (referred to as *mos Italicus*) of the medieval Commentators. A considerable part of the Humanists' work was concerned with the detection of the interpolations in the Justinianic codification as an important step towards uncovering the true character of classical Roman law.

The new school of thought was initiated in France by the Italian Andreas Alciatus (1492-1550) but its effects were felt all over Europe.[92] Among the most important representatives of this school, which included not only jurists, but also historians and philologists, were Jacques Cujas (Cuiacius, 1522-1590), Hugues Doneau (Donellus, 1527-1591), Guillaume Bude (Budaeus, 1467-1540), Ulrich Zasius (1461-1535), Antoine Favre

---

Pre-Reformation Germany, London 1972, 263; P. Stein, *Roman Law in European History*, Cambridge 1999, 88 ff; O. F. Robinson, T. D. Fergus, W. M. Gordon, *European Legal History*, London 1994, ch. 11; W. Kunkel/M. Schermaier, *Römische Rechtsgeschichte*, Cologne 2001, 234 ff.

[92] The centre of the Humanist school was the University of Bourges in France.

(Faber, 1557-1624), Charles Annibal Fabrot (Fabrotus, 1580-1659)[93] and Jacques Godefroy (Godofredus, 1587-1652).[94] The method adopted by the Humanist scholars in France for the study of Roman law became known as *mos gallicus* (in contradistinction with the *mos Italicus* of the Bolognese jurists) or *Elegante Jurisprudenz*. In general, however, the Humanist movement does not seem to have had much influence on the practice of law as the courts in France and elsewhere remained faithful to the Bartolist tradition. This was largely due to the fact that most Humanists were concerned chiefly with the historical analysis of Roman law and paid little attention to problems relating to the practical application of the law or the need to adapt Roman law to contemporary conditions. At the same time, however, the Humanists' approach to Roman law as a historical phenomenon helped jurists to appreciate the differences between Roman law and the law of their own times. By drawing attention to the historical and cultural circumstances in which law develops the Humanists prepared the ground for the eventual displacement of the *ius commune* and the emergence of national systems of law.[95]

The school of Natural law

In the seventeenth and eighteenth centuries European legal thought moved in a new direction under the influence of the school of Natural law. The new school challenged the supreme authority which medieval jurists had accorded to the codification of Justinian. It did so on the grounds that the *Corpus Iuris* was an expression of a particular legal order whose rules, like the rules of any other system of positive law, had to be assessed in the light of norms of a higher order, eternal and universally valid – the norms of

---

93 Fabrotus studied extensively the development of Byzantine law and published the *Basilica*.

94 It was Godofredus that gave the Justinianic codification the name *Corpus Iuris Civilis* by which it has become known.

95 On the influence of the Humanist movement see P. Stein, *Roman Law in European Legal History*, Cambridge 1999, 75ff; D. Maffei, *Gli inizi dell'umanesimo giuridico*, Milan 1956; D. R. Kelley, *Foundations of Modern Historical Scholarship: Language, Law and History in the French Renaissance*, New York 1970; O. F. Robinson, T. D. Fergus and W. M. Gordon, *European Legal History*, London 1994, ch. 10; M. P. Gilmore, *Humanists and Jurists*, Harvard UP 1963; F. Wieacker, *A History of Private Law in Europe*, Oxford 1995, 120 ff; H. J. Wolff, Roman Law, *An Historical Introduction*, U. of Oklahoma Press 1951, 209 ff; M. Kaser, *Römische Rechtsgeschichte*, Göttingen 1976, 257-8; W. Kunkel/M. Schermaier, *Römische Rechtsgeschichte*, Cologne 2001, 237-8.

Natural law. Natural law was understood as being rational in its content, since its norms could be discovered only by the use of reason, logic and rationality, common to all men of all times and of higher moral authority than any system of positive law. From this point of view, the Natural lawyers rejected certain 'irrational' features of the Roman system drawn attention to by the Humanists, such as the remnants of the old Roman formalism found in the *Corpus Iuris*, as being specific to the Roman system of social organisation and restricted in time. At the same time, however, they recognised that Roman law contained a large number of rules and principles which reflected or corresponded to the precepts of natural law – rules and principles which they regarded as the product of logical reasoning on the nature of man and society rather than the expression of the legal development of the Roman state. The Roman doctrine of *ius gentium* and *ius naturale*, in particular, seemed to lend support to their own theories, and many legal principles espoused by Roman jurists appeared to be suitable materials upon which to draw in building a rational system of law. As regards their methodology, the Natural lawyers, by relying on deductive reasoning, sought to derive from a small number of general concepts abstract principles of universal application which could then be used as a basis for developing an orderly and comprehensive system of law. Among the founders of the school of Natural law was the Dutch scholar Hugo Grotius (1583-1645), who in his work *De Iure Belli ac Pacis* (Concerning the Law of War and Peace) laid the foundations for the development of modern international law. Other noteworthy representatives of the school were Samuel Pufendorf (1632-1694), Christian Thomasius (1655-1728), and Christian Wolf (1679-1754). The Natural law school, with its system-building approach to law, gave rise to a renewed interest in codification as a means of integrating the diverse laws and customs of a national territory into a logically consistent and unitary system.[96]

---

[96] On the rise and influence of the School of Natural law see A. P. D'Entreves, *Natural Law: An Introduction to Legal Philosophy*, 2nd edn, London 1970; O. F. Robinson, T. D. Fergus and W. M. Gordon, *European Legal History*, London 1994, ch. 13; J. M. Kelly, *A Short History of Western Legal Theory*, Oxford 1992, ch. 6; F. Wieacker, *A History of Private Law in Europe*, Oxford, 1995, ch. 15; H. J. Wolff, *Roman Law, An Historical Introduction*, U of Oklahoma Press 1951, 213 ff; P. Stein, *Roman Law in European History*, Cambridge 1999, 107-10; D. Tamm, *Roman Law and European Legal History*, Copenhagen 1997, 231 ff.

The codification movement

The rise of nationalism and the consolidation of royal power in Europe in the seventeenth and eighteenth centuries led to an increased interest in the development of national law and this, in turn, precipitated the movement towards codification. The demand that law should be reduced to a code arose from two interrelated factors: the need for establishing legal unity within the boundaries of a nation-state, and the need for developing a rational, systematised and comprehensive legal system adapted to the conditions of the times. The school of Natural law, with its rationalist approach to institutional reform and its emphasis on comprehensive legal system-building, provided the ideological and methodological basis upon which the codification movement was to proceed. As a result of the unification of national law through codification, the *ius commune* was eventually displaced and Roman law ceased to be a direct source of law. But as the drafters of the codes relied heavily on the *ius commune*, elements of Roman law were incorporated in different ways and to varying degrees into the civil law systems of continental Europe.[97]

The first national codes aimed at achieving legal unity within one kingdom were compiled in Denmark (1683) and Sweden (1734). The process of codification continued in the late eighteenth and early nineteenth centuries with the introduction of the Bavarian, Prussian and Austrian Codes, completed in 1756, 1794 and 1811 respectively. The Natural law philosophy exercised a strong influence on both the contents and structure of these codes. But the most important codificatory event of this period was the enactment of the French Civil Code (*Code civil des francais*) under Napoleon in 1804. The chief aim of Napoleon's Code was to unify the law of France by fusing into one comprehensive system Roman law, customary law, royal ordinances and some laws of the revolutionary period, and in this respect it succeeded brilliantly. The importance of the Code lay not only in the fact that it brought about legal unity within France, but also in the fact that it was adopted, copied or adapted by many countries throughout the world. This was partly due to its clarity, simplicity and elegance, which made it a convenient article of exportation, and partly due to France's influence in the nineteenth century. Codes modelled on the

---

97 On the movement towards the codification of the civil law and the introduction of the early European codes see P. Stein, *Roman Law in European History*, Cambridge 1999, 110 ff; O. F. Robinson, T. D. Fergus and W. M. Gordon, *European Legal History*, London 1994, ch. 15; A. Watson, *The Making of the Civil Law*, Harvard UP 1981; F. Wieacker, *A History of Private Law in Europe*, Oxford 1995, Ch. 19; K. Zweigert and H. Kotz, *An Introduction to Comparative Law*, 2nd edn, Oxford 1987, ch. 7.

French Code were adopted in Italy, Belgium, Holland, Portugal, Spain, Quebec, Egypt, Louisiana and several other countries around the world.

In Germany the French Civil Code attracted a great deal of attention and, as Napoleon extended his rule over Europe, it came to be adopted in some parts of the country. But with the rise of German nationalism in the course of the wars of independence many scholars began to speak of the need for the introduction of one uniform code for Germany that could unite the country under one modern system of law and precipitate the process of its political unification. In 1814, Thibaut, a professor of Roman law at Heidelberg, expressed this view in a pamphlet entitled 'On the Necessity for a General Civil Code for Germany'. Thibaut, a representative of the Natural law movement, claimed that the existing French, Prussian and Austrian Civil Codes could serve as useful models for the German draftsmen. Thibaut's proposals were met with strong opposition by the members of the Historical School, headed by the influential jurist Friedrich Carl von Savigny (1779-1861).[98] Savigny's thesis, expressed in a pamphlet entitled 'On the Vocation of our Times for Legislation and Legal Science', was that law, like language, ethics and literature, was a product of the history and culture of a people, a manifestation of national consciousness (*Volksgeist*), and could not be derived by logical means alone from abstract principles of Natural law. From this point of view, Savigny argued that the introduction of a German Code should be postponed until the historical circumstances in which the law in Germany had developed were fully understood and the needs of the present were properly assessed.

Under the influence of the Historical School and, perhaps more importantly, because of the lack of an effective central government, the early proposals for codification were abandoned. At the same time scholarly attention turned from the largely ahistorical Natural law approach to the historical examination of the two main sources of the law that applied in Germany, namely Roman law and Germanic law, with a view to developing a true science of law. A group of scholars focused on the study of Germanic law, whilst others, including Savigny himself, concentrated on the study of Roman law, looking beyond the *ius commune* into the *Corpus Iuris* and other ancient sources. The latter jurists set themselves the task of studying Roman law with the aim of bringing to light its 'latent system', which could then be adapted to the needs and conditions of their own society. In carrying out this task the Pandectists, as these jurists became known, brought the study of the *Corpus Iuris*, and especially of the Digest,

98 The rise of the Historical School was one manifestation of the general reaction to the rationalism of the school of Natural law and the political philosophy associated with the French Revolution and the regime of Napoleon.

to its highest level, and produced an elaborate and highly systematic body of law (*Pandektenrecht*) for nineteenth century Germany.[99] Eventually, however, the Pandectists, convinced of the superiority and eternal validity of Roman law, came to adopt a largely ahistorical and primarily doctrinaire approach to law. Their chief objective was the construction of a legal system in which all particular rules could be derived from and classified under a set of clearly formulated juridical categories and abstract propositions. Although this way of thinking was met with severe criticism by other scholars, especially those belonging to the Germanist branch of the Historical School, the Pandectists played an important part in the process towards the codification of the civil law in Germany which began in 1874, three years after the political unification of the country under Bismark. The German Civil Code (*Bürgerliches Gesetzbuch* or *BGB*) was finally promulgated in 1896 and came into force in 1900. Its chief characteristics are its highly systematic structure and its conceptualism – in both these respects it owes much to the contribution of the Pandectist school. Like the French Code, the German Code has had a wide acceptance outside the frontiers of Germany. Codes influenced by it were adopted in Japan, Brazil, Hungary, Switzerland, Greece and Turkey.[100]

Concluding Note

Roman law has been one of the most important unifying factors in the development of the European civil law tradition. Despite the diversity in the responses of modern civil law systems to various legal issues, a considerable degree of uniformity throughout the civil law family still exists today. The most obvious element of unity is naturally provided by the fact that civil law systems are all derived from the same sources, and

---

99 Among the most important representatives of the Pandectists, as these jurists became known, were Puchta, Rudorff, Koetler, Ihering, Bekker, Brinz, Dernburg and Windscheid. On the German Historical School and the Pandectist movement see F. Wieacker, *A History of Private Law in Europe*, Oxford 1995, 280 ff; O. F. Robinson, T. D. Fergus and W. M. Gordon, *European Legal History*, London 1994, 262 ff; P. Stein, *Roman Law in European History*, Cambridge 1999, 115 ff; J. Whitman, *The Legacy of Roman Law in the German Romantic Era*, Princeton 1990.

100 The Code went through two drafts and took over twenty years to complete, partly due to the controversy between the Romanist and the Germanist jurists. For a closer look at its history and influence see F. Wieacker, *A History of Private Law in Europe*, Oxford 1995, 371 ff; K. Zweigert and H. Kotz, *An Introduction to Comparative Law*, 2nd edn, Oxford 1987, 149 ff.

that they have classified their legal institutions in accordance with a commonly accepted scheme which existed prior to their own development, and which at some stage in their growth they took over and made their own. The distinctive characteristics of the civil law systems become apparent when one considers the structure and language of the modern civil codes, legal methodology, the nature of judicial process and judicial reasoning, styles of legal thinking and argumentation, attitudes to legal education and the activities of lawyers and legal scholars in civil law countries. As Roman law forms an important part of the intellectual background of so many legal systems, its study is an integral part of the modern comparative study of legal systems and legal traditions. Roman law constitutes, above all, an essential part of the history of civilisation. If studied in its historical context it can offer valuable insights into the growth and progress of law as a social and cultural phenomenon.

Select Bibliography

Adcock, F. E., *Roman Political Ideas and Practice*, Ann Arbor, The University of Michigan Press, 1964, repr. 1975.

Alföldy, G., *The Social History of Rome*, London and Sydney, Croom Helm, 1985.

Bauman, R. A., *Lawyers in Roman Republican Politics, A Study of Roman Jurists In their Political Setting, 316-82 BC*, Munich, Beck, 1971.

Bauman, R. A., *Lawyers and Politics in the Early Roman Empire*, Munich, Beck, 1989.

Bauman, R. A., *Crime and Punishment in Ancient Rome*, London and New York, Routledge, 1996.

Bellomo, M., *The Common Legal Past of Europe, 1000-1800*, Washington DC, Catholic University of America Press, 1995.

Benke, N., *Juristenlatein*, Vienna, Manz, 2002.

Berger, A., *Encyclopedic Dictionary of Roman Law*, Philadelphia, APS, 1953.

Bleicken, J., *Staat und Recht in der Römischen Republik*, Wiesbaden, Steiner, 1978.

Boardman, J., Griffin, J. and Murray, O. (eds), *The Oxford History of the Roman World*, Oxford and New York, Oxford University Press, 1991.

Borkowski, A., *A Textbook on Roman Law*, London, Blackstone, 1994.

Buckland, W. W. and Stein, P., *A Textbook of Roman Law from Augustus to Justinian*, 3rd edn, Cambridge, Cambridge University Press, 1963, repr., 1975.

Burdese, A., *Manuale di diritto pubblico romano*, 3rd edn, Turin, UTET, 1987, repr. 1994.

Burdese, A., *Manuale di diritto privato romano*, 4th edn, Turin, UTET, 1993.

Bürge, A., *Römisches Privatrecht*, Darmstadt, Wiss. Buchges, 1999

Cameron, A., *The Later Roman Empire*, London, Fontana, 1993.

Cannata, C. A., *Profilo istituzionale del processo privato romano*, Turin, Giappichelli, 1982.

Cary, M. and Scullard, H. H., *A History of Rome*, 3rd edn, London, Macmillan, 1975.

Corcoran, S., *The Empire of the Tetrarchs*, Oxford, Clarendon, 1996.

Cornell, T. J., *The Beginnings of Rome*, London, Routledge, 1995, repr. 1997.

Cortese, E., *Il rinascimento giuridico medievale*, Rome, Bulzoni, 1992.

Crawford, M., *The Roman Republic*, 2nd edn, London, Fontana, 1992.

Crifò, G., *Lezioni di storia del diritto romano*, 3rd edn, Bologna, Monduzzi, 2000.

Crook, J. A., *Law and Life of Rome*, London, Thames & Hudson, 1967.

Crook, J. A., *Legal Advocacy in the Roman World*, London, Duckworth, 1995.

D'Ippolito, F., *I giuristi e la città, Naples*, Edizioni Scientifiche Italiane, 1978.

D'Ippolito, F., *Giuristi e sapienti in Roma arcaica*, Rome, Laterza, 1986.

D'Ippolito, F., *Aspetti di storia costituzionale romana*, Naples, Edizioni Scientifiche Italiane, 2001.

Daube, D., *Forms of Roman Legislation*, Oxford, Clarendon, 1956.

De Giovanni, L., *Introduzione allo studio del diritto romano tardoantico*, 4th edn, Naples, Jovene, 2000.

Declareuil, J., *Rome the Law-Giver*, London and New York, Routledge, 1996, (original edn 1927).

Delmaire, R., *Les Institutions du Bas-Èmpire romain, de Constantin à Justinien*, I, *Les Institutions palatines*, Paris, CERF, 1995.

Drew, K. F., *Law and Society in Early Medieval Europe. Studies in Legal History*, London, Variorum, 1988.

Evans Grubbs, J., *Law and Family in Late Antiquity*, Oxford, Oxford University Press, 1999.

Ferenczy, E., *From the Patrician State to the Patricio-Plebeian State*, Amsterdam, Hakkert, 1976.

Frier, B., *The Rise of the Roman Jurists*, Princeton, Princeton University Press, 1985.

Gardner, J. F., *Women in Roman Law and Society*, London, Routledge, 1986.

Garnsey, P., *Social Status and Legal Privilege*, Oxford, Clarendon, 1970.

Gioffredi, C., *I principi del diritto penale romano*, Torino, Giappichelli, 1970.

Giuffrè, V., *La repressione criminale nell' esperienza romana*, 4 th edn, Naples, Jovene, 1998.

Gruen, E. S., *Roman Politics and the Criminal Courts, 149-78 BC*, Harvard University Press, 1968.

Guarino A., *Storia del diritto romano*, 11th edn, Napoli, Jovene, 1996.

Guarino, A., *Diritto privato romano*, 12th edn., Naples, Jovene, 2001.

Harries, J., *Law and Empire in Late Antiquity*, Cambridge, Cambridge University Press, 1999.

Harries, J. and Wood, I. (eds), *The Theodosian Code: Studies in the Imperial Law of Late Antiquity*, London, Duckworth, 1993.

Honoré, T., *Tribonian*, London, Duckworth, 1978.

Honoré, T., *Emperors and Lawyers*, London, Duckworth, 1981.

Honoré, T., *Ulpian*, Oxford, Clarendon, 1982.

Honoré, T., *Law in the Crisis of Empire, 379-445 AD*, Oxford, Clarendon, 1998.

Jacques, F., and Scheid, J., *Rom und das Reich in der Hohen Kaiserzeit*, Stuttgart and Leipzig, B. G. Teubner, 1998.

Johnston, D., *Roman Law in Context*, Cambridge, Cambridge University Press, 1999.

Jolowicz, H. F. and Nicholas, B., *Historical Introduction to the Study of Roman Law*, 3rd edn, Cambridge, Cambridge University Press, 1972.

Jones, A. H. M., *Studies in Roman Government and Law*, Oxford, Blackwell, 1960.

Jones, A. H. M., *The Later Roman Empire*, Oxford, Blackwell, 1964.

Jones, A. H. M., *The Criminal Courts of the Roman Republic and Principate*, Oxford, Blackwell, 1972.

Kaser, M., *Das römische Privatrecht*, 2 vols, 2nd edn, Munich, Beck, 1971-1974.

Kaser, M., *Zur Methodologie der römischen Rechtsquellenforschung*, Vienna, Cologne and Graz, Böhlau, 1972.
Kaser, M., *Römische Rechtsgeschichte*, Göttingen, Vandenhoeck & Ruprecht,1976.
Kaser, M., *Ius gentium*, Cologne, Weimar and Vienna, Böhlau, 1993.
Kaser, M., *Das römische Zivilprozessrecht*, Munich, Beck, 1996.
Kelly, J. M., *Roman Litigation*, Oxford, Clarendon, 1966.
Kelly, J. M., *Studies in the Civil Judicature of the Roman Republic*, Oxford, Clarendon, 1976.
Kelly, J. M., *A Short History of Western Legal Theory*, Oxford, Clarendon, 1992.
Kennedy, G., *The Art of Rhetoric in the Roman World (300 BC - AD 300)*, Princeton, Princeton University Press, 1972.
Kunkel, W., *An Introduction to Roman Legal and Constitutional History*, 2nd edn, Oxford, Clarendon, 1973.
Kunkel, W., *Die Römischen Juristen*, Cologne, Weimar and Vienna, Böhlau, 2001.
Kunkel, W. and Schermaier. M., *Römische Rechtsgeschichte*, Cologne, Böhlau, 2001.
Levy, E., *West Roman Vulgar Law, the Law of Property*, Philadelphia, American Philosophical Society, 1951.
Lewis, A. D. E. and Ibbetson, D. J. (eds), *The Roman Law Tradition*, Cambridge, Cambridge University Press, 1994.
Lintott, A., *Judicial Reform and Land Reform in the Roman Republic*, Cambridge, Cambridge University Press, 1992.
Lintott, A., *Imperium Romanum: Politics and Administration*, London and New York, Routledge 1993.
Lintott, A., *The Constitution of the Roman Republic*, Oxford, Clarendon 1999.
Lupoi, M., *The Origins of the European Legal Order*, Cambridge, Cambridge University Press, 2000.
Merryman, J. H., *The Civil Law Tradition*, Stanford, Stanford University Press, 1969.
Metzger, E., *A New Outline of the Roman Civil Trial*, Oxford, Clarendon, 1997.
Millar, F., *The Emperor in the Roman World*, Ithaca, New York, Cornell University Press, 1977.
Mommsen, Th., *Römisches Strafrecht*, Leipzig, Duncker & Humblot, 1899, repr. Graz, Akademische Druck- und Verlaganstalt, 1955, and Darmstadt, Wissenschaftliche Buchgesellschaft, 1961.
Mommsen, Th., *Römisches Staatsrecht* I, Leipzig, Duncker & Humblot,1887, repr. Graz, Akademische Druck- und Verlaganstalt, 1971.
Monier, R., *Manuel élémentaire de droit romain*, Aalen, Scientia, 1977.
Nelson, H. L. W., *Überlieferung, Aufbau und Stil von Gai Institutiones*, Leiden, Brill, 1981.
Nicholas, B., *An Introduction to Roman Law*, Oxford, Clarendon, 1962, repr. 1991.
Nippel, W., *Public Order in Ancient Rome*, Cambridge, Cambridge University Press, 1995.
Radding, C. M., *The Origins of Medieval Jurisprudence*, New Haven and London, Yale University Press, 1988.

Rainer, J. M., *Einführung in das römische Staatsrecht*, Darmstadt, Wiss. Buchges, 1997.
Riggsby, A. M., *Crime and Community in Ciceronian Rome*, Austin, University of Texas Press, 1999.
Robinson, O. F., Fergus, T. D. and Gordon, W. M., *An Introduction to European Legal History*, 2nd edn, London, Butterworths, 1994.
Robinson, O. F., *The Criminal Law of Ancient Rome*, London, Duckworth, 1995.
Robinson, O. F., *The Sources of Roman Law*, London and New York, Routledge, 1997.
Santalucia, B., *Studi di diritto penale romano*, Roma, L'"Erma" di Bretschneider, 1994.
Santalucia, B., *Diritto e processo penale nell' antica Roma*, Milan, Giuffrè, 1989, 2nd edn 1998.
Schiller, A. A., *Roman Law: Mechanisms of Development*, The Hague and New York, Mouton, 1978.
Schulz, F., *Classical Roman Law*, Oxford, Clarendon, 1951.
Schulz, F., *History of Roman Legal Science*, Oxford, Clarendon, 1967 (original edn 1946).
Sherwin-White, A. N., *The Roman Citizenship*, 2nd edn, Oxford, Clarendon, 1973.
Stein, P., *The Character and Influence of the Roman Civil Law*, London, Hambledon, 1988.
Stein, P., *Roman Law in European History*, Cambridge, Cambridge University Press, 1999.
Strachan-Davidson, J. L., *Problems of the Roman Criminal Law* I, Oxford, Clarendon, 1912, repr. Amsterdam, Rodopi, 1969.
Syme, R., *The Roman Revolution*, Oxford, Clarendon, 1939.
Talamanca, M. (ed.), *Lineamenti di storia del diritto romano*, 2nd edn, Milan, Giuffrè, 1989.
Tamm, D., *Roman Law and European Legal History*, Copenhagen, DJOF, 1997.
Taylor, L. R., *Roman Voting Assemblies*, Ann Arbor, The University of Michigan Press, 1966.
Tellegen-Couperus, O. E., *A Short History of Roman Law*, London and New York, Routledge, 1993.
Urch, E. J., *The Evolution of the Inquisitorial Procedure in Roman Law*, Chicago, Ares Publishers, 1980.
Van Caenegem, R. C., *An Historical Introduction to Private Law*, Cambridge, Cambridge University Press, 1992.
Van der Wal, N. and Lokin, J. H. A., *Historiae iuris graeco-romani delineatio*, Groningen, Forsten, 1985.
Vinogradoff, P., *Roman Law in Medieval Europe*, Oxford, Clarendon, 1929.
Watson, A., *The Law of the Ancient Romans*, Dallas, Southern Methodist University Press, 1970.
Watson, A., *Law Making in the Roman Republic*, Oxford, Clarendon, 1974.
Watson, A., *Rome of the XII Tables*, Princeton, Princeton University Press, 1975.
Watson, A., *Legal Origins and Legal Change*, London, Hambledon, 1991.

Watson, A., *Roman Law and Comparative Law*, Athens, University of Georgia Press, 1991.

Watson, A., *The State, Law and Religion: Pagan Rome*, Athens, University of Georgia Press, 1992.

Watson, A., *The Spirit of Roman Law*, Athens, University of Georgia Press, 1995.

Wells, C., The Roman Empire, 2nd edn, London, Fontana, 1992.

Wenger, L., *Die Quellen des römischen Rechts*, Vienna, Holzhausen, 1953.

Wieacker, F., *Römische Rechtsgeschichte* I, Munich, Beck, 1988.

Wieacker, F., *A History of Private Law in Europe*, Oxford, Oxford University Press, 1995.

Williams, S., *Diocletian and the Roman Recovery*, London, Batsford, 1985.

Wolff, H.-J., *Roman Law: An Historical Introduction*, Norman, University of Oklahoma Press, 1951.

Index